# ETHICAL PROBLEMS
# IN THE
# PRACTICE OF LAW

# ETHICAL PROBLEMS
# IN THE
# PRACTICE OF LAW

**Lisa G. Lerman**
Professor of Law and Director, Law and Public Policy Program
The Catholic University of America Columbus School of Law

**Philip G. Schrag**
Professor of Law and Director, Center for Applied Legal Studies
Georgetown University Law Center

PUBLISHERS

111 Eighth Avenue, New York, NY 10011
www.aspenpublishers.com

© 2005 Aspen Publishers, Inc.

> Permissions
> Aspen Publishers
> 111 Eighth Avenue
> New York, NY 10011

Printed in the United States of America

1 2 3 4 5 6 7 8 9 0

ISBN 0-7355-2914-0

**Library of Congress Cataloging-in-Publication Data**
Lerman Lisa G.
   Ethical problems in the practice of law/by Lisa G. Lerman.
     p.cm.
   Includes index.
   ISBN 0-7355-2914-0 (hardcover)
   1. Legal ethics — United States. I. Title

KF306.A4L47 2005
174′.3 — dc22

2004030683

# About Aspen Publishers

Aspen Publishers, headquartered in New York City, is a leading information provider for attorneys, business professionals, and law students. Written by pre-eminent authorities, our products consist of analytical and practical information covering both U.S. and international topics. We publish in the full range of formats, including updated manuals, books, periodicals, CDs, and online products.

Our proprietary content is complemented by 2,500 legal databases, containing over 11 million documents, available through our Loislaw division. Aspen Publishers also offers a wide range of topical legal and business databases linked to Loislaw's primary material. Our mission is to provide accurate, timely, and authoritative content in easily accessible formats, supported by unmatched customer care.

To order any Aspen Publishers title, go to *www.aspenpublishers.com* or call 1-800-638-8437.

To reinstate your manual update service, call 1-800-638-8437.

For more information on Loislaw products, go to *www.loislaw.com* or call 1-800-364-2512.

For Customer Care issues, e-mail *CustomerCare@aspenpublishers.com*; call 1-800-234-1660; or fax 1-800-901-9075.

## Aspen Publishers
### A Wolters Kluwer Company

**To Sam and Sarah**
**who light up our lives**

# SUMMARY OF CONTENTS

# CONTENTS

# TABLE OF PROBLEMS

# FOREWORD

*by Peter R. Jarvis*

Three things are true about the rules of professional conduct or legal ethics rules. First, the rules provide a significant part of the glue that holds American lawyers together as a profession. Lawyers in a different state may have entirely different practices, but they are all subject to the same rules. In fact, and even though there are many state-to-state variations, the rules are generally more alike than different from one state to the next.

Second, the rules leave much — some would say too much — to interpretation or to the imagination. The rules often operate at a high level of abstraction, and the ability to travel back and forth between the abstract and the concrete is therefore critical. Put another way, the rules themselves do not provide a complete guide for lawyer conduct. They provide a starting point for analysis which ethical and successful practitioners must then learn to apply in the particular contexts of their own careers.

Third, most practicing lawyers care deeply about their own ethics and about the ethics of the profession. We understand that we play critical roles in the operation of our society and in the lives of our clients and others, and we want to play those roles to the best of our ability.

I have been a practicing lawyer for 28 years. My practice has emphasized attorney professional responsibility and risk management issues for 20 of those years. During that time, I have answered thousands of professional responsibility and risk management questions for lawyers throughout the country. There is an old joke to the effect that an optimist is someone who believes that we live in the best of all possible worlds while a pessimist is someone who fears that the optimist is correct. Through my practice, I have come to believe that we need to avoid both of these extremes.

Yes, we have our share of bad apples in the profession just as we have "good" lawyers who, for whatever reasons, may at times do "bad" things. But this is true of every profession and, for that matter, of humankind as a whole. And yes, too, the malefactors in the legal profession sometimes seek to justify aberrant behavior by asserting that they were only giving their clients the zealous representation that they often incorrectly assert our professional norms require. But once again, they are not alone. One need look no further than modern-day religious extremists to see similar ideas. Nevertheless, few of us would condemn all religions and religious beliefs because some are taken to an extreme.

I submit that the proper attitude towards the profession and towards lawyers' professional responsibility issues today is one of guarded optimism. There has never been a time in the past in which the professional responsibility rules were better than they are today. There also has never been a time when disciplinary enforcement has been as widespread or when as many practicing lawyers received continuing training in professional responsibility. And there has never been a time when bar membership was as diverse in terms of ethnicity, gender, sexual orientation, religion or other factors as it is today. We still have a lot of ground left to cover, but we have already covered a lot of ground. Contemporary professional responsibility professors and their students are privileged to stand on the shoulders of those who have come before.

There are limits on the extent to which professional responsibility as experienced in the field by practicing lawyers can truly be understood by law students. It is very hard to think through how to handle multiple would-be incorporators who would all like to become a lawyer's clients if one is not yet certain how to form a corporation or where and how future disagreements between the incorporators may arise. Similarly, there is only so much one can understand about client perjury or countless other problems until one has "been there" and "done that." Nor can purely theoretical classroom exercises fully inoculate future lawyers against the pressures that they will have to face from future colleagues, clients, adversaries, and judges.

On the other hand, a lot that can be learned — even in a single term course. One can come to a better understanding of the importance to society at large of how lawyers conduct ourselves. One can come to a better understanding of the interrelationships between the duties that lawyers owe to their clients, to non-clients, and to themselves. And one can come to a better understanding that our law of professional responsibility will continue to evolve as long as our society continues to evolve.

This is an outstanding book. The authors have avoided any hint of sanctimony or of talking down to practicing lawyers. They have covered issues that are of day-to-day and cutting edge importance to contemporary lawyers and have done so in a way that is both practical and professional. In addition, the method of presentation — principles first followed by factually oriented materials which call upon the students to apply the principles they have just learned — is particularly well-suited to this subject. When those of us in the "real world" are confronted by new or difficult questions of professional responsibility, we go back and forth between the rules and the facts in search of an appropriate balance — exactly what students must do here.

It is possible to be both ethical and successful just as it is possible to be both unethical and unsuccessful. The links between ethics and success include the ability to balance emotion and objectivity, pride of craft, love of the law and a decent respect for oneself and for the rights of others. Neither we nor any subsequent generation of lawyers will see an end to debate about the ethics of our profession. This is as it should be. How else can each new generation claim this essential but evolving body of law as its own?

*Peter Jarvis is a partner in the Portland, Oregon office of Hinshaw & Culbertson, LLP. Before joining Hinshaw in 2003, Jarvis was a partner at Stoel Rives, LLP, which he joined in 1976. He handled in-house ethics and risk avoidance issues at Stoel Rives for more than fifteen years. His practice focuses on attorney professional responsibility and risk management matters, as well as general contract and business matters. Jarvis is President of the Association of Professional Responsibility Lawyers and is Chair of the Planning Committee for the ABA National Conference on Professional Responsibility. He has authored or co-authored several books and articles on issues of attorney professional responsibility and risk management.*

# PREFACE FOR TEACHERS AND STUDENTS

Lawyers make, interpret and apply law, but the legal profession is also governed by law. This book is an introduction to the law that governs lawyers and to the legal profession.

Our principal goals in writing this book were to offer an overview of the law governing lawyers and to provide materials through which law students may explore some of the ethical problems that lawyers encounter in practice. Also we sought to provide opportunities for law students to consider the various professional roles that lawyers occupy and the moral quandaries that students will struggle with when they begin to practice law. For example, in negotiating a settlement for a client, a lawyer might say that his client would refuse to accept less than $100,000, even though the client has told the lawyer that he would be delighted to receive $50,000. This is deceptive, but lawyers commonly use this tactic to obtain favorable outcomes for their clients. Does the pervasiveness of this type of deception make it acceptable? Is a lawyer's only duty to get the best result for his client, or does he also owe his opposing counsel a duty of honesty?

This book provides an overview of the law that governs lawyers. The book does not include an encyclopedic analysis of every ethical rule, much less the entire body of law governing the legal profession. We focus primarily on the subjects that are most likely to arise during the first years of an individual's law practice. For example, many new lawyers become associates in law firms, so this book explores what an associate should do when a more senior associate or a partner asks the associate to do something that seems improper. Also, most new lawyers in private practice make frequent decisions about how to record their time for billing purposes. This book includes many problems that arise from everyday practice issues. Most of the examples and problems in this book involve lawyers who represent individuals or businesses in matters involving contracts, torts, criminal prosecution and defense, civil litigation, real estate, and family law. We have sought to develop problems and to select cases in which a student can understand the facts and the ethical issues regardless of whether the student has taken advanced courses in law school.[1]

This book offers opportunities to explore ethical dilemmas that have actually arisen in practice, some of which have resulted in published judicial decisions. While we have excerpted numerous important judicial opinions in the book, we have transformed a larger number of cases into problems for class discussion. Instead of reprinting the appellate opinions, we have presented the essential facts of these cases as one of those lawyers saw them, walking them backward in time to the moment at which that lawyer had to make a difficult choice based on both ethical and strategic considerations. Rather than reviewing the pre-digested legal analysis of a judicial opinion, we invite students to put themselves in the shoes of a lawyer who faces a difficult choice among possible actions. The dilemmas in most of our problems are based on tough situations that have confronted real lawyers.

Evaluating ethical dilemmas in class will help students to handle similar quandaries when they encounter them in practice. A student who has worked through the problems assigned in this course will know where in the law a particular issue might be addressed, how to begin to analyze the relevant rules and what questions to ask. Grappling with these problems also will increase students' awareness of ethical issues that otherwise might have gone unnoticed.[2]

We set out to write an introduction to the law governing lawyers that students will enjoy reading. Studies show that by the third year of law school, the class attendance rate is only about 60%, and that a majority of those students who do attend class read the assignments for the half or fewer than half of the classes they attend.[3] Increasingly, law students use their computers to play solitaire or write email during class.[4] This data suggests that law schools are failing in their efforts to retain the interest and attention of their students, particularly third year law students. We have sought to write a book whose content and methodology will capture and sustain the reader's interest. This aspiration is reflected in our choice of topics and materials, our concise summaries of the law, our challenging problems, and our use of graphic materials.

Here are some defining features of this book:

■ Compared to several other professional responsibility texts, this book is relatively short, so the reading assignments need not be burdensome.

---

1. An increasing number of law schools encourage students to take a course in Professional Responsibility during their first or second year. This makes it appropriate to use problems that can be understood by students who have not taken particular upper class offerings.

2. See Lisa G. Lerman, Teaching Moral Perception and Moral Judgment in Legal Ethics Courses: A Dialogue About Goals, 39 Wm. & Mary L. Rev. 457, 459 (1998) (explaining the reasons to use experiential methodology in professional responsibility classes); and Steven Hartwell, Promoting Moral Development Through Experiential Teaching, 1 Clinical L. Rev. 505, 527 (1995) (reporting on his empirical research which shows that professional responsibility students' moral reasoning skills made significant advances during a course in which students discussed simulated ethical dilemmas).

3. Mitu Gulati, Richard Sander, and Robert Sockloskie, The Happy Charade: An Empirical Examination of the Third Year of Law School, 51 J. of Legal Educ. 235, 244-45 (2001).

4. Ian Ayres, Lectures vs. Laptops, N.Y. Times, March 20, 2001, p. A25.

- We have begun almost every section of the book with a summary of the relevant doctrine which provides the legal background students need to analyze the problems that follow.
- We have included numerous judicial opinions, most of which will be familiar to teachers of professional responsibility. We have edited those opinions carefully and have provided brief summaries of others. However, as discussed above, we have presented many other cases that are widely taught in professional responsibility classes as problems rather than as opinions. We recount the facts of the cases in narrative form to allow students to analyze the issues as if they were the lawyers facing those dilemmas. We believe that this structure produces livelier discussion than does the autopsy method traditionally used in law classes, in which teachers invite post hoc dissection of judicial opinions. We have included more than seventy problems in this book. These may become the primary focus of class discussion.
- We have included the text of pertinent rules of professional conduct in the book so that students will not need to flip constantly back and forth between this text and a statutory supplement. When studying a particular rule, students will find it worthwhile to review the entire rule and comments in another published source or on the Internet.[5] However, this text is structured so that it can be read without constant reference to a supplement.
- We have included more than seventy problems in this book, which may provide the primary focus of class discussion.
- When we reproduce court opinions, we have inserted headings into them to help orient students to the logic of the opinions.
- We have included many bulleted lists and tables to clarify legal doctrines and other conceptual material.
- Most of the summaries of various aspects of the law governing lawyers is in question-and-answer format. This structure provides an ongoing roadmap, forecasting the content of the next subtopic and explaining why one might want to understand it. In addition, numerous concrete examples, set off from the text, illustrate the general doctrinal principles.
- We have included photographs, diagrams and cartoons. Some of these, like the photographs of some of the lawyers, parties, judges and scholars add important context. Others, like the cartoons, offer a change of pace from the textual narrative.[6]

We welcome your reactions to this book and your suggestions, small or large, for the next edition. Please send any comments or questions to lerman@law.edu.

*Lisa G. Lerman*
*Philip G. Schrag*

---

5. For example, students will find the full text of the Model Rules of Professional Conduct and the explanatory comments interpreting each rule at http://www.abanet.org/cpr/mrpc/mrpc_home.html (last visited Jan. 23, 2005).

6. Textbooks used in graduate programs in education, mathematics, medicine, psychology, and other fields make extensive use of graphic material; an increasing number of law books do so also.

# ACKNOWLEDGMENTS

Hundreds of law professors, practitioners, and judges have worked to regulate the practice of law, to study its regulation, and to publish their ideas. Decades of effort have gone into the drafting of successive model codes for lawyers, rules of state bars, and the Restatement. Academics have made countless contributions in the form of books and law review articles on the legal profession and papers delivered to conferences convened under the auspices of the American Bar Association, the Association of American Law Schools, the Keck Foundation, and other organizations. This book is in part a summary of many of those efforts.

We particularly want to acknowledge our intellectual debt to the authors of the Restatement and of the other treatises and textbooks that are used in courses on legal ethics and the American legal profession. We have consulted these books frequently in the course of writing this volume, and some of the materials we have used were called to our attention by other case book authors.

We have received invaluable encouragement and assistance from our editors at Aspen, especially Susan Boulanger, Richard Mixter, Lisa Wehrle, and Mei Wang. Several colleagues have reviewed various drafts of the book and have given us amazingly insightful and detailed comments and suggestions. These include: Russell Engler, Susan Saab Fortney, William Freivogel, Steve Goldman, Peter Joy, Ann Juergens, Arlene Kanter, Judith Maute, Ben Mintz, Ted Schneyer, and Brad Wendell. Many other people assisted us by answering questions and providing needed information. These include Nathan Crystal, Susanna Fischer, Art Garwin, Stephen Gillers, John Gleason, Bruce Green, James Grogan, David Luban, Carrie Menkel-Meadow, Nancy Moore, Lucian Pera, Jennifer Renne, John Rooney, Roy Simon, and Leah Wortham. We also benefitted from excellent research assistance by Dori Antonetti, Noel DeSantos, Jessica Kendall, Connie Lynch, Keith Palfin, Jason Parish, and Michael Provost. Special thanks go to Jason Parish, who cite-checked the entire manuscript and drafted the tables of cases, rules, and articles. He did all of this work with amazing precision and care.

We appreciate the support given us (in the form of leaves of absence from teaching and summer writing grants) by our employers, Catholic University and Georgetown University.

We would like to thank our teenagers, Samuel Schrag Lerman and Sarah Lerman Schrag (to whom the book is dedicated). Both of them are exquisitely sensitive to moral and ethical issues. Our understanding of ethical problems has been much advanced by our many conversations with them about the dilemmas that they have confronted. These conversations have informed our analysis of several problems in this book.[1] Besides being our ethics tutors, Sam and Sarah sat through an untold number of conversations about the book, at dinner, on vacations, and elsewhere. They also provided us with many good ideas about teaching and learning.

We thank these owners of literary and photographic rights for granting permission to reprint copyrighted material including excerpts from articles and books, photographs, and cartoons:

## Textual material

American Law Institute, Restatement of the Law Governing Lawyers. Copyright 2000 by the American Law Institute. Reproduced with permission. All rights reserved.

Michael Asimow, "Embodiment of Evil: Law Firms in the Movies, originally published in 48 UCLA L. Rev. 1339 (2001). Reprinted with permission.

Jon Bauer, The Character of the Questions and the Fitness of the Process: Mental Health, Bar Admissions, and the Americans with Disabilities Act, originally published in 49 UCLA L. Rev. 93 (2001). Reprinted with permission.

Scott Brede, A Notable Case of Exceptionally Unsafe Sex, Conn. Law Tribune, July 10, 2000. Reprinted with permission of the Law Tribune Newspapers.

Wayne D. Brazil, Views from the Front Lines: Observations by Chicago Lawyers About the System of Civil Discovery, 219 American Bar Foundation Research Journal 1980. Reprinted with permission of the University of Chicago Press and Wayne D. Brazil.

Stacy L. Brustin, Legal Services Provision Through Non-Profit Multidisciplinary Practice: Encouraging Holistic Advocacy While Protecting Ethical Interests. Reprinted with permission of the University of Colorado Law Review and Stacy L. Brustin.

California Bar Journal, Notice, John Wali Mustafa (suspended from the practice of law), June 2002. Reprinted with permission.

Douglas Campbell, Law firms do little pro bono, Business Journal of the Greater Triad Area, July 23, 2001. Reprinted with permission of the Business Journal of the Greater Triad Area.

Center for Law and Social Policy, Securing Justice for All (2003). Reprinted with permission.

Darryl van Duch, Best Snitches: Land of Lincoln Leads the Nation in Attorneys Turning in their Peers. Reprinted with permission of American Lawyer Media, Inc. from the January 27, 1997 issue of the National Law Journal.

Richard Dieter, With Justice for Few: The Growing Crisis in Death Penalty Representation. Reprinted with permission of the Death Penalty Information Center.

Sarah Helene Duggin, Internal Corporate Investigations: Legal Ethics, Professionalism, and the Employee Interview, 2003 Colum. Bus. L. Rev. 859. Reprinted with permission.

---

1. The ethical problems that lawyers encounter are often similar to those faced by non-lawyers, including adolescents; both kinds of problems involve issues such as loyalty, confidentiality, truthfulness, and conflicts of interest. For example, suppose that you are a teenager and that your friend tells you in confidence about a serious problem that she is having (e.g., with drugs or depression). Should you consult your parents despite your promise of confidence? What if your parents might inform your friend's parents who do not yet know about the problem? If your friend might pose a danger to others, should you tell the administration at your school, or talk directly to your friend's parents?

Florida Ethics Opinion 95-4. Reprinted with permission of the Florida Bar.

Charles Fried, The Lawyer as Friend: The Moral Foundations of the Lawyer-Client Relationship," 85 Yale L. J. 1060 (1976). Reprinted from the Yale Law Journal, vol. 85, pages 1060-1089 by permission of the Yale Law Journal Company and William S. Hein Company.

Stephen Gillers, "Can a Good Lawyer be a Bad Person," 84 Mich. L. Rev. 1011 (1986), revised and reprinted in 2 J. Inst. Study Leg. Ethics 131 (1999). Reprinted with permission.

Stephen Gillers, It's an MJP World, from the American Bar Association Journal, December 2002. Reprinted with permission of the American Bar Association Journal.

Martin Guggenheim, A Paradigm for Determining the Role of Counsel for Children, 64 Fordham L. Rev. 1399 (1996). Reprinted with permission.

Harvard Law School, Office of Public Interest Advising, Serving the Public: A Job Search Guide (14th ed. 2003). Reprinted with permission.

Michael Hertz, Large Law Firms: A Larger Role to Play, ProBono Net News, Oct. 1, 2003. Reprinted with permission of ProBono Net News.

Frances Gall Hill, Clinical Education and the "Best Interest" Representation of Children in Custody Disputes: Challenges and Opportunities in Lawyering and Pedagogy, 73 Ind. L.J. 605 (1998). Reprinted with permission of the Indiana Law Journal.

Jim Hoagland, Gadhafi's Lawyer, Washington Post, July 14, 1993. Copyright 1993 The Washington Post Writers Group. Reprinted with permission of the Washington Post Writers Group.

Lisa G. Lerman, Gross Profits? Questions about Lawyer Billing Practices, 22 Hofstra L. Rev. 645 (1994). Reprinted with permission of the Hofstra Law Review Association.

Lisa G. Lerman, Lying to Clients, 138 U. Pa. L. Rev. 659 (1990). Reprinted with permission of the University of Pennsylvania Law Review and William S. Hein & Co, Inc.

David Margolick, New York Court Shields Lawyers Who Report Dishonest Colleagues, N.Y. Times, Dec. 23, 1992. Reprinted with permission of the New York Times Company.

Carrie Menkel-Meadow Ethics, Morality and Professional Responsibility in Negotiation, published in Dispute Resolution Ethics: A Comprehensive Guide. Copyright 2002 American Bar Assocation. Reprinted with permission of the American Bar Association.

Robert L. Nelson, The Discovery Process as a Circle of Blame: Institutional, Professional and Socio-economic Factors that Contribute to Unreasonable, Inefficient, and Amoral Behavior in Corporate Litigation, 67 Fordham L. Rev. 773, (1998). Reprinted by permission.

Omaha World Journal, How Simpson Lawyers Bamboozled a Jury (editorial), Oct. 10, 1996. Reprinted with permission.

Deborah L. Rhode, Cultures of Commitment: Pro Bono for Lawyers and Law Students, 67 Fordham L. Rev. 2415 (1999). Reprinted by permission.

Patrick J. Schiltz, On Being a Happy, Healthy, and Ethical Member of an Unhappy, Unhealthy and Unethical Profession, 52 Vand. L. Rev. 871 (1999). Reprinted with permission of the Vanderbilt Law Review.

Ted Schneyer, Moral Philosophy's Standard Misconception of Legal Ethics, 1984 Wisc. L. Rev. 1529 (1985). Copyright 1984 by the Board of Regents of the University of Wisconsin System. Reprinted by permission of the Wisconsin Law Review and the Board of Regents of the University of Wisconsin System.

Carroll Seron, The Business of Practicing Law: The Work Lives of Solo and Small-Firm Attorneys. Used with permission of Temple University Press. Copyright 1996 by Temple University. All rights reserved.

Susan Shapiro, Tangled Loyalties: Conflict of Interest in Legal Practice. Reprinted with permission of the University of Michigan Press.

William Simon, Virtuous Lying: A Critique of Quasi-Categorical Moralism, 12 Geo. J. of Legal Ethics 433 (1999). Reprinted with permission of the Georgetown Journal of Legal Ethics.

Harry Subin, The Criminal Defense Lawyer's "Different Mission,": Reflections on the "Right" to Present a False Case, 1 Geo. J. of Legal Ethics 129 (1987). Reprinted with permission of the Georgetown Journal of Legal Ethics.

Margaret Graham Tebo, Fee Shifting Fallout, American Bar Association Journal, July 2003. Reprinted with permission of the American Bar Association Journal.

Paul Tremblay, On Persuasion and Paternalism: Lawyer Decisionmaking and the Questionably Competent Client, 1987 Utah L. Rev. 515 (1987). Reprinted with permission of the Utah Law Review and Paul Tremblay.

David Vladeck, Statement Before the ABA Commission on Non-lawyer Practice, June 25, 1993. Reprinted with permission.

Gregory F. Winter, Legal Firms Cutting Back on Free Services for Poor, N.Y. Times, Aug. 17, 2000. Reprinted with permission of the New York Times Company.

## Images

Frank H. Armani, photograph. Reproduced with permission of Frank H. Armani.

Michael Asimow, photograph. Reproduced with permission of Michael Asimow.

"Attention, please." Copyright The New Yorker Collection 1984 Leo Cullum from cartoonbank.com. All rights reserved. Reproduced with permission.

Francis Richard Belge, photograph. Reproduced with permission of Frances M. Belge.

Wayne D. Brazil, photograph. Reproduced with permission of Wayne D. Brazil.

Stacy Brustin, photograph. Reproduced with permission of Thomas Haederle.

Nancy Quattlebaum Burke, photograph. Reproduced with permission of Gray Plant Mooty.

Bus accident, photograph in Chapter 3. Reproduced with permission of dcfd.com.

Richard Dieter, photograph. Reproduced with permission of Margaret Ann Louden.

Sarah Duggin, photograph Reproduced with permission of Kirk Renaud.

Ellis County Jail, photograph. Photo courtesy of the Ellis County Museum.

Susan Saab Fortney, photograph. Reproduced with permission of Frank Ramos, Jr. and Texas Tech University.

Vincent Foster, photograph. Reproduced with permission of the Arkansas Democrat-Gazette.

Monroe H. Freedman, photograph. Reproduced with permission of Monroe H. Freedman.

William Freivogel, photograph. Reproduced with permission of Caroline Freivogel.

Robert Garrow, photograph. Reprinted from the Post-Standard (Syracuse, N.Y.). Reproduced with permission.

Daniel J. Gatti, photograph. Reproduced with permission of Gatti, Gatti, Maier, Krueger, Sayer and Associates.

Dominic Gentile, photograph. Reproduced with permission of Dominic Gentile.

Stephen Gillers, photograph. Reproduced with permission of Stephen Gillers.

Martin Guggenheim, photograph. Reproduced with permission of Martin Guggenheim.

"He's talking." Cartoon. Copyright The New Yorker Collection 1999 Liza Donnelly from cartoonbank.com. All rights reserved. Reproduced with permission.

Frances Gall Hill, photograph. Reproduced with permission of Brad Jacobs.

Webster Hubbell, photograph. Reproduced with permission of the Arkansas Democrat-Gazette.

"I never discuss." Cartoon. Copyright The New Yorker Collection 2004 Danny Shanahan from cartoonbank.com. All rights reserved. Reproduced with permission.

"I really love . . ." Cartoon. Copyright The New Yorker Collection 2004 Leo Cullum from cartoonbank.com. All rights reserved. Reproduced with permission.

Paula Jones, photograph. Reproduced with permission of the Arkansas Democrat-Gazette.

Lawyer-assisted suicide. Copyright The New Yorker Collection 1997 Roz Chast from cartoonbank.com. All rights reserved. Reproduced with permission.

Leslie Levin, photograph. Reproduced with permission of the University of Connecticut School of Law.

Ellen J. Messing, photograph by Joey Libby Photographers. Reproduced by permission of Messing, Rudavsky & Weliky, P.C.

Judith Maute, photograph. Reproduced with permission by the University of Oklahoma College of Law.

"Money? Ha!" Cartoon. Reproduced with permission of Stu Rees, www.stus.com.

Nancy J. Moore, photograph. Reproduced with permission by Mark Ostow.

Robert L. Nelson, photograph. Reproduced with permission by Neil Hamilton.

"My fees." Cartoon. Copyright The New Yorker Collection 1989 Leo Cullum from cartoonbank.com. All rights reserved. Reproduced with permission.

"OK Let's review." Cartoon. Copyright The New Yorker Collection 2002 Lee Lorenz from cartoonbank.com. All rights reserved. Reproduced with permission.

"Perhaps unethical was the wrong word . . ." Cartoon. Copyright William Hamilton. All rights reserved. Reproduced with permission.

Geoffrey Peters, photograph. Reproduced by permission of the Star-Tribune/Minneapolis-St. Paul 2004.

Joan Peterson, photograph. Reproduced by permission of David Warner.

Randy's Donuts and Legal Services, photograph by Walt Denson. Reproduced with permission from Walt Denson and Delta Dental of California.

Jennifer Renne, photograph. Reproduced with permission of Rebecca Roth.

Deborah Rhode, photograph. Reproduced with permission of David Weintraub.

Walter Rogosheske, photograph. Reproduced with permission of the Minnesota Historical Society.

Patrick J. Schiltz, photograph. Reproduced with permission of Neil Hamilton.

Ted Schneyer, photograph by Paul Kealey. Reproduced with permission of the University of Arizona College of Law.

Carroll Seron, photograph. Reproduced with permission of Carroll Seron.

Susan Shapiro, photograph. Reproduced with permission of Joanne Martin.

Harry Subin, photograph. Reproduced with permission of Carolyn Subin.

Paul Tremblay, photograph. Reproduced with permission of Paul Tremblay.

Uncle Bernie. Cartoon. Copyright The New Yorker Collection 1992 Danny Shanahan from cartoonbank.com. All rights reserved. Reproduced with permission.

David Vladeck, photograph. Reproduced with permission of Booth Gunter.

Howard Wieder, photograph. Reproduced by permission of Howard Wieder

Fred C. Zacharias, photograph. Reproduced by permission of Pablo Mason.

# ETHICAL PROBLEMS
# IN THE
# PRACTICE OF LAW

# INTRODUCTION

A. Ethics, morals, and professionalism

B. Some central themes in this book
  1. Conflicts of interest
  2. Truthfulness
  3. Lawyers' duties to clients versus their duties to the justice system
  4. Lawyers' personal and professional interests versus their fiduciary obligations
  5. Self-interest as a theme in regulation of lawyers
  6. Lawyers as employees: institutional pressures on ethical judgments

C. The structure of this book

D. The rules quoted in this book: a note on sources

E. Stylistic decisions

## A. Ethics, morals, and professionalism

### Why study the law governing lawyers?

The law governing lawyers is worth studying for two reasons. First, knowledge of this subject is an important element of your professional security. (That is, it will help you to stay out of trouble.) Second, you need to know the boundaries imposed by law on the conduct of the other lawyers you encounter so that you will recognize improper conduct and not allow your clients to be harmed by it.

This course is somewhat different from other courses in the curriculum because it has a very practical goal — to assist you in avoiding professional discipline, civil liability, and criminal charges. Some lawyers get into serious trouble, and others experience near-misses at some point during their careers. Many lawyers who have gotten into trouble made simple and avoidable mistakes. Some of the ethical and legal rules that govern lawyers are counter-intuitive, so an educated guess about what a rule provides is sometimes incorrect. A recent empirical study in New York concluded that "[v]ery few lawyers ever looked at the New York [professional responsibility] Code to resolve ethical issues they encountered in practice" and, in fact, "had not consulted it since law school."[1]

> **FOR EXAMPLE:**   Suppose that you are representing a plaintiff and are in the middle of a civil lawsuit. The other side offers to pay a preposterously low settlement. You are tempted to turn it down on the spot to demonstrate your contempt for the offer and to increase the pressure on your adversary to come up with a better one. But if you reject this offer without consulting your client, you are inadvertently violating an ethical rule. You could be disciplined, or your client might sue you for malpractice.

## Why study the history and sociology of the legal profession?

One reason to study the profession as well as its ethical rules is to acquire useful background knowledge about the various organizations that make and enforce the rules for lawyers.

> **FOR EXAMPLE:**   The American Bar Association writes many rules and opinions. What is this entity? Does it have some kind of governmental authority? What is its relationship to the bars of the 50 states?

Also, as a lawyer you need to be familiar with the various policy issues relating to the structure and regulation of the profession so that, through your state or local bar association or otherwise, you can participate in the improvement of the profession and the justice system.

> **FOR EXAMPLE:**   Should paralegals be allowed to provide some services to clients without being supervised by lawyers? Should lawyers be required to offer some services to clients who cannot afford to pay them? If you believe the answer to either of these questions is yes, you might become involved in advocacy to license paralegals or to mandate pro bono work.

---

1. Leslie C. Levin, The Ethical World of Solo and Small Law Firm Practitioners, 41 Houston L. Rev. 309, 368-369 (2004).

Even as a new lawyer, you will have opportunities to affect the ever-changing law of the legal profession. You may become a law clerk to a judge. You might be asked to draft an opinion on an appeal of a lawyer disciplinary matter or to advise your judge about proposed ethical rules. You could become involved in legislative policymaking as a staff member to a state or federal legislator, or even as an elected representative. Many recent law graduates serve on committees of state and local bar associations, which initiate or comment on changes in the rules that govern lawyers. Much of the impetus for law reform comes from the fresh perceptions of newcomers to a particular field of law who have not yet become fully accustomed to "business as usual."

## What is the difference between ethics and morals?

That depends on whom and in what context you ask. These two terms are sometimes used synonymously[2] and sometimes distinguished, but in varying ways. One scholar defines "morals" as

> values that we attribute to a system of beliefs that help the individual define right versus wrong, good versus bad. These typically get their authority from something outside the individual — a higher being or higher authority (e.g. government, society). Moral concepts, judgments and practices may vary from one society to another.[3]

We use the word "moral" to refer to the broad question of whether an act is right or wrong.

"Ethics" as a general concept is "also called moral philosophy, the discipline concerned with what is morally good and bad, right and wrong. The term is also applied to any system or theory of moral values or principles."[4] We use the term "ethics" or "ethical," however, to refer not to the field of moral philosophy, but to the field of legal ethics. The term "legal ethics" is defined as "principles of conduct that members of the profession are expected to observe in the practice of law. These principles are an outgrowth of the development of the legal profession itself."[5] When we ask if a particular act is "unethical," usually we are asking whether the act would violate the ethics codes that govern lawyers. We also invite readers to consider whether a particular response to a problem is moral or immoral. Often, but not always, the "right thing to do" in a particular situation also would comply with the ethical rules. Even so, it is important to ask both questions.

---

2. See, e.g., The Merriam-Webster On-Line Dictionary, *at* http://www.m-w.com/cgi-bin/dictionary?book=Dictionary&va=moral (last visited Nov. 13, 2004), which lists "moral" and "ethical" as synonyms.

3. Frank Navran, What Is the Difference Between Ethics, Morals and Values? *at* http://www.ethics.org/ask_e4.html (last visited Nov. 13, 2004).

4. "Ethics," Encyclopædia Britannica 2004, Encyclopædia Britannica Premium Service, *at* http://www.britannica.com/eb/article?eu=108566&tocid=0&query=moral&ct= (last visited Nov. 13, 2004).

5. "Legal Ethics," Encyclopædia Britannica 2004, Encyclopædia Britannica Premium Service, *at* http://www.britannica.com/eb/article?eu=109609 (last visited Nov. 13, 2004).

©William Hamilton

*"Perhaps 'unethical' was the wrong word; I meant sort of complex — legally complex . . ."*

The ethics codes reflect a fairly strong consensus within the legal profession about what lawyers should do when faced with certain kinds of pressures and dilemmas, but they may not correspond with an individual's judgment of whether a particular act is moral. On some issues, most lawyers would say that it is immoral as well as professionally improper to violate a state's code of ethics for lawyers. The rule prohibiting lawyers from lying to judges is probably in this category. On other issues, a lawyer might say it is not immoral to violate a particular professional rule.

**FOR EXAMPLE:** One rule bars litigating lawyers from helping indigent clients to pay their rent. While providing such assistance would violate the rule and could get a lawyer in trouble, few people would say that it would be immoral to do so.

The critical point here is that in evaluating any question in legal ethics, you must ask whether the conduct in question violates the ethics codes. (For the protection of both the lawyer and the client, you also must ask whether the conduct violates other law, such as criminal law or regulatory law.) Quite apart from the question of compliance with law, you should add a final question: "What is the right thing to do?"

## What difference does it make that lawyers are "professionals"?

The words "profession" and "professional," like the words "ethics" and "ethical," have multiple meanings. Some fields, such as medicine, law, and architecture, are considered "professions," while others are not. Members of most professions are permitted to do work that is forbidden to nonmembers. They must be licensed before they are allowed to ply their trades. To obtain licenses, they must receive extensive technical training. Governing bodies of professional associations develop standards for licensing professionals and for disciplining licensees who fail to meet the standards.

Second, a critical aspect of what it means to be a professional is a commitment to serving others. The training and licensing of lawyers is intended to promote the delivery of high-quality services, to expand the opportunities for people to have access to justice, and to foster support throughout society for the rule of law. Because the profession is essential to the protection of democratic government, and because lawyers, through the licensing process, have a monopoly on the service they provide, lawyers are expected to provide some service to clients who cannot afford to pay. They are also expected to participate in the improvement of the legal system.

Third, to be "professional," or do something in a professional way, means to do an unusually careful job. This sense of the word does not require advanced training, but it does imply a high degree of skill and care. One can do a professional job of any work, not just the work required of members of the "professions." Most people who consider themselves "professionals" have their own internal standards of performance. They want to perform at a high level at all times, even when no one is watching. They derive internal satisfaction as well as external rewards for doing excellent work.

A fourth aspect of becoming a professional is that a person joining a profession adopts a defined role and agrees to comply with articulated standards of conduct. This may lead the individual to make moral choices about his conduct that are justified by reference to the defined role.[6]

**FOR EXAMPLE:** A criminal defense lawyer might urge that it is proper to seek to exclude from evidence an exhibit that shows his client's guilt because the evidence was obtained improperly by the police. Even if the court's ability to discern the true facts is compromised by the exclusion of the evidence, the criminal defense lawyer would argue that it is consistent with his role.

---

6. For some of the many fine books and articles discussing professionalism among lawyers, see David Barnhizer, Profession Deleted, Using Market and Liability Forces to Regulate the Very Ordinary Business of Law Practice for Profit, 17 Geo. J. Leg. Ethics 203 (2004); Melissa L. Breger, Gina M. Calabrese & Theresa A. Hughes, Teaching Professionalism in Context, Insights from Students, Clients, Adversaries and Judges, 55 S.C. L. Rev. 303 (2003); Richard A. Posner, Professionalisms, 40 Ariz. L. Rev. 1 (1998); ABA Section of Legal Educ. & Admissions to the Bar, Teaching and Learning Professionalism 6 (1996); Mary Ann Glendon, A Nation Under Lawyers: How the Crisis in the Legal Profession Is Transforming American Society (1994); Anthony T. Kronman, The Lost Lawyer: Failing Ideals of the Legal Profession (1993); ABA Commission on Professionalism, In the Spirit of Public Service: A Blueprint for the Rekindling of Lawyer Professionalism (1986).

Some scholars have questioned whether this "role differentiation" is a justification for conduct that otherwise might be viewed as immoral.[7]

Most students are very excited by the prospect of joining a profession. Membership offers the opportunity to develop your skills and to evolve internal standards of performance, to challenge yourself to lifelong learning and improvement, and to serve others. And at least in law, after the first few years of training, no one but you will know the details of much of what you do. The external standards play an important role, but they often lie in the background. You must set most of your professional standards internally, especially those that relate to your treatment of clients and the quality of your work product.

Joining the legal profession requires mastery of a large and complex body of externally imposed ethical and legal standards. Many decisions are left to the professional discretion of the lawyer who is handling a particular matter, but the lawyer is expected to know which standards are discretionary and which are not. In this course, you will become acquainted with many external standards, and you will have opportunities to cultivate and refine your own internal standards.

## B. Some central themes in this book

Several themes come up repeatedly in this book. Perhaps they represent some fundamental questions about the practice of law and the legal profession.

### 1. Conflicts of interest

One common thread is that many ethical problems present conflicts of interest. One might define an ethical dilemma as a situation in which a person notices conflicting obligations to two or more people, one of whom may be herself. Chapters 5, 6, and part of Chapter 7 deal with the body of law that lawyers usually refer to when they are talking about "conflicts of interest," but many of the other topics could also involve conflicts between competing interests or obligations.

> **FOR EXAMPLE:** Suppose a client informs you that he was arrested in the course of planning a terrorist attack. The other conspirators have not been apprehended. You have a duty to protect the confidences shared with you by your client, but also you have a duty to your community to do your part to prevent the terrorist attack from taking place.

---

7. Richard Wasserstrom, Lawyers as Professionals: Some Moral Issues, 5 Hum. Rts. 1, 7-8 (1975).

**FOR EXAMPLE:**   Your firm will pay you a bonus of $25,000 if your annual billings exceed 2,300 hours.[8] You are working on one major memo, billing by the hour. You can achieve a very good result for the client in 30 hours, or you could do the "dissertation" version of the memo and bill 100 hours.

Try to look at the topics covered in this course through this "conflict of interest" lens. Sometimes you can see the problems more clearly by articulating the nature of the conflict.

## 2.  Truthfulness

Another central theme is the question of whether and to what extent a lawyer is obliged to be truthful. Rule 8.4 prohibits "dishonesty, fraud, deceit [and] misrepresentation." At first blush, this might seem like a very simple issue. In fact, however, very many ethical dilemmas involve a conflict about truthfulness. Some of the issues about truth and deception turn out to involve a conflict between a lawyer's personal interests and an obligation to a client, or a conflict between his duty to a client and to another person. These are two of the other recurrent themes.

**FOR EXAMPLE:**   Suppose you are conducting a direct examination of a client in court. Your client surprises you with a statement that you know is false. You have a duty to advance your client's interests, or at least not to harm them, and a duty to be truthful in dealing with the tribunal. If you tell the judge that your client lied on the stand (or if you persuade your client to correct his testimony), you are being fully truthful. If you conceal the information, however, you might better advance your client's interests.

**FOR EXAMPLE:**   A prospective client is considering hiring you to handle a large (that is, lucrative) matter involving toxic waste disposal. You once did a very modest amount of work on a matter involving similar facts. The client asks, "Do you have a lot of experience in this area?" A truthful answer probably will result in the client seeking representation elsewhere.

Many problems raise questions about whether a lawyer can lie or mislead someone, withhold information, shade the truth, or sit quietly and watch a client mislead someone. In an ideal world, we might aspire to unvarnished truthfulness in dealings with others, but the obligations of an advocate present many situations in which at least withholding information occasionally seems desirable.

---

8. Many law firms tie the amount they pay in bonuses to the number of hours worked and the number of years an associate has been with a firm. At Baker Botts, for example, senior associates who billed 2,300 or more hours in 2004 were eligible for bonuses of up to $25,000. Brenda Sapino Jeffreys, Big-Billables Bonus, Tex. Law., Apr. 26, 2004, at A3.

## 3. Lawyers' duties to clients versus their duties to the justice system

Lawyers differ in their perceptions of their role in society. Some lawyers see themselves as important cogs in the "adversary system" machine. These lawyers see their role almost exclusively to be the protection and advancement of client interests. As we discuss later in the text, the justification for this narrow view of lawyers' duties is strongest for criminal defense lawyers who represent indigent defendants. If there are substantial resources available for prosecution and few for defense, lawyers might properly focus their energies on the protection of their clients. Criminal defense lawyers in particular often urge that, by focusing on the representation of their clients, they *are* contributing to the improvement of the justice system.

At the other end of the spectrum are lawyers who believe their primary responsibility is to protect our system of justice, to ensure that proceedings are fair, that participants play by the rules, and so on. Lawyers who become judges or who work for judges are in this group. To a lesser degree, so are lawyers who work for government agencies, including prosecutors. In addition, some lawyers in private practice and in nonprofit organizations have a broad view of their public responsibilities. Sometimes lawyers' conceptions of their roles affect the fields in which they work. Some spend their lives, for example, trying to improve access to justice for disadvantaged groups. Sometimes this sense of responsibility affects lawyers' choice of types of work. A "public interest" lawyer might pursue class action litigation rather than individual cases or might work on legislation rather than litigation to produce broader results.

Although some lawyers define their roles closer to one end of the "client-centered" versus "public-centered" spectrum, most lawyers reside somewhere between those poles. Most lawyers take very seriously their duties to their clients, and simultaneously notice aspects of their work that might impact a broader group of people. Very many ethical dilemmas involve some conflict between the interests of a client and the interests of a larger community.

> **FOR EXAMPLE:** Suppose you are representing a client in a products liability suit involving a child's car seat that failed to restrain a child during a car accident because the straps came loose. You know that the defect that your client discovered in the car seat could endanger many other children. If you take the matter to trial, you will have the opportunity to publicize the problem and possibly to obtain an injunction requiring the manufacturer to correct the defect. However, the manufacturer has offered your client an attractive settlement, and your client prefers to accept the offer and put the episode behind her.

In this situation, a lawyer might advise the client of the other interests and considerations that point toward turning down the settlement. But the lawyer should defer to the client's wishes if she wants to accept the settlement. Even if the client wants to settle, there may be other steps that the lawyer could take independent of the work on the client's matter that would assist others who have purchased the same car seat. The perennial problem for many lawyers is that other clients' work awaits, and the possible law reform work is unlikely to generate fees.

This theme of the public interest versus a client's individual interest pops up throughout the text. In Chapter 1, for example, one case describes a lawyer who did not fulfill his duty to report the misconduct of another lawyer because his client did not want him to make a report. In Chapters 2 and 8, we discuss some circumstances in which a lawyer might have confidential information which, if revealed, could prevent or mitigate harm to others or could help to ensure a just outcome in litigation. In Chapter 10, we consider Evans v. Jeff D., an important case in which the Supreme Court made it easier for defendants in individual cases to pressure public interest lawyers into giving up court-awarded counsel fees that might support future public interest activities.

## 4. Lawyers' personal and professional interests versus their fiduciary obligations

Throughout the book are examples of situations in which a lawyers' own interests conflict in some way with her duties to a client. Chapter 7 addresses such conflicts directly, but they arise elsewhere also. In Chapter 2, for example, we discuss the tension between the duty to protect confidences and a lawyer's felt need to share aspects of her working life with her friends. In Chapter 10, we discuss the duty to provide services to clients who cannot afford to pay fees, which is in the public interest but may not be in the lawyer's financial self-interest.

## 5. Self-interest as a theme in regulation of lawyers

In the study of the rules that govern lawyers, especially the ethics codes, one often sees reflections of the drafters' concern for their own or other lawyers' interests. These concerns tend to predominate over attention to the interests of clients, adversaries, the public, or those who cannot afford to hire lawyers. For example, look at Rule 1.5(b), which explains lawyers' duty to inform clients about the basis of fees based on time spent:

> The scope of the representation and the *basis or rate* of the fee and expenses for which the client will be responsible shall be communicated to the client, *preferably* in writing, *before or within a reasonable time after* commencing the representation, *except* when the lawyer will charge a regularly represented client on the same basis or rate. Any changes in the basis or rate of the fee or expenses shall also be communicated to the client.

We italicize the various qualifiers in this rule. A client-centered rule might require disclosure of the amount to be charged before the client hires the lawyer. But this rule requires only disclosure of the "basis or rate" of the fee and expenses. The rule does not specify what must be disclosed, although the comments offer some details on disclosure of what expenses will be separately billed. This rule usually is understood to require disclosure of how much a lawyer plans to charge for each hour worked. It does not require disclosure of whether the lawyer plans to bill only for high-quality research and advocacy time, or whether the lawyer also intends to bill at that rate or some other rate for time spent doing administrative work, "thinking" time, airplane time, or time spent chatting with the client about their children's sporting events. Nor need the lawyer disclose how many hours the lawyer thinks the new matter might require. So a lawyer might comply with the rule but leave the client knowing almost nothing about the fees to be charged.

But there are more hedges. Need the lawyer make this paltry disclosure before the client hires the lawyer? No. The rule requires a lawyer only to inform the client of her hourly rate "before or within a reasonable time after" the lawyer begins the work. Need the lawyer make the disclosure in writing, so that the client has a record of what was said? The rule says no. Writing is preferred, but not required. Does the lawyer have to make a fee rate disclosure at the beginning of each matter undertaken for a client? No, this disclosure is required only if the lawyer has not regularly represented the client on the same basis.

The rule also requires a lawyer to tell the client if the basis or rate of the fee changes. But notice that the rule does not require the lawyer to consult with the client to get permission to raise his rates. Nor does the rule even require notice of an increase in the rate in advance of beginning to bill at a higher rate. A more consumer-oriented rule would disallow changes in the price of the service without the consent of the person charged. But not so for lawyers.

Why is this rule so hedged? One part of the answer is that it was drafted mainly by lawyers and then, in the states that adopted it, approved through a process in which most or all of the participants were lawyers. Perhaps we should not be surprised that many lawyers want maximum latitude and minimum regulation of their financial relationships with their clients.

This rule provides a vivid example of how lawyers' self-interest is expressed in the law governing lawyers. When reading rules and opinions, watch for other examples of rules that give primary attention to the interests of lawyers rather than of clients.

## 6. Lawyers as employees: institutional pressures on ethical judgments

One last theme that comes up often in the text involves lawyers as employees. Many ethical dilemmas are caused or exacerbated by conflicts between a lawyer's obligations under ethics rules or other law and the lawyer's felt duties to her employer. The felt duty to the institution might be to follow an instruction from a senior associate or a partner. Or it might be a felt obligation to keep private information about misconduct, which the rules require to be reported.

This tension is often most acute for lawyers who are recent graduates from law school. New lawyers often have good familiarity with the ethics rules. They may know what the rules say, and they may notice aspects of the work that seem to be inconsistent with what is required by the rules. But new lawyers often have little authority within the institutions where they work, and they have strong incentives to be diligent and loyal and not to criticize the conduct of their superiors. If they do raise questions about ethical problems, they may face retaliation through loss of raises, bonuses, attractive assignments, or promotions. They may even get fired.

In evaluating many problems in this text, you will encounter many ethical dilemmas that require action. In considering what to do, you will often find yourself caught between your duties as a member of the profession and your obligations to your employer institution. By exploring a large number of these problems, you will become more adept at distinguishing those that are serious enough to require action, even when that action might be considered disloyal. You will also develop a repertoire of methods by which you might fulfill your duties to the profession without placing yourself at risk of retaliation.

## C. The structure of this book

Chapter 1 identifies the institutions that make the law governing lawyers and the many relevant bodies of law. These provide an overview of regulation of lawyers. Then Chapter 1 explores a series of issues central to the regulation of lawyers, including admission to the bar, lawyer discipline, and the legal rights and duties of a lawyer in relation to misconduct by another lawyer.

Chapters 2 through 7 focus on lawyers' duties to clients and on lawyer-client relationships. Chapters 2 and 3 cover the lawyer's duty to protect client confidences and the evidence rules that protect attorney-client privilege and lawyer work product. These are related but distinct bodies of law, so Chapter 2 deals with the ethical duty and Chapter 3 deals with attorney-client privilege.

Chapter 4 explains the law of lawyer-client relationships. It covers the rules on how lawyers and clients begin and end their work together and lawyers' duties to clients, including the duties of competence, candor, and diligence. This chapter also examines the allocation of decision-making authority between lawyers and clients.

Chapters 5 and 6 and part of Chapter 7 explore the law on conflicts of interest, which involves questions of confidentiality and of loyalty. The law of conflicts, which is probably the most complex material in the book, includes ethical rules, liability rules, and disqualification rules. Chapter 5 addresses concurrent conflicts between the interests of two or more present clients. Chapter 6 examines conflicts between the interests of present clients and past clients, including conflicts of interest for present or former government lawyers and judges. Chapter 7 addresses conflicts between the interests of lawyers and their own clients, most of which involve money. It covers issues relating to fee arrangements and billing practices, the rules governing care of client money and property, and other issues that raise conflicts between the interests of lawyers and clients.

Chapter 8 looks at lawyers' duties to people who are not their clients. It explains the obligations of truthfulness to courts, adversaries, witnesses, and others. It considers the conflicts that arise between (a) protecting confidences and advocating for a client's interests, and (b) dealing honestly and fairly with everyone else.

Chapter 9 explores the history and composition of the legal profession in the United States. After a brief review of the evolution of the legal profession, we look at the gradual rise in the percentage of U.S. lawyers who are women or members of minority groups (or both). Then we offer some materials on the work environment and quality of life for lawyers in different work settings.

Chapter 10 examines questions about the delivery and distribution of legal services, including limitations on the activities of nonlawyers, limits on competition among lawyers, and the extent to which our society provides and limits legal services to disadvantaged people.

## D. The rules quoted in this book: A note on sources

This book quotes the text of numerous "rules of professional conduct" and their "comments." The American Bar Association (ABA) drafts and issues Model Rules of Professional Conduct and recommends that state courts adopt them as law. Most state courts have adopted the ABA's Model Rules, often with several variations reflecting local policy. Most law students study the Model Rules, not a particular state's variations, because most law schools are populated by students who will practice in many different states. The Model Rules are taught as a proxy for the state rules. Another reason why courses in professional responsibility focus on the Model Rules is that the states require applicants for admission to the bar to take the Multistate Professional Responsibility Examination (MPRE), which tests students on the Model Rules, not on the state variations.[9] One goal of many professional responsibility courses is to prepare the students for the MPRE.

Most law school textbooks on professional responsibility cite the ABA's Model Rules but do not quote them. The practice of not quoting the rules in the texts requires students to use two thick books while preparing for and attending class, the textbook and a supplement containing the text of the

---

9. The correct answers on the MPRE are "governed by the current ABA Model Rules of Professional Conduct." National Conference of Bar Examiners, "The MPRE," *at* http://www.ncbex .org/tests/mpre/mpre.htm (last visited Nov. 13, 2004).

rules. A conscientious student often must refer back and forth between the two books while reading a case or a problem. This is cumbersome. You should possess and consult a copy of the full text of the Model Rules of Professional Conduct, but it should be possible to read a textbook without constantly consulting the supplement. In this text, we quote the language of many of the rules that we discuss.

We asked the American Bar Association for permission to reprint some of the Model Rules and some of the comments in this text.[10] The ABA replied that it "cannot grant [the] request. It is the policy of the ABA and its Center for Professional Responsibility not to permit the reproduction of more than 25% of publications it is selling itself. Moreover, it is the policy of the ABA . . . not to permit reproduction of the Model Rules without the applicable Comments."[11]

The ABA indicated that if we submitted a request to use fewer rules, it might allow us to do so if we also would (a) pay a substantial fee and (b) agree to "reprint all the Comments contained in each Rule."

### Veasey does it

Law is not so easily privatized.[12] Soon after the ABA revised its Model Rules in 2002, Delaware adopted the Model Rules and their official comments as its own rules and comments, with the identical numbering system and with very few variations. Delaware moved more rapidly than the other states not because it is known as the "First State" (having been the first to ratify the Constitution), but probably because its chief justice at the time, E. Norman Veasey, chaired the ABA's Ethics 2000 Commission, which drafted the 2002 revision of the

---

10. Federal, state, and local law is not copyrightable but is considered to be in the public domain. The ABA claims a proprietary interest in the Model Rules even though these rules have official status and are more than mere models in three senses. First, most states have adopted them (with a few variations). Second, as noted above, state governments make study of the Model Rules a legal requirement in that their MPRE, which students must pass to become licensed, tests students on the ABA's Model Rules (not on state variations). Third, the U.S. Department of Education has made the ABA the accrediting body for law schools, and nearly all states require graduation from an ABA-accredited law school as a condition for becoming licensed to practice law. Exercising its federally delegated governmental authority, the ABA requires all law students to study its Model Rules:

> A law school shall require all students in the J.D. degree program to receive instruction in the history, goals, structure, duties, values, and responsibilities of the legal profession and its members, *including instruction in the Model Rules of Professional Conduct of the American Bar Association.* A law school should involve members of the bench and bar in this instruction. (Italics added.)

ABA, Section of Legal Education and Admissions to the Bar, Standards for Approval of Law Schools and Interpretations, Chapter 3, Program of Legal Education, Standard 302, Curriculum, subsection (b), *at* http://www.abanet.org/legaled/standards/chapter3.html (last visited Nov. 13, 2004).

11. Letter to Lisa Lerman from Nicole M. Maggio, Manager, Copyrights & Licensing, American Bar Association, Apr. 7, 2004. Ironically, the ABA posts this same document on the Internet for free public examination. We doubt that our textbook, which discusses only some of the rules and reproduces very few of the drafters' comments, actually competes with sales of ABA publications.

12. Veeck v. S. Bldg. Code Congress Intl., Inc., 293 F.3d 791 (5th Cir. 2002) (en banc) (reproduction of a jurisdiction's code, identifying it as the code of that jurisdiction, does not infringe the copyright of the organization that drafted a Model Code that the jurisdiction enacted).

rules. Many other states have more recently adopted the revised Model Rules and the ABA's comments as their own rules and official comments, again with minor variations. Since the Delaware and other state-adopted rules are in the public domain, we have in most cases quoted and cited state rules that match the Model Rules instead of citing the Model Rules.

Our citation to the rules should be understood as follows. When we reproduce particular rules, we are quoting the *Delaware Lawyers' Rules of Professional Conduct,* not the Model Rules. However, the rules and the comments that we quote from Delaware are *identical* in numbering and wording to the ABA Model Rules and comments. So, for example, where we provide the text of "Rule 1.2" without further elaboration of the citation, we are giving you Delaware Rule 1.2, which happens to be identical to the ABA's Model Rule 1.2.

In a few instances, we quote a rule for which Delaware did not adopt the ABA Model Rule verbatim. In those cases, we quote the Delaware rule and explain how it differs or specify the rule from another state that uses text identical to the corresponding Model Rule. In a few instances, we quote and compare two states' versions of a rule.

## E. Stylistic decisions

We use the following stylistic conventions:

- We indicate in the text which problems are based on real cases. In those problems, we change the names of the lawyers, clients, and other actors.
- In problems and examples, we refer to the lawyers, judges, clients, and other actors as "him," "her," or "him or her." In most cases, the male or female referent is chosen randomly. This is less cumbersome than to use the phrase "him or her" consistently.
- In excerpts from court opinions and articles, we eliminate citations and footnotes without inserting ellipses. We use ellipses where we omit text.
- In evaluating each problem, assume that the relevant jurisdictions have adopted the Model Rules. We do not repeat this point before each problem.
- When we refer to the "Restatement" without specifying a different Restatement (such as the Restatement of Contracts), we mean the American Law Institute's Restatement of the Law Governing Lawyers (Third) (2000).
- In cases, headings in brackets are those that we supply. The headings without brackets appear in the court's opinion.
- In tables that provide the language and brief explanations of ethical rules, the explanations are those of the authors, not of any official source.
- Our citations follow the format of the Association of Legal Writing Directors, ALWD Citation Manual: A Professional System of Citation (Aspen Publishers, 2d ed. 2003), rather than the format of the Blue Book. We have diverged from the ALWD format by putting all references in Roman type and by using the full word "comment" rather than "cmt" in our citations.

# 1 THE REGULATION OF LAWYERS

## A. Institutions that regulate lawyers
1. The highest state courts
2. State and local bar associations
3. Lawyer disciplinary agencies
4. The American Bar Association
5. The American Law Institute
6. Federal and state trial courts
7. Legislatures
8. Administrative agencies
9. Prosecutors
10. Malpractice insurers
11. Law firms and other employers
12. Clients

## B. The law governing lawyers
1. State ethics codes
2. Legal malpractice, breach of contract, and breach of fiduciary duty
3. Motions to disqualify for conflicts of interest
4. Contract law
5. Advisory ethics opinions
6. Research on ethics law

## C. Admission to practice
1. Requirements for admission
2. The bar examination
3. The character and fitness inquiry

## D. Professional discipline
1. The history and process of lawyer discipline
2. Grounds for discipline

E. **Reporting misconduct by other lawyers**
  1. The duty to report misconduct
  2. Lawyers' responsibility for ethical misconduct by colleagues and superiors
  3. Legal protections for subordinate lawyers

The legal profession is formally governed by the highest court in each state, but a large number of other institutions also play roles in the governance of lawyers. The law governing lawyers includes a wide range of ethics codes, statutes, case law, and regulations, as well as rules made by private individuals and organizations, such as clients. The first two sections of this chapter provide a brief guided tour of the primary institutions that govern lawyers and the primary sources of law that govern lawyers.

The third section of the chapter reviews the requirements for admission to the bar, with particular attention paid to the requirement that a person possess the requisite "moral character." This part of the regulatory system is of particular interest to law students, as the "moral character" test could obstruct or delay the admission of applicants to the bar because of certain past behavior. The next section explores the lawyer disciplinary system — the administrative process through which lawyers' licenses to practice are revoked or suspended, or lesser penalties are imposed. One important aspect of this system is the duty imposed on all lawyers to report misconduct by other lawyers.

In the last section of the chapter, we consider the rights of subordinate lawyers in relation to lawyer wrongdoing. Less experienced lawyers are often directed by more senior lawyers, so it is important to know what to do if a conflict arises between what one thinks the law requires and a supervisor's direction.

# A. Institutions that regulate lawyers

## 1. The highest state courts

### a. The responsibility of self-regulation

**Most law is made by legislatures, courts, and administrative agencies. Is this true of "lawyer law" also?**

Lawyers are subject to the law that governs the rest of society, so much of the body of "lawyer law" is created through normal legislative, judicial, or administrative processes.

However, the lawmaking process that produces the ethical rules governing lawyers is a bit different. The legal profession is largely self-regulated; it sets and enforces its own standards of conduct. In most states, the highest court of the state,[1] not the legislature, is responsible for adopting the rules of conduct that govern lawyers. In this respect, the high court performs a role usually played by a legislature. The state's highest court usually consults with the state's bar association in drafting these rules; it may also seek public comment. The bar association, in turn, may invite comment from its lawyer members. Most of the people involved in the writing of the ethical rules, then, are licensed lawyers. Also, the highest court in each state is ultimately responsible for enforcing its rules by disciplining lawyers who violate them. All the judges, of course, are lawyers. Similarly, lawyers bear primary responsibility for seeing that these rules are enforced. The ethical rules require lawyers to report misconduct (their own or that of another lawyer) to the disciplinary agency charged with enforcement of the rules.[2]

## Is the legal profession unique in having the responsibility to regulate itself?

Our society does not allow just any vocational group to make its own rules. For example, legislators and employees of government agencies draft most of the laws and regulations governing operators of auto repair shops and health spas. Some industries, such as the insurance industry, participate very actively in the development of the rules that govern them. But lawyers, like many other *professionals*, set and maintain their own standards of integrity and of performance. And the governmental regulation of lawyers is distinguished from other industries because the courts play such a prominent regulatory role.

## Is it a good idea to give lawyers such a dominant role in regulating their profession?

Maybe not. Many scholars and consumer advocates observe that the rules governing lawyers are more protective of lawyers and impose less regulatory constraint than they would if state legislatures wrote them.[3] We'll explain more about this when we describe the role of the American Bar Association in regulating the profession. But self-regulation is beneficial in that it provides the legal profession with some independence from the state. This is important because lawyers often challenge governmental actions in the course of representing clients. Lawyers raise questions about the validity of statutes and regulations, defend people charged with crimes by the state, and so on. If

---

1. The highest court in most states is called the supreme court. In some states, however, the highest court has a different name. In New York and Maryland, for example, the highest court is called the court of appeals.

2. Rule 8.3. The duty to report misconduct is explained later in this chapter.

3. Restatement (Third) of the Law Governing Lawyers § 1, comment d (2000). One organization that advocates on behalf of consumers of legal services is HALT, which describes itself as "an organization of Americans for legal reform." HALT, *at* http://www.halt.org (last visited Oct. 4, 2004).

lawyers were subject to greater control by the state, they might be restricted in representation of clients whose interests were contrary to those of the government.

> **FOR EXAMPLE:** Many lawyers who represent indigent clients in civil matters are employed by the federally funded Legal Services Corporation, and these advocates are more heavily regulated than most American lawyers. As we will see in Chapter 10, legal services lawyers used to be allowed to represent any client who met their income guidelines, and they could engage in legislative advocacy and class action litigation. However, Congress, wishing to avoid paying lawyers to achieve results that are contrary to federal policy, repeatedly has imposed restrictions on the work of legal services lawyers, prohibiting legislative advocacy, participation in class action suits, and many particular types of cases.

### How do state courts regulate lawyers?

The highest court in each state usually performs the following roles, though it sometimes delegates one or more to other government agencies. It

- adopts ethics codes and court procedural rules that govern lawyers;
- sets and implements standards for licensing of lawyers, including what educational and moral character requirements to impose (covered in more detail in Section C3); and
- supervises agencies that investigate and prosecute complaints of unethical conduct by lawyers; and
- supervises administrative judicial bodies that impose sanctions on lawyers who violate the ethics codes.

A license to practice law in one state does not entitle a lawyer to practice law across the border in the next state. Also, the ethical and procedural rules that govern lawyers vary from one state to another. So a lawyer who is licensed in both Wyoming and South Dakota is expected to know the rules of both jurisdictions. She is also expected to know when she is subject to the rules of one jurisdiction and when the other.[4]

## b. The inherent powers doctrine

The regulation of lawyers by courts is an exception to the usual principle that rules of law should be made by democratically elected representatives of the people. Under a traditional view of separation of powers, legislatures make law, the executive branch implements the law, and the courts interpret the law. At least with respect to ethical and procedural rules, the courts make the rules,

---

4. Actually, it isn't always possible to know which of two conflicting state rules applies, though this task is made much easier by Rule 8.5, which provides guidance for lawyers who are licensed in one state but undertake permitted activities in a state that has different ethical rules.

implement the rules, interpret the rules, enforce the rules, and hear challenges
to the validity of those rules.

| Roles of branches of government | | |
|---|---|---|
| **Branch of Government** | **Normal role** | **Role in governance of lawyers** |
| **Legislative branch** | Makes the law by adopting legislation | Passes some statutes that apply to lawyers |
| **Executive branch** | Implements the law through agency action | Adopts and implements some regulations and policies that apply to lawyers |
| **Judicial branch** | Interprets law and makes common law | Makes the law by adopting ethics codes, implements the law through delegation to bar associations, and interprets the law through court decisions in cases involving discipline, malpractice, disqualification, and other matters |

### Why are the courts mainly responsible for regulation of lawyers?

Courts claim the authority to regulate lawyers as an aspect of their authority
to administer the courts. In a few states, the state constitution expressly
assigns to the courts authority to regulate the conduct of lawyers.[5] In states
in which the constitution doesn't expressly delegate this power to the judiciary,
the courts claim that they have the inherent authority to regulate the
conduct of the lawyers as a matter of common law because the courts need
the authority to govern the conduct of those who appear before them. This is
the "inherent powers" doctrine.[6] The ethical rules govern both in-court and
out-of-court behavior, and they govern lawyer behavior even if the lawyer is
advising a client or assisting with a transaction or other work that is unrelated
to litigation.

### Can the legislature pass a bill to change a court rule, as it does when it wants to change the common law?

Not everywhere. Some state courts have asserted that their regulatory authority
over lawyers is *exclusive* of other branches of government. This version of the

---

5. Restatement § 1, comment c, reporter's note.

6. For discussions of the inherent powers doctrine, see, e.g., Benjamin H. Barton, An
Institutional Analysis of Lawyer Regulation: Who Should Control Lawyer Regulation — Courts,
Legislatures, or the Market? 37 Ga. L. Rev. 1167 (2003); Charles W. Wolfram, Toward a History
of the Legalization of American Legal Ethics II — The Modern Era, 15 Geo. J. Leg. Ethics 205 (2002);
Charles W. Wolfram, Lawyer Turf and Lawyer Regulation — The Role of the Inherent Powers
Doctrine, 12 UALR L.J. 1 (1989-1990).

inherent powers doctrine is called the "negative inherent powers" doctrine. Based on this rationale, some courts have invalidated legislation regulating lawyers.[7] The cases in this arena most often strike down laws allowing non-lawyers to engage in some activity that overlaps with the practice of law, such as drafting documents for the sale of real estate or handling hearings before administrative agencies.[8]

> **FOR EXAMPLE:** The legislature of Kentucky passed a statute that authorized nonlawyers to represent workers' compensation claimants in administrative hearings. But the state's supreme court said that the law violated the state constitution, which gave the supreme court exclusive power to regulate the practice of law.[9]

> **FOR EXAMPLE:** The Pennsylvania Supreme Court invalidated a statute that made it a misdemeanor offense for a lawyer to pay another person to recommend the lawyer's services to a prospective client.[10] The court said that the law intruded on the judicial authority to regulate lawyers because it was directed only to lawyers rather than to the general public (the latter would have been proper). That decision wasn't very significant, though, because the court's own ethics rules also prohibited lawyers from paying agents to solicit clients for them.[11]

## Do all state courts claim exclusive authority to regulate lawyers?

Even though some state courts say that their power to regulate lawyers is exclusive of other branches of government, some state court decisions acknowledge that, in fact, all three branches of government play roles in the regulation of lawyers.[12] Also, many statutes regulating lawyers have been adopted and implemented without objection. For example, the "negative inherent powers" doctrine has not been asserted to invalidate any of the recent state statutes authorizing law firms to reorganize as limited liability partnerships (LLPs) and thereby to protect lawyers from vicarious liability for some acts of their partners.[13] As statutes regulating lawyers proliferate, the courts may become more accepting of the idea that law is a business like many others, and that legislatures have a valid interest in protecting consumers of legal

---

7. Charles W. Wolfram, Modern Legal Ethics 27-28 (West 1986).

8. See the examples discussed in Nathan M. Crystal, Core Values: False and True, 70 Fordham L. Rev. 747 (2001) (urging that the negative inherent powers doctrine impedes the ability of legislatures to act to improve the availability of legal services to those who are not affluent).

9. Turner v. Kentucky Bar Assn., 980 S.W.2d 560 (Ky. 1998), discussed in Crystal, supra n. 8, at 766-767.

10. Commonwealth v. Stern, 701 A.2d 568 (Pa. 1997), discussed in Charles W. Wolfram, Inherent Powers in the Crucible of Lawyer Self-Protection: Reflections on the LLP Campaign, 39 S. Tex. L. Rev. 359, 376 (1998).

11. *Stern*, 701 A.2d at 571.

12. Restatement § 1, comment c, reporter's note.

13. See generally Wolfram, supra n. 10.

services. They may therefore become more reluctant to assert that their power to regulate lawyers is exclusive of other branches of government.

## 2. State and local bar associations

Most state bar associations are organized as private nonprofit organizations, but some have governmental functions. While the states' highest courts are formally responsible for the regulation of lawyers, some courts delegate lawyer regulatory functions to state bar associations. State bars often administer bar exams and review candidates for admission. Historically, the state bar associations had an important role in establishing lawyer disciplinary systems.[14] A state bar that accepts delegated functions from the state's highest court is called an integrated or unified bar rather than a voluntary bar. In unified state bars, membership is mandatory.[15]

A lawyer may be required to be a member of a bar association as a condition of obtaining a license to practice law.[16] Most bar associations have numerous committees that draft ethical rules, write advisory opinions interpreting the rules, and undertake law reform activities in many different fields of law.[17] Bar associations do not require their members to participate in association activities (except for continuing legal education), but many members choose to participate because they want to be involved in law reform work. Some lawyers participate in bar association activities for other reasons — to meet people, to keep up in their fields, or to obtain client referrals.

### Does each state have only one bar association?

No. In addition to the state organizations, there are many voluntary bar associations — city and county bar associations, bar associations for women and minorities, bar associations for lawyers in particular fields, and so on. With the exception of the patent bar, which has a separate licensing exam, a lawyer is not required to join any voluntary bar association to practice in a particular area.

## 3. Lawyer disciplinary agencies

Lawyer disciplinary agencies (often called bar counsel's offices or disciplinary counsels) bear the responsibility for investigating and prosecuting misconduct

---

14. See Wolfram, History of Legalization, supra n. 6, at 217.

15. See Levine v. Heffernan, 864 F.2d 457 (7th Cir. 1988), *cert. denied*, 493 U.S. 873 (1989) (finding no constitutional violation where lawyers licensed in a state were required to belong to a bar association).

16. This requirement was challenged as a violation of the constitutional right to free association, but the requirement was upheld in Lathrop v. Donohue, 367 U.S. 820 (1961).

17. The State Bar of Georgia, for example, lists among its committees one that helps indigents to access legal representation and another that helps convicted defendants on death row find

that violates the state ethics code. Possible sanctions include disbarment, suspension, and public or private reprimand. These agencies are usually run by the highest court in the state, by the state bar association, or by the court and the state bar. The disciplinary process is explained in detail in Section D of this chapter.

A large body of published opinions in disciplinary cases is helpful in interpreting and applying the ethics codes.[18] Many of these opinions are available on Lexis or Westlaw. Both services have databases organized by subject area. The relevant Lexis file is called "Ethics"; the relevant Westlaw file is called "Legal Ethics and Professional Responsibility."

> **FOR EXAMPLE:** One Maryland lawyer was suspended from practice after he was found to have spanked his secretaries and his clients at the office, sometimes putting them over his knees and baring their bottoms. This opinion was reported because the case was appealed.[19]

## 4. The American Bar Association

The American Bar Association (ABA) is a private nonprofit membership organization founded in 1878.[20] The state bar associations are independent of, not subordinate to, the ABA, although a majority of the membership of the ABA House of Delegates (the main governing unit) is selected by state and local bar associations.[21] Each ABA member pays an annual membership fee.[22] The ABA has over 400,000 lawyer members.[23] Although the primary drafter of lawyer ethics codes, the ABA has only limited governmental authority.[24] That's why

---

lawyers for postconviction proceedings. State Bar of Georgia, *at* http://www.gabar.org/committeeslist.asp?Header=Commspecial (last visited Oct. 4, 2004).

18. Many disciplinary committees and administrative disciplinary agencies (which handle appeals from the hearing committees) write opinions in all cases, but these opinions usually are not published. However, copies of unpublished opinions are often available by calling the disciplinary agency that handled a particular matter.

19. Atty. Grievance Commn. v. Goldsborough, 624 A.2d 503 (Md. 1993). Some disciplinary cases, like this one, involve conduct that violates the ethics code and other law. Other cases involve conduct that violates only the ethics code. See Sneed v. Bd. of Prof. Resp., 37 S.W.3d 886 (Tenn. 2000) (lawyer suspended for negligently failing to follow up on clients' cases).

20. Wolfram, supra n. 7, at 34.

21. ABA, ABA Leadership, House of Delegates, *at* http://www.abanet.org/leadership/delegates.html (last visited Oct. 14, 2004).

22. As of 2004, any lawyer with ten or more years of experience who wished to join the ABA paid annual dues of $350. A lawyer with fewer years of experience paid lower dues. For the first year after a lawyer is admitted to the bar, ABA membership is free. ABA, *at* http://www.abanet.org/members/join/ (last visited Oct. 14, 2004).

23. ABA, About the ABA, *at* http://www.abanet.org/about/home.html (last visited Oct. 14, 2004).

24. For example, the ABA is recognized by the U.S. Department of Education as the organization that provides accreditation to law schools. ABA, The ABA's Role in the Law School Accreditation Process, *at* http://www.abanet.org/legaled/accreditation/abarole.html (last visited Oct. 4, 2004).

the ABA ethics rules are called the Model Rules of Professional Conduct.[25] These rules have no legal force[26] unless they are adopted by the relevant governmental authority, usually a state's highest court.

### How are ethics rules written and adopted?

Usually, an ABA committee drafts a model rule or a set of revisions to the existing rules. Next the model rule is debated and approved by the ABA as a whole through its House of Delegates at one of its twice-yearly national meetings. Committees of the state bar associations then review these model rules, sometimes at the request of their state's highest court. The state bar committee or the court may solicit comments from members of the bar and from the public. Ultimately, the state's highest court accepts, rejects, or amends the rule. The court is under no duty to consider a rule just because it was proposed by the ABA or analyzed by a state bar association. However, the ABA's work strongly influences the views of most state bar associations, and courts.

Some ABA decisions about ethical rules are controversial, particularly when the Association appears to protect lawyers at the expense of clients. In fact, on some occasions when the ABA's House of Delegates has considered proposals by its committees to change the rules to better protect client interests, the House has rejected the proposals as being unnecessarily intrusive on lawyer discretion.[27]

## 5. The American Law Institute

The American Law Institute (ALI) is a private organization of 3,000 judges, lawyers, and law teachers that produces summaries of the law called Restatements. During the 1990s, the ALI wrote the *Restatement* (Third) *of the Law Governing Lawyers*, which summarizes the rules of law that govern lawyers. The Restatement includes rules governing malpractice liability to

---

25. Wolfram, supra n. 7, at 57. Wolfram explains that the word *Model* was added to the earlier version of the ABA rules as one term of a settlement of a lawsuit brought by the U.S. Department of Justice against the ABA. The Department of Justice had charged the ABA with attempting to regulate lawyers in a manner that violated the federal antitrust laws.

26. It is asserted sometimes that ethics codes do not have the force of law. See, e.g., Neisig v. Team 1, 76 N.Y.2d 363, 369 (1990) ("While unquestionably important, and respected by the courts, the [N.Y. Code of Professional Responsibility] does not have the force of law."). Despite the tradition of regarding ethical rules as "guidelines to be applied with due regard for the broad range of interests at stake," id., it is undeniable that compliance with ethical rules is mandatory for lawyers and that noncompliance leads in many cases to suspension or disbarment. The "force of law" is usually understood to refer to consequences for violation. Viewed in this light, the ethical rules — at least those that require or prohibit certain conduct — clearly have the force of law.

27. One example is the recent rejection by the House of Delegates of the ABA Ethics 2000 Commission's proposal that lawyers should be required to communicate the basis or rate of their fees to clients in writing. See ABA, Center for Professional Responsibility, Summary of House of Delegates Action on Ethics 2000 Commission Report, *available at* http://www.abanet.org/cpr/e2k-summary_2002.html (last visited Oct. 4, 2004) (reporting House of Delegates August 2002 adoption of an amendment to remove the writing requirement proposed by the Ethics 2000 Commission from Model Rule 1.5 on fees).

clients and third parties, rules governing disqualification of lawyers for conflicts of interest, and ethical rules for violation of which a lawyer may be subject to discipline. The Restatement also covers the evidentiary rules on attorney-client privilege, the criminal law governing lawyers, the law of unauthorized practice, and many other topics.

The Restatement includes black-letter rules, which often summarize the rule followed in a majority of jurisdictions.[28] The black-letter rules are followed by textual comments that explain them and by Reporter's Notes, which provide citations to court decisions, statutes, books, and articles on each topic addressed. A practicing lawyer is well advised to keep a copy of the *Restatement of the Law Governing Lawyers* for reference. The Restatement isn't law, but it includes much more information and reasoning than either the ABA Model Rules or the comments (annotations) on those rules.

### Is the Restatement consistent with the Model Rules?

Not always. In some instances, the Restatement's summary of the law appears at odds with a Model Rule or with a rule adopted by some states. In these instances, the comments in the Restatement usually note the discrepancy and explain why the authors of the Restatement take a different position. Sometimes the Restatement diverges from the ethical rules because the liability rules differ from the ethical rules, because the authors of the Restatement do not agree with the ABA about what the rule should be, or because the Restatement is more specific than the Model Rules. For example, in an ex parte hearing (one in which the adverse party is not present), Rule 3.3(d) requires a lawyer to reveal all material facts to the judge, even those adverse to her client. The rule does not explicitly create an exception for privileged information, but the Restatement takes the position that privileged information is exempt from this requirement.[29]

### When a state ethics rule and the Restatement are inconsistent, shouldn't a lawyer always follow the state rule?

It's not so simple. Many ethical questions are not addressed by the ethical rules or are addressed only in general terms. If a state ethics rule clearly requires or prohibits certain conduct, in most cases a lawyer should follow the rule. On rare occasions a lawyer might decide to violate a rule because compliance seems inconsistent with the lawyer's own ethical judgment. More often, a lawyer will find that the text of the state's ethical rule does not really provide guidance on the specific problem that the lawyer is facing. Then the lawyer must seek additional guidance from sources such as the commentary in the Restatement.

---

28. See Geoffrey C. Hazard Jr. & W. William Hodes, The Law of Lawyering § 1.19 (3d ed., Aspen L. & Bus. 2002). The mission of the ALI is "to promote the clarification and simplification of the law and its better adaptation to social needs." ALI, *at* http://www.ali.org (last visited Oct. 5, 2004).

29. Restatement § 112, comment b.

## 6. Federal and state trial courts

State and federal trial courts play important roles in the regulation of lawyers by setting rules for the conduct of lawyers in litigation, by sanctioning lawyers who violate those rules, and by hearing and deciding motions to disqualify lawyers who may have conflicts of interest that preclude their representation of particular clients.

A judge who becomes aware of lawyer misconduct in a matter before the court may sanction the lawyer directly under the federal or state civil procedure rules. For example, the court may hold a lawyer in contempt or may impose sanctions for obstructive behavior during discovery. Sanctions include fines, fee forfeiture, or other penalties. The judge must report the misconduct to the lawyer disciplinary agency if the misconduct violates an ethical rule that "raises a substantial question as to that lawyer's honesty, trustworthiness or fitness as a lawyer in other respects."[30]

Federal courts in each jurisdiction adopt their own standards of admission, and some adopt their own ethical rules.[31] Many federal courts adopt the same ethical rules that are in force in the states in which they are located. Some adopt additional rules of practice. Federal courts impose sanctions on lawyers who engage in misconduct in the course of federal litigation.[32]

### Is a member of a state bar automatically allowed to practice in the federal courts of that state?

No. Each federal district court and court of appeals requires lawyers to be admitted to practice before it. But applicants for admission to practice in the federal courts are not required to take another bar exam. Usually any licensed lawyer who applies and pays a fee is admitted to practice before the federal court.[33]

## 7. Legislatures

Despite the inherent powers doctrine, Congress and the state legislatures play a major role in the regulation of lawyers. Legislatures adopt constitutions and

---

30. Model Code of Judicial Conduct Canon 3(D)(2) (as amended, 2003). This language is in the rules that govern judges in most states. The rule requires judges to take "appropriate action" upon receiving information "indicating a substantial likelihood" that a lawyer has violated the rules of professional conduct. An accompanying comment states that "appropriate action" may include reporting the lawyer to disciplinary authorities.

31. Judith A. McMorrow & Daniel R. Coquillette, Moore's Federal Practice: The Federal Law of Attorney Conduct § 801 (3d ed., Matthew Bender 2001).

32. For a discussion of the sources of the federal courts' authority to regulate lawyers, see Fred C. Zacharias & Bruce A. Green, Federal Court Authority to Regulate Lawyers: A Practice in Search of a Theory, 56 Vand. L. Rev. 1303 (2003).

33. Some federal courts condition admission to practice before them on admission to the bar in the states in which the courts are located. Others condition admission to practice on admission before some other state or federal court. McMorrow & Coquillette, supra n. 30, at § 801.20[3].

statutes, including criminal laws, banking laws, securities laws, and so on, that apply to everyone doing business in the state, including lawyers.[34] Some state consumer protection laws explicitly govern lawyers, while others exempt lawyers.[35] In New York and California, statutory law governing lawyers is extensive and addresses some topics that are covered by the ethics codes in other states. Also, a majority of states have statutes that make it a misdemeanor to engage in the unauthorized practice of law (UPL).[36]

### Are lawyers who testify at legislative hearings or meet with legislators on behalf of clients required to comply with additional statutes and regulations?

Yes, in some cases. Usually a lawyer may appear at a legislative hearing without any "admission" process, but federal and some state law requires lawyers who engage in legislative advocacy for profit to register as lobbyists and to report financial and other information about their activities. Federal law imposes additional conflict of interest rules on those who engage in lobbying and requires a separate registration process for lobbyists who represent foreign nations.

---

34. Restatement § 8 (pointing out that with the exception of "traditional and appropriate activities of a lawyer in representing a client in accordance with the requirements of the applicable lawyer code," lawyers are subject to criminal law to the same extent as nonlawyers). See Bruce A. Green, The Criminal Regulation of Lawyers, 67 Fordham L. Rev. 327 (1998); Ted Schneyer, Legal Process Scholarship and the Regulation of Lawyers, 65 Fordham L. Rev. 33 (1996); Charles W. Wolfram, Lawyer Crime: Beyond the Law, 36 Val. U. L. Rev. 73 (2001).

35. See Manuel R. Ramos, Legal Malpractice: Reforming Lawyers and Law Professors, 70 Tul. L. Rev. 2583, 2599 (1996) (noting that most state consumer protection laws exempt lawyers because "the lawyers are supposedly regulating themselves"). Cf. Stewart Macaulay, Lawyers and Consumer Protection Laws, 4 L. & Socy. Rev. 115 (1979).

36. About 40 states have criminal statutes prohibiting UPL. See Attorneys' Liability Assurance Society, Inc., Statutes and Rules Limiting Multijurisdictional Law Practice from 51 United States Jurisdictions (compiled for the American Bar Association Symposium on the Multijurisdictional Practice of Law March 10-11, 2000), *available at* http://www.abanet.org/cpr/mjp-uplrules.html (last visited Oct. 6, 2004).

The UPL provisions of each state are found *at* http://www.crossingthebar.com/upl.htm (last visited Oct. 6, 2004). One example of a criminal UPL statute is California's, which provides in part that:

> (a) Any person advertising or holding himself or herself out as practicing or entitled to practice law or otherwise practicing law who is not an active member of the State Bar, or otherwise authorized pursuant to statute or court rule to practice law in this state at the time of doing so, is guilty of a misdemeanor punishable by up to one year in a county jail or by a fine of up to one thousand dollars ($1,000), or by both that fine and imprisonment. . . .

Cal. Bus. & Prof. Code § 6126 (West 1992 & Supp. 2004). In a few states, UPL may be prosecuted as a felony. See, e.g., S.C. Code Ann. § 40-5-310 (1991 & Supp. 2003). However, criminal prosecution for UPL is uncommon. See ABA/BNA Lawyers' Man. on Prof. Conduct 21:8008 (1984).

## 8. Administrative agencies

### Do lawyers need separate admission to practice before an administrative agency?

Generally speaking, lawyers admitted to practice in any state may appear before an agency of that state, and before any federal agency, without filing a separate application for admission.[37]

### Do administrative agencies impose additional ethical or procedural rules on lawyers who appear before them?

In many cases, the answer is yes. Some federal agencies, including the Securities and Exchange Commission, require lawyers who appear before them to comply with their administrative regulations, which may impose duties (such as responsibility to assure that material information is not omitted from papers filed before the agency)[38] in addition to the duties imposed by the ethics codes and other law. Lawyers who engage in misconduct in practice before these agencies may be subject to civil or criminal penalties.[39] Some agencies, such as the Justice Department's Executive Office for Immigration Review, also have their own ethical rules for practitioners.[40]

> **FOR EXAMPLE:** The large law firm of Kaye, Scholer, Fierman, Hays & Handler was the object of a 1992 administrative action by the Office of Thrift Supervision (OTS), a federal banking agency. The firm had assisted one savings and loan bank in reports to bank examiners. Those reports, the OTS alleged, included some misleading information and omitted some material information. OTS sought $275 million in compensation from the firm. When the administrative action was initiated, an order was issued freezing the firm's assets to prevent their transfer until the matter was resolved. The law firm settled the matter within a week after the charges by agreeing to pay $41 million to the OTS.[41]

## 9. Prosecutors

An increasing number of lawyers are indicted and prosecuted each year for crimes, some of which were committed in the course of practicing law.[42] Prosecutors have enormous discretion as to whether to file charges against a particular defendant. Prosecutors may once have been reluctant to charge lawyers as defendants, but any reservations about prosecuting lawyers

37. 5 U.S.C. § 500 (2004). See Wolfram, History of Legalization, supra n. 6, at 219 n. 48.
38. See, e.g., 17 C.F.R. § 205.3 (2004).
39. Id.
40. 8 C.F.R. § 1003.101-109 (2004).
41. Sharon Walsh, Law Firm Settles S & L Complaint, Wash. Post, Mar. 9, 1992, at A5.
42. See generally Green, supra n. 34.

evaporated in the last quarter of the twentieth century. The beginning of this cultural change was the Watergate scandal in which 29 lawyers, including high government officials, were convicted of felonies, named as unindicted co-conspirators, or otherwise disciplined for misconduct related to efforts to reelect President Nixon.[43] Ten years later, several prominent savings and loan associations collapsed, and lawyers were found to have participated in some fashion in the perpetration of massive financial frauds. The federal banking agencies, seeking to recoup some of the losses resulting from these frauds, indicted scores of lawyers and accountants who had served the savings and loan associations.[44] These events shattered public assumptions that lawyers would never be involved in criminal activity. At the same time, the disciplinary agencies were becoming better staffed and more effective, and some of the disciplinary investigations sparked criminal investigations. During the 1990s, prosecutors indicted a rising number of lawyers, including several affluent partners of large law firms.[45] One recent reflection of this trend was the establishment of a Justice System Integrity Division in the Los Angeles District Attorney's office. The primary mandate of this special unit is to prosecute crimes by police officers, judges, and lawyers.[46]

## 10. Malpractice insurers

The insurance industry doesn't merely sell insurance. Companies that provide malpractice insurance to lawyers set conditions for obtaining the insurance. These rules form a body of "private law" that governs lawyers who contract with those companies. A malpractice insurer may require a law firm that it insures to adopt a system to guard against conflicts of interest, or it may insist that senior partners must review all opinion letters that the firm sends to its clients. It may require a firm to have a "tickler" system to help prevent lawyers from missing deadlines. It may demand many other structures designed for the purpose of "loss prevention." This coy term refers to steps that can be taken to prevent a lawyer or a law firm from being held liable for malpractice. Many of the practices and procedures that prevent malpractice liability also promote compliance with ethical rules.

---

43. N.O.B.C. Reports on Results of Watergate-Related Charges Against Twenty-nine Lawyers, 62 A.B.A. J. 1337 (1976).

44. For an exploration of the roles of lawyers in the savings and loan scandal, see Symposium, The Attorney-Client Relationship in a Regulated Society, 35 S. Tex. L. Rev. 571 (1994); James O. Johnson Jr. & Daniel Scott Schecter, In the Matter of Kaye, Scholer, Fierman, Hays & Handler: A Symposium on Government Regulation, Lawyers' Ethics, and the Rule of Law, 66 S. Cal. L. Rev. 977 (1993); Susan P. Koniak, When the Hurlyburly's Done: The Bar's Struggle with the SEC, 103 Colum. L. Rev. 1236 (2003).

45. Some examples of such cases are discussed in Lisa G. Lerman, Blue-Chip Bilking: Regulation of Billing and Expense Fraud by Lawyers, 12 Geo. J. Leg. Ethics 205 (1999).

46. Richard Marosi & Anna Gorman, D.A. Gets Tough on Corrupt Lawyers, L.A. Times, Nov. 10, 2003, at B1; see also Los Angeles District Attorney's Office, Justice System Integrity Division, at http://da.co.la.ca.us/jsid.htm#attorney (last visited Oct. 6, 2003).

Some malpractice insurers provide advice to lawyers at the firms they insure. Some conduct audits to verify compliance with conditions of the insurance contracts. Often the advice given involves ethical or professional dilemmas that could mushroom into lawsuits or disciplinary proceedings. With careful management, these crises are often resolved. This guidance to and supervision of law firms by insurers is an important, though nongovernmental, form of regulation. Some scholars urge that the regulatory behavior of malpractice insurers has more impact on practicing lawyers than the prospect of discipline by a public agency.[47]

## 11. Law firms and other employers

While one responsibility of every organization that employs lawyers is to ensure compliance with ethical rules and other law, many employers have their own additional rules of practice. Some larger law firms have developed a comprehensive "ethical infrastructure" to provide lawyers and nonlawyers with training, offer expert advice about ethics and liability questions, and prevent conflicts of interest. Many such firms designate one or more lawyers to be "ethics counsel" or "loss prevention counsel," or both. Other large firms form ethics committees. These structures help to establish and maintain a positive ethical culture within the firms.[48]

Law firms and government agencies sometimes have stricter procedures to ensure confidentiality than those imposed by the state ethics code.[49] These complex procedures often implement confidentiality requirements that are nowhere mandated by law. Likewise, many firms have policies on file maintenance, consultation with other lawyers, time-keeping, and other issues. Like the "rules" made by malpractice insurers, these are a type of "private" law. They constrain lawyer employees as do rules of law, but they are imposed by a contract rather than by a licensing authority or legislature.

---

47. See, e.g., Anthony E. Davis, Professional Liability Insurers as Regulators of Law Practice, 65 Fordham L. Rev. 209 (1996); John Leubsdorf, Legal Malpractice and Professional Responsibility, 48 Rutgers L. Rev. 101 (1995); Ramos, supra n. 35, at 2591-2599; David B. Wilkins, Who Should Regulate Lawyers?, 105 Harv. L. Rev. 799 (1992).

48. Some of the recent articles chronicling this important development in private law practice include Elizabeth Chambliss & David B. Wilkins, Promoting Effective Ethical Infrastructure in Large Law Firms: A Call for Research and Reporting, 30 Hofstra L. Rev. 691, 710-711 (2002); Elizabeth Chambliss & David B. Wilkins, The Emerging Role of Ethics Advisors, General Counsel, and Other Compliance Specialists in Large Law Firms, 44 Ariz. L. Rev. 559 (2002); Susan S. Fortney & Jett Hanna, Fortifying a Law Firm's Ethical Infrastructure: Avoiding Legal Malpractice Claims Based on Conflicts of Interest, 33 St. Mary's L.J. 669, 690 (2002); Peter R. Jarvis & Mark J. Fucile, Inside an In-House Legal Ethics Practice, 14 Notre Dame J.L. Ethics & Pub. Policy 103 (2000); Ted Schneyer, A Tale of Four Systems: Reflections on How Law Influences the "Ethical Infrastructure" of Law Firms, 39 S. Tex. L. Rev. 245 (1998).

49. Students who work as externs at government agencies, for example, are sometimes prohibited from carrying documents out of the office or from talking with anyone about the substance of the matters that they are working on. See generally Alexis Anderson, Arlene Kanter & Cindy Slane, Ethics in Externships: Confidentiality, Conflicts, and Competence Issues in the Field and in the Classroom, 10 Clin. L. Rev. 473 (2004).

## 12. Clients

Many individual clients have very little ability to "regulate" their lawyers. Large corporations and government agencies, however, are major consumers of legal services. They have a great deal of bargaining power in dealing with law firms. A federal agency, for example, might make a policy prohibiting lawyers from doing "block billing" in which a lawyer records time worked on a matter in eight-hour blocks without specifying what tasks were performed during each block. An insurance company might impose a policy prohibiting outside counsel from billing more than ten hours of paralegal time on each case. Many institutional clients have lengthy and detailed policies. Law firms that work for those corporations must agree to comply with these policies as a condition of their employment. Institutional clients also may insist on some oversight of the lawyers who represent them. For example, some hire outside auditors to review the work performed and the bills submitted.[50]

Institutional clients, then, have a quasi-regulatory role in relation to the law firms that they employ. Like malpractice insurers, they sometimes set conditions that are similar to rules imposed by government agencies. Because law firms have strong incentives to attract and retain large institutional clients, they are motivated to comply with the guidelines articulated by these clients.

| Who Regulates Lawyers? | | |
|---|---|---|
| **Institution** | **Role of institution in regulating lawyers** | **Examples of regulatory function** |
| **Highest court in each state** | The states' highest courts have the inherent power to regulate lawyers (the inherent powers doctrine). | • Adopt codes of ethics<br>• Adopt court rules<br>• License lawyers<br>• Impose disciplinary sanctions on lawyers |
| **Other state courts** | Other state trial and appellate courts adopt procedural rules, impose sanctions for misconduct under their own rules of procedure, disqualify lawyers based on conflicts of interest, review and decide petitions for fees pursuant to fee-shifting statutes. | |
| **State bar associations** | States' highest courts delegate some functions to bar associations or to other organizations. | • Administer bar exams<br>• Some run disciplinary agencies<br>• Set up ethics committees to write opinions interpreting ethical rules |

---

50. See generally Roy Simon, Conference on Gross Profits: Gross Profits? An Introduction to a Program on Legal Fees, 22 Hofstra L. Rev. 625 (1994).

| Institution | Role of institution in regulating lawyers | Examples of regulatory function |
|---|---|---|
| Lawyer disciplinary agencies | Disciplinary agencies (often called offices of the bar counsel) investigate and prosecute alleged misconduct by lawyers. | |
| American Bar Association | The ABA is a private nongovernmental organization which produces model ethical rules and ethics opinions. | ABA Model Rules of Professional Conduct (see http://www.abanet.org) |
| American Law Institute | The ALI is a private organization of lawyers that produces summaries of the law called Restatements. | Restatement (Third) of the Law Governing Lawyers (1998) (see http://www.ali.org) |
| Federal courts | Federal courts admit lawyers to practice before them, adopt procedural rules and ethical rules, impose sanctions for misconduct under their rules, disqualify lawyers based on conflicts of interest, review and decide petitions for fees pursuant to fee-shifting statutes. | Federal Rules of Civil Procedure 11 and 26 include ethical standards and sanctions authority |
| Legislatures | Despite the inherent powers doctrine, much law adopted by legislatures governs lawyers. Also, legislative bodies may impose ethical or procedural rules on lawyers who appear before them. | |
| Administrative agencies | Federal and state agencies admit lawyers to practice before them without a separate bar exam. Some impose their own ethics regulations on lawyers. | |
| Prosecutors | Prosecutors have the authority (and the discretion) to bring criminal charges against lawyers for crimes committed in or out of practice. | |

*Continued*

| Institution | Role of institution in regulating lawyers | Examples of regulatory function |
|---|---|---|
| **Malpractice insurers** | Companies that provide malpractice insurance to lawyers set conditions for obtaining insurance. These rules form a body of 'private law' that governs lawyers who contract with those companies. | For example, a malpractice insurer may require a<br>• Conflicts checking system<br>• Review of opinion letters by senior people<br>• Tickler system |
| **Law firms and other employers** | Law firms and other organizations that employ lawyers adopt internal rules and standards of practice that regulate lawyers employed by each organization. | |
| **Clients** | Many clients (especially government agencies and large corporations) impose rules of conduct on the lawyers they employ. | For example, some institutional clients:<br>• Prohibit block billing<br>• Disallow billing for the time of a second or third lawyer at a deposition<br>• Use auditors to monitor the work of lawyers |

# B. The law governing lawyers

We have looked briefly at the institutions that govern lawyers. In the course of that discussion, we have referred to some of the bodies of law (such as the ethics codes and criminal law) that govern lawyers. In this section, we offer additional information about some of the statutes, rules, common law, and administrative rules that govern lawyers.[51]

---

51. Some of the bodies of law that govern lawyers, such as criminal law, court rules of procedure, administrative agency rules, and others, are discussed in Section A of this chapter. Except in the table at the end of this section, we do not reinventory them here but instead offer further discussion about those that don't fall neatly within the responsibility of a single institution. The ethics codes, for example, are created through processes that involve the American Bar Association, the highest state courts, and the bar associations.

# 1. State ethics codes

*Professor George Sharswood*

The American Bar Association (ABA) adopted its first set of Canons of Ethics in 1908.[52] These were mostly exhortations to lawyers of "best practices," based in large part on an ethics code that had been adopted in Alabama.[53] The Alabama ethics code, in turn, was derived in part from a set of lectures given by George Sharswood and published in 1854.[54]

Professor Sharswood's work was influenced by a set of "Fifty Resolutions" about ethical practice of law published in 1836 by a lawyer from Baltimore named David Hoffman.[55] While some states treated the canons as a set of mandatory rules, others treated them only as nonbinding guidance for lawyers.[56]

In the 1960s, Justice Lewis F. Powell, then in private practice, led a move within the ABA to rewrite the canons. This produced the ABA Model Code of Professional Responsibility, adopted by the ABA in 1969. This code was quickly adopted almost without change by courts in the vast majority of states, superseding the 1908 Canons.[57] Suddenly, the standards for lawyers became a lot more like binding "law."

*Justice Lewis F. Powell*

The adoption of the Model Code was an important step in the legalization of ethics rules. This is evident in the format of the Model Code, which for the first time separated binding disciplinary rules (DRs) from advisory ethical considerations (ECs). During the last half-century, the law governing lawyers has undergone

---

52. The 1908 code included 32 Canons. Fourteen more Canons were added between 1908 and 1969. Professional Responsibility: Standards, Rules and Statutes 649 (John S. Dzienkowski ed., 2002-2003 ed., West 2002).

53. Charles W. Wolfram, Modern Legal Ethics 54 n. 21 (West 1986). By the time the ABA undertook to write canons of ethics, ten states had adopted such codes. Most of the state codes also were modeled on the Alabama code. Id.

54. These lectures were published as a book called Professional Ethics. See Geoffrey C. Hazard & W. William Hodes, The Law of Lawyering § 1.9 (3d ed., Aspen L. & Bus. 2002). Sharswood was dean of the University of Pennsylvania's Law Department and later Chief Justice of Pennsylvania.

55. Thomas D. Morgan & Ronald D. Rotunda, Professional Responsibility: Problems and Materials 11 (7th ed., Found. Press 2000).

56. Restatement, § 1, comment b, reporter's note.

57. Wolfram, supra n. 53, at 56. One benchmark that illustrates the dramatic increase in lawyer regulation over the last decades of the twentieth century was a report in 1970 issued by an ABA committee chaired by former U.S. Supreme Court Justice Tom Clark. One conclusion of this report was that "disciplinary action [was] practically nonexistent in many jurisdictions; practices and procedures [were] antiquated; [and] many disciplinary agencies ha[d] little power to take effective steps against malefactors." ABA Special Committee on Evaluation of Disciplinary Enforcement, Problems and Recommendations in Disciplinary Enforcement, at 1 (1970), quoted in Mary M. Devlin, The Development of Lawyer Disciplinary Procedures in the United States, 7 Geo. J. Leg. Ethics 911, 921 (1994).

a gradual metamorphosis from a relatively general set of aspirational standards of ethics that were seldom enforced to a complex and sometimes quite specific set of rules of law that require, permit, or prohibit particular conduct. Violators often suffer serious consequences.[58]

The codification of the law governing lawyers in the 1960s marked a major change in the structure and content of the ethical rules. At the same time, new developments refined the law of malpractice, the criminal and regulatory law that applies to lawyers, and the law of disqualification.

### What is the history of the current ABA Model Rules?

Some critics observed that the Model Code was too focused on litigation-related issues and ignored some important problems that practitioners encounter. In 1977, the ABA appointed a committee called the Kutak Commission to rewrite the rules. The first drafts produced by the Commission met with substantial criticism from ABA members because the proposed rules limited client confidentiality, increased disclosure obligations, required pro bono work, and made other dramatic changes from the Model Code. By the time the House of Delegates adopted the Model Rules of Professional Conduct in 1983, the new code had been extensively amended to reduce the scope of the changes in the ethical rules initially proposed by the Commission.[59]

The states did not rush to adopt the Model Rules as they had done with the Model Code. They moved much more slowly to switch from their then-existing codes to the Model Rules. Also, most states made significant amendments to the ABA Model Rules before they adopted them. Twenty years later, some version of the Model Rules has been adopted by 44 states and the District of

Columbia,[60] but even among these states, the rules are much less uniform than they used to be. Some states have elected to retain and to update their Model Code–based versions of the ethics rules or to retain rules that do not follow either model.[61]

In 1997, the ABA undertook another revision of the Model Rules, delegating the research and drafting of changes to a committee that is usually referred to as the Ethics 2000 Commission. (Initially it contemplated completing its work in the year 2000.) The Commission's membership consisted of several of the legal profession's

*Professor Nancy J.*
~~Moore~~ Ugly

---

58. See Charles W. Wolfram, Toward a History of the Legalization of American Legal Ethics II — The Modern Era, 15 Geo. J. Legal Ethics 205, 206-210 (2002) (documenting the growth of lawyer regulation).

59. Wolfram, supra n. 53, at 61-62.

60. ABA, Center for Professional Responsibility, Dates of Adoption of the Model Rules of Professional Conduct, *available at* http://www.abanet.org/cpr/mrpc/chron_states.html (last visited Oct. 6, 2004).

61. The California Rules of Professional Conduct, for example, are influenced by the ABA codes, but less so than the ethical rules of other states. They are not modeled on either the Model Code or the Model Rules. ABA, supra n. 60.

leading experts on standards of professional responsibility, and much of the drafting work was done by the Commission's chief reporter, Professor Nancy J. Moore of Boston University Law School.

Between 2001 and 2003, the ABA House of Delegates accepted most, but not all, of the Commission's recommendations.[62] The states have begun to consider those amendments to the Model Rules, and some states have already adopted most or all of them.[63]

### How do the existing Model Rules relate to individual state ethics codes?

Early in the twenty-first century, the state ethics codes that govern lawyers are far more diverse and less uniform than they were thirty years before because so many states have amended the ABA Model Rules.[64] However, regardless of any amendments made, the primary functions of all state ethics codes are the same: (1) to guide lawyers in evaluating what conduct is proper in various situations and (2) to provide a basis for disciplining lawyers who violate the rules. Courts also consult the ethics codes for guidance in determining whether a lawyer has engaged in malpractice, charged an unreasonable fee, or should be disqualified from representation of a client because of a conflict of interest.[65] The ethics codes are a primary source of guidance for lawyers and judges about standards of conduct for lawyers. Also, many of the rules in the ethics codes are drawn from rules of tort law, contract law, agency law, and criminal law.[66]

### Do judges also have ethical rules?

Another important code drafted by the American Bar Association is the ABA Model Code of Judicial Conduct, which sets out ethical rules for judges. The development of the judicial ethics code has followed a course similar to the lawyer codes. The ABA adopted Canons of Judicial Ethics in 1924. Then, in 1972, the ABA House of Delegates adopted a much-expanded Code of Judicial Conduct, which has been adopted in some form in most states.[67]

---

62. ABA, Center for Professional Responsibility, Summary of House of Delegates Action on Ethics 2000 Commission Report, *available at* http://www.abanet.org/cpr/e2k-summary_2002.html (last visited Oct. 6, 2004).

63. Several states adopted comprehensive amendments to their rules of professional conduct during 2003, after the ABA had largely completed its revision of the Model Rules. (The ABA made further amendments to Model Rules 1.6 and 1.13 in August 2003.) These states include Arizona, Arkansas, Delaware, New Jersey, North Carolina, South Dakota, and Tennessee. Delaware's amendments are nearly identical to the 2002 amendments in the ABA Model Rules. The Tennessee revision was that state's first adoption of a format like the ABA Model Rules. Stephen Gillers & Roy D. Simon, Regulation of Lawyers: Statutes and Standards xx-xxvii (Aspen L. & Bus. 2004).

64. Every state posts its rules of professional conduct on the World Wide Web. The Cornell Legal Ethics Library, *at* http://www.law.cornell.edu/ethics/, has links to all of them. For a statutory supplement that includes the Model Rules and a good survey of the principal state variations, see Gillers & Simon, supra n. 63.

65. Restatement § 1, comment b.

66. Id.

67. The Model Code of Judicial Conduct has been revised several times. See ABA, Model Code of Judicial Conduct, *available at* http://www.abanet.org/cpr/mcjc/mcjc_home.html (last visited Oct. 6, 2004).

**Do other ethics codes apply to lawyers in specialized practice areas?**

Yes. Various bar organizations have recommend standards of conduct for lawyers in particular practice areas. Perhaps the most influential are the ABA Standards for Criminal Justice, which include standards of conduct for prosecutors and for criminal defense lawyers. These standards were adopted as a result of work initiated in 1964 by an ABA committee. The current version of the standards (extensively amended in the early 1990s) include separate sets of guidance for "The Prosecution Function" and "The Defense Function." Like other ABA recommendations, these ABA standards do not themselves carry the force of law, but more than 40 states have made changes in their criminal codes to incorporate some of these standards.[68]

Other ethics codes have been adopted by voluntary bar associations of lawyers who work for the federal government, lawyers who handle domestic relations matters, and others. These standards and codes also lack the force of law and are advisory in nature. However, lawyers and courts look to them for guidance, especially on issues not addressed by the mandatory ethics codes.

Many lawyers believe that, to understand the ethical rules, they need only read the ethical rules adopted by the highest court of their state and perhaps the official comments. *This belief is mistaken.* Although they were promulgated by courts rather than legislatures, the ethics rules have been subjected to interpretation, including judicial construction, as if they were statutes. The interpretations are found both in ethics opinions issued by state bars and in appellate decisions in disciplinary cases. In addition, a large number of statutes applicable to lawyers have been enacted by federal, state, and local legislative bodies. Aspects of the law regulating lawyers are found in decisions in malpractice cases, motions to disqualify lawyers from representing particular clients, appeals by criminal defendants who claim that they didn't receive competent representation, motions to sanction lawyers for violating court rules, challenges to lawyers' fees, and so on. Any time that you encounter a situation in practice in which you need to know your legal obligations, your research might begin with the ethical rules in your jurisdiction, but it should not end there.

## 2. Legal malpractice, breach of contract, and breach of fiduciary duty

A client seeking redress for some harm caused by a lawyer may complain to a disciplinary agency, in which case the client is a witness, not the plaintiff. The plaintiff is the state agency that prosecutes lawyers for violating the ethics rules. In addition, the client may sue the lawyer for legal malpractice, for breach of contract, or for breach of fiduciary duty.[69]

---

68. Stephen Gillers & Roy D. Simon, Regulation of Lawyers: Statutes and Standards 591 (Aspen L. & Bus. 2003); ABA, supra n. 67.

69. See Restatement § 48, comment c, § 49; John Leubsdorf, Legal Malpractice and Professional Responsibility, 48 Rutgers L. Rev. 101 (1995).

A tort claim of legal malpractice may involve either a claim of negligence or one of intentional misconduct.[70] The client must assert

- that the lawyer owed a duty to the plaintiff,
- that the lawyer failed to exercise "the competence and diligence normally exercised by lawyers in similar circumstances," and
- that the breach of duty caused harm to the plaintiff.[71]

Any mistake by a lawyer that would not have been made by an ordinarily competent and diligent lawyer in the same circumstances can form the basis for a malpractice claim. A lawyer, for example, who allows a statute of limitations to run without filing suit on behalf of a client may incur malpractice liability.[72] A lawyer who represents two clients with conflicting interests may be liable for malpractice if harm results.[73] A court may order the lawyer to pay damages for harm caused by malpractice, but it also could order compliance with an injunction, return of property, alteration or cancellation of a legal document, or other remedies.[74]

The ABA reported in 2001 that between 1996 and 1999, more than 35,000 claims of legal malpractice were made. About 5,900 of those concluded with a payment of more than $10,000 to the claimant. The most common practice areas in which malpractice claims occur are personal injury (claims against plaintiff's lawyers) (25 percent), real estate (17 percent), domestic relations (10 percent), and estate, trust, and probate cases (9 percent).[75]

Sometimes, malpractice claims are brought by nonclients to whom lawyers owe duties.[76]

**FOR EXAMPLE:** In one leading case, a lawyer was enlisted to help his brother-in-law to obtain a $1 million loan. To get the loan, the lawyer had to send the lender a letter attesting that he had searched and ascertained that there were no liens on the property to be pledged as loan collateral. The brother-in-law client told the lawyer there were no liens on the property in question (farm equipment), even though he knew that statement was false. The lawyer wrote the letter to the lender without checking whether any liens existed. The borrower later defaulted on the loan and then committed suicide. After most of the proceeds of the property were awarded to other creditors whose liens were found to have priority, the lender sued the lawyer for negligent misrepresentation. The

---

70. Thomas D. Morgan, Sanctions and Remedies for Attorney Misconduct, 19 S. Ill. U. L.J. 343, 349-350 (1995) (explaining that legal malpractice often has been characterized as a tort claim, but urging that the claim is more appropriately premised on the lawyer-client contract, which spells out the lawyer's duties).

71. Restatement § 48. See also Ronald E. Mallen & Jeffrey M. Smith, 5 Legal Malpractice § 33.9, at 75-85 (5th ed., West 2000).

72. See, e.g., Dixon Ticonderoga Co. v. Est. of O'Connor, 248 F.3d 151 (3d Cir. 2001).

73. See, e.g., Streber v. Hunter, 221 F.3d 701 (5th Cir. 2000).

74. Restatement § 6.

75. Stephen Gillers, Regulation of Lawyers 766 (6th ed., Aspen L. & Bus. 2002).

76. Restatement § 51.

lawyer argued that he owed no personal duty to the lender because his client was the borrower, not the lender. The Seventh Circuit upheld a judgment of $833,000 against the lawyer, finding the lawyer liable to the lender for negligent misrepresentation even though the lender was not his client.[77]

### Is a claim for breach of fiduciary duty different from a malpractice claim?

Yes and no. It is a separate cause of action that originates in the common law of fiduciary duty, which applies not only to lawyers but also to others who are deemed to be fiduciaries. A fiduciary is someone who assumes a position of trust in relation to another; examples include stockbrokers and financial advisors as well as lawyers. Fiduciaries owe special duties not to misuse property or information that has been entrusted to them,[78] must place the interests of the other above their own interests, and must act in good faith on the other's behalf.[79]

*Webster Hubbell,*

Brother to Andre the Giant

### Could a lawyer be disciplined, sued for malpractice, and criminally prosecuted all for one act of misconduct?

Yes, a lawyer who violates criminal law in the course of practicing law or who helps a client violate criminal law can be prosecuted in addition to being disciplined and sued for legal malpractice. As in other types of cases, defendants can be held both criminally and civilly liable. It is not common for lawyers to go to jail, but it does occasionally happen.

**FOR EXAMPLE:** Former associate attorney general Webster Hubbell was prosecuted for mail fraud and tax evasion because he engaged in billing and expense fraud while in private practice in Arkansas.[80] He was disbarred

---

77. Greycas, Inc. v. Proud, 826 F.2d 1560 (7th Cir. 1987), *cert. denied*, 484 U.S. 1043 (1988).

78. A person can become a fiduciary as a matter of law, such as in attorney-client or principal-agent relationships, or a fiduciary relationship can arise because one person justifiably places trust in another so that the other assumes a position of superiority and influence in relation to the first. Chou v. U. of Chicago, 254 F.3d 1347 (Fed. Cir. 2001).

79. See Restatement § 7, comment b, explaining that "The relationship between lawyer and client is one in which the lawyer generally owes the client rigorously enforced fiduciary duties, including duties of utmost good faith and fair dealing"; id. at § 16(3) (explaining that "a lawyer must . . . deal honestly with the client, and not employ advantages arising from the client-lawyer relationship in a manner adverse to the client"); id. at § 49 (explaining that breach of the fiduciary duty articulated in § 16(3) would render a lawyer civilly liable to a client if the breach causes injury to the client). The tort of breach of fiduciary duty is also discussed in Chapter 4.

80. See U.S. v. Hubbell, 530 U.S. 27 (2000).

for the same misconduct, and was also sued by his law firm for fraud, larceny, and embezzlement.[81]

## 3. Motions to disqualify for conflicts of interest

Another substantial body of "lawyer law" consists of the judicial opinions resulting from motions to disqualify lawyers because of conflicts of interest. These motions are often made by opposing counsel rather than by the lawyer's own clients.[82]

**In deciding motions to disqualify lawyers because of alleged conflicts of interest, do the courts simply interpret the state's ethical codes?**

No. In deciding these cases, the courts are influenced by the ethics rules on conflicts of interest, but the ethics rules articulate standards for discipline, not disqualification. Many courts follow their own common law standards, which may not be the same as those in the ethics rules. This issue is explored in Chapters 5 and 6.

## 4. Contract law

Another set of cases that create "lawyer law" are cases in which courts nullify contracts to which lawyers were parties or contracts negotiated by lawyers. If a lawyer negotiates an unfair fee agreement with a client through misrepresentation or overreaching, the fee agreement is voidable, just as is any contract so negotiated.[83] If a lawyer negotiates a settlement based on false representations, the settlement agreement is voidable even if it is embodied in a judgment.[84] Similarly, if a lawyer enters into a business transaction with a client without complete disclosure of the lawyer's interest in the transaction and her consequent inability to give disinterested advice, the transaction may be invalidated.[85]

## 5. Advisory ethics opinions

The ABA, the state bar associations, and the bar associations of some cities and counties have formed committees to write advisory opinions for lawyers seeking guidance on ethical questions. The committees are comprised of both lawyers and nonlawyers. Many ethics committee opinions are written

---

81. Rose Law Firm v. Hubbell, No. LR-C-96-212, Consent Judgment and Order (E.D. Ark., Oct. 28, 1996). For some other recent cases of theft by lawyers, see Lisa G. Lerman, Blue-Chip Bilking: Regulation of Billing and Expense Fraud by Lawyers, 12 Geo. J. Leg. Ethics 205 (1999).

82. Restatement § 6, comment i. See Chapter 5 for further discussion of this issue.

83. See, e.g., Restatement (Second) of Contracts, §§ 162, 164 (1981).

84. Fed. R. Civ. P. 60(b).

85. See, e.g., Abstract & Title Corp. v. Cochran, 414 So. 2d 284 (Fla. Dist. Ct. App. 1982).

in response to inquiries from lawyers, though some opinions are issued at the committees' own initiative. These opinions are published in local bar journals and in the Lawyers' Manual on Professional Conduct (described below). Many of them are also available on Lexis and Westlaw. The committees that write the advisory opinions are entirely separate from the bar counsel's offices that investigate complaints of lawyer misconduct. Advisory opinions are relied on by courts with increasing frequency.[86]

**What should a lawyer do if, after reading the ethics rules and cases, he still doesn't know whether a contemplated course of action is permissible?**

The lawyer might call the bar counsel or the bar's ethics committee. Sometimes off-the-cuff, nonbinding guidance is available from either the disciplinary counsel or from a staff lawyer from the ethics committee. The other alternative is to write a formal inquiry to the ethics committee, giving a detailed factual scenario in hypothetical form. However, it is not always practical to ask an ethics committee for advice if the issue requires speedy resolution. Ethics committees consist of volunteer lawyers, so often months go by between the receipt of an inquiry and the issuance of an opinion. Also, a lawyer may decide not to ask for advice, fearing that the ethics committee's answer will be excessively cautionary and will preclude a course of action that would be very helpful to her client.

## 6. Research on ethics law

When you research a legal ethics question, begin with the applicable state ethics code and the Restatement (Third) of the Law Governing Lawyers. Many states post their ethics rules and ethics opinions online, usually at the state bar Web site. Here is a list of some other useful resources.

> *ABA/BNA Lawyers' Manual on Professional Conduct*   This is a weekly looseleaf service published by the American Bar Association and the Bureau of National Affairs. Many law libraries maintain copies of this looseleaf service. It summarizes and excerpts case law, rules changes, advisory ethics opinions, and other materials on the law governing lawyers. It includes a list of Web sites that provide additional information. One volume of the Lawyers' Manual is organized by topic to allow quick access to information and references on many subjects.
>
> *The Georgetown Journal of Legal Ethics*   This scholarly journal publishes articles relating to the legal profession and the law governing lawyers. Likewise, the **Fordham Law Review** publishes an annual symposium issue on legal ethics issues, and the University of Alabama publishes the **Journal of the Legal Profession**. The **Notre Dame**

---

86. Peter A. Joy, Making Ethics Opinions Meaningful: Toward More Effective Regulation of Lawyers' Conduct, 15 Geo. J. Leg. Ethics 313, 319 (2002).

**Journal of Law, Ethics, and Public Policy** analyzes ethics issues "from a Judeo-Christian perspective."[87]

*Geoffrey C. Hazard Jr. & W. William Hodes, The Law of Lawyering (3d ed., Aspen L. & Bus. 2001)*    This two-volume treatise on the law governing lawyers, like the Lawyers' Manual, provides valuable description and analysis on many topics.

*Ronald E. Mallen & Jeffrey M. Smith, Legal Malpractice (5th ed., West 1996)*    This is a five-volume treatise on the law of legal malpractice.

*Stephen Gillers & Roy D. Simon, Regulation of Lawyers: Statutes and Standards (Aspen Publishers 2004)* (updated annually)    This comprehensive collection of lawyer codes includes helpful synthesis and reporting of new developments in the law governing lawyers. After each Model Rules, a section called "Selected State Variations" identifies which state rules diverge significantly from the Model Rules and explains each variation.

*Charles W. Wolfram, Modern Legal Ethics (West 1986)*    This one-volume treatise, although somewhat dated, is a lucid and erudite compendium of information on the law governing lawyers.

**Internet sites**    An increasing amount of legal research is conducted on the Internet. Not long ago, the best databases were those maintained by Lexis and Westlaw. Both companies have excellent databases on the law governing lawyers, but other public sites have emerged that are also very useful. Here are a few of them.

*Cornell Legal Ethics Library*    This database includes, among other things, the actual ethics rules adopted in many jurisdictions. http://www.law.cornell.edu/ethics/

*ABA Center for Professional Responsibility*    http://www.abanet.org/cpr/home.html

*ABA Bar Admission Information*    http://www.abanet.org/legaled/baradmissions/bar.html

*Findlaw*    http://www.findlaw.com/01topics/14ethics/index.html

*Legalethics.com*    http://www.legalethics.com/

*National Conference of Bar Examiners* (for information about the MPRE)    http://www.ncbex.org/tests.htm

*Jurist — Legal Profession*    http://jurist.law.pitt.edu/sg_prof.htm

*Washington University Legal Ethics Research Guide*    http://ls.wustl.edu/Infores/Library/Guides/legalethics.html

*National Law Journal*    http://www.nlj.com/

*The American Lawyer*    http://www.americanlawyer.com/

*U.S. Office of Government Ethics*    http://www.usoge.gov/

---

87. Notre Dame Journal of Law, Ethics, and Public Policy, *at* http://www.nd.edu/~ndjlepp/ (last visited Oct. 6, 2004).

**Greedy Associates** A conversation site for young lawyers in private practice and for those aspiring to join them. http://www.greedyassociates.com/

**Crossing the Bar** Information and commentary on the multijurisdictional practice of law. http://www.crossingthebar.com/upl.htm

This list is just the tip of the iceberg. A vast and rapidly growing amount of legal information is easily available on the Internet.

## What Law Governs Lawyers?

| Primary ethics codes | Description |
| --- | --- |
| State ethics codes | Rules governing the ethical conduct of lawyers. They usually become law by adoption by the states' highest courts. They are often based on the ABA Model Rules. |
| ABA Model Rules of Professional Conduct (as amended after Ethics 2000 Commission) | This new edition of the Model Rules makes a set of significant changes from the previous rules. It is being reviewed by the states for possible adoption. |
| 1983 ABA Model Rules of Professional Conduct | By 2003 the Model Rules had been adopted by 44 states and the District of Columbia with substantial variations in many rules. No state has adopted all of the Model Rules. |
| 1969 ABA Model Code of Professional Responsibility | By 1972, only a few years after adoption by the ABA, these rules had been adopted with few variations by the District of Columbia and all but 3 states. But in most states, the Model Code has been superseded by the state's version of the Model Rules. |
| 1908 Canons of Ethics | This was the first code of ethics adopted by the ABA. These were looked to for guidance by lawyers until they were superseded in 1969 by the ABA Code of Professional Responsibility. |
| ABA Model Code of Judicial Conduct | This code has been adopted by 19 states and the District of Columbia; 17 other states have adopted specific provisions of the code. Federal judges are governed by the Code of Conduct for United States Judges (1999). |
| Other ethics codes | Various voluntary bar organizations have adopted advisory codes to provide guidance to lawyers practicing in a particular area. These are sometimes relied on by courts. |
| ABA Standards for Criminal Justice | These were drafted by the ABA to provide guidance to prosecutors and defense lawyers on issues specific to criminal law practice. |

*Continued*

| Primary ethics codes | Description |
| --- | --- |
| Model Rules of Professional Conduct for Federal Lawyers | These were adopted by the Federal Bar Association and address issues that arise for lawyers employed by the federal government. |
| **Other law governing lawyers** | |
| Disciplinary law | This includes case law applying ethical rules to impose censure, reprimand, suspension, or disbarment. |
| Ethics opinions | The ABA and state and local bar ethics committees produce advisory opinions interpreting ethical rules, often in response to inquiries by lawyers. |
| Malpractice law | The law of legal malpractice is case law imposing civil liability on lawyers for misconduct. It is based on contract law, tort law, and fiduciary law. |
| Disqualification law | A lawyer who represents a client in litigation despite a conflict of interest may face a motion to disqualify him. The decisional law on disqualification is distinct from the ethics rules on conflicts of interest. |
| Criminal law | Criminal law applies to lawyers as to everyone else. Common charges against lawyers are mail fraud and tax fraud. |
| Court rules | Courts adopt rules of evidence and procedure. Lawyers are subject to sanctions for violation of these rules. |
| Regulatory law | Various federal and state agencies, such as the federal agencies that regulate banking and securities transactions, implement statutes and regulations that may impose disclosure and other requirements on lawyers as well as their clients. |
| Restatement (Third) of the Law Governing Lawyers | This summary of the law was adopted by the American Law Institute after its completion in 1998. |

# C. Admission to practice

## 1. Requirements for admission

### a. A short history of bar admission

The requirements to become a lawyer have changed a lot over the last century. In the colonial era, there were no law schools. A man who wished to become a lawyer had to first be an apprentice to another lawyer. The first law schools were law firms that did such a good job training their apprentices that they gave up practice to do more teaching. One of these was the Litchfield Law School in Connecticut, which trained two vice presidents, three supreme court justices, 28 senators, and 14 governors between its establishment in 1784 and its closure in 1833.[88] The early law schools were not founded as parts of universities, but they began to affiliate with universities in the 1820s.[89] In the first half of the nineteenth century, enthusiasm for formal legal education flagged for a while,[90] but around midcentury many law schools were established or reestablished, and legal education took root in American legal culture.[91]

By 1860, all but two states had established bar examinations, but the questions were administered orally and the process was fairly informal.[92] The states did not require attendance at law school as a condition of admission. Only nine of thirty-nine states required a defined period of apprenticeship as a precondition of admission to the bar.[93]

In the late nineteenth and early twentieth centuries, law school training was optional but not mandatory to practice law. By 1890, the number of states that required a period of apprenticeship increased to 23. Also during this period, many states began to require applicants to take written bar examinations.[94] As of 1900, 80-90 percent of lawyers had never attended college or law school.[95] Nor was college a prerequisite to law school. Some law students never even finished high school.[96] The majority of lawyers qualified for bar admission simply by completing a three-year apprenticeship.[97] Between 1870 and 1920, the legal education curriculum expanded in many universities from one year to three years. Only later did law become a course of graduate study.[98]

In the first half of the twentieth century, law school overtook apprenticeship as the primary, and later nearly exclusive, path of entry into the profession. By 1930, there were three times as many law schools as there had been in 1890.[99] The ABA urged that attendance at law school should be mandatory for bar admission.[100] Before 1927, no state required law school attendance to become a lawyer. The first state to make law school mandatory was West Virginia in 1928; it required one year of law school. By 1941, graduation

---

88. Robert Stevens, Law School: Legal Education in America from the 1850s to the 1980s at 3, 11 n. 9 (U.N.C. Press 1983).

89. Id. at 5.

90. Id. at 9-10.

91. Id. at 20-22.

92. Id. at 25.

93. Id.

94. Id.

95. Robert Stevens, Democracy and the Legal Profession: Cautionary Notes, Learning & Law (Fall 1976, at 15).

96. Stevens, supra n. 88, at 38.

97. Lawrence M. Friedman, A History of American Law 606 (2d ed., Simon & Schuster 1985).

98. Stevens, supra n. 88, at 36-37.

99. Herb D. Vest, Felling the Giant: Breaking the ABA's Stranglehold on Legal Education in America, 50 J. Leg. Educ. 494, 496 (2000).

100. The ABA pushed the states to require attendance at law school as a prerequisite to bar membership. Records of their discussions show that their goals were: (1) to raise standards; (2) to restrict numbers of lawyers; and (3) to keep out blacks, Jews, and other immigrants. Stevens, supra n. 95, at 16.

from an ABA-accredited law school was a prerequisite to sitting for the bar exam in all but a few states. This requirement is now imposed by nearly every state.[101]

## b. Contemporary bar admission requirements

In most states, the rules for admission to the bar are established by the highest court of each state. The licensing process is organized by state, so that a lawyer who wishes to practice law in New York and New Jersey must seek two separate bar admissions. In most states, the basic requirements for bar admission are

- graduation from an accredited undergraduate college (usually required for admission to law school);
- graduation from a law school that meets the state's educational standards (this usually means one accredited by the ABA);
- submission of an application for admission to the bar;
- obtaining a passing score on the bar examination administered by the state, usually including a state-specific section, the Multistate Bar Examination, and the Multistate Professional Responsibility Examination;[102]
- a finding that the applicant is of good moral character and is fit for the practice of law.[103]

Once admitted to the bar of a state, a lawyer must comply with various requirements to maintain her admission. These may include completion of a certain number of hours of continuing legal education every year, payment of annual dues, membership in a state bar association, and compliance with any requirements to maintain or submit records relating to the operation of a law office. Some states require that each member maintain an office in the state.[104]

If a lawyer has been admitted to practice in one state, the lawyer may gain admission in some other states without taking the bar examination, sometimes only after a specified number of years of practice. If a lawyer seeks admission to litigate only one case, the lawyer may be admitted *pro hac vice* by association with a lawyer admitted in the state. Most federal courts admit any licensed lawyers who apply for admission to appear before them.[105]

---

101. The few states that do not require graduation from an ABA-accredited law school in order to take the bar exam usually have additional, hard-to-meet requirements such as prior passage of another state's bar exam combined with practice as a lawyer in that other state for a number of years. See Vest, supra n. 99, at 497.

102. Some states also require passing scores on the Multistate Essay Examination or the Multistate Performance Test.

103. See ABA, Section on Legal Education and Admissions to the Bar, Overview on Bar Admissions, *available at* http://www.abanet.org/legaled/baradmissions/bo.html (last visited Oct. 4, 2004).

104. Restatement § 2, comment f.

105. Id. at comment b.

*"Attention, please. At 8:45 A.M. on Tuesday, July 29, 2008, you are all scheduled to take the New York State Bar Exam."*

## 2. The bar examination

Every state administers a bar examination to its applicants for admission, though some states allow candidates to "waive in" to the bar if they pay a fee, have practiced for a specified number of years in another state, and satisfy character and fitness requirements.[106] The bar examination usually consists of a combination of multiple choice and essay questions. Most candidates prepare for it by taking a six-week cram course from one of several private companies.

Critics charge that the bar examination favors those who can afford the time and money for the bar review course, tests nothing that has not already been tested through a law school's grading system, and discriminates against minorities and disabled persons.[107] One critic argues that "whether the

---

106. National Conference of Bar Examiners & ABA, Comprehensive Guide to Bar Admission Requirements 25-27 (2004).

107. Society of American Law Teachers Statement on the Bar Exam, 52 J. Leg. Educ. 446, 449-451 (2002) (bar exams disproportionately exclude people of color from the practice of law); Daniel R. Hansen, Do We Need the Bar Examination? A Critical Evaluation of the Justifications for

bar exam tests for legal skills or abilities related to lawyering is highly questionable."[108] Nevertheless, states continue to administer the examination because "no one has advanced a persuasive substitute."[109]

# 3. The character and fitness inquiry

How does a bar admissions authority evaluate the character and fitness of an applicant for admission to the bar? The point, obviously, is to try to assess whether the applicant will practice law in an honest and competent manner. This is a difficult exercise in prediction. If someone did something dishonest last year, will he do something dishonest next year? What should be the scope of the inquiry? What is relevant to the assessment of the "moral character" of a lawyer? Suppose the person has radical political views, an unusual lifestyle, or peculiar personal habits? What if the applicant has a history of mental illness? The political or moral biases of the members of the character committee might unfairly deny admission to an applicant. An overly broad question could demand that an applicant disclose highly sensitive personal information that may not be relevant to the individual's qualifications for admission to the bar.

## a. Criteria for evaluation

Most states require each bar applicant to fill out an application. This may require assembly and submission of a wide range of information, including residence and employment history, criminal records, traffic records, credit history, records of any litigation in which the applicant has been a party, and other information. The National Conference of Bar Examiners' standard moral character application form, which is used in many states and which runs 31 pages, asks for the following information, among many other things:

> List every permanent and temporary residence at which you have lived. If you are applying prior to your first bar admission: during the last ten years or since age 18, whichever period of time is longer. . . .
> List every job you have held. If you are applying prior to your first bar admission: for a ten-year period prior to the date of this application or since age 18, whichever period of time is shorter. . . . Include self-employment, clerkships, temporary or part-time employment and military service. Account for any period of time when you were unemployed for more than four months. . . .

---

the Bar Examination and Proposed Alternatives, 45 Case W. Res. L. Rev. 1191 (1995) (bar examinations do not test what lawyers must do). See Bartlett v. N.Y. Bd. of L. Examiners, 156 F.3d 321 (2d Cir. 1998) (New York bar exam administered without accommodations to reading-disabled applicant violated Americans with Disabilities Act).

108. Hansen, supra n. 107, at 1206.
109. Stephen Gillers, Regulation of Lawyers 696 (6th ed., Aspen L. & Bus. 2002).

> Have you ever been cited, arrested, charged, or convicted for any violation of
> any law other than as a juvenile? (Omit traffic violations.) Note: This
> should include matters that have been expunged or subject to a diversion
> program. If yes, complete form 5.
> Within the past five years, have you been diagnosed with or have you been
> treated for bi-polar disorder, schizophrenia, paranoia, or any other psy-
> chotic disorder? If you answered yes, complete forms 7 and 8.
> Within the past five years, have you ever raised the issue of consumption of
> drugs or alcohol, or the issue of a mental, emotional, nervous or behavioral
> disorder or condition as a defense, mitigation, or explanation for your
> actions in the course of any administrative or judicial proceeding or inves-
> tigation, any inquiry, or other proceeding; or any proposed termination by
> an educational institution, employer, government agency, professional
> organization, or licensing authority?[110]

About three-quarters of the state bar applications ask whether an applicant
has received outpatient treatment for any mental or emotional disorder or
condition.[111] As of 1995, nearly every state asked about whether an applicant
had ever been hospitalized for psychiatric reasons.[112] Likewise, nearly every
state asks some questions about abuse of drugs or alcohol and/or treatment
for substance abuse.[113] All states ask questions about past criminal conduct,
with some states seeking information not only about criminal convictions
but also about arrests or citations.[114] Some states include broad requests to
reveal any moral indiscretions. The South Carolina questionnaire, for example,
asks:

> Are there any other facts not disclosed . . . concerning your background,
> history, experience, or activities which in your opinion may have a bearing
> on your character, moral fitness, or eligibility to practice law in South
> Carolina and which should be placed at the disposal or brought to the atten-
> tion of the examining authorities? If yes, explain fully.[115]

Often applicants are asked to have lawyers write letters of recommendation for
their admission. Most states require that the dean of the law school attest to
moral character of applicants for the bar. Some state bars conduct personal
interviews with every applicant, while others interview only those applicants
whose questionnaire includes some problematic information. An application

---

110. National Board of Bar Examiners, Request for Preparation of Character Report, *available
at* http://www.ncbex.org/character/Standard01.pdf (last visited Oct. 6, 2004).

111. Donald H. Stone, The Bar Admission Process, Gatekeeper or Big Brother: An Empirical
Study, 15 N. Ill. U. L. Rev. 331, 332 (1995). But see Stanley S. Herr, Questioning the Questionnaires:
Bar Admissions and Candidates with Disabilities, 42 Vill. L. Rev. 635, 652 (1997) (noting that many
jurisdictions are narrowing or eliminating questions on both outpatient treatment and on hospitalization for mental disorders).

112. Stone, supra n. 111, at 335.

113. Id. at 337.

114. Id. at 341.

115. South Carolina Judicial Department, Bar Application, *available at* http://www.sccourts
.org/bar/BarWord2000.doc (last visited Oct. 6, 2004).

that raises significant problems of moral character may lead to an investigation by the bar and a formal hearing on the applicant's qualifications for admission.

## Does it make any sense for the bar examiners to ask every applicant to compile so much information about his or her personal history?

The moral character inquiry has been criticized as a fishing expedition into the background of applicants, one looking for any arguably problematic behavior. In most states, there is no published list of what conduct gives rise to an inquiry and no consistency in practice. The nature of the inquiry allows unfettered discretion to the biases of the examiners. The process asks examiners to make assessments of mental health, for which they have no qualifications.[116] The bar examiners tend to ask many questions that do not lead to investigation, such as where an applicant has lived for the last ten years. Do examiners really contact landlords to verify these residences or question applicants' past neighbors, as the FBI does when conducting security investigations? The examiners also ask about many matters that are unlikely to lead to denials of admission and that would be unlikely to lead to investigation of the person who already has been admitted to the bar.

In 1985, Professor Deborah Rhode reported after surveying bar examiners that "most states would investigate bounced checks (76%), marijuana possession (67%), involvement in litigation (52%), and high levels of debt (56%)[117] . . . [as well as] psychiatric treatment (98%), misdemeanor convictions arising from a sit-in (80%) and sexual conduct or lifestyle (49%)."[118] The lack of clear standards for what constitutes poor moral character results in a strikingly idiosyncratic body of case law, with an unusually high rate (43 percent as of 1985) of court reversals and remands of bar determinations on admission cases.[119]

The following table gives examples of actual cases deciding whether particular applicants satisfied the moral character requirement. It provides a sample of the range of issues that come up in moral character inquiries.

---

116. See Deborah L. Rhode, Moral Character as a Professional Credential, 94 Yale L.J. 491 (1985) (empirical study of the moral character evaluation process). Rhode concludes that "As currently implemented, the moral fitness requirement both subverts and trivializes the professional ideals it purports to sustain." Id. at 592.

117. [Authors' footnote.] There is something terribly ironic about bar examiners being suspicious of applicants who have high levels of debt since the vast majority of law students have enormously high levels of debt. See ABA, Commission on Loan Repayment and Forgiveness, Lifting the Burden: Law Student Debt as a Barrier to Public Service 20 (2003), available at http://www.abanet.org/legalservices/downloads/lrap/lrapfinalreport.pdf (last visited Oct. 13, 2004) (median college and law school educational debt at graduation of students who attend private law schools is $86,378).

118. Id. at 532.

119. Id. at 534.

## Recent court decisions on moral character

| Issue and citation | Synopsis of alleged disqualifying facts and conclusion | Reasoning and comments |
| --- | --- | --- |
| **International drug smuggling**: In re Prager, 661 N.E.2d 84 (Mass. 1996) | Applicant had organized an international marijuana smuggling operation that continued for six years, fled the U.S. upon indictment, and lived as a fugitive until extradition four years later; pleaded guilty, got five years probation, and completed extensive community service as a condition of probation. Graduated summa cum laude from law school, clerked for state supreme court justice. Admission denied, leave to reapply after five years. | Court found "seven years of a creditable work history, successful completion of law school, and compliance with the terms of a five-year probationary period, are insufficient to show good moral character when balanced against approximately sixteen years of marihuana use, international smuggling, and living as a fugitive." One justice dissented. |
| **Sexual relations with minors**: Vaughn v. Bd. of B. Examiners, 759 P.2d 1026 (Okla. 1988) | Applicant had been dismissed as a public school teacher after allegation that he had had sexual and/or romantic relationships with two 14-year-old students; criminal charges dismissed. Admission denied. | Court said, "we find his ethical value system deplorable. Vaughn has failed to demonstrate personal as well as professional ethics which are both imperative for bar admission." |
| **Declaration of bankruptcy**: Fla. Bd. of B. Examiners re S.M.D., 609 So. 2d 1309 (Fla. 1992) | Applicant lived on student loans and charged a wedding, a move, and other expenses to credit cards during law school. She filed for bankruptcy during her last semester of law school because of $109,000 of accumulated debt, most of which was nondischargeable student loans. Admitted when state supreme court overturned recommendation by board to deny admission. | Court said, "Board is rightly concerned over the morality of a person who continues to incur large debts with little or no prospect of repayment." But "we cannot agree that the evidence sufficiently demonstrates financial irresponsibility. . . ." |
| **Declaration of bankruptcy**: Application of Gahan, 279 N.W.2d 826 (Minn. 1979) | Law graduate's firm was to pay him $15,000 a year but had financial difficulties and did not pay him for two months. He resigned. While unemployed, he declared bankruptcy, which resulted in discharge of his $14,000 student loan. Court found no fraud or moral turpitude but denied him bar admission. | Court held that federal law prohibited denying him because he had exercised his federal rights but denied admission because his hardship was not "compelling." His failure to prepare to repay the student loans showed lack of good moral character. |

*Continued*

| Issue and citation | Synopsis of alleged disqualifying facts and conclusion | Reasoning and comments |
|---|---|---|
| **Shoplifting and misrepresentation of debt**: In re Tobiga, 791 P.2d 830 (Or. 1990) | Applicant arrested for shoplifting after leaving a store with a package of meat in his coat pocket; charge dismissed upon agreement to pay $100. Failed to disclose unpaid loans on bar application; claimed confusion. Many positive character witnesses. Admitted, applicant found to have proven moral character. | |
| **Copying another student's exam answers**: In re Widdison, 539 N.W.2d 671 (S.D. 1995) | Law student turned in an exam with answers nearly verbatim copies of the answers of another student. Also had been informally admonished for failure to cite sources on a law review note. Denied admission with leave to reapply if "able to rectify his character." | Respondent failed to disclose the law review incident on bar application. |
| **Plagiarism**: Radtke v. Board of B. Examiners, 601 N.W.2d 642 (Wis. 1999) | Applicant made misleading statements on bar application to conceal that he had been dismissed from a university teaching position because of plagiarism in a scholarly article. Denied admission; allowed to reapply after one year. | The underlying misconduct was unconnected to any legal work. |
| **Pattern of hostile and disruptive conduct**: In re Converse, 602 N.W.2d 500 (Neb. 1999) | Law student engaged in series of provocative acts, including display of a photo of a nude female's backside in his study carrel and production of a t-shirt showing a nude caricature of the dean sitting astride a hot dog (described by the student as "Deanie on a Weenie"); showed tendency to launch personal attacks in response to disputes. Application for admission denied. | Court found "such a pattern of acting in a hostile and disruptive manner as to render him unfit." The First Amendment did not preclude consideration of conduct relevant to moral character even if the conduct might be protected by the First Amendment. |

## b. The character questionnaire

Once you become a member of the bar, you might seek to participate in much-needed reform of the moral character inquiry process. In the coming year or two, however, your primary concern will be to successfully complete the moral character inquiry and gain admission to the bar. One hurdle is to realize that this is a complex and time-consuming process, so start early. Obtain a copy of the application forms and make a list of the information and records that you need to collect. It's worse if you confront this morass in April of your third year of law school or shortly after graduation.

**Is it risky to be too candid with the bar examiners? If you tell them too much, are you setting yourself up for rejection?**

Bar admissions committees, courts, and the Model Rules take the position that, in filling out questionnaire, you should be scrupulously honest in everything you say, even if your disclosures could delay or prevent your admission to the bar.[120] Bar examiners particularly dislike having applicants lie to them or conceal information. In one recent decision, the Florida Supreme Court denied admission to an applicant and barred him from reapplication for five years based on the following:

- Applicant failed to disclose that he had attended one law school for part of a semester, then withdrawn, and eventually enrolled in a different law school. (He claimed he had forgotten about it.)
- Applicant failed to disclose that he owed $1,700 to the law school from which he had withdrawn and eventually settled the debt by payment of $1,400.
- Applicant falsely stated that he had never been married or divorced.
- Applicant stated that he had never been charged with a traffic violation, when in fact he had received a speeding ticket about four years before his application.

In denying admission to this applicant, the court explained that "no qualification for membership in the Florida Bar is more important than truthfulness and candor."[121]

**What if you have something in your personal history that you think might raise the eyebrow of a bar examiner?**

You would be surprised how many law students have skeletons in their closets. If you are worried about something, get a copy of the character questionnaire from the state where you will apply for admission and read the questions carefully to see if the questionnaire requires you to disclose the past event.

---

120. Rule 8.1 requires that applicants for admission to the bar be honest and forthright with bar admissions authorities.

121. Fla. Bd. of B. Examiners re R.L.W., 793 So. 2d 918, 926 (Fla. 2001), quoting Fla. Bd. of B. Examiners re E.R.M., 630 So. 2d 1046, 1048 (Fla. 1994).

If the issue is potentially serious, you might seek expert advice well in advance about how serious the problem is and how to handle it. In some jurisdictions, you can initiate the moral character part of the review during your second year of law school. If you anticipate that your history may lead to an inquiry, you can avoid a delay in your ultimate bar admission by initiating this process early.

## What if the issue is something you should have disclosed on your application to law school?

The information you disclose on your bar application must be consistent with the information you disclosed on your law school application. If there is something that you need to disclose on your character questionnaire, review your law school application to see whether the law school asked a question that should have elicited the information at issue. Examine your answer. (If you don't have a copy of your law school application, you should be able to obtain a copy for review from your law school registrar.) If your earlier answer was incomplete, consider making a belated disclosure to the law school of the same information. You can write a letter to the relevant administrator explaining that in preparing your application for admission to the bar, you realized that you had omitted a piece of information on your law school application. If the information is so serious that it would have led to your being denied admission to the law school (such as a homicide conviction), the law school might take disciplinary action as a result of your disclosure. If, as is more common, the disclosure is of something minor (such as a misdemeanor arrest), the late disclosure probably won't lead to any disciplinary action.

**PROBLEM 1-1  POT**

> *This problem includes a question from the application form for admission to the Iowa state bar. The question was not concocted for this book; it is the actual question on the Iowa form.*[122]

You are a third year law student. Next summer, you plan to apply for admission to the Iowa bar. You have just received a copy of the application form, which begins with this statement:

IN THE SUPREME COURT OF IOWA
APPLICATION FOR THE IOWA BAR EXAMINATION

The contents of this application will be public information subject to the limitations of Iowa Code section 602.10141 [which provides that

---

122. Supreme Court of Iowa, Application for the Iowa Bar Examination, *available at* http://www.judicial.state.ia.us/regs/barinfo/barapp%20Aug%2003.doc (last visited Oct. 6, 2004).

a member of the five-person Board of Law Examiners 'shall not disclose information relating to the criminal history or prior misconduct of the applicant'].

Question 37 reads as follows:

37. Are you currently, or have you been in the last three years, engaged in the illegal use of drugs? _____ If Yes, give complete details below (or on an attached sheet).

_____

_____

"Illegal Use of Drugs" means the use of controlled substances obtained illegally as well as the use of controlled substances which are not obtained pursuant to a valid prescription or taken in the accordance [sic] with the directions of a licensed health care practitioner.

"Currently" does not mean on the day of, or even the weeks or months preceding the completion of this application. Rather, it means recently enough so that the condition or impairment may have an ongoing impact.

You have a right to elect not to answer those portions of the above questions which inquire as to the illegal use of controlled substances . . . [if] you have reasonable cause to believe that answering may expose you to the possibility of criminal prosecution. In that event, you may assert the Fifth Amendment privilege against self-incrimination. . . . If you choose to assert the Fifth Amendment privilege, you must do so in writing. . . . Your application for licensure will be processed if you claim the Fifth Amendment privilege against self incrimination. . . .

### RELEASE

. . . I . . . authorize and request every person . . . having . . . [information about me] to furnish to the Iowa Board of Law Examiners or their agents or representatives, any such information. . . .

_____ (signed and sworn to before a notary public)

Several times during each of your three years of law school, you and a few law school friends have smoked marijuana at parties. The last time you did this was three weeks ago. Now that you have read this question, you certainly won't smoke any more pot, at least not before you are admitted to the bar.

There is a rumor on campus that, a few years ago, a member of the bar admissions committee was asked what would happen to applicants who answered the question affirmatively, and he said that they would be denied admission to the bar.

How will you answer the question?

## c. Mental health of applicants

Should bar admissions authorities ask questions about the mental health of applicants? Perhaps some people who suffer from serious mental illness would disserve their clients because of their illnesses. Perhaps some applicants actually pose a danger to others. Such concerns have led bar examiners to ask a variety of questions. Until the 1980s and 1990s, many states asked very detailed and intrusive questions. Most states have now narrowed their questions to ask about mental illnesses that require hospitalization or that involve psychotic disorders. Which ones are those, you might ask? Is this the right place to draw the line? Consider the story of Rose Gower, as described in the following article.

### Jon Bauer, The Character of the Questions and the Fitness of the Process: Mental Health, Bar Admissions, and the Americans with Disabilities Act

49 UCLA L. Rev. 93 (2001)

[John Bauer is Clinical Professor of Law and Director of Civil Clinical Programs at the University of Connecticut School of Law.]

At the age of seventeen, during the summer after her graduation from high school, Rose Gower spent two weeks in the hospital for treatment of major depressive disorder. Over the next seven years, she went to college at Wesleyan University, worked in several jobs, and graduated from the University of Maine School of Law in 1998. There were no blemishes on her record of educational achievement or employment. After law school, she was admitted to the Maine bar (the application form there did not ask about mental health treatment or hospitalizations) and then moved to Connecticut after being offered a job as a Connecticut Superior Court law clerk. In February 1999, she took the Connecticut bar exam. On the bar application, she was required to respond affirmatively to the question that asked, "Have you ever been voluntarily or involuntarily committed to an institution for mental, emotional or nervous disorders?" As required, she described her diagnosis and identified the hospital, and authorized the bar examiners to obtain copies of her medical records.

In April 1999, Ms. Gower received a letter from the CBEC informing her that she had passed the bar examination, but that the committee would be conducting a further inquiry into her application. After hearing nothing for another five months, she wrote to the committee's staff to ask what was holding up her admission. In September, she received a letter informing her that the committee had reviewed her application back in May and determined that medical records should be requested. The hospital had not yet provided the records. Finally, in November, the records arrived. After reviewing them, the committee e-mailed a follow-up question: "Since your treatment at the [hospital], have you been engaged in any out-patient treatment programs?" Ms. Gower replied that she had received counseling, on-and-off, as needed, but had received no further treatment of a medical nature, nor had she taken any mood-altering medications since the time of her hospitalization. The CBEC asked her to elaborate on the circumstances of her treatment. Ms. Gower wrote back as follows:

Dear Committee Members:

I have received your request for further information concerning my mental health. I will attempt to provide sufficient detail. While I was a patient at [the hospital] following the death of my grandfather, the death of a classmate, and the attempted suicide of [somebody close to me], among other things, I was very briefly placed on an anti-depressant, but I became physically ill and the doctors discontinued administration of the drug. Other than that very brief time (literally a matter of days) I have never taken any drugs related to my mental health.

When I was at college, I sought therapy after I was raped. I also sought therapy once or twice a semester thereafter. I am currently in therapy because I am very strong now, and I want to confront issues I was unable to deal with while I was younger. I believe in health maintenance, both mental and physical, and I pay constant attention to my well-being.

There is no more information I can provide to you. I am, quite honestly, shocked that admission as a patient while I was a minor has provoked such intense scrutiny. I have provided all information that is necessary to a decision on my fitness to practice in this state. If the state of Connecticut wishes to deny admission to one of its own law clerks because I, unlike many, have made efforts to maintain my mental health and have recognized when I required help, so be it.

Consider my application complete, and please issue your decision as soon as possible.

Yours,
Rose M. Gower

The committee did not find this information sufficient. It asked for the names and addresses of Ms. Gower's current therapist and the therapists she saw while in college. Apparently not satisfied by Ms. Gower's assurance that she had not taken any drugs related to her mental health, the committee asked her to list all medications that she had been on since the time of her hospital stay. Rather than risk a denial of admission, Ms. Gower complied. On April 3, 2000, she provided the committee with the therapists' names and addresses and wrote, "The only medications I have taken since [my hospitalization] are antibiotics, antihistamines, contraceptive pills, and, rarely, over-the-counter medications such as ibuprofen, Tylenol, Pamprin, and cold medications." On May 25th, the CBEC sent a letter to Ms. Gower's most recent therapist, requesting a "report, narrating the following in detail: diagnosis, motivation for seeking treatment, treatment modality, duration of treatment, frequency of visits and prognosis at the time of discharge," and all records, including progress notes. The therapist sent back a brief report confirming that Ms. Gower had recently completed a five-month course of once-a-week psychotherapy to deal with mild symptoms of depression.

In the meantime, Ms. Gower had retained counsel, who wrote to the CBEC. The letter pointed out that Ms. Gower's admission had now been delayed for more than a year. During this time, Ms. Gower had been promoted to a supervisory position in the legal research office for Connecticut judges, as a result of her excellent performance as a law clerk. She had been offered, and would soon begin, a clerkship with a justice of the Maine Supreme Court. On June 12, 2000, the CBEC finally recommended her for admission to the Connecticut bar. Ms. Gower filed an ADA complaint with the U.S. Department of Justice and decided to speak publicly about her experiences. She was upset not only by the delay in her admission, but by the intrusiveness of the repeated demands for records and information, and by the tenor of distrust in the committee's dealings with her. "The whole experience was very insulting and invasive," she told the Hartford Courant. "I was hoping they would understand and see how long ago this was and that it isn't relative to my ability to practice law. . . . I'm proud that I got the treatment I did. I'm not ashamed of it. This is not something I want held against me."

## Questions about Rose Gower's Story

1. Why do you think that the bar admissions authorities believed that it was appropriate and necessary for them to ask for so much information about Rose Gower's mental health?

2. Which, if any, of the questions asked do you believe were appropriate and necessary, and why?

3. What reforms would you suggest to improve the bar examiners' process for evaluating character and fitness in Connecticut?

## d. Misconduct during law school

Many applicants report some misconduct committed earlier in their lives. One of the factors that affects decisions about prior misconduct is how long ago it occurred. What follows is a bar admission decision about a man who "borrowed" some money from a student organization during law school.

### In re Mustafa

631 A.2d 45 (D.C. 1993)

SULLIVAN, Associate Judge:
John W. Mustafa II, passed the July 1991 Bar examination and is an applicant for admission to the Bar of the District of Columbia. . . .

### I

In his third year of law school at the University of California at Los Angeles, Mustafa and Larry Brennan served as co-chief justices of the law school's moot court program, and shared access to and control over the program's checking account.[123] Over a five-month period, between October 1990 and February 1991, Mustafa wrote thirteen checks totaling $4,331, approximately $3,510 of which he converted to his personal use.[124] On at least seven occasions, he wrote checks to reimburse himself for expenditures which had been, or would be, reimbursed by the university's accounting department. At other times, he failed to make any notation about the use of the money or falsified the purpose of the checks.[125]

Mustafa admitted to Brennan on June 14, 1991, that he had taken $1,000 from the fund to pay his sister's bail and that he would repay the money from a loan he had arranged from his then-prospective employer. Several days later, Brennan discovered that less than $800 remained in the account, rather than the $1,300 he had expected; Brennan closed the account. On June 25th, Mustafa presented Brennan with a cashier's check for $2,200. On June 28th, Brennan disclosed Mustafa's misconduct to the law school dean; on the same day, Mustafa disclosed his misconduct to a law school professor and to the Committee. After an investigation, the university was satisfied that Mustafa had made full restitution and disposed of the matter by issuing a letter of censure to be placed in his confidential student discipline file for four years. As required by the university, Mustafa disclosed his misconduct to the law firm at which he is presently employed as a law clerk.

Following a hearing, the Committee found that Mustafa always intended to repay the sums taken from the fund, principally because he repaid $1,500 on January 2, 1991, kept an accurate mental record of how much he had taken from the fund, and made full restitution before there was any threatened action by the law school. The Committee was also impressed by Mustafa's honesty and forthrightness before the Committee and during the law school investigation. Moreover, Mustafa's references from two law school professors, three former members of the moot court program board, a former employer, and three partners and two associates from the law firm where Mustafa is employed, were, to the Committee, powerful testimony of his current good character. The Committee unanimously recommended that Mustafa be admitted to the Bar.

## II

In order to gain admission to the Bar, an applicant must demonstrate "by clear and convincing evidence, that the applicant possessed good moral character

---

123. [Court's footnote 1.] The account held student-paid dues of $25.00 each to cover moot court expenses not paid by the university.

124. [Court's footnote 2.] Mustafa explained that he used the funds principally to pay his rent and other bills, to pay a $1,000 bail for his sister, to lend another sister $750 so she could leave an abusive husband, and to pay expenses for a law student to compete in a Chicago moot court competition. Mustafa also assumed responsibility for approximately $811 which he claimed were legitimate moot court program expenses for which he could provide no documentation.

125. [Court's footnote 3.] In particular, on November 28, 1990, he wrote a check to himself for $1,500, stating falsely on the check stub that it was for air fare to a competition in New York. Mustafa returned this amount to the fund via a personal check on January 2, 1991. Again, on February 28, 1991, he wrote a check for $1,500, indicating on the stub that the check was for $75.00 for Girl Scout cookies.

and general fitness to practice law in the District of Columbia" at the time of the applicant's admission. . . . This court will "accept findings of fact made by the Committee unless they are unsupported by substantial evidence of record," will "make due allowance for the Committee's opportunity to observe and evaluate the demeanor of the applicant where relevant," and will "afford the Committee's recommendations some deference. . . ." In re Manville, 494 A.2d 1289, 1293 (D.C. 1985) (citations omitted) ("Manville I").

Mustafa candidly acknowledges that he, like few others in his position, was placed in a position of trust in handling others' money and that he "failed that test." As the Committee recognized, Mustafa's conduct, while it did not result in a criminal conviction, "was sufficiently serious to require analysis under the principles laid down in [Manville I]." Of particular significance is the Committee's finding that Mustafa's conduct "could be considered criminal in nature and would almost invariably have resulted in the disbarment of an attorney admitted to practice." There is no doubt that an attorney who mismanages the funds of a client will ordinarily face disbarment. . . . Similarly, an attorney convicted of a crime involving moral turpitude faces automatic disbarment. . . . A disbarred attorney would be ineligible to apply for reinstatement for five years. . . . While we do not hold as a matter of law that an applicant for admission to the Bar, like a disbarred attorney, must necessarily wait a minimum of five years from the date of proven misconduct before applying for admission to the Bar, we conclude that on the record here, particularly the relatively short period of time that has elapsed since the date of his misconduct, Mustafa has failed to establish that he has the good moral character required for admission to the Bar. . . .

In reaching this conclusion, we are mindful of Mustafa's outstanding law school record[126] and his appropriate conduct since the embezzlement: he cooperated with the university and the Committee; he has married; and he has volunteered in several community projects since coming to the District of Columbia. . . . Indeed, on the record here, it appears likely that Mustafa will be able to establish the requisite good moral character at some future time. At present, however, "[o]ur consideration of the entire record leaves us unpersuaded that [Mustafa] now possesses 'those qualities of truth-speaking, of a high sense of honor, of granite discretion, of the strictest observation of fiduciary responsibility, that have . . . been compendiously described as [the] "moral character"' necessary for the practice of law." . . . In sum, Mustafa has not demonstrated his present fitness for the privilege of membership in the District of Columbia Bar.

Accordingly we deny Mustafa's application for admission to the Bar of the District of Columbia. So ordered.

---

126. [Court's footnote 5.] Mustafa was a staff member and editor of the law review; he was one of two co-chief justices of the moot court program; was named one of twelve outstanding advocates during his second year of law school; and was one of three graduating law students selected by the law school Dean, Susan Westerberg Prager, to attend an annual donors' dinner. He also participated in several other law school activities.

## Question about *Mustafa*

Stop! Before reading further, decide whether you agree with the court that Mustafa should not have been licensed to practice law. Could his future conduct be predicted on the basis of his law school transgression? If not, is this sanction too severe?

### California Bar Journal

June 2002

John Wali Mustafa [#171355], 38, of Redondo Beach was suspended for five years, stayed, placed on five years of probation with an actual two-year suspension and was ordered to make restitution, take the MPRE and comply with Rule 955. The order took effect December 29, 2001.

Mustafa stipulated to misconduct in four matters.

He substituted into a civil matter, representing four clients against a music company, and filed a second amended complaint to his original federal filing without the court's permission. The defendants won $5,000 in sanctions, claiming Mustafa and his clients "had unreasonably and vexatiously multiplied the proceedings in the case."

In the meantime, his clients' former lawyer filed two attorney fee liens. The music company settled the case for $120,000 and issued a check payable to the four plaintiffs, the first lawyer and Mustafa, who had several conversations about the fee owed the first lawyer. Nonetheless, Mustafa negotiated the check without the other lawyer's endorsement and disbursed the funds to his clients and himself. When the other lawyer sued Mustafa for fraud and conversion, he sent the dispute to fee arbitration. He and his clients failed to appear at the fee arbitration hearing and the other lawyer was awarded $51,646.40 as his fee, plus reimbursement for costs and interest. The court also found that Mustafa had acted fraudulently when he converted the settlement funds, and ordered punitive damages of $50,000 against him.

He stipulated that he failed to report judicial sanctions to the State Bar and that he committed an act of moral turpitude by converting the settlement funds.

In another matter, Mustafa filed a wrongful termination complaint, representing his client on a contingency fee basis. He did not oppose any of four motions filed by the defendants, and the motions were granted. He also did not oppose a motion for monetary sanctions, nor did he appear in court for the hearing. The court ordered that the complaint be stricken and imposed sanctions of more than $6,300. Although Mustafa moved for reconsideration, he didn't appear at the hearing.

Over a period of several months, the client called Mustafa repeatedly, but he did not return the calls. He also did not respond to a State Bar investigator.

The third case involved a civil complaint against a mortuary for mishandling human remains. The complaint was filed on behalf of the deceased's three children. Mustafa did not return six phone calls from the clients over an eight-month period. He also did not cooperate with the bar's investigation.

Mustafa also commingled personal and business funds in his client trust account and wrote checks for personal expenses against the account.

In mitigation, he had family problems at the time of the misconduct and he cooperated with the bar's investigation.[127]

## Additional Notes and Questions about *Mustafa*

**1.** During 2002, while he was suspended from practice, additional charges were filed against Mustafa. Rather than respond to these additional charges, Mustafa resigned his bar membership.[128]

**2.** What, if any, connections do you see between the conduct alleged in the D.C. bar admission case and in the California disciplinary case? Are there significant differences between the two sets of allegations?

**3.** How do you suppose that Mustafa was admitted to the bar in California after he had been denied admission in D.C.? There is no published opinion discussing the California bar application, only the information that he was admitted in 1994. Do you think that the California bar examiners read the D.C. Court of Appeals opinion and reached a different conclusion? Do you think it is possible that they did not know that Mustafa had been denied admission in D.C.?

**4.** There seems to have been a great divergence of opinion about whether John Wali Mustafa was fit to practice law. The law school investigation resulted only in the placement of a letter of censure in his file — a relatively light sanction. The bar admissions committee in D.C. recommended Mustafa's admission to the bar, based in part on the committee's impression of his truthfulness and on his glowing character references. The D.C. Court of Appeals disagreed with this judgment, in part because of the short time that had elapsed since his law school misconduct, and denied him admission. A year later the California bar admissions authorities decided he was fit to practice. What might account for this divergence? Is the character and fitness review so subjective that consistent outcomes are not possible?

**5.** If you agree that the character and fitness review is too subjective and too inconsistent, do you believe that it should simply be abandoned? What would be the potential problems with abandoning this inquiry? If you believe that the review should be retained, how might it be improved?

## e. Law school discipline: A preliminary screening process

Most law schools have established internal disciplinary processes to evaluate student misconduct allegations and to impose sanctions. Sanctions range from

---

127. California Bar Journal, Disbarments, *available at* http://www.calbar.ca.gov/calbar/2cbj/02jun/attdisc.htm (June 2002) (last visited Oct. 6, 2004).

128. State Bar of California, Attorney Search, *at* http://members.calbar.ca.gov/search/member_search.aspx?ms=JOHN+WALI+MUSTAFA+ (last visited Oct. 6, 2004); Interview with NAME, Attorney Information Service Employee, California State Bar (Mar. 4, 2004).

asking the offending student to write a letter of apology to suspension or expulsion from law school. Sometimes the law school's sanctions include a transcript notation that bar examiners are certain to see. In other cases, as in Mustafa's, the sanction is noted only in the student's confidential record, which may or may not be reported to the bar by the law school. But the bar examiners often ask applicants to disclose any sanctions imposed by a law school, whether or not the law school considered them "confidential."

Some law school disciplinary boards are staffed entirely by students, others by students and faculty, and still others by faculty only. Likewise, some schools ask student or faculty volunteers to prosecute these cases, while a few have professional staff handle the prosecution of students. Student respondents are permitted to have counsel in these proceedings. Some schools allow nonlawyer advocates to assist respondents, and some allow or require faculty to represent the respondents. A student respondent may be represented by an outside lawyer of his choosing, but generally must pay the lawyer's fee himself.[129] The law school disciplinary systems tend to be structured like microcosms of the lawyer disciplinary system. The law schools perform a prescreening process for the bar examiners with respect to students who engage in misconduct while in law school.

## PROBLEM 1-2 **THE DOCTORED RESUME**

*The following problem is based on a true story, though some facts have been changed to protect the identity of the individual involved.*

You are a member of your law school Honor Board, a judicial body that does fact-finding and recommends disposition of allegations of misconduct by law students. The Board has the authority to recommend reprimand, suspension from law school, expulsion from law school, community service, or other sanctions. The law school administration generally adopts recommendations by the Honor Board. Any finding of violation of the law school Honor Code is reported to the bar to which a respondent applies for admission. The following matter has been presented to the board for review.

Erica Kass, a third-year law student, is charged with violation of the Honor Code because she included false information on her resume and then submitted the resume to law firms recruiting through the law school placement office. The law school Honor Code specifically prohibits students from "providing false or misleading information about their academic credentials, employment history, or other matters, to the law school, to prospective employers, or to anyone else."

---

129. See generally Elizabeth Gepford McCulley, Note, School of Sharks, Bar Fitness Requirements of Good Moral Character and the Role of Law Schools, 14 Geo. J. Leg. Ethics 839 (2001).

Erica came to the United States from Estonia a year before she began law school; her father is a diplomat and was sent to the United States. Her undergraduate degree is from Tartu University. Erica listed her undergraduate degree as having been "magna cum laude." Upon investigation, the Honor Board learned that Tartu University has never conferred Latin honors upon graduation — to Erica or to anyone else. Also, Erica was in the bottom quarter of her law school class. On her resume, she listed her law school class rank as "top third." Erica used white-out and a typewriter to make some corresponding changes in her actual law school transcript. Finally, during the year before she enrolled in law school, Erica worked at the Estonian Embassy in Washington. On her resume, she listed her position as Cultural Attaché. Her former employer informed an Honor Board investigator that Erica's position at the embassy was as receptionist.

A hearing was held, at which Erica admitted that all three of the alleged falsehoods on her resume were in fact false and that she had added this information to her resume in the hope of obtaining a good job in a law firm.

"I was new to the U.S., so even though I studied very hard, I didn't do very well on my exams. It seemed unfair to me that my grades were not good even though I worked harder than most of the other students. My normal English was pretty good by the time I started law school, but the technical language was very difficult for me.

"I have very high student loans — by the time I finish it will be above $100,000. My family is not wealthy — they cannot help me pay for this. Also the family is watching me to see whether I will succeed in the U.S. — I felt I must get a good position or else they would be ashamed of me.

"I tried applying for jobs but I wasn't getting any interviews. I talked with one of my American friends. He's another law student, I'd rather not say his name. He looked at my resume for me, and said I just needed to fix it up a little bit. He made some suggestions — I think the changes were all his ideas.

"At first I thought he was crazy — he was telling me to lie. He said they were just little white lies, and that if I wanted to succeed in America I had to stop being so prissy. He said at his college, no one ever wrote their own papers — they just copied over someone else's paper from the year before or downloaded one from the Internet. It's a free country, he said. I knew it wasn't right, but also I knew I needed to get a job, so I decided to take his advice. Obviously it was a mistake."

What sanction, if any, should the law school impose on this student? Should the alleged conduct preclude Erica from admission to the bar?

# D. Professional discipline

This section offers a detailed examination of the lawyer disciplinary system. One reason to examine the disciplinary system at this point is that a central focus of this course is the state ethics rules. Discipline is the intended sanction for violation of these rules, and understanding the structure of the enforcement system will aid you in understanding the rules.

## 1. The history and process of lawyer discipline

Before the twentieth century, a lawyer who engaged in misconduct might have been brought to court and charged with misfeasance (traditionally characterized as "conduct unbecoming a lawyer") by a client, another lawyer, or a bar association. The result might be for the judge to bar the lawyer from further practice in that court.[130] After the ABA adopted the 1908 Canons of Ethics, some courts began to refer to the canons as providing a basis for discipline of lawyers. Gradually, the states established administrative agencies to investigate and prosecute lawyer misconduct. Until the latter part of the twentieth century, however, many state disciplinary systems were extremely limited by lack of funding, by reliance on volunteer staffing, and so on.[131] More recently, the disciplinary systems have become "professionalized," with better funding, more staff, and greater ability to police lawyer misconduct.[132] Courts have established administrative hearing panels to make findings of fact and recommendations for sanctions. States have also adopted procedural rules for adjudication of lawyer discipline cases. Most of these are based on the ABA Model Rules for Lawyer Disciplinary Enforcement.[133]

**How does a disciplinary proceeding work? Where does it begin? What happens?**

In most states, the highest court runs the disciplinary system. An independent office set up by the court uses paid staff attorneys to investigate and prosecute charges against lawyers. Some of these disciplinary agencies are part of the state bar associations, but a majority are independent of the bar associations.[134]

---

130. Restatement ch. 1, tit. C, introductory note.

131. See Charles W. Wolfram, Modern Legal Ethics 84 (West 1986).

132. See generally Leslie C. Levin, The Emperor's Clothes and Other Tales About the Standards for Imposing Lawyer Discipline, 48 Am. U. L. Rev. 1 (1998) (chronicling this development and discussing contemporary problems with the lawyer discipline systems).

133. Restatement, supra n. 130.

134. Thirty-three states require lawyers to be members of the bar association as a condition of receiving a license to practice law. Of those states, twenty-two state bar associations run the lawyer disciplinary agencies under the supervision of the states' highest courts. The other eleven have independent disciplinary agencies. In the eighteen states in which bar membership is not mandatory, lawyers pay registration fees each year to agencies of the states' highest courts. Those agencies handle admission and discipline of lawyers. Mary M. Devlin, The Development of Lawyer Disciplinary Procedures in the United States, 7 Geo. J. Leg. Ethics 911, 933-934 (1994).

## How a disciplinary case proceeds

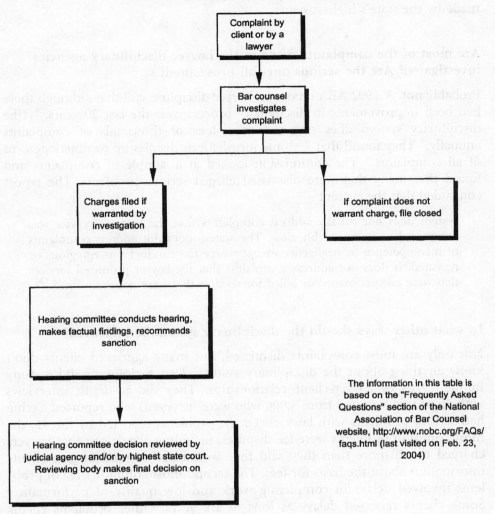

Complaint by
client or by a
lawyer

Bar counsel
investigates
complaint

Charges filed if
warranted by
investigation

If complaint does not
warrant charge, file closed

Hearing committee conducts hearing,
makes factual findings, recommends
sanction

The information in this table is
based on the "Frequently Asked
Questions" section of the National
Association of Bar Counsel
website, http://www.nobc.org/FAQs/
faqs.html (last visited on Feb. 23,
2004)

Hearing committee decision reviewed by
judicial agency and/or by highest state court.
Reviewing body makes final decision on
sanction

If a disciplinary agency thinks that a complaint against a lawyer appears warranted, it first presents the case to a hearing committee. The hearing committees often include two lawyers and a nonlawyer. In many states, those who serve on the hearing committees are volunteers. The hearing committees hear evidence, make findings of fact, and recommend sanctions.[135] The recommendations of hearing committees are then reviewed by a judicial

---

135. See Restatement, supra n. 130. Disciplinary proceedings used to be more heavily controlled by bar associations, but partly in response to the ABA's Model Rules for Lawyer Disciplinary Enforcement, these proceedings have become more independent of bar association influence. See Charles W. Wolfram, Toward a History of the Legalization of American Legal Ethics II — The Modern Era, 15 Geo. J. Leg. Ethics 205, 206 (2002).

agency and/or by the state's highest court. Final decisions on sanctions are made by the state's highest court.

### Are most of the complaints made to the lawyer disciplinary agencies investigated? Are the serious ones all prosecuted?

Probably not. A 1992 ABA report on lawyer discipline said that although there had been improvements in disciplinary process over the last 20 years, "[t]he disciplinary system does not address ... tens of thousands of complaints annually." They found that "[s]ome jurisdictions dismiss up to ninety percent of all complaints." The commission looked at a sample of complaints and found that many that were dismissed alleged serious problems. The report concluded that the current

> system does not usually address complaints that the lawyer's service was overpriced or unreasonably slow. The system does not address complaints of incompetence or negligence except where the conduct was egregious or repeated. It does not address complaints that the lawyer promised services that were not performed or billed for services that were not authorized.[136]

### In what other ways should the disciplinary system be improved?

Not only are most complaints dismissed, but many aggrieved clients don't know anything about the disciplinary system. Two sociologists did a study in the 1970s of lawyer-client relationships. They did in-depth interviews with 45 people (selected from 4,000 who were surveyed) who reported having had serious problems with lawyers. Of the problems reported by the 45, the most common problems were fee disputes, including allegations that lawyers charged much more than they said they would and refused to give clients information about the basis for fees. The second most common area of problems involved delays in completing work and low quality of performance. Some clients reported delays as long as six years. Other problems clients reported were conflicts of interest, failure to keep confidences, and failure to perform promised services. Of the 45 clients who had had serious problems with their lawyers, none had filed a grievance against the lawyer, and only one person had contacted the bar. Thirty-five of them did not know that a disciplinary system existed.[137]

---

136. ABA Center for Professional Responsibility, Commission on Evaluation of Disciplinary Enforcement, Lawyer Regulation for a New Century xv (1992). An earlier ABA investigation had found that when a client complained that a lawyer had stolen money from the client, the prosecutor would often offer to dismiss the complaint if the lawyer paid the client back. ABA Special Committee on Evaluation of Disciplinary Enforcement, Problems and Recommendations in Disciplinary Enforcement 78 (1970). The 1992 report indicated that these problems persisted.

137. Eric H. Steele & Raymond T. Nimmer, Lawyers, Clients, and Professional Regulation, 1976 Am. B. Found. Res. J. 917.

*Professor Leslie Levin*

Disciplinary agencies have made efforts in recent decades to be more visible to clients who might have complaints, but the disciplinary process remains secretive in most places. Historically, disciplinary agencies conducted business behind closed doors and provided very little information to the public.[138]

Professor Leslie Levin describes a few of the problems remaining with lawyer disciplinary systems:

There are over one million lawyers with active licenses in the United States. In 1996, state lawyer disciplinary agencies reported 118,891 complaints concerning alleged lawyer misconduct. The actual number of complaints was undoubtedly higher. Only about five percent of all complaints result in any sanctions against lawyers.

It appears the sanctions imposed on lawyers are often light and inconsistent. . . . Consider these facts: Private sanctions — the lightest form of discipline — are imposed almost twice as often as any other type of sanction. Lawyers often receive several private admonitions before they receive any public discipline. If a lawyer is suspended from practice, the period of suspension is frequently so brief that it does not interrupt a lawyer's practice.[139]

There are other problems too:

■ Most of the people disciplined are experienced sole practitioners,[140] even though there is reason to believe that some lawyers in firms, government lawyers, and lawyers who work for corporations also engage in serious misconduct.

---

138. Paula A. Monopoli, Legal Ethics and Practical Politics: Musings on the Public Perception of Lawyer Discipline, 10 Geo. J. Leg. Ethics 423, 424 (1997).

139. Levin, supra n. 132, at 8-9. Occasionally, the discipline imposed is so light and so late that it becomes a public issue. In 2004, the Virginia Bar made public disciplinary charges against one William P. Robinson, a former state legislator, who previously had been reprimanded four times by the bar and then held in contempt three times for not showing up in court. Twice the courts imposed suspended jail sentences. In addition, a court found that he had defaulted on four appeals, lied to his client by telling him that a case dismissed because of his negligence was still pending, and lied to another client, saying that the Virginia Supreme Court had dismissed his appeal. Even so, the court rejected the bar counsel's recommendation that Robinson be disbarred, instead suspending his license for only 30 days. The *Washington Post*, after reporting that Robinson had defaulted on eight other criminal appeals, asked, "What exactly does it take to get disbarred in Virginia? Mr. Robinson is an extreme example, but as our study has shown, he is far from the state's only defense lawyer who frequently tosses a client's rights away." Wash. Post, Editorial, A Lawyer's Tale, Aug. 6, 2004.

140. Patricia Manson, Solo Practitioners Draw Majority of Sanctions, Chi. Daily L. Bull., May 3, 2004, at 1 (reporting on the 2003 report of the Illinois Attorney Registration and Disciplinary Commission, which stated that 67 percent of the lawyers sanctioned were sole practitioners, even though only 19 percent of the licensed lawyers are sole practitioners). This pattern is observed throughout the United States. Ted Schneyer, Professional Discipline for Law Firms? 77 Cornell L. Rev. 1 (1992). But see Julie Rose O'Sullivan, Professional Discipline for Law Firms? A Response to Professor Schneyer's Proposal, 16 Geo. J. Leg. Ethics 1 (2002) (arguing that sole practitioners are not disproportionately disciplined).

■ Formal discipline is disproportionately imposed on members of minority groups.[141]

■ Most disciplinary complaints come from clients. Much lawyer misconduct is unknown to clients, so the types of misconduct that lead to discipline is skewed toward the problems that clients discover. (See discussion of reporting misconduct below.[142])

■ The disciplinary systems tend to impose sanctions that are more punitive than rehabilitative.[143]

## 2. Grounds for discipline

### Can a lawyer be disciplined for conduct that has nothing to do with the practice of law?

Yes. A lawyer may be disciplined for violation of the applicable ethics code whether or not the violation occurs in the course of law practice. Most ethical rules impose requirements on the conduct of law practice, but a lawyer may be disciplined also for any conduct that is dishonest or prejudicial to the administration of justice or that reflects lack of fitness to practice. Lawyers are often disciplined for conduct that was not part of their work as lawyers. Lawyers have been disciplined for domestic violence,[144] failure to pay child support,[145] drunk driving,[146] and even for putting slugs in parking meters.[147] One lawyer was disciplined because he sent flowers and a note offering legal assistance to the family of a deceased person, both of which were delivered to a funeral home.[148]

FOR EXAMPLE: One lawyer helped a former client (who was one of his buddies) to break into the home of the former client's wife. They ransacked the house, clogged the toilet, and stole some jewelry and other

---

141. Manson, supra n. 140 (reporting that the Illinois disciplinary data showed that "Black lawyers were disciplined in disproportionately larger numbers than their white counterparts." Eleven percent of the lawyers disciplined were black, but only about 4.9 percent of the lawyers who are admitted in Illinois are black).

142. See William T. Gallagher, Ideologies of Professionalism and the Politics of Self-Regulation in the California State Bar, 22 Pepp. L. Rev. 485, 612-614 (1995).

143. See Diane M. Ellis, A Decade of Diversion: Empirical Evidence that Alternative Discipline Is Working for Arizona Lawyers, 52 Emory L.J. 1221 (2003).

144. See In re Grella, 777 N.E.2d 167 (Mass. 2002) (lawyer suspended for two months after criminal conviction for domestic violence).

145. In 1996 Congress enacted a law requiring the states to suspend professional licenses of persons who failed to pay child support. 42 U.S.C. § 666(a)(16) (1997). Restatement § 5, comment b, reporter's note. But even before this federal law was passed, some lawyers were disciplined for nonpayment of child support. See, e.g., In re Wolfrom, 681 N.E.2d 1336 (Ohio 1997).

146. In re Conduct of McDonough, 77 P.3d 306 (Or. 2003) (lawyer suspended for 18 months for driving while intoxicated and other offenses).

147. Fellner v. B. Assn. of Baltimore City, 131 A.2d 729 (Md. 1957).

148. Norris v. Ala. St. B., 582 So. 2d 1034 (Ala.), cert. denied, 502 U.S. 957 (1991).

items. Most disturbing, the lawyer and his former client killed Max, the family kitten, in the microwave oven. The wife and her children found Max dead on the kitchen floor, smelling of champagne. The lawyer was indefinitely suspended from law practice with leave to apply for reinstatement after a year.[149]

*President Richard
M. Nixon*

Many lawyers who have held high public office have been disciplined for misconduct that related to their performance of their duties as public servants. Former president Richard Nixon was disbarred because of actions he took not while practicing law, but while president of the United States. The disciplinary committee concluded:

Unrebutted documentary evidence warrants sustaining charges against respondent, former president of the United States, that he improperly obstructed an FBI investigation of the unlawful entry into the headquarters of the Democratic National Committee; improperly authorized or approved the surreptitious payment of money . . . to prevent or delay . . . disclosure of information to federal law enforcement authorities; improperly attempted to obstruct an investigation by the U.S. Department of Justice of an unlawful entry into the offices of [a psychiatrist treating Daniel Ellsberg, leaker of the Pentagon Papers]; [and] improperly concealed . . . evidence relating to unlawful activities of members of his staff and of the Committee to Re-elect the president. . . . The failure of the respondent to answer the charges, to appear in the proceeding, or to submit any papers on his behalf must be construed by this Court as an admission of the charges and an indifference to the attendant consequences.[150]

Nixon was disbarred even though he was not acting as a lawyer in doing these things but was instead acting as the president of the United States. Many other members of the Nixon administration, including former vice president Spiro Agnew[151] and former attorney general John Mitchell, were also disbarred.[152] The creation of the law school course in professional responsibility was in significant part a response to the misconduct of lawyers involved in the Watergate scandal.

More recently, former president Clinton agreed to a five-year suspension for giving false testimony about his relationship with Monica Lewinsky in

---

149. Atty. Grievance Commn. of Md. v. Protokowicz, 619 A.2d 100 (Md. 1993).

150. Matter of Nixon, 385 N.Y.S.2d 305, 306 (App. Div. 1976).

151. Md. St. B. Assn. v. Agnew, 318 A.2d 811 (Md. 1974) (disbarment for willful tax evasion).

152. Mitchell v. Assn. of the B. of the City of N.Y., 351 N.E.2d 743 (N.Y. 1976) (summary disbarment of former attorney general John Mitchell after Watergate-related felony convictions).

a deposition in the lawsuit by Paula Jones.[153] Because lawyers are "officers of the court" and are expected to display exemplary integrity, respect for the law, and respect for the legal system, disciplinary agencies tend to be vigilant in prosecuting misconduct by lawyers who are in highly visible positions of public trust.

### Can a lawyer be disciplined for committing a crime?

Yes. A lawyer may be disciplined for the commission of any criminal act that violates an ethical rule or that reflects dishonesty, untrustworthiness, or lack of fitness to practice.

> **FOR EXAMPLE:** A part-time prosecutor was disciplined because he physically assaulted his ladyfriend and her daughter. This was viewed as raising concerns about his fitness to practice in light of his responsibilities as a prosecutor to the system of justice.[154]

### What if the lawyer has not been convicted of or even charged with the crime?

The predicate for discipline is the commission of such a criminal act. A lawyer may be disciplined for the act even if no criminal charge is filed or the lawyer is acquitted of a charge in a criminal proceeding. The purpose of criminal prosecution is to vindicate the interest of the state in prohibiting the act. The purpose of the disciplinary proceeding is to protect the public and the profession by disallowing practice by unfit lawyers. However, if a disciplinary action is filed based on conduct that is the subject of a pending criminal charge, the disciplinary action usually is stayed until the criminal proceeding is concluded.[155]

### Can a lawyer be disciplined based on the actions of an employee?

Yes. Suppose a lawyer tells a paralegal to shred a document that opposing counsel has requested in discovery. This lawyer may be disciplined for violating a rule by inducing or assisting another person to do something that violates the rules if done by a lawyer.

> **FOR EXAMPLE:** One lawyer got his partner to draft a codicil to his client's will leaving this client's property to himself. He was trying to get around a rule that bars lawyers from drafting legal documents for clients that transfer the client's property to themselves. He received a public censure.[156]

---

153. Correspondence and Agreed Order in the Settlement of Clinton's Case, N.Y. Times, Jan. 20, 2001, at A20.

154. In re Walker, 597 N.E.2d 1271 (Ind.), modified, 601 N.E.2d 327 (1992).

155. Restatement § 5, comment g.

156. In re Whelan, 619 A.2d 571 (N.H. 1992).

**Can a lawyer be disciplined for something she does outside the state in which she is licensed to practice?**

Yes. The lawyer may be disciplined for violation of the rules regardless of whether the violation occurs in the state in which the lawyer is admitted. So, for example, if a lawyer admitted in Idaho commits a crime in Nevada, she could be disciplined in Idaho for the criminal act in Nevada.[157]

**If a lawyer violates a rule in a state in which he is not licensed, can he be disciplined by the authorities in that state?**

It depends. Most ethics codes subject only lawyers admitted to practice in that state to discipline for violation of the rules. However, the ethics rules of California, the District of Columbia, and Maryland allow discipline of any lawyer who violates a rule of the jurisdiction, regardless of whether the person is licensed to practice in that state.[158]

**What if a lawyer is admitted to practice in several states but is suspended or disbarred in one of those states? Can the lawyer continue her practice in the other states?**

No. A lawyer who is admitted in more than one state must report to the other states where she is admitted if discipline is imposed in one of the states. If she does not comply with that obligation, she might get caught. The ABA maintains a National Regulatory Data Bank[159] that compiles information about discipline imposed around the country. Bar counsels periodically consult this data bank to see if any of their members have been disciplined in other states. Once a bar counsel learns of a sanction imposed on a member of the bar by another jurisdiction, the bar counsel may initiate a proceeding to impose "reciprocal discipline." A lawyer who is sanctioned in one jurisdiction often receives the same sanction in any other jurisdictions where the lawyer is admitted.[160]

**Are lawyers ever disciplined for conduct that occurs at a law school?**

Yes. Like lawyers who hold public office, law professors and deans occupy roles in which they are expected to set an example for other lawyers. Most law professors take that responsibility quite seriously. But, of course, there are some exceptions. Consider the following case, which was based on Minnesota's version of the Model Code of Professional Responsibility.

---

157. See Rule 8.5, which explains choice of law rules in such situations.

158. Restatement § 5, comment h.

159. ABA, Center for Professional Responsibility, National Lawyer Regulatory Databank, *at* http://www.abanet.org/cpr/databank.html (last visited Oct. 6, 2004).

160. Telephone Interview with John Rooney, District of Columbia Assistant Bar Counsel (Mar. 4, 2004).

# In re Peters

428 N.W.2d 375 (Minn. 1988)

PER CURIAM.

These proceedings are before the court on the petition of the Director of the Office of Lawyers Professional Responsibility for disciplinary action against respondent Geoffrey Peters, a lawyer charged with professional misconduct. . . . The petition alleged and the referee found that respondent, then dean of William Mitchell College of Law, repeatedly engaged in unwelcome physical contact and verbal communication of a sexual nature against four women employees, two of whom were also law students. The referee concluded that respondent's conduct adversely reflects on his fitness to practice law in violation of DR 1-102(A)(6) and recommended a public reprimand. We agree with the referee's conclusion. . . .

*Geoffrey Peters in the 1980s*

### [Some of the allegations of sexual harassment]

Joan Peterson was a Carleton College graduate who worked for a time before entering law school. At the time of the hearing in this matter she was an attorney in the office of a county public defender. She began law school in August 1982 and shortly thereafter was engaged as a research assistant for the respondent and for Associate Dean Melvin Goldberg.

The referee found that on four or five occasions between November 1982 and March 1983, respondent approached Peterson from behind, put his hands around her waist and squeezed it or pulled her sideways into his body. These incidents all occurred in the dean's suite at the college.

*Joan Peterson in 2004*

Peterson testified that following the first incident, to which she responded by firmly removing respondent's hand and attempting to put some distance between them, she began wearing more business-like clothes — suits and high-collared shirts — instead of the casual attire of many student researchers, because she wanted to make sure that she was not doing anything to encourage this type of behavior.

The referee found that in March 1983, while Peterson was conversing with a professor in the hallway at the college, respondent walked up to Peterson from behind, placed his hand on the back of her head, ran his fingers through her hair and down to her waist, letting his hand come to rest on the small of her back. . . . Because the gesture made the professor uncomfortable, as if he were interrupting some sort of intimate contact between Peterson and the respondent, and because Peterson appeared flustered, the professor walked away. A few days later Peterson apologized to the professor for the incident, explaining that she did not want him to get the wrong impression that she had a personal relationship with the dean.

The referee also found that in the spring of 1983 respondent put his hands on Peterson's waist and pulled her into his body and against a file cabinet in the office of respondent's administrative assistant. Respondent then asked if Peterson was returning to work for him in the fall.

In her testimony, Peterson distinguished between an unobjectionable brief touch on the arm or pat on the shoulder in the course of a discussion on a research project and the offensive and unwelcome touching of her waist and rib cage. Peterson testified that in response to respondent's physical contacts she froze up, ignored the misconduct, and removed respondent's hands if he did not remove them immediately. She attempted to communicate with respondent by notes rather than by speaking to him, and she stayed near the doorway when she entered his office. When asked why she did not report any of these incidents earlier, Peterson responded as follows:

> I felt that there would be strong repercussions that could potentially harm, disgrace or end my career. I was just a first-year student . . . and Dean Peters had all the power. . . . I had seen what the administration's reaction was when there were people who went to them with problems and it was generally retaliation for raising any problems, and I didn't want to become part of that. . . . I just wanted to get another job and get out without — without having to confront him directly and ruin my career. . . .

*Nancy Quattlebaum Burke in 2004*

Like Joan Peterson, Nancy Quattlebaum graduated from Carleton College, then worked the following year . . . before entering William Mitchell College of Law. She became a member of the law review and graduated with honors in 1984. She is now [in 1988] an associate in a large metropolitan law firm.

She began working for the respondent as a research assistant in June 1982, after having completed two years of a four-year program. The series of incidents affecting Quattlebaum began early in her employment. Quattlebaum testified that on her first day of work respondent put his arm around her and suggested that she spend the weekend with him at the law school's retreat center to work on a project. She declined the invitation. Respondent admitted extending the invitation but claimed that other senior administrators of the college would have been at the retreat center that weekend.

The referee . . . found that on at least three occasions between June 1982 and May 1983, while working with Quattlebaum in his office, respondent pulled his chair against hers and leaned over into her, sitting so close to her that his knee, leg, and arm were pressed against hers. Respondent did not deny that this occurred . . . but he stated that it was necessitated by the need for them to review documents simultaneously.

The referee found that in December 1982, at the dean's Christmas party, respondent put his arm around Quattlebaum, pulled her to him, and rubbed his hand up and down her rib cage while they were talking to several guests. . . .

Quattlebaum's response to this course of conduct was to attempt to avoid all situations where respondent could make such advances. . . . When asked why she did not report these incidents to anyone in an administrative capacity at the college until the following academic year when a faculty member asked whether she had encountered any problems while working for respondent, Quattlebaum made this reply:

> Professional suicide. It would have probably ruined my career. Dean Peters was
> a powerful man with a lot of influential friends. I couldn't take the risk. . . .

[*Authors' note: The opinion describes similar conduct by the dean toward one administrative assistant and toward the acting director of the library.*] The referee found that respondent's unwelcome touches and verbal communications substantially interfered with and created an hostile educational environment for two of the women and an hostile employment environment for all four of the women, and he concluded that these repeated physical contacts and verbal communications adversely reflected on respondent's fitness to practice law. . . .

### [Clear and convincing evidence of sexual harassment]

Sexual harassment is unlawful. . . . A formal adjudication that conduct is illegal is not prerequisite to a determination that conduct adversely reflects on a lawyer's fitness to practice law. DR 1-102(A)(3) expressly proscribes certain kinds of illegal conduct — illegal conduct involving moral turpitude. DR 1-102(A)(6) prohibits "any other conduct that adversely reflects on [a lawyer's] fitness to practice law." Indeed, this court has held that an attorney may be disciplined for actions which are illegal but do not result in criminal conviction. . . .

Neither can it be said that a lawyer's ethical obligations and professional responsibility are confined to conduct arising out of the attorney-client relationship. . . .

While it is true that discipline is seldom imposed for sexual misconduct unless the lawyer has been convicted of a crime or the conduct has arisen within the attorney-client relationship, . . . neither conviction for rape or child abuse nor the presence of an attorney-client relationship are necessary elements to a breach of ethical responsibility by reason of misconduct of a sexual nature. . . .[161]

---

161. [Court's footnote 4.] In re Miera, 426 N.W.2d 850 (Minn. 1988); In re Kirby, 354 N.W.2d 410 (Minn. 1984) (judge publicly censured for referring to female attorneys as "lawyerettes" in court); In re Snyder, 336 N.W.2d 533 (Minn. 1983) (public censure of judge pursuant to stipulation based on adulterous relationship with his secretary); In re Gould, 4 A.D.2d 174, 164 N.Y.S.2d 48, appeal denied, 4 A.D.2d 833, 166 N.Y.S.2d 301 (1957) (attorney disbarred for soliciting women who came to his office in response to help-wanted advertisements); Florida Bar v. Hefty, 213 So. 2d 422 (Fla. 1968) (attorney disbarred for sexual relations with his step-daughter, a minor).

[This is a] case of a demonstrated pattern of an employer's lamentable abuse of power grounded on discriminatory sexual harassment. . . .

Moreover, the respondent was . . . the dean of the law school in which two of the affected individuals were students — a status which made them singularly vulnerable to the dean's abuse of power. . . . A law student who wants to become eligible to practice law is a virtual captive of the law school. The law student can neither leave and go elsewhere to school nor risk retaliation which might take the form of expulsion or failing grades. . . . Sexual harassment in academic settings . . . surely set a pernicious example for the school's students and faculty and reflected adversely on the integrity and honor of the profession. . . .

A *public* reprimand is not only an appropriate but necessary response by this court to assure the public and warn the practicing bar that it cannot condone such conduct by an attorney — particularly one of the stature and influence of a law school dean.

Respondent Geoffrey Peters is publicly reprimanded. Respondent shall pay costs in the amount of $500.

## Notes and Questions about *Peters*

**1.** Peters was disciplined for conduct that did not lead to criminal charges. Should a lawyer be subject to discipline for alleged illegal conduct even if the lawyer was never arrested, charged, or convicted?

**2.** Peters was the dean of a law school. The women he harassed were not clients, but students and employees. Is such a case properly handled through the lawyer disciplinary system? Should Peters simply have been fired? What purpose is served by his being publically disciplined also?

**3.** The sanction imposed in this case was a public reprimand. This means that the case was made public and probably a notice was published in the bar journal announcing the decision. The ABA Model Rules for Lawyer Disciplinary Enforcement offer criteria by which disciplinary authorities should decide what sanction is appropriate for a particular offense.

> Factors to be Considered in Imposing Sanctions. In imposing a sanction after a finding of lawyer misconduct, the court or board shall consider the following factors, as enumerated in the ABA Standards for Imposing Lawyer Sanctions.
>
> > (1) whether the lawyer has violated a duty owed to a client, to the public, to the legal system, or to the profession;
> > (2) whether the lawyer acted intentionally, knowingly, or negligently;
> > (3) the amount of the actual or potential injury caused by the lawyer's misconduct; and
> > (4) the existence of any aggravating or mitigating factors.[162]

Do you think the sanction is too severe or not severe enough? Why?

---

162. American Bar Association Standing Committee on Professional Discipline, Model Rules for Lawyer Disciplinary Enforcement, Rule 10, sanctions, section c, *available at* http://www.abanet.org/cpr/disenf/rule10.html (last visited Oct. 6, 2004).

**4.** The disciplinary case mentions allegations by 4 women, 2 students and 2 staff. In fact, 11 women who said they had been harassed by Peters filed a complaint with the state's Department of Human Rights, and 3 of them filed suit against the university and some university officials. (The university was a defendant in part because Peters had been the dean and in part because when the women brought their complaints to the school's trustees, "they were met with disbelief."[163] Peters denied the allegations, and the university did not acknowledge the harassment either, but the suit was settled in 1984 for $300,000. The numbers don't really convey the suffering that some of the women reported. Harassment can be very debilitating.

Joan Peterson, for example, described how after the dean began grabbing her, she started wearing suits and putting her hair in a bun, and stopped wearing makeup to make sure she wasn't "sending out the wrong signals." She was afraid to confront the dean, quit, or complain for fear of ruining her career. Her other relationships were strained because she was regarded as the "dean's pet." One day she finally snapped and pushed him away, stormed out, and filed a complaint. After that, she went through months of stress related to the lawsuit, developed an eating disorder, and transferred to the University of Minnesota.[164]

Peters may have harassed more than 11 women. Twenty-three women attended one meeting of those potentially interested in participating in the lawsuit.[165] Peters's own lawyer characterized him as "the tactile dean."[166] The disciplinary case resulted in a published opinion that documented the harassment, but the harassment suit was settled, so there were no formal findings and no public record.

In addition, the *Minneapolis Star and Tribune* reported in 1983 that Geoffrey Peters had served as deputy director of the National Center for State Courts in 1979, before he became dean at William Mitchell. While there, several female employees made complaints that Peters had made unwanted sexual advances. One of the complaints was filed by Peters's secretary. When the secretary complained to other officials, "they told her she was whacko. They brought her in and told her they wanted her to leave but were willing to give her a good recommendation. . . . She left, changed her name and got psychological help."[167]

**5.** One of the problems with the lawyer disciplinary system is that some cases take years to get through the system. Peters's case is one example. The incidents described in the decision took place in 1982 and 1983. During

---

163. Douglas R. Heidenreich, With Satisfaction and Honor 273 (William Mitchell Coll. of Law 1999).

164. Pat Prince, Sexual Harassment Leaves Its Mark for Years, Star-Tribune, Jan. 29, 1989, at B1.

165. Cheryl Johnson, Victims Feel Vindicated at Last by William Mitchell Case Ruling, Star-Tribune, Aug. 27, 1988, at B1.

166. Prince, supra n. 164.

167. Dave Anderson, Earlier Sex Harassment by Law Dean Is Alleged, Minneapolis Star & Trib., Nov. 4, 1983.

1983, the women filed formal complaints with the Department of Human Rights and with the state bar disciplinary authorities.[168] The Minnesota Supreme Court did not issue its decision reprimanding Peters until August 1988.

**6.** So what happened to Geoffrey Peters? He was forced to resign from William Mitchell,[169] but he presently serves as president of an organization called Creative Direct Response.[170] In 2004 he was honored for his work with American Charities for Reasonable Fundraising Regulation Inc. The conference that honored him published his biography on the Internet, describing him, in pertinent part, as follows:

> Geoff W. Peters is a fundraiser, lawyer, and manager; has a J.D. degree, as well as an M.A. in social research and statistics. His A.B. degree is from Northwestern University. In addition to practicing law early in his career, he was a faculty member at Creighton University College of Law. After a period of time where he served as Deputy Director of the National Center for State Courts and as a member of the law faculty at William and Mary, he was, in 1980, appointed as the youngest dean of a major law school in the United States. [Notice that the bio doesn't mention the law school at which he was the dean, William Mitchell, 1980-1983.]
>
> Geoff has been the chief operating officer or chief executive officer of a national marketing research company, a national management consulting company, a $40 million insurance company, a commercial real estate development company, an international franchiser, an investment banking company, and an international World Trade Center. . . .
>
> Geoff's teaching credentials include more than eleven years of teaching at the graduate school level [and] presentations at more than 100 continuing education programs. He has also published more than 35 articles, book chapters, and monographs on various topics, and is a regular contributor to courses on fundraising, direct response marketing, the regulation of nonprofit organizations and their fundraisers, etc. He has made more than 25 formal presentations to charities and fundraisers in the past four years alone.[171]

**7.** Law professors who practice law may be disciplined for all the same practice-related misconduct that leads to charges against other lawyers. But some law professors, because of their teaching responsibilities, engage in

---

168. Heidenreich, supra n. 163, at 271 (Dept. of Human Rights); Address of complainant Joan C. Peterson to the National Lawyers' Guild (undated) (complaint to the Minnesota Professional Responsibility Board). The director of the Professional Responsibility Board initially dismissed the complaint on the ground that sexual harassment against a nonclient was not professional misconduct, but a member of the board reinstated the charges. At the hearing that followed, "the Dean's lawyer alleged that [complainant Peterson] had made [her] complaint in order to launch a public speaking career on the topic of sexual harassment." Id.

169. In his letter of resignation, Peters said he was leaving because of "the terrible pressures on my family caused by the unceasing harassment by the press." Heidenreich, supra n. 163, at 273.

170. Creative Direct Response, CDR Announces New President, Chairman of the Board, at http://www.cdr-nfl.com/articles/CDR_newpres.htm (last visited Oct. 6, 2004).

171. 2004 Washington Nonprofit Conference, Speaker Biographies, at http://dmany.convio.net/site/PageServer?pagename=Speakerbio& (last visited Oct. 6, 2004).

misconduct that is unique to their role.[172] Occasionally there are civil[173] or criminal cases,[174] or disciplinary actions against law professors.[175] Sometimes allegations of misconduct are investigated by the relevant dean's office[176] or by the law faculty. The Association of American Law Schools adopted a recommended code of conduct for law professors, but very few schools have formally endorsed it.[177]

Sexual harassment may be the most common category of law professor misconduct. In 2002, for example, Dean John Dwyer of Berkeley's Boalt Hall School of Law resigned in response to sexual harassment charges.[178] Here is a list of some other types of questionable conduct by law professors.

- ■ **Plagiarism:** Some law professors plagiarize the writing of their research assistants. Some plagiarize from case law or other published articles. Some claim credit toward tenure for work that was ghostwritten for them before they were law professors.[179]

---

172. Monroe H. Freedman, The Professional Responsibility of the Law Professor: Three Neglected Questions, 39 Vand. L. Rev. 275, 276 (1986).

173. See, e.g., Morris & Doherty, P.C. v. Lockwood, 2003 WL 22299123 (Mich. Ct. App., Oct. 7, 2003) (contract for referral fee allegedly owed to a law professor held unenforceable because professor had switched bar membership to "inactive" status and therefore was not able to practice law); Davis v. Goode, 995 F. Supp. 82 (E.D.N.Y. 1998) (lawsuit by C.U.N.Y. law student alleging unfair grading practices by a professor allowed to proceed over defendants' motion for summary judgment).

174. Elisabeth Franck, The Professor and the Porn, N.Y. Mag., June 23, 2003, at 41 (describing a criminal case against a New York Law School professor who was found to have assembled a large collection of child pornography images on the computer in his law school office).

175. See, e.g., In re Hager, 812 A.2d 904 (D.C. 2002) (ordering suspension of an American University law professor for settling a potential class action suit on terms favorable to himself without notifying or consulting his clients, and for other charges); see also James V. Grimaldi, Misconduct in Lice Case Puts AU Professor's Job in Jeopardy, Wash. Post, Mar. 10, 2003, at E1 (explaining the potential impact of the disciplinary action on the professor's position at the law school).

176. See John E. Montgomery, The Dean as a Crisis Manager, 34 U. Toledo L. Rev. 133 (2002).

177. Association of American Law Schools, Statement of Good Practices by Law Professors in the Discharge of Their Ethical and Professional Responsibilities, *available at* http://www.aals.org/ethic.html (last visited Oct. 6, 2004).

178. Deborah L. Rhode, Professor of Desire, National L.J., Jan. 27, 2003, at A17; Diana Walsh, Tanya Schevitz, & Harriet Chiang, Boalt Dean's Accuser Denies Saying Yes, San Fran. Chron., Dec. 3, 2002, at A1. For other examples of sexual harassment matters involving law professors, see Tonkovich v. Kan. Bd. of Regents, 159 F.3d 504 (10th Cir. 1998) (civil rights suit by law professor fired from state university law school based on allegations of sexual harassment); Murphy v. Duquesne U. of the Holy Ghost, 745 A.2d 1228 (Pa. Super. 1999) (holding that a university had properly terminated a tenured professor teaching law at Duquesne University after verification of allegations of sexual harassment). See generally ABA Commission on Women in the Profession, Elusive Inequality: Experiences of Women in Legal Education (1996).

179. See Lisa G. Lerman, Misattribution in Legal Scholarship: Plagiarism, Ghostwriting, and Authorship, 42 S. Tex. L. Rev. 467 (2001); Joan E. Van Tol, Detecting, Deterring and Punishing the Use of Fraudulent Academic Credentials: A Play in Two Acts, 30 Santa Clara L. Rev. 791 (1990); Bill L. Williamson, (Ab)using Students: The Ethics of Faculty Use of a Student's Work Product, 26 Ariz. St. L.J. 1029 (1994).

- **Neglect of teaching responsibilities:** Some law professors collect full-time teaching salaries while engaging in extensive (and lucrative) consulting or law practice.[180]
- **Manipulation of grades:** Some law professors use grades to punish or reward certain students for conduct unrelated to their performance in a course, perhaps giving good grades to a student who confers sexual favors or to reward a student who shares the professor's views. A professor sometimes may impose a disproportionate number of failing grades on a class for irrational reasons.[181]
- **Aggressive or discriminatory behavior:** Some law professors have temper tantrums in class or in dealings with colleagues or staff. Others show prejudice toward women, people of color, gays and lesbians, disabled people, and others, as reflected in their failure to call on members of certain groups in class, their interruptions of or disparaging responses to comments by members of certain groups, or their comments in class that directly disparage particular groups.[182] Some states explicitly prohibit discriminatory conduct in their disciplinary rules.[183] Others interpret more general rules to prohibit such conduct, some of them including a comment after Rule 8.4 explaining that some discrimination violates Rule 8.4(d).[184]

---

180. See Rory K. Little, Law Professors as Lawyers: Consultants, Of Counsel, and the Ethics of Self-Flagellation, 42 S. Tex. L. Rev. 345 (2001).

181. See ABA Commission on Women, supra n. 178; see also Davis v. Goode, 995 F. Supp. 82 (E.D.N.Y. 1998).

182. See ABA Commission on Women, supra n. 178.

183. Stephen Gillers, Regulation of Lawyers 867 (6th ed., Aspen L. & Bus. 2002). Among the states whose ethics rules prohibit discrimination by lawyers are California, Colorado, Florida, Illinois, Michigan, Minnesota, New Jersey, New York, Ohio, Texas, and the District of Columbia. Stephen Gillers & Roy D. Simon, Regulation of Lawyers: Statutes and Standards 421-427 (Aspen Publishers 2004).

184. Rule 8.4, Comment 3. In the mid-1990s, proposals were presented to the ABA to amend the Model Rules of Professional Conduct to prohibit discrimination. One of them, proposed by the Standing Committee on Ethics and Professional Responsibility, provided in part that it would be professional misconduct for a lawyer to "knowingly manifest by words or conduct, in the course of representing a client, bias or prejudice based upon race, sex, religion, national origin, disability, age, sexual orientation, or socio-economic status." The ABA Young Lawyers Division submitted a broader proposal that would have made it misconduct for a lawyer to "commit a discriminatory act prohibited by law or to harass a person on the basis of sex, race, age, creed, religion, color, national origin, disability, sexual orientation or marital status where the act of discrimination or harassment is committed in connection with a lawyer's professional activities." Gillers & Simon, supra n. 183, at 417-418. The latter proposal would have covered conduct by law professors toward law students. The former would not have done so. However, neither proposal was adopted, but the ABA House of Delegates instead passed a resolution condemning bias and prejudice by lawyers. Id. at 427. In 1998, two more such proposals were presented but withdrawn because the sponsors realized that they would not be adopted. However, in 1998 the House of Delegates adopted an amendment to the comments to Rule 8.4 that states that a lawyer who manifests bias or prejudice in the course of representing a client would violate Rule 8.4(d) if the conduct is prejudicial to the administration of justice. Id. at 419, Rule 8.4, Comment 3.

- **Dishonest behavior:** Some incidents involve professors who misrepresent their credentials or activities. This can take the form of plagiarism, but it can also involve resume fraud or other situations. Some law professors receive substantial sums for producing scholarship advocating a particular point of view and do not disclose in the published work that it was paid for by an interest group.[185]

**8.** Only a small number of law professors engage in various forms of misconduct, so we are not talking about very many cases. Why might the conduct of law professors be especially important?

**9.** Do you know of any examples of conduct by law professors that could be a basis for discipline? If you can think of an example, consider whether you or others reported or should have reported this conduct to the dean's office or to the bar counsel. If not, why not?

# E. Reporting misconduct by other lawyers

One theme of this text is to guide law students and new lawyers in evaluating whether they or other lawyers have committed misconduct. A cornerstone of the disciplinary system is the duty of lawyers to report serious misconduct by other lawyers, and the issue of whether an act must be reported comes up often in analysis of other ethical issues. Consequently, it is useful to explore this aspect of the system at an early stage of the study of professional responsibility.

This final section examines the legal protection available to subordinate lawyers who refuse to commit misconduct or who complain of the misconduct of others. We consider when a subordinate lawyer should or should not follow orders. We also look at the developing body of law that provides relief for lawyers fired for insisting on compliance with the ethical rules. If you encounter lawyer misconduct committed by your colleagues or superiors, and you take the reporting duty seriously, you run some risk of retaliation. If you are familiar with the law of wrongful discharge of lawyers, you will be better able to protect yourself should such a situation arise.

Many lawyers observe misconduct by other lawyers from time to time. Here are a few examples.

- A lawyer in a firm might notice that another lawyer in the firm is neglecting his work because of substance abuse, a personal crisis, or some other problem.
- A lawyer might encounter an opposing counsel who is deliberately obstructing the discovery process.

---

185. See Ronald K. L. Collins, A Letter on Scholarly Ethics, 45 J. Leg. Educ. 139 (1995) (urging that law professors should be more candid in disclosure of possible conflicts of interest in their scholarship); Richard B. Schmitt, Rules May Require Law Professors to Disclose Fees, Wall St. J., Jan. 31, 2000, at B1.

- A judge or a lawyer might observe another lawyer in court who is entirely unprepared for a hearing.
- A lawyer might be asked by a lawyer who supervises him to falsify time records.

These situations present various problems and dilemmas. Should the observing lawyer report the other lawyer? If so, to whom? To the firm management, a judge (if the matter is in litigation), a disciplinary agency, or the prosecutor's office? A second problem is whether the observing lawyer may be responsible (that is, subject to discipline or liability) for the other lawyer's actions. A third problem is what the lawyer should do if another lawyer is asking him to do something improper. And finally, what happens if the observing lawyer reports the other lawyer's misconduct and is fired from his job as a result?

## 1. The duty to report misconduct

One of the most important aspects of the lawyer self-regulatory system is that, in most states, lawyers are obliged to report other lawyers' misconduct to the disciplinary authorities. Rule 8.3 articulates this duty.

### Rule 8.3    Reporting Professional Misconduct

| Rule language* | Authors' explanation |
| --- | --- |
| (a) A lawyer who **knows** that another lawyer has **committed a violation of the Rules** of Professional Conduct that **raises a substantial question as to that lawyer's honesty, trustworthiness, or fitness as a lawyer in other respects, shall inform the appropriate professional authority.** . . . <br><br> [(b) Requires reporting misconduct by judges.] <br><br> (c) This Rule **does not require disclosure of information otherwise protected by Rule 1.6** or information gained by a lawyer or judge while participating in an approved lawyers assistance program. | A lawyer who "knows" of a violation by any other lawyer (an adversary, a public official, or a lawyer in own firm) must report it to the bar disciplinary agency. <br><br> Exceptions: <br><br> (1) Not all violations must be reported — only those raising a "substantial question" of the lawyer's "honesty, trustworthiness, or fitness." <br><br> (2) A report need not be made if it would reveal information *required* to be kept in confidence under Rule 1.6. A lawyer should encourage a client to waive confidentiality and permit reporting if that would not substantially prejudice the client. Comment 2. <br><br> (3) A lawyer assisting a lawyer who is in a treatment program (an "approved lawyers assistance program") is not required to report. Comment 5. |

*All emphasis added.

Most jurisdictions have adopted language that is similar or identical to Rule 8.3. A few states, however, have not adopted this standard. California imposes no such duty on lawyers. The Georgia rule says lawyers "should" (not "shall") report misconduct and specifies that violating the rule will not result in discipline. But most states require lawyers to report serious misconduct that is not confidential.[186]

### Must every lawyer in a state with a reporting rule report *serious* ethical violations by other lawyers?

Yes. The Restatement and most of the state ethics codes, however, do not require lawyers to report *every* violation of an ethical rule by another lawyer; they must report only those that raise "a substantial question as to that lawyer's honesty, trustworthiness, or fitness as a lawyer in other respects."[187] The duty is triggered by a lawyer's "knowledge" of another lawyer's misconduct. The standard for assessing knowledge is objective. The knowledge must be more than a mere suspicion that misconduct has occurred. The question is whether "a reasonable lawyer in the circumstances would have a firm opinion that the conduct in question more likely than not occurred."[188]

### Does this mean I have to blow the whistle on my boss if he does something unethical?

Yes. The reporting rule requires every lawyer to report serious misconduct by any other lawyer, whether the other lawyer is an adversary, a partner, a boss, or in some other relationship.[189] Associates have a duty to report misconduct by partners. A lawyer can't get off the hook by informing senior lawyers in a firm about the misconduct of another lawyer. The only exceptions from the reporting rule are for (1) information protected by the confidentiality rules and (2) information learned in the course of service on a lawyers' assistance program.[190] The confidentiality exception does not require that a lawyer get client approval before reporting misconduct of another lawyer. Neither does it allow a client to veto a lawyer's reporting of misconduct. The rule simply shields lawyers from reporting confidential client information.[191] Also, if a lawyer learns of misconduct during an adversary proceeding, the lawyer may

---

186. Stephen Gillers & Roy Simon, Regulation of Lawyers: Statutes and Standards 409-413 (Aspen Publishers 2004).

187. Rule 8.3(a).

188. Restatement § 5, comment i.

189. This rule applies, as well, to law professors who are members of the bar. In Section D, we suggest that law professors occasionally engage in misconduct that would be reportable under Rule 8.3 or its equivalent. If their colleagues are aware of such conduct but do not report it, those colleagues are violating the rule.

190. Rule 8.3(c).

191. Consider how important it is to be clear about what is confidential. Suppose, for example, that a lawyer is overbilling a client. Can this be reported without revealing confidences about the subject matter of the work at issue? Usually it is possible to report allegations of lawyer misconduct without revealing a client's secrets.

defer reporting the misconduct until the proceeding has concluded, if deferral is necessary to protect a client's interests.[192]

A lawyer who fails to report serious misconduct by another lawyer may be subject to discipline. While nearly every state has adopted a rule requiring lawyers to report misconduct of other lawyers, there are relatively few public reports of discipline of lawyers for not reporting. However, as the *National Law Journal* article excerpted below reports, even the possibility of discipline for not reporting misconduct has motivated many lawyers to come forward with reports of unethical behavior. This has led to the disclosure of some serious cases of misconduct that otherwise might have remained undetected and undeterred. However, the reporting rule has sometimes also been used as a weapon among rival lawyers in the same firm or in different firms.

## Daryl van Duch, Best Snitches: Land of Lincoln Leads the Nation in Attorneys Turning in Their Peers

Natl. L.J., Jan. 27, 1997, at A1

For years, the itch to snitch on a colleague gone bad has been greater among Illinois attorneys than anywhere else.

Information released last month by the Illinois Attorney Registration and Disciplinary Commission shows that whistleblowing by the state's attorneys on their colleagues in the 1990s, in many cases resulting in suspension or disbarment, continues to occur at an astounding rate.

According to the IARDC, Illinois attorneys filed nearly 600 complaints in 1995 against other attorneys here. During the previous four years, the IARDC now says, an average of more than 570 attorney-contra-attorney complaints had been received annually by the agency.

That's a benchmark no other state even approaches.

New York attorneys, for instance, have reported only "a handful" of colleagues to state authorities during the 1990s under its ethics rules, says one high-ranking New York disciplinary official.

In the District of Columbia, a snitch rule on the books since January 1991 has resulted in an average of about 30 reports by lawyers complaining about another's alleged misconduct, notes Leonard H. Becker, the district's deputy chief trial counsel.

Why the difference? No one knows for sure.

Maybe it's a question of incentive. Illinois became unique in 1988 when its highest court unequivocally sustained the suspension of a lawyer's license for failing to report another lawyer's misconduct and, in so doing, greatly narrowed the state's common law attorney-client privilege rule.

Whether such a "rat or pay the price" policy is good or bad continues to be debated both here and nationally.

---

192. Restatement § 5, comment i.

## Making of an Example

The uncommon Illinois experience began in 1983 when James H. Himmel, an eight-year veteran practicing law on his own in Palos Heights, Ill., agreed to help an 18-year-old motorcycle accident victim, a friend of his secretary, recover $23,000 in settlement monies her first lawyer allegedly had pocketed. The deal was that Mr. Himmel would get paid only if all the missing money was recovered.

During the course of 24 months, Mr. Himmel managed to induce the first lawyer to agree to a $75,000 settlement in return for a promise not to prosecute. The payment was not made. Mr. Himmel obtained a judgment, but not much more than $10,000 was returned to the client's wallet.

The client asked Mr. Himmel not to report the thievery to the IARDC for fear of upsetting ongoing recovery efforts.

In 1986, however, the IARDC charged Mr. Himmel with failing to report the serious misconduct of another lawyer and sought to suspend his license to practice for a year.

The Illinois Supreme Court in 1988 sustained the IARDC administrator in suspending Mr. Himmel, primarily because the evidence that had triggered concerns over his failure to report was not "privileged." The court found Mr. Himmel had talked to too many people about the other attorney's misconduct, including the client's own mother and an insurance company attorney. The court also found that, when the offending attorney signed a settlement agreement admitting his wrongdoing, any existing attorney-client privilege was lost.

The IARDC review board had recommended vindication because Mr. Himmel had been following his client's wishes not to report her old lawyer to authorities. But the high court said that was "irrelevant" in the face of the public's overriding right to bring wrongdoers to justice. In re Himmel, 533 N.E.2d 790 (Ill. 1988).

It's not as if Mr. Himmel hadn't been forewarned, says IARDC Chief Counsel James Grogan. Before Himmel, he notes, the long-standing model rules and model code adopted by most of the 50 states had cautioned that it was unethical not to report lawyers known to be engaging in serious misconduct.

On the other hand, broad exceptions had existed — both statutorily and under case law — for confidential and privileged matters. As a result, few lawyers in the United States reported one another, the model code and rules notwithstanding.

"Frankly, I never really thought of my obligations to the profession in this case," concedes Mr. Himmel. "I was just trying to help a client to be made whole after being harmed by another member of my profession."

## Taking the Hint

The state's legal community took the high court's cue seriously. In the year Himmel was decided, 154 attorneys reported wayward peers to the IARDC. That number jumped to 922 the following year.

Illinois lawyers, especially those in the biggest firms, became sensitized to the potential liability for not blowing the whistle on an attorney known to be doing serious harm to others, says IARDC administrator Mary Robinson.

Agrees University of Chicago Law School Prof. Albert Alschuler, "It's a reputational kind of thing. . . . It's bad enough to discover you have a sleaze in your high-class law firm . . . but the bad publicity generated from being accused of having sat on widespread misconduct would be even worse."

The advantage to obtaining an attorney's help in disciplining a peer, adds Mr. Grogan, is the allegations are more often proven.

Indeed, 18 percent of the formal charges filed with the IARDC against Illinois attorneys in 1995 can be traced to a complaint originally filed by another lawyer, IARDC's latest records indicate.

### Downside to "Himmel"

The public policy behind the Himmel rule, IARDC officials say, is to help break down the "conspiracy of silence" within the legal profession that arguably harbors wrongdoers.

And yet there are potential downsides to any snitch rule, Ms. Robinson and Mr. Grogan concede.

In 1990, they note, the Illinois Supreme Court had to make it unethical to threaten to snitch to the IARDC during pending civil litigation about opposing counsel's alleged misconduct because too many of the state's lawyers were using skeletons in their opponents' closets to gain negotiation leverage.

"The Himmel rule has given the unscrupulous the power to force other attorneys to not fully represent their clients for fear of being" exposed themselves, complains George B. Collins, a name partner at Chicago's Bargione & Collins, who helped represent Mr. Himmel on appeal.

Mr. Collins also has noted a dramatic rise in the number of the city's megafirms that have begun to tattle on their own. "There can be sharp rivalries between partners for the same business in the bigger firms," he says. "And what we're seeing is some of them using the pretense of reporting unethical behavior just to trash another partner and take over their business."

Indeed, it was partly because of fears about such "possible hidden agendas" that California decided in 1991 not to adopt a Himmel-like snitch rule, says Francis P. Bassios, deputy chief trial counsel for the State Bar of California. Even without such a rule, he notes, about 10 percent of the 5,000 complaints received by his agency each year come from lawyers against their peers.

Concludes Mr. Collins, "We haven't improved the morality of the profession . . . but . . . have simply made all of us more distrustful of each other."

### National Alert

Most state courts have indicated reluctance to follow the Himmel lead. Still, the case should teach lawyers everywhere to be more cautious when dealing with other attorneys accused of misconduct, says Mr. Grogan.

Another lasting impact of the Himmel debates is that they appear to have helped inspire disciplinary officials in a number of states to look for new ways to investigate and prosecute wayward lawyers.

In New York, a state that already had a Himmel-like snitch rule, the state's highest court arguably went the furthest last spring when it adopted a "law firm rule." That new rule appears to be the first and only official attempt to hold an entire law firm responsible for lawyer misconduct, even when an individual culprit cannot be identified, says Hal R. Lieberman, chief counsel for the 1st Judicial Department, which has jurisdiction over professionals in Manhattan and the Bronx.

Disciplining an entire firm can be a powerful anti-misconduct weapon, especially if used in tandem with the state's snitch rule, Mr. Lieberman notes. Indeed, some ethics lawyers say the law firm rule would have helped untangle the web of billings and tax fraud charges that led to the downfall of Harvey Myerson in 1992.

"The Harv," a former leading rainmaker at a series of leading New York firms during the 1980s, allegedly misled other partners about how he was billing clients. Part of his defense was that his modus operandi was no secret to the partners in the firm in which he worked, including Finley, Kumble, Wagner, Heine, Underberg, Manley, Myerson & Casey, which was eventually driven into bankruptcy.

It's still too early to judge the impact of the law firm rule, says Mr. Lieberman.

It can be said that large firms have been increasingly getting into trouble for the faux pas of their partners, even without a New York law firm rule. Pennsylvania insurance regulators, for instance, are now suggesting that Morgan, Lewis & Bockius L.L.P. should be held accountable for the $124 million insurance fraud allegedly committed by its former partner Allen W. Stewart. Mr. Stewart was charged . . . in a Philadelphia district court with bilking two insurance companies that he controlled and with causing their ultimate collapse in 1994.

### Big Firms Lead

Perhaps, then, it is no surprise that Chicago's biggest firms have been the biggest sticklers for adhering to the heightened ethical standards set forth in Himmel. The city's Winston & Strawn; Chapman and Cutler; Mayer, Brown & Platt; and Lord, Bissell & Brook all have since reported their own, IARDC officials say.

In the most celebrated case, Winston's former managing partner, Gary Fairchild, was reported for defrauding the firm and clients of in excess of $800,000. He not only was disbarred, but also . . . completed a two-year jail term after agreeing to a negotiated plea in a federal court here.

. . . Mr. Fairchild's wife, Maureen, was indicted by a Chicago federal grand jury for allegedly having defrauded her firm, Chapman and Cutler, as well as its clients, of more than $900,000. The IARDC also is seeking sanctions against her.

The reach of Himmel also arguably extended . . . to the Washington, D.C., office of Chicago's McDermott, Will & Emery, when the firm reported William Appler, a contract partner, for allegedly having diverted nearly $1 million in client fees. That firm-initiated investigation resulted in Mr. Appler's disbarment in December 1995, says Mr. Becker.

Mr. Himmel's parting advice on the dangers of not "Himmeling" a colleague who deserves it in Illinois:

"Don't risk making a wrong decision . . . and . . . make sure you have adequate malpractice insurance" before reporting another attorney against the wishes of a client.

---

In the years since the *Himmel* decision, a number of other attorneys have been disciplined for failure to report the misconduct of another lawyer. In most cases where a violation is found of Rule 8.3 or the state's counterpart, other misconduct is alleged as well. While imposition of sanctions for violation of Rule 8.3 is still rare, the duty to report misconduct is taken more seriously than it used to be.[193]

## 2. Lawyers' responsibility for ethical misconduct by colleagues and superiors

Ethical misconduct in legal organizations is not merely a problem for the individual transgressor. The Model Rules impose a limited amount of collective responsibility on other lawyers in the firm or other organization for the conduct of other lawyers and of nonlawyer employees. Rules 5.1, 5.2, and 5.3 address these issues.

- **Rule 5.1** explains the responsibility of a partner or supervising lawyer for ensuring compliance with the ethical rules by subordinate lawyers, and explains when a senior lawyer may be subject to discipline for the conduct of a subordinate lawyer.
- **Rule 5.2** explains when a subordinate lawyer is responsible for her own conduct, and under what circumstances she may follow orders without fear of discipline.
- **Rule 5.3**, using language nearly identical to that of Rule 5.1, explains the responsibilities of lawyers who supervise nonlawyer employees for ensuring that the employees comply with the rules of professional

---

193. See generally Nicki A. Ott & Heather F. Newton, A Current Look at Model Rule 8.3: How Is It Used and What Are Courts Doing About It?, 16 Geo. J. Leg. Ethics 747 (2003) (discussing *Himmel* and subsequent cases in which lawyers were sanctioned for failure to report the misconduct of another lawyer). The Illinois Supreme Court reaffirmed its view that the duty to report under Rule 8.3 is mandatory in Skolnick v. Altheimer & Gray, 730 N.E.2d 4 (Ill. 2000) (holding that a trial court's refusal to modify a protective order to allow a lawyer to report evidence of misconduct to the disciplinary authorities was not a reasonable exercise of discretion).

conduct, and explains when a lawyer may be subject to discipline based on the conduct of a nonlawyer employee.

We reprint Rules 5.1 and 5.2 below. We have not included Rule 5.3 because it is substantively so similar to Rule 5.1.

## Rule 5.1    Responsibilities of Partners, Managers, and Supervisory Lawyers

| Rule language* | Authors' explanation |
| --- | --- |
| (a) **A partner in a law firm**, and a lawyer who individually or together with other lawyers possesses comparable managerial authority in a law firm, **shall make reasonable efforts to ensure that** the firm has in effect measures giving reasonable assurance that **all lawyers in the firm conform to the Rules of Professional Conduct.** | Lawyer managers must set up systems to prevent ethical problems. These include procedures to check for conflicts of interest and to manage client funds. They must provide continuing education in legal ethics. In small firms of experienced lawyers, "informal supervision and periodic review" may suffice, while "more elaborate measures" may be needed in large firms. Comments 2 and 3. |
| | On its face, this rule applies only to partners and other managers "in a law firm," but Rule 1.0(c) and its Comment 3 defines "law firm" to include legal services organizations or the legal departments of corporations, government agencies, and other organizations. |
| (b) **A lawyer having direct supervisory authority** over another lawyer **shall make reasonable efforts** to ensure that the other lawyer conforms to the Rules of Professional Conduct. | If a subordinate lawyer commits an ethical violation, the supervising lawyer is not responsible for that violation if the supervisor did not direct or know about it. But the violation could reveal a breach of the supervisor's duty under Rule 5.1(b) to make reasonable efforts to prevent violations. Comments 6 and 7. |
| (c) **A lawyer shall be responsible for another lawyer's violation** of the Rules of Professional Conduct if: | A lawyer may be responsible for the conduct of a partner, associate, or subordinate. Partners have "at least indirect responsibility" for all work being done by the firm" as well as supervisory responsibility for work being done by subordinate lawyers on matters for which they are responsible. Comment 5. |
| (1) **the lawyer orders** or, with knowledge of the specific conduct, ratifies **the conduct** involved; or | A lawyer cannot avoid responsibility for violation of an ethical rule by ordering another lawyer to do the prohibited act. Comment 4 and Rule 8.4 (a). |

| Rule language* | Authors' explanation |
|---|---|
| (2) the **lawyer is a partner** or has comparable managerial authority in the law firm in which the other lawyer practices, **or has direct supervisory authority** over the other lawyer, **and knows of the conduct** at a time when its consequences can be avoided or mitigated **but fails to take remedial action.** | The directly supervising partner is not the only partner who may be responsible for a violation. Any partner in the firm who knows of the improper conduct and fails to take action to reduce or prevent the harm also commits a violation. In organizations that do not have partners, other lawyers with "comparable managerial authority" are equally responsible. |

*All emphasis added.

## Rule 5.2   Responsibilities of a Subordinate Lawyer

| Rule language* | Authors' explanation |
|---|---|
| (a) A lawyer is bound by the Rules of Professional Conduct **notwithstanding that the lawyer acted at the direction of another person.** | Like the foot soldier accused of committing a war crime, a lawyer is not excused from responsibility on the ground that she was just "following orders." However, if a supervisor directed the action, the subordinate lawyer may be able to prove that she did not actually know that the action was improper. Comment 1. |
| (b) A subordinate lawyer does not violate the Rules of Professional Conduct if that lawyer acts in accordance with a supervisory lawyer's reasonable resolution of an arguable question of professional duty. | Lawyers often disagree about whether proposed conduct would violate a rule. If the supervisor reasonably thinks the conduct is proper, the subordinate may undertake the action even if she believes otherwise. If the supervisor turns out to be wrong, however, the supervisor could be disciplined. Comment 2. If the supervisor was so wrong that her belief that the action was proper was not reasonable, the subordinate may also be disciplined. |

*All emphasis added.

### Are lawyers, then, only partially responsible for their colleagues' ethical violations?

In terms of disciplinary enforcement, these rules do make lawyers only partially responsible for each other's actions. The law does not allow discipline of all of the lawyers in a firm, or even of all of the partners, if one of the firm's associates violates a disciplinary rule. However, supervising lawyers are liable for the unethical acts of lawyers they are supervising if they direct the act or know of the proposed act and do not prevent it. Other managers of the organization are also responsible if they know of the proposed actions.

Subordinate lawyers may be held accountable for certain unethical actions that they were ordered to undertake (those in which the supervisor's decision was not a "reasonable resolution of an arguable question").

**Under Rule 5.2(b), a lawyer is off the disciplinary hook if the supervisor's instruction is a "reasonable resolution of an arguable question of professional duty." How can a lawyer know whether another lawyer's decision is reasonable?**

Suppose a partner tells an associate not to produce a particular document in discovery. The partner says it's not covered by the request. The associate thinks it is covered and that concealing it is unethical. If there were no Rule 5.2(b), the associate might refuse to follow the directions of his supervisor because he thought the instruction was improper or because he feared discipline for compliance. The partner, on the other hand, might fear discipline or malpractice liability if the firm produced an inculpatory document that was not called for by the discovery request. The result could be a standoff in which the associate would have to resign from the firm or would be fired for insubordination. The rule creates a safe harbor for junior lawyers who defer to the judgment of their superiors on questions that have more than one reasonable answer.

One scholar criticizes Rule 5.2, arguing that this rule discourages less experienced lawyers from raising and contesting ethical issues and thereby stifles ethical debate within law firms.[194] The existence of this rule means that the questioning associate would have a harder time arguing that he couldn't comply with the instruction because he might be disciplined. Still, he could argue that the instruction is not "reasonable." Rule 5.2, then, might have the unintended consequence of counseling associates to follow orders and not ask too many questions.

The limitations imposed by the ethical rules on one lawyer's responsibility for the conduct of others apply in the context of professional discipline. State tort law and judges who impose sanctions in litigation may not recognize them. For example, in a malpractice suit, an entire partnership may be held liable for the malpractice of any lawyer in the firm.[195]

**Can discipline be imposed on a whole law firm?**

In 1992, Professor Ted Schneyer argued that "large law firms are typically complex organizations. Consequently, their infrastructures may have at least

---

194. Carol M. Rice, The Superior Orders Defense in Legal Ethics: Sending the Wrong Message to Young Lawyers, 32 Wake Forest L. Rev. 887 (1997). Professor Rice points out that "no lawyer has ever successfully used Rule 5.2 as a defense in a reported disciplinary proceeding." Id. at 902.

195. See, e.g., Dresser Indus. v. Digges, 1989 WL 139234 (D. Md. Aug. 30, 1989) (holding that Edward Digges' partners were jointly and severally liable with him for misconduct he committed within the scope of the partnership). The extent of the partners' liability for the actions of other partners is affected by the organizational structure of the firm. Many firms reorganized as limited liability partnerships (LLPs) during the 1990s in an attempt to protect themselves from joint and several liability. See Chapter 7B5, for discussion of LLPs.

as much to do with causing and avoiding unjustified harm as do the individual values and practice skills of their lawyers." He urged, therefore, that in certain cases, state authorities should impose disciplinary sanctions, such as fines and suspension, on entire law firms.[196] The Ethics 2000 Commission initially embraced his suggestion but ultimately rejected it because it feared that imposing firm-wide responsibility for ethical violations would diminish individual accountability.[197] Many scholars, however, believe that the profession would be helped by allowing discipline of law firms.

In several cases in recent years, one partner was engaged in flagrant misconduct, and other partners evidently knew about it and did little to stop the misfeasance. Sometimes the other partners were being loyal. In other cases, they failed to act because they, too, were making money from their partners' wrongdoing.[198] These cases point to a need to allow disciplinary authorities to hold firms accountable for the misconduct of lawyers in certain circumstances.

In most states, only an individual lawyer may be disciplined for violation of ethical rules, but the rules of New York and New Jersey allow imposition of discipline on law firms for certain misconduct, such as failure to supervise employees or failure to maintain a system for checking new matters to identify conflicts of interest.[199]

## PROBLEM 1-3  **THE LITTLE HEARING**

*This problem is based on the experiences of a recent law school graduate. She accepted her first job as an associate of a sole practitioner of immigration law. After her second day on the job, she called Professor Lerman, who had been one of her law professors. The problem is based on what she told Lerman that evening.*

I started work this week at the law firm of Solomon Helman. He's a solo practitioner who does mostly immigration work. It looks like a very challenging position. He has so much more work than he can do that he's expecting me to take on the responsibilities of an experienced lawyer. I feel very fortunate to have gotten this job, given how bad the job market is. The only problem is, I'm not sure I can hack it.

Yesterday Helman told me that this morning, we'd take the train together and each handle separate hearings in Newark and New York. I said that was impossible — I'd never done immigration work and had never appeared at any kind of hearing. He said he had to conduct a

---

196. Ted Schneyer, Professional Discipline for Law Firms? 77 Cornell L. Rev. 1 (1992).

197. Margaret Colgate Love, The Revised ABA Model Rules of Professional Conduct: Summary of the Work of Ethics 2000, 15 Geo. J. Leg. Ethics 441, 470–471 (2002).

198. These cases are described in Lisa G. Lerman, Blue-Chip Bilking-Regulation of Billing and Expense Fraud by Lawyers, 12 Geo. J. Leg. Ethics 205 (1999).

199. N.J. Rules of General Application, Rules 1:20-1(a), 5.1(a), 5.3(a), & 5.4; N.Y. Code of Professional Responsibility DR 1-102(A), DR 1-104, DR 5-105(E); see also Schneyer, supra n. 196.

trial in federal court today, so there was no way he could go with me, and one of us had to show up. "It's just a little hearing," he said. I guess it seemed like I didn't have any choice but to go.

Needless to say, I was completely petrified since I knew nothing about immigration law or immigration hearings. I tried to get Helman to explain the case to me, but he said he had to leave. He said, "Don't worry, we can talk about it on the train tomorrow." So I met him at the train station this morning. I was all keyed up, and looking forward to getting some guidance about what the heck I was supposed to do. We got on the train, and he handed me the file and then sat across the aisle from me, putting his feet up on the empty seat next to him. I said, "Aren't we going to talk about the case?" He said, "Sorry, I need to sleep." He passed me a treatise and said, "Read the file. The hearing isn't until two. Anything you need to know about the law you will find in that book." I read the file on the train and skimmed through what I thought were the relevant parts of the treatise, but frankly, it didn't help much.

I got to the hearing office, and I had to ask the receptionist which of the people waiting there was my client. The client's English wasn't good, but she was happy to see me. Almost as soon as I got there, she started crying and begging me not to let them send her back to Rwanda. I was sweating; I didn't have a clue what to do. I tried to get her to explain the story, but it was hard to understand her.

The hearing started; the judge started asking questions to the client. We really needed an interpreter, but we didn't have one. I asked if we could get an interpreter, but the judge said no. We did the best we could. I felt really bad that I couldn't do more for her. The hearing was a disaster. I don't know which was worse, my insecurity or my lack of preparation. I kept wondering how much Mr. Helman was charging the client for my brilliant assistance. The judge said he would issue a decision in the next month. I took the train back, feeling really bad about the whole situation. I had thought it would be worse for me not to show up at all, but now I'm not so sure.

When I got back to the office, Mr. Helman's secretary gave me two more files and told me Mr. Helman wanted me to handle the hearings on those matters. Both hearings are scheduled for tomorrow, one in the morning, one in the afternoon. He wasn't around. I asked her why he is dumping all this work on me. She told me he has 1,500 active cases. There are more hearings scheduled each workday than Helman can attend.

I am troubled by the lack of prehearing preparation that seems to be the norm in this firm. I also noticed that the first rule in the ethics code, Rule 1.1, requires competent representation, and I don't think I am really competent to do this work. I asked Mr. Helman about it. He said that because these clients can't pay very much in the way of fees, the firm is in a stable but precarious financial condition. Also, if his firm took twice as long to work up each case, which is something he would eventually like it to be able to do, the firm would have to close its doors and go out of business. He said that he appreciated my concern, but now it was time to get back to work — pick up two more files, get down to the courthouse, and meet the clients in the waiting room.

What should Lenore do? Show up and do a bad job at two more hearings tomorrow? Quit her job tonight? Aside from her decision about staying in or leaving her job, is there anything else that she should or must do?

## 3. Legal protections for subordinate lawyers

Most associates in law firms are employees at-will. That means they do not have contracts for terms of years but may resign at any time for any reason or may be fired at any time for any reason. Well, almost any reason. Associates also are members of the bar. As such, they have independent obligations to comply with the law, including the ethical rules. Sometimes a lawyer's duties to his firm may conflict with his duties to the profession.

**FOR EXAMPLE:** Suppose an associate in a law firm sees a partner engage in behavior that "raises a substantial question as to that lawyer's honesty, trustworthiness or fitness as a lawyer in other respects." Under Rule 8.3 or its equivalent, the lawyer is obliged to "inform the appropriate professional authority." If the misconduct is serious, an associate is ethically obliged to blow the whistle on his boss or on another partner in the law firm. This, needless to say, puts the associate in an awkward position.

**FOR EXAMPLE:** Suppose instead that a partner instructs an associate to destroy a document that has been requested in discovery. If the partner's instruction is unethical and is not "a reasonable resolution of an arguable question of professional duty" (Rule 5.2(b)), then the associate would be subject to discipline for following orders.

A lawyer who is told to do something that the lawyer thinks is unethical has several options.

- Accept the directions of the superior
- Argue with the superior
- Discuss the problem with another superior
- Do more research or investigation to try to clarify the problem
- Ask to be relieved from work on the matter, or
- Resign (or be fired) from employment

Which of these options are available as a practical matter depends on the situation and the players. From time to time, an associate resigns or is fired because of his or her ethical qualms about something going on at work.

FOR EXAMPLE:   One of our students had a friend who had accepted a six-figure salary as an associate at a New York law firm. In one case he was helping to represent a doctor accused of malpractice for failure to make a timely diagnosis of cancer. The x-rays of the plaintiff's decedent showed a cancerous growth that the doctor had missed. The partner on the case told the associate to destroy the x-ray plate, saying "I'd rather have a missing documents case than have that picture come out at the trial." The associate resigned from his job.

## Does the law provide any protection for lawyers who are fired because they refuse to participate in unethical conduct or because they report misconduct of other lawyers to the disciplinary authorities?

Until recently, the law provided no such protection. Associates in law firms could be fired for any reason other than one expressly prohibited by law (for example, race). However, starting with the *Wieder* case in New York State, some courts have developed doctrine to protect attorneys who insist on ethical conduct or report breaches.

## David Margolick, New York Court Shields Lawyers Who Report Dishonest Colleagues

N.Y. Times, Dec. 23, 1992

New York State's highest court ruled yesterday that law firms cannot dismiss lawyers for doing what their professional disciplinary rules require — blowing the whistle on a dishonest colleague.

The court, the State Court of Appeals, has almost uniformly protected the rights of employers to dismiss almost any worker for almost any reason, at least when anti-discrimination laws do not apply. But given the role of lawyers as self-regulated officers of the court, the court held, in a 5-to-0 decision, that the rights of law firms must be read more narrowly.

The requirement that lawyers with evidence casting substantial doubt on "another lawyer's honesty, trustworthiness or fitness" inform disciplinary authorities is an implicit part of his employment contract with a law firm, the court held. When a firm discharges a lawyer for making such a report, it held, that firm can be sued for breach of contract.

### "Survival of the Profession"

Writing for the court, Judge Stewart F. Hancock Jr. said that no lawyer should have to choose between discharge for following the Code of Professional Responsibility or disbarment or suspension for failing to do so. He called the reporting requirement "nothing less than essential to the survival of the profession."

The ruling, which reversed two lower court decisions, came in the case of Howard L. Wieder, a lawyer who claims his former law firm, Feder, Kaszovitz,

*Howard Wieder*

Isaacson, Weber & Skala of Manhattan, dismissed him five years ago for insisting it report a dishonest colleague to disciplinary authorities. With the court's decision yesterday,[200] Mr. Wieder's lawsuit may now proceed to trial.

By protecting whistle-blowing lawyers against retaliatory discharge, the decision, apparently the first of its kind in the country, could compel the bar to police itself and weed out miscreants more conscientiously.

The decision also marked the court's most dramatic incursion to date into what has been, at least in New York, the largely sacrosanct right of employers to choose and lose employees at will. Those protections on the books in the state, for instance, for civil servants reporting official malfeasance, are there by statute, not court decision. . . .

### Ramifications Unclear

"Insisting that as an associate in their employ, plaintiff must act unethically and in violation of one of the primary rules," Judge Hancock wrote, "amounted to nothing less than a frustration of the only legitimate purpose of the employment relationship." . . .

Law firms, fearing the loss of clients, bad publicity or higher insurance premiums, have often been hard on any whistle-blowers.

"Study after study nationwide reflects that lawyers don't report misconduct by other lawyers," said Mr. Wieder's lawyer, David Vladeck of Public Citizen Litigation Group in Washington, D.C. "This decision basically opens the door for lawyers to fulfill their ethical and moral duty."

### Wrongdoing Acknowledged

In 1986 Mr. Wieder retained another lawyer in his firm, Larry Lubin, to handle the closing of his condominium. Mr. Lubin, he later charged, neglected his duties, then misled him to cover up that neglect. When Mr. Wieder complained to partners at Feder, Kaszovitz, he said, the firm made light of his experience.

Mr. Lubin subsequently acknowledged wrongdoing, and the firm reported him to the Departmental Disciplinary Committee of the Appellate Division of State Supreme Court in December 1987, three months after Mr. Wieder's complaint. The complaint was ultimately dismissed. So, too, was Mr. Wieder, in March 1988.

Mr. Wieder contends that the dismissal was retaliatory. The firm maintains that it dismissed him for his "poor work habits, unacceptable performance, inability to work with others and poor attitude."

---

200. [Authors' footnote.] Wieder v. Skala, 609 N.E. 105 (N.Y. 1992).

The 39-year-old Mr. Wieder, now a lawyer with the Manhattan firm of Harvis, Trien & Beck, said he was "delighted" by the ruling, but said his whistle-blowing days were over.

"I've been portrayed as crazed, eccentric and litigation-prone, I was unemployed for nine months, I've gone into massive debt," he said. "Even with this decision, any lawyer who pressures his or her law firm to do the right thing will still have to pay an immense price. But now maybe the travail will be considerably lighter than what I've had to face."[201]

## The Jacobson case: A contrary result

Lawyers fired for insisting on compliance with ethical rules are allowed to sue for wrongful discharge in some states but not others. Alan P. Jacobson was an associate in an Illinois firm. He realized that his firm was filing debt collection suits against consumers in violation of the venue provisions of the Federal Fair Debt Collection Act.[202] The act permits a debt collection suit to be instituted only where the consumer resides or where the consumer signed the contract on which the suit is based. Apparently the firm was filing such suits in other courts, which were less convenient for the consumer defendants.

Jacobson complained to a senior partner, urging that the firm was violating Rule 3.3 by representing falsely to the courts that the venue of the lawsuits was proper. Jacobson was told that the firm would change this practice. The practice did not change. Jacobson talked to the partner again. The partner assured him again that the firm would soon begin to file its cases in the proper venues. Again, the practice did not change. After Jacobson spoke to the partner for the third time, the firm fired him. He sued the firm, but the Illinois Supreme Court denied relief. The court agreed that the firm's practice violated the ethical rules. The court noted that Jacobson had a duty to report the unethical conduct to the bar disciplinary authorities and concluded that the duty to report was sufficient protection for the public against unethical behavior by lawyers. Therefore, the court concluded, there was no need to allow associates who were fired for insisting on compliance with ethical rules to sue law firms for wrongful discharge. The Chief Justice, dissenting, said that "today's opinion serves as yet another reminder to the attorneys in this state that, in certain circumstances, it is economically more advantageous to keep quiet than to follow the dictates of the Rules of Professional Responsibility."[203]

## The Strange Tale of Scott McKay Wolas

Scott McKay Wolas became a partner in the New York office of Hunton & Williams in 1989, after stints at two other large firms. A 1976 graduate of

---

201. Copyright 1992, N.Y. Times Co. Reprinted with permission.
202. 15 U.S.C. § 1692i (2004).
203. Jacobson v. Knepper & Moga, P.C., 706 N.E.2d 491 (Ill. 1998).

Fordham Law School, Wolas was the son of a liquor distributor. He was described as "disheveled, portly, a pit-bull litigator" who "took long lunches ... and came back with a glazed look."[204] Hunton & Williams, a large, elite, Richmond-based firm, where Supreme Court Justice Lewis Powell was once a partner, was the last place one would expect to find gross unethical conduct.

In 1991, three associates in the litigation department who worked with Wolas in the law firm began complaining that Wolas was billing many more hours than he was working. One noticed that Wolas was billing for simple debt collection work usually handled by associates. Another noticed that he had billed for reviewing a memo that the associate hadn't yet given him.[205] And so on. Wolas was a respected partner and a rainmaker. It took the firm 18 months to get around to investigating the associates' allegations. Eventually the firm held an all-day internal hearing. At the conclusion of this investigation, Wolas was cleared of any allegations of wrongdoing. Managing partner W. Taylor Reveley III told associates that the firm could not prove "beyond a reasonable doubt" that Wolas was engaged in fraudulent billing practices.[206] The managing partner said that Wolas was "a sloppy pig, not a dirty rat."[207] Case closed.

Then in 1995 Wolas disappeared with between $20 million and $40 million of other people's money. Apparently he spent very little time practicing law, but spent most of his time working on a Ponzi scheme, soliciting investors for a phony company that was to export Scotch whiskey to Japan. Some of Wolas's law partners at Hunton & Williams (some of the same ones who dragged their feet about the overbilling allegations) allegedly invested a total of about $775,000 in the export business.[208] After Wolas disappeared, the managing partner denied that Wolas's departure was triggered by the discovery of misconduct. He said, "Scott took a leave of absence after he advised us that he had to spend more time on family business matters," and "later in the summer, we mutually agreed his withdrawal from the firm would be appropriate, but it was for other reasons."[209]

This story isn't over yet. Wolas was disbarred from practice in New York in absentia in 1999.[210] In 2001 the Manhattan district attorney, as part of an effort to apprehend Wolas, unsealed a 119-count indictment of him, which included charges of grand larceny and securities fraud.[211] By then, Wolas had been "on the lam" for more than five years. At one point it was reported that he'd written a 500-page spy novel while in hiding, which he was trying to sell.[212] At another

---

204. Ann Davis, Scandal Embarrasses Virginia's Hunton, Natl. L.J., May 13, 1996, at A1.

205. Ann Davis, Firm's Handling of Allegations of Overbilling Brought Out in Suit, Wall St. J., June 16, 1997, at B6.

206. Id.

207. Edward A. Adams, Unsealed Papers Air Claims Against Firm, N.Y.L.J., Apr. 11, 1997, at 1.

208. Bruce Balestier, Indictment Unsealed in Effort to Catch Lawyer on the Lam, N.Y.L.J., Feb. 2, 2001, at 1.

209. Ann Davis, Scandal Embarrasses Virginia's Hunton, Natl. L.J., May 13, 1996, at A1.

210. Matter of Scott McKay Wolas, N.Y.L.J., Mar. 1, 1999, at A6.

211. Balestier, supra n. 208.

212. Ann Davis, While on the Lam Has Wolas Written a Spy Novel?, Natl. L.J., Nov. 16, 1996, at A4.

(22 April 2002)

## FORMER LAWYER, STOCK BROKER AND IDENTITY THEFT SUSPECT WITH TIES TO ORLANDO, FLORIDA WANTED BY FBI

**SCOTT WOLAS**

**DOB**: 04/18/1949, 02/05/1949, 03/18/1949.
**Also Known As**: Allen Lee Hengst, Allen Leem, Hengst, Scott J. Wolas, Scott M. Wolas, Robert F. McDowell, Scott J. McKay, Scott J. McKaywolas, Scott L Wolas, Robert McDowell, John McKay, Robert Francis McDowell.
**Race**: White; **Sex**: Male; **Height**: 5' 11", **Weight**: 205 pounds.
**Hair**: Gray; **Eyes**: Brown.
**Address Used**: 2110 W. Sabal Palm Place, Longwood, Florida, 240 West Sabal Palm Place #31, Longwood, Florida, 3311 Alba Way, Deerfield Beach, Florida, 3208 C.E. Colonial Drive, Orlando, Florida, P O BOX 1274 Anna Maria, Florida, 22 Pamela Road, Peekskill, New York, 22 Pamela Road, Westchester, New York, 22 Pamela Road, Cortlandt Manor, New York, 200 Park Avenue, New York, New York, Hunton Williams 43rd, New York, New York, 200 Park Avenue, New York, New York, 3340 Mirabella County Road, Boca Raton, Florida, 23440 Mirabella Circle South, Boca Raton, Florida, 3340 Mirabella Circle, Boca Raton, Florida, 200 Park Avenue 43rd, New York, New York, 101 Park Avenue, New York, New York, 5413 North State Road 7, Tamarac, Florida, 23440 Mirabella Circle, Boca Raton, Florida, 100 Park Avenue 10, New York, New York, 100 Park Avenue Florida 10, New York, New York, 100 Park Avenue, New York, New York, 101 Park, New York, New York.
**Vehicle Used**: 1999 Toyota Avalon, tan in color.

The above mentioned-person is currently as of February 28, 2002 wanted by the by New York, Police Department and by the FBI, Tampa, Florida for Grand Larceny and Flight to Avoid Prosecution.

The above-mentioned person is a single-state offender with prior arrests in Florida. His prior arrests include Resisting Law Enforcement Officer and Driving Under the Influence. He utilized a friends identity during the Seminole County Florida arrest.

The above-mentioned individual is an ex-lawyer who is accused of conning countless victims out of approximately $20,000,000.00 to $40,000,000.00 (twenty to forty million) dollars. Wolas has been named in a 119-count Grand Larceny and Fraud indictment case in New York.

A New York Judge took the unusual steps to unseal the 1997 charges against Wolas in hopes that someone would recognize him and turn him into authorities. Prosecutors believe that Wolas originally started stealing from his victims/clients from 1991 to 1995 when he was a partner in a Law Firm in New York.

His victims allegedly are family members, former law partners, clients, doctors, lawyers, reputed organized crime figures, Charity Organizations in Ocala, Florida and more. He is suspected of masterminding a variation of the "Ponzi Scheme". A scam in which money from a new investor is used to pay an earlier victim and that process is then repeated. He lured investors with promises of quick profits as high as 100% then used cash from his new recruits to pay off earlier victims and get them to reinvest. It is speculated that he had so many victims because he was a smooth talker and clients bought into the "get rich quick" scam because Wolas was so persuasive.

Once Wolas was disbarred he resurfaced as a stockbroker in southern Florida, first under the name of Robert Francis McDonald (stolen identity of his former classmate) and later changing his alias to Allen Lee Hengst (stolen identity of a Washington, D.C. Librarian.) While in Florida it is believed that that Wolas took on a new avenue to defraud and scheme. It is alleged that Wolas started running financial schemes by offering his investor's worthless gold certificates and phantom Caribbean liquor deals.

Investigators are under pressure to locate Wolas as losses continue to climb. The search has focused on a possible Cayman Island secret bank account. It is known that Wolas visited the Cayman Island by private jet several times before disappearing. He was last seen in mid-December 2000 at the Orlando, Florida Brokerage office where he was working.

A class-action suit of more than 100 plaintiffs is pending against Wolas in Brooklyn Federal Court. He has contacted a relative in Florida recently and may even be hiding out in Florida. Wolas is accustomed to living a lavish life style. He likes good living, fine women, fine wine and liquors, fine dining and dancing. He always had a girlfriend or two. He likes going out and drinking very expensive wines and knows them well. He likes to read good books. He doesn't mind spending money and frequents the best restaurants.

**Anyone with information on the location of Wolas is asked to contact their local law enforcement agency or:**

**Julian Yannotti**
**Senior Rackets Investigator**
**New York County**
**District Attorney's Office**
**New York, New York**
**(212) 335-9713, or**

**Lt. John Thorpe**
**Seminole County Sheriff's Office**
**Sanford, Florida**
**(407) 665-6610**

point Wolas was located in Florida, where he was working under a false name as a broker, but as yet he has not been arrested.[213] Some of the defrauded investors have sued the firm.[214] One of the investor suits alleged that if the firm had fully investigated the bill-padding allegations, it would have uncovered the fact that the hours falsely billed were spent on the fraudulent investment business.[215]

After the internal investigation and before Wolas disappeared, the three associates who had complained of overbilling were either fired or encouraged to leave the firm. Two of them subsequently sued the firm for wrongful discharge, claiming that their termination was in retaliation for their complaints about Wolas's billing practices. One of the associates was Peter Kelly.[216] His story paints a not-very-nice picture of what went on behind the scenes at his former firm. To understand the story, it is useful to know who is who.

| Associates | Partners Peter Kelly worked for | Partners who invested in Wolas's scheme | Present and former managing partners |
|---|---|---|---|
| Peter M. Kelly | Scott J. McKay Wolas | | B. Carey Tolley III (N.Y. office) |
| Joseph Saltarelli | (Ms.) Franklin Stone | Franklin Stone | James A. Jones III (former; N.Y. office) |
| Harold Geary | Christopher Mason | Christopher Mason | |
| | Kathy Robb | Kathy Robb | W. Taylor Reveley III (former; Richmond office) |

# Kelly v. Hunton & Williams

1999 WL 408416 (E.D.N.Y. 1999)

GLEESON, J.

Peter M. Kelly brought this diversity action against his former employer, the law firm of Hunton & Williams ("H & W"), alleging that H & W breached implied contractual obligations owed him when it terminated his employment with the firm. Specifically, plaintiff claims that H & W forced him to resign

---

213. Id.

214. See Hunton & Williams Settles Suit Involving Former Partner Wolas, Wall St. J., Dec. 23, 1998, at B11 (reporting that the firm had agreed to pay more than $6 million to settle one suit by about 20 investors, and mentioning a second suit of the same type).

215. Davis, supra n. 212.

216. The other associate who sued the firm was Harold Geary. His suit for breach of contract and fraud was dismissed. The trial court, whose order was affirmed by the New York Appellate Division, found that he had no cause of action based on termination because of his ethical concerns because he had not reported Wolas to the disciplinary agency, nor had he told the firm that he intended to do so. Geary v. Hunton & Williams, 257 A.D.2d 482 (N.Y. App. Div. 1999).

and implicitly threatened to withhold a favorable job reference, in order to impede and discourage him from reporting H & W partner Scott Wolas's billing fraud to the Disciplinary Committee. Hunton & Williams moves for summary judgment. The motion is denied.

## FACTS

There are many disputed facts in this case. . . . Set forth below are the central facts viewed in the light most favorable to plaintiff, resolving all credibility issues in his favor and drawing all inferences in his favor. . . .

### [A little trouble getting admitted to the bar]

In October 1990, plaintiff began working in H & W's New York office as an associate in the litigation department. Plaintiff took the New York bar examination in July 1990 and again in February 1991, failing both times. He passed on his third attempt, in July 1991. . . . Plaintiff did not complete his application for admission to the bar, however, until 1997. Several factors contributed to his delay, including difficulties in obtaining the required affirmations of employment from past employers, difficulties ascertaining all of his addresses since beginning college, and resolving a number of outstanding tickets, one of which had resulted in the issuance of a warrant for his arrest in California. Despite this delay, no one at H & W indicated to plaintiff that his failure to gain admission to the bar violated a condition of his employment at the firm. . . .

### [Kelly's first year at the firm: good reviews]

When plaintiff began with H & W in October 1990, . . . he worked primarily with Scott Wolas and Franklin Stone, who were partners, and with Christopher Mason, who became a partner in early 1992.

Plaintiff's first-year performance reviews, prepared in June and July of 1991, resulted in favorable ratings but expressed some concern over his not having passed the bar examination. In October 1991, Stone described plaintiff to another H & W partner as "a terrific associate — functioning well above his second year." The following month, when the favorable result of the bar examination was announced, partner Kathy Robb[217] wrote the following on plaintiff's first annual associate evaluation: "Typical 1st year. Strong 'goods.' Apply with vigor to work. Congratulations on passing the bar. Good potential here." Stone wrote: "Peter does excellent work and is a valuable asset to our team. He brings an intelligence and maturity to his work that is rare in a first year associate." Mason wrote: "Peter has good skills, indeed, very good skills in many ways. . . . I also have a good deal of confidence in his work, confidence beyond his first-year level." Plaintiff received the maximum pay raise for his class.

---

217. [Authors' footnote.] Robb is an environmental lawyer, not a litigator, but she was the New York office's representative on the firm's Associates Committee.

### [The associates notice Wolas's billing fraud]

Earlier in 1991, around April or May, plaintiff began suspecting Scott Wolas of billing fraud. Wolas had billed four hours per day over a two-week period for a particular matter, and plaintiff suspected that Wolas had not worked those hours. He shared those suspicions with another litigation associate, Joseph Saltarelli. In June 1991, Saltarelli informed plaintiff that Wolas had billed fictitious hours on a series of matters. Over the next several months, Saltarelli related to plaintiff other instances of Wolas's improper billing.

In November 1991, Saltarelli told plaintiff that Saltarelli was meeting with B. Carey Tolley, III, the managing partner of the firm's New York office, along with Stone, Mason, and Robb to discuss Wolas's billing practices. Soon after this meeting, Wolas organized a small gathering at the Lotos Club to celebrate plaintiff's passing the bar examination. Stone, Mason, and Robb also attended, as did Saltarelli. It was awkward; Wolas would not speak to Saltarelli, making everyone uncomfortable. . . .

In approximately June of 1992, plaintiff told Mason that Wolas was billing clients for time not worked. Unbeknownst to plaintiff, Mason had been investing heavily (and profitably) through Wolas for nearly two years. In addition to Wolas's status as a "rainmaking" partner at H & W, he solicited investments in his family's liquor business. These so-called investments were actually part of an alleged "Ponzi scheme" Wolas was conducting from his office at H & W. Wolas lent considerable credence to those allegations — in fact, everyone now seems to agree they are true — by absconding in 1995, leaving behind more than 100 investors who claim to have been defrauded of more than $30 million. Mason, however, was not one of the investors who were left holding the bag. To the contrary, he profited enormously from Wolas's scheme; in 1994 alone he earned $2 million. In any event, when plaintiff told him in June 1992 that Wolas was billing for time not worked, Mason responded curtly, telling plaintiff that things are not always what they seem, and that Wolas's billing was not plaintiff's concern.

### [The co-investor partners find fault with Kelly's work]

Before his conversation with Mason about Wolas's billing fraud, plaintiff had not received any substantial negative criticism of his work or work habits. However, shortly after the meeting, Stone began inquiring about plaintiff's whereabouts on mornings when he arrived late to the office. Stone, like Mason, invested heavily with Wolas from 1990 through 1995. In an e-mail to Robb, dated July 24, 1992, Stone wrote that plaintiff's "problems with basic logistics have gotten Scott [Wolas], Chris [Mason] and me pulling our hair out." Robb, like Mason and Stone, had invested substantial sums through Wolas. Four days later, in a July 28, 1992, e-mail to Stone, Wolas, and Mason, Robb mentioned that she had spoken to plaintiff about "his constant tardiness and other inattentions to the administrative aspects of practicing law (e.g., not pursuing finalizing his bar application in a timely fashion)." Robb continued, "I told him that all of you liked him enormously, think he is talented, and view him as having the potential to become an excellent lawyer, but that if he didn't take his inability to get to work consistently seriously, there was a good chance that you were going to boot him out of here."

### [The managing partner tells Saltarelli to help Wolas fix billing records]

Meanwhile, after putting Saltarelli off for months, Tolley finally reviewed Wolas's billing records. Tolley refused to approach Wolas for an explanation, but rather told Saltarelli in early August 1992 to raise it directly with Wolas, in a non-accusatory manner, under the guise of asking his help in explaining billing records that might raise questions when cases were settled or fee applications were made to courts. In essence, Tolley told Saltarelli to help Wolas repair billing records that Saltarelli believed were fraudulent.

### [Kelly's second-year review]

On September 10, 1992, Robb and Mason spoke further to plaintiff regarding his performance. As a result, plaintiff prepared a memorandum on September 16, 1992, listing ten steps he intended to take to improve his work habits. On November 10, 1992, plaintiff again met with Mason and Robb for his second annual associate evaluation. They informed him that he had received "needs improvement" ratings in several critical categories, that he displayed "poor attention to work" in general, and that his failure to gain admission to the New York bar put him behind his class because he could not "function independently." When plaintiff defended his performance, Robb responded by telling him that each of the New York litigation partners was billing more hours than plaintiff. Plaintiff asked, sarcastically, "Even Scott [Wolas]?" Robb responded, in an irritated tone, "Yes all the partners," which plaintiff understood as Robb's disagreement with plaintiff's accusation that Wolas was overbilling the firm's clients.

### [The associates report Wolas to another partner]

Over the following months, plaintiff, Saltarelli, and [Harold] Geary [another associate] encountered additional evidence of Wolas's systematic overbilling of clients. Sensing that Tolley was not going to deal with the problem, they approached James A. Jones, III, Tolley's predecessor as managing partner, in February of 1993. The three came forward as a group, prompted in part by the advice of a federal district judge whom Geary had served as a law clerk. The judge had further told Geary that he might have an ethical obligation to disclose the billing irregularities to the Disciplinary Committee if appropriate action were not taken by the firm.

Saltarelli, Geary, and plaintiff raised the issue of Wolas's improper billing with Jones in February 1993. Geary brought to Jones documentary evidence of Wolas's fraud. . . . The day following Geary's meeting with Jones, plaintiff met with Tolley to discuss Wolas's billing practices. In the ensuing weeks, plaintiff had additional meetings with Tolley, Jones, and Wolas himself to review Wolas's billing records. In late February, Tolley informed plaintiff that W. Taylor Reveley, the former managing partner of the firm's Richmond office, would be coming to New York to head the investigation into Wolas's billing.

### [Kelly researches his ethical obligations]

On February 4, 1993, plaintiff spent about four hours researching his and the firm's ethical duties with respect to Wolas's improper billing practices. According to plaintiff, H & W policy required him to record that time in his daily records in a non-billable account. Later that day, plaintiff encountered Stone, who demanded to know what he had been doing. Because plaintiff knew Stone was involved in the billing inquiry and believed she supported Wolas, plaintiff lied to her, saying that he had been at an interview with the Character and Fitness Committee of the state bar. He later recorded the four hours in his time record as an ethics interview.

### [The co-investor partners force Kelly to resign]

On February 25, 1993, Stone sent an e-mail to Mason and Robb. She stated, "I want to fire Peter Kelly NOW. He missed his deadline: 10:00 a.m. this morning to give me a draft. . . . Then Peter disappeared all day. He just returned and has nothing more for me. . . . I can't stand it anymore. We must get rid of him now." Plaintiff claims that, in fact, he met Stone's deadline, and that he had worked through the previous night to do so.

On March 1, 1993, the day before Reveley was scheduled to interview plaintiff about Wolas's billing activities, Robb and Mason told plaintiff that he had to leave the firm. They gave him a choice: he could (a) be fired immediately, without severance pay or a favorable job reference; or (b) announce his resignation and stay with the firm the next several months, which would gain him a favorable reference. This was not much of a choice. Plaintiff had no other employment lined up and no other source of income. He would face a difficult job search if he could not obtain a favorable reference from H & W. He would have to disclose on his application for admission to the bar that he had been fired. Consequently, plaintiff chose coerced resignation over being fired.

### [The Richmond partner "investigates"]

Before coming to New York to conduct his inquiry, Reveley spoke by telephone with Robb, who disparaged plaintiff and Geary. Stone admits that she "might have" told her partners (presumably including Reveley) before the billing investigation that plaintiff had concocted his allegations against Wolas in order to stretch out his employment at H & W. In any event, Reveley promptly rejected the accusing associates' claims. He interviewed them on March 2, 1993. He conducted a "hearing" nine days later. Present were the three accusers, Stone (whom Reveley insisted be present because she was "inextricably relevant" to the hearing), Mason, and Wolas. It was not much of a hearing. Reveley denied the accusing associates access to Wolas's written response to their charges and refused to permit them to question Wolas. Stone and Mason sat silently. They did not disclose their separate, investment-based financial interest in Wolas's continued membership in the firm. Indeed, Mason had invested $12,900 with Wolas the day before the hearing, and had received a $35,000 "return of principal" from him just ten days before that. Stone had received $96,200 in "repayments" from Wolas in the seven weeks before the hearing. Indeed, though Mason, Stone, and Robb were all integrally involved as H & W partners in exonerating Wolas and getting rid of plaintiff — Wolas's accuser — none of them revealed to Tolley, Reveley, or Jones their involvement as investors in Wolas's scheme. Indeed, if Mason, Stone, and Robb are to be believed, they never even discussed their financial stakes in Wolas among themselves until 1994 at the earliest.

It took Reveley only one day to decide that Wolas had not committed billing fraud, but he waited almost a month to meet with his accusers. On April 7, 1993, Reveley met with plaintiff, Geary, Saltarelli, and Tolley to discuss his findings. He told them that Wolas was a "sloppy pig, not a dirty rat." The three associates responded by presenting Reveley with additional evidence of fraudulent billing by Wolas. Reveley promised to continue his investigation.

### [The firm worries about reporting Wolas's misconduct]

On April 13, 1993, Tolley e-mailed Reveley. The subject was whether the firm or the accusing associates had an obligation to report the facts about Wolas's billing to the Disciplinary Committee. The e-mail made explicit reference to Wieder v. Skala. . . . Tolley opined that the firm's determination that fraud had not been clearly established extinguished the obligation to report not only for the firm, but for the associates as well. He sought Reveley's counsel on how to tell the associates that they had no obligation to report Wolas. On May 6, 1993, Reveley met with the accusing associates separately and told them they had no ethical obligation to take their accusations further. Although he added that each associate had to make that decision for himself, it was clear that anyone taking on Wolas before the Disciplinary Committee would be taking on H & W as well.

### [Kelly gets a bad reference, moves to Texas]

Plaintiff left H & W at the end of May 1993, although he remained on the firm's payroll for another month. In seven letters to prospective employers, dated July 27 through September 3, 1993, plaintiff stated that he left the firm "voluntarily." On November 11, 1993, a partner at another firm in New York contacted Stone seeking a job reference for plaintiff. Stone praised plaintiff's substantive abilities but mentioned that a series of personal problems had negatively affected plaintiff's job performance and attendance. According to Stone, the caller told her that plaintiff had mentioned that H & W let him go because he had blown the whistle on a partner's billing irregularities. Stone informed him that plaintiff's departure from H & W stemmed entirely from plaintiff's performance problems.

Unable to secure work in New York, plaintiff moved to Texas in 1994. On February 28, 1994, an attorney placement firm in Houston contacted Stone with regard to plaintiff. According to Stone, she told the placement firm that plaintiff "was very smart and a very good writer, but that he suffered from performance problems and family crises which severely affected his work."

Plaintiff was admitted to the Texas bar in 1994, and was finally admitted to the New York bar in the summer of 1997. On September 29, 1997, he brought this action.

### DISCUSSION ...

Plaintiff concedes that he worked at H & W as an employee-at-will, and that, under New York law, an employer may generally terminate such an employee at any time for any or no reason. . . . He contends that his termination fits within the narrow exception to that rule established . . . in Wieder v. Skala.

In *Wieder*, the court held that even though an associate at a law firm was an at-will employee, he had a valid claim against his firm for breach of contract based on the firm's discharging him for his insistence that the firm comply with the Code of Professional Responsibility by reporting to the Disciplinary Committee the professional misconduct of another associate. . . .

H & W argues that plaintiff cannot maintain the breach of contract claim established by *Wieder* because he was not admitted to the New York bar, or any bar for that matter, while he was at the firm. He was thus not subject to the disciplinary rules, the argument goes, and therefore a threat to take adverse action against him if he disclosed Wolas's fraud would not create the dilemma *Wieder* prohibits. Indeed, H & W argues, allowing plaintiff to assert a *Wieder* claim would be tantamount to expanding the scope of New York's disciplinary rules by imposing reporting obligations on non-lawyers, something only the New York Court of Appeals may do.

H & W contends that *Wieder* has other limitations as well. It argues that the cause of action *Wieder* creates is unavailable where the plaintiff has not overtly threatened to go to the Disciplinary Committee, and that *Wieder* does not affect a firm's right to condition favorable job references (as opposed to continued employment) upon an attorney's violation of DR 1-103(A). . . .

### A. The Availability of a *Wieder* Claim to an Associate
### Not Yet Admitted to the Bar

H & W is at pains on this motion to retroactively label plaintiff as a "law clerk," rather than as an "associate." . . .

It is difficult to conceive of H & W telling its clients what it is now telling me, i.e., that, as far as the firm is concerned, its unadmitted associates are not bound by the disciplinary rules and may knowingly act contrary to them without fear of professional sanction. More difficult still is imagining H & W telling that to the new class of law graduates that joins the firm as unadmitted associates each fall.

In any event, the question whether the *Wieder* cause of action would be extended by New York courts to unadmitted law graduates working as associates in law firms is easily answered. The answer is yes. . . . While associates not yet admitted to the bar are not officially attorneys, it would be anomalous to permit these associates to ignore unethical behavior that admitted associates are required to report. . . .

I reject H & W's contention that an unadmitted associate cannot, because he is unadmitted, face the dilemma of having to choose between continued employment at a firm and compliance with lawyers' disciplinary rules. The state bar may be unable to kick an unadmitted attorney off the roll of attorneys, but it certainly can keep him from getting on it. An associate at a law firm might reasonably believe that his knowing failure to disclose an attorney's fraud would cause the Character and Fitness Committee to recommend the denial of his application for admission to the bar. . . .

### B. The Other Claimed Limitations on the *Wieder* Cause of Action . . .

According to H & W, . . . as long as the associate is fired before he threatened to go to the Disciplinary Committee, and if only a favorable reference (i.e., not his job) is conditioned on his continuing violation of DR 1-103(A), . . . "[t]he *Wieder* case does not create a cause of action in that setting." (Transcript of Oral Argument, Mar. 19, 1999, at 12.) That perverse result is required, I am told, because *Wieder* "does not address that situation," and only the New York Court of Appeals can say it does. Id. I disagree. . . .

If a law firm fires an associate in retaliation for reporting a lawyer's misconduct to the firm, its action is inherently coercive and necessarily implies an effort to impede post-termination reporting to the Disciplinary Committee. Thus, a cause of action is available under *Wieder*. The associate's stated intention to go to the disciplinary authorities may be powerful circumstantial evidence of the firm's intent to punish and/or silence him or her, but it is neither dispositive nor necessary to the associate's claim. . . .

In sum, while I recognize that *Wieder* established a narrow exception to New York's at-will employment law, I decline to give it the crabbed construction advanced by H & W. If the jury resolves the disputed issues of facts in plaintiff's favor, it may properly conclude that H & W breached its employment contract with him. . . .

## Notes and Questions about *Kelly*

**1.** After summary judgment was denied, a trial was scheduled. On the last weekday before the trial was to begin, Hunton & Williams and Peter Kelly settled the case for an undisclosed amount. The settlement included an agreement to keep confidential the terms of the settlement.[218] During settlement

---

218. For a discussion of issues raised by promises to keep the terms of settlement agreements confidential, see Heather Waldbeser & Heather DeGrave, A Plaintiff's Lawyer's Dilemma: The Ethics of Entering a Confidential Settlement, 16 Geo. J. Leg. Ethics 815 (2003).

negotiations, the firm insisted on withholding income taxes from the amount to be paid to Kelly. The firm claimed that the payment was for back wages and that it was obliged to withhold taxes. The firm asked Judge Gleeson to issue an order declaring that its payment to Kelly of the settlement amount less taxes would satisfy its obligations. Judge Gleeson decided that the settlement payment was not "wages" because it related to a period during which Kelly was not employed by the firm.[219]

**2.** This decision offers a prospect of some protection for associates who complain about or report unethical conduct by other lawyers in the firm. However, most of us would want to avoid what Peter Kelly went through. Suppose you were aware of improprieties in your firm. What would you do? If you were a partner as opposed to an associate or a law clerk not yet admitted to practice, would you consider yourself more or less able to blow the whistle? To explore this question, consider the following problem.

## PROBLEM 1-4  THE PHOTOGRAPHER

*This problem is closely based on a situation that arose in a law firm in Washington, D.C.*

You are a junior partner in the Washington, D.C., office of a Texas law firm. You have observed some troubling behavior by your boss, the managing partner of the Washington office. You are wondering whether to bring it to the attention of the managing partner in the firm's main office in Texas.

You began your legal career as an assistant prosecutor in Ohio. Then you worked for seven years as a lawyer for the Federal Energy Regulatory Commission. You have a keen sense of ethical propriety, which you attribute to many factors, including having worked for so many years for government law enforcement and regulatory agencies.

You decided to join a private law firm, Sanders & Waldman, because the firm was expanding its energy practice. The Washington office had just begun work for a big new client, National Oil Corp.

For your first two years in the firm, you were an associate. You did regulatory work for National Oil with two partners, Donald Cavers (the senior partner who had brought National Oil to the firm) and Eldon Underwood, a mid-level partner.

After two years, you were made a partner. You have always recorded your hours carefully. After you were made a partner, and therefore routinely received the billing records of all members of the law firm, you noticed that Don Cavers was billing National Oil far more hours than he actually worked. He spent a lot of his time with office decorators, going out for long lunches, and pursuing his hobby of

---

219. Kelly v. Hunton & Williams, 1999 WL 759972 (E.D.N.Y. 1999).

photography. Cavers had a kind of photographic studio in his office; he would spread items of office equipment in patterns on his floor and photograph them. He spent hours on his hobby daily, including attending outside classes during the business day.

You checked your impression with Underwood. He agreed that Cavers was spending about three or four hours a day on client work, while billing National Oil for at least seven hours.

National Oil pays the firm's bills like clockwork. Nobody there has ever complained, visited the Washington office, or even asked a question about the hours that are billed. Of course, the large monthly bills (usually $50,000 to $75,000) that your office sends to National Oil are the life-blood of your office, but they are almost petty cash to a big company like National Oil. The general counsel at National Oil has a longstanding and close relationship with Cavers, which is the reason that National hired your firm.

For several weeks, you have been thinking that the D.C. Rules of Professional Conduct require you to report Cavers's conduct to the firm's managing partner in Texas. You asked Underwood to make the report with you. Underwood is encouraging you to report, but he is afraid to sign on. He mentioned that in the past years, two other partners reported other inappropriate conduct by Cavers to his senior partners in Texas. These lawyers are no longer with the firm.

You are a bit worried that Cavers or others within the firm might retaliate against you for reporting his misconduct, so you have done a little research. You have learned that your right to employment is governed by the partnership agreement, which does not have any explicit terms dealing with whistleblowing, either within the firm or to outside authorities. The agreement states that any dispute about the agreement must be settled by the courts in Texas. Texas has not yet had any cases involving retaliatory discharge of lawyers for whistle-blowing.

What will you do?

# 2 | THE DUTY TO PROTECT CLIENT CONFIDENCES

A. **The basic principle of confidentiality**
   1. Protection of "information relating to the representation of a client"
   2. Protection of information if there is a reasonable prospect of harm to a client's interests
   3. The bottom line

B. **Exceptions to the duty to protect confidences**
   1. Revelation of past criminal conduct
   2. The risk of future injury or death
   3. Client frauds and crimes that cause financial harm
   4. Revealing confidences to obtain advice about legal ethics
   5. Using a client's confidential information to protect the lawyer's interests
   6. Revealing confidences to comply with other law or a court order

C. **Use or disclosure of confidential information for personal gain or to benefit another client**

D. **Talking to clients about confidentiality**

E. **A concluding problem**

# A. The basic principle of confidentiality

One of the basic rules of client representation is that lawyers are obliged to keep clients' secrets. In fact, lawyers are required to keep confidential much of what they learn in the course of representing clients. This duty is expressed in the ethical rules; in the law of agency, which requires all agents to keep the confidences of their principals; and in the law of evidence, which protects lawyers and clients from being compelled to testify about confidential communications. This chapter explains the ethical and legal rules concerning the lawyer's obligation to protect client confidences, exploring what information must be kept confidential and under what circumstances a lawyer may or must reveal confidential information. Chapter 3 covers the related rules of evidence protecting attorney-client communications and the doctrine protecting the lawyer's work product.

## 1. Protection of "information relating to the representation of a client"

> **Rule 1.6(a)    Confidentiality of information**
> A lawyer shall not reveal information relating to representation of a client unless the client gives informed consent, the disclosure is impliedly authorized in order to carry out the representation, or the disclosure is permitted by paragraph (b) [which lays out some exceptions that are discussed later in the chapter].[1]

> **Comment 4**
> Paragraph (a) prohibits a lawyer from revealing information relating to the representation of a client. This prohibition also applies to disclosures by a lawyer that do not in themselves reveal protected information but could reasonably lead to the discovery of such information by a third person. A lawyer's use of a hypothetical to discuss issues relating to the representation is permissible so long as there is no reasonable likelihood that the listener will be able to ascertain the identity of the client or the situation involved.

Rule 1.6 requires lawyers to protect as confidential all information "relating to representation of a client."[2] This standard covers any information a

---

1. This is the text of the relevant Delaware Rule of Professional Conduct. Unless specified otherwise, all of this book's quotations from rules of professional conduct are quotations from the Delaware Rules of Professional Conduct. In a few instances, we quote from rules or from published proposed rules in other states. Except where we note otherwise, however, the text of all state rules that we quote is the same as the text of the ABA's Model Rules of Professional Conduct. See the note in the Introduction for a more detailed explanation. In Rule 1.6(a), the Delaware version has a comma after the second use of the word *representation* and the ABA version does not, but the difference between the Delaware version and the ABA version is purely stylistic.

2. The Restatement uses the same phrase, adding only that the definition excludes "information that is generally known." Restatement (Third) of Law Governing Lawyers § 59 (2000).

lawyer learns in connection with a matter the lawyer is handling for a client's case, regardless of whether the information was received from the client.[3] Here is a summary of what qualifies as confidential information.[4]

---

**Information that must be protected as confidential**

- All information relating to the matter on which the lawyer is representing the client is confidential, except information that is "generally known"
- Personal information relating to the client that the client would not want disclosed
- Information learned from the client, and information learned from interviews, documents, photographs, observation, or other sources
- Information acquired before the representation begins (such as during a preliminary consultation) and after the representation terminates
- Notes or memoranda that the lawyer creates relating to the matter

---

## What could happen if a lawyer fails to protect confidences?

MIf a lawyer improperly reveals confidences, her client might be harmed. For example, if a client who was in a car accident tells her lawyer that she believes she was at fault, and the lawyer tells her opposing counsel, the opposing lawyer might use this information to win a lawsuit against the client.

A lawyer who improperly reveals client confidences might suffer various legal or other consequences. The lawyer's client might fire the lawyer or refuse to pay the fee. The lawyer might be

- subject to professional discipline,
- liable in tort or contract for negligent or intentional breach of duty,
- disqualified from representation of one or more clients, or
- enjoined by a court from further revelation.

## What is the policy behind the confidentiality rule?

The primary purpose of the confidentiality rule is to facilitate open communication between lawyers and clients. Lawyers need to get accurate and complete information from their clients to represent them well. If lawyers were not bound to protect clients' secrets, clients might be more reluctant to share their secrets with their lawyers.

FOR EXAMPLE: A former client of Professor Lerman's got fired from his job as a hospital janitor because he broke a faucet on a sink with a two-by-four. He explained to Lerman that he got agitated because he had not

---

3. Id.
4. The information in the box is drawn from Restatement § 59, comments.

taken his prescription medication for an anxiety problem. The reason he hadn't taken his medication is that the hospital changed the location where employees were to pick up prescriptions, and he didn't know where to get it. He also told Lerman about other episodes of violence that occurred when he was not medicated. In fact, he once hijacked a plane. He had no weapon, but he bit the pilot.

Suppose Professor Lerman had had an option to tell his employer or other people about his violent history. He might not have told her about the other episodes.

### Isn't the recitation of those facts itself a violation of the rule on confidentiality?

It may be. Even though Professor Lerman is teaching now and not a practicing lawyer, she must still comply with the rules of confidentiality as to former clients. She has had no contact with this client in ages. He has not given her permission to talk about his story. But in recounting this tale, she hasn't mentioned his name, where he worked, when she represented him, or many other details that might enable the reader to identify him. Is that enough? It is hard to imagine any harm that could come to her former client from her having told just a few facts about his story. Is it relevant that these facts provide an interesting example of an important principle and therefore might have some value to readers? Perhaps a lawyer may reveal confidences if the lawyer keeps the client's identity sufficiently hidden, so long as no harm could result from telling the story. The language of Rule 1.6 does not say this, but the rule is widely understood this way.

### Is the fact that a lawyer is representing a particular client confidential?

Sometimes. Some clients don't care if it is known that they are clients. However, if a lawyer (with a certain client's permission) reveals that she is representing that client, she must then avoid disclosing confidential information about that client's matter. Some clients do not want anyone to know that they have consulted an attorney. In such cases, the fact of consultation or representation is confidential.[5]

> **FOR EXAMPLE:** Suppose a client is considering seeking a divorce but has not yet decided what to do. Revelation even of the fact that the client has consulted a lawyer could be personally or financially disastrous for the client.

Many of the problems involving the principle of client confidentiality arise out of its several exceptions. But before we turn to those exceptions, let's look

---

5. Lawyers may be able to avoid being compelled to reveal client identity under the attorney-client privilege. See Chapter 3C for a discussion of the application of the privilege to client identity.

at a very common problem involving the scope of the duty to protect confidences.

## PROBLEM 2-1  **YOUR DINNER WITH ANNA,**[6] **SCENE 1**

It is mid-August. You have just completed your first day as a lawyer in a law firm. For the first time, you are part of a legal team representing a client.[7]

You reach Chez Francois before Anna gets there. You settle down at an empty sidewalk table where you will see her when she arrives. You have known Anna since you were in a freshman seminar together in college. Your career paths have diverged, but today was Anna's first day at her first permanent job too. She has become a social worker on the children's ward of the city hospital. When you discovered last month that you would be starting work on the same day, you arranged to celebrate with Chez Francois's famous lobster thermidor and a bottle of good wine.

You order a sparkling water with lime while you keep a lookout for Anna. You feel pretty good about the firm. Some of your classmates will earn higher salaries than you, but probably they will have to work much longer hours. Everyone at Porter & Quarles seems pretty relaxed. Maybe that's just because it's summer. But maybe a firm with just 15 lawyers isn't as high-pressure as the bigger firms in town.

"Hey there," Anna calls. You get up and give her a hug. "You look great in your lawyer suit," she says.

"Well, it turns out I didn't have to dress up like this. The lawyers only dress up for clients and meetings, I gather. But heck, the first day, who knew? You look good too."

"So what's it like? Get any murderers off today?"

What can you say? In fact you spent the day working on a civil suit against the local police department on behalf of a client whose wrist was broken by a cop. Can you tell Anna this? What if anything can you tell her about the work that you have been doing?

---

Problem 2-1 asks you to think about the issue of confidentiality in very general terms. After you think about this open-ended question, consider the more contextualized version of the same question in Problem 2-2.

---

6. Cf. My Dinner with Andre (Saga Prod. 1981) (motion picture). In the film, as in this chapter, we eavesdrop on a dinner conversation between two friends.

7. You have not yet learned whether you passed the bar, so you are technically a law clerk and not yet a member of the bar. But for the purpose of this problem, assume that you are required to comply with the ethics rules. Although the rules may not formally bind lawyers not yet admitted, new lawyers are well-advised to comply with them. See Kelly v. Hunton & Williams, excerpted in Chapter 1E.

## PROBLEM 2-2 **YOUR DINNER WITH ANNA, SCENE 2**

Anna catches the waiter's eye and orders a Diet Kola.

"Don't you think we should get some wine?" you ask.

"Sure. I just need to cool off. Have you tried Diet Kola yet? It's new. I'm already addicted. You know I'm a diet soda freak."

"Yeah, I know." You consult the wine list and order a pricey bottle of red.

Anna tells you about her first day at work. She is part of a team that counsels parents of children with serious or terminal illnesses. Anna spent much of the day with the mother of an 11-year-old girl, Estella, who has cystic fibrosis. Anna's team knows that Estella probably will die within a few years. Her team is trying to help Estella to cope with her illness and with the possibility of death, and to prepare the family so that Estella's death will not devastate the rest of the family.

Anna's story makes you feel relieved that you decided to be a lawyer. It is hard to imagine having to deal with problems like Estella's every day.

"So what about your first day?" Anna asks.

"I have a kind-of police brutality case. Our client is this guy named Joey. I guess I better not say his last name. Not that it would mean anything to you, but you know, it's confidential. Late one night last fall, Joey was in a bar downtown, a place called The Alley. He'd had quite a lot to drink. There was a fight in the bar. The bartender called the cops, and Joey got arrested."

"Wait a minute. If Joey wasn't involved in the fight, why did he get arrested?"

"My boss, Arthur, thinks Joey may have been involved in the fight. You see, one of the other guys who was arrested for fighting is the live-in boyfriend of Joey's ex-wife."

"Hmmm ... so it seems a little weird that Joey got arrested for watching his ex-wife's boyfriend having a fight with someone else, right?"

"Right."

"Anyway, when it was all over, Joey had a broken arm. Joey says this big cop named Mallory broke the bone by twisting his arm. Mallory's report says Joey's arm got broken during the fight. It also says that Joey was resisting arrest. Joey denies it."

"Is Joey facing criminal charges?"

"Joey was charged with assault and with resisting arrest. But the charges were thrown out when Mallory didn't show up in court both the first time the case was called and the second."

"But if the charges were thrown out, why does he need a lawyer?"

"Joey wants to sue the police department for using excessive force. Which is a reasonable thing to do, if the cop really broke his arm. I have to find out more about what happened.

"Starting tomorrow, I'm supposed to read all the recent police brutality decisions in the state and write a memo on the legal standards for police liability. Then I'll go with Mason, our investigator, to talk to the bartender, and try to find some of the other guys who were in the fight. They all got arrested, so we should be able to locate them from the police records."

"Sounds interesting."

"Yeah. Pretty good for day one, don't you think?"

The wine arrives. As the waiter pours, you start to wonder: Have I just violated the principle of confidentiality on my first day as a lawyer? Have I told Anna too much?

---

## Notes and Questions

1. **Why talk?** If you were having dinner with Anna, why might you want to talk to her about your new case?

2. **Consider the text.** Did you violate Rule 1.6(a)? First, consider only the rule and not Comment 4. Do you think that any of the disclosures you made to Anna violated it?

3. **Keeping Joey's name out of it.** In her explanation of her reasons for talking about her former hospital employee-client, Professor Lerman suggests

that an implicit exception to Rule 1.6 permits lawyers to talk about their work so long as they don't reveal identifying information. In the conversation with Anna, Joey's last name was not revealed. Does this solve the possible problem about revealing confidential information?

**4. Possible exceptions.** Rule 1.6 (a) allows a lawyer to disclose confidential information if the client gives informed consent or if the client gives implied authorization. Does either of those exceptions allow your conversation with Anna?

**5. The comment.** Is the conversation with Anna permitted by Comment 4 following Rule 1.6? To begin with, does the comment permit any social conversations at all? If it does, does it permit this particular conversation?

**6. Cutting back.** Exactly which statements about your case might you have omitted to have better protected your client's identity?

## 2. Protection of information if there is a reasonable prospect of harm to a client's interests

The Restatement defines "confidential client information" similarly to the ethical rules,[8] but the Restatement prohibits revelation of such information only if "there is a reasonable prospect that doing so will adversely affect a material interest of the client or if the client has instructed the lawyer not to use or disclose such information."[9] Under this standard, you could discuss Joey's case with Anna if you didn't reveal any information from which his identity could be ascertained. (That wouldn't be a "disclosure.") Even if his identity could be ascertained, you could reveal the information if there was no "reasonable prospect" that your discussion with Anna would adversely affect Joey's interests.

The Restatement defines "adverse effects" to include frustration of the client's objectives in the representation; material misfortune, disadvantage, or other prejudice to the client; financial or physical harm to the client; or personal embarrassment to the client.[10] So the Restatement version of the rule imposes a lower standard of secrecy than do the ethical rules. In particular, while the Rule 1.6 appears to favor a bright line test barring almost all disclosure, the Restatement seems to distinguish between disclosures that could harm a client and those that could not.

### How do you know if there is a "reasonable prospect" of harm to a client's interests?

The Restatement says that whether there is a reasonable prospect of harm to a client depends on "whether a lawyer of reasonable caution, considering only

---

8. As mentioned above, § 59 defines confidential client information to include "information relating to the representation of a client, other than information that is generally known."

9. Restatement, § 60(1)(a). A comment to this section defines "disclosure" as a revealing information "in a form that identifies the client or the client matter either expressly or through reasonably ascertainable inference." It adds that "revealing information in a way that cannot be linked to the client involved is not a disclosure." § 60, Comment c(i).

10. Restatement § 60, comment c(i).

the client's objectives, would regard use or disclosure in the circumstances as creating an unreasonable risk of adverse effect either to those objectives or to other interests of the client."[11] This is a little circular, but the point is that a lawyer must make a judgment about whether a careful lawyer in his position would see a problem.

## More Questions about Problem 2-2

**7. The Restatement.** Under the Restatement standard, would your conversation with Anna be permissible?

**8. Swearing Anna to secrecy.** You have known Anna for a long time and know that she is very discreet. Could you solve the confidentiality problem by obtaining her agreement that she will keep confidential the information you tell her about your case?

**9. The walls have ears.** What about the fact that you are in a public place? Suppose you conclude that you can talk to Anna without stepping over the line. What about the people at the next table? Is your subjective assessment of the noise screen provided by the other diners' conversation an adequate basis for discussing sensitive information in a public place?

**10. Another consideration.** Suppose that your firm eventually assigns you to meet with Joey and you become the firm's primary contact with him. Suppose also that you become certain that Anna is not discussing your work with anyone else, nor will she do so in the future, and you talk further with her about the case even though you are not sure you are allowed to do so. Over time, you realize that Joey is cranky, demanding, somewhat mentally unstable, and even slightly paranoid. In a subsequent conversation with Anna, you say: "Joey is such a pain. He called me three times today, each time with another piece of neurotic minutia. I wouldn't be surprised if he wound up in a mental hospital. But if he keeps pestering me, I'm going to wind up in a mental hospital too." Apart from compliance with the duty to protect confidences, is it a betrayal of trust to talk this way about a client?

## 3. The bottom line

Unfortunately, there isn't a simple bottom line to the problem of informal discussions of client matters. Rule 1.6 does not seem to take into account the reality that lawyers, like most other people, talk to friends and family about their work, though they exercise varying amounts of caution in doing so. The Rule does not mention a "reasonable prospect of harm" test, though Comment 4 acknowledges that at least in some circumstances, a lawyer may talk hypothetically about a case so long as the identity of the client is protected.

A lawyer who wants to "play it safe" might decide never to discuss a client's case with anyone who is not at the lawyer's firm or otherwise involved

---

11. Id.

in the matter (such as an opposing counsel). This might have adverse personal or social consequences, but this lawyer would comply with the literal language of the rule.

A careful lawyer probably doesn't need to draw the line quite that sharply. The (relatively) permissive standard of the Restatement, which is probably closer to the norm of the profession, bars revelations if there is a "reasonable prospect" of harm to the client. However, it is difficult to apply the "reasonable prospect" standard in any particular case.

Two ethics gurus, Professors Hazard and Hodes, offer the following advice about protecting client confidences.

> In functional terms, the line between permissible and impermissible disclosure should probably be drawn at the point of anonymity: a lawyer may talk shop if she is virtually certain that the listeners could not ascertain the identity of the client or the situation involved. . . . To honor the rule of confidentiality, however, and to maintain its strength, lawyers should exercise self-restraint and resolve marginal cases in favor of nondisclosure.[12]

We add only that talking about cases with friends or family members involves some degree of risk. All lawyers must learn habits of discretion, avoid being casual about such conversations, consider the risks, and avoid or minimize them.

**"I never discuss my clients with their mothers."**

---

12. Geoffrey C. Hazard Jr. & W. William Hodes, The Law of Lawyering § 9.15 (3d ed., Aspen 2003).

# B. Exceptions to the duty to protect confidences

The duty to protect "information relating to the representation of a client" is very broad, but it is not absolute. The ethical rules identify several situations in which — depending on the rules of a particular jurisdiction — a lawyer *may* or, under certain circumstances, *must* reveal confidential information.

## Rule 1.6   Confidentiality of Information

| Rule language* | Authors' explanation of exceptions |
|---|---|
| (a) A lawyer shall not reveal information relating to the representation of a client unless | |
| the client gives **informed consent,** | |
| the disclosure is **impliedly authorized** in order to carry out the representation | |
| or the disclosure is **permitted by paragraph (b).** | |
| (b) A lawyer **may reveal** information relating to the representation of a client **to the extent the lawyer reasonably believes necessary:** | Before making a disclosure authorized by this rule, a lawyer should try to persuade a client to take action that will "obviate the need for disclosure." If a disclosure is made, it should be as narrow in content as possible and should be made to as few other people as possible.[13] |
| (1) to **prevent reasonably certain death or substantial bodily harm;** | "Such harm is reasonably certain to occur if it will be suffered imminently or if there is a present and substantial threat that a person will suffer such harm at a later date if the lawyer fails to take action necessary to eliminate the threat."[14] |
| (2) to **prevent the client from committing a crime or fraud that is reasonably certain to result in substantial injury to the financial interests or property** of another **and in furtherance of which the client has used or is using the lawyer's services;** | "The client can . . . prevent such disclosure by refraining from the wrongful conduct." Also, the rule does not require revelation, but other rules bar the lawyer from counseling or assisting the conduct in question, and may require the lawyer to withdraw from representation.[15] |

*Continued*

---

13. Rule 1.6, Comment 14.
14. Id. at Comment 6.
15. Id. at Comment 7.

| Rule language* | Authors' explanation of exceptions |
|---|---|
| (3) to **prevent, mitigate, or rectify substantial injury to the financial interests or property** of another that is reasonably certain to result or has resulted from the client's commission of a crime or fraud in furtherance of which the client has used the lawyer's services;[16] | This paragraph "addresses the situation in which the lawyer does not learn of the client's crime or fraud until after" the act occurred, and in which the loss can be prevented, rectified, or mitigated. The comment notes also that this paragraph does not apply when a person who has committed a crime or fraud "thereafter employs a lawyer for representation concerning that offense."[17] |
| (4) to **secure legal advice** about the lawyer's compliance with these rules; | This provision allows a lawyer to reveal otherwise confidential information to secure legal advice relating to compliance with the rules. |
| (5) to establish a **claim or defense** on behalf of the lawyer in a **controversy between the lawyer and the client,** to establish a **defense to a criminal charge or civil claim against the lawyer** based on conduct in which the lawyer was involved, or to respond to **allegations** in **any proceeding concerning the lawyer's representation of the client;** or | A lawyer may reveal confidences to the extent needed to collect a fee. Also, a client or a third party may allege that a lawyer has committed some wrongful act. In that event, a lawyer may reveal confidences to the extent necessary to respond to such an allegation. The lawyer need not wait for a complaint to be filed before the right to defend applies.[18] |
| (6) to **comply with other law or a court order.** | If a court order or other law requires a lawyer to reveal confidences, then if that other law supersedes the ethics rules, the lawyer may reveal the information.[19] |

*All emphasis added.

This section explores some of these exceptions to the duty to protect confidences. First, we take up the question of crime by a client. What if a client confesses to a lawyer that he has committed a murder? Is the lawyer supposed to keep that a secret? What if the client confesses that he is about to commit a murder, and the lawyer might be able to prevent it? Does it make a difference if the intended crime is a violent crime or a financial crime? These situations present a conflict between the lawyer's duty to protect his client and the lawyer's duty as a citizen or an officer of the court.

## 1. Revelation of past criminal conduct

A client who has committed a crime needs legal advice. To get good advice, the client may need to tell the lawyer all about the crime. This means the client

---

16. The ABA version of this section omits the comma after the word *mitigate*, but this is only a stylistic difference.

17. Rule 1.6, Comment 8. Delaware adds to its version of the comment an explicit statement that disclosure is permitted if the lawyer's services are used to commit a further crime or fraud such as obstruction of justice.

18. Rule 1.6, Comments 10 and 11.

19. See id. at Comments 12 and 13.

needs to be able to talk to the lawyer in confidence. This analysis has led to a broad consensus in the legal profession that information about most *past* criminal activity by clients should be kept in confidence. If the crime is over, the lawyer cannot prevent the harm by revealing it. Society, on the other hand, benefits by the fair administration of justice and by clients having unobstructed access to counsel.[20]

The rules require lawyers to keep information about past crimes by clients confidential.

## The Missing Persons Case: The Defense of Robert Garrow

In the 1970s in the Adirondack mountains of upstate New York, Frank Armani and Francis Belge, two local lawyers, were assigned by a judge to represent Robert Garrow, who was accused of murdering a teenager. In the course of representing this client, the lawyers became embroiled in an agonizing test of their duty to keep client confidences. In this section, we offer you some problems in which you may put yourselves in the shoes of the lawyers and explore the difficult choices that they faced. We also excerpt two court opinions that explore a conflict between a statute that requires disclosure of certain information and the ethical duty to protect confidences.

### PROBLEM 2-3  THE MISSING PERSONS, SCENE 1

*Put yourself in the shoes of attorney Francis R. Belge, who, along with Frank Armani, was a lawyer in the Adirondack mountains of upstate New York. The real case occurred in the 1970s, but assume that these events take place in the present and that you (like the actual Mr. Belge) are Mr. Armani's co-counsel. The following account is entirely based on the facts of the real case, except that you are written into the story as co-counsel and the story is told in the present tense.[21]*

Over the years, several teenagers or young adults have disappeared in your county. Their names are Philip Domblewski, Dan Porter, Susan Petz, and Alicia Hauck. Police officers have found the body of 16-year-

*Francis R. Belge*

old Philip Domblewski and have arrested Robert Garrow for murdering him. Garrow doesn't have enough money to pay for a legal defense, so the court assigned attorney Frank Armani to represent him. You have agreed to be Armani's co-counsel. You talk to Mr. Garrow, and he admits that he committed the murder. You advise Garrow that a

---

20. See id. at Comment 2.

21. The facts about the actual case, other than those in reported opinions, are drawn primarily from Tom Alibrandi with Frank Armani, Privileged Information (Dodd Mead 1984), and from the authors' correspondence with Mr. Armani.

verdict of not guilty by reason of insanity is his best chance of avoiding life imprisonment under harsh conditions. If the insanity defense is successful, Garrow would go to a mental hospital instead of to jail. Garrow instructs you to enter a plea of not guilty by reason of insanity.

The police discover the body of Dan Porter, 21, who was stabbed to death and tied up with the same type of rope found on Domblewski's body. Susan Petz, who had gone camping with Dan Porter, and Alicia Hauck, 16, are still missing. The distraught parents of these missing daughters begin to fear that Garrow killed their children too. The parents suspect that you know whether their daughters are dead or whether they are still alive, perhaps held captive somewhere.

The prosecutors have solid evidence that Garrow killed Domblewski. Your best chance of mercy for Garrow is to persuade the prosecutor to accept a plea of guilty by reason of insanity. But you know that the prosecution's psychiatrists will challenge an insanity claim. The prosecutor is the most likely to accept this deal if you provide him with information about Petz and Hauck, if Garrow has it.

When you explain this to Garrow, he admits that he has murdered Porter, Petz, and Hauck and authorizes you to try to make a deal with the prosecutor. He tells you that he dumped Petz's body in a certain mine shaft and hid Hauck's body in some tall grass in a distant cemetery (which he names). He has not yet authorized you to share these locations with the prosecutor, however. You are not certain whether Garrow is telling you the truth; he might be making up his claim about killing Petz and Hauck to seem more insane, to tantalize the prosecutor, or just to waste your time. For all you actually know, Petz and Hauck might still be alive somewhere.

---

## Questions

**1. What to do?** What would you do at this point? To help you think about this question, here is a menu of choices, but you may also suggest choices that are not listed here.

> **Option one.** Alert the police, the prosecutor, or the press of the location of the bodies.
>
> - If you are going to alert someone, whom will you alert?
> - Would you reveal that you are Garrow's lawyer or would you send an anonymous tip?
> - If you lean toward alerting someone, would you try to get Garrow to consent to the revelation of this information, or would you make the disclosure without consulting him?

■ If you ask for his permission to reveal the information and he says no, then what would you do?

**Option two.** Check on your client's tale by visiting the supposed sites of the bodies to see whether they are really there.

■ If you find the bodies where Garrow says he put them, how would that help you to decide what to do?

**Option three.** Do nothing about the missing girls. Just defend your client against the charge he is facing.

**2. Rule 1.6(b)(1).** Does this rule provide any argument that you could ethically reveal the location of the bodies?

**3. Rule 1.6(b)(6).** You know that a state health law requires reporting the discovery of bodies (so that they can be given a proper burial). Does Rule 1.6(b)(6) permit disclosure of the location of the bodies because such disclosure is necessary "to comply with other law or a court order"?

## PROBLEM 2-4  **THE MISSING PERSONS, SCENE 2**

*In the real case, Belge and Armani chose to check out their client's story.*

*Robert Garrow*

Suppose, like Belge and Armani, you conduct your own investigation. Garrow gives you instructions about where to find the hidden remains of the two girls. With great difficulty, because they are in fact well hidden, you find and photograph the remains without disturbing them. In the months that follow, Susan Petz's father, suspecting that you know more than you are saying, comes to your office and pleads with you to tell him whether his daughter is alive or dead. "Should we keep hoping and praying?" he asks.

What should you do now? Again, you consider options:

1. Tell the missing girls' parents (or the authorities, who will tell them) that they are dead.
2. Refuse to give Petz's father any information.

(If you choose either of these, Garrow is likely to be convicted of the Domblewski murder because the chance of prevailing with an insanity defense is not great. If you choose the second option, the bodies of the girls might never be found because the police have been searching fruitlessly for those bodies for a long time.)

3. Offer to give the prosecutor information that will help solve the two missing persons cases in exchange for a plea-bargained acceptance of Garrow's insanity defense.

Perhaps you can think of other options. Before you read on, pause here to think about what you would actually do.

---

## The Real Case

In the actual case, Belge and Armani initially decided not to reveal anything to the parents or to the authorities. They feared that if they led the authorities to the bodies, they would betray their client because the prosecutors would know that Garrow was guilty of additional murders. Also, evidence on the bodies might tie Garrow to the crimes. The prosecutors would almost certainly seek additional indictments, and the lawyers would lose all possible leverage for a plea bargain.

Several months later, the trial was approaching, and Garrow's prospects seemed poor. The lawyers changed course and tried to obtain a plea bargain by suggesting that they had information about the other missing children. The prosecutor rejected the offer. Garrow went to trial, and his lawyers tried to establish his insanity. During the trial, as part of his insanity defense, Garrow confessed to the multiple murders. However, he was convicted of the murder of Domblewski and sentenced to prison.

After the lawyers unsuccessfully tried to trade information for an insanity plea and Garrow confessed on the witness stand to the multiple murders, the prosecutor knew that the lawyers had known for months that Petz and Hauck were dead and where their bodies were located. The lawyers admitted as much since their admission could no longer adversely affect Garrow. At that point, public indignation directed at the lawyers became even more intense than it had been. Armani's law practice withered. He received death threats and a stream of hate letters. He purchased three guns for self-defense. His wife received obscene phone calls. She found a Molotov cocktail (an incendiary bomb) in the bushes next to her house. She and the Armani children moved to her parents' house.

Some people urged the prosecutor to indict Belge and Armani for obstruction of justice. The prosecutor did not do that but did charge Belge with a crime. A New York State public health statute required anyone who knew that a person had died without receiving medical attention to report that fact to the authorities. Belge was indicted for violating this statute. What follows is an excerpt of the county court opinion in that case.

### People v. Belge

---

372 N.Y.S.2d 798 (County Ct., Onondaga Co. 1975)

ORMAND N. GALE, J. . . .

#### [Belge's claim]

Defense counsel moves for a dismissal of the Indictment on the grounds that a confidential, privileged communication existed between him and Mr. Garrow, which should excuse the attorney from making full disclosure to the authorities. The National Association of Criminal Defense Lawyers, as Amicus Curiae succinctly state the issue in the following language: If this indictment stands, "the attorney-client privilege will be effectively destroyed." No defendant will be able to freely discuss the facts of his case with his attorney. No attorney will be able to listen to those facts without being faced with the Hobson's choice of violating the law or violating his professional code of Ethics.[22]

### [The importance of confidentiality]

The effectiveness of counsel is only as great as the confidentiality of its client-attorney relationship. If the lawyer cannot get all the facts about the case, he can only give his client half of a defense. This, of necessity, involves the client telling his attorney everything remotely connected with the crime.

Apparently, in the instant case, after analyzing all the evidence, and after hearing of the bizarre episodes in the life of their client, they decided that the only possibility of salvation was in a defense of insanity. For the client to disclose not only everything about this particular crime but also everything about other crimes which might have a bearing upon his defense, requires the strictest confidence in, and on the part of, the attorney. . . .

### [The Fifth Amendment privilege against self-incrimination]

A hue and cry went up from the press and other news media suggesting that the attorneys should be found guilty of such crimes as obstruction of justice or becoming an accomplice after the fact. From a layman's standpoint, this certainly was a logical conclusion. However, the constitution of the United States of America attempts to preserve the dignity of the individual and to do that guarantees him the services of an attorney who will bring to the bar and to the bench every conceivable protection from the inroads of the state against such rights as are vested in the constitution for one accused of crime. Among those substantial constitutional rights is that a defendant does not have to incriminate himself. His attorneys were bound to uphold that concept and maintain what has been called a sacred trust of confidentiality.

The following language from the brief of the Amicus Curiae further points up the statements just made:

> The client's Fifth Amendment rights cannot be violated by his attorney. There is no viable distinction between the personal papers and criminal evidence in the hands or mind of the client. Because the discovery of the body of Alicia Hauck would have presented a significant link in a chain of evidence tending

---

22. [Authors' footnote.] The National Association of Criminal Defense Lawyers apparently argued that Garrow's revelations were both "confidential" (the subject of this chapter) and "privileged" (the subject of Chapter 3). The attorney-client privilege protects lawyers and clients from being compelled to reveal private lawyer-client communications in which legal advice was sought or given. Lawyers usually don't invoke the privilege unless the government or a party to litigation asks for information about a lawyer-client communication. Here, no one had asked Belge for information about the missing persons, but a public health statute required revelation of the location of bodies without any official request. Belge claimed that he had no duty to report information protected by privilege. So the questions in this case were whether Belge was excused from reporting the location of the bodies by either the ethical duty of confidentiality or the attorney-client privilege.

to establish his guilt, Garrow was constitutionally exempt from any statutory requirement to disclose the location of the body. And Attorney Belge, as Garrow's attorney, was not only equally exempt, but under a positive stricture precluding such disclosure. Garrow, although constitutionally privileged against a requirement of compulsory disclosure, was free to make such a revelation if he chose to do so. Attorney Belge was affirmatively required to withhold disclosure. The criminal defendant's self-incrimination rights become completely nugatory if compulsory disclosure can be exacted through his attorney. . . .

### [Balancing Belge's duty to Garrow and his duty under the health law]

If the Grand Jury had returned an indictment charging Mr. Belge with obstruction of justice under a proper statute, the work of this Court would have been much more difficult than it is. . . . [But here] we have the Fifth Amendment right, derived from the constitution, on the one hand, as against the trivia of a pseudo-criminal statute on the other, which has seldom been brought into play. Clearly the latter is completely out of focus when placed alongside the client-attorney privilege. An examination of the Grand Jury testimony sheds little light on their reasoning. The testimony of Mr. Armani added nothing new to the facts as already presented to the Grand Jury. He and Mr. Belge were co-counsel. Both were answerable to the Canons of professional ethics. The Grand Jury chose to indict one and not the other. It appears as if that body were grasping at straws. . . . Both on the grounds of a privileged communication and in the interests of justice the Indictment is dismissed.

---

After the trial court dismissed the indictment, the prosecutor appealed.

## People v. Belge

376 N.Y.S.2d 771 (App. Div. 1975)

MEMORANDUM:

We affirm the Order of the Trial Court which properly dismissed the indictments laid against defendant for alleged violations of section 4200 (duty of a decent burial) and section 4143 (requirement to report death occurring without medical attendance) of the Public Health Law. We believe that the attorney-client privilege . . . effectively shielded the defendant-attorney from his actions which would otherwise have violated the Public Health Law. . . .

We note that the privilege is not all-encompassing and that in a given case there may be conflicting considerations. We believe that an attorney must protect his client's interests, but also must observe basic human standards of decency, having due regard to the need that the legal system accord justice to the interests of society and its individual members.

We write to emphasize our serious concern regarding the consequences which emanate from a claim of an absolute attorney-client privilege. Because the only question presented, briefed and argued on this appeal was a legal one with respect to the sufficiency of the indictments, we limit our determination to that issue and do not reach the ethical questions underlying this case.

## Questions about People v. Belge

1. **The prosecution of Belge.** Was it a proper exercise of prosecutorial discretion for the prosecutor to ask a grand jury to indict Belge for violation of the health law? Even if Belge committed a technical violation of law, did Belge do something wrong for which he deserved to be punished criminally?

2. **Obstruction of justice?** The courts dismissed the indictment. But suppose the statute had been more clearly applicable to these facts. For example, suppose that New York's obstruction of justice law declared that corpses are essential evidence in homicide investigations and made it a crime for any person with knowledge of the location of a dead body not to report that location to the police within four hours. Should the courts hold that such a statute overrides any obligations of confidentiality that a lawyer might otherwise have under Rule 1.6?

## PROBLEM 2-5 **THE MISSING PERSONS, SCENE 3**

*This problem, like these in scenes 1 and 2, is based on the events of the real case.*

Co-counsel Frank Armani's daughters Debbie and Dorina went to watch one day of Garrow's trial. In the courtroom, "Garrow dropped his hand from his face and turned toward [Dorina]. Their eyes locked for a moment, Garrow's hard penetrating stare frightening Dorina. His lips turned upward in a smile. 'Nice to see you again, Dorina.' The young woman's face froze in horror. She had to force herself to look away from Garrow's hypnotic stare. When she did, Dorina found herself looking into her sister's eyes. 'I didn't realize you knew Garrow,' Debbie said softly. 'I don't know him,' Dorina answered. Debbie's eyes widened. There was only one way Garrow could have known who Dorina was. He had to have been stalking her."[23]

*Frank Armani*

After Garrow's conviction, he was sentenced to prison for twenty-five years to life. He was sent to a maximum security prison. While in prison, he sued the State of New York for $10 million. In the course of

23. Alibrandi with Armani, supra n. 21, at 230.

capturing Garrow, the police had shot him. In the lawsuit, Garrow alleged that the state's doctors had caused him to become partially paralyzed because of their negligent treatment of these gunshot wounds. In exchange for his dropping the suit, the State transferred him to a medium security prison. State officials believed that he was unable to rise from a wheelchair because of his gunshot wounds. It turns out, however, that Garrow had been faking his paralysis.

Imagine, again, that you are Garrow's lawyer. It is now a year after Garrow has been convicted. The police come to see you. They tell you (as in real life they told Belge and Armani) that Garrow had scaled a 14-foot fence topped with barbed wire and made his escape, and that corrections officials had found a hit list with your name on it in Garrow's cell. The police ask you whether you have any idea where he might be hiding. Your first thought is to wonder whether, now that he's on the loose, Garrow will try to kill you or a member of your family.

You recall that Garrow once told you, in confidence, about where he hid before he was captured. Will you tell the police where he might be?

## Notes and Questions

**1. Duration of the duty to protect confidences.** Assume that after his conviction, Garrow ceases to be your client. Does the termination of the representation free you up to share information with the police?

**2. May you tell?** Under Rule 1.6, are you permitted to tell the police where Garrow sometimes hides?

**3. Will you?** In any event, what will you do?

**4. What really happened.** In the actual case, Armani told the police where Garrow had hidden in the past. The police followed Armani's lead and found Garrow. During the gunfight that ensued, the police shot and killed Garrow.

## 2. The risk of future injury or death

In the case that Armani and Belge handled, the lawyers became aware of deaths that had already occurred. Sometimes, lawyers learn about serious risks of future physical harm to others.

Under Rule 1.6, if the information relates to the representation of a client, the lawyer has a duty to protect the confidence, unless an exception applies. This is true whether the lawyer learned the information from a client or from another source.[24]

However, the rule allows a lawyer to reveal confidential information "to prevent reasonably certain death or substantial bodily harm." Under this

---

24. Rule 1.6, Comment 3.

standard, it doesn't matter whether the possible harm will be perpetrated by the client or by another person. What matters is what the lawyer believes to be the degree of possible harm and how likely the lawyer believes the harm is to occur. A comment explains that the purpose of the rule is to recognize "the overriding value of life and physical integrity." It explains that death or substantial bodily harm is "reasonably certain to occur if it will be suffered imminently or if there is a present and substantial threat that a person will suffer harm at a later date if the lawyer fails to take action necessary to eliminate the threat."[25]

The language discussed in the preceding paragraph was added to the Model Rules by the American Bar Association in 2002, and has been adopted in several states.[26] American lawyers have debated for decades how broad or narrow this exception should be.

DR 4-101 of the Model Code of Professional Responsibility, which preceded the Model Rules, allowed a lawyer to reveal "the intention of his client to commit a crime and the information necessary to prevent the crime." This language is substantively similar to text in the earlier ABA Canons of Professional Ethics. Many states retain this language, allowing a lawyer broad discretion in the face of any future criminal act by a client, but limiting the discretion to future acts that are criminal in nature.[27]

Before the 2002 amendment of Rule 1.6, the Model Rules provided that a lawyer may reveal confidences "to prevent the client from committing a criminal act that the lawyer believes is likely to result in imminent death or substantial bodily harm." This language allows revelation only when the harmful act is criminal in nature, the crime would be perpetrated by the lawyer's own client, the lawyer believes the crime is likely to kill or seriously harm another person, and the death or harm that would be caused by the crime is "imminent." This language, which remains in force in many states, is narrower than either the previous Model Code language or the current Model Rules language, which does not require that the contemplated harm be criminal.

Finally, some state ethics rules impose a *duty* on lawyers to reveal information about a threat of harm by a client to another person.[28] Illinois Rule 1.6(b), for example, states that "a lawyer *shall reveal* information about a client to the

---

25. Id. at Comment 6.

26. This language "to prevent reasonably certain death or substantial bodily harm," for example, has been adopted in the Rules of Professional Conduct of Delaware, Montana, North Carolina, and Tennessee. Proposals to adopt this and other language from the recent ABA amendments to the Model Rules are pending in many other states.

27. For information about which rules use this and similar language to allow revelation of certain confidences, see "Ethics Rules on Client Confidences," published in 2002 by the Attorneys' Liability Assurance Society, Inc., A Risk Retention Group (ALAS), reprinted in Thomas D. Morgan & Ronald D. Rotunda, 2003 Selected Standards on Professional Responsibility 134 (Found. 2003).

28. States that require revelation of confidences to prevent a client from committing a serious violent crime include Arizona, Connecticut, Illinois, Nevada, North Dakota, and Texas. Stephen Gillers & Roy D. Simon, Regulation of Lawyers: Statutes and Standards 73 (Aspen Publishers 2004).

extent it appears necessary to prevent the client from committing an act that would result in death or serious bodily harm" (emphasis added).

Because the state rules use such a wide range of language on when a lawyer may or must reveal confidences relating to possible future physical harm, it is essential to study the rule in the state in which you are admitted to practice.

## Spaulding v. Zimmerman

The 1962 case of Spaulding v. Zimmerman presents the issue of the lawyer's obligation when silence could lead to death. The case arose before Rule 1.6 was written. At the time, the Canons of Ethics required a lawyer "to preserve his client's confidences" except for an "announced intention of a client to commit a crime."[29] The Canons did not define the term "client's confidences."

The court doesn't explain very much about the events that led to this lawsuit. However, two law professors researched the case and learned some facts that are not in the opinion. Here's what happened.[30]

David Spaulding, 20, was riding home from work in the Zimmermans' car. The Zimmermans owned a road construction company; David was their employee. John Zimmerman, the driver of the car, was 19. Perhaps he and David Spaulding were friends since they were nearly the same age and worked together. There was a bad collision with another vehicle. Four other passengers were in the car. One of them, James Zimmerman, John's older brother, was killed in the accident. Another, Edward Zimmerman, John's father, suffered a broken neck.

Florian Ledermann, the driver of the other car, was 15. He had a "farm permit" to drive his father's car. He was driving his family to a county fair where Elaine, his 12-year-old sister, was to perform in a "4-H Dress Review." Elaine was killed in the accident. Florian's father's arm was seriously injured. As a result, he became unable to work as a farmer.

The accident occurred at the intersection of two country roads. There were no stop signs. Neither driver could see the approach of the other car because the drivers' view was blocked by corn in the fields surrounding the intersection. After this terrible accident, the Spauldings sued the Zimmerman and Ledermann families to get compensation for David Spaulding's injuries.

## Spaulding v. Zimmerman

263 Minn. 346 (1962)

GALLAGHER, Justice.

[This is an] appeal from an order of the District Court of Douglas County . . . [which vacated that court's] prior order . . . [in which the District Court had approved] a settlement made on behalf of David Spaulding on March 5, 1957, at which time he was a minor of the age of 20 years. . . .

---

29. Canons of Professional Ethics, Canon 37 (1908).

30. Roger C. Cramton & Lori P. Knowles, Professional Secrecy and Its Exceptions: Spaulding v. Zimmerman Revisited, 83 Minn. L. Rev. 63 (1998).

[The accident]

[An] action was brought against defendants by Theodore Spaulding, as father and natural guardian of David Spaulding, for injuries sustained by David in an automobile accident, arising out of a collision which occurred August 24, 1956, between an automobile driven by John Zimmerman, in which David was a passenger, and one owned by John Ledermann and driven by Florian Ledermann. . . .

[Medical examinations]

David's injuries were diagnosed by his family physician, Dr. James H. Cain, as a severe crushing injury of the chest with multiple rib fractures; a severe cerebral concussion, probably with petechial hemorrhages of the brain; and bilateral fractures of the clavicles. At Dr. Cain's suggestion, on January 3, 1957, David was examined by Dr. John F. Pohl, an orthopedic specialist, who made X-ray studies of his chest. Dr. Pohl's detailed report of this examination included the following:

> . . . The lung fields are clear. The heart and aorta are normal.

Nothing in such report indicated the aorta aneurysm with which David was then suffering. On March 1, 1957, at the suggestion of Dr. Pohl, David was examined from a neurological viewpoint by Dr. Paul S. Blake. [Dr. Blake concluded that David might possibly have permanent brain damage. He recommended that the Spauldings not settle the case for at least a year to make sure that such damage did not appear. But he did not find the aneurysm.]

In the meantime, on February 22, 1957, at defendants' request, David was examined by Dr. Hewitt Hannah, a neurologist. On February 26, 1957, the latter reported to Messrs. Field, Arveson, & Donoho, attorneys for defendant John Zimmerman, as follows:

> The one feature of the case which bothers me more than any other part of the case is the fact that this boy of 20 years of age has an aneurysm, which means a dilatation of the aorta and the arch of the aorta. Whether this came out of this accident I cannot say with any degree of certainty and I have discussed it with the Roentgenologist and a couple of Internists. . . . Of course an aneurysm or dilatation of the aorta in a boy of this age is a serious matter as far as his life. This aneurysm may dilate further and it might rupture with further dilatation and this would cause his death.
>
> It would be interesting also to know whether the X-ray of his lungs, taken immediately following the accident, shows this dilatation or not. If it was not present immediately following the accident and is now present, then we could be sure that it came out of the accident.

Prior to the negotiations for settlement, the contents of the above report were made known to counsel for defendants.

## [The settlement]

The case was called for trial on March 4, 1957 [when] neither David nor his father [was] aware that David was suffering the aorta aneurysm but on the contrary believed that he was recovering from the injuries sustained in the accident. On the following day an agreement for settlement was reached wherein, in consideration of the payment of $6,500, David and his father agreed to settle in full for all claims arising out of the accident.

Richard S. Roberts, counsel for David, thereafter presented to the court a petition for approval of the settlement, wherein David's injuries were described as: ". . . severe crushing of the chest, with multiple rib fractures, severe cerebral concussion, with petechial hemorrhages of the brain, bilateral fractures of the clavicles." . . .

At no time was there information disclosed to the court that David was then suffering from an aorta aneurysm which may have been the result of the accident. Based upon the petition for settlement and such affidavits of Drs. Cain and Blake, the court on May 8, 1957, made its order approving the settlement.[31]

## [David's belated discovery]

Early in 1959, David was required by the army reserve, of which he was a member, to have a physical checkup. For this, he again engaged the services of Dr. Cain. In this checkup, the latter discovered the aorta aneurysm. He then reexamined the X-rays which had been taken shortly after the accident and at this time discovered that they disclosed the beginning of the process which produced the aneurysm. He promptly sent David to Dr. Jerome Grismer for an examination and opinion. The latter confirmed the finding of the aorta aneurysm and recommended immediate surgery therefor. This was performed by him at Mount Sinai Hospital in Minneapolis on March 10, 1959. . . .

## [The holding of the Minnesota Supreme Court]

The court did not abuse its discretion in setting aside the settlement which it had approved on plaintiff's behalf while he was still a minor. . . . The seriousness of this disability is indicated by Dr. Hannah's report indicating the imminent danger of death therefrom. This was known by counsel for both defendants but was not disclosed to the court at the time it was petitioned to approve the settlement. While no canon of ethics or legal obligation may have required them to inform plaintiff or his counsel with respect thereto, or to advise the court therein, it did become obvious to them at the time, that

---

31. [Authors' footnote.] Civil cases are often settled by the parties without supervision or review by a court. In this case, however, there was there a "petition for settlement" and a court order approving it. The reason for court approval of the settlement in this case was that in Minnesota during the 1950s, if one of the parties was a minor, as in this case, the settlement had to be presented to a judge for approval before it became final. In *Spaulding*, the parties reached their settlement 16 days before David ceased to be a minor.

the settlement then made did not contemplate or take into consideration the disability described. This fact opened the way for the court to later exercise its discretion in vacating the settlement.

## Notes and Questions about *Spaulding*

**1. Who should decide about disclosure?** Apparently, Dr. Hannah sent a copy of his report to the defendants' lawyers, but he did not send a copy of his report to the Spauldings. The defendants' lawyers may have informed the defendants' insurance companies about David's aneurysm. However, they did not inform the Spauldings, the Zimmermans, or the Ledermanns. Probably the lawyers decided, without consulting their clients, not to disclose the existence of the aneurysm.[32]

Perhaps Dr. Hannah should have informed the Spauldings himself.[33] He may have thought that the defendants' lawyers would tell the Spauldings, or he may have deliberately left that decision to the defendants' lawyers. In any event, our primary focus is on what, if anything, the defendants' lawyers should have done, a question of legal ethics. To think about that question, note the sequence of events:

| | |
|---|---|
| August 1956: | Accident |
| Later in 1956: | Examination by plaintiff's family doctor |
| January 3, 1957: | Examination by plaintiff's orthopedist; aorta normal |
| February 22, 1957: | Examination by Dr. Hewitt, for defendant, who discovers that the aorta is enlarged |
| March 1, 1957: | Examination by Dr. Blake, plaintiff's neurologist, who does not discover the aorta damage but who recommends postponement of the settlement |
| Shortly thereafter: | Spauldings reject Dr. Blake's recommendation to postpone any settlement (perhaps because they needed the money to pay for the medical expenses or did not think that they could obtain a better settlement by waiting) |

**2. A little more history.** David Spaulding was lucky — the examination required by the army probably saved his life. However, the defendants' withholding of the information from him had real costs. The aneurysm could have

---

32. Cramton & Knowles, supra n. 30, at 94.

33. In 1999, the American Medical Association issued an opinion stating that a physician's examination of a person at the behest of a business or insurer represented a "limited patient-physician relationship" and that, in such a relationship, "the physician has a responsibility to inform the patient about important health information or abnormalities that he or she discovers . . . [and] should suggest that the patient seek care from a qualified physician. . . ." Am. Med. Assn. Op. E-10.03: Patient-Physician Relationship in the Context of Work-Related and Independent Medical Examinations, available at http://www.ama-assn.org/(last visited Oct. 14, 2004). Physicians retained by insurance companies in the 1950s may not have understood themselves to have duties to their examinees.

ruptured at any time during the two years after Dr. Hannah discovered it. Also, the surgery to repair the aneurysm at that point was expensive. As a result of the delay in the repair of the aneurysm, Spaulding suffered a permanent loss of most of his voice.[34]

David's family didn't know, even after the surgery, that the defendants had concealed knowledge of the aorta injury. At that point, David Spaulding (by then an adult) brought a new proceeding against the Zimmermans and Ledermanns to set aside the earlier settlement. His original complaint assumed that everyone had simply made a mistake about the extent of the damages. He relied on the contract doctrine of "mutual mistake" to try to vacate the earlier agreement and seek more money.[35] Amazingly, the defendants' response was that there had been no mutual mistake because they had known, from Dr. Hannah's report, that David had a life-threatening injury! (The fact that they admitted it suggests that perhaps they really believed that their duty as lawyers was not to reveal information that might lead their clients to have to pay a higher settlement amount.) This was how the Spauldings finally learned that the defendants had discovered David's aneurysm two years earlier but concealed it from them.[36]

At that point, the Spauldings amended their complaint, replacing the mutual mistake theory with the claim that the old judgment should be reopened because the defendants' lawyers should have told them about

the aortic injury.[37] Apparently, they argued that the defendants' lawyers should have revealed the lifesaving information they learned from Dr. Hannah.

The trial judge, Walter Rogosheske, did not agree with them. He seemed to blame the plaintiffs' lawyers for not asking about Dr. Hannah's examination and said that the defendants' lawyers had no obligation to disclose it during settlement negotiations. As quoted in the appellate decision, he said:

*Judge Walter Rogosheske*

> For reasons which do not appear, plaintiff's doctor failed to [spot the aneurysm]. By reason of the failure of plaintiff's counsel to use available rules of discovery, plaintiff's doctor and all his representatives did not learn that defendants and their agents knew of it. . . . Except for the character of the concealment in the light of plaintiff's minority, the Court would, I believe, be justified in denying plaintiff's motion to vacate, leaving him to whatever

---

34. Cramton & Lori P. Knowles, supra n. 30, at 127.

35. The doctrine of mutual mistake allows a party to avoid a contract if both parties are mistaken about a fact that was a basic premise of the contract. In addition, under modern contract doctrine, a party sometimes can avoid the contract if even that party alone was mistaken about such a fact. Restatement (Second) of Contracts §§ 152-153 (1981). At the time this case was litigated, it was possible to avoid a contract because of a unilateral mistake, but only if there was "concealment or, at least, knowledge on the part of one party that the other party is laboring under a mistake." Keller v. Wolf, 58 N.W.2d 891, 895 (Minn. 1953).

36. Cramton & Knowles, supra n. 30, at 71.

37. Id.

questionable remedy he may have against his doctor and against his lawyer. . . . There is no doubt of the good faith of both defendants' counsel. There is no doubt that during the course of the negotiations, when the parties were in an adversary relationship, no rule required or duty rested upon defendants or their representatives to disclose this knowledge.[38]

Note Judge Rogosheske's statement that "there is no doubt of the good faith" of defendants' counsel. He might have said, more directly, that the defendants' lawyers had no duty to disclose under the prevailing ethical rules. In an interview decades later, the judge recalled "that he had a high regard for, and personal relationship with, a senior partner of one of the defense lawyers involved in the case"; he did not want to embarrass his friend by "exposing the friend's partner to criticism." Also, just before oral argument on the motion to reopen the case, the judge admonished Robert Gislason, the Spauldings' lawyer, that "there is no need for comments on the ethics of the other attorneys involved." His sense of professional propriety and his dislike of criticizing other lawyers led him to tiptoe around the ethical issues.

Judge Rogosheske did reopen the Spauldings' case, albeit on the narrow ground that he had been required to approve a settlement in which all the facts were not known to him:

Once the agreement to settle was reached, it is difficult to characterize the parties' relationship as adverse. . . . The procedure took on the posture of a joint application to the Court. . . . It is here that the true nature of the concealment appears, and defendants' failure to [disclose was a] calculated risk that the settlement would be final. . . . [To permit it would] reward less than full performance of an officer of the Court's duty to make full disclosure to the Court when applying for approval in minor settlement proceedings.[39]

Then the Zimmermans appealed that decision. As you now know, the appellate court upheld the trial court's discretionary decision to reopen the case. Neither the trial court nor the appellate court squarely confronted the ethical problem that the Zimmermans' lawyer faced.

**3. Possible reasons for not using discovery.** The trial court mentioned that the Spauldings' lawyer did not engage in discovery. Presumably the Spauldings' lawyer could have asked for a copy of Dr. Hannah's report. The lawyer might not have asked for the report for any of several reasons.

- Perhaps he had little reason to think that it would contain anything his own doctors had not discovered.
- Discovery is used in only about half of civil cases — generally, the half involving the most money. Since this was a relatively small case, the lawyer may have believed that the case was not worth the considerable time and money that would have been required to draft and respond to discovery documents.

---

38. Spaulding v. Zimmerman, 263 Minn. 346, 351 (1962).
39. Id. at 352.

- David's family had just accumulated some heavy medical bills. They may have been eager to get a judgment or settlement, and discovery would have slowed down the process. Apparently, a trial date was available within days after Dr. Hannah's examination.
- The Spauldings' own neurologist, Dr. Blake, had just written a report counseling the Spauldings that the case should not be settled for at least a year so that the extent of the injury to David Spaulding's brain could be determined. If the Spauldings had asked for Dr. Hannah's report, the Zimmermans' lawyer probably would have routinely asked for Dr. Blake's report. If the judge had read Dr. Blake's recommendation, he might have rejected a prompt settlement, which all parties desired.[40]

**4. The availability of discovery as justification for nondisclosure.** Does the fact that the Spauldings' lawyer never asked for the report justify the Zimmermans' lawyer in deciding not to reveal the information?

**5. What should the Zimmermans' lawyer have done?** The Minnesota Supreme Court stated that "no canon of ethics or legal obligation may have required them to inform plaintiff." The case before it was, essentially, a civil procedure and contracts issue (whether to reopen a settlement), not a proceeding to discipline a lawyer, so the court did not have to look to the ethical standards to guide its decision. In principle, the court could have applied common law standards without considering the rules about proper lawyer behavior. The court's citation of ethical rules is an early example of a judge consulting the ethical rules to determine what lawyers should have done in cases arising from claims of malpractice, motions for disqualification, and other contexts.

As noted above, lawyers at the time had a duty to preserve "client confidences." The then-prevailing ABA Canons of Professional Ethics stated in pertinent part:

> It is the duty of a lawyer to preserve his client's confidences. . . . The announced intention of a client to commit a crime is not included within the confidences which he is bound to respect. He may properly make such disclosures as may be necessary to prevent the act or protect against whom it is threatened.

To make this problem more challenging, assume that Mr. Zimmerman was insured for only $10,000. Suppose further that if Mr. Zimmerman's lawyer did not disclose the aneurysm, he could expect to reach a settlement that would oblige Mr. Zimmerman to pay about $6,500, whereas if he disclosed, the settlement probably would be as much as $500,000, which would bankrupt Mr. Zimmerman. What should the lawyer in this situation have done, given the Canons as they existed at the time?

---

40. Cramton & Knowles, supra n. 30, at 74.

**6. David's age.** David was a minor at the time of the settlement, and that fact required court approval of the document. Therefore, according to the Minnesota courts, the defendants' lawyers had a duty to disclose the aneurysm when they asked for court approval. If David had been a month older at the time of the settlement, do you think that the courts would have imposed a duty to disclose the aneurysm? A duty to withhold the information? Or complete discretion with regard to this question?

**7. What if David had lost in the lower court?** If the lower court had declined to reopen the settlement in this case, would the appellate court have reversed?

**8. A strategic problem.** Imagine that you are the Zimmermans' lawyer. You have withheld Dr. Hannah's report and reached a settlement under which your client will have to pay only $6,500. You are about to present the settlement for court approval. Suppose that you could have anticipated the court's holding that because court approval is required, you must reveal the information at this point.

- If you make the revelation now, what is David Spaulding's lawyer likely to do?
- What does your conclusion suggest about Judge Rogosheske's statement that "when the parties were in an adversary relationship, no rule required or duty rested upon defendants or their representatives to disclose this knowledge"?

**9. Contemporary standards.** The *Spaulding* case was decided long before the current version of the Model Rules was written. If you were representing a modern-day Mr. Zimmerman (facing possible bankruptcy if the aneurysm were discovered), and your state had adopted Rule 1.6, what would you do?

## PROBLEM 2-6  YOUR DINNER WITH ANNA, SCENE 3

*Something like this actually happened to a lawyer who is a friend of one of the authors.*

Four months have passed since your first dinner with Anna, and you are on your way back to Chez Francois for another good meal and a chance to talk about your lives. You spent the whole day reading and summarizing documents that might be submitted in connection with the latest periodic report to the Food and Drug Administration (FDA) from one of your firm's clients, Twenty-First Century Foods. The files that you were reviewing pertain to that agency's review of the client's latest diet soda, called Diet Kola.

Diet Kola uses a new sweetening ingredient. When the FDA first approved this sweetener, all tests showed that it was risk-free. Nevertheless, the FDA required the company to continue testing to check for any long-range adverse effects of the product. You have been reviewing the latest tests on laboratory animals. The recent testing suggests that when female rats are given high concentrations of the sweetener, the rate of limb deformities in their offspring increases by ten percent. This could be a statistical fluke. The company wants the firm to help persuade the FDA to take no action until more test results are available. There is also some data showing that pregnant women who used a medication that contained a substance chemically similar to the sweetener in Diet Kola had miscarriages. This data is too limited to be statistically significant.

Anna is waiting for you when you arrive. She is reading a magazine and drinking a glass of Diet Kola. You are struck by the coincidence.

"Hey, Anna. It's been too long. You look great!"

"Thanks. You too."

"Want to order some wine?"

"No wine for me tonight," says Anna. "I'm sticking with Diet Kola. No more alcohol for a while, just Diet Kola and milk." She smiles knowingly.

"You mean . . ."

"I just learned last week—I'm almost two months pregnant!" She takes another sip of her drink.

---

## Questions

1. **Warn Anna?** Without violating Rule 1.6, can you say anything to her that would help to protect her child? Review the comments for guidance.

2. **Violate the rule?** However you answered the first question, suppose you think that rule precludes you from saying anything. Would you warn Anna anyway? Is it ever appropriate to violate an ethical rule?

3. **Your job.** If your law firm found out that you had warned Anna, what might be the repercussions for your job? Should that matter? If so, does it also matter that it is very unlikely that the firm would ever learn of your warning?

4. **More options?** Besides possibly warning Anna, is there anything you would do about the risk that you have learned about?

## 3. Client frauds and crimes that cause financial harm

Thus far, we have been concerned with harm to people—either past harm, as in the case of the buried bodies, or future harm, as in the case of David Spaulding's aneurysm. What if the harm to others is only to their property? Harm to the property interests of others might take the form of stealing or property destruction. Lawyers are sometimes involved in situations in which clients attempt to make money (or to avoid losing money) by lying or concealing information. Sometimes this conduct involves criminal behavior (such as in tax fraud or mail fraud). Lawyers are not permitted to assist clients in committing criminal or fraudulent acts,[41] but sometimes lawyers help clients file papers that include false information without realizing that the information is false.

Client fraud usually causes financial harm to others. Suppose a client tells a lawyer that he has defrauded people in the past or that he is planning to do so in the future. Or suppose (as is more likely) that a lawyer discovers in the course of reviewing documents that his client has perpetrated or plans to perpetrate a fraud. May the lawyer alert the intended victims or the law enforcement authorities?

## a. Enron and the Sarbanes-Oxley Act

Enron was a major energy corporation based in Houston. In October 2001, it was discovered that the company's officers, lawyers, and accountants had massively overstated its earnings, pocketing billions of dollars and causing corresponding losses to the company's stockholders. To prevent discovery of the fraud, the company's accounting firm, Arthur Andersen LLP, one of the largest accounting firms in the nation, destroyed documents to prevent Securities and Exchange Commission (SEC) investigators from finding them. It did so on the advice of Nancy Temple, its in-house lawyer. Andersen was convicted of obstruction of justice and went bankrupt.[42] During the same period, several other large corporations, including, for example, Imclone, Tyco, WorldCom, and HealthSouth, had similar financial collapses that also involved financial fraud.

In the aftermath of the Enron scandal, Congress passed the Sarbanes-Oxley Act to prevent further episodes of massive corporate fraud.[43] Section 307 of the new law authorized the SEC to promulgate tough new disclosure rules for professionals, including lawyers, who practice before the Commission and become aware of clients' frauds.

In introducing an amendment to add § 307, Senator John Edwards, its chief sponsor, said:

> If executives and/or accountants are breaking the law, you can be sure that part of the problem is that the lawyers who are there are involved and not doing their jobs. . . . What this amendment does [is to require that] [i]f you are a lawyer for a corporation, . . . you work for the corporation and . . . the shareholders. . . . This amendment is about making sure those lawyers . . . don't violate the law and . . . ensur[ing] that the law is being followed. . . . If you find out that the managers are breaking the law, you must tell them to stop. If they won't stop, you go to the board of directors, . . . and tell them what is going on.[44]

---

41. Rule 1.2(d).

42. The story is told in detail in Stephen Gillers & Roy D. Simon, Regulation of Lawyers: Statutes and Standards 1049-1072 (Aspen Publishers 2003).

43. Company Accounting Reform and Investor Protection (Sarbanes-Oxley) Act of 2002, Pub. L. No. 107-204, 116 Stat. 745 (2002) (codified as amended in scattered sections of 11 U.S.C., 15 U.S.C., and 28 U.S.C.).

44. Senator Edwards's statement is excerpted in Special Section: Sarbanes-Oxley Before the SEC, Stephen Gillers & Roy D. Simon, Regulation of Lawyers: Statutes and Standards 1002 (Aspen Publishers 2004).

The amendment to add § 307 passed, and the SEC promptly issued a rule that requires lawyers who practice before the Commission or who advise companies regulated by the Commission to report any information about securities fraud to the highest officials of the corporation.[45] The Commission also proposed a more stringent rule and published it for public comment, but it held that proposal in abeyance. Under that proposed rule, if a lawyer reported securities fraud to senior officials in a corporation, and those officials did not act promptly on the lawyer's internal report, the lawyer would be obliged to withdraw from representing the client and to notify the SEC that the lawyer was no longer representing the company "based on professional considerations." This action would blow the whistle on the company and trigger a government investigation.[46]

The chairman of the SEC suggested that the Commission might refrain from imposing this more drastic reporting obligation if the legal profession changed its official position on the disclosure of client fraud. Specifically, he suggested that further rulemaking would be influenced by action taken by the ABA.[47] In other words, if the ABA amended its Model Rules to permit lawyers to blow the whistle on their clients' frauds, the SEC might refrain from imposing even more stringent reporting obligations on lawyers.

### b. The ethical rules on revelation of client crimes and frauds

Even before Enron, most states had adopted ethical rules permitting or requiring lawyers to report clients' use of their services to commit fraud. The Model Rules of Professional Conduct, however, gave lawyers no discretion to reveal confidential information to prevent or mitigate the harm from client fraud. The Ethics 2000 Commission proposed to add language allowing lawyers to make such revelations, but the ABA House of Delegates rejected this proposal in August 2001.[48]

---

45. Id. at 745, § 307 (codified at 15 U.S.C. § 7245) (requiring the SEC to issue rules requiring securities lawyers to report violations of securities laws by company agents up the chain of command).

46. The regulation, proposed regulation, and related history are reported in depth in Gillers & Simon, supra n. 44, at 1001-1023.

47. ABA Task Force on Corporate Responsibility, Recommendation to Amend Rule 1.6(b) of the ABA Model Rules of Professional Responsibility (2003), *available at* http://www.abanet.org/leadership/2003/journal/119a.pdf (last visited Aug. 1, 2004). Specifically, the SEC's chair noted with approval the pending ABA proposal to change Rule 1.6 and had warned that "if the legal profession doesn't establish and enforce effective professional ethics for corporate attorneys, the federal government, including the Commission, will surely step in and fill the void." Harvey L. Pitt, Alan B. Levenson Keynote Address at the Securities Regulation Institute, Coronado, Cal., Jan. 29, 2003, *available at* http://www.sec.gov/news/speech/spch012903hlp.htm (last visited Oct. 14, 2004).

48. Lawrence Fox, a member of the Commission, introduced an amendment to delete the proposed language that would have allowed lawyers to reveal client fraud. His amendment was adopted by the House of Delegates. See ABA Center on Professional Responsibility, Summary of House of Delegates Action on Ethics 2000 Commission Report, *available at* http://www.abanet.org/cpr/e2k-summary_2002.html (last visited Oct. 14, 2004).

On August 14, 2001, Jeffrey Skilling, CEO at Enron, resigned after six months on the job, citing "personal reasons."[49] In the months that followed, the Enron scandal unraveled. By November 29, 2001, the company was on the brink of bankruptcy.[50] These developments led to a public outcry about lawyers' participation in various corporate scandals, so the ABA reconsidered its position on lawyers' responsibility to blow the whistle on client fraud. An ABA Task Force on Corporate Responsibility initially recommended mandatory disclosure of client crimes and frauds in which the lawyer's work was being used. But the task force later withdrew that proposal in the face of "strong criticism" from lawyers. The Task Force feared that if the rule made disclosure of client fraud mandatory, clients might be deterred from consulting lawyers "regarding close issues," fearing that the lawyers might feel compelled to disclose matters that were in reality "a matter of business judgment."[51] The Task Force substituted disclosure exceptions to confidentiality that allowed lawyers discretion to decide whether to reveal those crimes and frauds. In 2003, acting on the recommendation of the Task Force and the threat of more stringent federal regulation, the House of Delegates adopted the very same language that it had rejected two years earlier. It added exceptions (b)(2) and (3) to Model Rule 1.6. These exceptions apply to all lawyers in states that adopt the ABA's proposal; they are not restricted to the disclosure of frauds by publicly held companies, nor are they limited to lawyers who practice before the SEC.[52] (The House of Delegates also changed Model Rule 1.13 to require lawyers to report fraud by the employees of a client organization to more senior officials of the organization. We discuss this change in Chapter 5.)

---

49. Peter Behr, Citing Personal Reasons, Enron CEO Quits After Just Six Months, Wash. Post, Aug. 15, 2001, at E3.

50. Peter Behr, Deal to Take Over Enron Unravels; Once Proud Energy Trading Firm Left Near Bankruptcy; Market Impact Feared, Wash. Post, Nov. 29, 2001 at E1. For further discussion of the Enron scandal, see Roger C. Cramton, Enron and the Corporate Lawyer: A Primer on Legal and Ethical Issues, 58 Bus. Law. 143 (2002).

51. ABA Task Force on Corporate Responsibility, supra n. 47, at 16 n. 38.

52. As noted in Chapter 1, there are many instances when the ethics rules of particular states diverge from the Model Rules. On this topic, the divergence is particularly dramatic. For example, at least three states require (rather than permit) disclosure to rectify substantial loss from client crimes or frauds involving a lawyer's services. ABA Task Force on Corporate Responsibility, supra n. 47, at 14-15 n. 33. There are many variations among the states in the language used to authorize or require revelation of client fraud, so it is especially important for practicing lawyers to be familiar with the rules of their own jurisdictions. Also, although the SEC responded to the ABA's action by refraining from issuing more drastic rules, it might at a future date require lawyers to withdraw or disclose when they become aware of clients' frauds, particularly if existing SEC "reporting up" rules prove inadequate. One study of the operation of the new SEC rules concluded that they contain "a number of major loopholes [that] threaten to nullify the effectiveness of the reporting up requirement" and that "the reporting out obligation that remains pending before the SEC (usually referred to as 'noisy withdrawal') although of much less importance than correcting the deficiencies in the reporting up rules, remains a good idea." Roger C. Cramton, George M. Cohen & Susan P. Koniak, Legal and Ethical Duties of Lawyers After Sarbanes-Oxley, 49 Vill. L. Rev. 725 (2004).

Rule 1.6(b)(2) and (3) now permit a lawyer to reveal information relating to the representation of a client to the extent the lawyer reasonably believes necessary:

> **(2) to prevent the client from committing a crime or fraud that is reasonably certain to result in substantial injury to the financial interests or property of another and in furtherance of which the client has used or is using the lawyer's services;**
>
> **(3) to prevent, mitigate or rectify substantial injury to the financial interests or property of another that is reasonably certain to result or has resulted from the client's commission of a crime or fraud in furtherance of which the client has used the lawyer's services.**

The two subsections are similar, but subsection (b)(2) applies to situations where the client plans to commit or is committing the crime or fraud, and (b)(3) refers to the situation of a past crime or fraud. Under these rules, a lawyer may reveal client criminal or fraudulent conduct whether it is past, ongoing, or future, if

- there is a reasonable certainty that the client's conduct will result in financial injury or injury to the property of another person, and
- the client is using or has used the lawyer's services in committing the act(s), and
- the purpose of revealing confidences is to prevent the criminal or fraudulent act or to prevent, mitigate, or rectify the harm resulting from the act(s).

If the criminal or fraudulent conduct is past and the client has employed the lawyer for representation relating to that conduct, the lawyer is not permitted to reveal information under Rule 1.6(b)(3).[53]

In relation to physical harm, the rules focus on whether the act that would cause the harm is past or future and on the severity of the harm. In dealing with threats of financial harm, the distinction between past and future acts is not as distinct because a lie told last year about the financial status of a company may be relied upon next month by a stock purchaser.[54] Therefore the rules allow revelation of confidences about past, present, or future client fraud that has caused financial harm to another person. A lawyer is allowed to reveal such information, however, only if the lawyer's services were used in the perpetration of the criminal or fraudulent act. If lawyers were allowed to reveal all past or future criminal or fraudulent behavior, clients could have no confidence that they could safely talk to their lawyers about past wrongdoings. In the case of crimes and frauds that cause financial harm, however, lawyers

---

53. Rule 1.6, Comment 8.

54. There are instances in which a past act might cause physical harm in the future, such as situations in which a company has dumped carcinogenic material into a landfill or, as in the Garrow case, where an uncertainty about whether crime victims are living or dead causes severe anguish and perhaps accompanying physical harm to their families. But in most cases involving physical harm, the line between past and future harm is "brighter" than in cases of fraud.

whose services were used to commit the crimes or frauds do have some discretion.

The drafters of the new exceptions allowing revelation of financial crimes and frauds tried to balance three policies:

- To encourage frank communication between clients and lawyers
- To prevent harm to the public
- To protect the "integrity of the profession" by allowing lawyers to blow the whistle if their own work is being used to commit crimes or frauds[55]

In the balance struck by the rule as currently drafted, prevention of harm to the public is not alone sufficient to overcome the policy favoring protection of confidences, but when a lawyer's services have been used to assist a client's crime or fraud, the balance tips in favor of permissive disclosure.[56]

### Is a lawyer really free under the rules to decide not to reveal a client crime or fraud that will cause financial harm to another person?

The new exceptions to Rule 1.6 give the impression that a lawyer may choose not to reveal a client crime or fraud, even if her services have been used in its commission and even if it will cause harm to another person. However, another rule mandates such revelation in some circumstances. Rule 4.1(b) states: "In the course of representing a client a lawyer shall not knowingly . . . fail to disclose a material fact when disclosure is necessary to avoid assisting a criminal or fraudulent act, unless disclosure is *prohibited* by Rule 1.6" (emphasis added).[57] Rule 1.6 now permits revelation of confidential information to prevent, mitigate, or remedy some criminal and fraudulent client conduct. This means that in any situation in which a lawyer's failure to reveal would constitute "assisting a criminal or fraudulent act," Rule 4.1 now *requires* a lawyer to reveal the information.

Obviously, this is confusing. Why would the drafters write Rule 1.6 to give lawyers discretion to disclose or not, and then not mention in 1.6 that the discretion conferred by Rule 1.6 is restricted in situations covered by Rule 4.1? We are not sure.

---

55. ABA Task Force on Corporate Responsibility, Recommendation to Amend Rule 1.6(b) of the ABA Model Rules of Professional Responsibility 16-17 (2003).

56. Rule 1.13, discussed below, comes into play when a lawyer represents an organization such as a corporation, and it strikes a similar balance. It permits (but does not require) a lawyer to disclose confidences if despite the lawyer's efforts, the organization is violating a law, the highest authority in the organization acts or fails to act appropriately, and the violation of law is reasonably certain to result in substantial injury to the organization. Also, Rule 3.3, discussed in Chapter 8, may require a lawyer to disclose to a tribunal the fact that the lawyer's client or other witness has provided false testimony.

57. This is the text of Delaware Rule 4.1(b). The ABA Model Rule includes the phrase "to a third person" after the words "material fact."

## c. Fraud by a client, not assisted by a lawyer

### Can a lawyer reveal information about a client's crime or fraud if the lawyer had nothing to do with it?

Suppose a client tells her lawyer in confidence about a crime or fraud that the client has committed or is contemplating. The lawyer had absolutely no role in the commission of this act.

> **FOR EXAMPLE:** A lawyer is representing a criminal defendant on a charge of armed robbery. The defendant tells the lawyer that he has a little business, unrelated to the pending charge, in which he helps people with their taxes, falsely passing himself off as a certified public accountant.

Rule 1.6 does not allow a lawyer who has not assisted a client's financial crime or fraud to make a disclosure to protect another person from injury.[58] A lawyer may reveal confidences "to prevent reasonably certain death or substantial bodily harm"[59] regardless of whether the lawyer's work may have contributed to the harm. However, if the client has not used and is not using the lawyer's services to commit a fraud, the lawyer may not warn the intended victim of the fraud.[60]

## d. Fraud by a client, assisted by a lawyer

Let's start by considering an extreme case. Suppose a lawyer tutors a client in federal tax law so that the client can pass himself off (falsely) as an accountant. If the lawyer knows that the client plans to misrepresent his credentials, the lawyer might be criminally charged for abetting the client's fraud. The lawyer also would violate Rule 1.2(d), which provides: "A lawyer shall not counsel a client to engage, or assist a client, in conduct that the lawyer knows is criminal or fraudulent."[61] In addition, under Rule 1.6(b)(2), if the lawyer thinks that the client's plan was "reasonably certain" to cause substantial financial injury, the lawyer may disclose the client's plan to prevent that harm.

We term that example "extreme" because few lawyers deliberately set out to counsel clients on how to commit crimes, including crimes that involve fraud.

---

58. If a lawyer is employed or retained by an organization, however, the lawyer might have a duty to reveal information about economic crime or fraud by a client even if the lawyer's services had not been used in the commission of the crime or fraud. See Rule 1.13, discussed in Chapter 5.

59. Rule 1.6(b)(1).

60. Therefore, a client who commits an economic crime or fraud and then consults a lawyer (for example, for purposes of criminal defense) may do so with assurance that the lawyer will not disclose confidences, even to warn victims. Such a lawyer could not possibly have contributed to the client's offense because the client consulted the lawyer after the client completed the acts in question (though the effects of the fraud may be ongoing). See Rule 1.6, Comment 8.

61. For a discussion of lawyers' liability for *assisting* client fraud, see Donald C. Langevoort, Where Were the Lawyers? A Behavioral Inquiry into Lawyers' Responsibility for Clients' Fraud, 46 Vand. L. Rev. 75 (1993).

But there have been quite a few situations in which lawyers have stepped perilously close to the line. Such a situation might develop like this:

1. A lawyer helps a client to prepare documents that include false information, not knowing that the information is false.
2. The recipients of the documents rely on the statements in the documents and on the fact that the documents were prepared in part by a reputable lawyer or law firm.
3. The lawyer later discovers the falsity of the statements or that the client plans to use or has used the documents in a misleading way.

In this kind of situation, the lawyer may reveal the information to prevent the fraud. If the fraud has already occurred or is ongoing, the lawyer may reveal the information to prevent, mitigate, or rectify the harm. Revelation is also permitted in situations in which the client has used the lawyer's services to commit other crimes[62] against property, such as outright theft.

## Other ethics rules allowing or requiring revelation of confidences relating to criminal or fraudulent conduct

In addition to Rule 1.6, several other ethics rules define lawyers' duties in relation to client crimes and frauds. We explore these rules later in the book; here we simply identify them.

**Lawyers prohibited from committing or assisting fraud**    Rule 1.2(d) prohibits lawyers from assisting clients in criminal or fraudulent behavior. Rule 8.4(c) prohibits lawyers from engaging in any "dishonesty, fraud, deceit or misrepresentation."

**Duty of a lawyer representing an organization to call attention to crimes and frauds**    Rule 1.13, discussed in Chapter 5, addresses the duties of a lawyer representing an organization if the lawyer learns that someone associated with the organization is acting or intends to act in a manner that will violate the organization's duties or the law; these could involve criminal or fraudulent acts. The rule requires the lawyer to call the attention of corporate management to the wrongful conduct. If that doesn't work, the rule permits the lawyer to reveal the information to the extent necessary to prevent substantial injury to the organization.

**Duty to reveal client crimes or frauds to tribunals**    Rule 3.3, discussed in Chapter 8, may require a lawyer to disclose to a tribunal the fact that the lawyer's client or another witness has provided false testimony.

**Duty to reveal client crimes or frauds to certain third parties**    Rule 3.4, also discussed in Chapter 8, explains a lawyer's duties in relation to opposing

---

62. Fraud may be a crime, a tort, or a violation of any of a number of statutes. See discussion of fraud below.

counsel. It prohibits lawyers from hiding or destroying evidence or advising a witness to testify falsely. Rule 4.1 deals with obligations of truthfulness to third parties. It prohibits lying and, as noted above, requires a lawyer to disclose confidences to a third party if necessary to avoid assisting a criminal or fraudulent act.

**Duty to withdraw rather than assist client crime or fraud; discretion to withdraw if client crime or fraud**  Rule 1.16(a) requires a lawyer to withdraw from representing a client if continued representation would result in a violation of the rules. Rule 1.16(b) permits a lawyer to withdraw from representing a client who persists in criminal or fraudulent conduct.

### e. What is fraud? A primer

To comply with the rules listed above, a lawyer must understand what conduct is fraudulent. This is necessary to help the lawyer to avoid stepping over a not-so-clear line into conduct that could have adverse professional consequences (such as discipline or liability) and to be able to help clients to avoid stepping over that line. A lawyer also needs to understand what constitutes "assisting fraud," including whether or under what circumstances a failure to act could be viewed as assisting fraud. The next section offers some guidance on these questions.

Fraud refers to *deliberate deception*, but the term is defined somewhat differently in criminal law, tort law, contract law, and in the rules of legal ethics.

**States that have adopted the Model Rules**  Rule 1.0(d) defines fraud as "conduct that is fraudulent under the substantive or procedural law of the applicable jurisdiction and has a purpose to deceive." A comment explains that the drafters did not intend to include in this definition "merely negligent misrepresentation or negligent failure to apprise another of relevant information. For purposes of these rules, it is not necessary that anyone has suffered damages or relied on the misrepresentation or failure to inform."[63] The rules do not explain whether one should refer to criminal law, tort law, securities law, consumer law, or contract law, nor whether one should refer to state law or federal law. In some situations, it might be equally appropriate to apply a contract standard, a tort standard, a criminal standard, or a statutory standard. If an act is fraudulent under any substantive or procedural legal standard relevant to the act in question[64] in the applicable jurisdiction, it is reasonable to assume that it is fraudulent under the rules.

In addition to the problem of multiple relevant legal standards, there are situations in which it is not clear what legal standard should be used to evaluate a lawyer's conduct.

---

63. Rule 1.0, Comment 5.
64. By "relevant," we mean that one might refer to securities law for a definition of securities fraud, and to consumer law for a definition of consumer fraud.

FOR EXAMPLE: Suppose that you are representing a prominent client who is being interviewed by a federal prosecutor about a certain sale of stock. Suppose your client makes some statements during the interview that you believe are not truthful. You don't say anything. Have you committed a fraud under the definition in the rules? Should your conduct be analyzed under a criminal law fraud standard? Or might it be fraudulent under the rules even if it does not constitute fraud for which you could be indicted?

The point is that the new definition of fraud in the rules may not have succeeded in clarifying the meaning of this term.

**Torts**   A person may be liable for damages to another person for fraud if it is shown that he (1) intentionally made (2) a misrepresentation to the other of a fact, an intention, or of a law (3) with the intention of inducing the other person to act or to refrain from action in reliance on the misrepresentation, if the other person can demonstrate (4) financial loss as a result of (5) having relied upon the misrepresentation.[65]

**Criminal law**   Certain federal and state statutes make particular types of fraudulent actions criminal. Among these are laws on mail fraud, wire fraud, bank fraud, health care fraud, consumer fraud, securities fraud, and bankruptcy fraud.[66] Generally they require (1) intentional (knowing) (2) misrepresentation of (3) material facts in the context addressed by the statute.[67] Unlike tort law, criminal law does not require a showing of harm to find an act fraudulent.

**Contracts**   A contract may be voidable if one party was induced to sign it by a fraudulent (intentional) misrepresentation.[68] A contract may be voided also for a *material* misrepresentation even if it was not *intentional.*[69] While tort law and criminal law require that the misrepresentation was deliberate, contract law recognizes an action for rescission based on a misrepresentation that was significant for the transaction even if there was no intent to deceive.

---

65. See Restatement (Second) of Torts § 525 (1977).

66. See Courts Refine Elements of Federal Fraud Crimes, 7 (No. 3) Bus. Crimes Bull. 3 (2000).

67. See, e.g., Neder v. U.S., 527 U.S. 1, 23 (1999); U.S. v. Chandler, 98 F.3d 711, 716 (2d Cir. 1996); U.S. v. London, 753 F.2d 202, 206 (2d Cir. 1985); U.S. v. Regent Office Supply Co., 421 F.2d 1174, 1182 (2d Cir. 1970).

68. To be fraudulent, the person making the representation must (1) know or believe that it is false, or (2) must lack confidence that what he says is true, or (3) must know that he does not have a good basis for the stated facts. Restatement (Second) of Contracts § 162(1) (1981). A contract is voidable if a material misrepresentation (a misrepresentation important to the agreement) was made by the party who wants to enforce the agreement, if the party who wants to void the agreement was justified in relying on the misrepresentation. Restatement (Second) of Contracts § 164.

69. Restatement (Second) of Contracts § 162(1) (1981).

Normally a "misrepresentation" that would be a basis for rescission of a contract involves a statement, but a nondisclosure of a fact is "equivalent to an assertion that the fact does not exist" if, among other reasons, the person who is not disclosing:

> knows that the disclosure of the fact is necessary to prevent some previous assertion from being a misrepresentation or from being fraudulent or material . . . [or] he knows that disclosure of the fact would correct a mistake of the other party as to a basic assumption on which that party is making the contract and if non-disclosure of the fact amounts to a failure to act in good faith and in accordance with reasonable standards of fair dealing.[70]

A contract could be voidable for "fraud" even though the same "fraud" would not subject the actor to tort liability or to criminal sanctions.

### Under what circumstances might someone commit a fraud by failure to act or by omission?

Omissions and half-truths as well as false representations can constitute fraud. In many legal contexts, such as the sale of securities, material omissions, or "half-truths," are regarded as fraudulent. Under the Model Rules, a lawyer's omission may be fraudulent if the lawyer intended to deceive another person. For example, Rule 4.1(b) bars a lawyer from knowingly failing to disclose a nonconfidential material fact (that is, omitting such a fact) when disclosure is necessary to avoid assisting a client's fraudulent act. Comment 1 after Rule 4.1 makes it clear that partially true but misleading statements or omissions can be the same as false statements.[71]

### How can a lawyer know whether he is assisting a client fraud?

The ethics rules define a lawyer's obligations in relation to a present or future client crime or fraud differently depending on whether a lawyer is before a tribunal or dealing with a third party.

**Assisting a client crime or fraud before a tribunal**  In 1987, the ABA Ethics Committee explained the meaning of "assisting client fraud" in an opinion interpreting Rule 3.3, which deals with candor to tribunals. The committee said that if a lawyer had offered false testimony, failure to disclose that fact to the court would constitute "assisting fraud." Also, the Committee noted that "the language 'assisting a criminal or fraudulent act by the client' is not limited to the criminal law concepts of aiding and abetting or subornation. Rather, it seems clear that this language is intended to guide the conduct of the

---

70. Id. at § 161.

71. As noted above, Rule 4.1 imposes important disclosure obligations in many states that have confidentiality provisions allowing disclosures of frauds. The Restatement also takes the view that there is not much difference between false statements and deliberate deception by half-truths and omissions. It explains that "inaction (through nondisclosure) as well as action may constitute fraud under applicable law." Restatement § 67, comment d (2000).

lawyer as an officer of the court as a prophylactic measure to protect against client perjury contaminating the judicial process."[72]

**Assisting a crime or fraud by a client in dealing with a third party**    As noted above, Rule 4.1 requires disclosure of material facts when necessary to avoid assisting a client's criminal or fraudulent act "unless disclosure is prohibited by Rule 1.6." Rule 1.6 now *permits* disclosure of certain information about client crimes and frauds if the lawyer's services were used to commit the act in question. In some instances a lawyer can comply with Rule 4.1 by withdrawing and disaffirming the document he created.[73] Sometimes, however, a lawyer has to spill the beans.

A shady client won't tell her lawyer that the client wants help in defrauding someone. Rule 1.2 bars only assisting a client in conduct that the lawyer "knows" is fraudulent (which seems to exclude a lawyer's negligent and perhaps even reckless conduct from the prohibition). But a lawyer could be accused of fraud in connection with preparing a document even if the lawyer relied on his client and did not know of the falsity of the information in the document. Disciplinary authorities might infer from the circumstances that a lawyer did know that the legal assistance would be used for fraudulent purposes.[74] Also, standards of law other than the ethics rules might require a lawyer to check on the information that the client provides. For example, if a lawyer does not exercise the prevailing standard of care to discern client fraud, the victim of the fraud might sue the lawyer for negligence. In addition, a lawyer could be subject to discipline or criminal charges merely for advising a client to engage in criminal or fraudulent action, or for advising the client how to evade detection or prosecution, even if the lawyer prepared no documents containing misrepresentations.[75]

---

72. ABA Formal Op. 87-353. The formal opinion interpreted the recently deleted language that used to be Rule 3.3(a)(2), which stated that a lawyer shall not "fail to disclose a material fact to a tribunal when disclosure is necessary to avoid assisting a criminal or fraudulent act by a client." Although this language was deleted in the 2002 revision, the interpretation in the formal opinion probably is still valid. The reason why the ABA deleted Rule 3.3(a)(2) is that it replaced that subsection with the broader language of Rule 3.3(b), which requires "reasonable remedial measures, including, if necessary, disclosure to the tribunal" in a situation in which a lawyer is representing a client in an adjudicative proceeding and learns that *someone* (not just the client) "is engaging or has engaged in criminal or fraudulent conduct related to the proceeding." The previous language required action by the lawyer only upon learning of criminal or fraudulent conduct by a client. See ABA, Center for Professional Responsibility, Reporter's explanation of changes to Rule 3.3, *available at* http://www.abanet.org/cpr/e2k-rule33rem.html (last visited May 18, 2004).

73. Rule 4.1, Comment 3.

74. Rule 1.0(f). According to the Restatement, "a lawyer's intent to facilitate or encourage wrongful action may be inferred if in the circumstances it should have been apparent to the lawyer that the client would employ the assistance to further the client's wrongful conduct, and the lawyer nonetheless provided the assistance." Restatement § 94, comment c.

75. Restatement § 94, comment c, reporter's note, cites a case in which a lawyer was charged with obstruction of justice because he had advised a client to destroy documents, another in which a lawyer was disciplined for advising a client to conceal the identity of the owners of a business when applying for a liquor license, and a third in which a lawyer was disciplined for advising his client to leave the state to avoid prosecution. Just as you could be charged with a tort or a crime for conduct

A good rule of thumb is that a lawyer should become wary any time that a client's past or contemplated conduct appears to involve an intentional or knowing misrepresentation to another person. The client and, in some cases, the lawyer might be subject to criminal prosecution or civil liability because of the misrepresentation. If the misrepresentation occurs in the course of making a contract (including an agreement settling a lawsuit), the contract might be voidable because of the misrepresentation. In addition, the lawyer could be subject to discipline for committing a fraudulent act or for assisting a client in committing a fraudulent act. Legal consequences are more likely if the false statement concerns something important, if it is made to induce another person to act, if the other person acts in reliance on the statement, and if harm results.

### To the extent that the ethics rules give lawyers discretion to reveal client fraud, are lawyers protected from civil or criminal liability if they elect not to reveal?

No. The ethics rules articulate a standard of conduct that may result in discipline if violated by a lawyer. They do not set standards for civil or criminal liability.[76] Even when a lawyer would not be subject to discipline (under a rule that used the current language of Rule 1.6) for failure to disclose a client crime or fraud, a lawyer who does not disclose might face civil or criminal liability for his role in the criminal or fraudulent action.[77] The ethics rules are not a separate basis for civil or criminal liability, but neither do they protect a lawyer from liability if the lawyer participates with a client "as a co-principal or an accessory in the client's wrongful act."[78]

### If the lawyer decides not to disclose, does the lawyer have any other obligation under the rules?

Suppose a lawyer prepares a document that a client uses to obtain a loan from a bank. After the loan has been obtained, the lawyer discovers that some

---

that would not be assisting a fraud under the ethical rules, you could be subject to ethics discipline even if your conduct is not tortious or criminal. The Restatement explains that a lawyer might be subject to discipline for assisting client fraud even in situations in which criminal charges and civil liability would not be available. As an example, the Restatement points out that civil liability for fraud requires a showing of reliance on the fraud and damage resulting from the reliance. Neither reliance nor damages need be shown in a disciplinary proceeding. Restatement § 94, comment c.

76. In the Scope note at the beginning of the Rules, Comment 20 explains: "The Rules are designed to provide guidance to lawyers and to provide a structure for regulating conduct through disciplinary agencies. They are not designed to be a basis for civil liability."

77. See, e.g., Klein v. Boyd, 949 F. Supp. 280 (E.D. Pa. 1996), *vacated*, 1998 WL 55245 (3d Cir. Feb. 12, 1998) (holding that a lawyer may be liable to third party investors for material misstatements in a document prepared by the lawyer even if the lawyer did not sign or endorse the document). See also Restatement (Second) of Agency § 348 (1958) ("An agent who fraudulently makes misrepresentations . . . or knowingly assists in the commission of tortious fraud . . . by his principal . . . is subject to liability in tort to the injured person although the fraud . . . occurs in a transaction on behalf of the principal.").

78. Restatement § 66, comment g. See Restatement § 8, comment e, outlining a lawyer's potential criminal liability as an accomplice.

assertions in the document about the client's financial situation were incorrect. The client has used the lawyer's services to perpetrate a fraud. Suppose the lawyer then learns that the client intends to resubmit the document to get another loan.[79] The rules give the lawyer the discretion to reveal this information or not. However, if the lawyer decides not to disclose the specifics of the fraud, she must nevertheless withdraw from the representation. If the lawyer continues to represent the client, her ongoing representation may be understood by recipients of the client's resubmitted document to mean that the lawyer continues to affirm the accuracy of the document that contains the misinformation. Because under Rule 1.2(d) a lawyer is not allowed to assist a client in a criminal or fraudulent act, once the lawyer knows she has done so (unwittingly), she must withdraw. This is required by Rule 1.16(a)(1), which requires withdrawal if "the representation will result in violation of the rules of professional conduct or other law."[80] In the course of withdrawal, the lawyer may, short of actually revealing the fraud, simply "disaffirm" the document that she had prepared. This would involve notifying another person who might continue to rely on the document that the lawyer was no longer able to vouch for its accuracy. The disaffirmance is referred to as a "noisy withdrawal."

## PROBLEM 2-7  **REESE'S LEASES**

*This problem is based on a series of events that took place in New York City.*

After you finished law school, you started a law firm with three class-mates who are now your partners. The firm has done well, thanks largely to the work you do for one client, Executive Leasing Services. This company was founded by two of your childhood friends, Charlie Reese and Paula Suarez. Their company now does $17 million worth of business each year, and your legal work for them accounts for 60 percent of your law firm's monthly receipts. As they have prospered, so have you. Your firm now has three associates, a paralegal, and three secretaries. This pattern of growth is likely to continue if Executive Leasing continues to do well. If Executive Leasing Services were to fail, however, your law firm would have to lay off some staff immediately, and the firm would be unable to pay you or the other partners. The law firm probably would go out of business within a matter of months.

---

79. This is a variation on the situation that was addressed in ABA Formal Op. 92-366 (1992), in which the ABA Ethics Committee interpreted the rules (before the 2003 amendments) to require withdrawal and to permit disaffirmance of the document. This opinion has not been withdrawn or modified in the wake of the amendments, so one may assume that the analysis stands, especially since there has been no relevant amendment of Rules 1.2 and 1.16.

80. Similarly, Rule 1.16(b)(2) states that a lawyer may withdraw from representing a client if "the client persists in a course of action involving the lawyer's services that the lawyer reasonably believes is criminal or fraudulent."

Executive Leasing Services leases luxury cars to corporations for use by corporate managers. It started out by borrowing money from a bank to buy a few cars. Then it leased out those cars to its first corporate customers, using the promise of income under the leases as collateral to borrow more money and buy more cars to lease out.

Your firm's role was to draw up the paperwork for each lease, to supply legal opinions (for the benefit of the bank) affirming that Executive Leasing Services owned the cars that it was leasing, and, occasionally, to negotiate leases between the company and its corporate customers. As you and your partners did this work, you noticed that Executive Leasing Services was charging customers 15 percent less than other firms were charging for leasing comparable cars. You also noticed that the income from the leases was often smaller than repayments on the loans. You wondered why the bank kept giving your client larger and larger loans when the company seem to be losing money consistently.

Eventually, you learned the answer to your question. Executive Leasing's accountant asked if she could tell you something in confidence. You said that she could. She said that the firm's owners were leasing some cars, but that, in addition, they were creating some counterfeit leases for fictitious transactions. The counterfeit leases contained the vehicle identification numbers of cars that the firm actually did own, but that Executive Leasing had leased previously to the same customer or was already leasing to other customers.

"Why would they do that?" you inquired.

"Well," she said, "Charlie and Paula need more and more loans, so that they can expand their business by purchasing and leasing out additional cars, and also so that they can support their opulent lifestyles. (Charlie bought a mansion overlooking the river last year and Paula a house in Barbados.) To get the loans, they need collateral to give the bank. The higher volume of business they show, the larger the loans they can get. So the phony leases make their business look much bigger than it is."

"Wow," you say, not sure how else to respond to this astonishing news.

Today, you met with Charlie Reese privately. You told him that you were worried that the numbers didn't add up. You asked him straight out whether he had been cooking the books or somehow inflating the firm's value when it dealt with its bank. After some hemming and hawing, he admitted that the firm had submitted forged leases to the bank.

"How did you do it?" you asked, wondering what were the odds that Charlie or Paula would be facing criminal charges in the near future.

"It was pretty easy," Charlie said with just a hint of pride in his voice. "Once a month, Paula and I stayed late to go over the books. After the rest of the folks went home, we'd settle down in my office, modify the numbers on some existing leases, and generate some new leases."

"What do you mean, modify the numbers?" you asked.

"Well, sometimes, we would just add digits to the numbers in genuine leases to increase the number of cars being leased or the length of leases that the company supposedly received."

"If you also generated new leases in your office, you needed customer signatures. How did you do that?" you asked, starting to sweat.

Charlie smiled. "We always made the new leases seem to come from existing customers, so we just copied signatures we already had."

"That's not so easy," you observed.

"It's not so hard. I have a glass desktop. We turned off the lights, and I got down on the floor and shined a flashlight upwards through the last page of a real lease, which was covered by a fresh lease form. Paula traced the customer's signature onto the additional lease, which we then completed and sent to the bank."

"Wow," you say again.

"Don't worry," he replied. "The banks just add up the numbers. They don't check the signatures, call the customers to check out the transactions, or compare vehicle identification numbers in various leases. The money keeps rolling in."

Charlie noticed the sweat rolling down the side of your face. "Keep in mind that this is paying your mortgage as well as mine. Of course I'm telling you all this in the strictest confidence."

"I can't believe you have been doing this. And I wrote those opinion letters to the bank attesting to the validity of all the leases you submitted as collateral for the loan."

"No, your letters just said we had title to the cars, which was true. We really did buy the cars with the money we borrowed. Your nose is clean."

"Look, Charlie, this scheme is just too risky. It has got to stop, or all three of us could wind up in prison for a very long time."

Charlie stops looking smug. "I know it's risky. Paula and I have been worried all along. Last month after we got that last loan we decided it was enough. We won't fiddle with any more leases, I promise."

"I guess that might be the best we can do for right now," you reply.

---

## Questions

**1. Our little secret?** Consider the following possible actions. Which of them are permitted or required by the rules?

■ Reveal the fraud to the bank or the district attorney if Reese refuses to do so.

- Do not reveal the fraud but stop representing Executive Leasing Services.
- Do not reveal the fraud and continue to represent Executive Leasing Services, taking more care that the company does not engage in future fraud.

**2. Economic realities.** Keeping in mind that your own livelihood and the livelihoods of your partners and staff members depends on keeping Executive Leasing Services afloat, what would you actually do in this situation?

## 4. Revealing confidences to obtain advice about legal ethics

Rule 1.6(b)(4) permits a lawyer to reveal confidences to the extent necessary for the lawyer to obtain advice about complying with the rules of professional conduct. A lawyer may invoke this exception to consult another lawyer for advice. The other lawyer might be in another firm, or a law professor, or a bar official. This exception makes clear that compliance with the rules is even more important than protecting client confidences.[81]

## 5. Using a client's confidential information to protect the lawyer's interests

Rule 1.6(b)(5) allows lawyers to reveal confidential information to the extent necessary to protect their own interests.

Revelation of confidences is allowed if needed to defend the lawyer against any allegation of misconduct. It might be very hard for a lawyer to show that she acted properly unless she is allowed to reveal the substance of her work.

Rule 1.6(b)(5) also permits a lawyer to reveal a client's confidences so that the lawyer can collect a fee. This might be one of those instances in which the bar could be accused of putting its own interests ahead of everyone else's and dressing it up as "ethics." But perhaps this exception makes sense.

> **FOR EXAMPLE:** Imagine a client who falsely says that his lawyer didn't do any work at all. The work at issue consisted of writing a document based on confidential information. If the lawyer can't produce the document as part of her defense, the lawyer cannot prove that she did any work.

> **FOR EXAMPLE:** Suppose a lawyer tells a client, "If you don't pay every penny of my bill, I'll tell the local newspaper about all the crimes that you have confessed to me in secret and offer them the receipts you recently gave me that show the income that you didn't declare on last year's tax return." This lawyer's actions are not permissible under Rule 1.6(b)(5) because they are not "necessary to establish a claim or defense, . . . or to

---

81. Rule 1.6, Comment 9.

respond to allegations [against the lawyer]." This is a far-fetched example, but it shows the boundaries of the exception.

A comment to Rule 1.6 limits how much a lawyer can reveal, in her own defense or in other circumstances:

> Where practicable the lawyer should first seek to persuade the client to take suitable action to obviate the need for disclosure. In any case, a disclosure adverse to the client's interest should be no greater than the lawyer reasonably believes necessary to accomplish the purpose. If the disclosure will be made in connection with a judicial proceeding, the disclosure should be made in a manner that limits access to the information to the tribunal or other persons having a need to know it and appropriate protective orders or other arrangements should be sought by the lawyer to the fullest extent practicable.[82]

So if a lawyer needs to reveal confidences to protect her own interests, she must take steps to avoid the need for revelation, to limit its scope, or to limit the dissemination of the information.

**If a lawyer is about to be sued for malpractice, must he wait until the lawsuit is filed before he may reveal information to defend himself?**

No. The lawyer is allowed to respond to an assertion that he has engaged in wrongdoing by revealing information necessary to defend himself:

> The lawyer's right to respond arises when an assertion of such complicity [in wrongdoing] has been made. Paragraph (b)(5) does not require the lawyer to await the commencement of an action or proceeding that charges such complicity, so that the defense may be established by responding directly to a third party who has made such an assertion. The right to defend also applies, of course, where a proceeding has been commenced.[83]

Similarly, the Sarbanes-Oxley Act permits a lawyer practicing before the SEC who has reported a fraud to a client company's officials to use that report in connection with any investigation concerning the lawyer's compliance with the SEC's rules.[84]

**Does the exception in the ethical rules apply if a third party is making a claim against a client and the lawyer is accused of some minor role in a client's misconduct?**

The lawyer may be allowed to reveal confidences even if he is not alleged to be the primary wrongdoer:

> A charge [of wrongdoing that justifies revelation of confidences] can arise in a civil, criminal, disciplinary or other proceeding and can be based on a wrong allegedly committed by the lawyer against the client or on a wrong alleged by a

---

82. Rule 1.6, Comment 14.
83. Rule 1.6, Comment 10.
84. 17 C.F.R. § 205.3(d)(1) (2004).

third person, for example, a person claiming to have been defrauded by the lawyer and client acting together.[85]

This means that a lawyer may reveal confidences even if the "allegation" is made by an injured third party rather than by a client, and even if the lawyer is not the primary target of the allegation.

---

**When may a lawyer reveal confidential information in self-defense?**

- To establish a claim against a client for unpaid fees
- To defend against a claim of malpractice or other claim of civil liability against the lawyer
- To defend against a disciplinary proceeding
- To defend against a criminal charge

**When is revelation allowed?**

The lawyer need not wait for formal proceedings to be instituted but may reveal information to prevent such action.

**How much can a lawyer reveal?**

No more than necessary to vindicate the lawyer. The lawyer should minimize the number of people who learn the confidential information revealed and should seek a protective order or take other available steps to avoid the dissemination of the information.

**Should the lawyer inform the client before revealing confidential information?**

Yes. The lawyer should notify the client before using confidential information in self-defense and should seek solutions that do not require the lawyer to make the revelation, but the lawyer may use the information even if the client does not consent.

---

## 6. Revealing confidences to comply with other law or a court order

Rule 1.6(b)(6) permits a lawyer to disclose confidential information to comply with a court order or with other law. If a court orders a lawyer to disclose information, this rule makes clear that the court order trumps the obligation to protect confidences.[86] Also, if "other law" besides the ethics rules requires disclosure of confidential information, the "other law" trumps the ethics rules. For example, most states require anyone who knows of ongoing child abuse to report it to welfare agencies. Some states exempt lawyers from the

---

85. Rule 1.6, Comment 10.

86. However, a comment to Rule 1.6 urges lawyers to assert all nonfrivolous objections to the order and to consult with the client about the possibility of appealing the order. Rule 1.6, Comment 13.

reporting requirement; others do not. Whether a law really requires such reporting by lawyers is a matter of interpretation of that law, not of the rules of professional conduct.[87]

**FOR EXAMPLE:** In the Garrow case discussed earlier in this chapter, it was not self-evident that the law requiring members of the public to report knowledge of bodies that had not been buried properly was intended to override the usual rules of attorney-client confidentiality and privilege.

## Summary of exceptions to the rule against disclosing client confidences

| Situation | Scope of exception |
|---|---|
| **Client waives confidentiality** | Disclosure permitted if client gives informed consent. See terminology section of rules for definition of "informed consent." |
| **Disclosure needed to represent the client** | Disclosure permitted where it is "impliedly authorized" to carry out the representation. |
| **Past physical harms to people** | No exception permits disclosure. |
| **Threatened physical harms to people** | Disclosure permitted (but not required) by Rule 1.6(b)(1) to prevent "reasonably certain" death or bodily harm (whether or not by the client). |
| **Threatened or continuing client fraud or other economic crime** | Disclosure to prevent the crime or fraud permitted by Rule 1.6(b)(2) if it will result with reasonable certainty in substantial injury to someone's financial interests or property and the client used or is using the lawyer's services to commit the crime or fraud. Disclosure required under Rule 4.1(b) if those conditions are met and the revelation is necessary to avoid assisting a criminal or fraudulent act. |
| **Past client fraud or other economic crime** | Disclosure permitted by Rule 1.6(b)(3) to prevent, mitigate, or rectify substantial economic injury that has resulted or is reasonably certain to result in substantial financial injury, if the client used the lawyer services to commit the crime or fraud. |
| **Lawyer needs to obtain ethics advice from another lawyer** | Permitted by Rule 1.6(b)(4). |
| **Lawyer needs to prove work done to collect a fee or to defend against misconduct charge** | Permitted by Rule 1.6(b)(5). |
| **Court orders disclosure** | Permitted by Rule 1.6(b)(6). |

---

87. Rule 1.6, Comment 12.

# C. Use or disclosure of confidential information for personal gain or to benefit another client

If a lawyer acquires confidential information in the course of her legal work, she needs to be concerned not only about improper revelation but also about improper use of the information.

> **Rule 1.8(b)   Conflict of Interest: Current Clients: Specific Rules**
> A lawyer shall not use information relating to representation of a client to the disadvantage of the client unless the client gives informed consent, except as permitted or required by these Rules.

Comment 5 explains:

> Paragraph (b) applies when the information is used to benefit either the lawyer or a third person, such as another client or business associate of the lawyer. . . . The Rule does not prohibit uses that do not disadvantage the client. For example, a lawyer who learns a government agency's interpretation of trade legislation during the representation of one client may properly use that information to benefit other clients. Paragraph (b) prohibits disadvantageous use of client information unless the client gives informed consent, except as permitted or required by these Rules. . . .

### When is a lawyer permitted to use confidential information for personal gain?

Occasionally, a lawyer may have the opportunity to use confidential information that the lawyer obtains from a client for personal gain. Some — but not all — uses of confidential information from clients are considered improper.

> **FOR EXAMPLE:** Suppose a lawyer represents a publicly traded Internet start-up. The lawyer learns confidential information that suggests that this company's stock will escalate in value very dramatically over the next year. May the lawyer purchase stock based on this knowledge? No, because the purchase probably would be illegal insider trading, and the lawyer might be criminally prosecuted.

The following problem raises a similar issue that does not implicate the securities laws.

### PROBLEM 2-8   AN INVESTMENT PROJECT

You represent a company that is investigating possible sites for a new plant. Because you are privy to your client company's research, you learn that developers are acquiring contiguous parcels of land in a suburb called Lakeshore where they probably will build a shopping mall. One parcel of land remains to be sold. Your client has decided not to buy land in Lakeshore. The value of the Lakeshore property probably will rise either because the developers will want to buy it or as a result of its better proximity to shopping.

You would like to buy this parcel of land. Are you permitted to do so under Rule 1.8(b)? Does your answer change if your client has not yet decided whether to purchase the land?

---

### May a lawyer use confidential information to benefit another one of his clients?

Rule 1.8(b) provides that it is not prohibited for a lawyer to use confidential information obtained from one client to benefit another client so long as the first client either is not disadvantaged by the use of the information or gives informed consent. The Restatement recognizes that it is not always clear whether one use of confidential information will disadvantage the client on whose behalf the information was obtained. The Restatement prohibits use of confidences "if there is a reasonable prospect that [the use] will adversely affect a material interest of a client or if the client has instructed the lawyer not to use or disclose such information."[88] It gives an example of a permissible use of confidences on behalf of another client:

> [A] lawyer representing a plaintiff who has acquired extensive confidential information about the manner in which a defendant manufactured a product may employ that information for the benefit of another client with a claim against the same defendant arising out of a defect in the same product.[89]

## D. Talking to clients about confidentiality

*Professor Fred Zacharias*

A cornerstone of lawyer-client relationships is the lawyer's duty to keep client information confidential. But as we have seen, there are some circumstances in which a lawyer is permitted to reveal confidential information. There are also some situations in which a lawyer must reveal client confidences — if ordered to do so by a judge or if required to do so by a statute or by an ethical rule. Should a lawyer explain these exceptions to a client so that the client will not expect that the duty to protect confidences is absolute? What might be the adverse consequences of making such disclosures? Of not doing so?

Professor Fred C. Zacharias surveyed the lawyers in one county in New York State in the 1980s and reported

---

88. Restatement § 60.
89. Id. at comment j.

that most of the lawyers he surveyed say little or nothing to their clients about confidentiality. If they say anything at all, they just reassure their clients that whatever the clients tell them will be confidential. None of the lawyers interviewed told clients that the protection is not absolute or identified situations in which confidences would be revealed.

Zacharias also interviewed a set of clients in the same county to find out what they knew about the confidentiality rules. Most of the clients he interviewed had learned whatever they knew about lawyers' duties to keep confidences. They didn't know that there were situations in which lawyers were permitted or required to reveal confidential information.[90]

Zacharias studied lawyers in only one county in upstate New York. Perhaps other clients are better advised than the ones he interviewed. It seems clear, however, that if a lawyer might need to reveal confidential information in a particular matter, a client should know that. Most clients would prefer to have that information at the beginning of the relationship, before they reveal a great deal of sensitive, confidential information. On the other hand, a well-counseled client might be less open with his or her lawyer. Even if the lawyer wants to make such an advance disclosure, it's not so easy. The exceptions to the basic confidentiality rule are numerous, complex, and sometimes ambiguous.

# E.  A concluding problem

## PROBLEM 2-9  RAT POISON

*The following problem is based on a true story that was related to one of the authors by a lawyer. He was pleased to share the problem with you. He said that although more than a decade has passed, he still worries about what he should have done.*

You are a criminal defense lawyer. Your client, Harry Norton, operated a small extermination business from the back of his truck. Harry mostly treated homes for termites, cockroaches, and rodent infestation. He has been charged with involuntary manslaughter based on the death of a four-year-old boy who died after eating rat poison that Harry had placed in the basement of the boy's home. The powerful rat poison that Harry had used in the home was intended only for industrial use because of the danger to humans who might ingest it. Harry is out on bail while the charge is pending.

You noticed that Harry seemed kind and well intentioned, but not very smart. Since he graduated from high school, you assume that his IQ is normal.

---

90. Fred C. Zacharias, Rethinking Confidentiality, 74 Iowa L. Rev. 351, 379-392 (1989).

*Rat Poison*

During the first interview, now three months ago, you asked Harry whether he had put rat poison into other homes besides the one in which the child had died. Harry said he had. He wasn't sure how many other homes—perhaps 30 or 40. He said he had a file box with records of the services he had provided to each customer. You urged Harry to go through the box and find all of the other homes where he had put that type of rat poison, and to revisit those homes and remove it. Harry has not gotten around to doing this. You have offered several times to help Harry go through the files, but Harry insisted that he would do it himself.

You considered trying to approach the prosecutor to arrange an exchange of the information about the location of the other rat poison for a promise that the prosecutor would not file additional charges against Harry based on that information or any further harm discovered as a result of the revelation. Harry has been unwilling to allow you even to broach the subject with the prosecutor. He keeps saying he will revisit his former customers and get the rat poison out of there.

The prosecutor has not sought a warrant for Harry's records on services provided to other customers. You do not understand why he has not. You are worried that Harry may try to "solve" this problem by destroying his records.

A criminal law in your state provides that "any person who recklessly engages in conduct that creates a substantial risk of death or serious physical injury to another person is guilty of the misdemeanor of reckless endangerment."

What should you do? Would you actually do what you think you should do? Why or why not?

# 3 THE ATTORNEY-CLIENT PRIVILEGE AND THE WORK PRODUCT DOCTRINE

G.  **Waiver**
1.  Express waiver by client
2.  Waiver by inaction
3.  Waiver by revealing privileged communication to a nonprivileged person
4.  Waiver by putting privileged communication into issue
5.  Waiver as to a conversation by disclosure of part of it
6.  Compliance with court orders

H.  **The work product doctrine**
1.  Work product prepared in anticipation of litigation
2.  Origins of the work product rule
3.  Materials not created or collected in anticipation of litigation
4.  A qualified protection
5.  Protection of a lawyer's "mental impressions"
6.  Protection of work product, not underlying information

This chapter focuses on the law of attorney-client privilege. Generally speaking, the privilege gives lawyers and clients a right not to divulge what they say to each other, provided that the lawyer and client communicate in confidence outside of the presence of third parties for the purpose of delivery of legal services to the client.

We begin by distinguishing confidentiality from privilege. Then we lay out the elements of the attorney-client privilege. After that, we explain how the privilege applies when corporations rather than natural persons are clients. Next we examine rules that eliminate claims of privilege. These include exceptions to the privilege and waiver of the privilege. Finally, we explore the related work product doctrine.

# A.  Confidentiality and attorney-client privilege, compared

The law of attorney-client privilege is different from the ethics rules on confidentiality. Many law students (and lawyers) confuse these two, so we separate them into two chapters.

# 1. Ethics law versus evidence law

The most basic difference between confidentiality and privilege is that the duty to protect confidences is imposed by the ethical rules, violation of which can result in discipline. Privilege is "evidence law," which governs what kinds of evidence can be admitted in court. These sets of rules offer different but overlapping protection to lawyer-client communications. Privilege rules provide that neither lawyer nor client may be compelled to testify in court about protected communications. The ethical rules are more demanding because they require lawyers to protect confidential information whether or not someone is trying to compel the disclosure of information.

Both confidentiality and privilege are based on the idea that a legal system in which advocates speak for clients will work best if clients feel free to speak openly to their attorneys. In addition to encouraging open communication, the privilege helps to protect lawyers and clients from the prospect that an adversary might call a lawyer as a witness against the lawyer's own client.

**FOR EXAMPLE:**   Suppose a civil defendant told a certain secret to her lawyer. The lawyer is a "witness" to the defendant's revelation. Now suppose that the plaintiff subpoenaed the lawyer to testify about what the defendant said to the lawyer. The lawyer would say that his duty of confidentiality precluded the lawyer from revealing the secret. However, the court might override that duty. Rule 1.6(b)(6) allows revelation of confidences if necessary to comply with a court order. If the information is also covered by the attorney-client privilege, the court should not issue such an order. The privilege requires courts to refrain from ordering lawyers or clients to reveal the contents of certain conversations that they have with each other.

As we will see in Chapter 8, Rule 3.7 prohibits lawyers from acting as advocates and witnesses in the same trials, but there are exceptions to this rule. If a lawyer has relevant information and no privilege applies, the lawyer can be required to testify. Even when the privilege does not apply, courts usually try to avoid forcing lawyers to testify about information they learned from their clients in the course of representing them. Allowing testimony by counsel disrupts the adversary system, so several courts have said that a lawyer is required to testify only if the party who wants to question an adversary lawyer is able to show "a compelling and legitimate need."[1] With very rare exceptions, even a compelling need will not overcome the privilege.

# 2. Difference in scope

The duty of confidentiality is very broad, as we saw in the last chapter. It has some important exceptions, to be sure. But it covers all information "relating

---

1. Restatement § 108(4), comment l, reporter's note.

to the representation" that a lawyer obtains.[2] By contrast, the privilege covers only a relatively small part of that information: the part that involves communications between lawyer and client in which the client is seeking legal advice or other legal services.[3] In other words, the duty to protect confidences requires protection of nearly all information that is privileged and a great deal of additional information. Information covered by the privilege is only a subset of the confidential information.

> **FOR EXAMPLE:** If a lawyer interviews a witness to an accident that is the subject of a lawsuit, the information is confidential but not covered by the attorney-client privilege because the communication is not between attorney and client.[4] If the lawyer interviews her own client about the accident, neither of them can be compelled to testify about what they said during that conversation.

## 3. Different methods of enforcement

The confidentiality and privilege rules are implemented or enforced in different ways. If a lawyer violates a confidentiality rule, the lawyer might be subject to discipline. If a lawyer seeks information that another lawyer claims is privileged, that lawyer might move to quash a subpoena or object to compliance with a discovery request, claiming privilege.

Here is a table summarizing the differences discussed above between confidentiality and privilege.

| Differences Between Confidentiality and Privilege | | |
|---|---|---|
| | **Ethical duty to protect confidences** | **Attorney-client privilege** |
| **Source** | Ethical duty, Rule 1.6 | Common law evidence rule |
| **Scope** | Information relating to the representation of a client (obtained from any source) | Narrower scope: confidential communication between a lawyer and a client for the purpose of obtaining legal advice |
| **Method of enforcement** | Professional discipline | Quash subpoena or otherwise exclude the revelation from evidence |

---

2. Rule 1.6(a).

3. Other information (besides lawyer-client communications) that is not privileged but is protected by confidentiality rules includes, for example, much of the information a lawyer learns through interviews, discovery, and research, and information produced by experts hired by the lawyer. Geoffrey C. Hazard Jr. & W. William Hodes, The Law of Lawyering § 9.7 at 9-21 (3d ed., Aspen Publishers 2002). The obligation to protect confidences does not prohibit disclosure of information gathered by a lawyer that is drawn from public sources or is otherwise "generally known." Restatement § 59 and comment d.

4. The attorney's recollections and notes may be protected by the work product doctrine discussed at the end of this chapter, but that protection is more qualified than the attorney-client privilege.

## 4. When attorney-client privilege is invoked

Judges can force people to divulge information and can impose various penalties, including jail time for contempt, if they refuse. But if you have a "privilege" not to reveal the information, you can decline to comply with the order to reveal information, and you can't be penalized for invoking that privilege. The next table lists the occasions when a lawyer or a client might invoke the attorney-client privilege.

| Occasions When Attorney-Client Privilege Might Be Claimed* | |
|---|---|
| **Type of case** | **Privilege might be invoked as to arguably privileged material if:** |
| **Criminal cases** | • A lawyer or a client is subpoenaed to testify before a grand jury<br>• A lawyer is subpoenaed to testify before a petit (trial) jury<br>• A client is cross-examined during a trial<br>• A client's documents are seized pursuant to a search warrant |
| **Civil cases and administrative adjudications** | • Discovery is sought from a lawyer or a client through depositions, interrogatories, or a request for production of documents<br>• A lawyer is called to testify before a judge or jury at trial |
| **Legislative and administrative investigations** | • A lawyer or a client is subpoenaed to testify before a legislative committee or an administrative agency |
| **A reporting statute appears to compel a lawyer to disclose information even without an official request.** | • A lawyer seeks to avoid disclosure by preemptive proceeding (e.g., declaratory judgment or injunction) or invokes the privilege to defend against penalties for not having made disclosures (as in *Belge*[5]) |

*Note: Privilege may also be claimed only as to the parts of a communication that are privileged.

## 5. Why study a rule of evidence in a professional responsibility course?

Since the attorney-client privilege isn't an ethical norm and is not covered by the rules of professional conduct, you might wonder why it is covered in a course on legal ethics. Recall from Chapter 1 that the law regulating lawyers is much larger than the ethical rules. Some evidence courses include careful study of attorney-client privilege, but many do not. While the law of attorney-client privilege is somewhat technical, it is very important for every lawyer

---

5. People v. Belge, 376 N.Y.S.2d 771 (App. Div. 1975). This opinion is excerpted in Chapter 2B1.

to understand it. It is one of the many doctrines that govern lawyers that are not included in the rules of professional responsibility.

## 6. Source of the privilege

### Are the rules on attorney-client privilege the same in all the states and in the federal courts?

No. Privilege is a common law doctrine, so the exact scope of the privilege is somewhat different in each state. When federal courts apply state law (for example, in diversity cases), they also apply state privilege rules.[6] When federal courts apply federal law, they apply a federal common law of privilege, and there are slight variations in that law among the different circuits.[7] Nevertheless, the courts are in basic agreement about the scope of the privilege.

### Are the attorney-client privilege rules laid out somewhere?

Only unofficially. The drafters of the Federal Rules of Evidence attempted to create a uniform statement of the privilege, at least for the federal courts, when they proposed Rule 503. This rule was not formally adopted, but even so, it provides a good summary of the general rule. You may find it in your statutory supplement.[8] Also, the American Law Institute has summarized the rules on attorney-client privilege in the Restatement. We focus on the Restatement version to explain this set of rules.

# B. The elements of attorney-client privilege

## 1. Communication

The first element needed to claim attorney-client privilege is "communication" between lawyer and client. The privilege may be claimed for a face-to-face conversation or for other communicative acts; the "communication" could be a telephone call, a memorandum, a letter, a fax, an e-mail, an Instant Messenger exchange, or any other mode of exchanging information.[9] However, as we explain below, the privilege protects only against disclosure of the communication itself, not against disclosure of the underlying facts that might have been communicated.

---

6. Fed. R. Evid. 501.

7. See Brian M. Smith, Be Careful How You Use It or You May Lose It, 75 U. Det. Mercy L. Rev. 389 (1998) (comparing acts that may constitute a waiver of the attorney-client privilege in several jurisdictions).

8. It is included, for example, in Stephen Gillers & Roy D. Simon, Regulation of Lawyers: Statutes and Standards 627 (Aspen Publishers 2004).

9. Restatement § 69.

**What if the lawyer isn't yet the client's lawyer? Suppose a client is shopping around for a lawyer and reveals some important information to a lawyer but then chooses not to retain that lawyer?**

Communications with a prospective client or lawyer are privileged.[10] If there were no such privilege, it would be very hard for a client to tell a lawyer the information, in confidence, to enable the lawyer and client to decide whether the lawyer would represent the client.

## 2. Privileged persons

**Does the communication have to be with the actual lawyer, or is there privilege for communication with the lawyer's staff also?**

Most lawyers work closely with secretaries, paralegals, and investigators. Communications with these agents of a lawyer are privileged. Also, a lawyer's or secretary's notes of a privileged conversation are privileged, just as if the client had made her own notes and brought them to the lawyer in the form of a memorandum.

**Does the attorney-client privilege cover anyone besides lawyers, clients, and agents of the lawyer?**

If an interpreter is needed to translate the conversation between a lawyer and a client who does not speak English or who is hearing-impaired, the interpreter is covered, whether the interpreter was hired by the client or by the lawyer.[11] If a client needs another person to be present to enable or facilitate communication between the lawyer and the client or to provide psychological support during a lawyer-client interview, that person is also covered.[12] A client's psychologist, for example, could be present without destroying the attorney-client privilege.

If a minor child brings his parents to an interview with his lawyer, the parents have a legitimate role in helping the communication.[13] If a person who has been adjudicated incompetent (for example, a person with a very low IQ) is accompanied by someone appointed as her guardian, the guardian has an important role in assisting the communication.[14] A lawyer should not casually allow a third person to be present during a confidential communication because the person's presence could later be found to constitute a waiver of privilege. If a client brings a third person to a meeting with a lawyer, the lawyer should clarify the role of the third person.[15]

---

10. Restatement § 70, comment c.
11. Id. at comment f, illus. 2.
12. Id. at comment f.
13. Id. at comment f, illus. 4.
14. Id. at comment h, illus. 6.
15. Id. at comment e.

## 3. Communication in confidence

The third element is that the client must reasonably believe that the communication is confidential. Suppose a client shares some information with her lawyer in the crowded elevator of the lawyer's office building while they are heading for the cafeteria. Even if neither the lawyer nor the client knows anyone in the elevator, there is no privilege for communication that occurs in the presence of other people. The lawyer, the client, or one of the people on the elevator could be made to testify about what the client said because the circumstances of the communication were not reasonably private.[16] Perhaps you've seen signs in hospital elevators cautioning doctors not to discuss patient matters in public places. Lawyers are well advised to be equally careful, for the same reasons. Lawyers need to protect confidences to comply with their ethical obligation, to respect the privacy of their clients, and to avoid inadvertent waiver of attorney-client privilege.

**If a lawyer reveals information about a case to a friend, does the lawyer violate the rules of ethics *and* waive privilege as to that conversation?**

Yes. That revelation waives the privilege, regardless of whether the conversation took place in a public or private place. It is the disclosure to a third person of the contents of privileged communications that waives the privilege. This often is more of a theoretical problem than an actual problem because usually the opposing counsel would never find out that the lawyer had talked to a third person. But if he did find out, a subsequent claim of privilege probably would fail.

## 4. Communication for the purpose of seeking legal assistance

The last element is that communication is privileged only if the purpose was obtaining legal assistance. If a client asks for "business" advice (such as an investment tip), the conversation is not privileged.

> **FOR EXAMPLE:** Suppose that a lawyer's friend confesses to him that she caused an automobile accident and fled the scene. She tells him about this event because she needs his advice and support as a friend, not because she wants his legal help. The fact that he happens to be a lawyer does not render her admission privileged. He could be required to testify about what she told him.[17]

---

16. Application of the privilege does not require absolute privacy but only the reasonable expectation of privacy. An investigator's secret taping of a lawyer-client conversation through walls that normally block sound does not destroy the privilege attached to the communication. Restatement § 71, comment c, illus. 1.

17. Restatement § 72, comment c.

**If a lawyer doesn't bill a client (or a friend) for legal advice the lawyer provides, is the conversation privileged anyway?**

Yes. As we will see in Chapter 4, a promise or exchange of money isn't necessary to create a lawyer-client relationship.

**If a conversation with a lawyer is partly for the purpose of seeking legal advice and partly to obtain personal advice, is the whole conversation privileged?**

No. Only the part of the conversation that relates to the legal advice is privileged.

> FOR EXAMPLE: Suppose, as in the example above, the friend calls the lawyer and asks him for legal advice about the car accident. During the conversation, she also reveals that she is having an extramarital affair. The conversation about the car accident is privileged, but the conversation about the affair is not. If the friend also asks for legal advice about the affair, the whole conversation is privileged. Likewise, if she says that she caused the accident because she was speeding away to avoid being seen with her lover, the whole discussion probably is privileged.

**Does the privilege protect only what the client tells the lawyer, or does it protect also what the lawyer tells the client?**

The privilege protects communications from the client to the lawyer *and* from the lawyer to the client.[18] The privilege also protects a confidential memo a lawyer writes for his files or for a co-counsel that includes a record of a privileged communication with the client. Some cases have held that lawyer communication is protected only if it includes information about client communications. The Restatement favors broader coverage of confidential communications by lawyers.[19] The point is to create the conditions for a free-flowing communication between clients and lawyers. The rule reflects an assumption that, without the privilege, clients wouldn't consult lawyers so freely and therefore wouldn't get the advice they need. It is socially useful for clients to be well advised, partly because the advice may prevent some unlawful activity.

**Has it been proven empirically that without the privilege, clients are less open with their lawyers?**

Virtually no empirical data existed when the British common law courts evolved the privilege centuries ago, and not much more is available now. One study by Professor Fred Zacharias (also mentioned in Chapter 2), found that

---

18. See Kobluk v. University of Minnesota, 574 N.W.2d 436 (Minn. 1998) (drafts of documents by lawyer sent to client for review found privileged).

19. Restatement § 69, comment i.

60 percent of lawyers said that they told their clients about confidentiality in fewer than half their cases, that only about 26 percent explained confidentiality during the first lawyer-client conversation, and that 73 percent of clients say that their lawyers never told them about confidentiality.[20] Given these statistics it is unlikely that most clients are informed about the more complex concept of privilege. It is possible that more sophisticated clients' decisions about what to tell their lawyers are affected by understanding of the law of attorney-client privilege, but this study suggests that most clients don't know much about it.

**If a client tells a lawyer some factual information during a privileged conversation, is the client protected from being compelled to testify about those facts?**

No. The communication with the lawyer is privileged, but the underlying facts are not. The facts might be protected by a different privilege, such as the privilege against self-incrimination. But if other privileges don't apply (for example, if the prosecutor gives the client immunity and thus nullifies the privilege against self-incrimination), and the prosecutor then calls the client to testify, she must tell the truth about the facts.

> FOR EXAMPLE: A client meets with the lawyer who is defending her in a civil automobile accident case. The client confesses to the lawyer that she had taken more than the prescribed dose of a pain-killing drug that causes drowsiness before starting to drive on the day of the accident. Neither the lawyer nor the client could be compelled to testify about what the client told the lawyer. However, if asked whether she had taken the drug that day, and if so, how much she had taken, the client could not invoke the attorney-client privilege to avoid revealing those facts.

**If a client gives a lawyer a document (say, a copy of a contract) related to the matter on which the client seeks legal advice, does the document thereby become privileged?**

No. The document is a piece of evidence. The lawyer or the client could be compelled to provide a copy of the document to an adverse party. Lawyers are not allowed to hide evidence for clients. We return to this issue in Chapter 8.

**Does the attorney-client privilege protect any documents?**

Yes. Some papers are privileged, but only if the papers themselves are lawyer-client communications for the purpose of obtaining legal advice. For example, if a client prepares a summary of the facts of her case for her lawyer so that the lawyer can better advise her, that document is privileged. The mode of communication by the client is not important. It may be oral, written, or even

---

20. Fred C. Zacharias, Rethinking Confidentiality, 74 Iowa L. Rev. 351, 382-383 (1989).

nonverbal communication by the client in confidence to the lawyer. If the communication is a document, it must have come into existence at the same time as or later in time than the client's first communication with the lawyer.[21]

These tables summarize the scope of the attorney-client privilege.

## Scope of Attorney-Client Privilege[22]

| Requirements for attorney-client privilege | Comment |
| --- | --- |
| A communication between privileged persons | The communication may be oral, written, electronic, etc. Privileged persons include:<br>• Lawyers, clients, prospective clients, interpreters<br>• Others who participate in the lawyer-client conversation to facilitate the communication (such as parents of minors);<br>• Secretaries, paralegals, and other agents of the lawyer or the client[23] |
| which the client reasonably believes is confidential | The communication must be private, and if the lawyer or the client reports on the communication to nonprivileged persons, the privilege is waived. |
| and whose purpose is to seek or to provide legal advice or legal services | Business advice and personal advice are not covered by the privilege. Communication not related to legal advice or services is not privileged. |

## Consequences If a Communication Is Privileged

| Consequence | Comment |
| --- | --- |
| The lawyer can't be forced to testify. | The lawyer may not testify over the client's objection, even if he is willing to do so. The privilege belongs to the client. A lawyer may not waive privilege over her client's objection. |
| The client can't be forced to testify. | The client may waive the privilege, even if the lawyer objects. |
| Paper and electronic records of a privileged communication are also protected. | Only the communication, not the underlying information, is protected. |

---

21. Charles W. Wolfram, Modern Legal Ethics § 6.3.5 at 261 (West 1986).

22. Restatement §§ 68-72.

23. All of the "privileged persons" who are not lawyers are clients or others who facilitate the communication or the provision of legal advice or services.

PROBLEM 3-1 **THE CLANDESTINE VIDEOTAPE**

*This case is based on a problem that arose in California.*

You represent Dolores Snyder, who owns a small unincorporated business known as Jedi Rental Company. Jedi rented 12 large tables and 100 chairs to Wesley Windell for a surprise dinner party that he threw for his wife. During the dinner, one of the chairs collapsed because a rivet in one of its legs gave way. As a result, Elaine Dumont tumbled off the chair and over the edge of the patio in the Windells' garden. She fell several feet down into some dense bushes, injuring her spine. Dumont sued Snyder for negligent failure to inspect the chair before renting it to Windell. Dumont claims that ever since her release from the hospital, where she was treated for a spinal fracture, she has suffered long-term spinal pain.

After the litigation commenced, Snyder told you that she had heard from Wesley Windell that Elaine Dumont seemed to have resumed normal activities. Snyder suggested that you check it out, maybe even send someone out with a video camera to create evidence of her recovery.

You hired Spade and Archer, a firm of private investigators, to observe and videotape Dumont's activities. Miles Archer reported that he had followed her on a shopping excursion and that she did not seem to be in pain. He had discretely filmed her getting in and out of her car, climbing the stairs that led into the tanning parlor, and lifting some heavy ceramic pots into her trunk at the garden store. Despite Archer's efforts not to be observed while making the videotape, Dumont spotted him photographing her, and she guessed that he was doing so at your instruction. Her lawyer has served a notice for inspection and production of the video.

**Invoking the privilege.** May you resist inspection on the basis of the attorney-client privilege using any of these theories?

1. The videotape was made at Snyder's suggestion in the course of your representation of her.
2. The videotape is inextricably connected to your several communications to and from Archer.
3. Dumont's nonverbal behavior was a form of communication.

# C. Client identity

**May a lawyer be forced to reveal the identity of a client, or is that information privileged?**

In most jurisdictions and situations, the identity of a client is privileged, but the law is not entirely settled. Several cases state in dicta that client identity is not necessarily covered by the privilege but then go on to protect that information from disclosure.[24] A few cases hold that client identity is privileged when revelation of a client's identity represents the "last link" in a chain that shows that the client had committed a criminal offense. This exception has been criticized by some scholars as illogical.[25] A small number of cases balance public policy concerns against the application of the privilege and order disclosure.[26]

One situation of particular interest has involved clients who have committed crimes, have not been identified, and have asked lawyers to negotiate reduced penalties in exchange for their confessions. The clients wanted the lawyers to serve as go-betweens, employing the lawyers' negotiating skills but concealing their own identities until the deals had been secured.[27]

When prosecutors have sought to learn the clients' identities and the lawyers invoked the privilege, judges have sometimes required disclosure. However, there also are cases upholding the privilege under these circumstances. In 1960, the Ninth Circuit ruled in favor of a lawyer who sent the government a check for his anonymous client's back taxes, claiming that his client's identity was privileged.[28] A more recent case involved a lawyer who refused to disclose the identity of a client responsible for a hit-and-run accident. A lower court judge in Florida upheld the privilege.[29] On the other hand, some courts rule against lawyers who try to shield client identities.[30] The Restatement cites the Ninth Circuit case approvingly and takes the view that identity should be privileged when revelation of identity would reveal the content of lawyer-client communications.[31]

Although the scope of the privilege for clients' identities has been contested for two generations, it continues to generate controversy. In 2003, a court approved the Internal Revenue Service's request for an order to a Dallas law firm to disclose it with the names of 600 clients when the firm had advised to use a certain kind of tax shelter. The firm challenged the subpoena,

---

24. See, e.g., Dietz v. Doe, 911 P.2d 1025 (Wash. Ct. App. 1996); Matter of Kaplan (Blumenfeld), 8 N.Y.2d 214 (1960).

25. Charles W. Wolfram, The Secret Sharer, Manhattan Law., Apr. 11, 1989, at 13.

26. See, e.g., State ex rel. Friedman v. Provaznik, 668 S.W.2d 76 (Mo. 1984) (during grand jury investigation of lawyer double-billing, prosecutor could subpoena lawyers' records even though they contained names of clients).

27. See, e.g., Baltes v. Doe I, 57 U.S.L.W. 2268 (Fl. Cir. Ct. 1988); State v. Casby, 348 N.W.2d 736 (Minn. 1984); D'Alessio v. Gilberg, 617 N.Y.S.2d 484 (App. Div. 1994).

28. Baird v. Koerner, 279 F.2d 623 (9th Cir. 1960). Professor Wolfram characterized the lawyer as "serving as bagman for someone else's tax payment" and suggested that the client had not really obtained a "legal" service. Wolfram, supra n. 26.

29. Baltes v. Doe I, 57 U.S.L.W. 2268 (Fl. Cir. Ct. 1988). The judge in *Baltes* later rescinded his order to allow himself to reconsider his decision, and then the case became moot because the prosecutor discovered the offender. Wolfram, supra n. 26.

30. See, e.g., Edward A. Adams, Lawyer Ordered to Reveal Client's Name, N.Y.L.J., Oct. 1, 1992, at 1.

31. Restatement § 69, comment g. The Reporter's Note following the comment acknowledges that the Ninth Circuit case "has been extensively distinguished and limited."

arguing that compliance with a request for information defined in terms of both client identity and particular types of advice that the lawyers offered would reveal what advice the firm had given to particular clients, just the sort of information that the privilege was designed to protect. The government successfully countered that the privilege "does not protect the name, address, or whereabouts" of a client who receives tax advice, nor the amount of fees paid for the advice. A similar court battle ensued when the IRS demanded that the law firm of Sidley Austin Brown & Wood reveal the names of more than 600 clients who had purchased dubious tax shelters allegedly promoted by the firm. A federal judge upheld the government's subpoena but agreed to stay its ruling as to 48 clients pending an appeal.[32]

## D. The privilege for corporations

Corporate clients, like individual clients, may invoke an attorney-client privilege. However, the scope of the privilege for corporate clients has been controversial. For a long time, only the communications between the senior officers who controlled a corporation (the so-called control group) and the corporation's lawyers were thought to be privileged. In the late 1970s, federal law enforcement officials tried to learn about discussions between certain low-level employees and the general counsel for the Upjohn Company. The company claimed the privilege, even for communications involving those low-level employees. In the opinion excerpted below, the U.S. Supreme Court decided that — in federal proceedings applying federal law — corporate entities could claim attorney-client privilege and that the scope of the privilege should depend on the *subject matter* of the communication, not on who was doing the communicating.[33]

---

32. Jonathan D. Glater, Issue of Lawyer-Client Confidentiality, N.Y. Times, July 19, 2003; Lynnley Browning, Judge Backs I.R.S. in Tax Case, Then Accepts Request for a Stay, N.Y. Times, Apr. 30, 2004.

33. Although the decision has widely been acknowledged to have decided this question, the Court expressed some hesitancy in its opinion about whether it was actually ruling on the scope of the privilege. The Court explained:

> With respect to the privilege question the parties and various *amici* have described our task as one of choosing between two "tests" which have gained adherents in the courts of appeals. We are acutely aware, however, that we sit to decide concrete cases and not abstract propositions of law. We decline to lay down a broad rule or series of rules to govern all conceivable future questions in this area, even were we able to do so. We can and do, however, conclude that the attorney-client privilege protects the communications involved in this case from compelled disclosure. . . .

Upjohn Co. v. U.S., 449 U.S. 383, 386 (1981).

# Upjohn Co. v. United States

### 449 U.S. 383 (1981)

Justice REHNQUIST delivered the opinion of the court.

### [Upjohn's internal investigation]

Petitioner Upjohn Co. manufactures and sells pharmaceuticals here and abroad. [It] discovered that [its] subsidiary made payments to or for the benefit of foreign government officials in order to secure government business. . . . [Upjohn decided to conduct an internal investigation, so its] attorneys prepared a letter containing a questionnaire which was sent to "All Foreign General and Area Managers" over the Chairman's signature. . . . The letter indicated that the Chairman had asked [Gerard] Thomas, identified as "the company's General Counsel," "to conduct an investigation for the purpose of determining the nature and magnitude of any payments. . . ." The questionnaire sought detailed information concerning such payments. Managers were instructed to treat the investigation as "highly confidential" and not to discuss it with anyone other than Upjohn employees who might be helpful in providing the requested information. Responses were to be sent directly to Thomas. Thomas and outside counsel also interviewed the recipients of the questionnaire and some 33 other Upjohn officers or employees as part of the investigation.

On March 26, 1976, the company voluntarily submitted a preliminary report to the Securities and Exchange Commission disclosing certain questionable payments.[34]

[The Internal Revenue] Service issued a summons . . . demanding production of written questionnaires sent to managers of the Upjohn Company's foreign affiliates, and memorandums or notes of the interviews conducted in the United States and abroad with officers and employees. . . .

### [The decision of the Sixth Circuit]

[Upjohn contended that the questionnaire forms and interview notes were covered by the privilege. But the Sixth Circuit held] that the privilege [applied only to communications by the officials who were] responsible for directing Upjohn's actions in response to legal advice. . . . The court reasoned that accepting petitioners' claim for a broader application of the privilege would encourage upper-echelon management to ignore unpleasant facts and create too broad a "zone of silence." . . .

[The Sixth Circuit judges believed that] since the client was an inanimate entity . . . , only the senior management, guiding and integrating the several

---

34. [Authors' footnote.] The *New York Times* reported that Upjohn admitted that company officials had made payments of $4.1 million over a five-year period for the purpose of obtaining business. Upjohn Discloses Added Payments, N.Y. Times, Aug. 4, 1976.

operations, . . . can be said to possess an identity analogous to the corporation as a whole. . . .

[The Sixth Circuit limited the privilege to communications between counsel and senior corporate managers who were members of "the control group" — those responsible for the highest levels of decision making. The Supreme Court concludes that this definition of corporate privilege is too narrow.]

### [The purposes of the privilege]

Such a view, we think, overlooks the fact that the privilege exists to protect not only the giving of professional advice to those who can act on it but also the giving of information to the lawyer to enable him to give sound and informed advice. In the corporate context . . . it will frequently be employees beyond the control group . . . who will possess the information needed by the corporation's lawyers. Middle-level — and indeed lower-level — employees can . . . embroil the corporation in serious legal difficulties, and it is only natural that these employees would have the relevant information needed by corporate counsel if he is adequately to advise the client with respect to such actual or potential difficulties. . . . [Under the control group test, if the lawyer] interviews employees not having "the very highest authority," their communications to him will not be privileged. If, on the other hand, he interviews *only* those employees with "the very highest authority," he may find it extremely difficult, if not impossible, to determine what happened.

The control group test . . . frustrates the very purpose of the privilege by discouraging the communication of relevant information by employees of the client to attorneys seeking to render legal advice to the client corporation. . . . [It also] makes it more difficult to convey full and frank legal advice to the employees who will put into effect the client corporation's policy. [That test] also threatens to limit the valuable efforts of corporate counsel to ensure their client's compliance with the law. In light of the vast and complicated array of regulatory legislation confronting the modern corporation, corporations, unlike most individuals, "constantly go to lawyers to find out how to obey the law." Burnham, The Attorney-Client Privilege in the Corporate Arena, 24 Bus. Law. 901, 913 (1969). . . .[35] The very terms of the test adopted by the court below suggest the unpredictability of its application. The test restricts the availability of the privilege to those officers who play a "substantial role" in deciding and directing a corporation's legal response. Disparate decisions in cases applying this test illustrate its unpredictability.

---

35. [Court's footnote 2.] The Government argues that the risk of civil or criminal liability suffices to ensure that corporations will seek legal advice in the absence of the protection of the privilege. This response ignores the fact that the depth and quality of any investigations to ensure compliance with the law would suffer, even were they undertaken. The response also proves too much, since it applies to all communications covered by the privilege: an individual trying to comply with the law or faced with a legal problem also has strong incentive to disclose information to his lawyer, yet the common law has recognized the value of the privilege in further facilitating communications.

Compare, e.g., [one lower court case that held that the] control group includes managers and assistant managers of patent division and research and development department,[36] with [another decision holding that the] control group includes only division and corporate vice presidents, and not two directors of research and vice president for production and research.[37] . . .

### [Application of the privilege to this case]

Information, not available from upper-echelon management, was needed to supply a basis for legal advice concerning compliance with securities and tax laws, foreign laws, currency regulations, duties to shareholders, and potential litigation in each of these areas. . . .

### [The social cost of extending the privilege]

Application of the attorney-client privilege to communications such as those involved here . . . puts the adversary in no worse position than if the communications had never taken place.[38]

The privilege only protects disclosure of communications; it does not protect disclosure of the underlying facts by those who communicated with the attorney. . . . Here the Government was free to question the employees who communicated with . . . counsel. Upjohn has provided the IRS with a list of such employees, and the IRS has already interviewed some 25 of them. While it would probably be more convenient for the Government to secure the results of petitioner's internal investigation by simply subpoenaing the questionnaires and notes taken by petitioner's attorneys, such considerations of convenience do not overcome the policies served by the attorney-client privilege. . . . As Justice Jackson noted in his concurring opinion in Hickman v. Taylor, 329 U.S., at 516: "Discovery was hardly intended to enable a learned profession to perform its functions . . . on wits borrowed from the adversary." . . .

## Notes and Questions about *Upjohn*

1. **The actual burden on law enforcement officials.** The Court seems to imply that the government should have no problem obtaining the information if it would just do the necessary legwork. Toward the end of the opinion, however, in a section that we omitted, the Court noted: "The Government stresses that interviewees are scattered across the globe and that Upjohn has

---

36. [Authors' footnote.] The Supreme Court cited Hogan v. Zletz, 43 F.R.D. 308, 315-316 (N.D. Okla. 1967).

37. [Authors' footnote.] The Court cited Congoleum Indus., Inc. v. GAF Corp., 49 F.R.D. 82, 83-85 (E.D. Pa. 1969), aff'd, 478 F.2d 1398 (3d Cir. 1973).

38. [Authors' footnote.] This sentence contains a double negative. What the court means is that it's not so bad to make the government do its own investigation — it's in the same position it would have been in if Upjohn had never investigated itself.

forbidden its employees to answer questions that it considers irrelevant."[39] Except for this sentence, the Court paid scant attention to the considerable practical difficulty that government agencies or private plaintiffs sometimes have when they try to uncover corporate misdeeds. The corporation obviously has better access to personnel and records than does any outsider. The question is to what extent our society should require corporations to share that information with outsiders alleging corporate misconduct.

**2. The new test.** This case expanded the corporate attorney-client privilege in federal proceedings to communications between lawyers and low-level employees who talk with a corporation's lawyers, so long as the lawyers are gathering information to help guide the company's legal affairs.

Here is a table comparing the two leading alternative rules on corporate privilege.

### Scope of the Corporate Attorney-Client Privilege

| | |
|---|---|
| **Control group test** (still used in some states) | "limits the privilege to communications from persons in the organization who have authority to mold organizational policy or to take action in accordance with the lawyer's advice"[40] |
| **Subject matter test** (endorsed by the Supreme Court in *Upjohn* for cases based on federal law) | "extends the privilege to communications with any [management or] lower-echelon employee or agent[41] so long as the communication relates to the subject matter of the representation"[42] |

**3. State courts.** The *Upjohn* decision is not binding on the state courts because it articulates federal common law. The state courts make their own evidentiary rules. State courts may follow *Upjohn*, continue to use the control group test, or adopt a different standard to determine whether communications between counsel for a corporation and employees of the corporation are privileged. In fact, the states have done all of the above. As of 1997, 14 states had adopted the *Upjohn* test or a variant of its subject matter approach (which determines whether a communication is privileged not by who is talking but by the purpose of the communication). Eight states had adopted the control group test. Twenty-eight states had not decided (by state supreme court decision or adoption of a rule of evidence) as of 1997 what rule to follow.[43]

---

39. 449 U.S. at 392.

40. Restatement § 73, comment d.

41. To make a privileged communication, a person must be an agent of a corporation — this could include officers, employees, or independent contractors and may include directors; it does not include shareholders or creditors. The communication is privileged even if the agent was not specifically directed by the corporation to communicate with counsel. Id.

42. Id.

43. Brian E. Hamilton, Conflict, Disparity and Indecision: The Unsettled Corporate Attorney-Client Privilege, 1997 Ann. Surv. Am. L. 629, 633-640.

### 4. The need for a broad corporate privilege.

a. Justice Rehnquist stated in the *Upjohn* opinion that "The control group test . . . frustrates the very purpose of the privilege by discouraging the communication of relevant information by employees of the client to attorneys seeking to render legal advice to the client corporation." Do you agree that it was necessary to expand attorney-client privilege to ensure that corporate counsel would be able to learn what was really happening within a company?

b. Might corporate officers support a broader attorney-client privilege for some reasons other than the promotion of open communication with counsel?

c. What's the down side of the Court's decision? Is there any disadvantage to offering broad protection to corporations of their communications with counsel?

d. How might one investigate whether and to what extent broader privilege promotes open communication between clients and lawyers?

**5. Employees' incentives.** One justification for the broader corporate privilege is that this rule encourages employees who have engaged in wrongdoing to be candid. (The Court says that the limited control group test would "discourage" such communications.) Do you think broader privilege always induces employees to be candid with counsel? Suppose an employee who paid illegal bribes to get business for Upjohn is talking to the employer's counsel. If he knows that the conversation is protected by attorney-client privilege, will this ensure his truthfulness?[44]

**6. What about other organizations?** The *Upjohn* decision addresses the extension of the privilege to corporate entities. What about other types of organizations: unincorporated associations, partnerships, limited liability partnerships (a form favored by most large law firms). Should these entities also receive the protection of privilege? The Restatement urges that they should, that "neither logic nor principle supports limiting the organizational privilege to the corporate form."[45]

**7. Waiver.** The *Upjohn* opinion sets a policy favoring allowing corporations a fairly broad privilege to facilitate open communication with counsel, but in recent years, federal prosecutors investigating corporations have strongly encouraged corporations under investigation to waive the privilege, disclose the product of internal investigation, and be rewarded with lesser penalties for doing so. Professor Sarah Duggin explains this development.

---

44. These questions are explored in Elizabeth G. Thornburg, Sanctifying Secrecy: The Mythology of the Corporate Attorney-Client Privilege, 69 Notre Dame L. Rev. 163, 174-179 (1993).

45. Restatement § 73, comment b.

## Sarah Helene Duggin, Internal Corporate Investigations: Legal Ethics, Professionalism, and the Employee Interview

2003 Colum. Bus. L. Rev. 859, 862-865, 899-902, 907-912

[Professor Duggin is assistant professor of law at The Catholic University of America and previously served as the general counsel of the National Passenger Railroad Corporation (Amtrak) and as chief counsel of the University of Pennsylvania Health System.]

*Professor Sarah Helene Duggin*

At some point, almost every organization encounters troubling questions of real or suspected wrongdoing by officers, directors, or employees. Sometimes there are few, if any, repercussions. On occasion, however, unfolding events reveal a pattern of wrongdoing so pervasive that it destroys the organization itself and leaves many of its principals facing criminal prosecution. In an effort to help clients discover and deal with potentially serious misconduct, lawyers representing corporations routinely advise their clients to conduct internal investigations of suspected wrongdoing. Prosecutors and government agencies have encouraged this trend, and the highly publicized inquiries conducted by counsel retained by the boards of Enron, WorldCom and other major corporations have made the term "internal investigation" common parlance. Consequently, the internal investigation has become a hallmark of corporate legal practice.

An internal investigation is an inquiry conducted by, or on behalf of, an organization in an effort to discover salient facts pertaining to acts or omissions that may generate civil or criminal liability. Internal investigations are invaluable tools for addressing a wide variety of potential sources of corporate civil and criminal liability. The employee interview is the heart of the internal investigation. Documents, accounting ledgers, and other corporate records are important, but words and numbers come to life through the stories related by real people. . . .

For many employees, participation in an internal investigative interview is simply one more work obligation. For others, the investigative interview may lead to discipline, dismissal, or even criminal charges. In the current law enforcement environment, there is a significant possibility that information provided by corporate constituents in the course of internal investigative interviews will be disclosed to prosecutors or other government agents. United States Department of Justice ("DOJ") policy encourages prosecutors to seek disclosure of the fruits of corporate internal investigations before deciding whether to file criminal charges against corporate defendants, enter into plea negotiations, or take positions with respect to sentencing. "Voluntary" corporate disclosures often include material such as a lawyer's notes of employee interviews and communications with counsel that otherwise would be shielded by the corporation's attorney-client and work-product privileges. . . . [A]ttorneys conducting internal investigations may well be gathering information likely to end up in the hands of the government. Yet, even sophisticated employees often fail to appreciate that corporate counsel may metamorphose into de facto government agents. . . .

[L]awyers who conduct internal investigative interviews constantly confront the inherent tension between zealous representation of their corporate clients and fairness to corporate constituents. This tension gives rise to significant ethical issues for lawyers handling internal investigations for corporate clients, . . . [including] when and how to disclose to an interviewee that counsel represents the business entity, not the individual; what to say in response to questions such as "Do I need my own lawyer?"; and what to advise corporate clients with respect to government demands for privilege waivers, constituent requests for advancement of attorneys' fees, and related issues. . . .

### AN END-RUN AROUND *UPJOHN*: PRIVILEGE WAIVERS AS THE PRICE OF COOPERATION WITH THE FEDERAL GOVERNMENT . . .

As the risks of corporate criminal and civil liability began to increase, and the potentially staggering consequences became clear, more and more corporate defendants chose to settle with the government rather than litigate. From 1997 to 2000, close to ninety percent of all corporate defendants in federal criminal proceedings pled guilty; by 2001 the number had climbed to nearly ninety-three percent. The United States Sentencing Commission's *Organizational Sentencing Guidelines* . . . permit a corporation facing sentencing proceedings to lower its culpability score by showing that at the time the offense occurred the company had in place an "effective program to prevent and detect violations of the law," or by demonstrating "[s]elf-reporting, cooperation, and acceptance of responsibility" for the organization's wrongful conduct. . . . [T]he best opportunity for organizations to reduce criminal sanctions may well lie in the areas of "cooperation" and "corporate acceptance of responsibility" for [misconduct].

[T]he *United States Attorneys' Manual* . . . clearly set[s] forth the relevance of privilege waivers and corporate cooperation to the threshold decision whether to bring charges against corporate defendants, as well as determinations whether to grant amnesty or immunity to parties involved in government investigations. As the policy states:

> In determining whether to charge a corporation, that corporation's timely and voluntary disclosure of wrongdoing and its willingness to cooperate with the government's investigation may be relevant factors. In gauging cooperation, prosecutors should consider the corporation's willingness to identify the culprits within the corporation, including senior executives, to make witnesses available, to disclose the complete results of its internal investigation, and to waive the attorney-client and work-product privileges. . . .[46]

---

46. [Postscript from Prof. Duggin.] A series of amendments to the United States Sentencing Commission's Organizational Sentencing Guidelines effective November 1, 2004 . . . [states] that privilege waivers are not a prerequisite to reducing an organization's culpability score under the Guidelines "unless such waiver is necessary in order to provide timely and thorough disclosure of all pertinent information known to the organization." Despite the disclaimer, the provision clearly gives

The defense bar has repeatedly raised concerns about these policies, but with little effect to date. . . . In the words of one criminal defense lawyer, "the attorney-client privilege is under siege." . . .

The [DOJ] approach to privilege issues . . . severely compromises counsel's ability to rely on the attorney-client and work-product privileges to keep confidential any materials gathered, notes taken, or memoranda written in the course of an internal investigation. The government's policy very effectively undermines the Supreme Court's decision in Upjohn without the need for litigation. . . . Whether or not the public policy underlying the DOJ's strategy is sound, there is no question that it has dramatically affected the conduct of many internal investigations and the use of their findings.

## THE IMPACT OF FEDERAL CORPORATE COOPERATION POLICIES ON INDIVIDUALS INTERVIEWED IN THE COURSE OF INTERNAL INVESTIGATIONS OF POTENTIAL CRIMINAL VIOLATIONS

### Possible Loss of Fifth Amendment Protections

An employee asked to participate in an investigative interview has little choice. Refusal to do so may result in sanctions or even termination. In most states a refusal to cooperate with an internal investigation "constitutes a breach of an employee's duty of loyalty to the corporation and is good grounds for terminating his employment." Until the late 1990s, the Supreme Court's Upjohn decision provided some assurance for both corporations and their constituents that internal investigations were truly internal. The attorney-client privilege and work-product doctrine protected the materials counsel prepared in the course of their work, even if the corporation later engaged in voluntary disclosure or pleaded guilty to a criminal offense. That is no longer the case [because of the frequency of voluntary disclosure in response to criminal investigation.] . . . Consequently, if, in the course of an interview, "an employee responds to the corporate attorney in a manner which implicates him personally in criminal conduct, he may have unknowingly lost the value of his fifth amendment privilege against self-incrimination."[47] . . .

### Disclosures that May Embarrass the Employee or Superiors

In addition to the tension between sacrifice of constitutional protections and the loss of livelihood, employees may face intra-corporate political land mines, particularly if what the employee says turns out to embarrass the employee or her superiors. . . . It is . . . entirely possible that an unrepresented employee involved in questionable conduct may end up as a corporate

---

prosecutors license to determine necessity and will undoubtedly be invoked to encourage organizations to waive the attorney-client and work-product privileges. E-mail to the authors from Sarah Helene Duggin, Aug. 18, 2004.

47. [Duggin's footnote.] Kathryn W. Tate, Lawyer Ethics and the Corporate Employee: Is the Employee Owed More Protection Than the Model Rules Provide?, 23 Ind. L. Rev. 1, 3-4 & n. 6 (1990). . . .

scapegoat, particularly if the employee essentially confesses to engaging in some form of misconduct while a more culpable, but more legally sophisticated superior, manages to remain silent.

### Failure to Comprehend the Role of Investigating Counsel . . .

Counsel's first goal [in conducting an internal investigation] is to determine whether wrongdoing has occurred. If it has, it is in the corporation's best interest to show that an errant employee or agent acted on her own without either corporate encouragement or corporate authority. . . . [C]orporate counsel are ethically bound to choose the interests of the corporation over those of its constituents. The employee, however, may not realize his or her potential vulnerability. A corporate constituent may know and trust the lawyers conducting the interview and misperceive their role in the investigation. While this may be particularly true for lower echelon employees who lack legal sophistication, even senior employees are at risk. . . . [I]f the lawyers interviewing them are people they deal with regularly, managers may respond on the basis of existing personal connections without fully appreciating the true nature of the circumstances.

### Erroneous Expectations

In contrast, when the government approaches an employee directly, the elements of mutual trust and commitment are not present. Employees are far more likely to realize the personal risks inherent in the situation, and they have an opportunity to decline to participate without fearing job loss. Contacts by government agents may motivate employees to retain personal counsel or perhaps even request immunity in exchange for cooperation. . . . Employees at any level may have no idea that they are providing information likely to go to federal prosecutors, or that they may be forfeiting the Fifth Amendment's protection against self-incrimination by providing information to counsel conducting the interviews. . . .

If the corporation subsequently waives the attorney-client and work-product privileges with respect to the investigation, prosecutors are likely to garner all kinds of information — including potentially incriminating statements — from people who might otherwise decline to speak with prosecutors, FBI agents, or other government investigators.

## PROBLEM 3-2 **WORLDWIDE BRIBERY**

*This problem presents facts similar to those of the Upjohn case but asks you to consider how the analysis would be affected by the recent and controversial prosecution guidelines of the U.S. Department of Justice (discussed in Professor Duggin's article and quoted more fully below).*

You are the general counsel of the Horizon Corporation, a publicly traded company that manufactures cell phones and sells them worldwide. An employee told you that some officers of the corporation had been directing bribes to officials of foreign governments in violation of U.S. law. You directed the lawyers on your staff to interview officers and employees throughout the company. They verified that officers of the company had engaged in rampant bribery. Your staff compiled extensive records showing which company officials paid bribes, along with the dates, amounts, recipients, and benefits to the company from each bribe.

You reported the results of your investigation to Valerie Patel, the president of the company. You and she agreed to send a memo to all corporate employees directing them not to participate in bribery, even in countries where it is legal. You told her that the bribery could trigger criminal prosecution of the company and its officers. Also it could lead to drastic losses on the stock market. You and Patel therefore agreed that you would contact the U.S. attorney, admit in general terms that bribery had occurred, and offer to pay a civil fine to avoid criminal prosecution.

The U.S. attorney responded that she could not consider plea bargaining unless you first gave her the entire file from your internal investigation. She pointed out that her posture was consistent with the federal government's Guidance on Prosecution of Corporations.[48]

"By the way," she added, "now that I know that the company has broken the law, if you don't cooperate, we will open our own investigation, and you can expect to receive a grand jury subpoena."

After tearing out some of her hair, Patel asks you to advise her as to the pros and cons of turning over your investigative file.

# E. The crime-fraud exception

## 1. No privilege if a client seeks assistance with a crime or fraud

**Does the privilege cover a conversation in which a client asks a lawyer for advice or help in committing a crime or fraud?**

No. Even if a lawyer-client conversation satisfies all the criteria above for privilege, no privilege attaches if the client consults a lawyer for assistance in

---

48. U.S. Department of Justice, Principles of Federal Prosecution of Business Organizations, *available at* http://www.usdoj.gov/dag/cftf/corporate_guidelines.htm (Jan. 20, 2003) (last visited Oct. 14, 2004), which states: "In determining whether to charge a corporation . . . the prosecutor may consider the corporation's willingness to identify the culprits within the corporation, including senior executives, to make witnesses available, to disclose the complete results of its internal investigation, and to waive the attorney-client and work product privileges. . . . Such waivers permit the government to obtain statements of possible witnesses, subjects and targets, without having to

committing a crime *or* a fraud. Likewise, there is no privilege for a conversation if the client later uses the lawyer's advice or services to commit a crime or a fraud. (The bad act doesn't have to be both criminal and fraudulent; either one will do.)

**FOR EXAMPLE:**   If a client walks into the lawyer's office and asks where he could buy an unregistered gun with which to kill his wife, that communication is not privileged. This extreme example doesn't even reach the crime-fraud exception because the advice being sought isn't legal advice, so there's no basis for claiming privilege in the first place.

**FOR EXAMPLE:**   Suppose a client consults the lawyer after he shoots his wife and asks what countries he might escape to without risk that he will later be extradited to the United States. This question is a request for legal advice (Which countries do not have extradition treaties with the United States?), so this communication might be privileged. This conversation is *not* privileged, however, because the client is asking for advice about how to commit a crime. A federal statute makes it a crime to flee a jurisdiction to avoid prosecution.[49] The client's flight will violate that statute and might also constitute obstruction of justice under state law.

**FOR EXAMPLE:**   Suppose a client is planning to get his friends to put up money for a fraudulent investment scheme. This client wants his lawyer's advice about whether he can take the money, buy a mansion on the beach in Florida, and then declare bankruptcy without losing the mansion. He's heard that all the con artists do this. This is a request to the lawyer to help him commit fraud, so the communication is not privileged.

### What if a client asks for advice about a crime he plans to commit but does not ask the lawyer to give advice that assists him in the act?

Clients need to be able to talk in confidence with their lawyers before they commit crimes as well as afterward. Otherwise lawyers would not have the opportunity to dissuade the clients from committing the crimes. Consequently, a distinction is made between a request for advice that would help a client to commit a crime or to avoid apprehension, and a request for advice about whether a certain act is permitted under the law. In the latter case, the communication is privileged, at least in most states.[50]

---

negotiate individual cooperation or immunity agreements. In addition, they are often critical in enabling the government to evaluate the completeness of a corporation's voluntary disclosure and cooperation."

49. 18 U.S.C. § 1073 (2004). See United States v. Bando, 244 F.2d 833 (2d Cir.), *cert. denied*, 355 U.S. 844 (1957) (the statute is violated even if the offender fled the state prior to arrest or indictment).

50. There are important state variations in the law of attorney-client privilege, just as there are in the state rules governing confidentiality. For example, in 2003, California amended its law of attorney-client privilege to provide that the privilege does not protect otherwise confidential communications if the lawyer reasonably believes that disclosure is necessary to prevent a criminal act (by the client or anyone else) that is likely to result in death or substantial bodily harm. Cal. Evid. Code § 956.5 (2004).

**FOR EXAMPLE:** A Massachusetts lawyer was consulted by a client who talked about how he had been fired from his maintenance job and was to be evicted from the building where he lived and worked. He told the lawyer he was thinking of starting a fire at the building. The lawyer, after considerable deliberation and acting under a state ethical rule that allowed a lawyer to disclose the intention of a client to commit any crime, called the police. The police searched the building, found evidence of imminent arson (including gasoline poured on a hallway floor and disconnected smoke detectors), and arrested the lawyer's client for attempted arson. Later the lawyer was subpoenaed to testify about what his client told him. Although this communication was not protected as a confidence under the ethical rules, it was found to be protected by attorney-client privilege. The crime-fraud exception was found not to apply because the client was seeking advice from the lawyer about his threatened eviction but not assistance with the crime.[51]

### If a client asks his lawyer for advice about a past act that was criminal or fraudulent, is that communication privileged?

Yes, such communication is privileged so long as the past act is really past. If there is a continuing crime or fraud that results from a past act, there is no privilege. The crime-fraud exception does not apply to past crimes or frauds.

**FOR EXAMPLE:** Suppose the client in the example above already has committed the investment fraud and bought his mansion. He wants the lawyer to advise him only about the statute of limitations for criminal fraud in case the prosecutor is thinking of charging him. That question and the lawyer's answer are privileged. The lawyer would not be advising him how to commit a continuing or a future crime.

### What if a client consults a lawyer about a planned crime but doesn't know that the planned conduct is criminal? Is the consultation privileged?

No. The client's intention to perform a criminal or fraudulent act triggers the crime-fraud exception. It doesn't matter whether the client knows that the act is wrongful.[52]

**FOR EXAMPLE:** Suppose a client tells his lawyer that he has bought a substantial quantity of prescription medication from a friend at a low price. He says that he is planning to sell this medication to other people

---

51. Purcell v. District Atty. for Suffolk County, 676 N.E.2d 436 (Mass. 1997).
52. Restatement § 82, comment c.

at a profit and wants advice about how to minimize his tax obligations. He doesn't realize that it is a crime under state law to resell prescription medication. The lawyer advises him not to do it, but the client sells the drugs anyway. A prosecutor could make the lawyer reveal the contents of that discussion with her client.

## What if a client asks a lawyer for advice, learns that the planned conduct is criminal, and doesn't commit the crime? Is that conversation privileged?

It should be. In the example above, if the client takes the lawyer's advice and doesn't sell the drugs, the conversation should be privileged because one purpose of the privilege is to enable clients to get sound advice from lawyers and avoid committing criminal acts.[53]

## What if a client consults a lawyer about a plan that he knows involves a crime or fraud but conceals facts from the lawyer that would reveal the illegality of the scheme?

The lawyer's knowledge or intentions are irrelevant. Only the client's intentions are relevant. Such a conversation is not privileged because the client's planned transactions violate the law.[54]

> **FOR EXAMPLE:** Suppose that in the example above, the client doesn't tell his lawyer that the drugs are prescription drugs. He merely tells the lawyer that he's doing a business deal and asks if he can reduce his taxes by setting up a small corporation to handle his transactions. The lawyer has no idea that what the client is planning is criminal, but even so, there is no privilege for this conversation.

If, on the other hand, the lawyer has criminal intent and the client does not, the conversation is privileged. Only the client's intentions are relevant to the privilege.[55]

> **FOR EXAMPLE:** Suppose the client plans to sell merchandise legally, and the lawyer advises him about how to evade taxes on the transaction illegally. The lawyer does not tell the client that following his tax advice will violate the law. This conversation is privileged because the client has no intent to commit a crime or fraud.[56]

---

53. Id.
54. Id.
55. Restatement § 82, comment c, illus. 3.
56. However, in this case, the lawyer might be disciplined for violating Model Rule 1.2(d) (which prohibits a lawyer from assisting a client in committing a criminal or fraudulent act), and if the client took the lawyer's advice, the lawyer might be prosecuted as an accomplice or accessory.

## PROBLEM 3-3  **THE FATAL BUS CRASH**

*This problem is based on a case that occurred in a mid-Atlantic state in the 1980s.*

You represent the estate of Otto Crandell, who was severely injured in a bus crash in Europe. He lingered for a few weeks on life support systems, but after doctors said that he would never recover, his closest relative discontinued life support, and Crandell died.

As he passed through the airport on his way to Europe, Crandell bought a travel insurance policy from Phoenix Insurance. Under the policy, if Crandell died as the result of any accident that occurred while he was riding on a common carrier (train, plane, and so on) during his trip, his estate would be paid $300,000. The estate asked Phoenix to pay this sum, but Phoenix refused to pay the claim. On behalf of the estate, you wrote to Phoenix and asked its legal department to review the denial of the claim.

Phoenix is represented by a lawyer named Clara Tractenberg. Tractenberg wrote you a letter saying that she and other Phoenix officials had carefully reviewed the medical records. They had determined that the cause of Crandell's death was the disconnection of the life support systems, not the bus crash. You know from the medical records that Crandell's prospect for recovery from his injuries was hopeless, and you believe, therefore, that the true cause of death *was* the bus crash.

You have a theory about why Phoenix may have denied the claim. At the time Tractenberg wrote the letter, interest rates were at an all-time high. The longer Phoenix could wait before paying the $300,000, the longer it could earn interest on these funds. Even if a court eventually ordered Phoenix to pay the claim and awarded interest from the time of the accident, the interest rate used by the court would be far lower than what Phoenix could earn on the money in the meantime. So the longer the delay, the smaller its net loss from the claim.

You are convinced that Phoenix's real motive in denying the claim and sending the Tractenberg letter must have been to postpone the payment of damages. You sue Phoenix on behalf of Crandell's heirs for the $300,000, and for $2 million for the tort of intentional infliction of emotional distress.

Your suit does not charge Phoenix with fraud because state fraud law requires proof of reliance by the plaintiff on a deception by defendant. Your client did not rely on the truth of Phoenix's arguments, but actually sued Phoenix because of them.

During the litigation, you seek discovery of all letters, e-mails, and notes from meetings and phone calls between Tractenberg and Phoenix officials about the cause of death. Also, you seek to depose Tractenberg and the Phoenix official with whom she dealt about what happened during their conversations. (You have the actual medical records. You want to find out what Tractenberg and Phoenix officials *said* to each other about the cause of Crandell's death to prove intentional infliction of emotional distress.) Tractenberg resists on the basis of attorney-client privilege.

What are your best arguments to defeat the claim of attorney-client privilege? Consider any argument that Tractenberg will make. (There could be a claim of work product doctrine also, but simply focus on the attorney-client privilege here.)

## 2. Procedure for challenging the privilege on the basis of the exception

Suppose a lawyer writes a memo to a client that might or might not be privileged because the crime-fraud exception might apply. If the memo is requested in discovery, the lawyer will invoke the privilege on the client's behalf. How can the opposing lawyer know that such a memo exists or know enough about what is in the memo to prove that the document should not be found privileged because the crime-fraud exception applies?

The opposing lawyer must request documents based on guesses about what might exist or what it might contain. In the problem of the Fatal Bus Crash, for example, the plaintiff's lawyer might request any and all correspondence between Phoenix and the bus company relating to coverage of Crandall's claim. The lawyer could argue for in camera inspection of the correspondence (in which the judge reviews the documents privately to decide if they are privileged), urging that the inspection might show intention to commit a fraud.

A judge might agree to look at the documents in this case because there are some suspicious circumstances. The insurance company's defense was pretty outrageous. The lawyer conceded that both she and Phoenix officials had reviewed the medical file. The high interest rates suggested the possibility that the insurance company was just trying to delay paying the claim.

## 3. The tobacco litigation

The attorney-client privilege sometimes plays a central role in major litigation. During the 1990s, for example, many states sued companies that made tobacco products to recover the health care costs that they had expended over the years as a result of their residents' smoking-related illnesses. In the suits, they sought to discover the research that the companies had done over a period of decades, hoping to learn that the companies knew decades earlier that their products caused heart disease and cancer, and that they suppressed the research. Anticipating that adversary parties would try to pry open their secret research, they had put their general counsels in charge of the studies, so that all of the research would consist of employee or contractor reports to a tobacco company's lawyer. Then the companies resisted discovery by invoking the attorney-client privilege.

After extensive litigation of the issue, the tobacco companies' strategy failed. Courts found that the companies had used their attorneys and their privilege claims to defraud the public — essentially by releasing any studies that seemed to show little harm from smoking while burying in the lawyers' offices, perhaps forever, studies showing that tobacco products caused disease and death. The courts found either that the studies were not protected by the privilege to begin with or that they were covered by the crime-fraud exception.[57] As a result, the tobacco companies were forced into settlements under which they agreed to pay more than $200 billion to the states.[58]

---

57. Haines v. Liggett Group, Inc., 140 F.R.D. 681, 695 (D.N.J.), *rev'd on other grounds*, 975 F.2d 81 (3d Cir. 1992); Michael V. Ciresi, Roberta B. Walburn & Tara D. Sutton, Decades of Deceit: Document Discovery in the Minnesota Tobacco Litigation, 25 Wm. Mitchell L. Rev. 477 (1999) (reprinting excerpts from unpublished decisions by courts and special masters in the Minnesota tobacco litigation).

58. Id.

# F. The death of the client

## 1. Introduction

PROBLEM 3-4  **THE DEAD MURDERER**

*This problem is based on events that occurred in a southwestern state in the 1970s.*

Lawrence Giles was convicted of armed robbery and imprisoned in the state penitentiary two years ago. Shortly after his conviction, you began to handle his appeal. During the appellate proceedings, you visited him often in prison. Giles knew that he had cancer when you first visited him, and from month to month, he became more ill and feeble. During your last visit, he told you that he was dying.

Giles wanted to know whether he could ask you a question in confidence. You said he could. He then said that he had read in the newspaper that a man named Lucian Hammer had been arrested and would be put on trial for the murder of a convenience store clerk, Malcolm Browly, in a robbery that took place four years earlier. He told you that he had robbed and murdered Mr. Browly, that he had acted alone, and that Hammer had nothing to do with it. He told you the whole story, going into much more detail than the press reports provided. You were convinced that he was telling the truth.

Giles asked you whether, if he confessed to the crime, the state would put him on trial for murder or whether the prosecutor would not bother with him because he was dying anyway. You told him that you could not predict how the prosecutor would react. Even so, you advised him to confess so that Hammer, an innocent man, would not be convicted. He promised to think it over.

Two months later, Giles died without confessing. Hammer goes on trial next week.

## Questions

1. **Confidentiality**. Are you allowed to reveal Giles's confession, or is it confidential? If revelation is permitted, will you tell Hammer's lawyer about Giles's confession and offer to testify in Hammer's defense?

2. **Compelled testimony?** Suppose you decide not to talk about the conversation because you believe that you owe a duty to protect the confidences of your deceased client. Suppose further that Hammer suspects that Giles may have committed the murder and that he may have told you that he did it.

Could Hammer's lawyer subpoena you and force you to reveal what Giles told you?

## 2. The suicide of Vincent Foster

### a. Factual background

The Dead Murderer problem pits the right of the deceased person to maintain secrets against the right of a criminal defendant to use those secrets in his own defense. In a much-publicized case during the 1990s, the privilege of a deceased person conflicted with a different societal interest — the interest in a federal criminal investigation. In 1993, early in the Clinton administration, several employees of the White House travel office were fired after it was discovered that $18,000 of expenses were unaccounted for.[59] Senior Republicans in Congress called for appointment of an independent counsel and for congressional committees to investigate how the White House had handled the firings.[60]

*Vincent Foster*

Deputy White House Counsel Vincent Foster, who was a close friend of the Clintons from Arkansas, was involved in the decision to fire the travel office employees. After the Republicans called for an investigation of this matter, Foster met with a private lawyer named James Hamilton to seek legal advice. Hamilton took three pages of notes on the meeting. Nine days later, Foster committed suicide, leaving a mysterious, rambling note that said that the FBI had "'lied' in its report to Attorney General Janet Reno on its dealings with the White House counsel's office."[61] Later, at the request of the Independent Counsel, a federal grand jury issued a subpoena for Hamilton's notes. Hamilton resisted, asserting the attorney-client privilege.[62] A federal district judge examined the notes in camera and determined that the privilege applied. The U.S. Court of Appeals ordered the notes turned over, stating that the privilege for a dead client must give way when the information has substantial importance for an ongoing criminal investigation. Hamilton's firm appealed to the Supreme Court, which issued the following opinion.

---

59. Ruth Marcus, Clinton Aide Vincent Foster Dies in Apparent Suicide, Wash. Post, July 21, 1993, at A1; David Von Drehle, The Crumbling of a Pillar in Washington; Only Clinton Aide Foster Knew What Drove Him to Fort Marcy, Wash. Post, Aug. 15, 1993, at A1.

60. Ann Devroy & Helen Dewar, Republicans Seek Travel Office Probe, Wash. Post, June 12, 1993, at A5.

61. Michael Isikoff, Foster Was Shopping for Private Lawyer, Probers Find, Wash. Post, Aug. 15, 1993, at A20.

62. The attorney work product doctrine might also have been invoked, but as noted below, that protection is much weaker, and a judge might find that grounds existed for not applying it, particularly where a witness had died and was no longer available.

## b. The Supreme Court evaluates the privilege claim

### Swidler & Berlin v. United States

524 U.S. 399 (1998)

REHNQUIST, C.J. delivered the opinion of the Court. . . .

**[Historical justification for recognizing a posthumous privilege]**

Cases [from various states] addressing the existence of the privilege after death . . . uniformly presume the privilege survives. . . . For example, the Massachusetts Supreme Court concluded that survival of the privilege was "the clear implication" of its early pronouncements that communications subject to the privilege could not be disclosed at any time. The court further noted that survival of the privilege was "necessarily implied" by cases allowing waiver of the privilege in testamentary disputes. . . . [An historical exception to the attorney-client privilege allows revelation of a decedent's confidences to his or her attorney when several parties contest a will or other distribution of the decedent's property.] The rationale for . . . disclosure in litigation between the testator's heirs . . . is that it furthers the client's intent. . . .

**[Policy considerations]**

[The prosecutor argues that the exception for disputes among heirs] reflects a policy judgment that the interest in settling estates outweighs any posthumous interest in confidentiality. He then reasons by analogy that in criminal proceedings, the interest in determining whether a crime has been committed should trump client confidentiality, particularly since the financial interests of the estate are not at stake. . . .

The premise of his analogy is incorrect, since cases consistently recognize that the rationale for the testamentary exception is that it furthers the client's intent. There is no reason to suppose as a general matter that grand jury testimony about confidential communications furthers the client's intent. . . .

While the fear of disclosure, and the consequent withholding of information from counsel, may be reduced if disclosure is limited to posthumous disclosure in a criminal context, it seems unreasonable to assume that it vanishes altogether. Clients may be concerned about reputation, civil liability, or possible harm to friends or family. Posthumous disclosure of such communications may be as feared as disclosure during the client's lifetime. . . . Foster, perhaps already contemplating suicide, may not have sought legal advice from Hamilton if he had not been assured the conversation was privileged. . . .

**[The Court's holding]**

The prevailing caselaw . . . requires that the attorney-client privilege prevent disclosure of the notes at issue in this case.

Justice O'CONNOR, with whom Justice SCALIA and Justice THOMAS join, dissenting:

I do not believe that the attorney-client privilege should act as an absolute bar to the disclosure of a deceased client's communications. . . . Courts should be permitted to assess whether interests in fairness and accuracy outweigh the justifications for the privilege. . . . Where the exoneration of an innocent criminal defendant or a compelling law enforcement interest is at stake, the harm of precluding critical evidence that is unavailable by any other means outweighs the potential disincentive to forthright communication.

### Questions about *Swidler & Berlin*

**1. Create exceptions?** Suppose you were a member of the staff of the Judiciary Committee of the House of Representatives. The *Swidler & Berlin* decision is based only on common law — not on the Constitution — so it could be reversed by an Act of Congress. The chair of the committee wants your view on whether Congress should (a) let the decision stand, (b) create an exception in federal law for information from deceased persons needed for criminal investigation or defense, or (c) provide that, in cases based on federal law, the privilege terminates shortly after the client dies. California's legislature elected this third option based on the recommendation of the state's Law Revision Commission, which said "there is little reason to preserve secrecy at the expense of excluding relevant evidence after the estate is wound up and the [executor of the estate] is discharged."[63]

**2. History.** Sealing such privileged information in perpetuity affects not only the criminal justice system but also limits historians' access to information, even decades or centuries later. Should historians as well as prosecutors be allowed to obtain privileged information if they can show compelling needs? Or should the privilege as applied to lawyers' notes of their conversations with clients terminate after some period of years has passed? If so, how many years?

# G. Waiver

## 1. Express waiver by client

The attorney-client privilege can be waived. It can be expressly waived by a client. It can also be waived by the client's lawyer if the waiver has been authorized by the client.[64]

---

63. Cal. Evid. Code § 954 and official comment.
64. Restatement § 78.

## 2. Waiver by inaction

Suppose that a lawyer's client is being deposed by opposing counsel, who asks the client a question about a privileged communication. The lawyer could and should claim the privilege unless the client has authorized the lawyer to waive it.[65]

What happens if the lawyer does not realize that the question calls for privileged information, the lawyer does not object to the question, and the client answers the question? This series of events constitutes a waiver by inaction. No appeal can reverse the process, because the client would be held to have waived the objection.

## 3. Waiver by revealing privileged communication to a nonprivileged person

The privilege is waived if the client or the lawyer reveals the privileged information to a nonprivileged person.

> **FOR EXAMPLE:** Suppose that a client tells her lawyer, in the course of seeking legal advice, that she has forged a check. The lawyer asks her to write a statement for his files explaining exactly what she had done, and why, and she complies with this request.
>
> Feeling guilty, the client confidentially tells her minister about the forgery. The minister asks whether she has confessed to the police. She says that the only other person she has told is her lawyer, and she tells the minister what questions her lawyer asked her and what she told the lawyer. Her revelation of her lawyer-client conversation to her minister does not waive the privilege because communications made in confidence to members of the clergy are also privileged (as are some confidential communications to physicians, to spouses, and, in many states, to certain others such as psychologists).
>
> The client also tells her mother about the forgery, and she shows her mother the statement that she wrote for her lawyer. The nonprivileged communication to her mother waives the privilege. If a prosecutor seeks to compel the client, her mother, or the lawyer to testify about the communication, there is no attorney-client privilege.
>
> The client could still claim a separate privilege against self-incrimination provided by the Fifth Amendment of the U.S. Constitution, but this applies only to the client, not to her mother or her lawyer.

### Is the privilege lost if a lawyer represents two clients jointly?

No. If two clients hire a lawyer jointly, they are considered common clients with a common privilege.

> **FOR EXAMPLE:** Suppose a brother and sister work together on a scheme to forge checks. They jointly hire a lawyer to advise and represent them.

---

65. Restatement § 63, comment b.

The fact that each of them is present when the other tells the lawyer confidential information does not waive the privilege.

If these two clients hire the lawyer separately, and the lawyer wants the privilege to apply to conversations where both are present, the lawyer should obtain their agreement to participate in a "common" representation in which confidential information is shared among the three of them. That preserves the privilege.[66]

## 4. Waiver by putting privileged communication into issue

The privilege is also waived if the client puts the privileged communication into issue in a case.

> **FOR EXAMPLE:** If a client sues a lawyer for malpractice and asserts that the lawyer gave her certain incorrect advice, the lawyer may reveal the details of the relevant conversations for the purpose of self-defense.[67]

## 5. Waiver as to a conversation by disclosure of part of it

If a lawyer or client discloses part of an otherwise privileged lawyer-client communication, a judge might find that the partial disclosure was a waiver of the privilege as to the part of the conversation that relates to the subject matter on which the client volunteered testimony.[68] The reason for this subject matter test is to prevent the client from offering misleading testimony by revealing only a half-truth.

## 6. Compliance with court orders

If the lawyer thinks that her notes on a conversation with her client are privileged, but a judge says that the communication was never privileged or that the privilege was waived, the judge might order the lawyer to turn over the notes. At that point, the lawyer may turn over the information rather than withhold it because the lawyer's only alternative may be to go to jail for contempt of court.[69] (The same principle applies if a judge orders disclosure of information protected by the ethical rule on confidentiality.) Turning the

---

66. Restatement § 75, comment c. An exception exists for a subsequent adverse relationship between the co-clients unless they have agreed that the privilege continues to apply. Restatement § 75(2).

67. Restatement § 83(2).

68. Restatement § 79, comment f.

69. If the only way to obtain appellate review without first disclosing the information is to refuse to provide it, risking a ruling that the lawyer is in contempt of court, the lawyer may but is not required to commit the contempt. Restatement § 63, comment b.

information over in response to a court order does not waive the issue for purposes of appeal or of other litigation.

# H. The work product doctrine[70]

## 1. Work product prepared in anticipation of litigation

The work product doctrine is related to, but quite separate from, the attorney-client privilege. It protects notes and other material that a lawyer prepares "in anticipation of litigation" from discovery in pretrial civil proceedings.[71] The work product doctrine applies to documents that a lawyer prepares or collects while working on pending litigation or on a matter in which the lawyer knows that a lawsuit is about to be filed. For example, the doctrine usually protects statements that a lawyer obtains from witnesses. It protects some types of documents that are not covered by the attorney-client privilege because they do not relate to communications between lawyer and client.[72]

Protection of work product is not absolute. Courts are more likely to enforce it in the case of a witness statement to a lawyer if the lawyer asks questions and takes notes that reflect her strategic thinking in asking the questions rather than merely asking the witness to mail her a statement.

## 2. Origins of the work product rule

The work product doctrine was first recognized by the Supreme Court in the case of Hickman v. Taylor.[73] This doctrine is not grounded in the Constitution, any statute, or any rule of procedure. It is a (relatively) new common law rule that protects from compelled disclosure a lawyer's private notes and mental impressions. The work product rule was later expanded and codified in Federal Rule of Civil Procedure 26(b)(3) and in state rules of civil

---

70. The protection of attorney work product is referred to by many names. It is sometimes called a "doctrine," as in Frontier Ref. Inc. v. Commercial Union Assur. Co., 136 F.3d 695 (10th Cir. 1998). Many courts refer to it as a qualified "privilege." See, e.g., Pamida v. E.S. Originals, Inc., 281 F.3d 726 (8th Cir. 2002). The Restatement calls it an "immunity." Restatement § 87.

71. The Restatement explains that "Work product immunity is also recognized in criminal and administrative proceedings." Restatement § 87, comment c. The primary application of this doctrine is in civil proceedings because discovery is generally not available in criminal proceedings. Our explanation of this doctrine, like that in the Restatement, is limited to its primary application, which is in civil proceedings.

72. Professor Wolfram explains, "Work product extends to information prepared by a lawyer without regard to whether it was communicated to the lawyer in confidence and without regard to whether the lawyer's client or some other person was its source." The critical element for work product is possession of lawyer-generated information in the lawyer's mind or private files. Charles W. Wolfram, Modern Legal Ethics § 6.6.3 at 296 (West 1986).

73. 329 U.S. 495 (1947).

procedure. In addition, the common law doctrine is invoked in cases to which the federal rules do not apply (such as certain administrative law cases).

## 3. Materials not created or collected in anticipation of litigation

The work product doctrine does not protect materials that a lawyer creates or collects for reasons other than to prepare for litigation. Suppose the general counsel of a corporation routinely keeps records of the reasons for hiring or firing all employees. If one of those employees later sues for wrongful discharge, these records are not protected by this doctrine. On the other hand, if the lawyer does not routinely keep records of the reasons for all employee discharges but only collects information after discharged employees threaten to sue the corporation, the doctrine applies. In other words, it is only the lawyer's need to use the information in litigation that creates a degree of protection.[74]

Lawyers who work in the office of a corporate general counsel often collect information for more than one purpose. If certain information would have been collected routinely but was also collected because litigation was anticipated, most courts will deny protection to the information. The Restatement asserts that the work product doctrine applies in rulemaking proceedings as well as in litigation if the rulemaking is sufficiently adversarial, but it cites no authority for this proposition.[75]

**If a client gives a lawyer a set of documents that are relevant to impending litigation, are the documents protected by the work product doctrine?**

Not usually. If the lawyers can demonstrate that their "selection and compilation" of the documents reflects their litigation strategy, the documents may be protected. Absent such a showing, the work product doctrine does not apply.[76]

## 4. A qualified protection

Protection of work product is not absolute. A judge can order disclosure of written or oral information otherwise protected by this doctrine if the opposing party can show "substantial need" for the material and that the opposing party is "unable without undue hardship to obtain the substantial equivalent" of the material by other means.[77] This is a rather vague standard, so an attorney can never be certain that particular work product will, in the end,

---

74. Jack H. Friedenthal, Mary Kay Kane & Arthur R. Miller, Civil Procedure 396 (3d ed., West 1999).

75. Restatement § 87, comment h and reporter's note.

76. In re Grand Jury Subpoenas Dated Mar. 19, 2002, 318 F.3d 379 (2d Cir. 2003).

77. Fed. R. Civ. P. 26(b)(3).

be protected. In practice, an opponent may try to prove "undue hardship" by showing that a witness from whom an opposing attorney obtained information (for example, a witness statement) is unavailable (for example, dead) or hostile, or that through no fault of the seeking attorney, records of the event, other than those in the hands of the attorney asserting the protection of the work product doctrine, no longer exist.[78] This showing of substantial need or undue hardship can overcome a claim of work product immunity when the allegedly protected material is a witness statement or other "ordinary" work product. "Ordinary" work product is that which is compiled by the lawyer but does not contain the lawyer's "mental impressions."

## 5. Protection of lawyer's "mental impressions"

The doctrine gives stronger protection to work product that reveals the lawyer's thoughts, strategies, or mental impressions than it does to "ordinary" work product.[79] A lawyer's own notes of his own opinions, theories, observations, or feelings are immune from discovery. Some judicial opinions assert, usually in dicta, that even this information can be obtained by an adversary on a showing of "extraordinary circumstances."[80]

## 6. Protection of work product, not underlying information

The protection offered by the work product doctrine is not as powerful as it might seem at first blush. A lawyer often can get the information contained in protected documents from the original witnesses or sources. If an opposing counsel (as in *Upjohn*) collects questionnaires from a group of witnesses, a lawyer can develop her own questionnaire and contact the same witnesses (so long as contact is allowed under Rule 4.2 or the lawyer uses permitted discovery techniques). The doctrine prevents freeloading on an opponent's work, but it does not enable the opponent to close off a lawyer's sources of information by getting there first.

---

78. See, e.g., Thompson v. The Haskell Co., 1994 WL 597252 (M.D. Fla., Jun. 21, 1994) (psychological report prepared for plaintiff's lawyer was not privileged because it was the only one prepared promptly after plaintiff was fired; defendant could not reasonably have sought its own evaluation at that time because plaintiff did not bring suit until the following year).

79. See *Upjohn*, text at supra nn. 33 et seq.

80. Restatement § 89, comment d, reporter's note.

# 4 RELATIONSHIPS BETWEEN LAWYERS AND CLIENTS

**A. Formation of the lawyer-client relationship**
    1. Choosing clients
    2. Offering advice as the basis for a lawyer-client relationship

**B. Lawyers' responsibilities as agents**
    1. Express and implied authority
    2. Apparent authority

**C. Lawyers' duties of competence, honesty, communication, and diligence**
    1. Competence
    2. Competence in criminal trials
    3. Candor and communication
    4. Diligence
    5. Contractual duties

**D. Who calls the shots?**
    1. The competent adult client
    2. Contracts to change the duties owed to clients
    3. Clients with diminished capacity

**E. Terminating a lawyer-client relationship**
    1. Duties to the client at the conclusion of the relationship
    2. Grounds for termination before the work is completed

This chapter explores the basic elements of the lawyer-client relationship. We begin by describing how the lawyer-client relationship is established. Then we explain the application of agency law to the lawyer-client relationship. The chapter next reviews the duties of competence, candor, communication, and diligence, which are among the most important responsibilities of lawyers to their clients. (Recall that we explored the duty to protect confidences in Chapter 2. Chapters 5, 6, and 7 examine the duty of loyalty.)

In any lawyer-client relationship, some decisions are made by the lawyer, and some are made by the client. This chapter explores when a lawyer *must* consult with a client or defer to a client's wishes. If the client has a mental impairment or is a juvenile, the question of how much a lawyer should defer to a client is more complex. This chapter examines these questions as well.

We conclude with consideration of the rules that govern termination of lawyer-client relationships and the duties of lawyers toward clients at the end of those relationships.

## A. Formation of the lawyer-client relationship

### 1. Choosing clients

Many lawyer-client relationships begin in a very straightforward matter. A client comes to a lawyer's office, explains the problem, signs an agreement, and pays a fee; the lawyer then goes to work. But sometimes complications occur. A lawyer may be precluded from taking on the work because of a conflict of interest, a lack of expertise, or another problem. The lawyer may prefer not to represent the client because he dislikes the prospective client or disagrees with the goal of the representation. What happens then? The issues are discussed below.

**Is a lawyer permitted to accept legal work that requires knowledge of an area of law in which the lawyer has no experience?**

Yes, if the lawyer compensates for inexperience through study or affiliation with another lawyer. The ethics codes require lawyers to provide competent representation.

> **Rule 1.1 Competence**
> A lawyer shall provide competent representation to a client. Competent representation requires the legal knowledge, skill, thoroughness and preparation reasonably necessary for the representation.[1]

---

1. This is the text of the relevant Delaware Rule of Professional Conduct. Unless specified otherwise, all of this book's quotations from rules of professional conduct are quotations from the Delaware Rules of Professional Conduct. In a few instances, we quote from rules or from published proposed rules in other states. Except where we note otherwise, however, the text of all state rules that we quote is the same as the text of the ABA Model Rules of Professional Conduct. See the note in the Introduction for a more detailed explanation.

The question is whether a lawyer who has never handled a particular type of matter before can fulfill this duty. Comment 2 to Rule 1.1 explains that a lawyer can take on a matter in an unfamiliar field if the lawyer has the time and resources to get up to speed.

> A lawyer need not necessarily have special training or prior experience to handle legal problems of a type with which the lawyer is unfamiliar. A newly admitted lawyer can be as competent as a practitioner with long experience. . . . A lawyer can provide adequate representation in a wholly novel field through necessary study. Competent representation can also be provided through the association of a lawyer of established competence in the field in question.

**May a lawyer turn down a request for legal assistance if he lacks time, expertise, or interest in the matter?**

A lawyer may take on work in a new field if he does the necessary study. But what if he doesn't want to take on the matter? Is a lawyer obliged to help a client who wants to hire him? In general, lawyers are allowed to be picky; they don't have to accept any particular clients.[2] There are three caveats. First, Rule 6.1, to which we return in Chapter 10, addresses lawyers' duty to provide legal assistance to people who are not able to pay for it. The rule encourages lawyers to "aspire" to provide at least 50 hours per year of pro bono representation. This rule does not obligate a lawyer to represent or assist any particular poor person but urges lawyers to assist some indigent clients.

Second, a court may assign a lawyer to represent an indigent criminal defendant, even if the court does not have the resources to pay the lawyer for the work. Rule 6.2 directs lawyers to accept such an assignment except for "good cause." Rule 6.2 and court appointment also are discussed in Chapter 10.

Third, a lawyer may not discriminate on the basis of race, religion, nationality, sex, age, disability, or another protected category in her decisions about which clients to represent.[3]

## 2. Offering advice as the basis for a lawyer-client relationship

**To form a lawyer-client relationship, must the client sign an agreement or pay a fee?**

No. An agreement to pay a fee is not a necessary aspect of a lawyer-client relationship. Many lawyers represent clients without charging fees. Lawyers have the same duties to pro bono clients as they do to paying clients. Also, a person can become a client of a lawyer without signing a written agreement. If a

---

2. Restatement § 16, comment b.
3. See Nathanson v. Mass., 2003 WL 22480688 (Mass. Super. Ct., 2003) (affirming Mass. Commn. Against Discrimination order to female divorce attorney to refrain from refusing to accept male clients).

person seeks legal advice or legal services from a lawyer, and the lawyer gives legal advice or provides legal services, the person may thereby become a client. This means that it is important to be careful about what casual advice or assistance you provide to others. Consider the following case.

## Togstad v. Vesely, Otto, Miller & Keefe

291 N.W.2d 686 (Minn. 1980)

PER CURIAM . . .

In August 1971, John Togstad began to experience severe headaches and on August 16, 1971, was admitted to Methodist Hospital where tests disclosed that the headaches were caused by a large aneurism[4] on the left internal carotid artery. The attending physician, Dr. Paul Blake, a neurological surgeon, treated the problem by applying a Selverstone clamp to the left common carotid artery. The clamp was surgically implanted on August 27, 1971, in Togstad's neck to allow the gradual closure of the artery over a period of days.

The treatment was designed to eventually cut off the blood supply through the artery and thus relieve the pressure on the aneurism, allowing the aneurism to heal. It was anticipated that other arteries, as well as the brain's collateral or cross-arterial system would supply the required blood to the portion of the brain which would ordinarily have been provided by the left carotid artery. The greatest risk associated with this procedure is that the patient may become paralyzed if the brain does not receive an adequate flow of blood. In the event the supply of blood becomes so low as to endanger the health of the patient, the adjustable clamp can be opened to establish the proper blood circulation.

In the early morning hours of August 29, 1971, a nurse observed that Togstad was unable to speak or move. At the time, the clamp was one-half (50%) closed. Upon discovering Togstad's condition, the nurse called a resident physician, who did not adjust the clamp. Dr. Blake was also immediately informed of Togstad's condition and arrived about an hour later, at which time he opened the clamp. Togstad is now severely paralyzed in his right arm and leg, and is unable to speak.

Plaintiffs' expert, Dr. Ward Woods, testified that Togstad's paralysis and loss of speech was due to a lack of blood supply to his brain. Dr. Woods stated that the inadequate blood flow resulted from the clamp being 50% closed and that the negligence of Dr. Blake and the hospital precluded the clamp's being opened in time to avoid permanent brain damage. . . .

Dr. Blake and defendants' expert witness, Dr. Shelly Chou, testified that Togstad's condition was caused by blood clots going up the carotid artery to

---

4. [Authors' footnote.] This is the second case in this book that involves an aneurysm. Both are Minnesota cases. The coincidence of place and medical condition are just that — random coincidence. Both of these cases are leading cases on the issues they address. Both spellings of "aneurysm" are acceptable.

the brain. They both alleged that the blood clots were not a result of the Selverstone clamp procedure. . . .

### [The legal consultation]

About 14 months after her husband's hospitalization began, plaintiff Joan Togstad met with attorney Jerre Miller regarding her husband's condition. Neither she nor her husband was personally acquainted with Miller or his law firm prior to that time. John Togstad's former work supervisor, Ted Bucholz, made the appointment and accompanied Mrs. Togstad to Miller's office. Bucholz was present when Mrs. Togstad and Miller discussed the case.

Mrs. Togstad had become suspicious of the circumstances surrounding her husband's tragic condition due to the conduct and statements of the hospital nurses shortly after the paralysis occurred. One nurse told Mrs. Togstad that she had checked Mr. Togstad at 2 A.M. and he was fine; that when she returned at 3 A.M., by mistake, to give him someone else's medication, he was unable to move or speak; and that if she hadn't accidentally entered the room no one would have discovered his condition until morning. Mrs. Togstad also noticed that the other nurses were upset and crying, and that Mr. Togstad's condition was a topic of conversation.

Mrs. Togstad testified that she told Miller "everything that happened at the hospital," including the nurses' statements and conduct which had raised a question in her mind. She stated that she "believed" she had told Miller "about the procedure and what was undertaken, what was done, and what happened." She brought no records with her.

Miller took notes and asked questions during the meeting, which lasted 45 minutes to an hour. At its conclusion, according to Mrs. Togstad, Miller said that "he did not think we had a legal case, however, he was going to discuss this with his partner." She understood that if Miller changed his mind after talking to his partner, he would call her. Mrs. Togstad "gave it" a few days and, since she did not hear from Miller, decided "that they had come to the conclusion that there wasn't a case." No fee arrangements were discussed, no medical authorizations were requested, nor was Mrs. Togstad billed for the interview.

Mrs. Togstad . . . did not consult another attorney until one year after she talked to Miller. Mrs. Togstad indicated that she did not confer with another attorney [until a year later] because of her reliance on Miller's "legal advice" that they "did not have a case." [But by the time she saw another lawyer, the two-year statute of limitations for a suit against Dr. Blake and the hospital had run. Mrs. Togstad sued Miller's law firm for malpractice.]

### [The suit against Miller's law firm]

On cross-examination, Mrs. Togstad was asked whether she went to Miller's office "to see if he would take the case of (her) husband. . . ." She replied, "Well, I guess it was to go for legal advice, what to do, where shall we go from here? That is what we went for." Again in response to defense counsel's questions, Mrs. Togstad testified as follows:

Q. And it was clear to you, was it not, that what was taking place was a preliminary discussion between a prospective client and lawyer as to whether or not they wanted to enter into an attorney-client relationship?

A. I am not sure how to answer that. It was for legal advice as to what to do.

Q. And Mr. Miller was discussing with you your problem and indicating whether he, as a lawyer, wished to take the case, isn't that true?

A. Yes.

On re-direct examination, Mrs. Togstad acknowledged that when she left Miller's office she understood that she had been given a "qualified, quality legal opinion that (she and her husband) did not have a malpractice case." . . .

Miller's testimony was different in some respects from that of Mrs. Togstad. . . . According to Miller, Mrs. Togstad described the hospital incident, including the conduct of the nurses. He asked her questions, to which she responded. Miller testified that "[t]he only thing I told her [Mrs. Togstad] after we had pretty much finished the conversation was that there was nothing related in her factual circumstances that told me that she had a case that our firm would be interested in undertaking." . . . Miller stated that at the end of the conference he told Mrs. Togstad that he would consult with Charles Hvass and if Hvass's opinion differed from his, Miller would so inform her. Miller recollected that he called Hvass a "couple days" later and discussed the case with him. It was Miller's impression that Hvass thought there was no liability for malpractice in the case. Consequently, Miller did not communicate with Mrs. Togstad further.

On cross-examination, Miller testified . . . :

Q. You understood that . . . she was seeking legal advice from a professional attorney licensed to practice in this state and in this community?

A. I think you and I did have another interpretation or use of the term "Advice." She was there to see whether or not she had a case and whether the firm would accept it.

Q. We have two aspects; number one, your legal opinion concerning liability of a case for malpractice; number two, whether there was or wasn't liability, whether you would accept it, your firm, two separate elements, right?

A. I would say so.

Q. Were you asked on page 6 in the deposition, folio 14, "And you understood that she was seeking legal advice at the time that she was in your office, that is correct also, isn't it?" And did you give this answer, "I don't want to engage in semantics with you, but my impression was that she and Mr. Bucholz were asking my opinion after having related the incident that I referred to." The next question, "Your legal opinion?" Your answer, "Yes." Were those questions asked and were they given?

MR. COLLINS: Objection to this, Your Honor. It is not impeachment.

THE COURT: Overruled.

THE WITNESS: Yes, I gave those answers. Certainly, she was seeking my opinion as an attorney in the sense of whether or not there was a case that the firm would be interested in undertaking.

Kenneth Green, a Minneapolis attorney, was called as an expert by plaintiffs. He stated that in rendering legal advice regarding a claim of medical malpractice, the "minimum" an attorney should do would be to request medical authorizations from the client, review the hospital records, and consult with an expert in the field. John McNulty, a Minneapolis attorney, and Charles Hvass testified as experts on behalf of the defendants. McNulty stated that when an attorney is consulted as to whether he will take a case, the lawyer's only responsibility in refusing it is to so inform the party. He testified, however, that when a lawyer is asked his legal opinion on the merits of a medical malpractice claim, community standards require that the attorney check hospital records and consult with an expert before rendering his opinion.

Hvass stated that he had no recollection of Miller's calling him in October 1972 relative to the Togstad matter. He testified that:

A . . . when a person comes in to me about a medical malpractice action, based upon what the individual has told me, I have to make a decision as to whether or not there probably is or probably is not, based upon that information, medical malpractice. And if, in my judgment, based upon what the client has told me, there is not medical malpractice, I will so inform the client.

Hvass stated, however, that he would never render a "categorical" opinion. In addition, Hvass acknowledged that if he were consulted for a "legal opinion" regarding medical malpractice and 14 months had expired since the incident in question, "ordinary care and diligence" would require him to inform the party of the two-year statute of limitations applicable to that type of action. . . .

The jury found that Dr. Blake's negligence . . . was a direct cause of the injuries sustained by John Togstad; that there was an attorney-client contractual relationship between Mrs. Togstad and Miller; that Miller was negligent in rendering advice regarding the possible claims of Mr. and Mrs. Togstad; that, but for Miller's negligence, plaintiffs would have been successful in the prosecution of a legal action against Dr. Blake; and that neither Mr. nor Mrs. Togstad was negligent in pursuing their claims against Dr. Blake. The jury awarded damages to Mr. Togstad of $610,500 and to Mrs. Togstad of $39,000 [for loss of consortium]. . . .

### [The legal standard]

In a legal malpractice action of the type involved here, four elements must be shown: (1) that an attorney-client relationship existed; (2) that defendant acted negligently or in breach of contract; (3) that such acts were the proximate cause of the plaintiffs' damages; (4) that but for defendant's conduct the plaintiffs would have been successful in the prosecution of their medical malpractice claim. . . .

We believe it is unnecessary to decide whether a tort or contract theory is preferable for resolving the attorney-client relationship question raised by this appeal. The tort and contract analyses are very similar in a case such as the instant one,[5] and we conclude that under either theory the evidence shows that a lawyer-client relationship is present here. The thrust of Mrs. Togstad's testimony is that she went to Miller for legal advice, was told there wasn't a case, and relied upon this advice in failing to pursue the claim for medical malpractice. In addition, according to Mrs. Togstad, Miller did not qualify his legal opinion by urging her to seek advice from another attorney, nor did Miller inform her that he lacked expertise in the medical malpractice area. Assuming this testimony is true, as this court must do,[6] we believe a jury could properly find that Mrs. Togstad sought and received legal advice from Miller under circumstances which made it reasonably foreseeable to Miller that Mrs. Togstad would be injured if the advice were negligently given. Thus, under either a tort or contract analysis, there is sufficient evidence in the record to support the existence of an attorney-client relationship. . . .

Defendants argue that even if an attorney-client relationship was established the evidence fails to show that Miller acted negligently in assessing the merits of the Togstads' case. They appear to contend that, at most, Miller was guilty of an error in judgment which does not give rise to legal malpractice. However, this case does not involve a mere error of judgment. The gist of plaintiffs' claim is that Miller failed to perform the minimal research that an ordinarily prudent attorney would do before rendering legal advice in a case of this nature. The record, through the testimony of Kenneth Green and John McNulty, contains sufficient evidence to support plaintiffs' position. . . .

It was reasonable for a jury to determine that Miller acted negligently in failing to inform Mrs. Togstad of the applicable limitations period. . . . There is also sufficient evidence in the record establishing that, but for Miller's negligence, plaintiffs would have been successful in prosecuting their medical malpractice claim. Dr. Woods, in no uncertain terms, concluded that Mr. Togstad's injuries were caused by the medical malpractice of Dr. Blake. Defendants' expert testimony to the contrary was obviously not believed by the jury. Thus, the jury reasonably found that had plaintiff's medical malpractice action been properly brought, plaintiffs would have recovered.

---

5. [Court's footnote 4.] Under a negligence approach it must essentially be shown that defendant rendered legal advice (not necessarily at someone's request) under circumstances which made it reasonably foreseeable to the attorney that if such advice was rendered negligently, the individual receiving the advice might be injured thereby. See, e.g., Palsgraf v. Long Island R. Co., 248 N.Y. 339, 162 N.E. 99, 59 A.L.R. 1253 (1928). Or, stated another way, under a tort theory, "[a]n attorney-client relationship is created whenever an individual seeks and receives legal advice from an attorney in circumstances in which a reasonable person would rely on such advice." 63 Minn. L. Rev. 751, 759 (1979). A contract analysis requires the rendering of legal advice pursuant to another's request and the reliance factor, in this case, where the advice was not paid for, need be shown in the form of promissory estoppel. See 7 C.J.S., Attorney and Client, § 65; Restatement (Second) of Contracts, § 90.

6. [Court's footnote 5.] . . . [I]n determining whether the jury's verdict is reasonably supported by the record a court must view the credibility of evidence and every inference which may fairly be drawn therefrom in a light most favorable to the prevailing party.

Based on the foregoing, we hold that the jury's findings are adequately supported by the record. . . .

Affirmed.

## Notes and Questions about *Togstad*

**1. The importance of the relationship.** The court says, "a lawyer-client relationship is present here" and it spends some time justifying that conclusion. Why was it important that there was "a lawyer-client relationship"? The Togstads could have sued Miller for negligence if he'd run over them with his car, even if there had been no such relationship. Why couldn't the Togstads win their case against Miller for his negligent advice if the court had concluded that there was no lawyer-client relationship?

State negligence law usually asks whether the defendant had a duty to the plaintiff, whether the defendant breached the duty, whether the breach proximately caused the injury, and whether the plaintiff was damaged. In the case of automobile accidents or other events causing physical injury, the first subtest is satisfied because people are said to have a duty to use ordinary care so that they do not negligently kill or injure strangers on the street. However, in the case of purely economic harms (such as the harm caused by providing faulty information), the law of most states requires a relationship between the parties closer than that of strangers before it imposes liability for conduct that is merely negligent and not deliberate or willful.[7]

**2. Fair to Miller?** Mrs. Togstad asked Miller whether she had a case. He gave her his honest opinion that she did not. He never said he was her lawyer or was willing to become her lawyer, never signed any agreement with her, and never charged her a dime. Yet his firm ended up having to pay $649,500. Is this a fair decision?

**3. Mr. Togstad's claim.** Miller met Mrs. Togstad in his office. He never laid eyes on or spoke to her paralyzed husband. Yet apparently Mr. Togstad also became his client, and in fact, most of the judgment was awarded to him. When Mrs. Togstad consulted Miller, she was doing so on behalf of her paralyzed husband as well as on her own behalf. Miller had reason to know that Mrs. Togstad would communicate his advice to her husband, or that if she had been appointed her husband's legal guardian, she would act on the advice on his behalf. Miller's advice to Mrs. Togstad was advice to Mr. Togstad as well.

**4. What's the test of a lawyer-client relationship?** If someone can become your client (and can sue you for malpractice) even though you don't even discuss the terms of the representation, much less sign a written agreement, it is important to know exactly what conduct triggers the creation of a lawyer-client relationship. Where does this opinion draw the line?

**5. What could Miller have done?** How could Miller have avoided this liability?

---

7. See generally Restatement (Second) of Torts, § 282, annotations (1965).

## PROBLEM 4-1 THE CHAT ROOM

*The facts of this problem are hypothetical, but several recent ethics opinions have documented the increasing frequency of conversations in chat rooms between persons seeking legal advice and lawyers.*

You are a solo practitioner in Massachusetts. You mainly represent individual clients in personal injury, domestic relations, and estate matters. Some of your friends have found that a great way to get new clients is to visit Internet chat rooms and have casual conversations with people who need legal advice. You have started visiting chat rooms also, partly in the hope of getting new clients and partly because you like helping people.

Two or three evenings a week, you sign in to one of several Internet chat rooms. Your screen name is "Shaq54." (You are a basketball fan.) Sometimes you visit the Accident and Injuries Chat Room, where accident victims share their stories and grievances. This chat room gives participants the option to share their e-mail addresses with other participants. You have always disclosed your address.

Two months ago, that chat room added a "legal hour" on Thursday evenings to enable accident victims to chat with lawyers. To reach the screen for the legal hour, a user must first click through a screen on which the sponsor of the chat room has posted the following notice.

> *This chat room is for informational purposes only. Participating in this chat room does not establish an attorney-client relationship. This is a free service. You do not need to pay any subscription fee or make payments of any kind to participate in this chat room. If you agree to these terms, click the "I agree" button. You will not be able to proceed to the legal hour screen unless you click the "I agree" button.*

About a month ago, you started logging on to the legal hour as a lawyer. Each Thursday night, you and the two other lawyers in the chat room were deluged with legal questions.

Most of the questions were very general in nature, and you and the two other lawyers answered them in general terms. However, a few weeks ago one question (from "Swimmer," who did not disclose his or her e-mail address) was both poignant and specific:

> Swimmer: I live in Boston. Five years ago, I bought a can of Sierra hair spray. When I pressed the button on top, the pressurized can exploded. The spray and some of the metal spewed all over the place, some at my face. Something got in both of my eyes. I went to the doctor and he rinsed my eyes and gave me some treatments. I didn't need to go into the hospital, and the treatments ended within six months. My health insurance covered all the medical expenses. A year later, I thought the whole thing was over. But in the last year, my sight has been failing. The doctors think that although they got out all the metal, something in the chemicals must have caused slow,

long-term deterioration in both eyes. They think that I will go blind. Can I sue someone?

You didn't want to give Swimmer any false hope, so you wrote back:

> Shaq54: Swimmer, I am sorry to say that you won't be able to sue anyone. In Massachusetts, the statute of limitations for tort cases is only three years. Since this accident took place five years ago and you knew then that you had been injured, you would have had to bring any lawsuit several years ago. Unfortunately, the law imposes these sometimes artificial barriers to a fair recovery. I wish that I could be more encouraging.

The week after you had this conversation, you stumbled across an article that explained that California has an unusually long statute of limitations for products liability cases. Therefore, if perchance Swimmer's hair spray was manufactured in California, and if the statute of limitations applied to a suit against the manufacturer regardless of where the injury occurred, Swimmer might still have a viable claim. Swimmer hasn't logged into the chat room since that night, so you haven't been able to correct or clarify the information you provided.

## Questions

**1. Trouble for you?** Assuming that Swimmer's right to sue in California is not yet barred, are you in any potential trouble?

**2. Good policy?** Should you be at risk of liability for your comments in the chat room? If so, is that an example of the maxim that "no good deed goes unpunished"?

# B. Lawyers' responsibilities as agents

Lawyers are the "agents" of their clients who, in turn, are considered "principals" (the people in charge). Therefore, with very rare exceptions, a client is bound by what the lawyer does or fails to do, regardless of the client's own actions or culpability. The principles of the law of agency, which are much older than the modern legal profession, apply to clients, lawyers, and third parties.[8]

**FOR EXAMPLE:** If a lawyer fails to file a client's lawsuit within the statute of limitations period, the client loses her right to sue the defendant. This is true

---

8. Usually state agency law applies to lawyers and their clients because the lawyer-client relationship is a contractual relationship governed by state law. However, a few federal courts have concluded that when a lawyer acts in a federal forum on a client's behalf with respect to the client's rights arising under federal law, the court may deduce the pertinent principles of agency law applicable to the lawyer-client relationship from the governing federal substantive statute. See, e.g., Kinan v. Cohen, 268 F.3d 27 (1st Cir. 2001).

even if the client directed the lawyer to file the case on time and even if the lawyer falsely told the client that she had done so.[9] The client might sue the lawyer for malpractice under these circumstances. This imposes a terrible burden on a client and may not produce an adequate remedy, if, for example, the lawyer does not have good malpractice insurance and has less money than the original defendant.

These principles apply to lawyers' dealings on behalf of clients, in court and out of court. A client is bound by a lawyer's decisions to waive a defense or a privilege in court (even though these decisions are supposed to be made by the client), and also by a lawyer's agreement on behalf of the client to buy or sell property.[10]

The law of agency recognizes three different ways that a person can become an agent of another: express authority, implied authority, and apparent authority.

## 1. Express and implied authority

A client may explicitly give a lawyer "express" authority to act on the client's behalf. For example, a client could tell a lawyer, expressly and in explicit language, to sign a contract or to settle a case. Alternatively, a client may give a lawyer a general instruction that implicitly allows the lawyer to take certain actions on the client's behalf. In fact, just by asking a lawyer to represent him or her in a matter, a client impliedly authorizes the lawyer to take action that is reasonable and calculated to advance the client's interest.[11] Express authority and implied authority are both considered "actual" authority.[12] However, occasionally there are meaningful differences between them. In some jurisdictions, certain actions taken by lawyers are not valid unless the lawyers have express rather than implied authority. For example, lawyers may need express authority to settle disputes on behalf of their clients.[13]

---

9. See In re Crocket, 912 P.2d 176 (Kan. 1996) (lawyer suspended for a year, but appeal he filed too late was nevertheless untimely).

10. Inman v. American Home Furniture Placement, 120 F.3d 117, 118 (8th Cir. 1997) (default judgment against defendant affirmed, even if failure to respond to case was caused by lawyer's "personal problems," because "litigants choose counsel at their peril").

11. Restatement (Second) of Agency § 7, comment c (1958); Restatement (Third) of Agency § 2.01, comment b (2d tent. draft 2001).

12. Restatement § 26(1).

13. Geoffrey C. Hazard Jr., Susan P. Koniak & Roger C. Cramton, The Law and Ethics of Lawyering 475 (3d ed., Found. Press 1999). Because of this requirement, lawyers usually insist that settlement agreements be signed by the clients for both sides as well as by their attorneys. Id. In some jurisdictions, however, a lawyer may settle a case based on implied authority. See, e.g., Natare v. Acquatic Renovation Sys., 987 F. Supp. 695 (S.D. Ind. 1997) (applying Indiana law) (lawyer has implied authority to settle a case where, over a period of years, the client authorized the lawyer to participate in settlement negotiations and did not express reservations about a proposed settlement). Even in such jurisdictions, however, actual authority to settle is not implied from the mere fact that a client retains a lawyer to handle the litigation. Koval v. Simon Telelect, 693 N.E.2d 1299 (Ind. 1998).

## 2. Apparent authority

Even if an agent has neither express nor implied authority, she may have "apparent" authority. When a client tells a third party (such as the opposing party in a case) that the client's lawyer has the authority to settle a claim on his behalf, the third party may rely on the lawyer's subsequent actions, even if the client did not actually authorize those actions. Apparent authority also is sometimes found if a principal places an agent in a position that causes a third person reasonably to believe that the principal had given the agent express authority.[14] Some states apply this standard to conclude that merely by hiring lawyers to represent them in litigation, clients authorize their lawyers to settle cases.[15] In a few other states, express authority, not actual or apparent authority, is necessary to settle a case.[16] In most states, however, the mere fact that a lawyer represents a client in litigation does not provide apparent authority to allow the lawyer to *settle* the case.[17] Retaining a lawyer may confer apparent authority for many of the lawyer's other actions, both in transactions and in litigation.

Notice that a *lawyer's* statement to a third party that she is authorized to act does *not* constitute apparent authority. Only the acts or statements of a client (or another principal) can justify reliance by the third party.[18]

> **FOR EXAMPLE:** Suppose a client authorizes her lawyer to negotiate terms for the purchase of a building but privately instructs the lawyer not to enter into an agreement on her behalf. Suppose further that the client informs the seller of the building that her lawyer is acting on her behalf and that the seller should deal with the lawyer, not the client. If the lawyer violates the instructions and agrees that the client will buy the building for $1 million, the client would be held to have bought the building.[19] The seller relied on the lawyer's apparent authority. However, because of the doctrines applicable to clients' control over lawsuits, a court that recognized the lawyer's apparent authority to conclude the building purchase might not hold, based on similar client statements in litigation, that the lawyer had apparent authority to settle a case.

---

14. See Feltman v. Sarbov, 366 A.2d 139 (D.C. 1976), citing Drazin v. Jack Pry, Inc., 154 A.2d 553, 554 (D.C. 1959).

15. In these states, the mere fact that a client retains a lawyer for purposes of litigation imbues the lawyer with apparent authority to settle. Pembroke State Bank v. Warnell, 471 S.E.2d 187 (Ga. 1996); Nelson v. Consumers Power Co., 497 N.W.2d 205 (Mich. App. 1993) (apparent authority sufficient where the lawyer signed a written settlement agreement in court).

16. Pokorny v. Stastny, 186 N.W.2d 284 (Wis. 1971).

17. Restatement § 27, comment a; Koval v. Simon Telelect; 693 N.E.2d 1299 (Ind. 1998).

18. Restatement § 27 and comment c.

19. See Feltman v. Sarbov, 366 A.2d 137 (D.C. 1976) (facts similar to example, but involving a parking lot lease rather than a building sale).

## PROBLEM 4-2 **THE FIRED GUARD**

*This problem is closely based on some events that took place in an East Coast city at the turn of the twenty-first century.*

You work in the county attorney's office of Carlisle County. Your jurisdiction is one that permits lawyers to settle litigation based on express authority but not based on implied authority. It has never ruled on whether a case may be settled based on apparent authority.

Six years ago, the county decided to close one of its prisons, and it terminated the employment of several dozen guards, including Rose Salerno. Salerno had been complaining for months about the working conditions imposed by the Department of Corrections. She believed that she was fired because of sex discrimination and in retaliation for her complaints about work conditions, so she hired Caleb Green as her attorney and sued the county for damages and reinstatement. You were assigned to handle the case for the county.

The discrimination law required Salerno to exhaust her administrative remedies, so four years went by before the case was filed in federal court. At that point, the judge held a pretrial conference, which you, Green, and Salerno attended, during which he ordered both lawyers to meet with a magistrate judge to attempt to reach a settlement. The judge also mandated that "the parties shall either attend the settlement conference or be available by telephone."

All of the lawyers appeared for the settlement conference with the magistrate, but neither Salerno nor the relevant county official was present. About an hour into the settlement conference, based on standing instructions from county officials, you offered to settle the case by having the county pay Salerno $80,000. Green demanded $120,000. Another hour passed, during which the offers changed only slightly. The magistrate sent the attorneys out of the room to talk further. Green, Salerno's lawyer, went to the rest room twice during these breaks. The first time, he returned to the court room and said that his client would still not accept less than $120,000. The second time, he returned with his cell phone in his hand and said that his client would reluctantly accept $100,000 if the county would revise its records, which currently state that Salerno was discharged, to show that she had resigned. You agreed to the plaintiff's proposal, having received advance authority from your office to settle on those terms.

You and Green shook hands on the deal and jointly reported it to the magistrate in the courtroom. A few days later, you wrote up the agreement and sent it to Green. Green called you to report that Salerno refused to sign it. Green insisted that she had agreed to the settlement during a conversation on his cell phone.

The next day you received a letter from Salerno. She wrote that she had never agreed to settle for $100,000. She wrote that she had told

Green all along that she would never agree to any deal that did not include her being reemployed by the county. She says that she was on the phone with him during the settlement conference, that they discussed the various possible terms, and that she agreed as to the amount only if the settlement included an order of reinstatement (not merely a record that she had "resigned"). She reports that she has fired Green and will hire a new lawyer shortly. Meanwhile, she insists, there is no settlement.

You think that Salerno is telling the truth. You suspect that Green agreed to the settlement because he wanted to collect his contingent fee and be done with the case.

County officials regard Salerno as a troublemaker and do not want to rehire her. They do not want her lawsuit to go to trial because she might win reinstatement. You are thinking of making a motion to enforce the settlement agreement. Salerno, through her new counsel, would try to defeat such a motion.

### Questions

**1. Your case.** What arguments support your motion?

**2. Their case.** What arguments can you expect from Salerno's new lawyer?

**3. Prevention.** What might you have done at the time of the settlement conference to avoid having this problem now?

**4. Fairness.** You are pretty sure that Salerno never authorized the settlement that Green agreed to. Is it fair to Salerno for you to try to enforce the agreement? If not, should you do it anyway?

# C. Lawyers' duties of competence, honesty, communication, and diligence

This section explores lawyers' duties to act competently, deal honestly, keep clients informed of the progress of their matters, and perform work diligently in the interests of the client. Lawyers owe other duties to clients as well, such as the duty to protect confidences, the duty to avoid conflicts of interest, and the duty to charge reasonable fees. Some of these other duties are treated in depth elsewhere in this book. The duties discussed in this section are clustered together because they are critically important, interrelated obligations.

## 1. Competence

Earlier in this chapter you reviewed Rule 1.1 on competence, which states: "Competent representation requires the legal knowledge, skill, thoroughness and preparation reasonably necessary for the representation."[20] Comment 2, elaborates:

> Some important legal skills, such as the analysis of precedent, the evaluation of evidence, and legal drafting, are required in all legal problems. Perhaps the most fundamental legal skill consists of determining what kinds of legal problems a situation may involve. . . .

The comments to Rule 1.1 identify various other features of competent lawyering. Lawyers without experience in an area must get training or assistance to enable them to perform competently. If the work is complex or technical, the amount of study or supervision required is greater than if the matter is a simple one. Competent representation is in some part a question of study and training, but competent performance also requires diligence and thoroughness. Comment 5, on "thoroughness and preparation," explains that to handle a matter competently, a lawyer must inquire into and analyze the factual and legal elements of the problem.

Some scholars have pointed out that the definition of competence in the ethics rules offers only "limited guidance."[21] A more rigorous definition of competent lawyering was developed by an ABA task force that explored some of the shortcomings of legal education as preparation for practice. This task force recommended that law school curricula give more attention to the development of lawyering skills and values.[22] The report of the task force, referred to as the MacCrate Report, lists ten lawyering skills and four lawyering values as ones with which "a well-trained generalist should be familiar before assuming ultimate responsibility for a client."[23]

**Ten Fundamental Lawyering Skills**
1. Problem-solving
2. Legal analysis and reasoning
3. Legal research
4. Factual investigation
5. Oral and written communication
6. Counseling
7. Negotiation
8. Litigation and alternative dispute resolution procedures
9. Organization and management of legal work
10. Recognizing and resolving ethical dilemmas[24]

---

20. Rule 1.1.

21. Alexis Anderson, Arlene Kanter & Cindy Slane, Externships and Ethics: A Primer on Confidentiality, Conflicts and Competency Issues in the Field and in the Classroom, 10 Clin. L. Rev. 473 (2004).

22. ABA, Section of Legal Education and Admissions to the Bar, Report of the Task Force on Law Schools and the Profession: Narrowing the Gap (Robert MacCrate ed., 1992) (hereinafter MacCrate Report). Excerpts of the MacCrate Report are available online at http://www.abanet.org/legaled/publications/onlinepubs/maccrate.html (last visited Oct. 18, 2004).

23. Id. at 125.

24. Id. at 138-140. The report also notes that the acquisition of substantive knowledge of the law is important to competent practice.

**Four Fundamental Lawyering Values**

1. As a member of a profession dedicated to the service of clients, a lawyer should be committed to the values of attaining a level of competence in one's own field of practice; maintaining a level of competence in one's own field of practice; [and] representing clients in a competent manner.

2. As a member of a profession that bears special responsibilities for the quality of justice, a lawyer should be committed to the values of: promoting justice, fairness, and morality in one's own daily practice; contributing to the profession's fulfillment of its responsibility to ensure that adequate legal services are provided to those who cannot afford to pay for them; [and] contributing to the profession's fulfillment of its responsibility to enhance the capacity of law and legal institutions to do justice.

3. As a member of a self-governing profession, a lawyer should be committed to the values of: participating in activities designed to improve the profession; assisting in the training and preparation of new lawyers; [and] striving to rid the profession of bias based on race, religion, ethnic origin, gender, sexual orientation, or disability, and to rectify the effects of these biases.

4. As a member of a learned profession, a lawyer should be committed to the values of: seeking out and taking advantage of opportunities to increase his or her knowledge and improve his or her skills; [and] selecting and maintaining employment that will allow the lawyer to develop as a professional and to pursue his or her professional and personal goals.[25]

Other skills are relevant also to competent lawyering. A lawyer who reads well and remembers well will perform better than one who does not. A lawyer who has strong interpersonal skills will perform better than one who does not. A lawyer who is tenacious, diligent, careful, and creative will perform better than one who is not. In other words, all the basic skills that people need to do good work are essential to good lawyering also.[26]

Before you read further, take a minute to assess your own progress in developing these essential skills. You could rate your competency on the MacCrate skills list on a scale of zero to five. Then consider which of those skills are most likely to be important to your performance in whatever professional path you hope to pursue. Finally, think about what steps you can take to fill any gaps in your professional skill development. If you are not in your last semester of law school, you could enroll in a course or two to focus on the development of these skills. If you are about to graduate, you could avail yourself of one of the many skills training programs for lawyers that are sponsored by bar associations, law schools, and other organizations.

When lawyers are charged by disciplinary agencies with lack of competence, they often face other charges as well — neglect of client matters, failure to communicate, and others. Often such cases come to the attention of the

---

25. Id. at 138-140.

26. These and other lawyering skills and methods of developing them are discussed in J. P. Ogilvy, Leah Wortham & Lisa G. Lerman, Learning from Practice: A Professional Development Text for Legal Externs (West 1998); see also Gary Bellow & Beatrice Moulton, The Lawyering Process: Ethics and Professional Responsibility (Found. Press 1981).

disciplinary authorities because of a string of complaints by clients. And in some cases, the lawyer's failure of performance is related to alcohol or drug abuse, depression, or some other serious personal problem. What follows is one such case.

# Matter of Neal

### 20 P.3d 121 (N.M. 2001)

PER CURIAM.

[This is a disciplinary action against a lawyer.]

### [The lawyer's inaction]

Respondent was trial counsel for a defendant convicted of first degree murder, conspiracy to commit murder, and other related crimes. The judgment [was appealed] to this Court.

Rule 12-201(A)(2) NMRA 1999 requires that the notice of appeal be filed within thirty days after the judgment was filed in the district court clerk's office. Respondent failed to file the notice of appeal within the thirty-day period. On August 20, 1999, thirty-one days after the judgment was filed, without having filed a notice of appeal in district court, respondent attempted to file via facsimile a motion for extension of time to file the statement of issues in this Court.

Respondent was contacted by the chief deputy clerk for the New Mexico Supreme Court. Respondent told the clerk he had not filed a notice of appeal because he did not think it was required since the appeal was an automatic appeal. Rule 12-202(A) states that an appeal permitted by law as of right is taken by filing a notice of appeal with the district court clerk within the time allowed by Rule 12-201. The clerk informed respondent that it was necessary for him to fulfill the notice of appeal requirements.

Almost one month later, on September 16, 1999, respondent filed a motion for untimely filing of notice of appeal with the district court clerk. Although the motion was granted the same day, respondent did not file the notice of appeal with the district court clerk until October 4, 1999.

[Another rule] requires the appellant in a criminal case to serve copies of the notice of appeal on the appellate court, the appellate division of the attorney general, the appellate division of the public defender, the trial judge, trial counsel of record for all other parties, and the tape monitor or court reporter who took the record. . . . [Neal sent a copy to the district attorney but not to these other people.]

[Still another rule] requires that, within thirty days of filing the notice of appeal, the appellant shall file a docketing statement if the appeal is before the court of appeals, or a statement of issues if the appeal is before the Supreme Court. Rule 12-208(A) provides that the statement of issues is the duty of trial counsel. After filing the notice of appeal on October 4, 1999, respondent attempted on October 19, 1999, to file a pleading denominated "Docketing

Statement" with the clerk of the Supreme Court. The chief deputy clerk once again contacted respondent and informed him that he must file a "Statement of Issues" not a "Docketing Statement." The clerk specifically advised respondent to read the Rules of Appellate Procedure. . . .

On December 15, 1999, respondent attempted to file a statement of issues without a motion for extension of time, which motion was required because the pleading was more than thirty days overdue. The chief deputy clerk called respondent and informed him that a motion for extension was required because the statement of issues was untimely. Respondent faxed a motion for extension of time to file that same day. Both the motion for extension of time and the statement of issues were filed on December 15, 1999. . . .

[The New Mexico Supreme Court dismissed the appeal of the murder case because the appeal hadn't been filed properly. Neal telephoned the clerk and stated that the public defender was now handling the case. The clerk advised him to file a motion to reinstate the appeal, but Neal didn't do so. Instead, he filed a motion in the district court to ask that the public defender be appointed to handle the appeal, but he didn't send the public defender any of the documents. The public defender eventually got notice of the case from Neal or from the court and took over representation of the defendant. Neal also didn't comply with the rule requiring him to send to the district court a list of the transcript pages that he wanted the appellate court to read. Finally, about six months after the required documents should have been filed, Neal sent the list of pages, and the public defender was able to obtain the statement of issues that Neal had prepared and deliver it to the district court. At that time, the public defender got the appeal reinstated.]

Prior to this case, respondent had never handled a criminal appeal, except to the district court from rulings of the metropolitan court of limited jurisdiction. In response to supplemental inquiries from disciplinary counsel concerning this matter, he stated as follows:

> My understanding was that "automatic appeal" meant just that, an automatic appeal. In retrospect, it would have been better to consult the rule prior to making any assumptions.

### [The punishment]

By reason of his failure to properly pursue his client's appeal, respondent violated Rule 16-101, by failing to provide competent representation to his client. . . .

The disciplinary charges also alleged that significant aggravating factors were present in respondent's case. Respondent engaged in a pattern of misconduct by failing to comply with numerous requirements of the Rules of Appellate Procedure. Respondent committed multiple violations of the Rules of Professional Conduct. Respondent's client was especially vulnerable to respondent's misconduct because the matter at issue concerned a criminal sentence equal to life imprisonment, the client was incarcerated during the time of respondent's misconduct, and the client was without resources sufficient to hire another attorney. All of these factors are recognized by the ABA Standards for Imposing Lawyer Sanctions Section 9.2, and all are present in this case and properly considered in formulating the appropriate disciplinary sanctions.

In addition, the disciplinary charges alleged that respondent had refused to acknowledge the wrongful nature of his conduct, which is another recognized aggravating factor. At a hearing, respondent maintained that he did acknowledge the wrongful nature of his conduct. Nonetheless, his testimony included lengthy recitations of the difficulties he encountered in defending his client, from the very small fee he collected, the withdrawal of co-counsel on the eve of trial, through the completion of the sentencing process. Respondent also testified that he assumed that an automatic appeal would not require the same amount of attention as another appeal, and that he assumed the transcript and record would be automatically prepared. Although respondent may not have thought his recitations evinced a failure to accept responsibility, the hearing committee did. Even respondent's own counsel expressed concern that respondent was still engaging in a certain amount of denial. We share the concerns expressed about respondent's level of cognition and acceptance of his responsibilities and the extent to which he was derelict in discharging them.

Rule 16-101 of the Rules of Professional Responsibility defines competent representation as requiring "the legal knowledge, skill, thoroughness and preparation reasonably necessary for the representation." Respondent's eight years of experience practicing law should have been sufficient for him to know not to operate on his assumptions about the meaning of an automatic appeal, and if it was not, then the wording of Rule 16-101 should have provided him with the necessary guidance. Research, analysis and timeliness are fundamental in the legal profession. No lawyer should approach any task without knowledge of the applicable statutes, court rules, and case law, especially in matters with which one is not intimately familiar. Regardless of how well respondent may have served his client at the trial level, he was completely incompetent in discharging his appellate duties. That the client eventually received the appeal to which he was entitled is in no measure a result of respondent's representation; only the diligence of the Clerk of this Court and her staff, as well as that of the appellate public defender, preserved this appeal. If respondent fails to fully accept how profoundly he failed his client in this appeal, he is unlikely to benefit from the opportunity to learn provided by the discipline being imposed. . . .

In response to the formal disciplinary charges filed against him, respondent alleged in mitigation that he had been diagnosed with depression eight years previously. He stated he had not remained faithful to the treatment because he did not understand that he needed to remain on medication. Respondent also alleged that shortly before the formal disciplinary charges were filed, he had resumed treatment for depression. Respondent's depression cannot be considered a mitigating factor because he failed to demonstrate a prolonged period of rehabilitation, which is the standard for considering a mental health condition as a mitigating factor as set forth in the ABA Standards for Imposing Lawyer Sanctions Section 9.3. . . .

After raising the issue of his previously-diagnosed depression, respondent agreed to undergo a psychological evaluation. The resultant report diagnosed an alcohol abuse issue as well as mental health issues. . . .

[The court suspended Neal from practicing law for two years. However, it deferred the suspension and allowed Neal to keep practicing, provided that he comply with several conditions. To keep practicing, he had to obey all professional responsibility rules, confer with a court-appointed supervising attorney at least once a month, pay for the services of the supervising attorney, refrain from using drugs or alcohol, participate in an alcohol treatment program, allow reports of his progress in the program to be sent to the court's disciplinary counsel, pay for the treatment program, have approximately two years of psychotherapy, submit to and pay for random drug and alcohol screens within eight hours of a request for testing, and pay the costs of the disciplinary proceeding.]

## Questions about *Neal*

**1. Incompetence.** Until 2001, Neal was a successful trial lawyer and former public defender who specialized in criminal defense and the defense of people accused of driving while intoxicated. (A LEXIS search reveals 52 *Albuquerque Journal* stories about his cases.) He had never before handled the appeal of a first degree murder case. He knew that an appeal in a case of this type was "automatic."[27] In an automatic appeal, the defense attorney is required to file various papers, but the court considers the appeal even if the lawyer fails to file the papers on time. Neal told the clerk that he did not file papers in the murder case on time because he did not realize that he was required to do so for an automatic appeal. Does this prove a lack of competence?

**2. Self-defense.** Neal tried to persuade the court that one reason that he made mistakes in this case is that he was being paid only a very small fee. He also mentioned that his co-counsel withdrew on the eve of trial and offered some other extenuating circumstances.

   a. Should lawyers be held to the same standard of performance regardless of whether they are being paid well, poorly, or not at all?

   b. The court was not persuaded by Neal's explanations and regarded his attempt to excuse his conduct as further evidence of his culpability. Was this fair?

**3. Supervision.** The court deferred Neal's suspension from practice and set up an elaborate set of requirements that, if met, could allow Neal to keep

---

27. This is how certain criminal appeals are commonly referred to in New Mexico. See Fritz Thompson, Desnoyers Gets Life Sentence for Killing NMU Student, Albuquerque J., Apr. 21, 2000, at A1 ("Thursday's action is the latest in the southern New Mexico murder case. Desnoyers' defense attorneys, Gary Mitchell and Carmen Garza, said they will prepare for an automatic appeal before the state Supreme Court.").

practicing law. These included getting help in managing his law practice, avoiding drugs or alcohol, getting treatment for depression and alcoholism, and allowing monitoring of his compliance with these conditions. Is it appropriate for courts to become this involved in managing the details of rehabilitation for lawyers who are disciplined?[28]

## PROBLEM 4-3 THE WASHING MACHINE

*The facts of this problem are adapted from a case that Professor Lerman supervised in a law school clinic.*

You are a general practitioner in a small town in your state. A new client, Nasser Kamath, comes to your office because he is being sued by Hallmart, a very reputable chain of retail stores. He had bought a new washing machine on an installment contract. After he had made two of his twelve $60 monthly payments (that is, $120 of the $720), Kamath was laid off from his job and could no longer afford to make payments. The store called him at home several times, saying that his credit record would be spoiled if he did not pay. But he was simply unable to make the third payment, so the store sued him. Kamath can't afford to pay your fee, but you agreed to represent him anyway. Kamath's daughter is on the same soccer team as your daughter, and he's the coach, so you feel you owe him a favor. You thought you could handle this matter without spending a lot of time.

A term in the contract provided that if the buyer missed a payment, the buyer was in "default" and the seller was entitled to sue for the entire remaining balance (in this case, $600 minus a bit of interest that hadn't yet accrued), plus the seller's attorneys' fees. So Hallmart sued for about $600 plus its attorneys' fees.

When he learned about the lawsuit, Kamath called the store and offered to return the washing machine. The store's credit department said that the store had no use for a used machine and that he should pay the money.

A week ago, you filed papers informing Hallmart's lawyer and the court that you are representing Kamath. This morning, Hallmart's lawyer called to ask if your client wanted to set up a "payment plan."

---

28. "Although most jurisdictions treat alcohol abuse as a mitigating factor in disciplinary actions, no uniform national standard exists to explain how or to what degree alcoholism should mitigate a lawyer's incompetence. As a result, there is a great deal of inconsistency among jurisdictions. . . . " Nathaniel S. Currall, The Cirrhosis of the Legal Profession: Alcoholism as an Ethical Violation or Disease within the Profession, 12 Geo. J. Leg. Ethics 739 (1999). The ABA has helped state bars to establish lawyers assistance programs to provide intervention and peer counseling to assist lawyers who have mental health or chemical dependency problems. See ABA Commission on Lawyer Assistance Programs, News, *at* http://www.abanet.org/legalservices/colap/ (last visited Oct. 18, 2004).

The lawyer offered to settle the case for an agreement under which your client would pay $25 per month for 26 more months. Under this plan, your client would pay the store an additional $650. This means he would end up paying a total of $770 for the washing machine ($50 more than under the original contract), but each payment would be much smaller.

You called Kamath. He said that he could probably pay $25 per month, but not $60 per month. He said that the proposed payment plan seems like a good solution.

What should you do?

## 2. Competence in criminal trials

Dissatisfied clients seek recourse against lawyers in various ways. Some complain to their lawyers and object to paying the legal fee. Some complain to bar disciplinary authorities. Some file malpractice suits against their former lawyers. Some clients who were convicted in criminal cases file appeals urging that the conviction should be reversed because the trial lawyer was incompetent. Such a defendant would claim that he was denied the "effective assistance of counsel." The Sixth Amendment requires that a criminal defendant be provided with a lawyer whose work meets at least the minimum standard of being "effective." A state could provide a higher degree of protection to its criminal defendants than the constitutional minimum, but this constitutional right may be claimed in every state regardless of any variation in state law or state ethics rules.

Many judges are very reluctant to overturn a criminal conviction because a different lawyer might have done a better job for a defendant. Therefore, it is unlikely that a defendant can win an ineffective assistance appeal unless his lawyer's performance was really awful. Furthermore, a defendant appealing a conviction must prove not only that the assistance was unusually poor, but also (as in civil malpractice cases) that better representation would have made a difference. The leading case is Strickland v. Washington.

## Strickland v. Washington

466 U.S. 668 (1984)

O'CONNOR, J., delivered the opinion of the court.

### [Mr. Washington's claim]

[Washington committed several crimes, including three gruesome murders. After his accomplices were apprehended, he surrendered. The state appointed William Tunkey, an experienced criminal lawyer, to represent him in a capital case. Against Tunkey's advice, Washington confessed to having committed murder, and he pleaded guilty. Also he agreed to testify against a co-defendant. Thus there was no trial, but Washington was entitled to a hearing on whether he would receive the death penalty or life imprisonment. At the hearing, he had the right to present "mitigation" evidence, including a psychiatric report, to justify a life sentence. Tunkey did not meet with Washington's wife or mother, did not seek out character witnesses, did not obtain a psychiatric evaluation of Washington, and did not introduce evidence about Washington's prior criminal record. Tunkey hoped that the judge would be merciful because Washington had expressed remorse, had stated on the record that he had been under great stress, had no significant criminal record, and had surrendered, confessed, and agreed to testify against a co-defendant. In addition, Tunkey knew that the judge had a reputation for dealing fairly with people who took responsibility for their crimes.]

In the plea colloquy, respondent told the trial judge that, although he had committed a string of burglaries, he had no significant prior criminal record and that at the time of his criminal spree he was under extreme stress caused by his inability to support his family. . . . He also stated, however, that he accepted responsibility for the crimes. . . . The trial judge told respondent that he had "a great deal of respect for people who are willing to step forward and admit their responsibility" but that he was making no statement at all about his likely sentencing decision. . . .

[At the sentencing hearing, however, the judge relied heavily on the presence of "aggravating factors" such as the cruelty of the crimes and the fact that the motive was robbery. He found that Washington was not suffering from extreme mental or emotional disturbance, and he imposed the death penalty. Washington appealed, arguing that his lawyer's assistance had been ineffective.]

He asserted that counsel was ineffective because he failed . . . to request a psychiatric report, to investigate and present character witnesses, [or] to seek a presentence investigation report. . . . Respondent submitted 14 affidavits from friends, neighbors and relatives stating that they would have testified if asked to do so [and two psychological reports] stating that respondent, though not under the influence of extreme mental or emotional disturbance was "chronically frustrated and depressed because of his economic dilemma" at the time of his crimes. . . .

### [The standard for ineffective assistance of counsel]

A convicted defendant's claim that counsel's assistance was so defective as to require reversal of a conviction or death sentence has two components. First, the defendant must show that counsel's performance was deficient. This requires showing that counsel made errors so serious that counsel was not functioning as the "counsel" guaranteed the defendant by the Sixth Amendment. Second, the defendant must show that the deficient performance prejudiced the defense. This requires showing that counsel's errors were so serious as to deprive the defendant of a fair trial, a trial whose result is reliable. Unless a defendant makes both showings, it cannot be said that the conviction or death sentence resulted from a breakdown in the adversary process that renders the result unreliable. . . .

Representation of a criminal defendant entails certain basic duties. Counsel's function is to assist the defendant, and hence counsel owes the client a duty of loyalty, a duty to avoid conflicts of interest. See Cuyler v. Sullivan, [446 U.S.] at 346. From counsel's function as assistant to the defendant derive the overarching duty to advocate the defendant's cause and the more particular duties to consult with the defendant on important decisions and to keep the defendant informed of important developments in the course of the prosecution. Counsel also has a duty to bring to bear such skill and knowledge as will render the trial a reliable adversarial testing process. . . .

Judicial scrutiny of counsel's performance must be highly deferential [to the attorney in question]. . . . The availability of intrusive post-trial inquiry into attorney performance or of detailed guidelines for its evaluation would encourage the proliferation of ineffectiveness challenges. . . . Counsel's performance and even willingness to serve could be adversely affected. . . .

Strategic choices made after less than complete investigation are reasonable precisely to the extent that reasonable professional judgments support the limitations on investigation. In other words, counsel has a duty to make reasonable investigations or to make a reasonable decision that makes particular investigations unnecessary. In any ineffectiveness case, a particular decision not to investigate must be directly assessed for reasonableness in all the circumstances, applying a heavy measure of deference to counsel's judgments. . . .

An error by counsel, even if professionally unreasonable, does not warrant setting aside the judgment of a criminal proceeding if the error has no effect on the judgment. . . . It is not enough for the defendant to show that the errors had some conceivable effect on the outcome of the proceeding. Virtually every act or omission of counsel would meet that test. . . . The defendant must show that there is a reasonable probability that, but for counsel's unprofessional errors, the result of the proceeding would have been different. A reasonable probability is a probability sufficient to undermine confidence in the outcome. . . .

### [Application of the standard to this case]

The conduct of respondent's counsel . . . cannot be found unreasonable. . . . Even assuming the challenged conduct of counsel was unreasonable, respondent suffered insufficient prejudice to warrant setting aside his death sentence. . . . Respondent made a strategic choice to . . . rely as fully as possible on respondent's acceptance of responsibility for his crimes [and on his claim of emotional distress]. . . . The decision not to seek more character or psychological evidence than was already in hand was likewise reasonable. The trial judge's views on the importance of owning up to one's crimes were well known to counsel. . . . Restricting testimony on respondent's character to [the statements during the plea colloquy] ensured that contrary character and psychological evidence and respondent's criminal history, which counsel had successfully moved to exclude [at an earlier stage] would not come in. . . .

With respect to the prejudice component . . . [a psychological report and character witnesses] would barely have altered the sentencing profile presented to the sentencing judge. . . . Indeed, admission of the evidence respondent now offers might even have been harmful to his case: his "rap sheet" would probably have been admitted into evidence, and the psychological reports would have directly contradicted respondent's claim that the mitigating circumstance of extreme emotional disturbance applied to his case. . . .

MARSHALL, J., dissenting:

To tell lawyers and the lower courts that counsel for a criminal defendant must behave "reasonably" and must act like "a reasonably competent attorney," is to tell them almost nothing. In essence, the majority has instructed judges called upon to assess claims of ineffective assistance of counsel to advert to their own intuitions regarding what constitutes "professional" representation, and has discouraged them from trying to develop more detailed standards governing the performance of defense counsel. . . .

I agree that counsel must be afforded "wide latitude" when making "tactical decisions" regarding trial strategy, but many aspects of the job of a criminal defense attorney are more amenable to judicial oversight. For example, much of the work involved in preparing for a trial, applying for bail, conferring with one's client, making timely objections to significant, arguably erroneous rulings of the trial judge, and filing a notice of appeal if there are colorable grounds therefor could profitably be made the subject of uniform standards. . . .

[Also], it seems to me senseless to impose on a defendant whose lawyer has been shown to have been incompetent the burden of demonstrating prejudice. . . . When defense counsel fails to take certain actions, not because he is "compelled" to do so, but because he is incompetent, it is often equally difficult to ascertain the prejudice consequent upon his omissions. . . .

[As for this case], it is undisputed that respondent's trial counsel made virtually no investigation of the possibility of obtaining testimony from respondent's relatives, friends, or former employers pertaining to respondent's character or background. Had counsel done so, he would have found several persons willing and able to testify that, in their experience, respondent was a responsible, nonviolent man, devoted to his family, and active in the affairs of his church. Respondent contends that his lawyer could have and should have used that testimony to "humanize" respondent, to counteract the impression conveyed by the trial that he was little more than a cold-blooded killer. Had this evidence been admitted, respondent argues, his chances of obtaining a life sentence would have been significantly better. Measured against the standards outlined above, respondent's contentions are substantial. Experienced members of the death-penalty bar have long recognized the crucial importance of adducing evidence at a sentencing proceeding that establishes the defendant's social and familial connections.[29] [While the decision not to present such evidence] might have been [a reasonable one] after counsel had fairly assessed the potential strength of the mitigating evidence available to him, counsel's failure to make any significant effort to find out what evidence might be garnered from respondent's relatives and acquaintances surely cannot be described as "reasonable." Counsel's failure to investigate is particularly suspicious in light of his candid admission that respondent's confessions and conduct in the course of the trial gave him a feeling of "hopelessness" regarding the possibility of saving respondent's life. . . .

Florida sentencing judges and the Florida Supreme Court sometimes refuse to impose death sentences in cases "in which, even though statutory mitigating circumstances do not outweigh statutory aggravating circumstances, the addition of nonstatutory mitigating circumstances tips the scales in favor of life imprisonment." Barclay v. Florida, 463 U.S. 939, 964 (1983) (Stevens, J., concurring in judgment). If counsel had investigated the

---

29. [Authors' footnote.] The Court cited Goodpaster, The Trial for Life: Effective Assistance of Counsel in Death Penalty Cases, 58 N.Y.U. L. Rev. 299, 300-303, 334-335 (1983).

availability of mitigating evidence, he might well have decided to present some such material at the hearing. If he had done so, there is a significant chance that respondent would have been given a life sentence. In my view, those possibilities, conjoined with the unreasonableness of counsel's failure to investigate, are more than sufficient to establish a violation of the Sixth Amendment and to entitle respondent to a new sentencing proceeding. I respectfully dissent.

## Questions

**1. Who's right?** Do you agree with the majority or with Justice Marshall as to the standards to be applied and their application to this case? Should Washington have been given another chance to avoid execution by being granted a resentencing hearing at which his new lawyer could present to the sentencing judge some evidence about his character and his psychological state at the time he committed the crimes?

**2. What's going on out there?** If most criminal defense attorneys do an excellent job of investigating the law and facts, a strong degree of deference to the decisions of trial counsel is warranted. If that is the case, the cost, in time and other resources, of holding hearings on ineffective assistance claims and of reversing convictions based on those claims might be disproportionate to the social value of allowing challenges based on poor representation. Try to guess the answers to the following questions. Then compare your guesses with the statistical information in the final footnote of this chapter on page 278.

> a. In the Phoenix metropolitan area, in what percentage of criminal cases do defense lawyers interview all of the prosecution witnesses who testify at the trial?
>
> b. In the Phoenix area, in what percentage of felony cases do defense lawyers interview all of the defense witnesses before engaging in plea negotiations?
>
> c. In what percentage of homicide cases in New York City do defense lawyers do any legal research (for example, for possible motions to suppress confessions or other evidence)?
>
> d. In what percentage of felony cases in New York City do defense lawyers talk to the defendant's family before sentencing to learn about the defendant's character and background and to explore whether the defendant might qualify for a treatment program rather than incarceration?
>
> e. In the five years after the *Strickland* decision, in what percentage of the 702 reported cases did defendants prevail in their claims of ineffective assistance of counsel?

**3. Relationship to standards of professional responsibility.** You are a member of the disciplinary committee of the Florida State Bar. Assume that from his cell, Washington has filed a complaint accusing his lawyer of having violated the state version of Rule 1.1. What discipline, if any, should you impose on the lawyer? Does it matter to you, as it did to the Supreme Court, whether different tactics might have led to a different result?

## 3. Candor and communication

### a. Is it ever okay to lie?

Is lying to another person ever acceptable? Many philosophers and religions urge that lying is wrong.[30] But most people, including lawyers, believe that in some circumstances, lying is justifiable. A few examples:

- **White lies.** One line of a song in the musical *Into the Woods* explains, "Everyone tells tiny lies; what matters, really, is their size."[31] The idea is that some fibs are so small and harmless that they don't matter. Among these are little lies told to avoid embarrassment or to avoid hurting another person's feelings.
- **Lies to protect people.** Suppose you are representing a wife in a divorce, and the husband's attorney gives you copies of some documents in which the husband says some really nasty things about her. These assertions will not have any impact on the divorce settlement. If your client asks what was in the document, can you tell her "nothing you would care about"? Or suppose you learn in confidence from a client's physician that the client is dying, and the physician says that it would harm his patient to learn this fact. If the client asks you whether the doctor said that his disease was terminal, may you lie?[32]
- **Lying to protect your own privacy.** Suppose you have a nosy client who asks intrusive questions about your private life and who won't let you off the hook by your just refusing to answer. He asks, for example,

---

30. St. Augustine and Immanuel Kant take the position that people have a duty always to be truthful; all lying is wrong regardless of whether a particular lie causes any harm. St. Augustine set up a hierarchy of lies, from the least pardonable (those uttered in the teaching of religion) to the most pardonable (those that harmed no one and helped someone), and urged that while all were wrong, the degree of wrong differed. See Sissela Bok, Lying: Moral Choice in Public and Private Life 35-36 (Pantheon 1978). According to Kant, "[t]ruthfulness in statements which cannot be avoided is the formal duty of an individual to everyone, however great may be the disadvantage accruing to himself or to another. . . . Thus the definition of a lie as merely an intentional untruthful declaration to another person does not require the additional condition that it must harm another. . . . For a lie always harms another; if not some other particular man, still it harms mankind generally, for it vitiates the source of law itself." Immanuel Kant, Critique of Practical Reason and Other Writings in Moral Philosophy 346-350 (L.W. Beck trans. & ed., U. Chi. Press 1949), quoted in Bok, at 286.

31. Stephen Sondheim & James Lapine, Maybe They're Magic, Into the Woods (RCA Victor 1987).

32. Comment 7 to Rule 1.4 states that a lawyer may "withhold" a psychiatric diagnosis of a client when an examining psychiatrist indicates that disclosure would harm the client but the comment does not expressly address whether the lawyer may lie about the diagnosis if the client frames a direct question to the lawyer.

"Have you ever slept with one of your clients?" If the true answer is yes, but it's none of your client's business, can you simply say, "No, of course not"?

Although some people believe that one should never ever tell a lie, others conclude that in some of these or similar circumstances, it is permissible to lie. Questions that might be relevant in assessing whether a lie is justifiable include the following.

- Is the subject lied about either trivial or private?
- Is anyone harmed by the lie?
- Is the purpose of the lie to protect someone?
- Does the person lied to have a right to know (or a strong interest in knowing the truth)?
- If there is a reason to tell a lie, can the problem be solved without lying?
- If you tell this lie, will you need to tell other lies to cover up the first one?

As you consider whether lawyers are ever justified in lying or deceiving others, consider also whether lawyers should be guided by the same moral principles that guide other people. Or are there aspects of the lawyer's role that make lying or deception more or less justifiable than it is for nonlawyers?

## b. Lying versus deception: Is there a moral distinction?

Some philosophers say that in evaluating the morality of a statement, the important question is not whether there is a false statement but whether the speaker intends to deceive the other person.[33] If the speaker intends to deceive, an evasive statement that withholds information is arguably morally identical to a false statement. Each accomplishes the same deceptive purpose. But perhaps it is not as bad to deceive another person if one does it without saying anything false or misleading. If the deceiver manages just to keep silent, is the withholding of information immoral? This question is pretty complicated because so much depends on the circumstances. Like lies, some deceptions may be justifiable. In other cases, however, a deception accomplished without making a false statement is just as bad as telling a lie.

FOR EXAMPLE:    Suppose you are representing the wife in a divorce. She fills out a financial statement disclosing her assets, but she confesses to you privately that she has not listed in her assets one bank account where she deposits most of her very substantial consulting fees. If you transmit the financial statement to your opposing counsel without saying a word, you have not told a lie, but you are perpetrating a deception. If your

---

33. Moral philosopher Sissela Bok defines a lie as "any intentionally deceptive message which is stated." She defines deception more broadly, as encompassing "messages meant to mislead others . . . through gesture, through disguise, by means of action or inaction, even through silence." Bok, supra n. 30, at 14.

opposing counsel asks, "Are there any assets not listed on the financial statement?" and you say, "No, they are all listed," have you done anything more morally culpable than you did by simply transmitting the financial statement?

As we explore the ethical rules on deception here and in Chapter 8, you will notice that many rules, including, for example, Rules 3.3 and 4.1, are more categorical in their prohibition on the telling of lies than they are in their prohibition of deceptions accomplished by withholding information. There are many circumstances in which an advocate's role requires withholding information or presenting information selectively or in the best light. Because of this, many lawyers believe that deception is problematic only if it is accomplished by making a false statement. As you study this section of the chapter, consider your own views on this question.

### c. Truth versus truthfulness

Another important distinction in considering questions about dishonesty is the one between "truth" and "truthfulness." Is it dishonest to make a false statement that you believe to be true? We think not, unless you had some reason to know that you might have been mistaken. Similarly, if a lawyer is competent and does diligent research or investigation, she might still miss some information or obtain some incorrect information, which she might then report to her client. But if she is diligent and is honest with her client about what she does learn, she is being truthful even if she makes a mistake.

### d. Honesty and communication under the ethics rules

**Do the ethical rules ever allow lawyers to lie to or deceive their clients?**

The ethics rules explicitly direct lawyers not to lie to tribunals or to persons other than clients.[34] Curiously, the portion of the rules dealing with the "Client-Lawyer Relationship" does not explicitly require lawyers to be honest with their clients. Probably the reason for the failure to impose a specific duty of truthfulness to clients is that most lawyers assume that lawyers will be truthful with clients, and that a lawyer is more likely to deceive someone else on a client's behalf. However, a careful reading of the rules makes it clear that the drafters intended that lawyers should generally be truthful, and this intention extends to clients as well as to others.

Rule 8.4(c) prohibits a lawyer from engaging "in conduct involving dishonesty, fraud, deceit, or misrepresentation." A lie to a client might not amount to "fraud" because the ethics rules limit "fraud" to conduct that is

---

34. Rules 3.3(a) (tribunals) and 4.1 (third persons). Rule 4.1 does not bar lying to clients because clients are not "third" persons. Rules 3.3 and 4.1 are discussed in Chapter 8.

fraudulent under the state's substantive or procedural law.[35] As noted in Chapter 2, however, definitions of fraud vary from state to state and also depend on whether the fraud is being asserted as part of a claim in tort contract or criminal law. Even if a lie is not "fraud," however, it may amount to deceit or misrepresentation and therefore be a ground for professional discipline under Rule 8.4(c).[36]

In addition, Rule 1.4 requires that a lawyer shall provide information to a client about matters that require informed consent, about which a client must make a decision, about the status of a matter, and about matters on which the client has requested information. Perhaps the duty to keep clients informed implies the duty to give accurate rather than false information. Comment 1 notes that "reasonable communication between the lawyer and the client is necessary for the client effectively to participate in the representation." It would be a stretch to think that "reasonable communication" could include lies by lawyers to their clients. On the other hand, Rule 1.4 does not deal with every type of communication between lawyer and client, nor does it require lawyers to communicate every minor event that occurs during the course of a representation.[37]

Whether or not Rule 1.4 prohibits lying to clients, it certainly requires a lawyer to inform clients about important developments in their cases.

## Rule 1.4   Communication

| Rule language* | Authors' explanation |
| --- | --- |
| (a) A lawyer shall:<br><br>(1) promptly **inform the client** of any **decision or circumstance** with respect to which the client's **informed consent**, as defined in Rule 1.0(e), is required by these Rules; | • Requires communication with clients when another rule requires the lawyer to obtain "informed consent."<br>• Example: Another rule prohibits lawyers from representing two clients concurrently, if the clients have adverse interests, but permits the representation if several conditions are met, including the informed consent of both clients.[38] |

*Continued*

---

35. Rule 1.0(d).

36. See Iowa Sup. Ct. Bd. Prof. Ethics & Conduct v. Jones, 606 N.W.2d 5 (Iowa 2000) (lawyer's unintentionally false statement persuading a former client to make a loan to a current client did not amount to "fraud" but resulted in suspension for misrepresentation).

37. Rule 7.1 may also be relevant. It prohibits lawyers from making false or misleading communications about themselves or their services. While Rule 7.1 was drafted with an eye to lawyer advertising, the language of this rule is broad enough to apply to all communications about legal services.

38. Rule 1.7, discussed in Chapter 5.

| Rule language* | Authors' explanation |
|---|---|
| (2) **reasonably consult** with the client **about the means** by which the client's objectives are to be accomplished; | Rule 1.2 gives the lawyer some discretion about the "means" to be used to carry out the representation (as opposed to the "objectives," which clients are entitled to decide). But lawyers must consult with clients about these means. |
| (3) **keep the client reasonably informed** about the status of the matter; | • "Status" includes "significant developments affecting the timing or substance of the representation." Comment 3.<br>• Example: If the court's schedule delays resolution of a case for six months, the lawyer should inform the client. |
| (4) promptly **comply with reasonable requests** for information; and | • If the lawyer cannot respond promptly, he should explain when a response may be expected. Comment 4.<br>• Client telephone calls "should be promptly returned or acknowledged." Comment 4. |
| (5) **consult** with the client about any relevant **limitation on the lawyer's conduct** when the lawyer knows that the client expects **assistance not permitted** by the Rules of Professional Conduct or other law. | Example: If client asks lawyer to claim a tax deduction that the client is not entitled to claim, the lawyer should explain that he cannot do that. |
| (b) A lawyer shall **explain a matter to the extent reasonably necessary** to permit the client to make **informed decisions** regarding the representation. | The lawyer should give the client enough information "to participate intelligently" in decisions about objectives and means. But a lawyer "ordinarily will not be expected to describe trial or negotiation strategy in detail." Comment 5. |

*All emphasis added.

## e. Civil liability for dishonesty to clients

The prohibition on lying to clients is not limited to exhortations that are stated or implied in the ethical rules. A client injured by a dishonest lawyer may sue the lawyer in tort for fraud or for breach of the lawyer's fiduciary responsibilities to the client. To fulfill his fiduciary duties to a client, a lawyer must

> comply with obligations concerning the client's confidences and property, avoid impermissible conflicting interests, deal honestly with the client, and not employ advantages arising from the client-lawyer relationship in a manner adverse to the client.[39]

---

39. Restatement § 16(3). Restatement § 49, comment b, explains that the duties specified in the quoted section constitute a lawyer's fiduciary duties to a client.

Breach of fiduciary duty, in the context of a lawyer-client relationship, is the lawyer's failure to act consistently with the trust that a client reposes in a lawyer because the lawyer has special skills and knowledge. Professors Ray Anderson and Walter Steele explain the fiduciary nature of the lawyer-client relationship as follows:[40]

> Although definitions of an attorney's fiduciary duty to her client abound, they are framed in quite general terms. The following is typical: "[T]he relationship between attorney and client has been described as one of uberrima fides, which means, 'most abundant good faith,' requiring absolute and perfect candor, openness and honesty, and the absence of any concealment or deception."[41] Fiduciary obligation is shaped by the discretionary control that an attorney usually has over a significant aspect of the client's life or assets, and by the fact that very often the interests of the lawyer are not always the same as, and may be in conflict with, those of the client. One court explained the special nature of a relationship that gives rise to fiduciary obligation in this way:
>
> > There is no invariable rule which determines the existence of a fiduciary relationship, but it is manifest in all the decisions that there must be not only confidence of the one in the other, but there must exist a certain inequality, dependence, weakness of age, of mental strength, business intelligence, knowledge of the facts involved, or other conditions, giving to one advantage over the other.[42]

Most cases of breach of fiduciary duty result from disloyalty (for example, undisclosed conflicts of interest), which are treated as "constructive frauds," but the tort can result from actual fraud as well. For example, a male lawyer representing a female client in a divorce told her that he wanted to have a sexual relationship with her and stated that he was divorced. In response to her request, he told her that he was willing to have a monogamous relationship with her. Later, he conceded that he was only separated, not divorced. The client then called her lawyer's wife and learned that the lawyer had been married for 20 years, had been living with his wife the entire time, and was still living with her. The court held that client's complaint stated a valid claim for breach of fiduciary duty.[43] Similarly, an attorney who "willfully and deliberately lied to, misled, and stole from his clients," could be sued for punitive as well as compensatory damages,[44] although punitive damages are not available for the ordinary negligence-based tort of malpractice.

---

40. Ray Ryden Anderson & Walter W. Steele Jr., Fiduciary Duty, Tort, and Contract: A Primer on the Legal Malpractice Puzzle, 47 SMU L. Rev. 235 (1994).

41. [Article's footnote 26.] Perez v. Kirk & Carrigan, 822 S.W.2d 261, 265 (Tex. App. — Corpus Christi 1991, writ denied).

42. [Article's citation.] Garrett v. BankWest, 459 N.W.2d 833, 838 (quoting Yuster v. Keefe, 90 N.E. 920 (Ind. App. 1910)).

43. Walter v. Stewart, 67 P.3d 1042 (Utah App. 2003).

44. Anand v. Allison, 55 Va. Cir. 261 (2001).

## PROBLEM 4-4  **LYING TO CLIENTS**

*Professor Lerman interviewed 20 lawyers to learn whether and when they deceived their clients. Many of the stories they told were about billing practices, which are discussed in Chapter 7. But her subjects reported that several other types of client deception were fairly common. Some examples are listed below.*

As we explained above, Rule 8.4(c) prohibits lawyers from engaging in any "dishonesty, fraud, deceit and misrepresentation" in relation to clients and everyone else. But is all deception of clients a breach of the ethical rules?

Which, if any, of the following examples do you think are ethically permissible? Specifically, consider whether each (a) involves wrongful conduct, (b) violates the disciplinary rules, (c) can reasonably be justified, and (d) would be acceptable conduct if engaged in by nonlawyers.

**Exaggerating expertise.** One law firm partner told a prospective client that he was familiar with a field in which he actually had no experience. He knew that others in the firm did have the relevant expertise, but he felt he had to claim that he had this knowledge. He thought that the client would hire the firm only if he promised to work on the matter.[45]

**Lowballing.** One personal injury lawyer explained that in talking to a new client, he often underestimates the value of the case so that the eventual settlement will look good. He said, "Clients have misconceptions from the newspapers. They think they won the lottery when they get hurt. ... I understate what is likely. ... If I tell them [honestly] what I think the case is worth, then they think they got what was coming to them [and that I didn't do any work to justify my fee]."[46]

**"I never reviewed this document."** Sometimes lawyers are asked to sign off on documents or arrangements that are illegal or dishonest. Especially for an in-house corporate lawyer, there may be pressure to give the desired answer. One lawyer, asked to review some deceptive advertising copy, claimed never to have seen it to avoid either approving it (which he couldn't) or disapproving it (which could have had adverse consequences for him). He said, "It just seems normal in a corporation that when the shit hits the fan everybody ducks. ... When something goes wrong, nobody ever saw the document and nobody ever approved it."[47]

**Who did the work?** Several lawyers reported that they wrote memos or other documents that were sent to a client or elsewhere under the names of other lawyers besides the drafters. Sometimes this was said to

---

45. Lisa G. Lerman, Lying to Clients, 138 U. Penn. L. Rev. 659, 722 n. 261 (1990).
46. Id. at 734.
47. Id. at 727.

reflect who was "taking responsibility" for the contents of the document, but in some cases the objective was to give clients the impression that a senior lawyer had done work that in fact had been done by a junior lawyer. In some cases the concern was not to let the client know that more than one or two lawyers worked on the matter.[48]

**Covering up mistakes.** One lawyer missed a deadline on an answer to a motion. He filed and argued for an extension of time and won but did not report any of these events to the client. He explained: "If you tell the client, the client will panic, and might fire you. . . . In a divorce case, the client might go off the deep end. . . . Half of the job is keeping [an] agitated clientele happy."[49] Maybe it is acceptable not to tell the client about a mistake like this one if the client doesn't ask. (No harm, no foul?) But what if the client asked whether the lawyer had answered the motion on time?

**Blaming others for mistakes.** One lawyer sent a package to a client and inadvertently included a document intended for someone else. The client called and said, "Did you really want to send me this?" The lawyer's response was (more or less), "It's so hard to get good help these days," implying (falsely) that his secretary had made the error.[50]

## 4. Diligence

One fundamental duty of lawyers toward clients is to do the work that they have been hired to do, and to do it without undue delay. Rule 1.3 puts it this way: "A lawyer shall act with reasonable diligence and promptness in representing a client." Many disciplinary cases include charges that lawyers have neglected client matters — they may have failed to return phone calls or to file court papers on time. These are charged as violations of this rule. Comment 1 states that a lawyer should pursue a matter for a client despite opposition or personal inconvenience and take "whatever measures are required" to vindicate a client's cause. The lawyer must act "with zeal in advocacy upon the client's behalf." Comment 3 notes that "perhaps no professional shortcoming is more widely resented than procrastination."

The Model Code of Professional Responsibility (which preceded the Model Rules) included a canon[51] stating that a lawyer should represent a client "zealously within the bounds of the law."[52] This exhortation was dropped from the

---

48. Id. at 730-732.
49. Id. at 728.
50. Id.
51. "Canons" were "statements of axiomatic norms, expressing in general terms the standards of professional conduct expected of lawyers."
52. Model Code Prof. Resp. Canon 7 (as amended 1980).

Model Rules and most of the state rules because of a concern that it encouraged unethical behavior.[53] Even though the Model Code directed lawyers to treat opponents and opposing counsel with courtesy and consideration,[54] some lawyers used and still use the requirement of zealous advocacy to justify pursuing every possible argument or advantage in litigation. These "scorched earth" litigation tactics dragged out lawsuits, ran up costs, and contributed to the negative public opinion about lawyers. The Model Rules replaced the requirement of zeal with one of "diligence" and demoted the language on zeal to the comments.

The present formulation of the comment reflects ambivalence about aggressive lawyering. Comment 1 urges zealous advocacy, but it states that a lawyer is "not bound . . . to press for every advantage that might be realized." It says that the rule does not "require" the use of offensive tactics or "preclude" a lawyer from treating all persons with courtesy and respect. (This locution is really peculiar. It would make more sense for the comment to *prohibit* offensive tactics and *require* respectful treatment.)

The opposite of diligent representation is total neglect of clients' cases. Any search of recent lawyer disciplinary decisions turns up examples in which lawyers ignored their clients' cases. In some of these decisions, the lawyer had never filed the case, and the statute of limitations had passed. In others, the lawyer had filed a case but allowed it to languish. Often, neglect is caused or compounded by substance abuse, as in *Matter of Neal*, discussed above.

Lawyers are responsible for paying attention to all matters for which they accept responsibility by virtue of making agreements with clients or filing appearances with courts. In cases they initiate, they are not excused from the duty of diligence if they leave a law firm, unless they formally withdraw from representation.

FOR EXAMPLE: In one case, a client hired a firm to bring an employment discrimination case. One of the firm's partners signed the complaint as an accommodation to his partner who was actually handling the case, but he never met the client or worked on the case. The partner supposedly handling the case, to whom all papers were routed by the firm's secretaries, neglected the case, and unbeknownst to the partner who signed the complaint, it was dismissed. The partner eventually left the firm. Years later, he was formally (though privately) reprimanded for having neglected the case, for which he had responsibility because he'd signed the complaint.[55]

---

53. Some jurisdictions retain the requirement of zealous representation in their rules. D.C. Rule 1.3, for example, states that "a lawyer shall represent a client zealously and diligently within the bounds of the law." Massachusetts Rule 1.3 provides that a lawyer shall act with reasonable diligence and promptness but adds that the lawyer "should represent a client zealously within the bounds of the law."

54. Model Code Prof. Resp. DR 7-101(A)(1) (as amended through 1980).

55. Matter of Anonymous, 724 N.E.2d 1101 (Ind. 2000).

## 5. Contractual duties

In addition to duties imposed by the law (such as the rules of professional responsibility and tort law), lawyers undertake contractual duties to their clients. Some of these set more demanding standards of performance than those required by the rules. For example, Rule 1.4 requires that a lawyer keep a client "reasonably informed," but a lawyer and client might agree that the lawyer would give the client weekly reports. Similarly, Rule 1.5 requires that fees be "reasonable" and that a lawyer should inform a client as to the basis on which the fee will be determined. By contract, however, a lawyer may agree to provide detailed billing statements on a specified schedule. If a lawyer violates duties that are imposed only by contract, the lawyer may be subject to discipline for those contractual violations.[56]

# D. Who calls the shots?

## 1. The competent adult client

Which decisions may a lawyer make without consulting a client, and which decisions require client consultation? To resolve a legal matter, whether in court or privately, a lawyer often must make hundreds of decisions. They range in significance from the obviously momentous (for example, the decision whether to file suit or to sign a contract) to the apparently trivial (such as whether, in order to seek an extension of time within which to file a brief, the lawyer should telephone opposing counsel, write a letter, or send a fax). Even apparently unimportant choices can have a significant impact on the outcome of a case. For example, a lawyer asking for an extension often telephones opposing counsel rather than writing a letter. This saves time, but if later on there is a dispute about whether the opposing counsel agreed to the extension of time, there may be no written record of the conversation. Also a phone call opens the door for opposing counsel to make a counter-request (perhaps for information about the case) and to negotiate about both requests. In either case, a small decision could have substantive consequences.

Suppose a lawyer consults a client about a particular decision and they then disagree about what should be done. Who gets to call the shots? Does it depend on what the issue is?

Because a lawyer is his client's agent, one might argue that *all* decisions should be a matter of consultation and ultimately should be left to the client. However, this is impractical. Some decisions, such as the decision whether to make an objection to a question during a hearing, must be made instantly.

---

56. Restatement § 16, comment f. The cases cited by the Restatement impose discipline for violations of Model Code DR 7-101 (an earlier version of Rule 1.3).

In addition, legal work involves so many decisions that for the client to be involved in all of them, the client would practically have to live in the lawyer's office while the lawyer was working on the case.[57]

On the other hand, lawyers must consult with clients about some decisions about how to proceed in the case. Some decisions that lawyers make have profound consequences for clients. Also agency law imputes lawyers' decisions to clients, so a client could face liability for a decision made by his lawyer. Rule 1.2 offers guidance on which decisions a lawyer must make after consultation with the client. The standard is necessarily somewhat vague because of the enormous variety of types of decisions that lawyers and clients make during the course of representation.

### Rule 1.2   Scope of Representation and Allocation of Authority Between Client and Lawyer

| Language of rule | Authors' explanation |
|---|---|
| (a) Subject to paragraphs (c) and (d), a lawyer shall abide by a **client's decisions** concerning the **objectives** of representation and, as required by Rule 1.4, **shall consult** with the client as to the **means** by which they are to be pursued. A lawyer may take such action on behalf of the client as is impliedly authorized to carry out the representation. **A lawyer shall abide by a client's decision whether to settle** a matter. In a **criminal** case, the lawyer shall abide by the **client's decision**, after consultation with the lawyer, as to a **plea to be entered**, whether to **waive jury trial** and whether the **client will testify.** | • Client decides objectives of representation.<br>• Lawyer must consult client as to means used to pursue objectives.<br>• Civil case: Client decides whether to settle.<br>• Criminal case: Client decides whether<br>—to plead guilty,<br>—to waive jury trial,<br>—to testify. |
| (b) A lawyer's **representation** of a client, including representation by appointment, does **not constitute an endorsement** of the client's political, economic, social or moral views or activities. | Example: A lawyer might represent the American Nazi Party even if he thought its goals were objectionable. |
| (c) A lawyer may **limit the scope of the representation** if the limitation is reasonable under the circumstances and the client gives informed consent. | A lawyer and a client may agree that the lawyer will provide less than the full range of services. The client may prefer this arrangement to reduce costs or for other reasons. |

*Continued*

---

57. Many published descriptions of civil litigation capture the quality of the constant decision making in which lawyers engage. See, e.g., Jonathan Harr, A Civil Action (Random House 1995).

| Language of rule | Authors' explanation |
|---|---|
| (d) A lawyer **shall not counsel a client to engage, or assist a client, in conduct that the lawyer knows is criminal or fraudulent,** but a lawyer may discuss the legal consequences of any proposed course of conduct with a client and may counsel or assist a client to make a good faith effort to determine the validity, scope, meaning or application of the law. | Although placed in a rule about the scope of the lawyer's representation, this provision bars lawyers from advising or assisting clients in illegal or fraudulent activity.[58] |

Both Rule 1.2 and the communication requirements of Rule 1.4, discussed above, allocate decision making between lawyers and clients. A lawyer must keep the client "reasonably" informed about the "status" of a matter.[59] The lawyer must also explain the work to the extent "reasonably necessary" to permit the client to make "informed decisions" regarding the representation.[60] Once consulted and informed, the client has the right to make decisions concerning the "objectives" of the representation and the explicit right to make four particular decisions: in a civil dispute, to settle or refuse to settle; and in a criminal case, to decide on the plea to be entered, whether to waive a jury trial, and whether to testify.[61]

Rule 1.2 does not define "objectives." Nor does Rule 1.2 say much about what decisions the lawyer may make, except the obvious point that the lawyer may take actions that are "impliedly authorized." The rule does not explain what types of decisions a client impliedly authorizes the lawyer to make. Comment 2 states that "clients normally defer to the special knowledge and skill of their lawyer with respect to the means to be used to accomplish their objectives, particularly with respect to technical, legal, and tactical matters." The Comment explains also that lawyers usually defer to clients with respect to "questions such as the expense to be incurred and concern for third persons who might be adversely affected." But, when lawyers and clients disagree about the means to be employed, "the rule does not prescribe how such disagreements are to be resolved."

The Restatement provides more guidance than the ethics rules. It states that except for decisions reserved for clients and in the absence of an agreement on these matters, a lawyer may take "any lawful measure within the scope of representation that is reasonably calculated to advance a client's objective."[62] For example, the lawyer may decide whether

- to move to dismiss a complaint and what discovery to pursue or resist,
- to accommodate reasonable requests of opposing counsel,

---

58. See the discussion in connection with the problem on Reese's Leases in Chapter 2.
59. Rule 1.4(a)(3).
60. Rule 1.4(b).
61. Rule 1.2(a).
62. Restatement § 21, comment e.

■ to object or waive objections to questions during hearings, or
■ to decide what questions to ask a witness.[63]

The Restatement suggests that unless a lawyer and client have agreed otherwise, the lawyer, not the client, should make decisions that "involve technical legal and strategic considerations difficult for a client to assess."[64]

Both the ethics rules and the Restatement leave unanswered many questions about what lawyers can do in the absence of specific authorization from their clients or in the face of specific opposition from their clients. May a lawyer transfer a case to another lawyer in his law firm? Although a lawyer may not settle a case without the client's permission, may she make a settlement offer to see how the other side responds? If she does this, must she disclose that she has not yet discussed the offer with the client? May a lawyer decide without consulting a client or over a client's objection to waive a technical defense or a jury trial in a civil case?

May a lawyer decline to press a weak legal argument that he thinks will not prevail and that he thinks will signal the court that his whole case is very weak? The following case explores this issue. As you have seen in other cases, when the issue arises in a criminal context, the ordinary issues of legal ethics are overlaid with a set of issues relating to the constitutional rights of criminal defendants.

## Jones v. Barnes

463 U.S. 745 (1983)

Chief Justice BURGER delivered the opinion of the Court.
We granted certiorari to consider whether defense counsel assigned to prosecute an appeal from a criminal conviction has a constitutional duty to raise every nonfrivolous issue requested by the defendant.

### [The conviction]

... In 1976, Richard Butts was robbed at knifepoint by four men in the lobby of an apartment building; he was badly beaten and his watch and money were taken. Butts informed a Housing Authority detective that he recognized one of his assailants as a person known to him as "Froggy," and gave a physical description of the person to the detective. The following day the detective arrested respondent David Barnes, who is known as "Froggy." Respondent was charged with first- and second-degree robbery, second-degree assault, and third-degree larceny. The prosecution rested primarily upon Butts' testimony and his identification of respondent. During cross-examination, defense counsel asked Butts whether he had ever undergone psychiatric treatment; however, no offer of proof was made on the substance or relevance of the

---

63. Id.
64. Id.

question after the trial judge sua sponte instructed Butts not to answer. At the close of trial, the trial judge declined to give an instruction on accessorial liability requested by the defense. The jury convicted respondent of first- and second-degree robbery and second-degree assault.

## [The appeal]

The Appellate Division [New York's appellate court] assigned Michael Melinger to represent respondent on appeal. Respondent sent Melinger a letter listing several claims that he felt should be raised. Included were claims that Butts' identification testimony should have been suppressed, that the trial judge improperly excluded psychiatric evidence, and that respondent's trial counsel was ineffective. Respondent also enclosed a copy of a pro se brief he had written. In a return letter, Melinger accepted some but rejected most of the suggested claims, stating that they would not aid respondent in obtaining a new trial and that they could not be raised on appeal because they were not based on evidence in the record. Melinger then listed seven potential claims of error that he was considering including in his brief, and invited respondent's "reflections and suggestions" with regard to those seven issues. The record does not reveal any response to this letter.

Melinger's brief to the Appellate Division concentrated on three of the seven points he had raised in his letter to respondent: improper exclusion of psychiatric evidence, failure to suppress Butts' identification testimony, and improper cross-examination of respondent by the trial judge. In addition, Melinger submitted respondent's own pro se brief. Thereafter, respondent filed two more pro se briefs, raising three more of the seven issues Melinger had identified.

At oral argument, Melinger argued the three points presented in his own brief, but not the arguments raised in the pro se briefs. . . . [Barnes' conviction was affirmed.] . . .

## [Barnes' complaint about his appellate lawyer's conduct]

On August 8, 1978, respondent filed a pro se petition for a writ of habeas corpus. . . . Respondent raised five claims of error, including ineffective assistance of trial counsel. . . . Respondent [later added a] claim of ineffective assistance by appellate counsel. The District Court . . . dismissed the petition, holding that the record gave no support to the claim of ineffective assistance of appellate counsel. . . . The District Court concluded: "It is not required that an attorney argue every conceivable issue on appeal, especially when some may be without merit. Indeed, it is his professional duty to choose among potential issues, according to his judgment as to their merit and his tactical approach." . . . A divided panel of the Court of Appeals reversed. . . . Laying down a new standard, the majority held that when "the appellant requests that [his attorney] raise additional colorable points [on appeal], counsel must argue the additional points to the full extent of his professional ability." . . . In the view of the majority, this conclusion followed from Anders v. California, 386 U.S. 738 (1967). In *Anders*, this Court held that an appointed attorney must advocate his client's cause vigorously and may not withdraw from a nonfrivolous appeal. The Court of Appeals majority held that, since *Anders* bars counsel from abandoning a nonfrivolous appeal, it also bars counsel from abandoning a nonfrivolous issue on appeal. . . .

The court concluded that Melinger had not met the above standard in that he had failed to press at least two nonfrivolous claims: the trial judge's failure to instruct on accessory liability and ineffective assistance of trial counsel. The fact that these issues had been raised in respondent's own pro se briefs did not cure the error, since "[a] pro se brief is no substitute for the advocacy of experienced counsel." . . . We reverse. . . .

### [Why lawyers should decide which issues to argue on appeal]

There is, of course, no constitutional right to an appeal, but . . . the Court [has] held that if an appeal is open to those who can pay for it, an appeal must be provided for an indigent. It is also recognized that the accused has the ultimate authority to make certain fundamental decisions regarding the case, as to whether to plead guilty, waive a jury, testify in his or her own behalf, or take an appeal. . . . In addition, we have held that, with some limitations, a defendant may elect to act as his or her own advocate, Faretta v. California, 422 U.S. 806 (1975). Neither *Anders* nor any other decision of this Court suggests, however, that the indigent defendant has a constitutional right to compel appointed counsel to press nonfrivolous points requested by the client, if counsel, as a matter of professional judgment, decides not to present those points. . . . This Court, in holding that a state must provide counsel for an indigent appellant on his first appeal as of right, recognized the superior ability of trained counsel in the "examination into the record, research of the law, and marshaling of arguments on [the appellant's] behalf." . . . Yet by promulgating a per se rule that the client, not the professional advocate, must be allowed to decide what issues are to be pressed, the Court of Appeals seriously undermines the ability of counsel to present the client's case in accord with counsel's professional evaluation.

Experienced advocates since time beyond memory have emphasized the importance of winnowing out weaker arguments on appeal and focusing on one central issue if possible, or at most on a few key issues. Justice Jackson, after observing appellate advocates for many years, stated: "One of the first tests of a discriminating advocate is to select the question, or questions, that he will present orally. Legal contentions, like the currency, depreciate through overissue. The mind of an appellate judge is habitually receptive to the suggestion that a lower court committed an error. But receptiveness declines as the number of assigned errors increases. Multiplicity hints at lack of confidence in any one. . . . [Experience] on the bench convinces me that multiplying assignments of error will dilute and weaken a good case and will not save a bad one." Jackson, Advocacy Before the United States Supreme Court, 25 Temple L.Q. 115, 119 (1951). Justice Jackson's observation echoes the advice of countless advocates before him and since. An authoritative work on appellate practice observes: "Most cases present only one, two, or three significant questions. . . . Usually, . . . if you cannot win on a few major points, the others are not likely to help, and to attempt to deal with a great many in the limited number of pages allowed for briefs will mean that none may receive adequate attention. The effect of adding weak arguments will be to dilute the force of the stronger ones." R. Stern, Appellate Practice in the United States 266 (1981). . . .

There can hardly be any question about the importance of having the appellate advocate examine the record with a view to selecting the most promising issues for review. This has assumed a greater importance in an era when oral argument is strictly limited in most courts — often to as little as 15 minutes — and when page limits on briefs are widely imposed. . . . [65] Even in a court that imposes no time or page limits, however, the new per se rule laid down by the Court of Appeals is contrary to all experience and logic. A brief that raises every colorable issue runs the risk of burying good arguments — those that, in the words of the great advocate John W. Davis, "go for the jugular." Davis, The Argument of an Appeal, 26 A.B.A.J. 895, 897 (1940)[66] — in a verbal mound made up of strong and weak contentions. . . . [Except for decisions allocated to the client in the ethical rules,] an attorney's duty is to take professional responsibility for the conduct of the case, after consulting with his client. . . .

*Anders* recognized that the role of the advocate "requires that he support his client's appeal to the best of his ability." Here the appointed counsel did just that. . . . Reversed.

Justice BLACKMUN, concurring.

As an ethical matter, an attorney should argue on appeal all nonfrivolous claims upon which his client insists. Whether or not one agrees with the Court's view of legal strategy, it seems to me that the lawyer, after giving his client his best opinion as to the course most likely to succeed, should acquiesce in the client's choice of which nonfrivolous claims to pursue. . . .

However, . . . my view . . . of the ideal allocation of decisionmaking authority between client and lawyer . . . [does not assume] constitutional status where counsel's performance is "within the range of competence demanded of attorneys in criminal cases," McMann v. Richardson, 397 U.S. 759, 771 (1970), and

---

65. [Court's footnote 6.] [Under the ABA's Model Rules] with the exception of [three] specified fundamental decisions, an attorney's duty is to take professional responsibility for the conduct of the case, after consulting with his client.

66. [Authors' footnote.] John W. Davis is famous for, among other things, having argued South Carolina's case (against desegregation) in Brown v. Board of Education. See Anthony G. Amsterdam, Telling Stories and Stories About Them, 1 Clin. L. Rev. 9 (1994). He was the Democratic Party's nominee for President in 1924.

"[assures] the indigent defendant an adequate opportunity to present his claims fairly in the context of the State's appellate process," Ross v. Moffitt, 417 U.S. 600, 616 (1974). I agree that both these requirements were met here. . . .

Justices BRENNAN and MARSHALL, dissenting. . . .
The Sixth Amendment provides that "[in] all criminal prosecutions, the accused shall enjoy the right . . . to have the *Assistance* of Counsel for his defence" (emphasis added). I find myself in fundamental disagreement with the Court over what a right to "the assistance of counsel" means. The import of words like "assistance" and "counsel" seems inconsistent with a regime under which counsel appointed by the State to represent a criminal defendant can refuse to raise issues with arguable merit on appeal when his client, after hearing his assessment of the case and his advice, has directed him to raise them. . . .

It is undeniable that in most criminal prosecutions defendants could better defend with counsel's guidance than by their own unskilled efforts. But where the defendant will not voluntarily accept representation by counsel, the potential advantage of a lawyer's training and experience can be realized, if at all, only imperfectly. To force a lawyer on a defendant can only lead him to believe that the law contrives against him. . . . Personal liberties are not rooted in the law of averages. The right to defend is personal. The defendant, and not his lawyer or the State, will bear the personal consequences of a conviction. It is the defendant, therefore, who must be free personally to decide whether in his particular case counsel is to his advantage. And although he may conduct his own defense ultimately to his own detriment, his choice must be honored out of "that respect for the individual which is the lifeblood of the law." Illinois v. Allen, 397 U.S. 337, 350-351 (Brennan, J., concurring). . . .

From the standpoint of effective administration of justice, the need to confer decisive authority on the attorney is paramount with regard to the hundreds of decisions that must be made quickly in the course of a trial. Decisions regarding which issues to press on appeal, in contrast, can and should be made more deliberately, in the course of deciding whether to appeal at all. . . .

The Court argues that good appellate advocacy demands selectivity among arguments. That is certainly true — the Court's advice is good. It ought to be taken to heart by every lawyer called upon to argue an appeal in this or any other court, and by his client. . . . The Constitution, however, does not require clients to be wise, and other policies should be weighed in the balance as well.

It is no secret that indigent clients often mistrust the lawyers appointed to represent them.[67] See generally Burt, Conflict and Trust Between Attorney and Client, 69 Geo. L.J. 1015 (1981). There are many reasons for this, some perhaps unavoidable even under perfect conditions — differences in

---

67. [Authors' footnote.] For a discussion of client mistrust of lawyers in civil cases, see Gerald P. Lopez, The Work We Know So Little About, 42 Stan. L. Rev. 1 (1989).

education, disposition, and socio-economic class — and some that should (but may not always) be zealously avoided. A lawyer and his client do not always have the same interests. Even with paying clients, a lawyer may have a strong interest in having judges and prosecutors think well of him, and, if he is working for a flat fee — a common arrangement for criminal defense attorneys — or if his fees for court appointments are lower than he would receive for other work, he has an obvious financial incentive to conclude cases on his criminal docket swiftly. . . . A constitutional rule that encourages lawyers to disregard their clients' wishes without compelling need can only exacerbate the clients' suspicion of their lawyers. . . . I am not willing to risk deepening the mistrust between clients and lawyers in all cases to ensure optimal presentation for that fraction of a handful in which presentation might really affect the result reached by the court of appeals.

Finally, today's ruling denigrates the values of individual autonomy and dignity central to many constitutional rights, especially those Fifth and Sixth Amendment rights that come into play in the criminal process. . . .

Until his conviction becomes final and he has had an opportunity to appeal, any restrictions on [a defendant's] individual autonomy and dignity should be limited to the minimum necessary to vindicate the State's interest in a speedy, effective prosecution. The role of the defense lawyer should be above all to function as the instrument and defender of the client's autonomy and dignity in all phases of the criminal process. . . . The Court subtly but unmistakably adopts a different conception of the defense lawyer's role — he need do nothing beyond what the State, not his client, considers most important. In many ways, having a lawyer becomes one of the many indignities visited upon someone who has the ill fortune to run afoul of the criminal justice system. I cannot accept the notion that lawyers are one of the punishments a person receives merely for being accused of a crime. . . .

## Notes and Questions about Jones v. Barnes

**1. What got settled?** Did Jones v. Barnes settle the question of whether lawyers should let their clients decide which issues to raise?

**2. What would you do?** What do you think of Justice Brennan's view that since clients bear the consequences of lawyers' decisions, lawyers should defer to their clients' judgments? If you are appointed to represent a criminal defendant, should you follow your client's guidance in raising issues (at trial or on appeal), against your better judgment and your advice to your client?

**3. A wealthy client.** Suppose you are representing a really wealthy criminal defendant — someone like Martha Stewart, perhaps. Might you be more deferential to the wishes of such a well-heeled client? If so, why?

**4. Paid representation.** In principle, if the defendant can pay, he could fire you and get a new attorney. In practice, that option may not really be available. If the client has already given you a retainer of some thousands of dollars, the client may not have enough money to start over again with a new lawyer. Even if the client has the money, it is often impractical to change lawyers in the middle of a case because of the time required for another lawyer to become familiar with the matter. The court may not be willing to delay the case if the defendant changes lawyers. Does this suggest that a criminal defense lawyer should be very deferential to a client regardless of his financial resources?

**5. Civil cases.** The consequence of losing a civil case does not include loss of liberty, but a plaintiff might face loss of compensation for a serious injury. A defendant might face extensive monetary liability or other consequences. Given this, perhaps a lawyer should be just as deferential to a client in a civil case as in a criminal case. Alternatively, perhaps the degree of deference should depend more on the context of a particular case than on whether it is civil or criminal.

**6. The client's brief.** Justice Jackson (quoted in the majority opinion) wrote that "One of the first tests of a discriminating advocate is to select the question, or questions, that he will present orally." If you think that as a lawyer you should sort through the arguments and present the best case to the court, should you, like Melinger, *also* file the brief that your clients wrote, which presents the arguments that you did not want to present?

**7. Ends and means.** Rule 1.2(a) appears to distinguish between the "objectives" of the representation (which are for the client to decide) and the "means by which they are to be pursued," as to which lawyer must consult the client. Is this distinction clear? For example, was Barnes's desire to present his issues to the appellate court one of his "objectives," or was it only a "means" to the end of having his conviction reversed?

**8. Collaboration.** In an article published shortly after the decision in Jones v. Barnes, Professor Judith Maute contended that the Model Rules embody a "collaborative joint venture model" of lawyer-client decision making. She sees the vagueness of the rules as a virtue: "By providing only general guidance, the Rules promote genuine dialogue between interdependent persons."[68] The interdependence results from the fact that the client will suffer if she discharges a lawyer who has already put substantial work into a matter, and the lawyer will suffer the economic losses after such a discharge.

Professor Maute's optimism about lawyer-client dialogue may not be justified. When she addresses decisions by lawyers that the rules do not clearly allocate to either the lawyer or the client, she finds that case law supports a fairly traditional lawyer-centered approach. With respect to civil litigation, she reports that:

> Upon hiring a lawyer for litigation representation the client relinquishes control over procedural and tactical issues. The cases are replete with references to the lawyer's plenary powers in litigation. . . . The lawyer's broad authority

---

68. Judith L. Maute, Allocation of Decisionmaking Authority Under the Model Rules of Professional Conduct, 17 U. Cal. Davis L. Rev. 1049, 1059, 1066 (1984).

is justified. . . . A retainer to litigate a matter may impliedly authorize a lawyer to accept service of process, to waive jurisdictional defects, to waive technical filing errors . . . or to consent to a preliminary injunction. . . . Stipulations and concessions by counsel present dilemmas and often fall within the overlap zone of authority. . . . The [few decisions in civil] cases confer principal authority over the litigation process to the lawyer [but] also reflect an ambivalence toward procedural decisions [by lawyers] that threaten clients' substantive interests.[69]

## PROBLEM 4-5 **THE PACKAGE BOMBER**

*This problem is based on the problem facing defense counsel in a highly publicized prosecution in the late 1990s.*

You are an experienced public defender. You are well known for your vehement opposition to capital punishment. The court has appointed

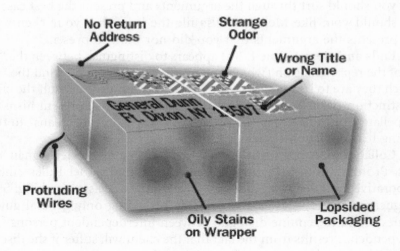

you to represent Gabriel Stroessler, who has been charged with mailing package bombs to university professors over a period of nearly 20 years. The bombs, mailed to offices at Yale, the University of California, and corporations concerned with technology, have killed three people and injured many others. Stroessler's alleged motive was that by killing his victims, he was fighting the spread of technological culture. The prosecutor is seeking the death penalty. The judge probably appointed you to defend Stroessler because of your extensive

---

69. Id. at 1089-1093, 1107.

record of careful and often successful representation of defendants in capital cases.

Stroessler, a former professor who had become a recluse, was captured after a nationwide manhunt that lasted for several years. He was identified only because his brother turned him in after recognizing his writing style in a manifesto that the bomber sent to newspapers. The FBI searched his rural cabin and found a great deal of physical evidence, including his private diary, which contained thousands of pages describing how he made the bombs.

After you interviewed Stroessler and other witnesses and reviewed the evidence and the applicable law, you scheduled a meeting with Stroessler to lay out realities and options. You explained to him that his chance of acquittal was exceedingly poor, and that even his chance of being sentenced to life in prison, rather than death, was not good. There were only two possible avenues for a defense.

First, there were some arguable flaws in the procedure through which the FBI obtained authorization to search his cabin. If the search were shown to be illegal, the evidence that was seized, which was the basis of the prosecution case, could be suppressed. Such motions rarely succeeded. In this case, however, the chance that a judge would declare the search illegal was vanishingly small because the bomber had committed acts of terrorism during nearly 20 years of mail bombings. He was one of the most wanted criminals in the nation.

The second and more promising defense strategy was to argue that when he committed the crimes, Stroessler's mental status was impaired — not so badly as to render him incapable of criminal activity[70] but badly enough to preclude a verdict of first degree murder, a crime for which the death penalty could be imposed. If he were convicted only of second degree murder, he would be jailed but could not be executed.

As part of your preliminary research on the case, before your meeting with Stroessler, you consulted with some psychiatrists whom you had used as expert witnesses in previous capital cases. These experts thought that an evaluation, if Stroessler were to permit one, might well result in their finding that Stroessler was mentally impaired. They based this judgment on their knowledge of the nature of Stroessler's crimes, the rambling nature of his manifesto, and his personal history of alienation and loneliness.

You recommended to Stroessler, therefore, that he submit to psychiatric testing because expert testimony that he was mentally impaired could save his life. This strategy depended on Stroessler agreeing to be examined.

---

70. For Stroessler to be incapable of any criminal activity, he would have to prove that at the time of his acts, he had a "severe mental disease or defect" rendering him "unable to appreciate the wrongfulness of his acts." 18 U.S.C. § 17(a) (2004).

Stroessler reacted angrily to your counseling. He urged that an excellent strategy would be to attack the legality of the search of his cabin. He believed that the court should invalidate the search because of the procedural errors. He was confident — much more confident than you — that the judge would not be improperly influenced by the public outcry over this case or by the fact that the arguably unlawful search revealed unequivocal evidence of his guilt.

Stroessler also said that if the evidence was not suppressed, he wanted to defend his bombings as justified to prevent a greater threat to society from ever-advancing technology. He hoped he could persuade the jury that he was acting to save humanity, not to harm it. You thought that his attempt to justify his crimes would only make matters worse.

Stroessler was totally opposed to raising any mental health defense. Later, from his cell, Stroessler wrote you a letter. "I categorically refuse to use a mental-status defense," he said. In another letter shortly thereafter, he wrote that psychiatry was an element of the technological society that he had devoted his life to fighting. He wrote, "I am bitterly opposed to the development of a science of the human mind."

You believe that Stroessler is competent to stand trial and to make decisions about whether he wants to keep you as his counsel. However, you also believe that he is probably suffering from a mental impairment, perhaps a mild case of schizophrenia, which clouds his judgment and his perceptions even though it does not prevent him from functioning. If you could prove that, you might save his life. Indeed, a mental health defense appears to be the *only* way to save his life. You might be able to establish this defense even without expert psychiatric testimony, though the best bet would be to have him evaluated by a psychiatrist. But Stroessler steadfastly refuses to submit to such an examination.

You identify these three options and have the following thoughts about the odds of success as to each option.

a. **Option One: Stroessler's proposal**. Raise only the suppression-of-evidence defense. When that fails, allow Stroessler to try to persuade the jury that his bombings were necessary to warn and protect society from a greater disaster. This strategy will fail and will lead to a death sentence. It also may subject you to ridicule and severe criticism from your colleagues who represent capital defendants. This is what Stroessler wants you to do, but he does not appreciate the fact that it is a hopeless plan.

b. **Option Two: Despite Stroessler's objection, ask the judge to order a psychiatric evaluation**. Move to suppress the evidence. This motion probably will fail. Also try to persuade the court that you (the expert lawyer), rather than your client, are entitled to make decisions about what defenses to raise. Ask the court to order a psychiatric evaluation even if your client objects. (If you decide to introduce psychiatric testimony, the government also will be able to obtain its own psychiatrist interview and tests.) This strategy is also unlikely to succeed. The judge may refuse to order a psychiatric examination over Stroessler's objection. Also, Stroessler may fire you as his lawyer when he hears that you are trying to divest him of the power to make a key strategic decision.

c. **Option Three: A possible compromise.** The third option is rather complicated. You would ask the court to suppress the evidence seized from the cabin. At the same time, anticipating the failure of that motion, you would try to persuade Stroessler that he should submit to a psychiatric examination. You would tell Stroessler that the results will be used only under two circumstances:

i. If tests show that he is mentally unimpaired, the results will be used to show the public that his well-publicized views on technology are not the ravings of a madman.
ii. If tests show that he is mentally impaired, they would be used only if he is found guilty. They would *not* be used during the "guilt" phase of the trial for the purpose of showing that he was impaired. If Stroessler is found guilty, the court would hold a second, "penalty" phase of the trial. You would tell Stroessler that in the penalty phase, the test results will be used to show mitigating circumstances and avoid the death penalty. You think Stroessler might agree to an examination if he thought that any finding of mental impairment would be used only during a penalty phase. He might agree to this because he believes that he will be acquitted and that therefore there never will be a penalty phase.

In fact, if Stroessler allows the examination, and it shows him impaired, you would use the psychiatrist's findings to persuade the judge to let you make the strategic decisions in the case. Then you would present the psychiatric evidence to the jury during the first phase of the trial despite Stroessler's objection. Essentially, you would trick Stroessler into allowing the psychiatric examination that could show that he did not commit first degree murder. This strategy seems to be the only one that has a chance of saving his life.

As you decide among these strategies, take into account that Stroessler could fire you and take over his own defense. But clients aren't allowed to fire appointed counsel on the eve of trial if that would cause undue delay. The trial is approaching in two months, and the judge might not let Stroessler fire you if Stroessler waits until the trial is about to start. Also, Stroessler knows that he isn't well informed about legal procedure. You doubt he will try to take over his defense.

## Questions

**1.** Do the ethics rules or Jones v. Barnes suggest that any of the three options is professionally improper?

**2.** If none of these options would violate the rules of professional conduct, which one would you actually follow?

**3.** If you oppose the death penalty, would you be willing to help your client pursue the self-destructive course of action he favors? Would you participate in a process through which you, your client, and the state collaborate in helping Stroessler die at the hands of the state?

## 2. Contracts to change the duties owed to clients

We have already seen that by contract, lawyers may undertake duties to clients in addition to those imposed by the ethics rules. Lawyers and clients may also agree that lawyers do not owe clients some of the duties otherwise imposed by the rules.[71] One permissible type of restriction on the lawyer's duties involves the range of legal services the lawyer will provide. A lawyer might agree, for example, to undertake legislative advocacy but not litigation. Or the lawyer might agree to attempt to negotiate a settlement but not to file a lawsuit.

A client might want to limit the legal services to be provided to limit the size of the lawyer's fee or for other reasons. When a client hires a lawyer to handle a certain matter, the client can expect that the lawyer will explore all plausible options that might be available to address the client's problem. However, if the client wants to pay for only specific types of investigation, research, or action, or wishes to limit the number of hours that the lawyer spends on a project, the lawyer and client may agree to such limitations under Rule 1.2(c).

> **FOR EXAMPLE:** A client could direct the lawyer to attempt to reach a settlement but not to initiate a lawsuit, even if negotiations fail. A client might ask a lawyer to investigate recovery under an insurance policy but, if that effort fails, not to spend the time and money necessary to see whether the client also has a valid tort claim.

In Chapter 10, we return to the subject of limited legal representation. There we consider whether it is good policy to encourage the practice of offering limited, low-cost services so that more clients could afford the benefit of receiving some legal advice. Here, however, we consider only the degree to which, under current rules, lawyers and clients may agree to limit the scope of representation.

---

71. As in other bodies of law, some of the ethical rules are default rules, which means that they are imposed unless the parties agree otherwise. For example, some of the rules prohibiting representation of a client in the face of a conflict of interest or against using information to the detriment of a client may be waived if a client gives informed consent. See, e.g., Rules 1.7(b) and 1.8(b). Other rules are mandatory and may not be waived or altered by contract.

Certain limitations are not permissible. A lawyer may not enter into an agreement waiving the duty of competent representation. However, a limitation on the scope of the representation "is a factor to be considered when determining the legal knowledge, skill, thoroughness and preparation reasonably necessary for the representation."[72] If a client asks a lawyer to perform a limited service, the lawyer would not be found incompetent for having failed to do work that he was not asked to do. A lawyer also is barred from making "an agreement prospectively limiting the lawyer's liability for malpractice unless the client is independently represented in making the agreement."[73]

## Can a client waive his rights to be kept informed or to be consulted about settlement offers?

In ordinary representation, a lawyer must keep a client apprised of important developments in a matter and absolutely must consult the client before responding to settlement offers. But what about in lawsuits designed to challenge institutional practices or to develop new law? In many such cases, the lawyer is really the driving force behind the case and the client willingly offers his or her name to the case as a nominal plaintiff.

**FOR EXAMPLE:** Some of the school desegregation cases filed in the 1950s and 1960s dragged on for a decade or more. Parents whose young children were the named plaintiffs didn't expect to hear from the civil rights lawyers handling the cases until the cases were over. By the time the cases were finally won, some of the children who had been in elementary school when the suits were filed were eligible to be hired as teachers in the newly desegregated school systems.[74]

**FOR EXAMPLE:** In contemporary fair housing litigation, African American "testers" are employed by fair housing organizations to see whether landlords will rent them vacant apartments. If the landlord refuses to rent, civil rights lawyers sue the landlord in the name of the tester, but the real instigators of the litigation are the civil rights organization and its lawyer. The testers often have very little personal interest in the cases.[75]

The ethical rules were written with a broad range of lawyers and clients in mind. Although in a few places the drafters made special rules for criminal

---

72. Rule 1.2, Comment 6.

73. Rule 1.8(h)(1).

74. One desegregation case, Briggs v. Elliot, 98 F. Supp. 529 (D.S.C. 1951), which was argued together with and reversed by the famous case of Brown v. Board of Education, 349 U.S. 294 (1955), wasn't fully resolved until a costs and fees proceeding was upheld in Brown v. Unified Sch. Dist. No. 501, 56 F. Supp. 2d 1212 (D. Kan. 1999), almost four decades years later. Flax v. Potts, 204 F. Supp. 458 (N.D. Tex. 1962), filed well after *Brown* was decided, was not resolved until Flax v. Potts, 915 F.2d 155 (5th Cir. 1990).

75. See Leroy D. Clark, Employment Discrimination Testing: Theories of Standing and a Reply to Professor Yelnosky, 28 U. Mich. J.L. Reform 1, 19 (1994).

defense lawyers, they may not always have considered the special issues that arise in law reform cases or in class actions. The extent to which lawyers and their clients may knowingly agree to unusual arrangements (such as less consultation) in such cases is a matter of conjecture. One looks in vain for case law resolving these issues.

## 3. Clients with diminished capacity

Lawyers are often called upon to represent children and persons with mental disabilities. A client with diminished capacity may be unable to make wise judgments about legal matters. The ethics rules address this issue in Rule 1.14.

> Rule 1.14    Client with diminished capacity
>
> (a) When a client's capacity to make adequately considered decisions in connection with a representation is diminished, whether because of minority, mental impairment or for some other reason, the lawyer shall, as far as reasonably possible, maintain a normal client-lawyer relationship with the client.
>
> (b) When the lawyer reasonably believes that the client has diminished capacity, is at risk of substantial physical, financial or other harm unless action is taken and cannot adequately act in the client's own interest, the lawyer may take reasonably necessary protective action, including consulting with individuals or entities that have the ability to take action to protect the client and, in appropriate cases, seeking the appointment of a guardian ad litem, conservator or guardian.
>
> (c) Information relating to the representation of a client with diminished capacity is protected by Rule 1.6. When taking protective action pursuant to paragraph (b), the lawyer is impliedly authorized under Rule 1.6(a) to reveal information about the client, but only to the extent reasonably necessary to protect the client's interests.

Subsection (a) of the rule encourages lawyers to maintain "normal" lawyer-client relations with clients who may have some degree of diminished capacity. Subsection (b) acknowledges that in some situations, a lawyer needs the flexibility to assume a more paternalistic role to protect the client from some harm. In such cases, a lawyer may ask a court to appoint a third party who would make some legal decisions on behalf of the client. This raises several issues. Is a lawyer supposed to assess whether and to what extent a client suffers from diminished mental capacity? Most lawyers are not expert in psychological evaluation. How can a lawyer make such an assessment? Is a lawyer who has doubts about a client's mental capacity supposed to send the client for a psychological evaluation? Comment 6 to Rule 1.14 suggests that a lawyer can and should make some assessment of a client's mental capacity. It urges lawyers to

> consider and balance such factors as: the client's ability to articulate reasoning leading to a decision, variability of state of mind and ability to appreciate consequences of a decision, the substantive fairness of a decision, and the consistency of a decision with the known long-term commitments and values

of the client. In appropriate circumstances, the lawyer may seek guidance from an appropriate diagnostician.

The rule assumes that, in at least some cases, a lawyer would know that a client's mental capacity is diminished. In such a case, what should the lawyer do? The rule contemplates that the lawyer may consult about the matter on which the lawyer is representing the client with "individuals or entities" other than the client, such as members of the client's family or public agencies. But it does not explain how the lawyer should know whether to do so. This judgment is important because such contact will involve divulging some client confidences and it will reduce client autonomy.

## a. Clients who may have mental disabilities

A lawyer who represents a client who has an intellectual impairment or a diagnosis of mental illness has several options.

- She might simply follow the client's instructions, to the extent possible.
- She might impose her own ideas of what is best, either because the client is unable to provide instructions or gives instructions that the lawyer believes could cause harm to the client.
- She might invite others (the client's friends or family members, social welfare agencies, or courts) to provide substitute guidance.

Also, the lawyer might limit her focus to the matter for which she has been retained, or she might try to help the client with problems other than the particular matter for which the lawyer has been retained. For example, the lawyer (or a third person consulted by the lawyer) might investigate whether the client is able to take care of himself, whether anyone else can care for him, and whether someone else should be given legal authority to do so. If it seems necessary to give someone else legal authority over the client, the lawyer might petition the court to appoint a guardian ad litem, a conservator, or a guardian for the client.

- A **guardian ad litem** is empowered to speak for the client (even contrary to the client's expressed wishes) in a particular legal matter.[76]
- A **conservator** is given power to manage the financial affairs of the client, who thereby loses the power to buy, sell, and hold property.[77]
- A **guardian** has even more authority. The guardian manages the client's financial affairs and may make medical and other personal decisions for the client, who is thereafter the guardian's "ward."[78]

---

76. Black's Law Dictionary (Bryan A. Garner ed., 7th ed., West 1999).
77. Id.
78. Id.

The following excerpt explains the choices that lawyers face when they represent mentally impaired clients.[79]

## Paul R. Tremblay, On Persuasion and Paternalism: Lawyer Decisionmaking and the Questionably Competent Client

1987 Utah L. Rev. 515

[Paul Tremblay is Clinical Professor of Law at Boston College Law School. He supervises students in a clinical setting at the Boston College Legal Assistance Bureau and teaches a course on lawyers' ethics.]

The lawyer's great difficulty in proceeding with representation of a confused client should be apparent. The most obvious problem is the considerable tension between the ethical requirement that the lawyer permit the client to make decisions and the lawyer's consid-

*Professor Paul R. Tremblay*     ered judgment that to do so not only would fail to achieve the purposes of the representation but also would be to follow an instruction that the client would not give in more lucid times. . . .

### A. THE ANTIPATERNALISM OPTION: TREAT THE CLIENT AS COMPETENT

Strictly following the client's wishes [and refusing] to intervene in extreme cases of distraught self-destructive behavior (the most obvious example is a depressed individual's suicide attempt) is arguably morally wrong. . . . If the lawyer correctly determines (1) that the client's competence has failed, (2) that the client has chosen a course of conduct contrary to his values, and (3) that in fact he would choose differently if he were competent, then the lawyer's decision to try to achieve what the client actually values is not disloyal behavior. It may be disloyal vis-à-vis the client's present wants, but not vis-à-vis the client's enduring values. So when the lawyer correctly perceives incompetence, some intervention is appropriate. . . . The types of intervention that are justifiable must be identified. The next sections address that issue.

---

79. The discussion assumes that at the moment that the client becomes a client, the client is not so disabled as to be unable to form a lawyer-client relationship. If the client were that disabled, no contract could or should be made. The typical cases in which the problem of mental disabilities arise are those in which (a) the client is fully competent to begin with but becomes less competent after the lawyer-client relationship is formed; (b) the client is not fully competent to begin with, but is sufficiently competent to form a lawyer-client relationship; and (c) the lawyer is appointed to represent a client who is not fully competent, and therefore the relationship is not based on a consensual contract.

## B. THE GUARDIANSHIP CONUNDRUM

Appointment of a guardian is generally recognized as a drastic and virtually complete deprivation of civil rights, [depriving the ward of the] right to make legally binding decisions, to vote, to own property, to choose his place and manner of living, to make medical decisions, and so on. . . . Because of the deprivation of rights and liberties, a prospective ward is often entitled to counsel for purposes of opposing the petition. Thus a lawyer who is the petitioner is "suing" her own client, who must have other counsel to oppose the petition. All this is just an interlude of sorts, after which the lawyer probably intends to continue representing her client in the matter that caused her to seek a guardian in the first place. . . . Viewed from its harshest perspective, the process looks like this: the client hires the lawyer to serve as his loyal agent and confidante; the lawyer promises him that those expectations are warranted and will be fulfilled; the lawyer then uses her client's confidences to bring a court proceeding that will deprive him of all his rights, and will require him to obtain another lawyer to defend against it; and all the while the lawyer plans to resume representing him once this distraction is over. This representation is obviously full of direct ethical violations.

The serious professional responsibility concerns that inevitably arise in this scenario, however, do not necessarily mandate banning this approach. The consequences of not intervening, and the harm to the client, may well warrant overriding the usual ethical considerations. . . . [But labeling one's client as mentally ill] can hardly be beneficial or even neutral . . . [and] guardianship petitions tend to be granted [because judges do not want to be responsible for harm befalling a potential ward]. . . . Thus, referral actually creates the guardianship. . . . [Also the lawyer usually doesn't tell the client that she played a role in obtaining the guardianship, and this secrecy is itself disloyal.][80]

## C. RELIANCE ON "NATURAL GUARDIANS" FOR PROXY CONSENT

Reliance on family members . . . is preferable to unilateral lawyer usurpation of authority because it requires the lawyer to articulate the considerations involved in the decision, just as she would with a competent client. Second, it is likely to provide a more accurate gauge of substituted judgment [and relying on family members rather than appointed guardians] is less expensive, less permanent, and involves fewer ethical conflicts. But . . . in many

---

80. [Authors' footnote.] In 1996, the ABA issued Formal Opinion 96-404, which provided, in part, that "although not expressly dictated by the Model Rules, the principle of respecting the client's autonomy dictates that the action taken by a lawyer . . . should be the action that is reasonably viewed as the least restrictive action under the circumstances. The appointment of a guardian . . . ought not to be undertaken if other, less drastic, solutions are available." In 2000, when the ABA revised the Model Rules, it had the opportunity to codify this guidance in Rule 1.14 but it did not do so. Instead, Comment 7 directs the lawyer to "be aware of any [state] law that requires the lawyer to advocate the least restrictive action on behalf of the client."

jurisdictions the family has absolutely no lawful authority to give consent [and the law offers] no guidance on how to resolve conflicting family sentiment or how to prioritize among family members. . . .

## D. DE FACTO GUARDIANSHIP

[Tremblay criticized a former sentence in a Comment to Rule 1.14 that stated that the lawyer "often must act as de facto guardian." He pointed out that states granted lawyers no authority to play this role, and that the role permitted unbridled paternalism. The sentence was removed from the comment in 2002, but it persists in the comments in many states.]

## E. THE DIALOGUE: PERSUASION, MANIPULATION, AND "FRATERNAL CORRECTION" . . .

A lawyer should ordinarily refrain from expressing an opinion regarding the relative merit of any choice available to [a fully competent] client. To guide the client's decision by doing so is inconsistent with the policy of informed consent because clients are unlikely to resist lawyer influence, which results in lawyer-centered rather than client-centered decisions. Although perhaps not exactly a breach of ethics, such a practice is tactically inappropriate. . . . [But] lawyers ought to be permitted greater latitude to use persuasive dialogue with a confused client than with a more coherent one. . . . If the only objection to persuasion is paternalism, it is the least objectionable of all the available options. . . .

Actively exploring the clients' reasons have two beneficial effects: the client may learn that his decision is inconsistent with his values; or the lawyer may learn that the client has arrived at an apparently "insane" decision by means of a rational process. . . .

Persuasion cannot be used with clients who cannot comprehend the dialogue and who, therefore, cannot give consent. The distinction between persuasion and coercion is critical; with such severely impaired clients, however, the process of persuasion can be a test of competence. . . . If the client's response to the lawyer's arguments is continued reliance on delusions, with no appreciation of the actual facts and circumstances, then the lawyer can appropriately determine that competence is in question. . . . [Tremblay says that the form of the lawyer's statements is important. It is acceptable for a lawyer to advise that, "You will lose your home if you do not ask a judge for help, and you have always told me that you do not want to lose your house." But it is not acceptable for the lawyer to make a "persuasive threat" such as, "You really should file that lawsuit."] . . .

Lawyers and the ethical rules that govern them . . . must acknowledge and counterattack their natural attraction to dominance and manipulation. The trick is to assist clients while restraining lawyers. It is not an easy balance to strike. [This article suggests that] guardianship is legitimate in extreme cases, that reliance on family may be appropriate, that noncoercive persuasion is justified in less extreme cases, and that unilateral usurpation of client autonomy is never appropriate except in emergencies. . . .

## PROBLEM 4-6  **VINYL WINDOWS**

*The facts of this problem are drawn from a real case in which the client was represented by students in a law school clinic. The case was supervised by the authors.*

You are a staff attorney at the civil legal assistance office. A few days ago, your office was called by Mary McCabe, who had just been sued. McCabe said that she needed legal help, but she was too old to come to your office. You went to see her at her home.

McCabe turned out to be a small, frail woman. During your first conversation, she volunteered that she was 83 years old. Her house was a large, Tudor-style home, which she and her husband had bought nearly 50 years ago. She had been a widow for 8 years. The house appeared to be in good condition, although the living room was very cluttered.

McCabe told you that two salesmen for a company called Stormguard had come to her door about a year ago and talked with her about getting new vinyl windows for her house. She didn't think that she needed new windows, but after conversing with them over a cup of tea, she agreed to let them put some windows in. She signed some papers, and the salesmen asked for some money. She didn't have a checking account or any credit cards, so she went with them to the bank, withdrew money from her account, and gave them a bank check. At the time, she had most of her life savings, $14,000, in that account. She also owns the house. Two weeks later, work on the windows started. Each time the men came to work on the windows, they asked her to go to the bank with them and have the teller give them another bank check for a portion of the amount due.

Eventually the windows were completed, but when the men asked her to pay the last $900, McCabe complained that one of the window frames leaked, and they had damaged one wall while installing one of the windows. She refused to make the last payment. Now the company has sued her for $900. She showed you the complaint from the small claims court, in which Stormguard says that she agreed to pay $8,900 but never paid the final $900 installment.

McCabe was quite confused about how much money she already paid, or when. When you asked to see any contracts, receipts, or other documents the company's men or the bank might have given her, she got distracted and started talking about "those crazy boys" who were putting in the windows. She told you that the red-headed one made a lot of jokes and that the tall one never seemed quite well. She smiled as she remembered how much they liked the brownies that she made for them. You started wondering whether your client bought the windows because she enjoyed her visits with "those crazy boys." However, McCabe thinks that one of the insallers stole $400 in cash from underneath her mattress.

You laid out the options for McCabe. You told her that you know from prior experience with Stormguard's lawyer (whose name was on the summons) that when he gets to court, he offers to settle for about 50 percent of the amount stated in the complaint. If he takes this course, she could probably terminate the lawsuit by paying $450. You told her that she could

- pay the full amount now;
- wait until trial and be prepared to accept an offer to pay about $450;
- defend against the lawsuit (you immediately saw possible defenses based on duress, unconscionability, and misrepresentation);
- try to get some or all of her money back by filing a counterclaim for damages (based on the windows leaking, on the damage to the wall, and on the fact that Stormguard is apparently unlicensed, and on a local case holding that unlicensed contractors may not collect any money before completing their work); or
- try to make the company repair the window frame that leaks and repair the wall that was damaged (this might be accomplished as part of a settlement or through a counterclaim for specific performance).

McCabe understood that she was required to respond to the lawsuit, but she had a hard time figuring out what she wanted to do. Whenever you tried to get her to make a decision, she went on about "those crazy boys." During your first meeting with her, McCabe signed your organization's standard form retainer in which you agreed to represent her in her dispute with Stormguard without charging her a fee.

You asked McCabe if she had any living relatives. She does not; her only brother died a year ago. You asked if there were any friends or neighbors whom she knew well. All of her old friends had passed away, but she said she was friendly with her next-door neighbor, Mrs. Houston, whom she sees every week or two.

The Court does not require a written answer if McCabe plans to appear and offer defenses against the claim. You tend to favor fairly aggressive strategies, so you think that she should not pay any more money and should counterclaim. If she wants to file a counterclaim, however, you must file it within a few days. The trial date is in one week, though you probably could obtain a short continuance. You will be seeing McCabe again this afternoon. If she still can't decide how she wants to respond to the lawsuit, what should you do?

The Vinyl Windows problem presents issues about the role of clients and lawyers in making decisions when the lawyer's own interests or emotions, or larger public interests, are not directly involved. In the next problem, again based on a real case, the lawyer must consider whether to consider how, if at all, these other considerations should affect the balance of decisionmaking between lawyer and client.

## PROBLEM 4-7 **TIGHTENING THE KNOT**

*This problem is very closely modeled on a problem faced by a law student in a clinic. The student was being supervised by Professor Paul Reingold of the University of Michigan Law School.*

You work as a lawyer at a nonprofit organization called the Community Mental Health Law Center. Under a foundation grant, you and your colleagues provide representation for people who are allegedly mentally ill, have been picked up by the police, and are being committed involuntarily, in civil proceedings, to the state mental institution. To assure fairness for the persons being committed, the hospital calls your institute when these proceedings are initiated to enlist your services. When the hospital asks the Center to represent its patients, it does so routinely under its grant, without being appointed by the court.

Your boss has accepted representation of Thomas Criddon and has assigned you to do the work. Two days ago, Criddon was picked up by the police after allegedly threatening passersby. In four days, the city will argue to a judge that Criddon should be committed for at least six months, with periodic reviews thereafter.

When you study the city's commitment petition, you discover a technical error. The statement of the police officer who observed Criddon's conduct was not notarized as required by state law. Regardless of his current mental condition, you may be able to get your client released at the end of the hearing because of this mistake.

You go to meet with Criddon at the mental hospital. He is nearly seven feet tall and seems to be perpetually angry. You tried some small talk, which didn't really work, so you are about to try to talk with him about the upcoming proceedings. Suddenly, he starts raging at you, "Get me out of this hell hole, you [expletive]. You people are all worms and maggots. You all deserve to die." He leans over, grabs your tie, and starts to pull on it. He looks you in the eye and says, "When you wear one of these, do you ever think about someone tightening it, slowly, slowly, until you can't breathe any more?" You start to choke on the knot in your tie. He lets go and laughs. He says, "I can do that any time I want."

You had been just about to tell Criddon that you had found an error in the legal papers that the city had filed and that you hoped to obtain his release very soon. Will you do so?

## b. Juveniles

Rule 1.14 applies the same standards to minors that it applies to adults with mental impairments. This means that lawyers should maintain normal lawyer-client relationships with minors to the extent possible. Comment 1 notes that "children as young as five or six years of age, and certainly those of ten or twelve, are regarded as having opinions that are entitled to weight in legal proceedings concerning their custody." The rule makes no distinctions among the various types of proceedings in which minors may be involved. These include delinquency cases (in which the minor has been charged with an offense), custody or adoption proceedings, abuse and neglect proceedings (in which the state is attempting to terminate a parent's custody of a child and remove the child to institutional care or a foster home), or other civil cases (such as personal injury suits by or against minors). Although the ethics rules posit a single rule to cover all these situations, lawyers who represent minors tend to observe norms that are specific to the proceedings involved.

**Delinquency cases**   When they represent children who are charged with juvenile offenses, lawyers typically represent older children, and the cases resemble criminal cases. Therefore, as the following excerpt explains, most lawyers follow norms of representation similar to the norms they follow when representing adults in court.

### Martin Guggenheim, A Paradigm for Determining the Role of Counsel for Children

64 Fordham L. Rev. 1399, 1423 (1996)

*Professor Martin Guggenheim*

[Martin Guggenheim is a Professor of Clinical Law at New York University, where he directs a clinical program that represents juveniles.]

[In re Gault, 387 U.S. 1 (1967), held] that children possess the same autonomy rights to resist coercive intervention based on alleged criminal activity that adults enjoy. Although children continue to be denied equivalent self-determination authority in most other legal matters, they enjoy it in delinquency and criminal cases.

From this newly recognized power of children follows both the need for and, ultimately, the role of counsel. Because the right to remain silent requires the state to prove its case by presenting evidence in court, the Supreme Court turned its attention to enhancing the fairness of the judicial process. The Court concluded that "fundamental fairness" requires that the evidence presented be competent, holding that children have the right to cross-examine and confront adverse witnesses. Once it is a requirement in these proceedings that children be given the opportunity to challenge adverse evidence, it is easy to appreciate why the Court concluded that unassisted children rarely could effectively use their right to test the state's witnesses. Accordingly, the Court required lawyers. In addition, the Court eventually clarified the strength of the state's case necessary to convict, holding that the evidence must be beyond a reasonable doubt.

From this, then, we can only conclude that young children are empowered to set the objectives of their criminal case to the same degree as an unimpaired adult. . . . Unless children are allowed by lawyers to set the objectives in their cases, they would not only be effectively deprived of a number of constitutional rights, they would be denied procedures that are fundamental to the rule of law. The lawyer, not the child, would decide whether the child should forgo his or her right to remain silent. The lawyer, not the trier of fact, would effectively decide what outcome is in the child's best interests.

What, then, is the role of counsel in criminal proceedings involving children? The same as it is in criminal proceedings involving adults. By this I do not mean there are no differences. Lawyers for children need to be particularly good communicators. They need to be keenly sensitive to the risk that their clients will put too much faith in their advice because the lawyer has even more power to persuade a child client to agree to a particular result than an adult client. In addition, the sentencing structure for juvenile proceedings is dramatically different from their adult counterpart and, as a result, lawyers for children need to pay careful attention to these differences. But these differences are all a matter of detail. The sense in which I mean there are no differences in the representation between children and adults is in the underlying purposes and goals of the representation.

---

**Custody, abuse, and neglect proceedings**    Although lawyers are supposed to play essentially the same role as representatives of juveniles in delinquency proceedings that they do for adults who are charged with crimes, their role in other proceedings involving children may be less shaped by the traditional model of the lawyer-client relationship. One difference is that most juveniles who are charged with criminal offenses are teenagers, whereas children in some other types of proceedings may be much younger. A second difference is that although the substantive law may permit or require children to have their own lawyers in delinquency cases, it may afford them fewer rights in certain other types of proceedings.

Should a lawyer representing a young child in a child custody matter advocate for the child's stated wishes or the child's "best interests"? Does a lawyer who represents the parents in a matter in which the child has no separate lawyer have duties to the child also? It is problematic for any lawyer in a custody matter to advocate only the child's wishes, on the one hand, or

*"He's talking now, but only through his attorney."*

what the lawyer thinks are the child's best interests, on the other. A child might be too young to state goals or too emotionally immature to have the knowledge and judgment needed to evaluate what he or she would prefer to do. On the other hand, if lawyers are free to make their own judgments of what is in their juvenile clients' best interests, the outcome may depend more on who is the lawyer (and what are his presuppositions, biases, and so on) than on the wishes of the child. Also, many lawyers who represent children have large caseloads and do not have time to investigate fully the child's family situation. So the lawyer's judgment might not be fully informed.

While Rule 1.14 lumps representation of children with representation of other persons who have limited mental capacity, other advisory standards, including the one that follows, provide more precise guidance on the role of lawyers in representing children.

## ABA, Standards of Practice for Lawyers Representing a Child in Abuse and Neglect Cases (1996)[81]

### [DEFINITION] A-1. THE CHILD'S ATTORNEY

The term "child's attorney" means a lawyer who provides legal services for a child and who owes the same duties of undivided loyalty, confidentiality, and competent representation to the child as is due an adult client.

---

81. The ABA Standards are available online *at* http://www.abanet.org/child/childrep.html (last visited Oct. 18, 2004). ABA Standards are intended to provide guidance for lawyers, but unlike the

## Commentary

These Standards explicitly recognize that the child is a separate individual with potentially discrete and independent views. To ensure that the child's independent voice is heard, the child's attorney must advocate the child's articulated position. . . .

## [DEFINITION] A-2. LAWYER APPOINTED AS GUARDIAN AD LITEM

A lawyer appointed as "guardian ad litem" for a child is an officer of the court appointed to protect the child's interests without being bound by the child's expressed preferences.

## Commentary

In some jurisdictions the lawyer may be appointed as guardian ad litem. These Standards, however, express a clear preference for the appointment as the "child's attorney." . . .

## [STANDARD] B-4. CLIENT PREFERENCES

The child's attorney should elicit the child's preferences in a developmentally appropriate manner, advise the child, and provide guidance. The child's attorney should represent the child's expressed preferences and follow the child's direction throughout the course of litigation.

## Commentary

The lawyer has a duty to explain to the child in a developmentally appropriate way such information as will assist the child in having maximum input in determination of the particular position at issue. . . . The lawyer for the child has dual fiduciary duties to the child . . . which must be balanced. On one hand, the lawyer has a duty to ensure that the child client is given the information necessary to make an informed decision, including advice and guidance. On the other hand, the lawyer has a duty not to overbear the will of the child. While the lawyer may attempt to persuade the child to accept a particular position, the lawyer may not advocate a position contrary to the child's expressed position except as provided by these Abuse and Neglect Standards or the [ethical rules]. . . . [However, if] the child's attorney determines that the child's expressed preference would be seriously injurious to the child (as opposed to merely being contrary to the lawyer's opinion of what would be in the child's interests), the lawyer may request appointment of a separate guardian ad litem and continue to represent the child's expressed preference, unless the child's position is prohibited by law or without any factual foundation.

Model Rules, they are not intended to be promulgated by state courts as formal disciplinary rules. The ABA regards the standard as current guidance, but it predates the 2002 revision to Model Rule 1.14, which instituted the idea that clients may be of "diminished capacity" and do not simply have or lack a disability.

Some jurisdictions use the model described above. A lawyer represents the child's expressed preferences, but a separate guardian ad litem, sometimes a lawyer and sometimes a nonlawyer who is represented by a second lawyer, may represent what the guardian believes are the child's best interests, especially in cases in which there appears to be a conflict between the two.[82] In other jurisdictions, however, a lawyer serves as a guardian ad litem and tries to navigate between what she perceives to be the child's best interests and the child's preferences. This is quite different from a conventional lawyer-client relationship.

### Frances Gall Hill, Clinical Education and the "Best Interest" Representation of Children in Custody Disputes: Challenges and Opportunities in Lawyering and Pedagogy

73 Ind. L.J. 605, 621-624 (1998)

*Professor Frances Gall Hill*

[When she wrote this article, Professor Hill was Director of the Child Advocacy Clinic at Indiana University School of Law–Bloomington.]

GAL representation of children has come under attack in recent years. [Professor Hill refers to the model in which, in many states, a guardian ad litem, who may be a lawyer, is appointed to represent a child's interests in custody or child abuse proceedings.] Critics charge that the best-interest role of the GAL is paternalistic and has the potential for cultural bias and middle-class imperialism, does not empower or give true voice to the child, and is vague and impossible to forecast. Further, it is suggested that GAL representation usurps the judicial role of determining best interest and is easily abused by judges who give GALs unfair procedural latitude or afford them undue credibility. . . . With regard specifically to attorneys who serve as GALs, the complaint is raised that attorneys are not trained to determine the best interest and that GAL representation requires counsel to function outside of the traditional ethical boundaries of the attorney-client relationship. . . .

The GAL model may not be perfect, but it is preferable to the attorney-client model. The attorney-client relationship is based on the ability of the client to identify the goals of the litigation and direct the attorney consistent with those goals. The adaptation of this relationship to young children who lack the cognitive skills, maturity, and desire to direct the litigation places the attorney in the awkward role under Rule 1.14 . . . of continually assessing the extent of the child's disability and deciding which decisionmaking the child should participate in or control. The concern with this adaptation is . . . that it is labeled "attorney-client" and that therefore the child and the other

---

82. See D.C. Bar, Legal Ethics Comm., Op. 295, Restriction on Communications by a Lawyer Acting as Guardian Ad Litem in a Child Abuse and Neglect Proceeding n. 1 (2000).

participants in the litigation may reasonably expect . . . zealous representation of stated desires, confidentiality, and client-directed litigation.

Aside from the criticisms of the attorney-client model, the GAL model of representation has some affirmative strengths. Best-interest representation is consistent with society's notion that children have not attained the full measure of cognitive skills, maturity, and judgment necessary for autonomous decisionmaking. Children need and generally expect that an adult will oversee the major events of their lives. Perhaps in this sense GAL representation is paternalistic, but the negative connotations often associated with paternalism are not inherent within the GAL model of representation. GAL representation allows the child to fully express his needs, concerns, and desires, but screens the child's position for accuracy and investigates the child's situation from the broader perspective of the family system and the long-range interests of the child. . . . The ability of the GAL to disclose information and act in the child's best interest seems advantageous when compared to the moral dilemma of an attorney who is prohibited by his child client from disclosing information of abuse or self-harming behaviors.

Finally, although it may be impossible to forecast best-interest for a particular child, the GAL model of representation provides the greater opportunity to investigate the interests and needs of the child and anticipate what would be better for the child. . . . The GAL investigation garners information regarding the child and the parents that would not be offered as evidence by either parent. More information, appropriately screened for accuracy and relevance, increases the likelihood that the judge's custody or visitation order will "better" meet the needs of the child, even though it does not ensure that the best interest is truly obtained. . . . Commonly held values on parenting (if clearly identified by the GAL as the basis of a recommendation), statutory factors, and current behavioral research are tools that increase the predictability of what is best for the child. When these are combined with a thorough investigation of the child's situation and an appropriate appreciation of the child's desires, there is a likelihood the GAL's recommendation will approximate the best, or at least better, options for the child.

Sorting out what a lawyer's role should be in relation to a child client can be very challenging as a conceptual matter. But it can be even more difficult for a lawyer to sort through these questions in relation to a particular client.

## PROBLEM 4-8 **THE FOSTER CHILD**

*This problem is closely based on a case that was handled by Jennifer Renne, an Adjunct Professor of Law at Georgetown University, when she worked for a legal aid organization.*

You are a staff attorney for the Legal Aid Society, which represents children who are in child abuse and neglect proceedings. For a year and a half, you have been representing Grace, who is now eight years old, and you are preparing to participate in a court hearing to determine her placement. You are not a guardian ad litem, and no guardian ad litem has been appointed for Grace.

*Professor Jennifer Renne*

When you were first assigned to represent Grace, the Department of Social Services had filed a petition to remove her from the care of her mother, Rhonda Mason. You first met Grace on the day she was taken from her mother. The court had scheduled a hearing to decide a temporary placement for Grace. This hearing was to begin a few hours after you were called to meet with her.

Before that meeting with Grace, you read the documents that the Department had filed in court. According to Grace's teachers, Grace had been showing up at school with red welts on her arms and legs. A social worker had investigated and had learned that Mason had been using a variety of drugs and had been beating Grace with a wooden spoon whenever she misbehaved. Grace has two younger brothers, but the Department has not charged her with abusing them. (For the last year and a half, they have continued to live with Mason.)

You met with Grace, that first time, in a private office at the court house. You tried to have a conversation with her about the case, but her mind was elsewhere. She told you that butterflies were really angels who had come to earth. She did not seem to understand that officials were proposing to separate her from her mother.

At the end of that first hearing a year and a half ago, Grace was placed in temporary foster care with Valerie Waite. You visited Grace twice during the 30 days before the next hearing to find out what she wanted you to do at that hearing, but still it was not possible to get her to focus on her abuse and neglect case. In fact, she seemed to be out of touch with reality. At the second hearing, the judge determined that her mother had been abusive, and he issued an order that Grace should remain in temporary foster care. Under the law, a hearing to review Grace's case is scheduled every six months. The court may change her placement at any time.

In the following eight months, the Department arranged for Grace to be seen by a psychiatrist, who concluded that she had a psychotic disorder. He prescribed anti-psychotic medication and saw her once a week. Her condition improved considerably.

You know Grace's foster mother, Waite, not only because you have visited Grace in her home several times but also because one of your former clients had been placed in her care. Waite is 70 years old. Like Grace, Waite is African American. She has taken care of foster children all her life, has worked with several hundreds of them over the years, and has adopted two of them. You have seen her with Grace. Grace is difficult to handle and has massive temper tantrums. Waite is almost saintly in her patience, and she is always able to calm Grace down. Although she has a lifetime of foster care experience, Waite has had no formal training in taking care of children with special needs.

A year after Grace was first placed in foster care, she was able to have real conversations with you. You see her about once a month. You often ask her how she feels about her life and what she wants to happen. Most of the time, she tells you that she wants to return to her mother's house because her younger brothers need her to take care of them, and she misses them. You ask her if she is afraid of her mother. She says no. You ask if she remembers her mother hitting her. She says she does not remember.

Sometimes Grace changes her mind about going home. Her mother's boyfriend, Ray, stays at her mother's house some of the time and then leaves town for periods of time. When Grace hears from her mother (who calls and visits her sometimes) that Ray is there, Grace expresses a preference to stay at Waite's home.

There is some truth to Grace's perception of her brothers' needs. You know from conversations with a Department of Social Services parent aide assigned to work with Grace's mother that Mason functions at a very low level and has few child-raising skills. She was ordered to attend parenting classes and a drug and alcohol abuse course, but her attendance has been very poor. She also was ordered to work with a parent aide who would help her with the younger children. The parent aide reports that often, when she arrives at Mason's home for her scheduled appointments, no one is home.

At the hearing that will be held in a few days, the judge will determine whether Grace should remain in Waite's care or be placed elsewhere. The Department of Social Services is proposing that the court place Grace with Mr. and Mrs. Drew Langerfeld. They are a white, childless couple in their late 20s. They have taken an intensive, government-approved course in foster care for children with special needs. Their household has been approved as a "therapeutic foster home." If a foster child with special needs like Grace is placed with them, they have agreed that one of them will be with the child at all times when she is not in school. Because of their training and this commitment, the state will pay them $25,000 per year, three times the rate paid to other foster parents.

In preparation for this hearing, you have talked to Grace, her mother, her maternal grandmother Adelaide, who lives nearby, the Langerfelds, and Grace's psychiatrist. This is what each of them says:

■ *Grace* knows that Ray is currently in another city. Consistent with her previously stated preferences when Ray is away, she wants to return to her mother. You asked, "If the judge didn't allow you to go home, where would you want to go?" She answered that her next choice would be to live with her Grandmother Adelaide.

■ *Rhonda Mason and Adelaide (Grace's mother and grandmother)* want Grace returned to her mother. If that isn't possible, they want Grace to be placed with Adelaide. Adelaide has shown some interest in Grace and has called her a few times and visited her twice. But Grace has never lived with Adelaide, and Adelaide has no training in taking care of children with special needs.

■ *The Langerfelds* want Grace to be placed with them. They have invested a lot of effort in being trained as therapeutic foster parents, and they are certain that they can provide Grace with both a warm, loving home and the special support that she needs.

■ *Dr. Hsiu,* Grace's psychiatrist, says that the best thing for Grace would be either to keep her with Waite, where she has made so much improvement, or place her with the Langerfelds. He believes that if she is returned to her mother, she probably will not be given her medication on a regular basis. Even if she gets her medication, he says, she will regress. You asked him whether she is capable of knowing what she wants, and he said that she was.

Based on your own observations of Waite's care, you think it would be best for Grace to remain with Waite. You believe that her long-term interests and her chances for a healthy and productive life would be best served by leaving her where she is, at least for the next year or so.

You think that placement with her mother or with the Langerfelds would not be nearly as good. Her mother has not made much of an effort to learn parenting skills, and there is no reason to believe that she would not again respond to Grace's misbehavior by beating her. As for the Langerfelds, you have seen too many idealistic white foster parents give up on children with special needs after a few months. Also, you think Waite is much better for Grace because they are both African Americans. A federal law prohibits the government from taking race into account when placing children in foster care, but you are not a federal employee. You would prefer living in a society in which race didn't matter, but you think that, realistically, it will help Grace to thrive if she lives with an African American adult. Because of the federal law, you aren't certain whether it would be a good idea to mention this factor in court.

Should you advocate for a particular placement for Grace at the upcoming hearing? If so, which placement?

# E. Terminating a lawyer-client relationship

## 1. Duties to the client at the conclusion of the relationship

Most lawyer-client relationships end when all the work on the relevant matter has been completed.[83] When the work is finished, the lawyer must return to the client "any papers and property to which the client is entitled" and must return any unearned payment that the client may have made.[84] The relationship is not entirely over at this point because the lawyer has a duty to protect client confidences, a duty that continues indefinitely.[85]

The ethics rules do not specify what types of papers must be returned to a client or whether they must be delivered to the client even if the client does not request them. The Restatement is more specific about a lawyer's duties to a client, both during and after the representation. Section 46 explains:

> (2) On request, a lawyer must allow a client *or former client* to inspect and copy any document[86] possessed by the lawyer relating to the representation, unless substantial grounds exist to refuse.
>
> (3) Unless a client or former client consents to non-delivery or substantial grounds exist for refusing to make delivery, a lawyer must deliver to the client or former client, at an appropriate time and *in any event promptly after the representation ends,* such originals and copies of other documents possessed by the lawyer relating to the representation as the client or former client reasonably needs [emphasis added].

A comment identifies certain types of documents that may be withheld from a client or former client.

> A lawyer may refuse to disclose to the client certain law-firm documents reasonably intended only for internal review, such as a memorandum discussing which lawyers in the firm should be assigned to a case, whether a lawyer must withdraw because of the client's misconduct, or the firm's possible malpractice liability to the client. The need for lawyers to be able to set down their thoughts privately in order to assure effective and appropriate representation warrants keeping such documents secret from the client involved. ... The lawyer's duty to inform the client can require the lawyer to disclose matters discussed in a document even when the document itself need not be disclosed.[87]

---

83. A lawyer does not have a continuing duty to inform former clients about changes in the law pertinent to the former representation. If the lawyer continues to represent the client on the matter or on other matters, a court might eventually infer such a duty, but there are as yet no holdings on point. Restatement § 33, comment h and reporter's note.

84. Rule 1.16(d).

85. Rule 1.6, Comment 18.

86. [Authors' footnote.] Restatement § 46, comment a, explains that "a document includes a writing, drawing, graph, chart, photograph, phono-record, tape, disc, or other form of data compilation." Comment d explains that "The client should have an original of documents such as contracts, while a copy will suffice for such documents as legal memoranda and court opinions."

87. Restatement § 46, comment c.

## If a client has not paid the bill at the end of the representation, may the lawyer keep the client's documents until the client pays?

If the client has not yet fully paid the lawyer's fee, or the fee is disputed, the lawyer may retain the documents that the lawyer created for the client for which compensation has not been received, unless retention would "unreasonably harm the client."[88] In all but a few states, statutes and court rules permit a lawyer to withhold even the client's *original* client documents, such as birth certificates, marriage records, and passports, when the fee is unpaid or disputed. The authors of the Restatement strongly criticize that right, called a "retaining lien," on the ground that it may "impose pressure on a client [to pay a disputed bill or a bill that a client cannot afford to pay] disproportionate to the size or validity of the lawyer's fee claim."[89]

### PROBLEM 4-9  THE CANDID NOTES

*This problem is based on a situation that arose in a law school clinic. We have changed the setting to a law firm and changed the text of the "candid notes."*

You are a partner in a small law firm that has three partners, four associates, and three paralegals. The lawyers have instructed the paralegals to make thorough notes of their work, and especially to record their candid impressions of clients whom they interview, so that the lawyers know what to expect when they encounter these clients.

A few months ago, you represented Winnie Bryzanski in an unsuccessful administrative proceeding to require the local school board to admit her daughter Leona to a special education program. Bryzanski decided not to take the matter to court because she did not have enough money to continue to retain you. At that point, she paid for the work that your firm had performed, and your representation ended. You returned to Bryzanski all of her original documents such as Leona's birth certificate.

Yesterday, you received a letter from Bryzanski asking for a copy of "my entire file," because she is about to retain another less costly lawyer to take the case to court. Before sending it, you reviewed the file. In it, you found several memoranda from one of your paralegals to one of your associates reporting on the paralegal's initial interviews with Bryzanski and Leona. Most of the information was of a factual nature, but the memoranda were sprinkled with the paralegal's

---

88. Restatement § 43, comment c.

89. Restatement § 43, comment b. Section 46(3) declines to follow the majority practice, but it bows to the inevitable and allows a lawyer to assert a retaining lien in jurisdictions that permit it "by statute or rule." Restatement §§ 46(4), 43(1). Therefore, even by the Restatement's own terms, such liens are permitted in a majority of jurisdictions, though the Restatement implies that judges who have recognized such liens as a matter of common law have reached the wrong result.

impressions and observations, some of which were derogatory. In particular, the memoranda included these passages:

> This interview took much longer than expected because Ms. Bryzanski is very long-winded and pushy. She insists on having her own way 100 percent. I don't think that she will make a good witness and might even argue with or antagonize the judge. . . .
>
> Leona certainly should win this case and be placed in the special education program. Her social worker says that she is severely emotionally disturbed, and I can confirm that from what I saw of her. She can't seem to sit still and she constantly interrupted both me and her mother. . . .
>
> Although I have related the story of Ms. Bryzanski's encounter with the school principal just as she told it, I should add that I don't think that it is entirely accurate. Sometimes I have the feeling that Ms. Bryzanski exaggerates her accounts because she feels so strongly that the school system has wronged her daughter.

Assume that since there is no ethics rule to the contrary, your jurisdiction would follow the Restatement standard. Must you send copies of the memoranda to Bryzanski? If you must send her the documents, should you redact (that is, delete) your paralegal's impressions?

## 2. Grounds for termination before the work is completed

Sometimes, lawyers are required or permitted to end the representation of a client before the work is completed. Rule 1.16 distinguishes between situations where early termination is mandatory and those where it is permissive.

### a. When the client fires the lawyer

A lawyer must withdraw if the client fires the lawyer.[90] A client always has the right to change lawyers except that a client for whom a lawyer has been appointed may not change lawyers without the court's permission. Also, a court may refuse to permit a substitution that would unduly delay a case. A lawyer also must withdraw if the lawyer's illness or loss of capacity would materially impair the representation.[91]

### b. When continued representation would involve unethical conduct

A lawyer also must withdraw if representation will require the lawyer to violate the law, including the state's rules of professional conduct.[92] A sudden

---

90. Rule 1.16(a)(3). However, most clients are unable to afford to fire their lawyer and start anew with someone else.

91. Rule 1.16(a)(2).

92. We have already considered one application of this requirement in the problem on Reese's Leases in Chapter 2.

withdrawal because the representation entailed a possible violation of law may call adverse attention to the client. During litigation, a lawyer's withdrawal may cause the court to become suspicious about the client. Even so, a lawyer is required to withdraw rather than violate the law.

If the client has already used the lawyer's services to commit a crime or fraud but continued representation will not result in a new or continuing crime or fraud, the lawyer may withdraw but is not required to do so.[93] Similarly, if the client persists in a course of action that the lawyer reasonably believes is a crime or fraud, and the lawyer's services are being used to assist this action, the lawyer may withdraw, even if the actions have not yet been adjudicated to be criminal or fraudulent. Finally, if the client insists on action the lawyer finds "repugnant," the lawyer may withdraw.[94]

### c. When the lawyer wants to terminate the relationship

A lawyer may withdraw from representing a client in other circumstances also. Rule 1.16(b)(1) offers the broadest opportunity for exit. The lawyer may withdraw if it is possible to do so "without material adverse effect on the interests of the client." On the eve of trial, or just before closing a complex business deal, material adverse effect is likely. If the matter is complex and the lawyer has done extensive work, the client might not be able to change lawyers without substantial additional cost. However, when time is not of the essence and in a matter that is not too complex, it may be possible for a client to hire new counsel who will obtain the prior lawyer's records and become familiar with the matter. If the client is indigent and the lawyer is working without a fee, the option to withdraw depends on the availability of another lawyer to take over.

### d. Matters in litigation

If a lawyer has filed suit on behalf of a client or entered an appearance in a matter in litigation, the lawyer generally cannot withdraw from representation of the client without permission from the court that is to hear the case. Rule 1.16(c) acknowledges this by requiring that "A lawyer must comply with applicable law requiring notice to or permission of a tribunal when terminating a representation."

A court may be reluctant to permit withdrawal if the case will be delayed or if a substituted lawyer for the client has not been arranged. Although forcing

---

93. Rule 1.16(b)(3).

94. Rule 1.16(b)(2), (b)(4). For an example of "repugnant" conduct, see Plunkett v. State, 883 S.W.2d 349 (Tex. App. 1994), in which the court allowed an attorney to withdraw during a jury trial because the client had (without using the services of the lawyer) bribed several jurors.

the lawyer to remain in the case may be economically ruinous, a lawyer may not be able to count on a court's granting permission to withdraw.[95]

### e. When the client stops paying the fee

A lawyer may withdraw if the client doesn't pay the lawyer's fee, but the lawyer must first warn the client that nonpayment will lead to withdrawal.[96] This can be very complicated. Sometimes when a client doesn't pay a lawyer's fee, the client is satisfied with the service but doesn't have the money or doesn't want to spend the money. In many cases, however, clients fail to pay lawyers' bills because they are dissatisfied with the service or because they believe that the fees are too high. (This is a common problem if a client has agreed to an hourly fee and has not been given an accurate estimate of the total cost of the work.) If the client doesn't have the money to cover the fee, a lawyer should consider reducing the fee to make the representation affordable for a client with limited means.[97] If a client has a complaint about the service or the fee, usually it is best to sit down with the client and work out a resolution of the dispute rather than simply withdrawing from representation.

### f. When the case imposes an unreasonable financial burden on the lawyer

If a case turns out to impose an unreasonable financial burden on the lawyer, the lawyer may withdraw. This might arise in any matter that turned out to be more complex than the lawyer originally anticipated.[98]

### g. When the client will not cooperate

A lawyer may withdraw if the client makes continued representation by the lawyer "unreasonably difficult." For example, if the client repeatedly fails to show up for scheduled meetings or hearings or if the client refuses to divulge to

---

95. See, e.g., In re Withdrawal of Attorney, 594 N.W.2d 514 (Mich. App. 1999), in which a court repeatedly refused to allow a firm to withdraw from representing prisoners in a class action against the Department of Corrections, even though one of the firm's lawyers had spent ten months doing nothing but observing other lawyers take testimony on behalf of other parties in the case and had been given no date by which she could expect to begin presenting her witnesses, the firm had not been appointed to represent any party, and the firm was not collecting any fees from the prisoners whom it had agreed to represent.

96. Rule 1.16(b)(5).

97. See Rule 6.1, which articulates lawyers' professional obligation to spend part of their time providing services to clients who cannot afford to pay their fees.

98. For an extreme example of such problems, consider the plight of the lawyer in Jonathan Harr, A Civil Action (Random House 1995), in which the lawyer did *not* withdraw, even when on the verge of bankruptcy.

the lawyer the identities of witnesses who could help the case, the lawyer may withdraw.[99] Finally, Rule 1.16 permits withdrawal for "other good cause."[100]

**Postscript:**

Here are the answers to the questions on page 230.[101]

---

99. Rule 1.16(b)(6). See Bailey v. Virginia, 568 S.E.2d 440 (Va. App. 2002) (permitting appointed counsel to withdraw from representing a defendant who insisted that his lawyer communicate with him only in writing).

100. Rule 1.16(b)(7). See, e.g., Greig v. Macy's Northeast, 1996 U.S. Dist. LEXIS 22142 (D.N.J. 1996) ("other good cause" existed for allowing withdrawal, where the lawyer doubted the validity of the client's federal civil rights claim against Macy's for "being wrongfully targeted as a shoplifter" and the mutual failure of lawyer and client to "sustain adequate communication" had caused a "deterioration of the attorney-client relationship").

101. (a) 32% (Source: A Study of the Fact Investigation Practices of Criminal Lawyers in Phoenix, Arizona, 1981 Ariz. St. L.J. 447, 537 (1981)); (b) 39% (Source: Id. at 579); (c) 39% (Source: Michael McConville & Chester L. Mirsky, Criminal Defense of the Poor in New York City, 15 N.Y.U. Rev. L. & Soc. Change 581, 767 (1987)); (d) 12% (Source: Id. at 773); (e) 4% (Source: Martin C. Calhoun, Note, How to Thread the Needle: Toward a Checklist-Based Standard for Evaluating Ineffective Assistance of Counsel Claims, 77 Georgetown L.J. 413, 458 (1988)).

# 5 | CONCURRENT CONFLICTS OF INTEREST

## A. Studying conflicts of interest
1. Why lawyers need to understand conflicts
2. Why the study of conflicts is difficult
3. How the conflicts rules are organized

## B. General principles in evaluating concurrent conflicts
1. Rule 1.7
2. How to evaluate conflicts
3. Nonconsentable conflicts
4. Informed consent
5. Withdrawal and disqualification
6. Imputation of concurrent conflicts

## C. Conflicts between current clients in civil litigation
1. Suing a current client
2. Cross-examining a current client
3. Representation of co-plaintiffs or co-defendants in civil litigation
4. Representing economic competitors in unrelated matters
5. Conflicts in public interest litigation
6. Taking inconsistent legal positions in litigation

## D. Conflicts in nonlitigation matters: Representation of both parties to a transaction

## E. Conflicts in representation of organizations
1. Who is the client?
2. Representation of the entity and employees
3. Duty to protect confidences of employees

# A. Studying conflicts of interest

A lawyer in Chicago has this to say about conflicts of interest:

> When I was young . . . if a law firm — or in those days, really, a lawyer — had two important clients that got into a dispute, the most natural thing for them to do would be both of them would go in, see their lawyer and hash it out with them. . . . And they'd reach an agreement. Maybe it would be worked out in writing, maybe it was a handshake. We can sit back and say, "How unethical that guy was! Here he is collecting a fee from two people who had adverse interests. It's cutting across the lines of loyalty and duty and everything else." But that's not how it was viewed in the '40s and '50s and maybe even into the early '60s. It was: they went to their lawyer; their lawyer is a professional; he's an ethical man; he understands his obligations to both sides, and he can be trusted in that situation. And I think the change that you see is today, what we are saying is, "no, nobody can be trusted in that situation! . . . People have a right to independent counsel. People have a right to have a lawyer that's just thinking about their best interests. You know, the adversary system, hooray, hooray!"[1]

## 1. Why lawyers need to understand conflicts

Lawyers are supposed to avoid conflicts of interest. What defines "conflicts of interest" may have changed over time, as the lawyer quoted above points out, but a basic principle of ethical practice is, and has been, to avoid conflicts. When a lawyer undertakes representation of a client, the lawyer owes that client a duty of loyalty and a duty to protect confidential information. In

---

1. Susan Shapiro, Tangled Loyalties: Conflict of Interest in Legal Practice 58 (U. Mich. Press 2002), quoting an interview with a Chicago lawyer in a firm with more than 100 lawyers.

some situations, it is disloyal for the lawyer to agree to represent another client whose interests are adverse to the first. Also, in the course of representing the second client, the lawyer might (intentionally or accidentally) use or reveal confidential information learned from the first client.

---

**Some possible consequences of representing a client in the face of a conflict:**

**Legal sanctions:**

- Disqualification
- Discipline
- Malpractice liability
- Injunction against representation (transactional case)
- Fee forfeiture

**Business repercussions:**

- Client may reatin a different lawyer
- Client may mistrust you
- Your professional reputation may suffer

---

The conflicts rules guide lawyers on how to distinguish which conflicts are so serious that the lawyer should turn down the second client (or withdraw, if the lawyer already has begun representation), which conflicts are adequately addressed by obtaining informed consent from the clients affected, and which ones are not serious enough even to require informed consent.

One of the most important skills that you will need as a lawyer is to learn to identify and analyze conflicts. Some large firms have one or more expert lawyers whose main role is to evaluate potential or actual conflicts,[2] but most lawyers screen their own cases for conflicts. You can get into real trouble if you don't notice and address conflicts. A lawyer who proceeds in the face of a conflict might be disqualified by a judge, enjoined from further representation,[3] sued for malpractice, or charged with violation of disciplinary rules. The lawyer might forfeit a fee for the conflicted work. The lawyer might even be indicted for ignoring a conflict of interest. The most common type of litigation

---

2. Many large firms have concluded that having an ethics advisor in the firm to screen conflicts and to help build "ethical infrastructure" helps to avoid professional liability and other problems. Elizabeth Chambliss & David B. Wilkins, The Emerging Role of Ethics Advisors, General Counsel, and Other Compliance Specialists in Large Law Firms, 44 Ariz. L. Rev. 559 (2002); Elizabeth Chambliss & David B. Wilkins, Promoting Ethical Infrastructure in Large Law Firms: A Call for Research and Reporting, 30 Hofstra L. Rev. 691 (2002); Susan Saab Fortney, Are Law Firm Partners Islands unto Themselves? An Empirical Study of Law Firm Peer Review and Culture, 10 Geo. J. Leg. Ethics 271 (1996).

3. If the matter is in litigation, a lawyer might be disqualified. If the representation is transactional, a client aggrieved by conflicting work for another client might seek an injunction prohibiting the lawyer from continuing the work in question. See Maritrans GP Inc., v. Pepper, Hamilton & Scheetz, 602 A.2d 1277 (Pa. 1992).

over conflicts involves one firm moving to disqualify another that has an apparent conflict of interest. Proceeding in the face of conflicts has been the basis for malpractice suits. Any of these consequences are possible.

Even leaving these various disaster scenarios aside, you need to be able to evaluate potential conflicts to know whether you can take on a particular matter. If you take on a matter that raises a conflict without remedying it, a client may feel betrayed, a real problem even if the client doesn't fire you or sue you. Your role as a lawyer puts you in a position of trust with each client. Maintaining that trust and inspiring confidence in your loyalty and judgment are essential to your practice.

Competency in conflict evaluation also is important to your financial interests. If you doze through these difficult chapters on conflicts of interest, you might take on a matter that you shouldn't and wind up losing more than one client as a result. Or, in an abundance of caution, you might turn down a matter that you would be permitted to take on if you obtained client consent. If you plan to work in a law firm, you may not be responsible at the beginning of your time in practice for client intake decisions. But even if you are not responsible, a good working knowledge of conflicts rules is useful. Suppose, for example, that you get a job in a small firm that does criminal defense work, and you notice that the firm routinely undertakes joint representation of criminal defendants. Perhaps the partners graduated from law school in the 1960s, when there was no course in professional responsibility. New lawyers often wind up educating their elders about the rules of professional conduct and the other law that governs lawyers.

## 2. Why the study of conflicts is difficult

Most students find this material more difficult than the other subjects addressed in this course. Here are some of the reasons why studying conflicts of interest can give you a headache.

- **Technical lingo.** Lawyers and judges who deal with conflicts use many terms of art and make many conceptual distinctions. How do you determine whether there is "direct adversity" or whether there is a "substantial relationship" between one matter and another? What is an "imputed conflict"?
- **Conflicts with whom?** A lawyer can have conflicts caused by her obligations to a present client, a former client, or to some other person. A lawyer can have conflicts because of the obligations of other lawyers with whom the lawyer works or used to work. A lawyer also can have conflicts between her clients' interests and her own interests.
- **A dizzying array of scenarios.** A conflict might be identified when a lawyer is considering taking on a new client. Another might be triggered by one client company merging with another. A third might develop because a firm hires an associate from another firm. Conflicts arise in many situations.

■ **At intake or midstream.** A conflict can be evident at the outset of the representation of a client, or it might emerge when work on a matter is well under way. It is not sufficient for a firm to have a good system for reviewing incoming matters to check for conflicts. It also must have a system to monitor for emerging conflicts.

■ **Factual context is everything.** Conflicts problems tend to be very fact-specific, so it is difficult to come up with meaningful generalizations about them. A conflict can relate to the relationship between two clients, to the subject matter at issue in a case or to some specific issue that arises in litigation.

■ **Special rules for particular types of work.** The constitutional rights of criminal defendants, for example, impose a separate set of rules in criminal conflicts situations. Policy considerations have produced some different rules for government lawyers and for law students who work in law firms.

■ **Complex solutions.** When a conflict arises, several different remedial options are available. Choosing one of them is usually a complex decision. If a conflict is very serious, for example, a lawyer sometimes needs to withdraw from representing one or more clients. (This is a big deal; the clients lose a valued lawyer and may have to pay additional fees to get another lawyer up to speed. The lawyer loses a client and the fees that would have been earned for the remainder of the work.) In other instances, a lawyer must decline to take on representation of a new client. Some conflicts are "consentable" — a lawyer may proceed if clients give informed consent.[4] Other conflicts are remedied by making an agreement with one or more clients to limit the scope of representation. Still others are remedied by imposing a "screen" (a communication barrier) between the conflicted lawyer and the one taking on the problematic work.

---

**Possible remedies for conflicts between clients:**
- Withdrawing or declining to represent a new client
- Obtaining clients' informed consent
- Signing agreements that limit representation
- Screening

---

■ **Inconsistent rules.** Another problem in studying conflicts is that the rules on what is permissible vary. You might well begin your conflicts analysis by looking at the ethical rules, which would be the applicable

---

4. The word "consentable" may have entered the English language through scholars of legal ethics. The official Reporters of the Restatement apparently coined the terms "consentable" and "non-consentable" in relationship to conflicts of interest. Thomas D. Morgan, Conflicts of Interest in the Restatement: Comments on Professor Moore's Paper, 10 Geo. J. Leg. Ethics 575, 576 (1997).

standards in a disciplinary proceeding against a lawyer. But if the matter is before a judge on a malpractice claim, the judge will follow prior case law on civil liability for malpractice. If the matter is before a judge on a motion to disqualify, the judge will follow precedent on disqualification.[5] These other bodies of law are often in harmony with the ethical rules, but not always. For example, some jurisdictions recognize screening as an acceptable method of resolving conflicts for the purpose of disqualification even if their ethical rules do not allow solving conflicts problems by screening.[6] And, as we have seen in other contexts, the ethical rules vary from one state to another.

■ **Fuzzy standards.** Perhaps the most serious problem is that the rules draw broad, fuzzy lines and therefore do not answer many questions definitively.

The goal of this chapter is to acquaint you with the various categories of conflicts, to teach you which questions you need to ask about which types of conflicts, and to give you a start on developing the judgment required to arrive at useful answers to those questions.

## Light in the tunnel

At the end of the last century, the American Law Institute (ALI) completed the Restatement (Third) of the Law Governing Lawyers. This work is the most comprehensive synthesis of the law that governs lawyers, on conflicts and other issues. Then the ABA Ethics 2000 Commission completed a report that, among other things, updated the conflicts rules to take account of the ALI's work. Although some confusion and ambiguity remain, there has been significant progress in pulling together the body of law that governs lawyers, in general, and the conflict of interest rules, in particular.

In the material that follows, we do our part in providing a partial antidote to any remaining ambiguity by offering a conceptual outline of each topic and then providing examples and illustrative problems for each. A starting point is to become familiar with how the rules are organized and to learn the terminology used in the rules to refer to different types of conflicts.

---

5. Perhaps the divergence is not as serious as it might seem. For example, if a judge decided not to disqualify a lawyer for proceeding in the face of a conflict, it is unlikely that a bar counsel would decide to bring charges against that lawyer for a conflict that a judge had cleared. On the other hand, disciplinary charges often are brought against lawyers whose misconduct may involve criminal activity but who have not been indicted. (One spectacular example is that former President Richard M. Nixon was charged with disciplinary violations for his conduct in the Watergate scandal and resigned his New York law license, even though he was never indicted. Bruce A. Green, The Criminal Regulation of Lawyers, 67 Fordham L. Rev. 327, 350 (1998).

6. See Chapter 6 for an explanation of the concept of "screening" a disqualified lawyer from other lawyers in that lawyer's firm, and a discussion of the limited situations in which the rules of professional conduct in most states accept screening as a device to prevent disqualification of the entire firm.

## 3. How the conflicts rules are organized

---

**Categories of Conflicts**

**Concurrent conflict: Rules 1.7, 1.8.** This is a conflict between two present obligations of a lawyer or between one present client and one prospective client. Sometimes a lawyer seeks informed consent from the affected clients to waive a concurrent conflict. In some cases, representation is prohibited even with consent.

**Successive conflict of interest: Rule 1.9.** This is a conflict between an obligation to a present client and an obligation to a former client. A lawyer may proceed despite a successive conflict if the affected client consents.

**Imputed conflict: Rule 1.10.** This is a conflict between an obligation of one lawyer to a client and an obligation of an affiliated lawyer. One lawyer is "infected" by a conflict because one of his partners would face a conflict in taking on a particular client. The conflict could be between a client of lawyer A and a client of one of A's partners (concurrent). There could be a conflict between a client of A and a past client of A's partner (successive); the former client might have been represented by the same firm or the former firm. An imputed conflict may be waived by a client under the conditions stated in Rule 1.7.

**Conflicts for government lawyers: Rule 1.11.** Rule 1.11 addresses both successive and imputed conflicts of interest for lawyers who move between jobs in government and the private sector. These include successive conflicts, if a lawyer's new clients' interests conflict with the interests of his former employer, and imputed conflicts, where work done by other lawyers in a firm conflicts with the interests of a lawyer's former employer. Many such conflicts are resolved by informed consent.

---

The Model Rules and the state rules based on them address first the most immediate conflicts and then the more remote conflicts. The most immediate ones involve simultaneous representation of conflicting obligations by one lawyer or firm. The more remote conflicts are those that involve one current and one former client and may involve another lawyer or firm. The following table illustrates this point.

| Conflicts spectrum: Overlap in time, lawyers, and firms | | | | |
|---|---|---|---|---|
| Type of conflict | Simultaneous or sequential representation | Conflict between two clients of one lawyer[7] or not | Lawyer(s) in same firm or formerly in same firm | Lawyer may proceed if client(s) give informed consent[8] |
| **Concurrent** | Simultaneous | One lawyer | Same firm | Sometimes |
| **Successive** | Sequential | One lawyer | Same firm | Always |
| **Imputed** | Simultaneous or sequential | Two or more lawyers | Currently or formerly in same firm | Sometimes |

## How the conflicts discussion is organized

The material on conflicts of interest is more voluminous and more complex than the other topics in this book.[9] Consequently, we divide this material into three chapters. The rest of this chapter covers concurrent conflicts of interest. These are conflicts that involve a lawyer's conflicting obligations to two current clients, or to one present and one prospective client. We begin by presenting some basic principles about how to analyze concurrent conflicts. We then examine concurrent conflicts that arise in civil litigation and in transactional settings, and in the representation of organizations. Finally, we consider some issues that arise in the joint representation of clients in criminal, domestic relations, estate planning, insurance, and class action cases.

In Chapter 6, we explore successive and imputed conflicts, and conflicts for judges. Successive conflicts are those that involve one present and one past obligation (e.g., between a present client and a former client). Lawyers who work or worked for governmental organizations are subject to different successive conflicts rules. These are also explained in Chapter 6, as are the rules on when conflicts are imputed to other lawyers and how a firm may prevent or remedy imputation. Chapter 7 considers conflicts between the interests of a client and a lawyer's own interests. That chapter covers fee arrangements

---

7. A conflict presented between two clients of one lawyer is described here as a one-lawyer conflict. An imputed conflict occurs because of one lawyer's present or former association with another lawyer, not because one lawyer is representing conflicting interests.

8. In some cases, a lawyer needs the consent of both clients to proceed; in others, the lawyer needs consent from only one client. For example, if work on behalf of a new client might involve adverse use of confidences received from a former client, the lawyer needs consent from the former client but not the new client.

9. The volume of this material reflects its bulk in the Model Rules; nearly a third of the pages of the Model Rules and their comments are devoted to the subjects covered in Chapters 5, 6, and 7 of this book. Likewise, many practicing lawyers who are the resident legal ethics experts in their firms would tell you that the majority of their time is devoted to evaluating possible conflicts of interest.

between lawyers and clients,[10] business transactions between lawyer and client, gifts from clients, and other issues.

# B. General principles in evaluating concurrent conflicts

## 1. Rule 1.7

Rule 1.7 first explains what is considered to be a problematic conflict between two present clients (or one present and one prospective client). It then explains that for some, but not all, of these conflicts, a lawyer may seek informed consent from the affected clients and may proceed if consent is obtained.

### Rule 1.7    Conflicts of interest: current clients[11]

| Rule language* | Authors' explanation |
| --- | --- |
| (a) Except as provided in paragraph (b), a lawyer **shall not** represent a client if the representation involves a **concurrent** conflict of interest. A concurrent conflict of interest exists if: | A concurrent conflict is one between two current obligations of the lawyer — two clients, a client and another person, or a client and the lawyer's own interests. |
| (1) the representation of one client will be **directly adverse** to another client; or | "Directly adverse" means that a lawyer is acting directly against the interests of one of his own clients. (See box below.) |
| (2) there is a **significant risk** that the **representation** of one or more clients will be **materially limited** by the lawyer's **responsibilities to another** client, a former client or a third person or by a **personal interest** of the lawyer. | Even if there is no direct adversity, there is a conflict if there is a significant "likelihood that a difference in interests will eventuate and, if it does, [that] it will materially interfere with the lawyer's independent professional judgment." Comment 8. |

*Continued*

---

10. Most books on professional responsibility do not include issues about legal fees in the materials on conflicts of interest. We cover them for two reasons. When a lawyer charges a fee to a client, there is usually a conflict of interest, in the ordinary if not the technical sense of the term. The lawyer would like the fee to be higher. The client would like it to be lower. Also, most of the issues that are conventionally thought of as involving lawyer-client conflicts are about money, so we placed all the lawyer-client money issues in one chapter.

11. This is the text of the relevant Delaware Rules of Professional Conduct. Unless specified otherwise, all of this book's quotations from rules of professional conduct are quotations from the Delaware Rules of Professional Conduct. In a few instances, we quote from rules or from published proposed rules in other states. Except where we note otherwise, however, the text of all state rules that we quote is the same as the text of the ABA's Model Rules of Professional Conduct. See the note in the Introduction for a more detailed explanation.

| Rule language* | Authors' explanation |
|---|---|
| (b) **Notwithstanding** the existence of a concurrent conflict of interest under paragraph (a), a lawyer **may represent** a client if: | Even if a conflict is found under Rule 1.7(a), in most cases a lawyer may represent the conflicting interests if he obtains the clients' informed consent. But in some cases (listed below) the lawyer may *not* ask for client consent. |
| (1) the lawyer **reasonably believes** that the lawyer will be able to provide **competent and diligent representation** to each affected client; | A lawyer may not ask for consent "if in the circumstances the lawyer cannot reasonably conclude that the lawyer will be able to provide competent and diligent representation." Comment 15. |
| (2) the representation is **not prohibited by law;** | "For example, in some states substantive law provides that [even if the clients consent] the same lawyer may not represent more than one defendant in a capital case." Comment 16. |
| (3) the representation does **not** involve the assertion of a **claim by one** client **against another client** represented by the lawyer in the **same litigation or other proceeding before a tribunal; and** | A lawyer can't represent adverse parties in litigation even with their consent. This means, for example, that a lawyer cannot represent both plaintiff and defendant in a lawsuit requesting an amicable divorce. |
| (4) **each affected client gives informed consent**, confirmed in writing. | To get informed consent, a lawyer must explain to each affected client the "ways that the conflict could have adverse effects on the interests of that client." Comment 18. Sometimes this requires disclosure of the confidences of another client, which depends on the other client's consent. Comment 19. |

*All emphasis added.

Rule 1.7 addresses how a lawyer should analyze conflicts between two present clients. Under Rule 1.7, a lawyer is prohibited from representing a client if one of the conflicts described in 1.7(a) exists, unless as per 1.7(b) the conflict is waivable by the client and the client gives informed consent to allow the lawyer to continue with the representation despite the conflict. Rule 1.7(a) outlines two types of conflicts that might preclude representation of a client: One client's interests might be directly adverse to those of another client, or there might be a "significant risk" that a representation will be "materially limited" by another obligation of the lawyer — to another client, to a former client, or to a third person. A representation also could be materially limited by a conflict between the lawyer's interests and the client's interests.[12] If a conflict is present, a lawyer

---

12. The Restatement subsumes both the "direct adversity" and "material limitation" conflicts into one category and asserts that:

A conflict of interest is involved if there is a substantial risk that the lawyer's representation of the client would be materially and adversely affected by the client's own interests or by the lawyer's duties to another current client, a former client, or a third person.

should evaluate under 1.7(b) whether she may continue to represent the affected clients if they give informed consent after learning about the conflicts. A lawyer may seek consent to resolve many, but not all, conflicts.

## a. Direct adversity

A conflict is said to involve "direct adversity" to the interests of a client if the lawyer's conduct on behalf of one client requires the lawyer to act against the interest of another current client. The most obvious example is a lawyer who files suit on behalf of one client against another of his own clients. If, in the course of representing one client, the lawyer takes action that could directly harm another client, there is direct adversity. Both litigation and nonlitigation situations can involve direct adversity.

---

**Direct Adversity: Common Situations**

- A lawyer who represents client A in one matter sues client A in a second matter on behalf of client B. (Someone else might be representing client A in the second lawsuit.)
- The lawyer acts adversely to a client in litigation (e.g., by cross-examining him).
- Outside of litigation, a lawyer is asked to undertake adversarial negotiation against another client. (Rule 1.7, Comments 6 and 7.)

---

## b. Material limitation

Even if there is no direct adversity, a conflict exists if representation of one client would be "materially limited" by another responsibility of the lawyer. The "other responsibilities" that might materially limit a lawyer's representation of a client include obligations to

- another present client;
- a former client;
- someone else to whom a lawyer owes a duty (e.g., if the lawyer has fiduciary obligations because the lawyer is a trustee, an executor, or a member of a corporate board of directors);
- someone other than the client who is paying the lawyer's fee;
- the lawyer's own financial, employment, personal, or other interests.

FOR EXAMPLE: Comment 8 to Rule 1.7 explains that "a lawyer asked to represent several individuals seeking to form a joint venture is likely to be materially limited in [his] ability to recommend or advocate all possible

---

Restatement § 121. The language used by the Restatement sounds more like the "material limitation" language of Rule 1.7. However, there is not a significant substantive difference between the standards articulated by the Restatement and the Model Rules. "Direct adversity" conflicts are in fact a subset of a larger group of conflicts in which the lawyer's representation could be materially limited by another obligation. The conflicts that involve direct adversity often are the most serious conflicts.

positions that each might take because of the lawyer's duty of loyalty to the others."[13]

If a client would receive less vigorous representation from a lawyer because of a lawyer's other responsibilities, there might be a "material limitation" conflict. A "mere possibility" of harm is insufficient to present a conflict. To evaluate whether a conflict is present, a lawyer must ask two questions.

- How likely is it "that a difference in interests will eventuate"?
- If there likely is such a divergence, would it "materially interfere" with the lawyer's advice to or representation of a client?[14]

If there is a conflict that presents either direct adversity or material limitation, the conflict must be evaluated under Rule 1.7(b) to see whether the lawyer may seek informed consent from the affected clients or whether the conflict is nonconsentable.

## 2. How to evaluate conflicts

To resolve a concurrent conflict under Rule 1.7, a lawyer must

1. clearly identify the client or clients;
2. determine whether a conflict of interest exists;
3. decide whether the representation may be undertaken despite the existence of a conflict (i.e., whether the conflict is consentable); and
4. if so, consult with the clients affected under paragraph (a) and obtain their informed consent, confirmed in writing.[15]

Some conflicts are apparent at the time a lawyer undertakes to represent a client; others emerge later because of changes in circumstances or information learned in the course of representation. The rules encourage lawyers to "adopt reasonable procedures, appropriate for the size and type of firm and practice, to determine in both litigation and non-litigation matters the persons and issues involved" for the purpose of identifying conflicts.[16]

If a consentable conflict is identified before a client is accepted, and the affected client gives informed consent after being fully advised by the lawyer about the possible problems that the conflict might generate, the lawyer may go forward despite the conflict. If the conflict is not consentable, the lawyer must decline to accept representation of one or more clients. If a nonconsentable conflict emerges after a lawyer has undertaken representation, the lawyer might be able to avoid the conflict by withdrawing from the representation of one of

---

13. Later in this chapter, you will see examples of several types of situations that have been found to present a conflict in which the lawyer's representation of a client would be materially limited by the lawyer's responsibility to another client or to someone else.
14. Rule 1.7, Comment 8.
15. Rule 1.7, Comment 2.
16. Id. at Comment 3.

the affected clients.[17] Sometimes, however, the lawyer will have to give up both clients.

## 3. Nonconsentable conflicts

Most conflicts are consentable — it is the unusual case in which a court might say that even with the consent of all parties, the lawyer should not go forward. But some conflicts are considered so problematic that a lawyer may not continue the representation in the face of them, even if the client wishes the lawyer to do so. To determine whether a conflict is consentable, Rule 1.7(b) directs a lawyer to ask

- whether she "reasonably believes that [she] will be able to provide competent and diligent representation" to the relevant clients;
- whether "the representation is . . . prohibited by law"; and
- whether the representation involves litigation in which the lawyer is representing one client against another client whom the lawyer is representing in that matter.

### a. The lawyer's reasonable belief

In evaluating a conflict, a lawyer must consider "whether the interests of the clients will be adequately protected if the clients are permitted to give their informed consent to representation burdened by a conflict of interest."[18] The question is whether the lawyer can "reasonably conclude that [he] will be able to provide competent and diligent representation."[19] The inquiry is not whether the lawyer has the subjective impression that the conflict is consentable. The question is what a reasonable lawyer would think.[20]

In considering whether a conflict may be waived by consent, the lawyer should ask: Would there be an adverse effect on the *relationship* with either client? Also, would there be an adverse effect on the *representation* of either client? In addressing these questions, a lawyer should consider the following questions.

- Are the conflicting representations related or unrelated? If the matters involved are not factually interrelated, the conflict may be waivable.[21]

---

17. Id. at Comment 5.

18. Id. at Comment 15.

19. Id. The Restatement formulates this question a little differently, explaining that "if a reasonable and disinterested lawyer would conclude that one or more of the affected clients could not consent . . . because the representation would fall short in either respect, the conflict is nonconsentable." Restatement, § 122, comment g(iv).

20. Rule 1.7, Comment 15. The Restatement uses similar language, stating "a lawyer may not represent a client if . . . it is not reasonably likely that the lawyer will be able to provide adequate representation to one or more of the clients." Restatement, § 122(2)(c).

21. Restatement § 122, comment g(iv).

- Does the problem involve joint representation of two parties with very divergent interests? If so, it may not be possible to pursue the interests of one without harming the other.[22]
- Is the conflict between two present clients or between one present and one former client? In the latter case, all conflicts are consentable.[23]
- Does the lawyer have a friendship or a bond of professional loyalty toward one of the two clients? If so, the lawyer might be unable to provide competent and diligent representation to the other, especially if the interests of the two are divergent.[24]
- How sophisticated is the client? If the client is a sophisticated user of legal services, the client's consent is likely to solve the problem. For example, in a practice in which the clients are large institutional clients with general counsels advising them, nearly all conflicts may be waived by consent.[25]

## b. Representation prohibited by law

Some conflicts are not consentable because the representation of a client in the face of some conflicts is prohibited by statute or by case law.

**FOR EXAMPLE:** A federal statute prohibits a federal government lawyer from representing a client against the United States regardless of whether the government consents.[26]

**FOR EXAMPLE:** Some state statutes provide that even with client consent, a lawyer may not represent more than one co-defendant in a capital case.[27]

## c. Suing one client on behalf of another client

A final category of nonconsentable conflicts are cases in which a lawyer is asked to represent two parties who are "aligned directly against each other in the same litigation."[28] A lawyer may not represent "opposing parties in the same litigation, regardless of the clients' consent."[29]

**FOR EXAMPLE:** Can a lawyer represent both husband and wife in a divorce? Some jurisdictions allow two spouses to hire one lawyer to

---

22. Id.
23. See Rule 1.9; Restatement § 122, comment g(iv).
24. Id.
25. Restatement, § 122, comment g(iv).
26. 18 U.S.C. § 205 (2004).
27. Restatement § 122, comment g(i).
28. Restatement § 122, comment g(iii).
29. Rule 1.7, Comment 23.

help them work out the property settlement and other issues. Under this rule, however, the lawyer could not file a divorce action in which the lawyer represented both plaintiff and defendant. The parties might agree, however, that after the lawyer assisted both of them in negotiating terms, the lawyer could represent one of them in the litigation.[30]

## 4. Informed consent

If the conflict is consentable, a lawyer may ask the affected clients whether they would like to waive the conflict by giving informed consent. If the client declines to give consent, the lawyer cannot take on or continue the conflicting work. A lawyer seeking such consent must communicate to a client all the information needed to understand the possible adverse effects that might befall the client if she waives the conflict. The Model Rules define "informed consent" to refer to an "agreement to a proposed course of conduct after the lawyer has communicated adequate information and explanation about the material risks of and reasonably available alternatives to the proposed course of conduct."[31]

### How much information does a lawyer have to give a client to obtain informed consent?

The lawyer must orally explain to the client the risks, advantages, and possible alternatives to the lawyer going forward with the representation. A client's oral consent must be "confirmed in writing" by the lawyer. Specifically, the client must sign a waiver of the conflict of interest, or the lawyer must, within a reasonable time, send the client a document memorializing the oral communication.[32] Although the client is not required to sign the document, a client must explicitly indicate consent to the conflict. A lawyer may not merely explain the conflict in a letter and state that she will assume consent if the client does not respond.[33]

---

30. This example is based on Restatement § 122, comment g(iii), illus. 8. The Restatement notes that some jurisdictions restrict joint representation in situations involving the interests of children. See the discussion below of conflicts in domestic relations matters.

31. Rule 1.0(e). The Restatement uses similar language, stating that to give informed consent, a present or former client must "have reasonably adequate information about the material risks of such representation to that client or former client." Restatement § 122(1).

32. See Rule 1.7, Comment 20.

33. Restatement § 122, comment c(i).

*Dr. Susan Shapiro*

Much of our knowledge about how lawyers actually handle conflicts of interest comes from a sociological study undertaken by Dr. Susan Shapiro, a Senior Research Fellow at the American Bar Foundation. She interviewed 128 lawyers in Illinois to explore the conflicts of interest that arise in different arenas of law practice and to examine how the lawyers think about and evaluate conflicts. She reports the results in Tangled Loyalties: Conflict of Interest in Legal Practice (U. Mich. Press 2002). This study is the most comprehensive empirical study to date on how American lawyers think about conflicts of interest. (Shapiro lists some of the other studies, all narrower in scope, on page 20.)

Shapiro talked to lawyers from large and small law firms, and to lawyers who worked in large cities and small towns. Id. at 29. She talked with lawyers who specialize in many different areas of practice. Id. at 51. Ninety-four percent of the lawyers interviewed were men. Id. at 52. They ranged in age from late 20s to late 70s. Id. at 53. She chose to interview only Illinois lawyers to avoid finding differences in the lawyers' analyses of conflicts that were the product of differences among the state rules. Some aspects of the lawyers' thinking may reflect Illinois legal culture, but the range of her exploration covers the gamut of types of private law practice. Ninety-two percent of the firms randomly selected consented to allow Shapiro to conduct one or more interviews. This makes it unlikely that her data is atypical because of a nonresponse bias. Id. at 28.

We appreciate Dr. Shapiro's willingness to allow us to illustrate conflicts of interest by quoting her research.

**When clients are asked to consent to conflicts, do they usually agree?**

Many clients give consent to waive conflicts, especially if they perceive the conflicts to be technical and believe that it will not harm their interests for the lawyers to pursue the conflicting work. But clients' actions are not always predictable. Some clients decline to waive even technical conflicts. Susan Shapiro talked to one lawyer who told the following story:

> Did some work for a bank in a smaller town in Illinois — for their trust department. We had a client in the firm that wanted to sue the bank with regard to mishandling of a commercial loan. It had nothing to do with their trust department. This bank is represented by every lawyer in . . . their town. So that, from the point of view of finding someone to defend them, they had no legitimate gripe. From the point of view of my knowing anything that would have any bearing upon this suit, they had no legitimate gripe. We thought it would be nice to ask them anyway. And they said no, that they absolutely did not want us representing anybody who was suing them. . . . That was a very surprising reaction.[34]

---

34. Susan Shapiro, Tangled Loyalties: Conflict of Interest in Legal Practice 61 (U. Mich. Press 2002).

### How can a lawyer make adequate disclosure without revealing confidences of one client to another?

Often the lawyer will need to disclose some confidential information about client A's case to client B so that client B has enough information to know whether he wants to consent. This disclosure may be necessary to help the client to understand the nature of the conflict.

> **FOR EXAMPLE:** Suppose client A proposes to purchase a video rental business from client B, and both want a single lawyer to handle the transaction. The lawyer knows that client B is leaving the video business to become an evangelical minister. Client A has told the lawyer that he intends to expand the store to include X-rated films. The lawyer might need to disclose this to client B because if client B knew this information, he might not want to sell to client A, much less share a lawyer with client A.

To obtain informed consent from the seller in this example, the lawyer must share confidential information from the buyer. Before doing this, the lawyer must ask the buyer's permission to disclose confidences to the seller. If the buyer declines to allow the lawyer to disclose the relevant confidences, the lawyer may not proceed with the representation because the lawyer will not be able to obtain informed consent from the seller.

### If the client already knows the information needed to give consent, does the lawyer have to explain it anyway?

No. The lawyer must assure that the client has the relevant information, but if the client receives the information from another source, the lawyer doesn't have to provide it also. For example, if the client has a separate lawyer to advise her about the risks involved in waiving a particular conflict, the client might need less information from the lawyer than one who did not.[35]

### If a client gives informed consent to a conflict, and things turn out worse than expected, can the client change her mind and withdraw consent?

Suppose two clients give informed consent to a lawyer's continued representation of both of them in making a business deal. They begin negotiations, and things go badly. It appears that one of them may file suit against the other. Are they stuck with a common lawyer? Clearly not. A client always has the right to fire a lawyer. A client who has waived a conflict may revoke the waiver.[36]

If a client justifiably revokes consent, her lawyer might need to withdraw from representing both clients, or the lawyer might be able to continue to

---

35. Restatement § 122, comment c(i).

36. A client may always revoke his consent to a conflict, but the revocation may or may not preclude the lawyer from continuing to represent other involved clients. This will depend on whether the revocation is justified, for example, because of a material change in circumstances, and on whether there would be material harm to the client or to the other lawyer if the lawyer ceases representation of other clients. Restatement § 122, comment f.

represent one of them. This depends on the nature of the conflict that has arisen, what if any circumstances have changed, and what harm might result from continuing to represent one of the clients.[37] If a client revoked consent arbitrarily, a lawyer might be permitted to continue to represent another client who had relied on the earlier consent in hiring this lawyer.[38]

During the informed consent process, a lawyer may ask whether if a conflict arises, the lawyer could continue to work with one of the clients, and if so, which one? If there is disclosure and consent to a contingency plan, it is more likely that the lawyer may continue to represent one of them if a conflict arises.

### Can a client give consent early in the representation to possible conflicts that might arise in the future?

Does a client have to give informed consent at the point at which a conflict arises, or can a client consent to waive conflicts when the client engages the services of the lawyer? Like so many conflicts questions, the answer is, "It depends." Certainly a lawyer may seek advance waivers from clients, but the validity of those waivers depends on

- how well the client understands the risks of the possible future conflicts;
- the thoroughness and specificity of the lawyer's disclosure of possible future conflicts before the waiver was given;
- the client's experience with respect to the legal services being provided and the nature of the conflicts that could arise;
- whether the client received independent legal advice before giving the advance waiver; and
- whether the conflict that arises is one that can be solved by consent (if it is nonconsentable, the waiver will not be valid as to that particular conflict).[39]

**FOR EXAMPLE:** A law firm has an office in New York and one in Chicago. The firm does commercial collection work for one sophisticated institutional client in New York and gives tax advice to many Chicago clients. The law firm might obtain valid advance consent from the New York client to conflicts that would arise if the firm were to file a collection matter against one of its Chicago clients.[40] (The Chicago client would have a different lawyer for the collection matter.) In the event of such a suit, the firm would need consent from the tax client also.[41]

---

37. Rule 1.7, Comment 21.
38. Restatement § 122, comment f.
39. Rule 1.7, Comment 22. One scholar recommends amending Rule 1.7 to reduce uncertainties about the effectiveness of advance waivers, by expressly encouraging and permitting lawyers and clients to sign agreements defining direct adversity and substantial relatedness for the lawyer's work involving that client. Richard Painter, Advance Waiver of Conflicts, 13 Geo. J. Leg. Ethics 289 (2000).
40. The firm would not represent the tax client in the collection matter.
41. This example is based on Restatement § 122, comment d, illus. 2.

## 5. Withdrawal and disqualification

Suppose a lawyer discovers a nonconsentable conflict or the relevant client declines to consent to the lawyer's continued work on the matter. In this case, the lawyer must withdraw from representation. (See Rule 1.16.) The lawyer might take this action (to seek consent and withdraw if consent is not forthcoming) on his own initiative, or he might be prompted to act by his opposing counsel. If a lawyer is representing a client in the face of a conflict without obtaining consent, the lawyer's opposing counsel may file a motion to disqualify the lawyer from continuing the work.

Some motions for disqualification are motivated by concerns that the conflicted representation will affect another party, but sometimes they are filed to obstruct litigation or to obtain a strategic advantage by requiring an adversary to spend time and money to change lawyers. Courts review motions to disqualify filed by adversaries with care to ensure that they are not being enlisted to assist in such tactics.[42]

There may be many cases in which law firms simply turn away clients because the firms have been interviewed by the adverse party. Susan Shapiro notes that "Major corporations [and individual clients] needlessly [engage] law firms in order to strategically conflict out a firm possessed of rare expertise that might be used against them."[43] One of the Chicago lawyers whom Shapiro interviewed explained that

> in the divorce area ... there are people who deliberately shop around for lawyers, in order to create conflicts so that their spouses can't hire those lawyers.... Obviously, I think it's unethical.... And there are also ... people [who] have been through a divorce ... who ... will encourage friends ... going through a divorce — to "go see five, six lawyers before you ... sign with the one you intend to sign with, so that your [spouse] can't ... see those lawyers."[44]

### Do the rules of professional conduct apply in determining disqualification motions?

Although the ethics rules were written primarily to be a basis for discipline of lawyers who violated them, the courts have come to rely on, or at least give substantial weight to, the rules in various other types of proceedings, including motions to disqualify lawyers because of conflicts of interest or other unethical behavior.[45] Some courts evaluating disqualification motions have looked not at the conflicts rules in the applicable jurisdiction but at the ABA Model Rules,

---

42. ABA, Annotated Model Rules of Professional Conduct 116-117 (5th ed. 2003). See also the Preamble to the Model Rules, ¶ 20.

43. Shapiro, supra n. 34, at 74.

44. Id. at 74-75. Note, however, that the conduct described may not actually be "unethical," as the rules of professional conduct do not explicitly prohibit this tactic.

45. Annotated Model Rules, supra n. 42, at 4-5.

and sometimes at the Restatement, as evidence of "national standards" for evaluation of conflicts of interest.[46]

## 6. Imputation of concurrent conflicts

A lawyer can have a conflict of interest because he represents two clients whose interests conflict or because he represents one client whose interests conflict with those of a client represented by his partner. We discuss imputed conflicts in greater depth in Chapter 6. Here we introduce the rules on imputation of conflicts between current clients.

> **Rule 1.10   Imputation of Conflicts of Interest: General Rule**[47]
> **(a) While lawyers are associated in a firm, none of them shall knowingly represent a client when any one of them practicing alone would be prohibited from doing so by [Rules] 1.7 or 1.9, unless the prohibition is based on a personal interest of the prohibited lawyer and does not present a significant risk of materially limiting the representation of the client by the remaining lawyers in the firm. . . .**
> **(c) A disqualification prescribed by this rule may be waived by the affected client under the conditions stated in Rule 1.7.**

Rule 1.10(a) takes the position that "a firm of lawyers is essentially one lawyer for purposes of the rules governing loyalty to the client. . . ."[48] If one lawyer has a conflict, then so do all the other lawyers in the firm. Both partners and associates are "lawyers" in the firm. This rule applies to all conflicts involving a lawyer's obligations to a client. Some conflicts between a client's interest and a lawyer's personal interest are not imputed to other lawyers in the firm.[49]

While the range of conflicts imputed to all lawyers within a firm is very broad, Rule 1.10 provides that such conflicts may be waived by a client affected by the conflict, subject to the restrictions articulated in Rule 1.7(b).[50] A few jurisdictions allow law firms to avoid imputation of conflicts by "screening" the conflicted lawyer from any contact with the matter that presents the problem.[51] In these jurisdictions, if an adequate screening process has been implemented, the firm need not get the client's consent to proceed. Except in

---

46. Annotated Model Rules, supra n. 42, at 9, citing several cases that have relied on the Model Rules or the Restatement.

47. Ariz. R. Prof. Conduct, ER 1.10. (The language of the quoted sections of this rule is identical to that in the corresponding sections of the Model Rules of Professional Conduct.)

48. Ariz. Rule 1.10, Comment 2. See Section B3 for an explanation of which conflicts are not consentable.

49. The exemption of some personal interest conflicts is discussed in Chapter 6.

50. Rule 1.10(c).

51. See, e.g., Schiessle v. Stephens, 717 F.2d 417 (7th Cir. 1983). Forty-four of the 51 U.S. jurisdictions do not allow screening as a remedy for problems of imputed disqualification. Seven states do allow screening, as do some federal courts. Federal courts sometimes follow their own precedent on standards for disqualification rather than following the state ethics rules. See Attys' Liab. Assurance Socy., Inc., Chart on Lawyer Screening (2002), reprinted in Thomas D. Morgan & Ronald D. Rotunda, 2003 Selected Standards on Professional Responsibility 173 (Found. Press 2002).

very limited circumstances, however, the Model Rules do not permit screening as an alternative to client consent to avoid imputation of a conflict within a firm. In Chapter 6 we explain when screening is allowed and discuss the mechanics of implementing a conflicts screen.

## What is a "firm" for the purpose of imputing conflicts?

This rule applies to lawyers in a "firm." A comment explains that this term includes "lawyers in a law partnership, professional corporation, sole proprietorship or other association" as well as "lawyers employed in a legal services organization or the legal department of a corporation or other organization."[52] This rule applies to firms of two lawyers and to firms of 1,500 lawyers, and to firms with offices in many cities or on different continents. The conflicts of a lawyer in Chicago are imputed to another lawyer in the Hong Kong office of the same firm. This remains so even if the Chicago lawyer and the Hong Kong lawyer (a) have never spoken, (b) practice in different fields, (c) represent different clients, and (d) will never come into contact with one another. Right away one can see that this principle multiplies the number of conflicts that must be evaluated and for which consent must be sought. The larger the firm, the larger the number of conflicts. Large firms must use sophisticated computer programs, among other methods, to identify actual or potential conflicts.

Lawyers who have separate practices but who share office space may be considered to be a law firm for conflicts purposes if their file management and communication is such that one lawyer in a suite might have access to confidential information about a matter being handled by another lawyer.[53] This rule covers all practicing lawyers except those who work for governments; the imputation rules for government lawyers are stated in Rule 1.11.

## Are conflicts imputed to temporary lawyers and nonlawyer employees?

The imputation rules apply to conflicts presented by all lawyers in a firm (including associates) but do not apply to conflicts presented by law clerks, paralegals, secretaries, or other nonlawyer employees.[54] Perhaps present or former clients do not have the same expectations of loyalty from nonlawyer employees. However, nonlawyers are required to protect client confidences in the same way that lawyers are. If a conflict is presented by work done by a nonlawyer, a comment to Rule 1.10 explains that the conflicted person "ordinarily must be screened from any personal participation in the matter...."[55] (This is one of the exceptions to the rules' general disapproval of screening as a remedy for conflicts.) A firm must maintain a conflicts-checking system that lists the clients and former clients of lawyers and nonlawyer employees to identify cases in which screening is necessary.

---

52. Rule 1.10, Comment 1.
53. See Rule 1.0, Comment 2.
54. Rule 1.10(a) also does not apply to conflicts that are presented by one lawyer because of work that that person did before she became a lawyer. Rule 1.10, Comment 4.
55. Id.

## PROBLEM 5-1 **THE INJURED PASSENGERS, SCENE 1**

Jill and Reema are passengers in a taxicab taking them from the airport to each of their homes. They don't know each other. The taxi driver is a fast driver. He changes lanes and ignores speed limits. He crashes into another car. Both Jill and Reema sustain significant injuries.

You are a personal injury lawyer in the town where the accident occurred. Jill and Reema come to see you together. They want you to represent both of them in a lawsuit against the cab driver and the cab company. Jill suffered whiplash, which is not too serious but will require physical therapy. Reema suffered several fractures and some abdominal injuries. She was hospitalized for five weeks. If you were to represent them, you would charge contingent fees. The fee for each one would be calculated as one-third of the amount received by that passenger in a settlement or a judgment.

### Questions

**1.** Can you represent both Jill and Reema? What other information do you need to know to be able to answer this question?

**2.** Might there be a nonconsentable conflict in this case?

**3.** Do you need to get informed consent before undertaking the joint representation?

**4.** Assuming that you need to obtain informed consent, what would you need to disclose to the clients to obtain their consent?

---

Having provided a general overview of the process for analyzing concurrent conflicts, we next explore the standards by which a lawyer judges whether a conflict exists between the interests of two clients. We examine conflicts as they arise in civil litigation, in transactional work, in criminal litigation, and in the representation of organizations.[56]

# C. Conflicts between current clients in civil litigation

## 1. Suing a current client

Suppose lawyer A is representing a husband, Fred, in a divorce. While that work is progressing, a new client, Mona, asks lawyer A to sue a driver who rammed into her car at a stop sign. The ramming driver turns out to be lawyer A's client Fred. If lawyer A sues Fred on behalf of Mona while he represents Fred in another matter, this situation involves direct adversity. This is true even though the cases are unrelated.[57] It is direct adversity even if a different lawyer represents Fred in the accident case.[58]

---

**Case 1: Divorce**

| | | |
|---|---|---|
| Fred | v. | Wife |
| (lawyer A) | | (lawyer B) |

**Case 2: Car accident**

| | | |
|---|---|---|
| Mona | v. | Fred |
| (lawyer A) | | (lawyer C) |

If lawyer A represents Fred in case 1 and Mona in case 2, there is a conflict of interest that involves direct adversity.

---

56. This organizational structure is informed by the organization of the concurrent client conflicts material in the Restatement.

57. "Unrelated" in this context means that "no work done for, or information learned in, one representation would be relevant to the other." Thomas D. Morgan, Suing a Current Client, 9 Geo. J. Leg. Ethics 1157, 1157 n. 1 (1996).

58. See Rule 1.7, Comment 6.

### How often does this come up?

One of the large firm lawyers interviewed by sociologist Susan Shapiro said, "That comes up all the time. . . . I'll bet that probably once a week, we're invited to get into a situation where we'd be adverse to a current client."[59]

### Are lawyers allowed to sue current clients?

In nearly every state, the ethics rules provide that a lawyer cannot file suit against another present client unless the lawyer reasonably believes that she can represent both without adverse impact on either and unless both clients give informed consent.[60] Many court decisions reach the same conclusion.[61] The general rule is that you cannot sue a current client without consent.[62]

### Do practicing lawyers think the rule is too restrictive?

Many lawyers would decline to accept a matter that involved suing a current client, regardless of what the rules say. One lawyer at a large firm who talked to Susan Shapiro said:

> If two clients are fighting, we try to stay out. . . . We're just going to lose. . . . If we represent somebody who's really adverse to another client, we're guaranteed to lose that other client. I mean, it's like no question! Because if you do as good a job as you can possibly do for the client you're staying with, you're just going to tick the other side off. So, that's a no-brainer; no-win situation.[63]

## Questions about Suing a Current Client

**1.** The rule makes sense in the context of an individual client and an individual lawyer because the client would perceive the lawsuit as a breach

---

59. Susan Shapiro, Tangled Loyalties: Conflict of Interest in Legal Practice 59 (U. Mich. Press 2002).

60. ABA/BNA Lawyers' Manual on Professional Conduct Reference Manual, Conflicts of Interest, Representation Adverse to Existing Client 51:101 (1998). Comment 8 to Rule 1.7(a) explains that "[a]bsent consent, a lawyer may not act as an advocate in one matter against a person the lawyer represents in some other matter, even when the matters are wholly unrelated." But this prohibition doesn't apply if the relevant clients consent. Restatement, § 128, comment e.

Texas does not require consent for a matter unrelated to the one on which the lawyer is representing the client. Ohio's rule has been interpreted similarly. William Freivogel, Freivogel on Conflicts, Current Conflicts and Direct Adversity, at http://www.freivogelonconflicts.com/new_page_22.htm (last visited Oct. 19, 2004).

61. See, e.g., IBM v. Levin, 579 F.2d 271 (3d Cir. 1978) (a lawyer cannot sue a present client on behalf of another client even if the lawyer is not working on a matter for the defendant client at the time of the lawsuit unless the client consents to be sued).

62. See, e.g., ABA Comm. on Ethics & Prof. Resp., Formal Op. 93-372 (1993); ABA Comm. on Ethics & Prof. Resp., and Formal Op. 95-390 (1995) (Fox, dissenting); In re Dresser Indus., Inc., 972 F.2d 540, 545 (5th Cir. 1992) (stating that "the national standards of attorney conduct forbid a lawyer from bringing a suit against a current client without the consent of both clients").

63. Shapiro, supra n. 59, at 60.

of trust, a betrayal. Does this rule also make sense for a law firm, with hundreds of lawyers and several offices in different cities, that represents a large corporation in a tax matter? Should this law firm be barred from representing a plaintiff who wants to sue the corporation on a products liability matter?[64]

2. Likewise, should a long-time client who has an ongoing relationship with a lawyer be required to hire new counsel simply because she wants to sue someone for whom the firm is providing modest service?[65] What if the potential defendant is a large corporation that has hired each of the major firms in town precisely to preclude their being sued by any of those firms?[66] Then the potential defendant could simply decline to waive the conflict, thereby insulating itself from suit by particular firms.

## PROBLEM 5-2 I THOUGHT YOU WERE *MY* LAWYER!

*This problem is based on a case that arose in the western United States in the 1970s.*

You are the ethics lawyer for Shelton & Cadenas. It is your job to advise the firm on any ethics problems that it has, particularly conflicts problems.

One of the firm's clients, Dori Hathaway, was hit by a bus while she was crossing the street. On her behalf, Shelton & Cadenas is suing the bus company. The firm has already put a lot of work into the case.

While that case was pending, Shelton & Cadenas accepted another client, Kevin Bielaski, who is suing his wife for divorce. Because Dori Hathaway has a different last name, the firm didn't realize that she is Bielaski's wife.

Kevin was not involved in the bus accident. Both Dori and Kevin want to go ahead with the divorce. They have no children, but they do have some property, and there may be a dispute about the property division.

The lawyer handling the divorce has just discovered that Hathaway is a firm client.

## Questions

1. Your firm has signed contracts agreeing to represent Dori in the accident case and Kevin in the divorce case. What, if anything, should you advise the firm to do? Evaluate this conflict under Rule 1.7.

---

64. This question is raised by Professor Thomas Morgan in Suing a Current Client, supra n. 57, at 1157.

65. Id. at 1161-1162.

66. Id. at 1162.

**2.** What if the law firm has two offices in different cities. If one office is handling Dori's case and the other office is handling Kevin's case, does the analysis change?

**3.** Assume you decide that the firm cannot represent both Kevin and Dori. Can the firm represent one of them? If so, can the firm choose which client to drop?

## 2. Cross-examining a current client

A lawyer can have an adverse relationship to a current client in litigation even if the client is not a defendant in the case. One common problem is that a lawyer might be called upon to cross-examine one of her clients in a trial of charges against another of her clients.

> FOR EXAMPLE: Suppose a lawyer represents Henry, a criminal defendant who is accused of robbing a convenience store. The same lawyer represents Roger, who is facing an unrelated arson charge. But Roger is also a prosecution witness in the robbery case against Henry because he was involved in the robbery. The lawyer would cross-examine Roger to show that Roger drove Henry to the store and insisted that Henry hold up the store to get cash to pay Roger for drugs that Roger supplied to Henry. The cross-examination of Roger could show that Henry was coerced but could lead the prosecutor to file new charges against Roger. In this situation, the lawyer's cross-examination of Roger would be directly adverse to Roger, his own client. It might not affect the arson matter, but still it could raise the odds that Roger would go to prison.[67]

---

**State v. Henry (robbery) (Roger participated)**
(lawyer A)

**State v. Roger (arson)**
(lawyer A)

Henry charged with robbing convenience store.
Roger, who had a role in the robbery, is a prosecution witness.

Lawyer A represents Roger in a separate arson matter.
Lawyer A is acting directly adverse to Roger if, while defending Henry, he cross-examines Roger about Roger's role in the robbery.

---

This kind of conflict can arise before a criminal case is tried. It is very common for criminal defendants to try to get lighter penalties or early release from prison by offering statements that assist the prosecution in obtaining conviction of other defendants. Especially in small communities, it often turns out that a lawyer who represents one defendant also is also defending or has

---

67. See Rule 1.7, Comment 6.

previously defended others who might incriminate him. One small-town criminal defense lawyer shared the following story with Susan Shapiro:

> I was trying a murder case here. And, on the eve of trial, two of my clients that I had represented previously . . . made statements against a third client of mine in the murder case. . . . I really found myself in quite a dilemma. . . . [O]n the one hand, I'm still in active representation of a client who's charged with murder. . . . [O]n the other hand, these guys are making statements . . . that, if they make 'em, the likelihood of them coming out of [prison] alive is not great. [The implication is that the statements were more incriminating of the speakers than they realized, and that they might exculpate the murder defendant.] And, obviously, law enforcement's not telling them that. But I was almost in a catch-22 situation. I couldn't get to them to say, "Guys, it's probably not in your interest to say this. And then I almost have a conflict by saying that, because I'm really trying to help my other client.[68]

## 3. Representation of co-plaintiffs or co-defendants in civil litigation

For a lawyer to sue one client on behalf of another presents perhaps the most serious type of conflict of interest. If a lawyer jointly[69] represents two clients who are both either plaintiffs or defendants in a lawsuit, their relationship is not one of direct adversity, but their interests might conflict anyway. Possible problems include the following.

- One client might have a potential claim against the other.
- If the clients are co-plaintiffs, they might be suing a defendant whose limited assets would make it impossible to satisfy both their claims.
- If a settlement is proposed, the two plaintiffs might have different views on whether to settle. The defendant might try to trade one client's claim off against the other.
- If a lawyer represents two defendants who each have some responsibility for the harm that is the subject of the suit, then each might seek to avoid liability by asserting that the other is responsible.
- If the clients are plaintiffs in a lawsuit seeking injunctive relief as well as damages, they might disagree as to what the remedy should be.[70]

Joint representation often occurs in accident cases in which two passengers or a passenger and driver in one car sue the driver of the other car that was involved in the accident. Several cases have held that a driver and passenger have sufficiently divergent interests that they may not be represented by a

---

68. Shapiro, supra n. 59, at 72.
69. The discussion of these issues often refers to the representation of two plaintiffs or two defendants as "joint representation" or "multiple representation." These terms are interchangeable.
70. Restatement § 128, comment d.

single lawyer.[71] The Restatement, however, takes the position that this type of conflict may be waivable by the client after full disclosure.[72]

### PROBLEM 5-3  THE INJURED PASSENGERS, SCENE 2

Let's return to the accident in which both Jill and Reema were injured in an accident while they were passengers in a taxicab. Recall that Reema's injuries are much more serious than Jill's. Assume that you concluded that you could represent them both, and that you have obtained their informed consent. You have filed suit on behalf of each of your clients and done some discovery. The attorney for the taxicab company contacts you to discuss settlement. During settlement negotiations, the attorney for the cab company hints that he may soon offer $350,000 to settle Reema's claim if you'll accept only $50,000 for Jill's claim.

### Questions

1. How should you respond?
2. Suppose that you are able to continue representing both clients, and they both reject the settlement offer. During your deposition of the driver, he states that Jill was very drunk when she got into the car and that the accident occurred while Jill was swearing at him for going too fast. You ask Reema about Jill's behavior in the cab, and she confirms what the driver told you. How does this information affect your work on behalf of Jill and Reema?

## 4. Representing economic competitors in unrelated matters

Suppose a lawyer represents the owner of one shop that develops photos in its negotiation of a new ten-year lease with its landlord. While this work is going

---

71. In re Thornton, 421 A.2d 1 (D.C. 1980). Thornton represented driver and passengers in an accident case despite the fact that the judge expressed concern about the conflict. The judge referred the matter to the bar counsel. In response to an inquiry from bar counsel, Thornton submitted a document that purported to reflect the informed consent of the driver and the passengers. This document was found to be "patently unbelievable." Thornton was suspended from practice for one year. See also Restatement § 128, comment d.

72. Restatement § 128, comment d. Another common situation is one in which an employer and an employee are sued for damages. If the employer agrees to cover any damages awarded against it or the employee, the possible conflicts are limited enough that the courts generally allow both defendants to be represented by one lawyer. Smith v. N.Y.C., 611 F. Supp. 1080 (S.D.N.Y. 1985) (corporation counsel properly undertook to represent both the city and police officers in an action alleging misconduct by the officers).

on, the owner of the town's other photo shop asks the lawyer to represent him in a suit for damages by an employee claiming wrongful discharge. The two clients are economic competitors, but the lawyer is not representing one of them against the other. Comment 6 to Rule 1.7 states that "simultaneous representation in unrelated matters of clients whose interests are only economically adverse ... does not ordinarily constitute a conflict of interest. ..." However, at least one court stated that even if representation of economic competitors does not violate the rules of professional conduct, it may be a breach of a lawyer's fiduciary duty to avoid representation that involves conflicting interests.[73]

---

**Lawyer's matter #1:**
**Lawyer represents photo shop 1:    Negotiate new ten-year lease.**

**Lawyer's matter #2:**
**Lawyer represents photo shop 2 (competitor of photo shop 1):**
**Defend photo shop 2 against suit by former employee.**

A lawyer may represent these two competitors in different matters without a conflict.

---

73. Maritrans GP Inc. v. Pepper, Hamilton & Scheetz, 602 A.2d 1277 (Pa. 1992), quoting Tri-Growth Centre City, Ltd. v. Silldorf, Burdman, Duignan & Eisenberg, 216 Cal. App. 3d 1139, 1150

## 5. Conflicts in public interest litigation

Many of the examples of conflicts that we have encountered so far involve either criminal co-defendants or parties who have some type of economic conflict with each other. Conflicts or potential conflicts may also arise in public interest litigation because different groups interested in the litigation may have opposing goals. Sometimes those goals can be reconciled, but sometimes one group's success necessarily defeats another group's aspirations. For example, in litigation in Atlanta during the 1960s and 1970s to enforce Brown v. Board of Education, some African American parents and groups that supported them wanted to press for genuinely integrated schools. Other African American parents and groups wanted the courts to order the public school system to hire many African American administrators and teachers, regardless of whether many white children remained in the system.[74] Both groups could not prevail.

PROBLEM 5-4 **THE PRISONERS' DILEMMA**

*This problem is closely based on a situation that arose during litigation in New England.*

---

You are a lawyer at the Legal Assistance Program (LAP), the only program of free civil legal services for the poor in the entire state. You are managing a class action on behalf of Joyce Pelligrino and 22 other named and hundreds of unnamed female prison inmates.

The state has no women's prison, so some women prisoners are housed in county jails that were never intended for long-term incarceration. The county jails have virtually no exercise areas, libraries, or other basic facilities. The state also contracts with women's prisons in other states to house some of its women prisoners. Consequently, some female prisoners are sent far away from their children and their lawyers. Your equal protection class action seeks to force the state to build a women's prison. This case is called the "Pelligrino" case after the first named plaintiff.

---

(1989), to define a fiduciary relationship:

> A fiduciary or confidential relationship can arise when confidence is reposed by persons in the integrity of others, and if the latter voluntarily accept or assume to accept the confidence, they cannot act so as to take advantage of the others' interests without their knowledge or consent. The attorney/client relationship is a fiduciary one, binding the attorney to the most conscientious fidelity.

74. Tomiko Brown-Nagin, Race as Identity Caricature: A Local Legal History in the Salience of Interracial Conflict, 151 U. Pa. L. Rev. 1913 (2003).

*A county jail*

A different lawyer, at a different office of LAP, is the lead counsel in another class action challenging the conditions at the Piper State school, the state's only institution for people with mental retardation. This one is referred to as the "O'Connor" case. LAP's objective in that action is to close down the 1,200 bed facility and to require the state to provide housing for the inmates in individual or group homes. The state defended against the O'Connor case vigorously, but even so, the court gave the plaintiffs most of what they wanted. However, the court has been unwilling to close down the institution completely. Specifically, the court has ordered a gradual reduction in the number of people housed at Piper. By the time the Pelligrino case heats up, there are still about 200 people, the most severely retarded individuals, housed in Piper. The case is still formally open.

After several years of dogged opposition to the Pelligrino litigation, the state's lawyers appear to recognize that they will lose that case. But the governor and the voters don't want to pay for the construction of a new prison. Two weeks before the Pelligrino case is to go to trial, the state's lawyers offer you a deal. Under this proposal, the state will not build a new women's prison. What they will do is to move another 100 people out of Piper, leaving only 100 retarded patients there. Then they will have 1,100 beds free at Piper. They will move all the women prisoners now in the county jails to that facility, build fences and perform extensive renovations, and designate it the State Women's Prison.

What should you do when you receive this offer?

## 6. Taking inconsistent legal positions in litigation

**If a lawyer makes a legal argument on behalf of one client in one case that is contrary to the interests of another client who is not involved in the case, does that situation present a conflict?**

Although it is a conflict to advocate on behalf of one client against another client, normally a lawyer may make inconsistent arguments on a legal issue in different courts at different times without running afoul of the conflicts rules.[75] This situation is called a positional conflict. It is usually less problematic than other types of conflicts. Whether a positional conflict presents a serious conflict of interest, however, depends on the likelihood that one client would be materially harmed by a lawyer's making an argument in another case that was contrary to the client's interest. Comment 24 following Rule 1.7 states, in part:

> The mere fact that advocating a legal position on behalf of one client might create precedent adverse to the interests of a client represented by the lawyer in an unrelated matter does not create a conflict of interest. A conflict of interest exists, however, if there is a significant risk that a lawyer's action on behalf of one client will materially limit the lawyer's effectiveness in representing another client in a different case; for example, when a decision favoring one client will create a precedent likely to seriously weaken the position taken on behalf of the other client. . . . If there is significant risk of material limitation, then absent informed consent of the affected clients, the lawyer must refuse one of the representations or withdraw from one or both matters.

The comment following Rule 1.7 and the Restatement identify factors to be considered in making this assessment:

- Whether the issue is before a trial or appellate court
- Whether the issue is substantive or procedural
- The temporal relationship between the matters
- The practical significance of the issue to the immediate and long-run interests of the clients involved
- The clients' reasonable expectations in retaining the lawyer[76]

An ABA ethics opinion on this issue concluded that it was not very significant whether the relevant matters were at the trial or appellate level. The committee urged that a lawyer evaluating a positional conflict should consider whether the decision in one case is likely to affect the decision in the other, and whether the lawyer might be inclined to "soft-pedal" or otherwise alter one or another argument to avoid affecting the other case.[77]

---

75. See Rule 1.7, Comment 24 quoted below.
76. Restatement § 128, comment f.
77. ABA Comm. on Ethics & Prof. Resp., Formal Op. 93-377 (1993).

FOR EXAMPLE:   A lawyer may argue in California on behalf of an insurance company in defense of a state statute setting a cap on damages in personal injury cases. That same lawyer may also argue in Indiana on behalf of a personal injury plaintiff that a similar statute is invalid or inapplicable. Then again, if the California insurance client did extensive business in Indiana and would be adversely impacted by the invalidation of the Indiana law, the Indiana matter might present a conflict.

---

California case: personal injury plaintiff v. defendant (and insurer)
  Lawyer A (representing insurer) defends California statute setting cap on damages.

Indiana case: personal injury plaintiff v. defendant (and different insurer)
  Lawyer A (representing plaintiff) challenges Indiana statute setting cap on damages.

---

## PROBLEM 5-5  **TOP GUN**

*Events very much like those described in this problem occurred in a large New York law firm in 2004.*

You are a partner at a large urban law firm. In your city, gun violence has killed many people. The mayor has long decried this

 violence. At his request, the city's legal department approached your firm and asked it to help the city to bring a novel lawsuit against the nation's major gun manufacturers.

The city needed a large law firm to take the lead in this case because the gun manufacturers were expected to have a large number of very experienced lawyers. The legal department sought help from your firm because your firm does not represent any gun manufacturers.

Two years ago, after extensive discussion among the partners, the firm agreed to represent the city in this matter and to do the work without charging a fee. For the last two years, you, two of your partners and a dozen associates have been working on the case. The trial will be held six months from now.

The lawsuit names four major gun manufacturers as defendants. It alleges that these companies support an illegal market in the guns that criminals use to murder residents of the city. The legal argument is that the manufacturers are creating a "public nuisance" in violation of common law. You are seeking an injunction to prohibit those manufacturers from selling guns to dealers who are known to have supplied them to criminals.

The day before yesterday, one of your partners received a call from Aaron Cavalier, the general counsel of Global Pharmaceuticals, one of your firm's largest clients. Cavalier said that the general counsel of one of the defendant gun manufacturers had called him and had persuaded him that if the city won the gun case, it could create a precedent that would hurt Global. Here's his analysis.

Global used to produce a prescription painkiller drug called Zorenal that many misguided people used for recreational purposes. Dozens of people who became addicted to Zorenal died from overdoses. There were rumors that it was easy to fill even a forged prescription for Zorenal at certain drug store chains.

A court decision holding the gun manufacturers liable for shooting deaths could result in Global being held liable for the deaths of people who bought the drug from such pharmacies because Global sold Zorenal to those pharmacies even after company officials heard the rumors. Even absent actual liability, such a precedent could damage Global's credit rating, significantly raising the interest rate that it would have to pay to borrow money.

Cavalier told your partner that, in his view, the firm had a conflict of interest and should withdraw from representing the city in the lawsuit against the gun manufacturers. He mentioned that Global can choose to obtain legal services from many different large firms in a competitive market. He said that the management at Global would not feel right about remaining a client of a firm that was helping to set precedents that would hurt its business.

This afternoon, a partnership meeting will be held to decide whether to withdraw from the gun suit.

## Questions

**1.** Must the firm withdraw from representing the city against the gun manufacturers?

**2.** Even if the firm is not required to withdraw because of the alleged conflict, should it withdraw to avoid making one of its most important clients uneasy?

# D. Conflicts in nonlitigation matters: Representation of both parties to a transaction

Suppose you are approached by the buyer and seller of a business. They want you to represent both of them in drawing up the documents of sale. Are you allowed to do this? In most circumstances, the answer is yes, but in many such cases, you would need to provide the clients with information about the possible downsides of the joint representation and to obtain their consent.[78] This rule, permitting representation but usually requiring consent, applies whenever a lawyer is approached by two clients seeking legal assistance with a common goal. The clients might be forming a corporation, settling a dispute without litigation, doing estate planning, and so on. Not every such case presents a possible conflict.

> **FOR EXAMPLE:** If two domestic partners seek legal assistance to purchase the house in which they will live, there is usually no conflict.[79] If there is no apparent possible conflict, the lawyer may undertake the work without obtaining informed consent.

On the other hand, there are all sorts of ways that the interests of two parties to a transaction might conflict. One lawyer whom Susan Shapiro interviewed said that representing two parties to a transaction was like "handling a porcupine."[80] Another of her lawyer informants gave this example involving representation of both a buyer and a seller:

> [Consider] two parties who come in and just want to use one lawyer for a property transaction. . . . I think that's almost impossible to do without conflicts. Although people ask you to do it all the time. . . . But it's to the seller's benefit to pro-rate taxes at the current levels. Or to the buyer's benefit to pro-rate taxes at an estimated 110 percent level of previous taxes. Inspection clauses, who's going to pay for repairs if they're required? . . . [T]here's just absolutely no way you can — aggressively, anyway — represent both sides. You always have to kind of compromise in the middle. And I think that's a real, real conflict.[81]

### How does a lawyer know whether she needs to obtain informed consent?

The relevant question is whether there is an actual or potential conflict that is "reasonably apparent" to the lawyer. If the clients' interests appear entirely harmonious, there may be no need to obtain consent. If, on the other hand, the clients have some divergent interests or goals, or some tension is apparent in the communication between them, the lawyer should obtain their consent to be sure they understand the possible disadvantages of being represented by a single lawyer.[82]

---

78. William Freivogel, Freivogel on Conflicts, Joint/Multiple Representation, *at* http://www.freivogelonconflicts.com/new_page_8.htm (last visited Oct. 19, 2004).
79. Restatement § 130, comment b.
80. Susan Shapiro, Tangled Loyalties: Conflict of Interest in Legal Practice 66 (U. Mich. Press 2002).
81. Id. at 65.
82. Restatement § 130, comment c.

### Can a lawyer solve the possible conflict by undertaking just to draft documents without giving advice?

No. If a lawyer undertakes joint representation of parties to a transaction, the lawyer should not regard himself as a "mere scrivener" who is simply recording their preferences. He instead should endeavor to provide the same range of services to each of the two clients as he would if he were representing only one of them.[83]

### Can a lawyer keep confidences learned from one client from the other client?

A lawyer owes both clients a duty of loyalty, which might be compromised if the lawyer keeps secrets from either one of them.

> FOR EXAMPLE: Suppose one of the domestic partners pays three-quarters of the price of the house that they purchase jointly but receives only half the ownership interest. The other partner confides to the lawyer that he is unsure how long the partners' relationship will last. Especially if the transaction is not completed, the lawyer may have an obligation to reveal this confidence to the partner who is paying more. (The lawyer has an obligation to keep each client informed and to render candid advice under Rule 1.4.) Alternatively, the lawyer may be obliged to withdraw because she cannot continue the representation without violating a rule.

Although there is no attorney-client privilege shielding information from either of the clients when they are jointly represented (unless the clients have agreed otherwise),[84] the ethical duty to protect confidences is less clear. However, Comment 31 to Rule 1.7 suggests that a lawyer usually should not keep confidences from one joint client received from the other:

> The lawyer should, at the outset of the common representation and as part of the process of obtaining each client's informed consent, advise each client that information will be shared and that the lawyer will have to withdraw if one client decides that some matter material to the representation should be kept from the other. In limited circumstances, it may be appropriate for the lawyer to proceed with the representation when the clients have agreed, after being properly informed, that the lawyer will keep certain information confidential. For example, the lawyer may reasonably conclude that failure to disclose one client's trade secrets to another client will not adversely affect representation involving a joint venture between the clients and agree to keep that information confidential with the informed consent of both clients.

---

83. Id. at comment b.
84. Restatement § 75.

**If the two clients wind up in litigation against one another, does the lawyer have to withdraw altogether, or can the lawyer represent one against the other?**

If a conflict develops that will lead to litigation, a lawyer may not continue to represent both (or all) of the clients because that would involve the lawyer in suing one client on behalf of another in an adversarial situation. If the lawyer withdraws from representing one client, the other becomes a former client. In this case, the lawyer usually cannot represent one client in a lawsuit against a former client because the suit would be (per Rule 1.9) "the same or a substantially related matter" and its initiation would be materially adverse to the interests of the former client.[85] In such a situation, representation is allowed only with the consent of the former client.[86] A lawyer might be able to continue to represent one (or fewer than all) of the clients if the lawyer obtained a valid advance waiver of this conflict from the clients at the outset of the representation. As part of the informed consent process, the lawyer should work out with the clients what would happen if litigation develops and whether they would consent to the lawyer representing one (or fewer than all) of them against the other.[87]

# E. Conflicts in representation of organizations

Lawyers used to spend most of their professional lives representing individual persons. This is no longer the case. These days the majority of legal services are delivered to organizations rather than persons.[88] Most of these organizations are for-profit corporations, which since the late nineteenth century have been accorded the status of legal personhood.

This section of the chapter explores some of the questions that arise when a lawyer is representing an organization. For example:

- Who is "the client" of a lawyer who represents an organization?
- May a lawyer represent an organization and its employees, members, and affiliates?
- If a lawyer is representing an organization, may the lawyer take on representation that might be adverse to an employee, member, or affiliate of the organization? If the conflict may be waived by the clients, who can give consent to waive a conflict on behalf of an organization?
- What if one member of an organization seeks to act in a manner contrary to the interests of the organization?

---

85. Restatement § 132.
86. See Chapter 6 for discussion of former client conflicts.
87. Restatement § 130, comment c.
88. In Chapters 9 and 10, we discuss the legal profession's increasing emphasis on the representation of organizations and wealthy individuals. See particularly John P. Heinz & Edward O. Laumann, Chicago Lawyers: The Social Structure of the Bar (Amer. B. Found., 2d ed. 1994).

# 1. Who is the client?

## Does the lawyer represent only the corporation, or are the officers, subsidiaries, and other affiliates of the corporation also clients?

If a lawyer is engaged to represent a corporation, usually the lawyer's client is the corporation itself, not the officers or shareholders of the corporation, and not other corporations owned (in part or whole) by the corporation. Rule 1.13(a) provides that "A lawyer employed or retained by an organization represents the organization acting through its duly authorized constituents." Sometimes, however, the lawyer has obligations toward other individuals or organizations affiliated with a client organization, especially if financial consequences toward the other person or organization will impact the client organization.[89]

Many lawyers who represent corporations develop close and cooperative working relationships with the corporate representatives with whom they deal. The persons who communicate with the lawyer about the work often seem like "the client." They give instructions to the lawyer, they pay the bills, and they may be responsible for selection of outside counsel on various matters. This means that they may decide whether the lawyer will continue to receive work from the corporation. But the lawyer's obligations run to the organization itself.[90]

The question of who is the lawyer's client comes up in various contexts. Here are a few examples.

- A person or entity related to the primary client organization (such as the chief executive officer) might seek legal advice or services, or might seek to impose liability on a lawyer for advice or services provided.
- Another client of the lawyer might ask the lawyer to file suit against a subsidiary or other entity related to a corporate client of the lawyer. The question is whether the lawyer is precluded from undertaking this work.
- The corporate representative might ask the lawyer to do something that is in that person's individual interest (for example, shred documents that are embarrassing or incriminating) but that is not in the interest of the organization as a whole.

**FOR EXAMPLE:** Suppose that on behalf of a client, a lawyer wants to sue a subsidiary of a corporation that she also represents. The question is whether the subsidiary is a client for conflicts purposes. To figure out whether the subsidiary might be viewed as her client, the lawyer might consider the following questions.

---

89. See Rule 1.7, Comment 34; Restatement § 121, comment d; ABA Formal Op. 95-390 (1995) (concluding that a lawyer for a corporation does not represent affiliates unless the client has a reasonable expectation of representation); Charles W. Wolfram, Corporate Family Conflicts, 2 J. Inst. Study Leg. Ethics 295 (1999).

90. See Restatement § 131, comment e. Regarding the attorney-client privilege for such communications, see Chapter 3 and Restatement § 73, comment j.

## Factors affecting whether a related entity is a client

| Related entity more likely to be a client if: | Related entity less likely to be a client if: |
| --- | --- |
| The lawyer received confidential information from or provided advice to the subsidiary | The lawyer no longer represents the initial corporate client |
| The entity was controlled and supervised by the parent organization | The two entities became linked (e.g., by a merger) after the lawyer began representation of the corporation |
| The original client could be materially harmed by the suit against the subsidiary | |

The case law is not consistent on this question. Some courts examine the particular circumstances, using the criteria listed in the table.[91] The important thing to remember is that if you represent an entity, you need to obtain information about other organizations and individuals that are related to the entity (owners of, owned by, officers and directors of, and so forth) so that if you are asked to take on a matter adverse to one of the related persons or entities, you can evaluate whether there is a conflict.

## 2. Representation of the entity and employees

### Can a lawyer who represents a corporation provide legal services to individual employees of the organization?

A lawyer in private practice[92] who represents an organization may represent a member or an employee of the organization unless the interests of the organization and the individual conflict.[93] If consent for such a conflict is required, a designated corporate official can give consent, so long as that person is not the one to be represented by the lawyer.[94] Suppose an organization is accused of misconduct — for example, of grossly overstating its earnings for a few years running. An individual who participated in the decisions to do this might also be accused of wrongdoing. A lawyer may not be able to represent both the

---

91. Restatement § 121, comment d, reporter's note.

92. A lawyer who works in the general counsel's office of a corporation may not be permitted to represent a corporate employee. In general, a lawyer who is an employee of the corporation may represent the corporation but may not undertake representation of others, such as customers of the corporation, in matters involving their own interests. Authority is divided about whether a lawyer who works for an insurance company may represent insured persons. Restatement § 4, comment e and reporter's note to comment e.

93. Restatement § 131 puts it this way: Absent consent, "a lawyer may not represent both an organization and a director, officer, employee, shareholder, owner, partner, member or other individual or organization associated with the organization if there is a substantial risk that the lawyer's representation of either would be materially and adversely affected by the lawyer's duties to the other."

94. Rule 1.13(e) [Delaware Rules]; 1.13(g) [ABA Model Rules].

organization and the individual because each would have an interest in pointing the finger at the other to avoid responsibility.[95] On the other hand, if the individual and the organization would assert the same defense to the accusation, there might be no serious conflict in the lawyer representing them both, but the possibility of divergence down the road requires that the lawyer obtain informed consent from both the organization and the individual.[96]

> **FOR EXAMPLE:** Suppose a citizen who claims to be the victim of police brutality files suit against the town where he was allegedly beaten and against the individual officers who were involved. Can the lawyer for the city also represent the police? If the city admits that the police were acting within the scope of their duties when the incident occurred, one lawyer may represent both of them, but if the town takes the position that the police were acting outside the scope of their duties, the town and the officers probably need separate lawyers.[97]

**In a derivative suit, may a lawyer for an organization represent both the organization and the officers and directors named as defendants?**

Sometimes shareholders of an organization file "derivative suits" alleging that officers or directors of the organization have breached a duty to the organization. Usually the organization is an involuntary plaintiff and the officers or directors are defendants. The suit is brought for the benefit of the organization. In most cases, a lawyer for the organization should not undertake to represent the defendants, even with client consent. In this kind of situation, some courts have held that the lawyer for the corporation should represent the officers or directors, and the corporation should hire a separate lawyer.[98] The exception is that "if disinterested directors conclude that no basis exists for the claim[s]" and all relevant persons consent, the lawyer may represent the organization and the defendants.[99]

## 3. Duty to protect confidences of employees

**If an employee of a corporation discloses information to the corporation's lawyer in confidence, does the lawyer have an obligation to the employee to protect the confidence?**

As usual, it depends.[100] If the lawyer represents only the organization and not any employee, the lawyer generally has no duty to protect confidences of employees.

---

95. Restatement § 131, comment e.

96. Id. at illus. 3.

97. See Coleman v. Smith, 814 F.2d 1142 (7th Cir. 1987); Dunton v. Suffolk County, 729 F.2d 903 (2d Cir. 1984).

98. See Cannon v. U.S. Acoustics Corp., 398 F. Supp. 209 (N.D. Ill. 1975), *aff'd in relevant part*, 532 F.2d 1118 (7th Cir. 1976); Forrest v. Baeza, 67 Cal. Rptr. 2d 857 (Cal. App. 1997).

99. Restatement § 131, comment f.

100. See generally Sarah Helene Duggin, Internal Corporate Investigations: Legal Ethics, Professionalism and the Employee Interview, 2003 Colum. Bus. L. Rev. 859. An excerpt of this article appears in Chapter 3.

If an employee approaches the lawyer and the lawyer perceives a potential conflict of interest, the lawyer must advise the employee that a potential conflict exists and that discussions between the employee and the lawyer are not confidential. The lawyer should decline to represent the employee and should suggest that the employee obtain independent representation.[101] If the lawyer fails to give such a warning and behaves in a manner that would justify the employee in her expectation of confidentiality, then the lawyer might have inadvertently created a lawyer-client relationship with the employee, with an attendant duty to protect confidences and a possible concurrent conflict of interest to boot.[102]

A related issue — the scope of the attorney-client privilege accorded to corporations — is addressed in Chapter 3.

## 4. Responding to unlawful conduct by corporate officers and other employees

**What should a lawyer do if an officer or employee of an organization threatens to do something illegal or something that would harm the organization?**

In the course of representing organizations, a lawyer sometimes learns that an officer or employee has done something or is planning to do something that is illegal or that would cause harm to the organization.

> **FOR EXAMPLE:** Suppose that the chief executive officer is planning to use funds belonging to the organization to purchase a luxury car for his mistress.[103] Or suppose that the chief financial officer is planning to include material misinformation in a report that is to be filed with a state regulatory agency.

The lawyer's duty is to the organization, not to the senior executives. Rule 1.13 requires the lawyer to serve the interests of the organization. In the first instance, this usually means that the lawyer should report the misconduct to higher authority within the organization and, if need be, to the highest authority that can act (for a corporation, the board of directors or its audit committee).[104] If the highest authority refuses to act properly, and the lawyer believes that the misconduct will result in substantial injury to the organization, the Model Rules now permit the lawyer to reveal the misconduct to public officials.[105]

---

101. Rule 1.13, Comment 7 [Delaware Rules]; Comment 10 [ABA Model Rules].

102. Restatement § 131, comment e; see also Restatement § 15, comment c; § 103, comment e.

103. This example is adapted from Restatement § 96, illus. 1.

104. Rule 1.13(b).

105. ABA Model Rule 1.13(c). Not all states permit "reporting out" to officials. The Delaware Rules, for example, do not condone reporting to officials. They merely permit (but do not require) the lawyer to resign. Delaware Rule 1.13(c). The Model Rules do not permit revelation to outside entities if the organization retained the lawyer to investigate the misconduct or to defend the organization or its employees against a claim arising out of an alleged violation of law. ABA Model

It is risky for a lawyer to report proposed or past misconduct by senior officers to the president or board of directors. For one thing, senior officials whose conduct is reported might fire the lawyer.

If the lawyer is fired for reporting to higher authorities within or outside the organization, or if the lawyer withdraws because the lawyer has become aware of misconduct of an officer, the Model Rules direct the lawyer to inform the organization's highest authority of the discharge or withdrawal.[106] Even if the most senior officers address the misconduct, they might not rehire the lawyer who reported it.

## 5. Entity lawyers on boards of directors

**Is there a conflict of interest if a lawyer sits on the board of directors of a corporation that the lawyer represents?**

Lawyers are not forbidden to sit on the boards of directors of organizations that they represent, and some lawyers do so. In many instances, there is no conflict between the two roles. However, there are circumstances when the obligations of a director conflict with the obligations of counsel. For example, the directors might ask the lawyer to give an opinion on payment of bonuses to a group of corporate officers. If the lawyer would be one of the recipients of the bonus, his judgment might be affected by his personal interests.[107] A lawyer-director might be accused of wrongdoing in a derivative suit; in this case, the lawyer may not represent the organization in the suit.[108]

If a conflict arises that presents "a substantial risk that the lawyer's representation of the client would be materially and adversely affected" by the lawyer's obligations as a director, the lawyer should cease to represent the corporation on that matter unless the organization waives the conflict.[109] Alternatively, the lawyer could resign from the board of directors to resolve the conflict.[110] If such conflicts are likely to be frequent and serious, a lawyer should not take on the dual roles.[111] If a lawyer is also a director of an organization, communications with him may not be protected by attorney-client privilege.[112]

---

Rule 1.13(d). In these cases, the importance of serving the corporation apparently outweighs the importance of disclosure. If the client's activities are regulated by federal agencies such as the Securities and Exchange Commission, federal law may impose additional obligations on the lawyer. See, e.g., the discussion in Chapter 2 of the regulations and proposed regulations under the Sarbanes-Oxley Act.

106. ABA Model Rule 1.13(e).
107. Restatement § 135, comment d, illus. 3.
108. See, e.g., Harrison v. Keystone Coca-Cola Bottling Co., 428 F. Supp. 149 (M.D. Pa. 1977).
109. Restatement § 135.
110. Rule 1.7, Comment 35.
111. Id.
112. Restatement § 135, comment d, reporter's note; Rule 1.7, Comment 35.

**Do the principles that apply to representation of for-profit corporations also apply to representation of nonprofit corporations and other organizations?**

Yes. Rule 1.13 applies the same principles whether the lawyer is representing a business or another type of organization.

## PROBLEM 5-6  MY CLIENT'S SUBSIDIARY

Let's return to consider the representation of Dori Hathaway, who was hit by a bus while crossing the street. (You may recall that your firm took on representation of her soon-to-be ex-husband in a divorce action while it was representing Hathaway in a personal injury suit relating to the accident.) Hathaway was quite seriously injured in the accident. She had several fractures in her legs and pelvis, spent some weeks in the hospital, and had to have four different surgeries to repair the damage. As a result of the accident, she suffers from chronic pain, and one of her legs is about an inch shorter than the other.

Hathaway has hired Shelton & Cadenas to represent her in the accident case. (Assume that her husband found a different law firm to represent him in the divorce.) You are still the ethics advisor to Shelton & Cadenas. The firm filed a lawsuit against the bus driver and against Pearl Bus Co., Inc., the company that owns the bus.

A couple of months after the suit is filed, you discover that Pearl is owned by Transport, Inc., which is an active client of the law firm. Your firm's conflicts-checking system doesn't always capture information about companies that own or are owned by client companies. You were not aware of this connection, and you have never had any contact with any Pearl officials. You send an e-mail to the other lawyers at Shelton & Cadenas, and it seems no one at the firm has ever done any work for Pearl.

You call Jason Kerr, the president of Transport, to get more information. He says the corporation purchased the bus company many years ago. In recent years, Transport has had to take over many management functions because the bus company managers kept making costly errors. A couple of times, Transport has had to shell out tens of thousands of dollars to cover damage awards in excess of Pearl's insurance coverage. After the last one, Kerr says he insisted that Pearl massively increase its insurance coverage. Pearl agreed to this after Kerr agreed to help cover the increased cost of the insurance. Kerr hopes to prevent another cash drain from Transport.

"Anything else you can tell me about this?" you ask.

Kerr pauses. "Well, I guess it might be relevant that my son is the president of Pearl. He just took over a couple of years ago, after we discovered that the former president was embezzling funds from the company. Why do you want to know all this, anyway?"

Must the firm withdraw from representing Hathaway, or may it continue? Is continued work on her behalf contingent on obtaining Transport's consent?

---

# F. Joint representation in particular practice settings

We have explored the general principles raised by conflicts between the interests of two clients. There are some practice settings in which conflicts are especially common. These include a lawyer's representation of criminal co-defendants, of spouses in domestic relations matters and in estate planning, and of insured persons and their insurance companies. All these situations have in common the problem of a lawyer attempting to represent two clients who have some common interests, but who may have some divergent interests. In an ideal world, perhaps each person confronting a legal problem would have his or her own lawyer. This would avoid the possible compromise of the interests of one client on behalf of another.[113] In the real world, however, legal representation is very expensive, so many clients manage the expense by sharing counsel with someone else who has common interests. This is not always a bad thing, but sometimes it causes problems.

## 1. Representation of criminal co-defendants[114]

As we have seen, representation of co-plaintiffs or co-defendants in a civil matter can be complicated. While at first glance they may appear to have more common interests than conflicting ones, there may be sufficient divergence in their interests that a lawyer should not even ask the clients to consent to allow her to represent them both. Or the conflict could be such that the lawyer may proceed, but only with informed consent.

---

113. This assumes that the ideal representation is one in which a lawyer would pursue the interests of a single client with undivided loyalty. If one assumes that pursuit of self-interest is the name of the game, this looks like a good model. However, sometimes this model foments controversy where compromise would have been possible. If the goal is to resolve conflicts in a way that attends to the interests of all parties instead of helping one party to win every possible advantage, then perhaps one lawyer representing two parties with overlapping interests can be more beneficial than detrimental. See generally Carrie Menkel-Meadow, The Silences of the Restatement of the Law Governing Lawyers: Lawyering as Only Adversary Practice, 10 Geo. J. Leg. Ethics 631 (1997).

114. A criminal lawyer may encounter concurrent client conflicts through representation of co-defendants or in other circumstances. One example was presented above, where a criminal defense lawyer was called upon to cross-examine his own client, albeit in a different case. The general rule is that a lawyer may not represent a criminal defendant and simultaneously represent either a prosecution witness or the prosecutor. See, e.g., Castillo v. Estelle, 504 F.2d 1243 (5th Cir. 1974).

## a. The costs and benefits of joint representation of co-defendants

In criminal cases, the stakes are higher than in civil cases since the defendants may face imprisonment if they are convicted. As in civil cases, many co-defendants wish to be represented by a single lawyer because neither one can afford to hire separate counsel.[115] More important, criminal co-defendants' best chance of avoiding conviction may lie in cooperation with each other. If

*Professor Kenneth Mann*

neither one confesses or provides information to the prosecutor, the prosecutor may be unable to convict either of them. As Professor Peter Tague explains, "any group of clients might benefit from united opposition to the government. If none cooperates . . . the government may be unable to indict any client because no other credible sources possess enough admissible information."[116] Kenneth Mann, a lawyer and a sociologist,[117] surveyed more than 1,000 defense attorneys in New York and interviewed and observed 29 of them who defended white-collar criminals. In the rich, remarkable book that resulted from his studies, Mann reports:

> When the defense attorney uses his position to facilitate noncooperation on the part of more than one person in an investigation . . . it was not uncommon for an attorney to say, "I am stonewalling," meaning that he was conducting a defense in which he was attempting to keep all persons holding inculpatory information from talking to government investigators and thereby defeat the criminal investigation. There are many benefits . . . including close coordination of statements given to investigators, early warning of investigatorial contacts with third parties, and the making of uniform legal arguments.[118]

Mann also points out that because only a witness is allowed into a grand jury room (and even the lawyer for that witness must remain outside, although the witness may consult with the waiting lawyer frequently), the best way for a lawyer to know what questions a prosecutor asked in that proceeding, and how the witnesses said they answered, is to represent all of those witnesses — in other words, to represent more than one co-defendant.

---

115. Criminal defendants who cannot afford to hire lawyers can get court-appointed counsel, but many defendants strongly prefer to hire private lawyers. Many public defenders must represent 200 or more clients at any given time, so they may not be able to devote as much time to each case as a private lawyer can.

116. Peter W. Tague, Multiple Representation of Targets and Witnesses during a Grand Jury Investigation, 17 Am. Crim. L. Rev. 301 (1980).

117. Mann did this research for his Ph.D. dissertation in sociology at Yale. Later he became a law professor and the chief public defender of Israel.

118. Kenneth Mann, Defending White Collar Crime: A Portrait of Attorneys at Work 166 (Yale U. Press 1985).

Mann notes that sometimes, when permitted by law, defense lawyers can manage the conflicts through informed consent, to the advantage of some, and occasionally all, co-defendants:

> [If] the government has just enough evidence to consider asking for an indictment against each, but not enough to dismiss the option of granting immunity to one client in order to get determinative evidence against the other . . . it is difficult for an attorney to act without compromising one of the clients' interests. If he advises neither to make a deal because he believes that he may be able to win the case for both, he is sacrificing a certain success for one of them. And he clearly cannot advise one to make a deal against the other's interest. Some attorneys are able to obtain informed consent in this situation, after explaining the implications of the multiple representation. They then continue to represent all clients in a strategy based on total noncooperation [in which all defendants invoke their privilege against self-incrimination]. It is often the case that no client is willing to voluntarily become an informer against other clients. The stonewall defense continues until the government decides to force immunity on one of the clients, at which time the attorney will then have to divide representation. . . . [If the prosecution has less information to begin with,] both clients may be able to hold out and save each other the humiliation and embarrassment of becoming either an informant or the subject of a criminal prosecution.[119]

Although it may be more efficient or strategically appealing for one lawyer to represent multiple plaintiffs or defendants, joint representation could ultimately involve a significant sacrifice of the interests of one client on behalf of another. When multiple people are charged in connection with one crime, the stone wall they initially erected may crumble, and one or more of them may seek to reduce any potential penalty by offering to give the prosecutor inculpatory information about another defendant.

*Maher Hawash*

**FOR EXAMPLE:** Prosecutors charged Maher Hawash, a software engineer, with terrorism for aiding the Taliban government of Afghanistan. He could have faced more than 20 years in jail. Later, in exchange for his plea of guilty to a conspiracy charge and his promise to testify against six other suspects, authorities dropped the terrorism charge. As a result, Hawash expects to serve only 7 to 10 years in jail.[120] If Hawash's lawyer had also represented one or two of the other suspects, his facilitation of Hawash's cooperation would have helped one client while harming another.

---

119. Id. at 170.
120. Blaine Harden, Ore. Man Pleads Guilty to Helping Taliban, Wash. Post, Aug. 7, 2003.

## b. Case law and ethics rules on joint representation of co-defendants

### Are lawyers permitted to represent criminal co-defendants?

Case law, ethics rules, and scholarly commentary[121] all discourage joint representation of co-defendants by a single lawyer. The comments to the Model Rules take a fairly strong stand against representation of two or more criminal defendants on charges arising out of a single occurrence. Comment 23 to Rule 1.7 states: "The potential for conflict of interest in representing multiple defendants in a criminal case is so grave that ordinarily a lawyer should decline to represent more than one co-defendant." Likewise, the ABA guidelines for criminal defense lawyers urge that, except for bail hearings and other preliminary matters, a firm that does criminal defense work should not take on more than one co-defendant unless there is no conflict. The standards make clear that the "no conflict" situation is the rare exception.[122]

The Restatement says that a lawyer may not represent criminal co-defendants unless the clients give informed consent and it is "reasonably likely that the lawyer will be able to provide adequate representation to . . . the clients."[123] The Restatement provides the following illustration:

> A and B are co-defendants charged with a felony offense of armed robbery. They are both represented by Lawyer. The prosecutor believes that A planned the crime and was the only one carrying a weapon. The prosecutor offers to accept B's plea of guilty to a misdemeanor if B will testify against A. Lawyer's loyalty to A causes Lawyer to persuade B that the prosecutor's proposal should be rejected. Following a trial, both A and B are convicted of the felony. When plea negotiations involving B's separate interests began, B should have received independent counsel. In the circumstances, Lawyer could not properly represent A and B even with the informed consent of both clients.[124]

If a lawyer proposes to represent two criminal defendants in a federal court case, the judge must hold a hearing and advise both defendants of their right to separate counsel.[125] In other courts, judges may not be required to inquire about possible conflicts in joint representation of criminal defendants unless a conflict is apparent to the judge.[126] Even if an inquiry into a possible conflict is not required, it may be advisable.[127]

---

121. See, e.g., Peter W. Tague, Multiple Representation and Conflicts of Interest in Criminal Cases, 67 Geo. L.J. 1075 (1979).

122. Standards for Criminal Justice: Prosecution Function and Defense Function, Standard 4-3.5(c), Conflicts of Interest (3d ed. 1993).

123. Restatement §§ 122, 129.

124. Restatement § 129, comment c, based on Alvarez v. Wainwright, 522 F.2d 100 (5th Cir. 1975).

125. Fed. R. Crim. P. 44c.

126. Geoffrey C. Hazard, Jr., Susan P. Koniak & Roger C. Cramton, The Law and Ethics of Lawyering 618 (3d ed., Found. Press 1999).

127. Restatement § 129, comment c, reporter's note.

**Do criminal defense lawyers often represent multiple co-defendants?**

In some communities, representation of criminal co-defendants is fairly common. Some lawyers who represent multiple defendants are disqualified or disciplined for proceeding in the face of a conflict.[128] Joint representation of criminal defendants also can lead to a conviction being reversed.[129]

Most public defenders avoid multiple representation of defendants. A survey published in 1978 indicated that 70 percent of public defender offices had strong preferences against multiple representation in criminal cases, and that 49 percent of the offices surveyed never represent more than one defendant in a multiple defendant case.[130] These offices hire criminal defense lawyers in private practice to represent one defendant in a matter in which the office is representing another.

## c. The Sixth Amendment and joint representation

**Does joint representation of criminal co-defendants violate their Sixth Amendment right to counsel?**

Joint representation of criminal defendants may violate the conflict of interest rules and also may violate the Sixth Amendment right to counsel of a defendant. If a defendant is represented by a lawyer who has a conflict of interest, he may challenge his conviction on the basis that he was denied the effective assistance of counsel.[131] However, not all conflicts that violate Rule 1.7 are so serious that they prompt a court to reverse a conviction.[132]

If a lawyer objects to jointly representing defendants with conflicting interests and a court nevertheless requires the lawyer to continue to represent them, any resulting conviction may be overturned. In Holloway v. Arkansas, for example, a criminal defense lawyer made a timely objection that he could not adequately represent three co-defendants. The judge declined to appoint separate counsel and refused to allow the lawyer to cross-examine any of the three co-defendants on behalf of the other two. In 1978, the U.S. Supreme Court overturned the resulting conviction, stating that "whenever a trial court improperly requires joint representation over timely objection reversal is automatic."[133]

If no one objects to joint representation of defendants, a resulting conviction may be overturned if the conflict significantly affected the representation. In Cuyler v. Sullivan, three co-defendants in a murder case were tried separately but were represented by a single lawyer. No one objected to the multiple

---

128. See id. (disqualification); Atty. Grievance Comm. v. Kent, 653 A.2d 909 (Md. 1993) (lawyer disbarred after he represented two defendants in a murder case whose conflict was non-consentable).

129. Holloway v. Arkansas, 435 U.S. 475 (1978); Kentucky v. Holder, 705 S.W.2d 907 (Ky. 1986).

130. Gary T. Lowenthal, Joint Representation in Criminal Cases: A Critical Appraisal, 64 Va. L. Rev. 939, 950 n. 40 (1978), cited in Cuyler v. Sullivan, 446 U.S. 335, 346 n. 11 (1980).

131. The Sixth Amendment to the U.S. Constitution provides: "In all criminal prosecutions, the accused shall enjoy the right . . . to have the Assistance of Counsel for his defense."

132. See the discussion of Strickland v. Washington in Chapter 4, Section C2.

133. Holloway v. Arkansas, 435 U.S. 475, 488 (1978).

representation. The Supreme Court decided that if a defendant who was jointly represented is convicted, and there was no objection to the joint representation at the time, to overturn the conviction on Sixth Amendment grounds, the defendant must show that there was "a conflict of interest [that] actually affected the adequacy of his representation."[134] The Court held that the defendant need not demonstrate prejudice but only an adverse impact in the representation.[135]

In Mickens v. Taylor,[136] a capital conviction was challenged because the court-appointed counsel for a defendant in a murder case had represented the murder victim on unrelated criminal charges. The lawyer did not object when he was appointed to represent the defendant in the murder case, but the judge knew or should have known that he had been the lawyer for the victim until the day before she appointed him to represent the defendant.[137]

The lawyer who represented Mickens at the murder trial apparently believed that he had no further obligation to the victim because the victim was dead.[138] It was asserted that the attorney had not learned any confidences from the victim that would be relevant to the defense of the murder suspect.[139] The postconviction defense lawyer discovered evidence that Hall, the murder victim, was a male prostitute, and that the defendant and the victim might have engaged in consensual sex before the homicide. If this had been proven, Mickens could not have been sentenced to death.[140] Saunders, the trial attorney, did not offer this evidence for reasons that are unknown. Perhaps he felt an obligation to protect the reputation of his former client or had no knowledge of the evidence.

The Supreme Court decided the case 5-4 and held that if "the trial judge is not aware of a conflict (and thus not obligated to inquire) . . . prejudice will be presumed only if the conflict has *significantly affected* counsel's performance — thereby rendering the verdict unreliable."[141] Habeas corpus was denied because there was no such proof of significant impact.[142]

---

134. Cuyler v. Sullivan, 466 U.S. 335, 348-349 (1980).

135. Id.

136. 535 U.S. 162 (2002).

137. She had signed a docket sheet on the victim's case after he died that listed "BRYAN SAUNDERS" in large, handwritten letters, as counsel for the decedent on assault and battery charges and a concealed weapon charge. Id. at 190 n. 1 (Souter, J., dissenting). This fact was significant because the majority opinion premised that the duty to prove adverse impact from the representation is greater if no objection to the conflict was proffered at the trial. Justice Souter questioned why, if the judge should have known of the conflict, the making of an objection would be important. He urged that in the face of a finding that the judge knew or should have known of the conflict and did nothing about it, the conviction should have been overturned. Id. at 190.

138. Once murdered, the victim became a former client. When he was appointed to represent Mickens, the lawyer should have evaluated the conflict under Virginia's standards for handling successive conflicts.

139. *Mickens*, 535 U.S. at 177-179 (Kennedy, J., concurring).

140. Id. at 181 (Stevens, J., dissenting). The death penalty could not have been imposed without a finding of forcible sodomy, so if the sexual contact was consensual, this penalty would not have been available.

141. Id. (emphasis added).

142. Id.

This decision makes it less likely that a criminal conviction will be overturned on the basis that the defense attorney had a conflict of interest.[143]

### If a criminal defendant wants to waive a conflict, can the judge disqualify the lawyer anyway?

The constitutional guarantee of right to counsel might be trampled on if the conflicts rules intrude too far into a criminal defendant's right to be represented by counsel of his own choosing. In general, a criminal defendant is entitled to give a knowing waiver of a conflict created by his lawyer's representation of another co-defendant in the same case.[144] A defendant who waives a conflict is foreclosed from challenging a subsequent conviction on the basis of the conflict.[145] But where there is a great risk of prejudice resulting from a conflict, a judge may disqualify counsel from representing co-defendants even if the co-defendants want to waive the conflict.[146]

### PROBLEM 5-7 **POLICE BRUTALITY, SCENE 1**

*This problem is based on a real case that took place in New York in the 1990s.*

Several police officers were indicted in connection with a brutal assault against a man named Louis Alston. Alston was taken into a bathroom after he was arrested and sexually assaulted with a broken broomstick. Officer Tom Babbage pleaded guilty to charges arising out of this incident, but the victim says that at least one other officer participated in the assault. Two other officers, Chip Stone and Bob Morton, are facing charges that they participated in the assault. The Policeman's Benevolent Association (PBA), which provides lawyers for officers who face charges in connection with their work, has asked you and your law partner to represent these two co-defendants.

---

143. Justice Breyer, dissenting, questioned whether in this or other similar cases, at the post-trial stage, it would be possible to prove whether the trial lawyer's conflict of interest actually affected the lawyer's judgment about what strategy to pursue, what witnesses to call, what arguments to make, and so on. Id. at 210 (Breyer, J., dissenting).

144. U.S. v. Curcio, 680 F.2d 881 (2d Cir. 1982); U.S. v. Garcia, 517 F.2d 272 (5th Cir. 1975).

145. Id.

146. See, e.g., U.S. v. Flanagan, 679 F.2d 1072 (3d Cir. 1982). In Wheat v. U.S., the defendant wanted to have the same lawyer as two other defendants whose charges arose out of a common situation but who were to be tried separately. The district court denied this request because of the possibility that the various defendants would be witnesses at each other's trials. Wheat appealed to the Supreme Court, which held that a court may disqualify a lawyer on the basis of an actual or potential conflict even if the defendant prefers to waive the conflict. The Court held that such disqualification would not violate a defendant's Sixth Amendment right to be represented by the counsel of his choice. The Court pointed out that conflicts are hard to anticipate and that judges need broad discretion in such judgments in part because less ethical attorneys are more willing to seek waivers. 486 U.S. 153 (1988). In California, the defendant has the ultimate call on choice of lawyer. Alcocer v. Superior Ct., 254 Cal. Rptr. 72, 75 (1988).

If you agree to represent Stone and Morton, the PBA would pay your fees. Rule 1.8(f) states that a lawyer may not accept compensation from a third person unless the represented client gives informed consent, "there is no interference with the lawyer's independence of professional judgment or with the lawyer-client relationship," and confidences are protected.

## Questions

1. What potential conflicts should you consider in deciding whether you can represent Stone while your partner represents Morton?
2. Are these potential conflicts so serious that you must not represent both defendants even if you obtain their consent?

### PROBLEM 5-8  POLICE BRUTALITY, SCENE 2

Assume that your firm has agreed to represent both clients. Meanwhile, Alston has filed a civil suit against the PBA, alleging a conspiracy among several officers to injure him and a failure of the association leadership to provide adequate supervision of the officers.

A few months later, the PBA offers your firm a two-year contract for $10 million to handle representation of all PBA members. The PBA would pay an agreed portion of the money at the outset and the remainder in regular installments. The PBA could cancel the contract at any time if it was dissatisfied with the work of your firm.

Meanwhile, another co-defendant has been indicted in the Alston case, Officer Tony Gutman. Like Stone and Morton, Gutman denies having been present during the assault. The whereabouts of all of the other officers in the station at the time can be accounted for. Consequently, if Alston is telling the truth, one of those three men participated with Babbage. Gutman is being represented by a lawyer from another firm. However, Gutman is a member of the PBA and an elected member of the PBA Board.

## Questions

1. If Stone, Morton, and the PBA all consent, can your firm accept the attractive PBA contract?
2. Assume that you conclude that you may seek waivers from your clients. How might your disclosure of the potential conflicts to the two criminal defendants be affected by your desire to obtain the PBA contract?

**3.** If you ask your clients to waive the potential conflicts and they refuse, what are your options? Can you take on the PBA contract and ask the PBA to get new counsel for Stone and Morton?

### PROBLEM 5-9    POLICE BRUTALITY, SCENE 3

Assume that the firm has signed the PBA contract. You are representing Chip Stone, who is charged with having participated in the assault. One of your partners is representing Morton. Stone consents in writing to waive any conflicts caused by your partner's representation of Morton and by your contract with the PBA. In court, the judge goes over the potential conflicts again, and Stone again states that he wants to waive them. As the case proceeds, statements from other officers to police investigators suggest that Gutman (the PBA board member), not Stone or Morton, was the second police officer in the bathroom. Alston cannot personally identify the second officer, but some of the other officers have stated in interviews that they saw Gutman going toward the bathroom with Alston. If you introduce testimony from these officers in defending Stone, it could exonerate your client Stone, but the testimony could be used against Gutman. Also, this testimony could be relevant to the civil suit against the PBA because implicating other officers would help Alston in the civil suit. The PBA might retaliate against you by canceling your contract.

---

### Questions

**1.** Should you present the testimony of the officers who say that they saw Gutman going toward the bathroom with Alston?

**2.** Suppose you don't introduce the testimony of the other officers. Instead you decide to rely on the theory that Officer Babbage acted alone. Babbage has already pleaded guilty. Stone is then convicted. He appeals, claiming that your representation of him was "ineffective" because of your conflicting obligations to the PBA and its board member Gutman, and that despite his consent to your representation, the judge should have disqualified you to prevent the violation of his Sixth Amendment right to effective counsel. Is he likely to prevail?

## 2. Conflicts in representing family members

### a. Representing both spouses in a divorce

Domestic relations lawyers often are asked to represent both spouses in a divorce. Technically this would involve the lawyer in filing a lawsuit on behalf of one client against another client. However, if both parties want to get divorced and have no disagreement about child custody or property division, then perhaps there is no actual adversity, only technical adversity.

### If the spouses want help drawing up a separation agreement, can a lawyer agree to it?

Some states allow a lawyer to represent both parties in an uncontested divorce. Others do not allow the lawyer to represent both husband and wife in the suit for divorce, but allow a lawyer to assist both parties in preparing a settlement agreement, as long as the clients agree and the resulting settlement seems fair.[147] But some jurisdictions do not allow a lawyer to represent both husband and wife in any divorce action, even with the consent of both spouses.[148] This prohibition is motivated in part by a concern that even if there is no apparent disagreement between the parties, they may in fact have conflicting financial or other interests that would emerge if they were separately advised. A lawyer who improperly represents both spouses in a divorce may be subject to malpractice liability[149] or discipline.[150]

## b. Representing family members in estate planning

It is quite common for lawyers to draft wills for husbands and wives, and for the beneficiaries of the wills to be other family members. This can be a harmonious process, but a number of problems can arise.[151] What if one spouse has a secret from the other? What if a parent wants to secretly change her will to disinherit a child? Does the lawyer have a duty to disclose this information to the other family member? Does it matter if the other person is formally a client? The following excerpts illustrate the kinds of conflicts that arise in this arena.

Some authorities urge that joint representation of two clients should include an agreement that information shared by one is not to be held in confidence from the other. What happens, then, if the lawyer doesn't have this conversation with the clients, and then "something comes up"? The following advisory ethics opinion explores that issue.

---

147. See, e.g., Klemm v. Superior Ct., 142 Cal. Rptr. 509 (Cal. App. 1977).

148. Id.

149. See, e.g., Ishmael v. Millington, 50 Cal. Rptr. 592 (Cal. App. 1966) (defendant had represented both husband and wife in divorce, failed to learn about some of the husband's assets, and produced a settlement that gave the wife far less than her share of the property; allegations found to state a claim for malpractice).

150. See, e.g., In re Houston, 985 P.2d 752 (N.M. 1999) (lawyer suspended from practice after representing both husband and wife in a divorce while simultaneously representing the husband on charges of domestic violence and sexual abuse of a child).

151. The conflicts that arise in estate planning matters are thoroughly explored in Teresa S. Collett, Disclosure, Discretion or Deception: The Estate Planner's Ethical Dilemma from a Unilateral Confidence, 28 Real Prop., Prob. & Tr. J. 683, 743 (1994); Teresa S. Collett, And the Two Shall Become as One . . . Until the Lawyers are Done, 7 Notre Dame J.L. Ethics & Pub. Policy 101 (1993); Geoffrey Hazard, Conflict of Interest in Estate Planning for Husband and Wife, 20 Prob. Law. 1 (1994).

## Florida Bar Opinion 95-4 (1997)

Lawyer has represented Husband and Wife for many years in a range of personal matters, including estate planning. Husband and Wife have substantial individual assets, and they also own substantial jointly-held property.

Recently, Lawyer prepared new updated wills that Husband and Wife signed. Like their previous wills, the new wills primarily benefit the survivor of them for his or her life, with beneficial disposition at the death of the survivor being made equally to their children (none of whom were born by prior marriage). . . .

Several months after the execution of the new wills, Husband confers separately with Lawyer. Husband reveals to Lawyer that he has just executed a codicil (prepared by another law firm) that makes substantial beneficial disposition to a woman with whom Husband has been having an extra-marital relationship. Husband tells Lawyer that Wife knows about neither the relationship nor the new codicil, as to which Husband asks Lawyer to advise him regarding Wife's rights of election in the event she were to survive Husband. . . .

### DISCUSSION

From the inception of the representation until Husband's communication to Lawyer of the information concerning the codicil and the extra-marital relationship (hereinafter the "separate confidence"), there was no objective indication that the interests of Husband and Wife diverged, nor did it objectively appear to Lawyer that any such divergence of interests was reasonably likely to arise. . . .

[T]he central issue presented . . . is the application of the confidentiality rule in a situation where confidentiality was not discussed at the outset of the joint representation. A lawyer is ethically obligated to [protect confidences but] . . . also has a duty to communicate to a client information that is relevant to the representation. . . . Which duty must give way? We conclude that, under the facts presented, Lawyer's duty of confidentiality must take precedence. Consequently, if Husband fails to disclose (or give Lawyer permission to disclose) the subject information to Wife, Lawyer is not ethically required to disclose the information to Wife and does not have discretion to reveal the information. To the contrary, Lawyer's ethical obligation of confidentiality to Husband *prohibits* Lawyer from disclosing the information to Wife. . . .

It has been suggested that, in a joint representation, a lawyer who receives information from the "communicating client" that is relevant to the interests of the non-communicating client may disclose the information to the latter, even over the communicating client's objections and even where disclosure would be damaging to the communicating client. The committee . . . rejects this "no-confidentiality" position. . . .

Significantly, existing Rule 4-1.6(c)(1) allows the joint clients' lawyer to share information received from one client with the other client, without the need to obtain consent from the communicating client, when such disclosure is reasonably necessary to further the interests of the joint representation. . . . [But if a conflict arises,] any "community of interests" has been damaged or destroyed. . . .

The second basis advanced for a no-confidentiality rule is the law governing the evidentiary attorney-client privilege. . . . Communications relevant to a matter of common interest between joint clients generally are not privileged as a matter of law. . . .

There are different purposes underlying the concepts of confidentiality and privilege. . . . The committee is of the opinion that the law of privilege does not, and should not, set the ethical standard of lawyer-client confidentiality.

It has been argued . . . that the usual rule of lawyer-client confidentiality does not apply in a joint representation and that the lawyer should have the *discretion* to determine whether the lawyer should disclose the separate confidence to the non-communicating client. This discretionary approach is advanced in the *Restatement*, § 112, comment *l.* . . . The *Restatement* itself acknowledges that no case law supports the discretionary approach. . . .

The committee further concludes that Lawyer must withdraw from the joint representation under the facts presented. An adversity of interests concerning the joint representation has arisen. This creates a conflict of interest. Many conflicts can be cured by obtaining the fully informed consent of the affected clients. Rule 4-1.7. Some conflicts, however, are of such a nature that it is not reasonable for a lawyer to request consent to continue the representation. . . .

In withdrawing from the representation, Lawyer should inform Wife and Husband that a conflict of interest has arisen that precludes Lawyer's continued representation of Wife and Husband in these matters. Lawyer may also advise both Wife and Husband that each should retain separate counsel. As discussed above, however, Lawyer may not disclose the separate confidence to Wife. The committee recognizes that a sudden withdrawal by Lawyer almost certainly will raise suspicions on the part of Wife. This may even alert Wife to the substance of the separate confidence. Regardless of whether such surmising by Wife occurs when Lawyer gives notice of withdrawal, Lawyer nevertheless has complied with the Rules of Professional Conduct and has not violated Lawyer's duties to Husband.

## Questions about Florida Bar Opinion 95-4

**1.** Do you think that the Florida Ethics Committee decided this question correctly?

**2.** What options are available to the lawyer in this situation under Rule 1.6?

PROBLEM 5-10 **REPRESENTING THE McCARTHYS**

*The facts of this problem are very similar to those of a case that was litigated in a northeastern state.*

You are a partner in the law firm of Kenney & Drogula. Your specialty is estate planning. About 18 months ago, you were approached by Hugh and Joline McCarthy, who wanted you to assist them in planning their estates. You undertook to represent them jointly, drafting a will for each that left his or her property to the other.

At the outset of the representation, you asked each of them each to sign a letter that explains the possible conflicts of interest inherent in this type of joint representation. The letter explained that one effect of a will leaving property to the other spouse is that he or she could then dispose of the property as she pleased. Also, the letter explained that information disclosed to the firm by one spouse could become available to the other. The McCarthys signed this disclosure statement.[152]

The wills were written and finalized over the next few weeks. The wills provided that each spouse left part of his or her estate to the other spouse, and part of it in trust for the children of both spouses. After the wills were finalized, the McCarthys signed a continuing retainer agreement providing that for a small annual fee, the firm would continue to represent the McCarthys, providing periodic advice on changes in tax law that might affect the disposition of the property.

The firm maintained a database to check for possible conflicts of interest. The clerk who opened the file on the case and entered the data in the firm's conflicts database unfortunately misspelled the McCarthys' last name, writing it as "MacCarthy."

Six months later, a woman named Maureen Carr retained Kenney & Drogula to file a paternity suit on her behalf against Hugh McCarthy. She claims that Hugh is the father of her newborn baby daughter, so she wants to sue him for child support. Gus Kenney, a partner in the family law department, accepted the matter. He did not know that Hugh was a client of the firm. The conflicts check did not identify him as a client because of the misspelling in the database.[153]

Before long, Kenney sent a letter to Hugh McCarthy about Carr's paternity claim. It didn't occur to Hugh to object to the fact that the firm that had written his will was representing Carr, since he's not a lawyer and has no training in conflicts of interest. He did not tell you about the matter, not being eager to talk about it with anyone. Instead, he hired another lawyer, Charlie Bucci, to represent him in connection with the paternity claim. Hugh denied that he was the father of the child, but he agreed to voluntary DNA testing, which would have been ordered by the court if he had not agreed. The DNA test indicated that he *was* in fact the father of Carr's child.

The conflict came to light when Maureen Carr's lawyer, Kenney, asked Bucci for information about Hugh's assets. Bucci politely informed Kenney that Kenney & Drogula already had the relevant financial information. (Hugh had told him that a lawyer at Kenney & Drogula had written his will.) He suggested that Kenney check

---

152. For sample letters to clients disclosing various types of conflicts of interest and requesting consent, see Freivogel on Conflicts, at http://www.freivogelonconflicts.com/new_page_38.htm (last visited Oct. 20, 2004).

153. This really happened, although the misspelling was, obviously, of a different name.

Hugh's file in the firm's estate department and then call him back if he needed anything else.

---

## Questions

**1.** You (the McCarthys' estate planning lawyer) just got off the phone with your partner, Gus Kenney, who told you he is representing Maureen Carr in a paternity suit against Hugh McCarthy. Now what? Does the firm have a conflict of interest under Rule 1.7? If so, is it consentable? If so, from whom would the firm need consent?

**2.** Assume that the conflict is not consentable. May Kenney & Drogula continue to represent one or two of these clients, or must it withdraw from representation of all three?

**3.** You are pretty sure that Joline McCarthy has no idea that her husband is allegedly the father of an illegitimate child. Assume that even if you have made a decision to withdraw, you have not done so yet, so Joline is still your client. What if any obligation do you have to disclose this information to her?

## 3. Representing insurance companies and insured persons

Insurance policies usually provide that when the insured person is sued over an event covered in the policy, such as a car accident, the insurance company will provide the insured person with a lawyer to defend him or her. If damages are awarded, the insurance company will cover the damages up to the amount of the insurance policy. The lawyer who defends the insured person may work at a private law firm paid by the insurance company to handle claims against its insured. The lawyer's contact at the insurance company usually is an insurance adjuster, who evaluates each claim and determines what, if anything, the insurance company should agree to pay.

The lawyer has some obligations to the insurer, who pays the fee and who will probably pay any damages awarded, and some obligations to the insured. Sometimes the interests of insurers and their insureds conflict. This section explains how such conflicts should be handled.

### Who is the client of the insurance defense lawyer?

The insurance defense lawyer's dilemma is fundamentally about money. The lawyer is being paid by one client (the insurer) to represent both itself and another client (the insured). While this relationship is governed in part by contract law and by insurance law,[154] the ethical rules provide useful guidance as well.

---

154. The Restatement takes the position that because of the other applicable law, the relationship between a lawyer, and insurance company and an insured is beyond the scope of the restatement. See Restatement § 134, comments a and f.

**Rule 1.8(f)**

(f) A lawyer shall not accept compensation for representing a client from one other than the client unless:

(1) the client gives informed consent;

(2) there is no interference with the lawyer's independence of professional judgment or with the client-lawyer relationship; and

(3) information relating to representation of a client is protected as required by Rule 1.6.

If acceptance of payment from someone other than the client "presents a significant risk that the lawyer's representation of the client will be materially limited by the lawyer's own interest in accommodating the person paying the lawyer's fee or by the lawyer's responsibilities to a payer who is also a co-client," there is a conflict under Rule 1.7(b); the lawyer must assess whether the conflict is consentable and seek informed consent from the client.[155]

But the tricky question in the case of the insurance company and the insured is "who is the client?"[156] The Restatement says that it is "clear in an insurance situation that a lawyer designated to defend the insured has a client-lawyer relationship with the insured. The insurer is not, simply by the fact that it designates the lawyer, a client of the lawyer."[157] The insurance company may be a client, depending on the contract and on state law. But the insured is always a client. Even so, the Restatement continues, communications between the insurer and counsel for the insured "should be regarded as privileged" and the insurer may sue the lawyer for negligence.

### When is there a conflict between the interests of the insurer and the insured?

Much case law takes the position that a lawyer may represent both the insurer and the insured so long as there is no conflict between their interests. If, for example, any claim will be covered entirely by the insurance policy, then perhaps the insurer and insured's interests are largely aligned. If, however, it appears that a damage award may exceed the amount covered by an insurance policy, a conflict may be more likely. The more likely a conflict, the more careful a lawyer should be about consulting with the insurer and insured to obtain informed consent before proceeding.[158]

### Can a lawyer accept direction from an insurer as to how much to spend on discovery and other aspects of litigation?

If a lawyer represents an insured but his fee is paid by the insurer, the lawyer owes the client a duty of competent representation. However, as to

---

155. Rule 1.7, Comment 13.

156. For one of many explorations of the conflicts faced by insurance defense lawyers, see Geoffrey Hazard, Triangular Lawyer Relationships: An Exploratory Analysis, 1 Geo. J. Leg. Ethics 15 (1987); John Leubsdorf, Pluralizing the Lawyer-Client Relationship, 77 Cornell L. Rev. 825 (1992).

157. Restatement § 134, comment f.

158. Id.

duties that go beyond a duty of competency, the contract between the insurer and the insured may delegate to the insurer the authority to make decisions about discretionary efforts or expenses in litigation.[159] However, if the insured might incur liability exceeding the policy limits, the lawyer may not follow a direction by the insurer that would substantially increase the risk of such liability.[160]

## Can the lawyer reveal confidential information from the insured person to the insurer?

Suppose a lawyer is assigned by an insurer to represent an insured on a fire insurance claim. Suppose the insured person reveals to the lawyer that he caused the fire by smoking in bed. This information probably would lead the insurer to decide to contest coverage of the claim. Can the lawyer tell the insurer? The answer is no, even if the insurer also is a client of the lawyer and even if "the insurer has asserted a 'reservation of rights'" in this matter and informed the insured that it may refuse to pay the claim.[161] In one case, a lawyer learned that an assault on a child had been intentional and therefore would not be covered by the insurance policy.[162] The lawyer was held to be obliged to keep the information confidential and to withdraw from representing the parties. If, in this circumstance, the lawyer used the information to benefit the insurer, the company was estopped from denying coverage.

## If a conflict of interest arises between the insured and the insurer, what is the lawyer supposed to do?

If there is a conflict, the lawyer should act in the best interests of the insured, except that the lawyer may not assist client fraud. If the insured is also the lawyer's client, the lawyer should try to act in the best interests of both clients. If that is not possible, the lawyer is required to withdraw from representation of both clients.[163] Many insurance policies provide that in the event of a claim, the insured person and the insurer will be represented by a single lawyer, but that if there is a conflict between the interests of the insured and the insurer (for example, if the insurer asserts that the claim is not covered), the insurer will pay the cost of hiring a separate lawyer for the insured.[164] Most jurisdictions have held (as an insurance law matter) that if an insurer contests coverage, the insurer has to pay for a lawyer selected by the insured unless

---

159. Id. at illus. 5.
160. Id. at comment f.
161. Restatement § 60, comment l.
162. Parsons v. Continental Natl. Am. Group, 550 P.2d 94 (S. Ct. Ariz. 1976).
163. Id.
164. See, e.g., Nandorf, Inc. v. CNA Ins. Cos., 479 N.E.2d 988 (Ill. App. 1985). If the insurer selects the alternate lawyer, the insured must give informed consent. See, e.g., N.Y. St. Urb. Dev. Corp. v. VSL Corp., 738 F.2d 61 (2d Cir. 1984).

the insured has agreed or agrees to be represented by a lawyer selected by the insurer.[165]

### What if the insurer and the insured disagree about whether to settle?

What if the insurer wants to settle and the insured does not? Although an insured person can agree by contract to allow the insurer to control some aspects of her defense, the lawyer's professional obligations to the insured should govern the lawyer's conduct in the event of a dispute about settlement.[166] ABA Opinion 96-403 (1996) concludes that if the insurer and the insured disagree about whether to settle, the lawyer must withdraw from representing both of them in that matter. Once the insured is a former client, the lawyer still cannot assist the insurer in settling the matter against the interests of his former client.[167] Of course, the lawyer's proposed withdrawal after the lawsuit has been partly litigated usually will create a practical problem for the insured, who will have to hire a new lawyer, probably (in this case, unlike if coverage is denied) at her own expense.

On the other hand, what if the plaintiff offers to settle the claim within the policy limits, the insured wants to do so, and the insurer insists on turning down the settlement? If the insurer turns down a settlement and then damages are awarded in excess of the policy limits, the insurer often is required to cover those costs.[168]

### PROBLEM 5-11 TWO MASTERS

*This story is one of many told to Professor Lerman by "Nicholas Farber."[169] "Nicholas Farber" told these stories because he was troubled by many things that had happened at this law firm. He agreed to publication of the stories only if neither he nor the firm would be identified because some of the stories involve serious misconduct.*

"Nicholas Farber" worked for a couple of years at an insurance defense firm in a big city on the East Coast. The firm had about 50 lawyers. Farber explained that it can be difficult for insurance company lawyers to understand who they are supposed to be representing:

"We handled lots of cases for an insurance company. As to those cases, I didn't know who the client was until I had been at the firm three or four months. I thought the clients were the individuals we represented. But from my firm's perspective, the client was the insurance company because the company paid their bills. You are serving two masters. I thought it bordered on malpractice that they didn't

---

165. Restatement § 134, comment f, reporter's note.
166. Id.
167. Id.
168. Parsons v. Continental Natl. Am. Group, 550 P.2d 94 (S. Ct. Ariz. 1976).
169. Others are found in Lisa G. Lerman, Scenes from a Law Firm, 50 Rutgers L. Rev. 2153 (1998), and in Chapter 7.

explain that very carefully and then supervise me until I was comfortable with that relationship.

"I started at the firm at the end of September, and by early November, I had 80 files on my desk. . . . They dumped on my desk the caseload of a fifth-year associate who left on maternity leave. Their thought was, 'Well, who else is going to do it?' I got 70 or 75 files from her, and I was involved in 5 or 6 others with a partner.

"There was one specific incident I will never forget. I was told by 'my client,' the defendant [that is, the insured person], that I was not to settle a case without her permission. . . . She said, 'I don't give a damn what that adjuster says. The contract says they can't settle anything without getting my permission first.'

"I remember calling the adjuster from the judge's chambers and saying, 'I need to know how much authority I have to settle this case.' He said he thought $5,000. I remember saying, 'I need to call my client.' They said, 'No you don't.' I said, 'Yes I do. She told me that she didn't care what the insurance company said, we need her permission.' And he said, 'I'll deal with her. You settle the case.'

"[I didn't settle.] I caught all sorts of hell for that later on. Not from the defendant, . . . [b]ut it ruined my relationship with that adjuster, and the partners were not happy with me because I wasn't making their client happy. . . . It was awful."

---

## Questions

**1.** If the damages were to be paid by the insurance company, why might the defendant have been so adamant that the claim should not be settled without her approval? Was she being unreasonable?

**2.** Why might the partners in Farber's firm have been unhappy that he wanted to consult the insured person before agreeing to a settlement of a claim against her?

## 4. Conflicts in representation of a class

You will recall how many conflicts can arise if a lawyer represents two plaintiffs or defendants in a lawsuit. Imagine, then, a lawyer representing a class of thousands of plaintiffs seeking relief through a class action suit.[170] Some of the possible conflicts are between the members of the class, while others are conflicts between the clients' interests and the lawyer's personal interests. "Examples of potential conflicts include (a) a greater concern for the interests

---

170. A similar array of issues may be raised if a lawyer is representing a group of clients who are not certified as a class, but whose claims are settled jointly. See Restatement § 128, comment d(i).

of the class representatives than for the unnamed members of the class; (b) a prior relationship with the named defendants in the class action; (c) a greater concern for receiving a fee than for pursuing the class claim; and (d) the settlement of claims by collusion rather than through a fair process where class members' interests are adequately represented."[171]

Suppose you represent 40 individual clients who were seriously injured because they took a drug that had dangerous side effects about which the manufacturer had failed to give proper warning. You realize that at least a thousand other people have suffered similar injuries after taking the drug. Is it a problem to seek class certification and join all the aggrieved individuals? On your end, it's a lot more work to litigate a class action, and the case probably will take much longer to resolve, but the potential attorneys' fees are enormously higher. (This means there may be a conflict between your interests and your clients' interests in prompt resolution.) In addition, a class suit might deplete the defendant's resources, and a court will supervise any class action settlement, so your individual clients might recover less than they would if you pursue lawsuits on behalf of them alone. Alternatively, if the class action falters, you might later be tempted to settle for fewer dollars per class member, so that the clients you know well, and from whom you will receive 33 percent contingent fee recoveries, will collect more. A lawyer considering pursuing a class action must discuss the potential risks and benefits in detail with individual clients. In addition, the lawyer should consider carefully whether the matter is appropriate for a class action. If the clients' concerns and desired remedies are more common than conflicting, and the size of the claim makes it too expensive to litigate them separately, a class action could be a proper strategy.[172]

The existence of class actions as a category of litigation in our system reflects that our justice system does not insist that each litigant have an advocate whose loyalty is undivided. Instead, there is a balance between the ideal of an unconflicted advocate, on one hand, and the goal of allowing citizens access to the courts to get remedies for harm. Sometimes the best vehicle for that remedy might be a lawyer who has never laid eyes on most of his clients and who will advocate in their collective interests, even if that means his loyalties are spread over a large group.

However, the traditional principles for preventing conflicts of interest, as embodied in Rule 1.7, don't fit very well with the class action device. Class actions often involve the kinds of conflicts that we would not permit in individual lawsuits, at least not without the consent of all parties, and actual consent from all of the members of a large class is impracticable, although

---

171. Gregg H. Curry, Conflicts of Interest Problems for Lawyers Representing a Class in a Class Action Lawsuit, 24 J. Legal Prof. 397 (1999). For discussion of these issues, see Samuel Issacharoff, Class Action Conflicts, 30 U.C. Davis L. Rev. 805 (1997) (discussing F.R.C.P. 23 in depth but not even mentioning Rule 1.7); Deborah Rhode, Class Conflicts in Class Actions, 34 Stan. L. Rev. 1182 (1982).

172. Restatement § 128, comment d(iii).

in suits for money damages, class members are notified of the lawsuit and permitted to withdraw from it to preserve their right to sue individually.[173] Perhaps because Rule 1.7 is ill-suited to the analysis of lawyers' roles in class actions, judges rarely apply it, even when a party (usually a party opposing the class action) complains to a court about a conflict. Instead, the courts usually resolve the conflict by applying the court's class action rules, particularly the rules requiring lawyers for the class to be adequate representatives of the class as a whole.[174]

---

173. Fed. R. Civ. P. 23.
174. Curry, supra n. 171, at 408-410.

# 6

# Conflicts Involving Former Clients, Government Lawyers, and Judges

A. **The nature of conflicts between present and former clients**

B. **Duties to former clients**

C. **Distinguishing present and former clients**
   1. Maintaining contact
   2. Hiring and firing lawyers to create or eliminate conflicts
   3. Former in-house counsel

D. **Evaluating successive conflicts**
   1. Questions to ask
   2. The same matter
   3. Substantial relationship
   4. Confidential information
   5. Variations in the definition of "substantial relationship"
   6. Material adversity

E. **Practice issues relating to former client conflicts**

F. **Particular applications of Rule 1.9**
   1. Suing former clients
   2. Representing the competitor of a former client

G. **Conflicts between the interests of a present client and a client who was represented by a lawyer's former firm**
   1. Analyzing former firm conflicts
   2. Using or revealing a former client's confidences

This chapter begins by examining conflicts that involve the interests of former clients. It looks at what duties lawyers owe to former clients and what lawyers should do if those duties conflict with those of current or new clients. The chapter then examines successive conflicts of government lawyers who have gone into private practice as well as lawyers who have left private practice to work in government. Last, it briefly discusses conflicts involving judges and judicial law clerks and those involving prospective clients.

# A. The nature of conflicts between present and former clients

Sometimes a lawyer wants to take on work that poses a conflict with the interests of a person or an organization that the lawyer represented in the past. Or sometimes a conflict with a former client's interests develops or becomes apparent after a lawyer is well into some work on behalf of a current client. In a former client/present client situation, a lawyer might betray the interests of the former client or the present client. A lawyer might

- betray confidences of a former client to a present client,
- make *adverse use* of confidences that the lawyer learned during the representation of the former client,

- attack or challenge work that the lawyer did on behalf of the former client, or
- engage in work that is in some other way disloyal to the former client or at least causes the former client to feel betrayed.

If the interests of the former and present clients conflict, a lawyer might also be less zealous on behalf of the present client because of an obligation to the former client. For example, suppose the lawyer knows information from the former representation that could help the present client, but does not use or reveal that information because of his duty to protect confidences. His advocacy on behalf of the new client is somewhat compromised by his duties to the former client.

A lawyer who perceives a conflict between her duties to a present client and a former client might favor her current client because the latter is paying current fees. But previous financial relationships, the expectation of future work, or continuing emotional ties might cause a lawyer to favor her former client and thus to be a less vigorous advocate for her present one.

### If a conflict involves a present client and a former client, which ethical rule applies?

Protections for all present clients are provided in Rule 1.7, which is discussed fully in Chapter 5. If a present and former client's interests conflict, a lawyer would refer to Rule 1.7 for guidance on protection of the interests of the present client. Rule 1.7(a)(2) defines a concurrent conflict to include a situation in which "there is a significant risk that the representation of one or more clients will be materially limited by a lawyer's responsibilities to another client, *a former client*, a third person or by a personal interest of the lawyer" (emphasis added). Comment 9 explains that "a lawyer's duties of loyalty and independence may be materially limited by responsibilities to former clients under Rule 1.9."

Protections for former clients are provided by Rule 1.9. If a situation involves possible compromises of the interests of both the new client and the former client, a lawyer should look to both rules (1.7 and 1.9) for guidance. The following table illustrates this point.

## Which rule to apply to conflicts involving present and former clients

| Situation | Possible interest harmed | Can this conflict be waived? | Rule |
|---|---|---|---|
| Lawyer knows (or might have had access to) information from a former client that could be used adversely to the former client. | Breach of commitment to keep confidences of **former client** | Yes, by informed consent of former client | 1.9 |

*Continued*

| Situation | Possible interest harmed | Can this conflict be waived? | Rule |
|---|---|---|---|
| New client wants lawyer to sue lawyer's former client, whom lawyer represented for years on a variety of matters. | • Possible adverse use of confidences of **former client**, depending on subject matter<br>• Lawyer's advocacy on behalf of **new client** might be compromised by relationship to former client | Yes, by informed consent of present and former clients, unless the conflict is so severe that the lawyer could not reasonably believe that he could provide competent and diligent representation to the new client | 1.9<br><br><br><br><br><br>1.7 |

Notice, then, that in a conflict between a present and former client, there may be a "former client problem," that is, one that would impact the former client, and a "present client problem" if the relationship with the former client might impair the representation of the present client.

### Are the ethical rules less restrictive as to successive conflicts than they are as to concurrent conflicts?

Yes. The ethics rules reflect an assumption that the problems relating to former clients may not be quite as serious as those with present clients. A lawyer's duties to a former client are limited mainly to protecting confidences, avoiding side-switching, and refraining from attacking the work the lawyer did for the former client.[1] The passage of time often reduces the likelihood that a lawyer will deliberately or inadvertently misuse information she received from one client while representing another client.[2] In addition, the legal profession does not want to hamstring lawyers by imposing lifetime loyalty obligations to former clients that would preclude too broad a range of future work.[3]

Although the rules on former clients are not as restrictive as those on current client conflicts, they do preclude a lawyer from proceeding in many situations without the consent of the former client.

---

1. Some authorities assert that there is no separate duty of loyalty to a former client, but the duties described here are in fact a set of limited duties of loyalty.

2. Although the rules assume that lesser protection is needed to avoid harm from conflicts involving former clients, some former client conflicts problems might be more serious than those between present clients. For example, in some cases, lawyers might be likely to misuse information from former clients because they do not feel any present loyalty to the former clients. A lawyer might make inadvertent misuse of confidential information received from a former client without realizing where she got the information.

3. Restatement § 132, comment b. While the profession is reluctant to impose lifetime *loyalty* obligations, Rule 1.6 does impose a lifetime *confidentiality* obligation.

# B. Duties to former clients

## What duties does a lawyer owe a former client?

The primary duty that lawyers owe to former clients is to protect their confidences.[4] A lawyer must decline any new matter that presents a substantial risk that the lawyer would make material adverse use of the former client's confidences, unless the former client consents. Rule 1.9 articulates the standards against which lawyers should evaluate successive conflicts. (Later in this chapter, we explain its terms in some detail.)

---

### Rule 1.9 Duties to former clients[5]

| Rule language* | Authors' explanation |
|---|---|
| (a) A lawyer who has **formerly represented a client** in a matter **shall not** thereafter **represent** another person in **the same or a substantially related matter** in which that person's interests are **materially adverse** to the interests of the former client **unless the former client gives informed consent, confirmed in writing.** | This section explains how to evaluate a conflict between a *particular lawyer's former client* and a present or new client. |
| (b) A lawyer **shall not** knowingly **represent** a person in the **same or a substantially related matter** in which **a firm with which the lawyer formerly was associated had previously represented a client** | This section applies to conflicts between a present or new client and *a client of the lawyer's previous firm*. |
| (1) whose interests are **materially adverse** to that person; **and** | |
| (2) about whom the lawyer had **acquired information protected by Rules 1.6 and 1.9(c)** that is **material** to the matter; | |
| unless the former client gives informed consent, confirmed in writing. | |

*Continued*

---

4. See, e.g., Analytica v. NPD Research, 708 F.2d 1263 (7th Cir. 1983).

5. This is the text of the relevant Delaware Rule of Professional Conduct. Unless specified otherwise, all of this book's quotations from rules of professional conduct are quotations from the Delaware Rules of Professional Conduct. In a few instances, we quote from rules or from published proposed rules in other states. Except where we note otherwise, however, the text of all state rules that we quote is the same as the text of the ABA Model Rules of Professional Conduct. See the note in the Introduction for a more detailed explanation.

| Rule language* | Authors' explanation |
|---|---|
| (c) A lawyer who has **formerly represented** a client in a matter **or whose present or former firm has formerly represented** a client in a matter **shall not** thereafter: | This section bars *use or revelation* of confidences of former clients or clients of a former firm to the same extent as such use or revelation is barred for present clients. |
| (1) **use information relating to the representation to the disadvantage of the former client except** as these Rules would permit or require with respect to a client, or when the information has become **generally known;** or | |
| (2) **reveal** information relating to the representation except as these Rules would permit or require with respect to a client. | |

*All emphasis added.

Under Rule 1.9(a), a lawyer may not do work on behalf of a new client if that work involves "the same or a substantially related matter" as a former representation *and* the new client's interests are "materially adverse to the interests of the former client, *unless* the former client gives informed consent, confirmed in writing" (emphasis added). One obvious difference between the rule on concurrent conflicts and this rule is that in dealing with conflicts that might *adversely impact former clients,* a lawyer is *always* permitted to proceed with the new work if the lawyer can secure informed consent from the former client. However, as discussed in Chapter 5, a conflict that could *adversely impact a present client* might not be waiveable.[6]

Conflicts that impact present clients may be problematic regardless of the subject matter of the two representations. Conflicts that impact former clients, on the other hand, raise a problem only if there is a "substantial relationship" between the work done for the former client and the new matter.

## C. Distinguishing present and former clients

### How do you know if a client is a present client or a former client?

This sounds like a dumb question, but it isn't. A concurrent conflict involves two present clients or one present and one prospective client. A successive conflict involves one present or prospective client and one former client. But some clients a lawyer regards as former clients may consider themselves present clients. In some cases, their beliefs may be reasonable. As conflicts

---

6. Rule 1.7(b).

*William Freivogel*

expert William Freivogel notes, things would be simpler if every lawyer, upon completion of a piece of work (such as writing a will), wrote a letter to a client saying: "This matter has concluded. We plan to do no further work for you, and you are no longer our client."[7]

The problem, says Freivogel, is that, "Lawyers hate to write letters like that. A truly effective letter may offend the client. Moreover, the lawyer wants to maintain a bond with the client so that it will send more business. Thus, these letters are rarely written."[8]

One Chicago lawyer, for example, puts it this way:

> Do you think that anyone in their right mind is going to . . . send a letter to that client [for whom a deal had been handled] saying, "It was a pleasure working for you. We don't work for you any more. We consider our relationship terminated. Very truly yours?" No. They might send a letter . . . saying "It's been a pleasure handling this deal. We look forward to working with you again."[9]

If there is not a clear statement by the lawyer or the client or in the contract between them confirming that the relationship is over, the Restatement says the lawyer's representational authority can also end "because the lawyer has completed the contemplated services."[10]

This question of who is a present client and who is a former one is fraught with practical pressures. As firms grow larger and as institutional clients increasingly tend to use multiple firms, the problems multiply. On one hand, there is "business pressure" to treat any client for whom the work has been completed as a former client. This reduces the number of prospective clients whose interests conflict with those of other current clients (because more of them are treated as former clients). On the other hand, taking on work that conflicts with the interests of an arguably former client (who might still think she is a present client) without that person's consent can have negative fallout, either ethically or practically. Susan Shapiro elaborates:

> As monogamous general counsel relationships are increasingly being transformed into promiscuous one-night stands with special counsel, law firms can ill afford to shelter their uncommitted paramours from the former-client category. As many respondents observe, they face both potential ethical and

---

7. William Freivogel, Former Client: The Substantial Relationship Test, at http://www.freivogelonconflicts.com/new_page_34.htm (last visited Oct. 22, 2004).

8. Id.

9. Susan Shapiro, Tangled Loyalties: Conflict of Interest in Legal Practice 192 (U. Mich. Press 2002), quoting an interview with a Chicago lawyer in a firm with over 100 lawyers.

10. Restatement § 31(2)(e). Comment h states that this question depends on examination of the course of dealing between the parties. The comment notes that "Because contracts with a client are to be construed from the client's viewpoint, the client's reasonable understanding of the scope of representation controls."

financial consequences when they consider one-shot patrons former clients and financial consequences when they do not.[11]

# 1. Maintaining contact

**What if a lawyer has a long-term client, but the lawyer has not done anything for that client in a year or more?**

If a lawyer has not formally concluded representation of the client, a court might still find that the client is a present one and that a conflict with another client should be evaluated as a concurrent conflict.[12]

One Chicago lawyer raises the following question:

> Ours is primarily a transactional practice. A client may call you up to do one thing. It is completed. The firm continues to send a newsletter to the client. Lawyers occasionally make a sales call to them.[13] How does this fit into the assessment of whether someone is a former client?[14]

PROBLEM 6-1 **KEEPING IN TOUCH**

You work for a law firm that five years ago did some work for Almond Enterprises, a small business. The firm's prior work for Almond was to provide an opinion on the tax consequences of purchasing certain bonds. This work took one day. Almond paid $2,500. Your firm sends its annual newsletter to all of its previous clients as well as its current clients. The newsletter alerts recipients to changes in tax law and other laws that might affect small businesses. One purpose of sending the newsletter is to encourage small-business clients to contact and retain the law firm for more specific advice about the implications of these changes. The firm also called Almond several times over the years to ask if it needed additional services. Almond always declined.

Now Star Information Systems, Inc., a computer service company, wants to hire the law firm to sue Almond to collect unpaid bills for

---

11. Shapiro, supra n. 9, at 195.

12. Restatement § 132, comment c, reporter's note, citing Shearing v. Allergan, Inc., 1994 WL 396139 (D. Nev. May 1994) (lawyer had represented a client for 13 years but had not done any work for that client in more than a year — still found to be a current client).

13. [Authors' footnote.] Under the ethics rules in most jurisdictions, there are some restrictions on in-person or telephonic solicitation of business from new clients, but once a client has engaged the services of a firm, the firm may contact the client to suggest additional services that the firm could provide. See, e.g., Rule 7.3.

14. Shapiro, supra n. 9, at 192, quoting a Chicago lawyer in a firm with between 50 and 99 lawyers.

40 hours of consulting services it provided when Almond was installing a new e-mail system. The computer consulting services have nothing to do with the bond purchase five years ago. The firm's senior partner wants to know whether Almond is a current client, because if so, the more stringent restrictions of Rule 1.7 would apply.

Is Almond a current client?

---

## 2. Hiring and firing lawyers to create or eliminate conflicts

Sometimes both lawyers and clients try to either form or terminate lawyer-client relationships to create conflicts problems or to solve them. Sometimes lawyers try to turn present clients into former clients to avoid concurrent client restrictions. Likewise, sometimes clients hire firms solely for the purpose of precluding their adversaries from hiring those same firms.

**If you withdraw from representing a client to solve a potential conflict, does the "fired" client become a former client for the purpose of evaluating conflicts?**

> FOR EXAMPLE:  What if you have just agreed to represent client A in a small transaction, and then client B wants to retain you for a great deal of money to do work on a major transaction (a different one) that would be adverse to client A? Can you drop client A and turn a concurrent conflict into a less serious successive conflict?

The work for client B would be much more substantial (and lucrative) than the work for client A, but their interests are adverse. Can you withdraw from client A, thereby turning A into a former client, so that the conflict may be analyzed as successive rather than concurrent? In general, the answer is no. If the withdrawal is premature and motivated by a desire to dump client A so that the lawyer can work for client B, the lawyer's withdrawal represents a breach of the lawyer's duty to client A. One court put it this way: "A firm may not drop a client like a hot potato, especially if it is in order to keep happy a far more lucrative client."[15]

So a lawyer can't fire a client to lower the conflicts bar on a new client. On the other hand, if one of the following conditions is satisfied, the lawyer may use the more lenient successive conflict standards to evaluate the conflict.

- The lawyer withdraws at the natural end point in the representation.
- The client fires the lawyer for reasons other than the impending conflict.
- The client triggers a conflict for the lawyer by some action (for example, acquiring a company that is a defendant in a matter in which the lawyer

---

15. Picker Intl., Inc. v. Varian Assocs., 670 F. Supp. 1363, 1365 (N.D. Ohio 1987).

represents the plaintiff) that was unforeseeable to the lawyer.[16] In this case, the lawyer's withdrawal makes this client a former client.

■ The lawyer withdraws for some other good reason (for example, if the client insists that the lawyer assist in committing a fraud or if the client refuses to pay the fees it owes).[17]

**Can a client preclude an adversary from hiring certain firms by hiring those firms for small, continuing matters, thereby creating concurrent conflicts for the firms if the adversary approaches them?**

It is possible for a client to preclude an adversary from hiring certain lawyers by hiring them. Since a law firm may not drop a client like a hot potato and then become its adversary, law firms are vulnerable to this practice, referred to by some lawyers as "sabotage."[18] However, at least one state bar ethics committee concluded that it is unethical for a lawyer to suggest or participate in this practice.[19] Meanwhile, some law firms realize that new clients hiring them for small matters may be trying to set up conflicts for them. They may refuse the business or attempt to avoid the conflicts by asking the new clients for advance waivers of future conflicts of interest. At least in some jurisdictions, such advance waivers are effective.[20] Comment 22 to Rule 1.7 explicitly condones advance waivers of conflicts under some circumstances, particularly if the client is an "experienced user . . . of legal services" and the client signing the waiver is familiar with the type of conflict waived.[21]

## 3. Former in-house counsel

**If a lawyer used to work in the law department of a corporation, is the corporation his former client on all matters that were going on during his employment?**

Not necessarily. Former in-house counsel have been disqualified for such conflicts in several cases,[22] but the mere fact of employment does not make a lawyer the corporation's lawyer on every matter. If a lawyer worked on a matter (more than a trivial amount) on behalf of his employer corporation, the

---

16. Restatement § 132, comment j, reporter's note, citing Gould, Inc. v. Mitsui Mining & Smelting Co., 738 F. Supp. 1121 (N.D. Ohio 1990). This type of conflict is sometimes referred to as one "thrust upon" a lawyer by the client. See D.C. Bar, Legal Ethics Comm., Op. 292 (1999).

17. Restatement § 132 comment c.

18. Lincoln Caplan, Skadden: Power, Money, and the Rise of a Legal Empire 84 (Farrar 1993).

19. Indiana State Bar, Op. 2 (2000), available at http://www.inbar.org/content/pdf/Legal%20Ethics/2000.pdf (last visited Oct. 23, 2004) (improper for divorce lawyer to suggest that client consult a firm so that the firm will be disqualified from representing his spouse).

20. Kennecott Copper Corp. v. Curtiss-Wright Corp., 449 F. Supp. 951 (S.D.N.Y. 1978), aff'd and rev'd, 584 F.2d 1195 (2d Cir. 1978), discussed in Richard W. Painter, Advance Waiver of Conflicts, 13 Geo. J. Leg. Ethics 289, 297-298 (2000).

21. Rule 1.7, Comment 22.

22. See, e.g., NCK Org., Ltd. v. Bregman, 542 F.2d 128 (2d Cir. 1976).

corporation is his former client as to that matter. However, the corporation may not be the lawyer's former client as to matters that were going on during the lawyer's employment if the lawyer did not work on them and received no confidences regarding those matters.[23]

## Analyzing Successive Conflicts Under Rule 1.9

```
┌──────────────────┐                    ┌──────────────────┐
│ Does the work for│                    │ Is the matter    │
│ the current      │                    │ "substantially   │            ┌──────────────┐
│ client constitute│                    │ related" to the  │            │ No conflict  │
│ the "same matter"│──── NO ──────────▶ │ matter handled   │─── NO ───▶ │ under        │
│ as the work      │                    │ for the previous │            │ Rule 1.9     │
│ handled for the  │                    │ client?          │            └──────────────┘
│ previous client? │                    └──────────────────┘                   ▲
└──────────────────┘                             │                             │
        │                                        │                             │
       YES                                      YES                           NO
        │                                        │                             │
        └──────────────┬─────────────────────────┘                            │
                       ▼                                                       │
            ┌──────────────────────┐                                          │
            │ Are the new client's │                                          │
            │ interests            │                                          │
            │ "materially adverse" │──────────────────────────────────────────┘
            │ to the former        │
            │ client's interests?  │
            └──────────────────────┘
                       │
                      YES
                       │
                       ▼
            ┌──────────────────────┐                    ┌──────────────────┐
            │ Has the former client│                    │ Conflict is      │
            │ given informed       │──── YES ──────────▶│ waived. Rule 1.9 │
            │ consent in writing?  │                    │ is no bar to     │
            └──────────────────────┘                    │ representation   │
                       │                                └──────────────────┘
                      NO
                       │
                       ▼
            ┌──────────────────────┐
            │ Rule 1.9 bars        │
            │ representation       │
            └──────────────────────┘
```

# D.  Evaluating successive conflicts

## 1.  Questions to ask

The critical question about conflicts between present and former clients is whether the conflict is serious enough that the lawyer may not go forward with the new work without the former client's informed consent. To answer this

---

23. ABA Comm. on Ethics & Prof. Resp., Formal Op. 99-415 (1999).

question, the lawyer, applying Rule 1.9, must ask two things about the new matter:

- Is it the "same matter" as the previous one?
- If not, is it "substantially related" to the previous one?

Beware! Both these questions use terms of art that must be understood to answer them correctly.

- If one of the two questions above is answered "yes," the lawyer must ask whether the new client's interests are "materially adverse to the interests of the former client."
- If the matter is the same or substantially related and there is material adversity, the lawyer may not go forward with the new representation without the former client's informed consent.
- There must be written confirmation of the consent.

The discussion that follows explores each of these steps. Keep in mind that if the conflict might adversely impact your representation of a current client, you must also do a separate analysis of the conflict under Rule 1.7.

## 2. The same matter

### When is one matter "the same matter" as a previous one?

First of all, what is a "matter"? A matter can be anything that is the subject of representation: a litigation, a transaction, a subject on which a client requests advice.[24] A conflict may occur between a former matter that did not involve adversarial advocacy — perhaps the client just sought advice — and a subsequent, more adversarial matter.[25]

The most obvious "same matter" is a single transaction or lawsuit. In addition, it is the "same matter" if the new representation involves a document that the lawyer was involved in producing — the subject matter is the same.[26]

Under Rule 1.9, a lawyer may not switch sides in the midst of a negotiation or a litigation (same matter, materially adverse interests) unless the former client gives written consent, which would be unlikely.[27] Likewise, a lawyer may not "switch sides" and attack an instrument that the lawyer drafted.

> **FOR EXAMPLE:** A lawyer drafts a will for a client who wishes to disinherit his eldest son. After the client dies, the eldest son asks the lawyer to represent him to challenge the validity of this will. The lawyer may not take on this work.

---

24. Restatement § 132 comment d(iii).
25. Id. at comment d(iii), reporter's note.
26. Id. at comment d(ii).
27. Id. at comment d(i).

## 3. Substantial relationship

### When is there a "substantial relationship" between one matter and another?

A commonsense application of this test requires one to ask if there is some connection between the earlier matter and the new matter. There are many possible connections: Two matters might involve the same parties, the same lawsuit, the same legal issues, or the same (or overlapping) facts. The legal definition of "substantial relationship," however, is far narrower and focuses on likely access to relevant confidential information.

The dominant legal definition of "substantial relationship" asks whether the lawyer, in the course of her work in the first matter, would normally have learned information that could be used adversely to the former client in the second. Comment 3 to Rule 1.9 explains:

> Matters are "substantially related" for purposes of this Rule if they involve the same transaction or legal dispute or if there otherwise is a substantial risk that confidential factual information as would normally have been obtained in the prior representation would materially advance the client's position in the subsequent matter.[28]

The Seventh Circuit explained it this way:

> [T]he determination of whether there is a substantial relationship turns on the possibility, or appearance thereof, that confidential information might have been given to the attorney in relation to the subsequent matter in which disqualification is sought. The rule thus does not necessarily involve any inquiry into the imponderables involved in the degree of relationship between the two matters but instead involves a realistic appraisal of the possibility that confidences had been disclosed in the one matter which will be harmful to the client in the other. . . . [I]t is not appropriate for the court to inquire into whether actual confidences were disclosed.[29]

The comments to Rule 1.9 offer a couple of examples of what is a substantial relationship. Let's consider them.

> A lawyer who has represented a businessperson and learned extensive private financial information about that person may not then represent that person's spouse in seeking a divorce.[30]

During the first representation, the lawyer learned specific information about the husband's assets that could be helpful in representing the wife in the divorce. What if the husband tried to conceal some assets during the divorce

---

28. The Restatement defines substantial relationship very similarly. Id. at comment d(iii).

29. Westinghouse Elec. Corp. v. Gulf Oil Corp., 588 F.2d 221, 224 (7th Cir. 1978). This well-articulated definition of the term is quoted in Restatement § 132, comment d(iii).

30. Rule 1.9, Comment 3.

proceeding? His former lawyer might know of those assets and tell his current client, the wife. This would be improper, of course, because the lawyer learned about the assets in confidence and is not allowed to use this information adversely to his former client. Even if the lawyer makes a mental commitment not to use the information, a substantial relationship still exists. It doesn't matter if the information *would be used;* the question is whether the information could be *useful.* If the new representation also involves "material adversity" toward the former client (obviously true of this divorce), the lawyer may not represent the wife in the divorce without the consent of the husband, his former client. Unless the divorce is an entirely harmonious one, the odds that the husband would consent are low.

Here's another example:

> A lawyer who has previously represented a client in securing environmental permits to build a shopping center would be precluded from representing neighbors seeking to oppose rezoning of the property on the basis of environmental considerations; however, the lawyer would not be precluded, on the grounds of substantial relationship, from defending a tenant of the completed shopping center in resisting eviction for nonpayment of rent.[31]

Because the lawyer got the environmental permits, he possesses confidential information on the environmental features of the property that might be at issue in the new matter. For example, he might know how much solid waste the shopping center produces annually. These facts could help the neighbors to oppose rezoning. There is a substantial relationship between these two matters because the lawyer *would have had access* during the first matter to confidences that could be used adversely to his former client in the second matter. The environmental information is (presumably) irrelevant to the eviction case. Since there would be no opportunity to make adverse use of the confidential information, there is no substantial relationship.[32]

---

31. Rule 1.9, Comment 3.

32. Suppose the lawyer did this analysis, drew this conclusion, and accepted representation of the tenant in the eviction case. Suppose further that upon interviewing the tenant, the lawyer learned that the tenant had stopped paying rent because toxic waste seeping into her ground floor space had forced her to leave the building. If the "environmental issues" the lawyer learned about in the first representation included information about toxic wastes at the site, the lawyer would conclude that there was a substantial relationship after all. Since there is material adversity, the lawyer would need to withdraw unless the former client consented to his continued work. In contrast, see Silver Chrysler Plymouth, Inc. v. Chrysler Motors Corp., 370 F. Supp. 581 (E.D.N.Y. 1973), *aff'd,* 518 F.2d 751 (2d Cir. 1975). As an associate at his previous firm, the lawyer had helped to defend Chrysler Motors against an antitrust claim brought by a taxicab company. He was not disqualified from representing a Chrysler dealer suing Chrysler Motors in a dispute about the terms of a real estate lease. The two matters were found not to be substantially related. This case was decided before either the Model Code or the Model Rules had been promulgated.

# 4. Confidential information

### What types of confidential information create conflicts? What if the information provided by the former client consists only of general information about its business operations?

If a lawyer possesses only general knowledge that has only slight relevance to the new matter, such knowledge may not create a substantial relationship between the two matters.[33] Comment 3 to Rule 1.9 explains:

> In the case of an organizational client, general knowledge of the client's policies and practices ordinarily will not preclude a subsequent representation; on the other hand, knowledge of specific facts gained in a prior representation that are relevant to the matter in question ordinarily will preclude such a representation.

FOR EXAMPLE: A lawyer, once general counsel to a corporation, now works in private practice. Another company asks the lawyer to file an antitrust suit against the lawyer's former employer. The suit is predicated on events that occurred after the lawyer left the corporation. However, the allegations involve a pattern of business practices that extend back through the period when the lawyer was general counsel. Unless the former client (the corporation) consents, the lawyer may not handle the antitrust suit because he knows too much about the operations of the defendant company.[34]

### What if the lawyer knows information about how the former client approaches legal disputes?

Suppose a lawyer has represented a client in several lawsuits or nonlitigation matters unrelated to the new client's matter. As a result of the prior representation, the lawyer knows how the client tends to react to legal problems — disposition toward settlement, attitude about cooperation with discovery requests, and so on.[35] This type of knowledge might give the lawyer and his new client an advantage in subsequent litigation against the former client. Whether such knowledge amounts to a substantial relationship depends on the range of information that a lawyer could be expected to have learned during the former representation. If the lawyer represented the former client

---

33. Restatement § 132, comment d(iii).

34. This example is based on Restatement § 132, comment d(iii), illus. 3, which is based on Chugach Elec. Assn. v. U.S. Dist. Ct., 370 F.2d 441 (9th Cir. 1966). See also In re Corrugated Container Antitrust Litig., 659 F.2d 1341, 1346 (5th Cir. 1982) (more recent case, similar facts). But see ABA Comm. on Ethics & Prof. Resp., Formal Op. 99-415 (1999), criticizing the *Chugach* opinion as overbroad. Restatement § 132, comment d(iii), reporter's note, refers to some cases that say possession of general information is an insufficient basis for disqualification.

35. Professor Charles Wolfram refers to this type of knowledge as a "playbook view" of the former client. Charles W. Wolfram, Former Client Conflicts, 10 Geo. J. Leg. Ethics 677 (1997).

for a long period of time, it is more likely that the lawyer's prior representation would be found to be substantially related to the new matter.[36]

### What if the information that the lawyer learned in the previous representation has become public or is obsolete?

If the confidential information that a lawyer learned from the former client has become public, the lawyer is not precluded from representing the new client by the possession of that knowledge. Similarly, if the information learned in the previous representation is so out-of-date that it is not relevant, it is unlikely that the new matter would be found to be substantially related to the old one.[37]

The law governing when two matters are substantially related seems maddeningly complex and indeterminate. William Freivogel places the following notice near the beginning of his summary of this body of law:

> *Warning*: More cases deal with former client issues than just about any other issue relating to conflicts of interest. The cases also tend to be more fact-specific than those in other areas — particularly as to what is "substantially related." Thus, many of them have relatively little value as precedent.[38]

As you study the application of this slippery standard, then, focus on exploring the facts of a problem and on what a lawyer might have learned during the first matter that could be used adversely to the former client in the second.

## 5. Variations in the definition of "substantial relationship"

The purpose of the substantial relationship standard articulated in Rule 1.9 is to evaluate whether a lawyer should be disciplined for representing a client whose interests are in conflict with those of a former client, not to set a standard for whether the lawyer should be disqualified from handling a particular case. However, much of the case law on successive conflicts of interest involves motions to disqualify lawyers.[39] In ruling on motions to disqualify lawyers because of conflicts of interest, the courts are not bound to use the

---

36. William Freivogel, Former Client: The Substantial Relationship Test, at http://www.freivogelonconflicts.com/new_page_34.htm (last visited Oct. 22, 2004).

37. Rule 1.9, Comment 3.

38. See Freivogel, supra n. 36.

39. A motion to disqualify a firm from representing a current adversary is the most common remedy for conflicts involving former clients. Nathan M. Crystal, An Introduction to Professional Responsibility 101 (Aspen L. & Bus. 1998). In fact, a wide variety of litigation occurs in which one party seeks some remedy for an alleged conflict of interest of the lawyer for another party. As lawyer and professor Richard Flamm explains,

> The use of the ABA conflict rules as a cudgel, rather than as a compass, has not been confined to a single type of proceeding. On the contrary, claims that a lawyer has engaged in conflicted representation, or failed to disclose such a conflict, have supplied the basis for breach of contract actions, legal malpractice claims, and lawsuits filed for the express purpose of enjoining the challenged attorney or firm from continuing to engage in conflicted representation,

ethics rules as standards.[40] As a result, the courts have articulated various versions of the substantial relationship rule.[41]

Most courts take the position that the relationship between the two matters depends on whether there is *factual information* learned during the first matter that could be used adversely to the first client during the second representation. The inquiry is not about common legal issues, but about common facts. Under this interpretation, a lawyer who becomes expert in a legal topic (say, the law of escheat) in one matter may use that *legal knowledge* in any subsequent representation that does not present a conflict based on the facts. On the other hand, a few courts define "substantial relationship" to include matters that involve common legal issues.[42]

# 6. Material adversity

## What does it mean for a matter to be "materially adverse" to the interests of a former client?

If a new representation is substantially related to a previous one *and* presents "material adversity" to the interests of a former client, the lawyer may not pursue the new matter without the consent of the former client. Neither Rule 1.9 nor the comments that follow it defines "material adversity." The apparent intention of the rule is to require consent if the use of the former client's confidences *might* harm the former client's interests. If the subsequent use of the confidences would not harm the former client's interests, consent is

---

as well as for proceedings seeking to preclude a "conflicted" lawyer or firm from collecting a fee, or to affirmatively "disgorge" fees that have already been paid.

Richard E. Flamm, Looking Ahead to Ethics 2015: Or Why I Still Do Not Get the ABA Model Conflict of Interest Rules, 19 N. Ill. U. L. Rev. 273 (1999).

40. The possible divergence between the conflicts standards on discipline and disqualification don't make too much difference in cases in which courts conclude that there is no conflict. If a judge *denies* a motion to disqualify a lawyer because of a conflict, it is unlikely that a bar counsel would impose discipline. If a judge *grants* such a motion, discipline would not necessarily be initiated, and in fact the matter usually ends there. But it is not out of the question that the disciplinary authorities would go forward with an investigation.

Representing a client in a matter that is substantially related to one handled for a former client also can be a basis for a malpractice claim. See Damron v. Herzog, 67 F.3d 211 (9th Cir. 1995). It also can be the basis of a claim of breach of fiduciary duty. See, e.g., Maritrans GP Inc. v. Pepper, Hamilton & Scheetz, 602 A.2d 1277 (Pa. 1992). If a court finds that a lawyer has breached his fiduciary duty to a client by representing a client in the face of a conflict of interest, a court may order "the disgorgement of fees paid or the forfeiture of fees owed." Id. at 1285.

41. Because of the variations in state law, it is important to study the law of the jurisdiction in which you intend to practice. However, since the Ethics 2000 Commission definition of "substantial relationship" and the Restatement definition are so similar, perhaps we will see a greater degree of uniformity in future cases.

42. Crystal, supra n. 39. The Restatement suggests that the better analysis is to look at overlapping facts and to ask whether "there is a substantial risk that representation of the present client will involve use of information acquired in the course of representing the former client." Restatement § 132 and comment d(iii). Professor Crystal concurs in this view. Crystal, supra n. 39, at 101.

not required. One court held that "adversity is a product of the likelihood of the risk and the seriousness of its consequences."[43]

**FOR EXAMPLE:** A lawyer was to depose a former client in a lawsuit related to the prior representation. A federal court found this situation to present material adversity under Rule 1.9 because of a slight risk that the former client would be exposed to liability or would suffer harm to her business reputation if the lawyer were permitted to depose her. The court said that the former client "has a right to expect that her credibility and integrity will not be impugned by her former attorney in a substantially related matter."[44]

Authorities differ as to the meaning of the phrase "material adversity." The ABA Ethics Committee once urged that "material adversity" in Rule 1.9 should be read to refer only to "direct adversity" as defined in Rule 1.7.[45] The Restatement, on the other hand, concludes that material adversity is limited to potential harm to the type of interests that the lawyer sought to advance on behalf of the former client. If the new matter were adverse to the interests of a former client unrelated to the lawyer's previous work, this, under the Restatement analysis, would not create material adversity.[46]

**FOR EXAMPLE:** Suppose a lawyer negotiates a lease for office space for a company that manufactures shower curtains. In the course of the representation, the lawyer does not learn anything about the manufacturing process but is solely concerned with securing favorable terms in the lease. At a later time, the lawyer is approached by a new client who wants the lawyer to assist with a patent application for a new process to create material that would be used for shower curtains. The new client could pose competition for the old client. Under the Restatement definition, the new representation would not present material adversity because it does not relate to the interests sought to be advanced in the prior representation. Under the ABA Ethics Committee definition, this work would not present material adversity because it involves neither a suit against the old client nor participation in some similarly adversarial process. Consent would not be required under either approach.

---

43. Natl. Med. Enters., Inc. v. Godbey, 924 S.W.2d 123 (Tex. 1996).

44. Selby v. Revlon Consumer Prods. Corp., 6 F. Supp. 2d 577 (N.D. Tex. 1997) (noting also that there is "a paucity of authority" on the meaning of "material adversity" as it is used in Rule 1.9).

45. ABA Comm. on Ethics & Prof. Resp., Formal Op. 99-415 (1999). However, the committee reached this conclusion based on a sentence in Rule 1.9, Comment 1, which read, "The principles in Rule 1.7 determine whether the interests of the present and former client are adverse." This sentence was struck from the comments by the Ethics 2000 Committee. The opinion dealt with disqualification of former in-house corporate counsel from matters handled by the legal departments of their former employers.

46. Restatement § 132, comment e. This analysis would appear to effectively narrow the substantial relationship test so that a lawyer need not obtain consent unless the lawyer could have learned adverse facts in representing the first client that could be used against that client in the new representation *and* the new representation would attack the interests of the former client that were at stake in the first representation.

# E. Practice issues relating to former client conflicts

**If a lawyer discovers a conflict between a former client and a present client, what courses of action are available to the lawyer?**

A lawyer who encounters a conflict that impacts a former client might choose one of three courses of action, depending on the lawyer's analysis of the conflict.

- The lawyer might conclude that the two matters are unrelated and simply proceed with the new matter without seeking consent.
- The lawyer might conclude that there is a substantial relationship between the matters and material adversity and tell the new client that the firm cannot accept the matter.
- The lawyer might disclose the problem to the former client and ask for consent.[47]

Even though the critical question is whether consent is required to proceed, lawyers don't often seek consent from former clients. More often, they either decide they don't need consent or they decide not to go forward.

One can speculate about the problems that might be associated with asking for a conflicts waiver from a former client. A lawyer is bound to protect the confidences of both the new client and the former client from each other, so disclosure of that information would require client permission. If the lawyer asks for this consent, the new client might decide to hire a different firm rather than to allow disclosure of confidences. If a lawyer seeks consent from a former client to represent a new client whose interests conflict with those of the former client, the former client (a) would have little reason to give consent, (b) might claim that it was a current rather than a former client, or (c) might later claim that the request for a waiver constitutes an admission that a waiver was needed. It may be that lawyers don't seek consent from former clients very often because of these complexities.[48]

**Can a lawyer make a reliable assessment of a successive conflict?**

Many lawyers have difficulty evaluating whether a new matter is substantially related to an old one. When a new case comes in, a law firm must make this assessment to decide whether the consent of a former client is needed. If a lawyer decides there is no substantial relationship and goes forward

---

47. See Rule 1.7. If the conflict affects the interests of current clients, both parties must consent (if the conflict is consentable). In a successive conflict situation, if the only person potentially adversely affected is the former client (a Rule 1.9 issue), then only the former client must consent. But if, in addition, the present client's interests might be compromised by a lawyer's duties to the former client, then the lawyer must obtain the consent of the present client under Rule 1.7 and of the former client under Rule 1.9.

48. See e-mails from William Freivogel to Lisa Lerman, June 17, 2004, and June 21, 2004 (on file with authors). Freivogel reports that he had no data on the frequency of requests for conflicts waivers from former clients, but he wrote: "I cannot recall counseling a firm on it in 16+ years of doing this." Id.

without consent, she may face a motion to disqualify. Susan Shapiro notes that a "number of respondents . . . shared troubling memories of instances in which they guessed wrong and were disqualified from a matter that a judge considered substantially related to a prior representation."[49] Some of the lawyers Shapiro interviewed expressed frustration that there seemed to be no "reliably predictive formula by which to classify matters as related or unrelated."[50]

In some cases, common sense and gut judgment seems useful. One large-firm Chicago lawyer suggested that the length and depth of the firm's relationship with the former client was the key:

> A law firm knows so much about the inner workings of that particular company that judges will say, "Maybe this case has nothing to do with any of the work you did for that former client. But you were so close to that client and you defended so many cases that had issues that were touched on . . . that you just got into their skin and bones. And until more time has passed, you can't be an adversary."[51]

### If a former client moves to disqualify a lawyer from working on a new matter, does she have to reveal the relevant confidences to make the case?

No. That would defeat the purpose of the motion. The former client may give a general description of the lawyer's previous services, and a judge may draw inferences about the type of confidences that ordinarily would be learned in that type of representation.[52] By examining "the general features of the matters involved," the judge can assess "the likelihood that confidences were imparted by the former client that could be used to adverse effect in the subsequent representation."[53] In evaluating a motion to disqualify a lawyer, a judge does not learn details on the confidences at issue or inquire into whether relevant confidences actually were disclosed in the first representation. She evaluates only "the possibility that confidences had been disclosed in the one matter which will be harmful to the [former] client in the other."[54]

The test is not whether the lawyer *actually* learned information in the first matter that could later harm that first client. If actual knowledge were the test, a disqualification motion might require the former client to get on the stand and testify about what she told her lawyer, thereby violating her right to confidentiality.

Nor is the test "whether the lawyer could possibly have learned" information harmful to the first client while representing that client. That test would disqualify too many lawyers. Instead, the test is an objective one. One looks at

---

49. Susan Shapiro, Tangled Loyalties: Conflict of Interest in Legal Practice 195 (U. Mich. Press 2002).
50. Id. at 196.
51. Id.
52. Id.
53. Restatement § 132, comment d(iii).
54. Westinghouse Elec. Corp. v. Gulf Oil Corp., 588 F.2d 221, 224 (7th Cir. 1978).

the type of information that might ordinarily be disclosed in the course of the prior representation. For example, in a divorce or estate matter, the client normally would provide the lawyer with financial information. If such information could be used adversely to the client in the subsequent matter, the two matters are deemed substantially related. The analysis depends on assumptions about what might have occurred in the ordinary course of business.

## PROBLEM 6-2  **THE DISTRICT ATTORNEY**

*This is a problem that arose for a prosecutor in a city in New England.*

You are the district attorney of your city. Twelve years ago, when you were in private practice, you represented Zeke Brick, then 5 years old, who was injured in an automobile accident. Brick suffered a concussion and three fractures in the accident. You negotiated a good settlement for him. You don't remember anything about the case, and you haven't looked at the file since the case was settled.

Last month, Brick (now 17) was arrested and charged with murder. His lawyer, the public defender, has served notice that he plans to rely on a defense of "mental disease or defect." In the letter, the lawyer demanded that you disqualify yourself from prosecuting him because you previously represented him in the automobile accident case.

Your old firm has already turned over Brick's case file to the public defender, and you haven't asked for or received a copy.

Under Rule 1.9, should you withdraw from representing the state in the prosecution of Brick, or may you proceed?

# F.  **Particular applications of Rule 1.9**

## 1.  **Suing former clients**

**May a lawyer (on behalf of a new client) sue a former client, without the former client's consent, in a matter that is not substantially related to the previous representation?**

Yes. No consent is required unless the new matter is "the same or substantially related" and the new representation is "materially adverse" to the interests of the former client.

FOR EXAMPLE:  A law firm had represented the publisher of the *Village Voice* in a defamation case. Subsequently, the same firm filed suit against the publisher on behalf of an employee who had been fired. The newspaper moved to disqualify the firm in the second case. The court denied the motion.[55] Other cases involving unrelated suits against former clients have been resolved similarly.[56]

### Is it a good idea to sue a former client?

It depends. Although a lawyer is permitted to sue a former client on an unrelated matter, it may be a bad idea.

> **FOR EXAMPLE:** Suppose a lawyer in a small community represented a family-owned business for 25 years in various corporate matters. The business switched lawyers without acrimony; the son wanted to hire a close friend. Two years later the lawyer is asked to sue the company in a matter unrelated to any prior representation. Even if the lawyer *may* do this, the lawyer might choose to refer the client to a different lawyer. His former client might be dismayed to find this lawyer on the other side of a case. If the client feels betrayed, the client might not refer others to the lawyer or might damage the lawyer's reputation in the community. Also, a lawyer's sense of professional duty might counsel against suing this former client even if the lawyer isn't likely to lose business as a result.

## 2. Representing the competitor of a former client

### May a lawyer represent the competitor of a former client?

It depends. A comment to Rule 1.7 states that ordinarily representation of economic competitors poses no serious conflict of interest.[57] If it is not a conflict to represent economic competitors concurrently, one would think it would be less problematic to represent the economic competitor of a *former* client.

However, if the firm learned a great deal about the operation of the former client and that information could be used on behalf of a competitor to the disadvantage of that former client, the firm could have a serious conflict.

Consider the following case involving labor lawyer J. Anthony Messina, which illustrates this problem. The opinion also provides a clear summary of the relationship between common law duties, violation of which could lead to liability, and duties under the ethical rules, violation of which could lead to professional discipline.

---

55. Nichols v. Village Voice, Inc., 417 N.Y.S.2d 415 (App. Div. 1979).

56. See examples listed in Restatement § 132, comment d(iii), reporter's note.

57. Comment 6 states that "simultaneous representation in unrelated matters of clients whose interests are only economically adverse, such as representation of competing economic enterprises in unrelated litigation, does not ordinarily constitute a conflict of interests and thus may not require consent of the respective clients."

## Maritrans GP, Inc. v. Pepper, Hamilton & Scheetz

602 A.2d 1277 (Pa. 1992)

PAPADAKOS, Justice.

### [Pepper's representation of Maritrans]

In February, 1988, Maritrans brought an action for preliminary and permanent injunctive relief, as well as for compensatory and punitive damages, against [Pepper, Hamilton & Scheetz and its partner J. Anthony Messina], its former attorneys of more than ten years. Maritrans' action arises out of Pepper's representation of Maritrans' competitors. . . . [The trial court enjoined the firm from continuing to represent the competitors except for one upcoming trial. The firm appealed, and the injunction was overturned. That decision was appealed, and after some preliminary denials, an appeal was made to the Supreme Court of Pennsylvania.] The matter is now on full appeal to this Court. For the reasons explained below, we reverse [and reinstate the injunction]. . . .

Maritrans is a Philadelphia-based public company in the business of transporting petroleum products along the East and Gulf coasts of the United States by tug and barge. Maritrans competes in the marine transportation business with other tug and/or barge companies, including a number of companies based in New York. . . . Pepper represented Maritrans . . . in the broadest range of labor relations matters for well over a decade . . . [and] in a complex public offering of securities, a private offering of $115 million in debt, a conveyance of all assets, and a negotiation and implementation of a working capital line of credit. Over the course of the representation, Pepper was paid approximately $1 million for its labor representation of Maritrans and, in the last year of the representation, approximately $1 million for its corporate and securities representation of Maritrans.

During the course of their labor representation of Maritrans, Pepper became "intimately familiar with Maritrans' operations" and "gained detailed financial and business information, including Maritrans' financial goals and projections, labor cost/savings, crew costs and operating costs." This information was discussed with Pepper's labor attorneys, and particularly with Messina, for the purpose of developing Maritrans' labor goals and strategies. In addition, during the course of preparing Maritrans' public offering, Pepper was furnished with substantial confidential commercial information in Maritrans' possession . . . including projected labor costs, projected debt coverage and projected revenues through the year 1994, and projected rates through the year 1990. Pepper, during the course of their decade-long representation of Maritrans, came to know the complete inner-workings of the company along with Maritrans' long-term objectives, and competitive strategies in a number of areas including the area of labor costs, a particularly sensitive area in terms of effective competition. In furtherance of its ultimate goal of obtaining more business than does its competition, including the

New York-based companies, Maritrans analyzed each of its competitors with Pepper. These analyses included an evaluation of each competitor's strengths and weaknesses, and of how Maritrans deals with its competitors.

### [Pepper's representation of the competitors]

Armed with this information, Pepper subsequently undertook to represent several of Maritrans' New York-based competitors. Indeed, Pepper undertook to represent the New York companies in their labor negotiations, albeit with a different union, during which the New York companies sought wage and benefit reductions in order to compete more effectively with, i.e., to win business away from, Maritrans.

In September, 1987, Maritrans learned from [outside] sources . . . that Pepper [was] representing four of its New York-based competitors in their labor relations matters. Maritrans objected to these representations, and voiced those objections to many Pepper attorneys. . . . Pepper took the position that this was a "business conflict," not a "legal conflict," and that they had no fiduciary or ethical duty to Maritrans that would prohibit these representations.

To prevent Pepper from taking on the representation of any other competitors, especially its largest competitor, Bouchard Transportation Company, Maritrans agreed to an arrangement proposed by Pepper whereby Pepper would continue as Maritrans' counsel but would not represent any more than the four New York companies it was then already representing. In addition, Messina — the Pepper attorney with the most knowledge about Maritrans — was to act not as counsel for Maritrans but, rather, as counsel for the New York companies, while two other Pepper labor attorneys would act as counsel for Maritrans; the attorneys on one side of this "Chinese Wall"[58] would not discuss their respective representations with the attorneys on the other side. Maritrans represented that it agreed to this arrangement because it believed that this was the only way to keep Pepper from representing yet more of its competitors, especially Bouchard.

Unbeknownst to Maritrans, however, Messina then "parked" Bouchard and another of the competitors, Eklof, with Mr. Vincent Pentima, a labor attorney then at another law firm, at the same time that Messina was negotiating with Pentima for Pentima's admission into the partnership at Pepper. . . . [Despite] Pepper's specific agreement not to represent these other companies, Messina for all intents and purposes was representing Bouchard and Eklof, as he was conducting joint negotiating sessions for those companies and his other four New York clients. On November 5, 1987, Maritrans executives discussed with

---

58. [Authors' footnote.] American lawyers have used the term "Chinese Wall" to refer to a set of restrictions to prevent communication of confidential information possessed by some lawyers in a firm to other lawyers who would remain ignorant of this information and would handle a new and possibly conflicting matter. The lawyers on the new matter also are barred from access to the records from the conflicting matter. The term "Chinese Wall" refers metaphorically to the (impassable) Great Wall of China. The term does not appear to have any pejorative meaning, but even so, some lawyers became concerned that it would be interpreted as an ethnic slur. Therefore the phrase gave way to the term "screen" and the gerund "screening."

Pepper attorneys, inter alia, Maritrans' plans and strategies of an aggressive nature in the event of a strike against the New York companies. . . . [O]n December 2, 1987, Pepper terminated its representation of Maritrans in all matters. . . . [O]n December 23, 1987, Pepper undertook the representation of the New York companies. Then, on January 4, 1988, Mr. Pentima joined Pepper as a partner and brought with him, as clients, Bouchard and Eklof. In February, 1988, Maritrans filed a complaint in the trial court against Pepper and Messina.

Discovery procedures produced evidence as follows: (i) testimony by principals of the New York companies . . . that . . . the type of information that Pepper possess[es] about Maritrans is . . . confidential commercial information [of a type that they would not reveal to their competitors]; (ii) . . . that they were desirous of obtaining Maritrans' confidential commercial information; (iii) . . . that labor costs are the one item that make or break a company's competitive posture; (iv) an affidavit . . . attesting that . . . Maritrans' labor contracts are not on file with the Department of Labor and thus not available under the Freedom of Information Act. . . .

In reconsidering sua sponte the initial decision not to enjoin Pepper and Messina, the trial court held . . . that a substantial relationship exists between Pepper and Messina's former representation of Maritrans and their current representation of the competitors, entities whose interests are materially adverse to the interests of Maritrans in the current representation. The trial court also found that Pepper breached its obligation, which was fortified by a specific promise, to keep from Messina that which was learned after the erection of the "Chinese wall." . . .

The Superior Court reversed stating that the trial court erred by issuing a preliminary injunction based upon Pepper's alleged violation of the [Pennsylvania] Rules of Professional Conduct[59] without making any independent finding that Pepper's conduct was actionable. . . . The Superior Court then held that an attorney's conflict of interest in representing a subsequent client whose interests are materially adverse to a prior client in a substantially related matter is not "actionable" in Pennsylvania. As already noted, we reverse.

**[The legal bases of lawyer liability and their
relationship to one another]**

## I. Actionability and Independent Fiduciary Duty at Common Law of
Avoiding Conflicts of Interest — Injunctive Relief . . .

Activity is actionable if it constitutes breach of a duty imposed by statute or by common law. Our common law imposes on attorneys the status of fiduciaries

---

59. [Court's footnote 2.] The Superior court noted that the Pennsylvania Code of Professional Responsibility, and not the Pennsylvania Rules of Professional Conduct, were in effect at the time Pepper began representing the New York Companies. 392 Pa. Superior Ct. 153, 572 A.2d 737, 741. However, the analysis of Pepper's conduct is the same under both Code and Rules. In any event, the disciplinary rules prohibiting attorneys from engaging in former-client conflicts of interest do nothing but reaffirm pre-existing substantive law, therefore, making it irrelevant whether the trial court was guided by the Rules rather than the Code.

vis à vis their clients; that is, attorneys are bound, at law, to perform their fiduciary duties properly. Failure to so perform gives rise to a cause of action. It is "actionable." Threatened failure to so perform gives rise to a request for injunctive relief to prevent the breach of duty.

At common law, an attorney owes a fiduciary duty to his client; such duty demands undivided loyalty and prohibits the attorney from engaging in conflicts of interest, and breach of such duty is actionable. . . .[60]

Our courts clearly have the power to enjoin an attorney from breaching his duty to a client:

> While the breach by a lawyer of his duty to keep the confidences of his client and to avoid representing conflicting interests may be the subject of appropriate disciplinary action, a court is not bound to await such development before acting to restrain improper conduct where it is disclosed in a case pending in that court. . . .

Accordingly, the trial court's preliminary injunction was a proper mechanism to abate an unlawful and actionable breach of fiduciary duties to Maritrans where the facts support such a conclusion.

## II. An Attorney's Common Law Duty Is Independent of the Ethics Rules . . .

[The Superior Court was] correct in saying that the trial court's finding of violation of the ethical rules concerning misuse of a client's confidences is not as such a basis for issuing an injunction. . . .

However, the Superior Court then stood this correct analysis on its head. That court held that the trial judge's reference to violations of the rules of ethics somehow negated or precluded the existence of a breach of legal duty by the Pepper firm to its former client. The court also held that the presumption of misuse of a former client's confidences, developed in the law of disqualification, is inapplicable because the present case involves an injunction. . . .

Long before the [ethics codes] were adopted, the common law recognized that a lawyer could not undertake a representation adverse to a former client in a matter "substantially related" to that in which the lawyer previously had served the client. . . . [This rule was articulated in cases in the 1930s and 1950s involving motions for disqualification and in one case in which a client defended against his lawyer's suit for fees by alleging that the lawyer had misused confidences.]

The legal obligation of a lawyer to refrain from misuse of a client's confidences goes even further back, predating the ABA Canons of Professional Ethics promulgated in 1908 [case cited from 1899]. . . . The threatened

---

60. [Court's footnote 3.] The Tri-Growth court explained the concept of a fiduciary relationship as follows: "A fiduciary or confidential relationship can arise when confidence is reposed by persons in the integrity of others, and if the latter voluntarily accept or assume to accept the confidence, they cannot act so as to take advantage of the others' interests without their knowledge or consent. The attorney/client relationship is a fiduciary one, binding the attorney to the most conscientious fidelity." 216 Cal. App. 3d at 1150, 265 Cal. Rptr. at 334-335 (citations omitted).

violation of this duty thus has been recognized as the basis for an injunction for at least virtually a century. . . .

The Superior Court seems to have the idea that because conduct is not a tort simply because it is a disciplinary violation, then conduct ceases to be a tort when it is at the same time a disciplinary violation. This is an inversion of logic and legal policy and misunderstands the history of the disciplinary rules. . . .

### III. Scope of Duties at Common Law . . .

Attorneys have always been held civilly liable for engaging in conduct violative of their fiduciary duties to clients, despite the existence of professional rules under which the attorneys could also have been disciplined.

Courts throughout the country have ordered the disgorgement of fees paid or the forfeiture of fees owed to attorneys who have breached their fiduciary duties to their clients by engaging in impermissible conflicts of interests. . . .

Courts have also allowed civil actions for damages for an attorney's breach of his fiduciary duties by engaging in conflicts of interest. . . .

Courts throughout the United States have not hesitated to impose civil sanctions upon attorneys who breach their fiduciary duties to their clients, . . . [quite] apart from professional discipline. What must be decided in this case is whether, under the instant facts, an injunction lies to prohibit a potential conflict of interest from resulting in harm to Appellant Maritrans. . . .

### IV. Equity

Injunctive relief will lie where there is no adequate remedy at law. The purpose of a preliminary injunction is to preserve the status quo as it exists *or previously existed before the acts complained of,* thereby preventing irreparable injury or gross injustice. . . .

### [Pepper's conflict]

Whether a fiduciary can later represent competitors or whether a law firm can later represent competitors of its former client is a matter that must be decided from case to case and depends on a number of factors. One factor is the extent to which the fiduciary was involved in its former client's affairs. The greater the involvement, the greater the danger that confidences (where such exist) will be revealed. Here, Pepper's involvement was extensive as was their knowledge of sensitive information provided to them by Maritrans. We do *not* wish to establish a blanket rule that a law firm may not later represent the economic competitor of a client in matters in which the former client is not also a party to a law suit. But situations may well exist where the danger of revelation of the confidences of a former client is so great that injunctive relief is warranted. This is one of those situations. There is a substantial relationship here between Pepper's former representation of Maritrans and their current representation of Maritrans' competitors such that the injunctive relief granted here was justified. It might be theoretically possible to argue that Pepper should merely be enjoined from revealing the confidential material they have acquired from Maritrans but such an injunction would be difficult, if not impossible, to administer. . . .

## Conclusion . . .

[T]he relationship between the attorney and his client is a fiduciary relationship. . . . "[T]he concept of 'fiduciary relation' by *definition* does not permit conflicts of interest." This prohibition extends to attorneys.[61] . . . [A] fiduciary who breaches his duty of loyalty to his principal is liable to his principle (sic), and an injunction is a proper remedy for the breach.

Obviously, there are some disciplinary rules . . . which, if violated, may not give rise to civil liability. . . . [T]here is an independent cause of action available to a client whose attorney engaged in impermissible conflicts of interest vis a vis that client. The violator is subject to civil liability as well as injunctive relief. . . .

The order of the Superior Court is reversed and the order of the Court of Common Pleas granting a preliminary injunction is reinstated. . . .

NIX, Chief Justice, dissenting.

In the instant matter the majority has concluded that appellee . . . ("Pepper"), was properly enjoined from representing Maritrans' competitors because of the significant risk of the disclosure of confidential information. The majority finds the creation of the relationship which harbors this risk to be a breach of Pepper's fiduciary duty to Maritrans. . . . [I]n reaching this result, the majority overlooks the significant body of case law that has developed in this area, as well as a key factor that renders its conclusion unreasonable.

The Chinese wall defense[62] is set forth in the Model Rules of Professional Conduct, Rule 1.11.[63] The procedure established is one whereby a single attorney or group of attorneys who has represented a particular client is

---

61. [Court's footnote 4.] § 394 of the Restatement (Second) of Agency states: "Unless otherwise agreed, an agent is subject to a duty not to act or to agree to act during the period of his agency for persons whose interests conflict with those of the principal in matters in which the agent is employed." Comment d to § 394 provides in pertinent part: "Unless an attorney makes full disclosure to his client, it is improper for him, in court proceedings or otherwise, to act for two clients whose interests conflict."

62. [Dissent's footnote 1.] The procedure set forth in Rule 1.11 ABA Model Rules of Professional Responsibility, applies specifically to former government attorneys. But see infra note 3 [of my dissenting opinion].

63. [Dissent's footnote 2.] In Pennsylvania, the same procedure is found at Rule 1.10(a) and (b) of the Rules of Professional Conduct. That Rule provides as follows:

> (a) While lawyers are associated in a firm, none of them shall knowingly represent a client when any one of them practicing alone would be prohibited from doing so by Rules 1.7, 1.8(c), 1.9 or 2.2.

isolated from another attorney or attorneys within the same firm who represent a client whose interests are substantially related but materially adverse to those of the initial client. The goal . . . is to minimize the potential for the transmission of confidential information between attorneys representing clients with competing interest.

The Chinese wall defense is asserted in the following manner. First, in attempting to have an attorney disqualified, the former client must show that matters embraced within a pending lawsuit, in which his former attorney appears on behalf of an adversary, are substantially related to matters wherein the attorney had previously represented the former client. Once . . . the "substantial relationship test" is met, and the complainant has shown that the former representation exposed the attorney to confidences or secrets arguably pertinent in the present dispute, a rebuttable presumption arises that those confidences were shared.

To overcome this presumption, the Chinese wall defense is asserted, and the attorney and firm must demonstrate sufficient facts and circumstances of their particular case to establish the probable effectiveness of the wall. The factors to be considered in the acceptance of the Chinese wall defense are the substantiality of the relationship between the attorney and the former client, the time lapse between the matters in dispute, the size of the firm and the number of disqualified attorneys, the nature of the disqualified attorney's involvement, and the timing of the wall. Relevant features of the wall itself include the following:

a. the prohibition of discussion of sensitive matters
b. restricted circulation of sensitive documents
c. restricted access to files
d. strong firm policy against breach, including sanctions, physical and/or geographical separation. ABA Opinion 342, 62 ABA J. 517, 521 (1976).[64]

Applying these factors to the instant matter, we would be inclined initially to agree with Maritrans' assertions that the wall in this case was probably defective. Despite the size of the firm and the number of attorneys involved, the timing of the wall was delayed in relation to the existence of the conflict. The relationship between Maritrans and Pepper was substantial, as was

---

(b) When a lawyer becomes associated with a firm, the firm may not knowingly represent a person in the same or substantially related matter in which that lawyer, or a firm with which the lawyer was associated, had previously represented a client whose interests are materially adverse to that person and about whom the lawyer had acquired information protected by Rules 1.6 and 1.9(b) that is material to the matter unless:

(1) the disqualified lawyer is screened from any participation in the matter and is apportioned no part of the fee therefrom; and
(2) written notice is promptly given to the appropriate client to enable it to ascertain compliance with the provisions of this rule.

64. [Dissent's footnote 3.] Although the ABA opinion limits its application of the Chinese Wall to situations where the private-firm attorney's conflict exists because of prior government employment, case law indicates that the concept has wider applicability.

Messina's involvement with Maritrans. Of particular significance is the fact that the conflict existed not merely within the firm as a whole but within a single attorney who sought to represent competing clients.

These factors reveal serious concerns which must have been patently obvious at the time the conflict arose. Nevertheless, *Maritrans was informed of this peculiar arrangement and consented to it.* It is well-settled in the field of legal ethics *that a client's consent,* upon full disclosure of a conflict of interest, *is sufficient to permit the attorney to continue the otherwise objectionable representation.* Thus, while Maritrans' concerns may have been legitimate, their initial acquiescence must be construed as a forbearance of any objections based upon the *potential* for breach of confidentiality. Having consented to the arrangement, they are now bound by their consent until such time as an actual breach of confidentiality occurs. . . . [N]o actual disclosure of confidential information has occurred.[65] Maritrans' prior consent amounts to a waiver of their right to an objection based upon the fear of disclosure. Accordingly, I dissent.

## Notes and Questions about *Maritrans*

**1.** According to the majority opinion in *Maritrans*, when does representation of an economic competitor constitute a conflict? Does this analysis conflict with the assertion in the ethics rules that a lawyer may represent economic competitors of a client or a former client?

**2.** This case involves a successive conflict, in that Maritrans is a former client at the time the representation of the competitors is challenged. Is there an argument that this is really a concurrent conflict situation?

**3.** The court concluded that the law firm's representation of Maritrans's competitors was substantially related to its representation of Maritrans, but it didn't explain exactly why. Review the facts and explore whether you agree with the court's conclusion and why.

**4.** The Pennsylvania ethics rules allow lawyers to remedy conflicts with former clients by screening the lawyers who know confidences from discussion of these with the lawyers handling the new matter.[66] Why didn't this solve the problem?

---

65. [Dissent's footnote 4.] Although Maritrans repeatedly insists that it has no way of knowing whether confidences have actually been disclosed because attorney-client privilege makes that fact difficult, if not impossible, to ascertain, it does not deny conceding the absence of disclosure at the prior proceeding before this Court. Moreover, the majority in the instant appeal concedes that the concern is not that actual disclosure has occurred, but that the circumstances create significant potential for such disclosure.

66. Pennsylvania is one of only seven states whose ethics rules allow screening as a remedy for imputed conflicts. Some federal courts also have adopted standards for disqualification that recognize screening as a legitimate remedy for a conflict of a former client represented by a lawyer while he was at a previous law firm. See Attys.' Liab. Assurance Socy., Inc., Chart on Lawyer Screening (2002), reprinted in Thomas D. Morgan & Ronald D. Rotunda, 2003 Selected Standards on Professional Responsibility 173 (Found. Press 2002). See discussion of screening in the section on imputed conflicts below.

# G. Conflicts between the interests of a present client and a client who was represented by a lawyer's former firm

So far we have discussed successive conflicts that involve a single lawyer. But what if the former client was not represented by the lawyer personally, but by another lawyer at a law firm where one of the lawyers in the firm used to work?

**FOR EXAMPLE:** A lawyer named Hank used to work at the firm of Barr & Thornburgh. While Hank worked there, some other lawyers at Barr & Thornburgh represented The Toy Chest, Inc., a small chain of toy stores, in employment matters. Hank didn't work on any Toy Chest matters. Now Hank works at Reno & Days. Hank has been asked to represent a new client, Jenny, in a suit against her former employer, The Toy Chest.

---

**T1:**
Hank works for B & T
Other B & T lawyers defend The Toy Chest in employment cases
**T2:**
Hank works for R & D
Jenny wants Hank to sue The Toy Chest for wrongful discharge

---

This is just like the successive conflicts cases we have discussed above except that the prior representation was not handled by Hank personally but by other lawyers at his former firm. Rule 1.9(b) addresses this type of situation.

**Rule 1.9(b)**
A lawyer shall not knowingly represent a person in the same or a substantially related matter in which a firm with which the lawyer formerly was associated had previously represented a client
        (1) whose interests are materially adverse to that person; and
        (2) about whom the lawyer had acquired information protected
    by Rules 1.6 and 1.9(c) that is material to the matter;
unless the former client gives informed consent, confirmed in writing.

The analysis is similar to the questions raised by Rule 1.9(a): Is the matter the same or substantially related? Is there material adversity? If so, you need informed consent. But there is a critical difference. Under (b), which applies to lawyers whose former firms represented the prior client, consent is not required unless "the lawyer had acquired information protected by Rules 1.6 and 1.9(c) that is material to the matter." Under 1.9(a), one asks whether the lawyer *could have acquired* confidential information in the first representation that might be used adversely to the former client's interests. Here, by contrast, one asks whether the lawyer *actually acquired* material confidential information.

Like the other conflicts rules, this one attempts to strike a balance among competing values — protection of confidences shared by former clients, provision of relative freedom to clients in their choice of counsel, and assurance of relative freedom to lawyers in moving from one firm to another and in taking on new clients. Several decades ago, most lawyers stayed in one law firm for their entire careers.[67] In the last couple of decades, a new pattern has emerged. Many lawyers change law firms several times, both early in their careers and later on. Similarly, many clients used to employ one lawyer or one firm to service all their legal needs. Not so any more. Many institutional clients employ multiple law firms at any given time and switch lawyers often. This rule attempts to protect client interests from harmful conflicts while avoiding undue interference with the desire of both lawyers and clients to play "musical law firms."[68]

## 1. Analyzing former firm conflicts

**If a lawyer switched firms, how would anyone other than the lawyer know what confidences he had acquired at the first firm?**

It can be difficult to figure out whether a lawyer who has changed firms acquired material confidences about a particular matter at her old firm. Susan Shapiro comments that possible conflicts with "baggage left behind" (meaning the lawyer's former firm's clients) is "insidious because it is harder to inventory (and remember) everything on which the lateral hire actively worked, in which he or she was only tangentially involved, or that he or she inadvertently overheard."[69]

To know if a lawyer has acquired material confidences, one must analyze the specific facts relating to the lawyer's access to or information about the relevant matter. Comment 6 after Rule 1.9 directs analysts to use certain assumptions. For example, a lawyer who had management responsibility at a former firm may be presumed to have received confidential information about all firm matters. This is because firm managers often have access to all client files and often are involved in discussions about many different matters. On the other hand, one might assume that a junior lawyer with no management duties had access to or information about only the matters that she worked on or perhaps only matters handled by her department. She would not be presumed to have information about other matters.[70]

---

67. Marc Galanter & Thomas Palay, Tournament of Lawyers: The Transformation of the Big Law Firm, 24 (U. Chi. Press 1991).

68. See Rule 1.9, Comment 4.

69. Susan Shapiro, Tangled Loyalties: Conflict of Interest in Legal Practice 208 (U. Mich. Press 2002).

70. Rule 1.9, Comment 6.

A party seeking to disqualify opposing counsel based on this type of successive conflict may not have access to information about exactly what the lawyer worked on or learned about at the former firm. Therefore, the comment to Rule 1.9 urges that the firm whose disqualification is sought (in the example above, Hank's current firm) should have the burden to prove that the lawyer who changed firms does not possess confidential information that is material to the new matter.[71] Proving a negative is difficult, but it would be unfair to make the opposing party prove that Hank did possess confidential information.

## 2. Using or revealing a former client's confidences

The duty to protect client confidences does not end when the representation is concluded but continues indefinitely. Rule 1.9(c) explains the nature of this duty to former clients.

> **Rule 1.9(c)**
> A lawyer who has formerly represented a client in a matter or whose present or former firm has formerly represented a client in a matter shall not thereafter:
>> (1) use information relating to the representation to the disadvantage of the former client except as these Rules would permit or require with respect to a client, or when the information has become generally known; or
>> (2) reveal information relating to the representation except as these Rules would permit or require with respect to a client.

A lawyer must protect confidences of his own present and former clients, of other present and former clients of law firms where he works or used to work, and of prospective clients. If a lawyer represents an organization and receives information about a member or a subsidiary entity, the lawyer has a duty to the client organization to protect those confidences. In any situation in which there is a substantial risk that the lawyer would normally have obtained confidences in a former matter that could be used adversely to the former client in a subsequent matter, the lawyer may not be able to handle the second matter unless the former client consents. But regardless of whether the possible receipt of confidences in a prior matter precludes representation of a new client, Rule 1.9(c) prohibits the *revelation* of confidences received from former clients and prohibits the *adverse use* of such confidences.

Rule 1.9 exempts from protection any confidences that may or must be revealed pursuant to other rules. So, for example, if a former client sues a lawyer for malpractice, the lawyer is permitted under Rule 1.6(b)(3) to reveal confidential information to the extent necessary to defend herself against the action. Also, as explained in Chapter 2, a lawyer is not barred from all use of

---

71. Rule 1.9, Comment 6.

client confidences, just from uses that would adversely impact the client on whose behalf the lawyer learned them.

Rule 1.9(c) includes one additional exception to the mandate to protect confidences of former clients. If the information received in confidence has since become generally known, the lawyer need not keep it confidential.

## PROBLEM 6-3  A DYSFUNCTIONAL FAMILY BUSINESS

*This problem is loosely based on a case that arose in a southern state.*

For many years, you represented a family-owned retail clothing business. The business consisted of two corporations created after the family's patriarch Henry Elliston Rice, Jr., bequeathed his assets to his sons. One corporation was called "HER, Inc." (This company name is derived from the founder's initials.) The other was called HER Fashions, Inc. HER, Inc. owned a factory and three retail clothing outlets. HER Fashions, Inc. owned a larger factory and one retail clothing outlet.

Until a few years ago, two brothers, Henry Elliston Rice III and Joseph Rice, jointly owned both corporations. At the time, they were on good terms. You were the general counsel for both corporations, and each paid half your salary. Among other things, you handled an application to register a trademark consisting of a drawing of a fashionably dressed teenage girl that was the company emblem. The trademarks were issued in the name of HER, Inc., but the public was unaware that there were two separate companies and thought that there was simply a company called "HER." The drawing became the recognized symbols of both companies.

The original concept for these two companies, which started in the 1960s, was to design and manufacture tasteful and stylish clothing for girls and women aged 15 to 30. Henry III was distressed by the styles (ranging from way-too-short skirts to disheveled rags) prevalent in the sixties. He wanted to provide a positive alternative. More recently, his brother Joseph began authorizing production of clothing designs that featured bare midriffs and outerwear that looked like underwear. Henry was horrified; he felt that Joseph was undermining the entire purpose of the business. After many attempts to work out these problems, the brothers decided they had to split the business.

In the wake of the fraternal dispute, the family business was reorganized. Henry obtained ownership of HER, Inc., which still owned the smaller factory and two of the retail outlets. Joseph obtained sole ownership of HER Fashions, Inc., which now owned the other factory and the other two retail outlets.

When the company split, you realized that with so much enmity and rivalry between the brothers, you could not represent both companies.

You resigned as general counsel of HER, Inc. (Henry's company) but continued as general counsel of HER Fashions, Inc. (Joseph's company).

After the split, both corporations continued using the HER trademarks, although at the time of the split, there had been no discussion of whether both companies would continue to use them. Henry just assumed that Joseph would commission a new logo for HER Fashions. But Joseph, being aware of the good reputation and brand-name recognition of HER, continued to use the registered drawing.

Then Henry's company sued Joseph's company for an injunction to prohibit HER Fashions from using the trademark. In this lawsuit, you entered your appearance as the lawyer for HER Fashions, the defendant. Henry's new lawyer telephoned you immediately and asked you to withdraw from representing Joseph's company. He claimed that your participation would violate Rule 1.9. He said that if you refused to withdraw, he would move to disqualify you. But Joseph has told you that using the logo is very important to his business, and he very much wants you to help him fight the suit.

Must you withdraw?

---

# H. Imputation of former client conflicts to affiliated lawyers

In Chapter 5, we examined conflicts between current clients and the imputation of such conflicts from one lawyer in a firm to another. Here we address a related question: To what extent are conflicts caused by work done for former clients imputed to other lawyers in a firm?

Rule 1.10 (which we also encountered in Chapter 5 when we considered concurrent conflicts) explains the rules on imputation for private sector lawyers. (Rule 1.11 covers government lawyers, for whom slightly different standards apply.)

---

### Rule 1.10   Imputation of Conflicts of Interest: General Rule[72]

| Rule language* | Authors' explanation |
|---|---|
| (a) While lawyers are associated in a firm, **none** of them shall knowingly **represent a client when any one** of them practicing alone **would be prohibited** from doing so by Rules 1.7 or 1.9 | General rule on imputation—if one lawyer in a firm has a conflict, all are precluded. |

*Continued*

---

72. Note that this Delaware rule has a subsection c that does not appear in the corresponding ABA Model Rule.

| Rule language* | Authors' explanation |
|---|---|
| **unless** the prohibition is based on a **personal interest** of the prohibited lawyer and **does not present a significant risk of materially limiting the representation** of the client by the remaining lawyers in the firm.[73] | This part of section (a) exempts from imputation conflicts that do not involve client loyalty or protection of confidences, but involve only a personal interest of the lawyer (such as his political beliefs). Comment 3. |
| **(b) When a lawyer has terminated an association with a firm**, the firm is **not** prohibited from thereafter representing a person with interests **materially adverse to those of a client represented by the formerly associated lawyer** and not currently represented by the firm, **unless:** | If a lawyer leaves a firm, his former firm should use this rule to evaluate new business that conflicts with the former lawyer's work at the firm. Conflict leaves the firm with the lawyer unless: |
| **(1) the matter is the same or substantially related** to that in which the formerly associated lawyer represented the client; and | the matter is the same or substantially related *and* |
| **(2) any lawyer** remaining in the firm has **information protected by [Rules] 1.6 and 1.9(c) that is material** to the matter. | a remaining lawyer knows material confidential information. |
| (c) When a lawyer becomes associated with a firm, no lawyer associated in the firm shall knowingly represent a client in a matter in which that lawyer is disqualified under Rule 1.9 unless: (1) the personally disqualified lawyer is timely screened from any participation in the matter and is apportioned no part of the fee therefrom; and (2) written notice is promptly given to the affected former client. | This subsection is part of Rule 1.10 as promulgated in Delaware, but the ABA Model Rule has no corresponding section. Model Rule 1.10 does not permit screening to solve the problem of an imputed successive conflict. |
| (d)[74] A disqualification prescribed by this rule **may be waived** by the affected client under the conditions stated in Rule 1.7. | Most imputed conflicts may be waived. See ABA Model Rule 1.10, comment 6. |
| (e)[75] The disqualification of lawyers associated in a firm with the former or current government lawyers is governed by Rule 1.11. | |

## Delaware Rule 1.10 above refers to "screening," a concept also discussed in *Maritrans*. What is screening?

Rule 1.0(k) explains that "screening" refers to isolating a lawyer from any participation in a matter through "procedures . . . reasonably adequate . . . to protect information that the isolated lawyer is obligated to protect."

---

73. Rule 1.10(a) is discussed in Chapter 5.
74. This subsection is lettered "c" in ABA Model Rule 1.10.
75. This subsection is lettered "d" in ABA Model Rule 1.10.

In practice, firms that attempt to erect screens take the following actions as soon as the conflict is identified.

- Tell all other lawyers in the firm not to discuss the matter with the isolated former government lawyer
- Prohibit all discussion of the matter in the presence of the lawyer
- Bar lawyers from allowing the isolated lawyer to have access to any relevant documents
- Keep all relevant documents in a locked file cabinet
- Control the keys to the cabinet so that only lawyers and staff members working on the matter have access to it
- Use passwords to limit access to relevant computer files
- Bar the isolated lawyer from receiving any profits from the case (such as a share of the fees)[76]

**When can conflicts be remedied by screening?**

Screening generally is not permitted as a remedy for conflicts between two present clients in a firm or for conflicts between a present and former client of the same firm. Screening is permitted in some states and by some federal courts as a remedy for conflicts that involve a lawyer who has switched firms and whose former firm represented a client with a conflicting interest.

The ABA Ethics 2000 Commission proposed to amend Rule 1.10 to include language allowing screening as a remedy for these imputed successive conflicts. This proposal was controversial and much debated. Lawrence J. Fox, a partner at Drinker, Biddle & Reath LLP, proposed an amendment to delete the language allowing screening from Rule 1.10. He argued that if screening is allowed, "the client gets no choice at all when a lawyer goes to a firm on the other side." The ABA House of Delegates approved the Fox amendment and rejected screening by a vote of 176 to 130.[77]

The table above shows that Delaware has adopted language allowing screening of imputed successive conflicts. Several other states that have amended their rules to take account of changes in the Model Rules that were adopted in response to the Ethics 2000 Commission also have decided, notwithstanding the ABA's rejection of the device, to permit screening in this situation.[78]

# 1. Imputation of the conflicts of an entering lawyer who is "infected"

To understand how conflicts may travel with a lawyer who changes firms, consider a variant of the problem we encountered earlier. Recall Hank, the

---

76. This list of screening devices is described in LaSalle Natl. Bank v. County of Lake, 703 F.2d 252 (7th Cir. 1983) (screening procedures adopted six months too late).

77. Model Rules: ABA Stands Firm on Client Confidentiality, Rejects "Screening" for Conflicts of Interest, 17 ABA/BNA Lawyers' Manual on Professional Conduct 492 (Aug. 15, 2001).

78. See, e.g., N.C. Prof. Conduct R. 1.10(c)(2004); Ariz. R. Prof. Conduct ER 1.10(d)(2)-(3) II (2003); Mont. R. Prof. Conduct 1.10(c) (2004).

lawyer in the hypothetical situation posed on page 373, Hank used to work at the firm of Barr & Thornburgh. Barr & Thornburgh used to defend The Toy Chest in employment matters, and it still does so, but Hank didn't work on any Toy Chest matters. On the other hand, Hank often chatted with his colleagues about their cases. Suppose that Hank learned in passing that one of the personnel managers at The Toy Chest, who later left the company, believed that women were good cashiers and wholesale buyers but were poor executives. Now Hank works at Reno & Days. Reno & Days has been asked to represent Jenny in a suit against her former employer, The Toy Chest. The firm would like several of its other lawyers (but not Hank) to work on Jenny's case. Hank has never discussed any Toy Chest matters with the lawyers who would work on the case, and he doesn't plan to do so. May Reno & Days accept Jenny as a client?

---

**T1:**

Hank works for B & T

Other B & T lawyers defend The Toy Chest in employment cases

Hank knows about these cases but does not work on them

**T2:**

Hank works for R & D

R & D wants its lawyers — but not Hank — to sue The Toy Chest for wrongful discharge

Hank has not discussed The Toy Chest with these lawyers

---

As with conflicts involving present clients, the general rule is that a former client of one lawyer in a firm is imputed to the other lawyers in the firm. If one lawyer can't take on a matter, neither can the other lawyers in the firm, unless conflict is consentable and the relevant clients give informed consent. The situation becomes more complicated when conflicted lawyers leave or enter a firm. As discussed below, if a conflicted (or we might say "infected") lawyer leaves the firm, the remaining lawyers are no longer infected by the ex-lawyer's conflict unless the new matter is substantially related to the old matter and one of the remaining lawyers possesses material confidences learned as a result of the ex-lawyer's previous work.[79]

If an infected lawyer enters a firm, the outcome depends on whether the jurisdiction allows screening to solve the problem or whether, following the lead of the ABA Model Rules, it rejects screening. In addition, most imputed conflicts may be solved by client consent. The exception is that if the conflict is nonconsentable under Rule 1.7, other lawyers in the firm may not solve the conflict by obtaining consent.[80]

Applying these rules to the hypothetical about Hank, the other lawyers at Reno & Days probably would be allowed to represent Jenny in Delaware if Hank were screened from the matter. (We say "probably" because even in

---

79. Rule 1.10(b).
80. Rule 1.10, Comment 9 (Delaware Rule) or 6 (ABA Model Rule).

states where the rules allow screening, courts may impose more stringent limitations when deciding motions to disqualify lawyers.[81]) In states that follow the ABA Model Rules, Hank would not be allowed to represent Jenny because he has information protected by Rule 1.6 that is material to the prospective employment litigation against his old firm's client. He would therefore be barred under Rule 1.9. Because Hank would be barred, ABA Model Rule 1.10(a) also would bar all of the lawyers at his new firm from undertaking the matter unless The Toy Chest consented.

Even the more strict ABA version of this rule makes an exception for law students, so as not to discourage law firms from hiring lawyers who, as students, had summer jobs at other firms. Paralegals, secretaries, and other nonlawyer assistants who formerly worked at a firm that represented a client whose interests are adverse to a client of their present firm, and law students who worked at such a firm before joining the bar, are barred from personal participation in work for the client of the new firm. In addition, they must be screened so that any confidential information they learned at the former firm is not passed along to lawyers at the current firm. If these precautions are taken, their conflicts are not imputed to other lawyers in the firm. This is one of only three situations in which the Model Rules permit screening to solve a problem.[82]

## 2. Imputation of the conflicts of a departed lawyer to his former firm

**When a lawyer has left a firm, are her conflicts still imputed to her former firm?**

> **FOR EXAMPLE:** Suppose that while she was at firm A, a lawyer named Allyson represented a printing company called Ink, Inc. When she moves to firm B, Ink wants her to continue as its lawyer, so it moves its legal business to firm B. After Allyson and Ink are gone, can firm A accept work that would conflict with the interests of Ink?

Rule 1.10(b) addresses this question. The analysis is conceptually similar to analysis prescribed by Rule 1.9(b). Firm A can take on a new client whose interests are materially adverse to those of Ink, unless the matter is substantially related to the work that Allyson did for Ink while at firm A and a lawyer who still works at firm A has material confidential information learned in connection with the work done for Ink. In that case, consent is required. In both cases, lawyers in the firm that seek to take on the new work should determine whether there is (a) material adversity, (b) substantial relationship,

---

81. Delaware Rule 1.10, Comment 6.

82. Rule 1.10, Comment 4. The other two situations in which the Model Rules allow screening, discussed later in this chapter, involve former government lawyers and lawyers in firms in which another lawyer received confidential information from a prospective client who did not become an actual client.

and (c) possession of material confidences by a lawyer in the firm. If the answer is yes to all three questions, the firm can't take on the work without the consent of the affected client.

Many lawyers and law students find these two rules maddeningly similar and therefore very confusing. One antidote to this confusion is to reread Rules 1.9(b) and 1.10(b) and then reread the two preceding paragraphs. Focus on *when* each of these rules applies. Both rules deal with conflicts precipitated by a lawyer changing jobs. Rule 1.9(b) examines whether the lawyer brings the old firm's conflicts with her. Rule 1.10(b) looks at whether the old firm retains the conflicts created by the work of the moving lawyer. This point may be diagrammed as follows:

---

**Lawyer moves from firm A to firm B.**
To analyze conflicts **brought into firm B:** 1.9(b).
To analyze conflicts **remaining at firm A:** 1.10(b).

---

## 3. Client waiver of imputed conflicts

Rule 1.10 explains that a conflict imputed to one lawyer from another often may be resolved by obtaining the informed consent of the affected client to the new representation. The analysis for waiver of imputed conflicts is the same as that for concurrent conflicts under Rule 1.7(b). (See discussion of conflict waiver in Chapter 5.) If an imputed conflict is waiveable, the lawyer must make the appropriate disclosures and the necessary consent must be in writing.

## 4. Imputation of conflicts among lawyers sharing office space

If lawyers are practicing as a law firm, it is obvious that the imputation rules apply among them. It doesn't matter whether the firm is organized as a partnership, a professional corporation, a limited liability corporation, or some other way. It doesn't matter if the lawyers involved are partners, associates, or counsel. It doesn't even matter whether one lawyer is the most senior partner in the New York office and the other lawyer is the most junior associate in the Moscow office.[83] If they are practicing in a firm, their conflicts are imputed to one another.

But some lawyers share office space without any formal association of their practices. Consider the following situation.

---

83. Westinghouse Elec. Corp. v. Kerr-McGee Corp., 580 F.2d 1311 (7th Cir. 1978).

PROBLEM 6-4   **THE FATAL SHOT**

*This problem is closely based on a case that arose in a northeastern state in the 1990s.*

Chad Collingwood and Moji Kaplan are two sole practitioners. Both lawyers do criminal defense work. They share a suite of offices to cut down on expenses and to avoid the isolation of practicing alone. They each operate a separate business. The door has separate signs, one for each of them. The suite has a common waiting area, and the two lawyers share one secretary-receptionist. The lawyers have separate phone lines, and the secretary screens calls for both of them. Although they conduct separate practices, they often have lunch together and consult each other about cases. Each gives files to the secretary for typing and filing. Sometimes the secretary joins the lawyers for lunch, leaving the phone to be answered by a machine.

During a gang battle, an innocent bystander was shot dead. Boris Lubinski was arrested. He told the police that although he was present at the shooting, his associate in drug trafficking, Carmine Bellavia, actually shot the gun. Bellavia was arrested; he claimed that Lubinski fired the shot. Both Lubinski and Bellavia were charged with murder. The only other eyewitness knew that both Lubinski and Bellavia had been at the scene, but he was so far away that he could not tell which of them fired the fatal shot.

Lubinski's family contacted Collingwood, who agreed to represent Lubinski. During their first meeting in the jail, Lubinski told Collingwood that Bellavia would also need a lawyer. Collingwood recommended that Bellavia hire Kaplan.

## Questions about the Fatal Shot

1. May Kaplan agree to represent Bellavia?
2. Assume that Kaplan concludes after analysis of the possible conflicts, and after both clients give informed consent, that she may represent Bellavia and begins to do so. The arraignment of Bellavia is scheduled, but Kaplan is trying another case that day. Kaplan asks Collingwood to stand in for her at the arraignment and enter a "not guilty" plea for Bellavia. She suggests that Collingwood explain to the court that Kaplan is Bellavia's lawyer and that Collingwood is entering the plea because of Kaplan's schedule conflict. Collingwood would not have to ask Bellavia any questions, either in public or in private. The arraignment probably will take one or two minutes. If the cases later come to trial, Collingwood may have to cross-examine Bellavia to show that Bellavia, not Lubinski, was the gunman. If the judge permits the stand-in arrangement, may Collingwood ethically substitute for Kaplan at the arraignment?

**3.** Separate trials for Lubinski and Bellavia have been scheduled. Meanwhile Collingwood and Kaplan each of whom represents one defendant, have decided to become law partners. May they do so before the trials occur?

**4.** Suppose that Collingwood and Kaplan do not become partners until after the trials end. The defendants accuse each other of firing the fatal shot. Each jury believes the accuser and convicts its defendant of first degree murder. Each of them appeals. A different lawyer is handling Bellavia's appeal. May the newly formed Collingwood-Kaplan partnership handle the appeal for Lubinski?

# I. Successive conflicts of present and former government lawyers

If a lawyer works for a government agency for a period of years and then joins a private law firm, some of the lawyer's previous work may conflict with her new practice. A standard successive conflict problem, right? Right. Logically, all successive conflicts would be governed by the standard articulated in Rule 1.9. Government lawyers are expected to comply with the applicable rules of professional conduct just as are lawyers in private practice.[84] However, Rule 1.11 imposes less stringent standards regarding successive conflicts that arise from a lawyer's present or past government service. The main reason for the different rule is that too-stringent conflict standards would make it more difficult for government lawyers to obtain positions in law firms because their government work might preclude the firms from representing many clients. This bar, in turn, might unduly discourage lawyers from serving in the government. Likewise, if conflicts barriers were higher, government agencies might be precluded from hiring lawyers from private practice because of prior conflicting work.

In recent years, the gap between government and private sector salaries has widened, making it more difficult for government agencies to compete with the private sector in hiring lawyers.[85] Many lawyers work in government in part to gain expertise to use later in private practice. Especially in light of the growing salary gap, it is important not to impose conflicts rules that discourage movement between the private and public sectors.[86]

---

84. See Rule 1.11, Comment 1. There has been some dispute about whether prosecutors are subject to Rules 4.1 and 4.2, which restrict lawyers and their agents from falsifying their identities and communicating directly with persons known to be represented by counsel. This issue is discussed in Chapter 8.

85. See discussion of the salary gap between the public and private sectors in Chapter 9.

86. There are several statutes governing conflicts of interest for government lawyers that do not apply to other lawyers. See, e.g., 18 U.S.C. § 205 (2004) (prohibiting current officers and employees of the United States from bringing claims against the United States or representing any party before any agency or court in connection with a matter in which the United States has a direct and substantial interest); 18 U.S.C. § 207 (2004) (prohibiting, for two years, former officers and employees of the United States from bringing claims against the United States or helping others to bring claims in which the United States is a party or has a direct and substantial interest and in which the former officer or employee participated personally and substantially while a federal employee).

The successive conflicts rules for present and former government lawyers, articulated in Rule 1.11, differ in two principal ways from the rules that apply to other lawyers. One is a slightly narrower standard for what constitutes a conflict. Instead of a "substantial relationship" between the two matters (the standard used in Rule 1.9), the question is whether the lawyer was "personally and substantially involved" in a matter in the former work. In the case of a former government lawyer, one must ask also whether the lawyer possesses "confidential government information" that could be used adversely in private practice. The second major difference between Rules 1.9 and 1.11 is that the conflicts of former government lawyers are not imputed to other lawyers in a firm if the former government lawyer is screened from contact with the conflicting matter. This is the second of the three situations in which the Model Rules permit screening to solve a conflicts problem.

# 1. Conflicts of former government lawyers in private practice

Rule 1.11(a) articulates the standard by which former government lawyers are to evaluate potential conflicts between prior government work and subsequent work:

> **Rule 1.11(a)**
> Except as law may otherwise expressly permit, a lawyer who has formerly served as a public officer or employee of the government:
>> (1) is subject to Rule 1.9(c); and
>> (2) shall not otherwise represent a client in connection with a matter in which the lawyer participated personally and substantially as a public officer or employee, unless the appropriate government agency gives its informed consent, confirmed in writing, to the representation.[87]

Recall that under Rule 1.9, the general successive conflicts standard precludes representation (absent informed consent) if a new client's interests are "materially adverse" to those of the former client and the matter is "the same or . . . substantially related." Rule 1.11(a), in contrast, precludes a former government lawyer from representing a client in "a matter in which the lawyer participated personally and substantially" while in government service. The rule requires no inquiry about the degree of adversity between the new client's interests and the government's interests. If the lawyer participated personally and substantially in the matter, the lawyer may not take on the subsequent work unless the government agency gives informed consent. The following table illustrates the similarities and differences in the two successive conflicts rules.

---

87. An additional conflict standard is stated in Rule 1.11(c); this is discussed below.

### Comparison of Rule 1.9(a) and Rule 1.11(a)

| Rule and conflicts subject to rule | Lawyer may not represent a new client without the consent of the former client in: | Differences between the rules |
|---|---|---|
| **Rule 1.9(a):** Applies to all successive conflicts except those related to former government work | "the same or a substantially related matter" if the new client's interests are "materially adverse" to those of the former client | |
| **Rule 1.11(a):** Applies to conflicts related to former government work | "a matter in which the lawyer participated personally and substantially" | • Applies only to the same matter as the previous work<br>• No requirement of material (or other) adversity[88]<br>• Lawyer's involvement must have been personal and substantial |

If the matter is the same and the lawyer's participation was personal and substantial, then the relevant agency must give its informed consent before the lawyer can take on the matter. Rule 1.11(b) also addresses imputation of such conflicts to other lawyers. It directs a lawyer to ask: When the firm took on a matter that posed a conflict for the former government lawyer, was the former government lawyer screened from participation and the relevant agency notified? If so, the conflict is not imputed to other lawyers in the firm.

### a. What is a "matter"?

Whether a representation involves the same "matter" as a previous one sounds like a commonsense assessment, but it's not always so simple.

FOR EXAMPLE:  Suppose a lawyer at the Department of Justice helped to defend the government against a lawsuit by a group of citizens challenging the validity of a rule on toxic waste cleanup. After leaving DOJ, the lawyer went to work at a private firm. Consider which of the following work by the firm would constitute the "same matter":

■ Representation of the citizen group on an appeal of the lawsuit
■ Representation of the citizen group in a petition to modify the rule that was challenged in the lawsuit
■ Representation of a different organization in a petition to modify the rule

---

88. Rule 1.11, Comment 3, explains that the reason why the prohibition does not require adverseness is that the purpose of this rule is "not only to protect the former client, but also to prevent a lawyer from exploiting public office for the advantage of another client."

■ Representation of the citizen group or the other organization in lobbying Congress for legislation to overturn the rule

Suppose instead that the lawyer was not involved in any prior litigation over the rule but assisted in drafting the rule. Can he or the firm later participate in litigation over the validity of the rule?

All of these questions turn on whether the new work is part of the same matter that the lawyer worked on while in the government. If the work does involve the same matter, Rule 1.11 might bar the former government lawyer from participation absent agency consent and might bar the firm from participation absent screening and notice to the agency.

Rule 1.11(e) gives a definition of the term "matter" for the purpose of this rule.

> **Rule 1.11(e)**
> **As used in this Rule, the term "matter" includes:**
> **(1) any judicial or other proceeding, application, request for a ruling or other determination, contract, claim, controversy, investigation, charge, accusation, arrest or other particular matter involving a specific party or parties, and**
> **(2) any other matter covered by the conflict of interest rules of the appropriate government agency.**

The comments offer two further explanations:

> [P]aragraphs (a)(2) and (d)(2) [disqualify lawyers only from work on] matters involving a specific party or parties, rather than extending disqualification to all substantive issues on which the lawyer worked.[89]

> For purposes of paragraph (e) of this Rule, a "matter" may continue in another form. In determining whether two particular matters are the same, the lawyer should consider the extent to which the matters involve the same basic facts, the same or related parties, and the time elapsed.[90]

On one hand, what is the same matter is not necessarily defined by the boundaries of one litigation or other proceeding. If the citizen group lost the case and six months later started a petition to achieve the same result through regulatory or congressional action, perhaps the second round would be regarded as the same matter. On the other hand, if five years elapse, the players change, and another initiative is undertaken to change the rule, then the new initiative probably is not the same matter.

## b. Personal and substantial participation

The comments to Rule 1.11 do not define "personal and substantial participation." However, the language is borrowed from the federal conflict of

---

89. Rule 1.11, Comment 3.
90. Id. at Comment 10.

interest laws;[91] the regulations implementing the federal statute offer some guidance.[92]

> The restrictions of section 207(a) apply only to those matters in which a former Government employee had "personal and substantial participation," exercised "through decision, approval, disapproval, recommendation, the rendering of advice, investigation or otherwise." To participate "personally" means directly, and includes the participation of a subordinate when actually directed by the former Government employee in the matter. "Substantially," means that the employee's involvement must be of significance to the matter, or form a basis for a reasonable appearance of such significance. It requires more than official responsibility, knowledge, perfunctory involvement, or involvement on an administrative or peripheral issue. . . . [T]he single act of approving or participation in a critical step may be substantial. It is essential that the participation be related to a "particular matter involving a specific party."[93]

Although this definition is relevant only by analogy, it is helpful in understanding the likely intended scope of the restriction imposed by Rule 1.11.

---

**Bases for disqualification of former government lawyers:**
- Subsequent work involves a "matter" in which the government lawyer was "personally and substantially involved" while in the government. (This can be cured by agency consent.) Rule 1.11(a) (type 1).
- Subsequent work could involve use of "confidential government information" about a person known to the lawyer in a way that would materially disadvantage that person. (This cannot be cured by consent.) Rule 1.11(c) (type 2).

---

### c. Screening of former government lawyers

In reviewing Rule 1.10, you learned that, as a general rule, if one lawyer in a firm has a conflict of interest based on previous legal work (in other words, not a conflict with the lawyer's personal interests), the ethical rules impute that conflict to all other lawyers in the law firm. Other lawyers in the firm are prohibited from handling the conflicting work unless the affected client gives informed consent.[94] The Model Rules and the rules of most states do not allow the conflicted lawyer to be screened from involvement in or communication about the conflicting work as a solution to this problem. So if one asks, "Can imputation of client-related conflicts be solved by screening

---

91. See 18 U.S.C. § 207 (2004).

92. While federal regulations implementing a criminal statute cannot be considered a dictionary for the ethical rules, they offer helpful guidance.

93. 5 C.F.R. § 2637.201(d) (2004).

94. See Rule 1.10(a) and (c).

the conflicted lawyer?," the answer in most cases is no. If the conflict is with work that a lawyer did while employed by a government agency, however, the answer changes from no to yes. Rule 1.11(b) explains how to avoid imputation of a conflict of a former government lawyer who had been personally and substantially involved in a matter (type 1 on the table above).

> **Rule 1.11(b)**
> When a lawyer is disqualified from representation under paragraph (a), no lawyer in a firm with which that lawyer is associated may knowingly undertake or continue representation in such a matter unless:
>
> > (1) the disqualified lawyer is timely screened from any participation in the matter and is apportioned no part of the fee therefrom; and
> >
> > (2) written notice is promptly given to the appropriate government agency to enable it to ascertain compliance with the provisions of this rule.

Under this rule, the former government lawyer's firm must screen the former government lawyer from any contact with the work and see that he earns no part of the fee except if it is part of a regular salary or partnership share.[95] The firm need not seek consent from the government agency as a prerequisite to taking on the conflicting work, but must simply notify the government agency about its work on the matter.[96]

## d. Confidential government information

Even if a former government lawyer is not precluded from representing a client because of "personal and substantial participation" in a "matter," the lawyer might be precluded because, while in the government, she learned "confidential government information" about a person; the new matter could involve material adverse use of that information. Rule 1.11(c) imposes this restriction, defines "confidential government information," and permits screening to avoid imputation of conflicts resulting from possession of such information.

> **Rule 1.11(c)**
> Except as law may otherwise expressly permit, a lawyer having information that the lawyer knows is confidential government information about a person acquired when the lawyer was a public officer or employee, may not represent a private client whose interests are adverse to that person in a matter in which the information could be used to the material disadvantage of that person. As used in this Rule, the term "confidential government information" means information that has been obtained under governmental authority and which, at the time this Rule is applied, the government is prohibited by law from disclosing to the public or has a legal privilege not to disclose and which is not otherwise available to the

---

95. See Rule 1.11, Comment 6.
96. The notice should include "a description of the screened lawyer's prior representation and of the screening procedures employed." Rule 1.11, Comment 7.

public. A firm with which that lawyer is associated may undertake or continue representation in the matter only if the disqualified lawyer is timely screened from any participation in the matter and is apportioned no part of the fee therefrom.

Government law enforcement and other agencies have the power to collect information not normally available to members of the public. One concern underlying this rule is to prevent the use of governmental power in aid of private interests. Another is to avoid giving an unfair advantage to a party whose lawyer has confidential government information about individual citizens.[97] If a former government lawyer has actually learned information[98] about a person that was obtained under governmental authority and that could be used to the material disadvantage of that person in a new representation, the former government lawyer cannot take on that work. This type of conflict cannot be cured by obtaining consent.

The definition of "confidential government information" covers a wide range of "information that has been obtained under government authority" that is prohibited by law from disclosure or privileged, and that is not publically available. However, Rule 1.11(c) defines such conflicts only to include confidential government information "about a person."

In the case of a conflict that results from the former government lawyer's possession of confidential government information (type 2 in the box above), the imputation rule is explained in Rule 1.11(c), quoted above. The requirements to avoid imputation of this type of conflict are the same as under Rule 1.11(b) except that the firm need not notify the government agency about its work on the matter.

## PROBLEM 6-5  THE FORMER GOVERNMENT LAWYER

Colonel Moammar Gadhafi seized power in Libya in 1969. An ABC News biography explains: "Throughout the 1970s, his regime was  implicated in subversive and terrorist activities in both Arab and non-Arab countries, and for giving support to various revolutionary movements. By the mid-1980s, he was widely regarded in the West as the principal financier of international terrorism." He once said that "American soldiers must be turned into lambs and eating them is tolerated."[99]

*Col. Moammar Gadhafi*

---

97. Rule 1.11, Comment 4.

98. Rule 1.11, Comment 8, explains that a former government lawyer is precluded by this section only by having "actual knowledge" about a person, and that knowledge cannot be imputed to her.

99. ABCNEWS.com, Biographis, Moammar Gadhafi, at http://abcnews.go.com/reference/bios/gadhafi.html (last visited May 15, 2004).

*Abraham D. Sofaer*

Abraham D. Sofaer is one of the most distinguished American lawyers of his generation. Before going into private practice, he was a professor at Columbia Law School, a federal district judge, and the legal advisor (general counsel) to the U.S. Department of State. After he left the government and went into private practice, he agreed to represent the government of Libya.

Read the following article, and then consider the questions that follow.

### Jim Hoagland, Gadhafi's Lawyer, Wash. Post, July 14, 1993

Consider it the Washington lawyer's version of the "Indecent Proposal" Robert Redford made on-screen to Demi Moore: If Moammar Gadhafi offered you half a million dollars to represent the Libyan government in the bombing of Pan Am 103, would you do it?

Make it more interesting: Would you represent Gadhafi even if you had once worked as the State Department's top lawyer, developing the legal justification in 1986 for economic sanctions against Libya and for the U.S. air raid on Tripoli that experts believe the Libyans sought to avenge with the Pan Am massacre?

Would you do it even if ungenerous souls would inevitably suspect that the Libyans wanted to hire you precisely because of your high profile on and intimate knowledge of their troubles with the Reagan and Bush administrations, at a moment when the Clinton administration wants to turn the screws more tightly on Libya?

You would if you were Abraham Sofaer, ex-legal adviser to secretaries of state George Shultz and James Baker. Beginning July 1, Sofaer has taken on a job that astonishes and pains many who have long admired him as a staunch conservative in U.S. politics and a strong supporter of Israel.

Sofaer has agreed to represent Libya in the Pan Am 103 case for a fee he declines to disclose.

The attack on Pan Am 103 in December 1988 cost the lives of 259 passengers and crew members, most of them Americans. Two Libyan intelligence agents were indicted by a U.S. grand jury in November 1991 for mounting the attack. But Gadhafi has refused the demands of the United States and the United Nations that the two alleged terrorists be handed over for trial in the United States or in Britain.

Bill Clinton promised the families of the victims of Pan Am 103 last fall to pursue and punish Gadhafi more vigorously. The Libyans seem worried that Clinton may mean it. They have mounted an intensive campaign in recent months to hire Washington lobbyists and lawyers.

Several attorneys were offered $500,000 retainers for starters. Even so, they refused after talking to Yussef Dibri, the shadowy head of Libya's National

Security Service, which Western intelligence agencies have implicated in terrorist acts. Dibri is also the point man in Gadhafi's effort to mend relations with the United States.

In a telephone conversation, Sofaer confirmed he had taken the job. He declined three times to discuss my information that the Libyans were offering half a million up front for a prestigious U.S. lawyer, saying only that his New York-based international law firm, Hughes, Hubbard & Reed, would "charge for its services in our normal way. It will be well within the range charged by major law firms. This is not pro bono."

Sofaer preemptively dismissed the possibility the Libyans were hiring him as a way to gain influence, or the impression of influence, in Washington. "This is strictly for legal services, for arranging a consensual resolution of the Pan Am 103 case, in regard to the case brought by the government or civil suits by families. If we are able to do that, we will have accomplished something worthwhile."

The former State Department legal adviser failed to see any irony in his going on the payroll of a government he had worked hard to undermine in the past. To be able to work for the Libyans, Sofaer had to get a special license from the Treasury Department's Office of Foreign Assets Control exempting him from the trade embargo that Sofaer had played a key role in crafting for President Reagan in 1986.

That was about the same time that he quickly provided Shultz with a legal justification for the April 1986 U.S. air raid that almost killed Gadhafi. The raid was mounted to punish Libya for bombing a West Berlin discotheque frequented by American soldiers.

Sofaer refused to confirm my information that he had met with Dibri in Geneva recently to discuss the contract. He acknowledged knowing Dibri's identity as Gadhafi's national security chief and head of the Libyan government's Committee to Resolve the Pan Am 103 Dispute.

Dibri's idea of resolving the dispute is to make sure that the two [indicted Libyan] agents do not undergo interrogation that would lead to their conviction in a U.S. court or to their naming names of higher-ups involved in the bombing, according to one American who has talked to Dibri about working for Libya.

Sofaer suggested, without being precise, that he may be able to get Gadhafi to change his spots at long last: "I will not compromise my values and beliefs. It is significant that Libya has retained someone who has always been against terrorism and is still strongly against terrorism, and who continues to support Israel strongly."

I know people who have spent a professional lifetime waiting for Gadhafi to change his spots. And I know people in the Middle East who will see the Libyans' hiring Sofaer as a sign that Gadhafi is more secure and influential, not more likely to change. Sofaer's appointment, announced in a press release Monday night after I told him I was working on this column, will dishearten the anti-Gadhafi resistance movement that exists outside Libya, I am reliably told.

Sofaer has no qualms about commingling his previous existence as Libya-accuser with his current role as Libya-adviser. Demi Moore at least anguished over the proposal made to her before accepting it.

Assume that the current Rule 1.11 had been in effect at the time that Mr. Sofaer took on this representation.[100] Also assume (as was found by a court) the following:

(a) After Pan Am flight 103 was destroyed, and before Libya was implicated in the bombing, some of the victims' relatives sued Pan Am. Pan Am served a subpoena on the government, seeking documents that might show that the government had advance notice that the flight would be bombed. (Pan Am hoped to show that the government was at fault for failing to warn the airline.) Pan Am's CEO then was given a private, confidential meeting with the secretary of state to discuss Pan Am's theory that the government might have had warning.

The State Department moved to quash the subpoena, but in case the subpoena was not quashed, it was also preparing a witness to testify about what the State Department knew before the bombing occurred. Because the meeting between the CEO and the secretary was very confidential, the State Department witness had not been told about it. Sofaer was involved in a decision about whether to reveal information about this meeting to that witness. The subpoena was later quashed, and the witness never testified.

(b) A few months after Mr. Sofaer was involved in this decision, he left the State Department and went into private practice.

(c) While Sofaer was in the State Department, Iran and Syria, rather than Libya, were suspected of having planted the bomb. Within a few weeks after Sofaer left the government, however, Libya was implicated in the bombing. Three years later, facing international pressure and sanctions, Libya sought to hire Mr. Sofaer to represent it and to try to negotiate an out-of-court settlement. During his work at the State Department on the Pan Am case, Sofaer had received no classified information about Libya's involvement in the bombing; Libya had not yet been implicated.

(d) Sofaer did not request permission from the State Department before accepting Libya's invitation to him to serve as its counsel in this matter.

## Questions about the Former Government Lawyer

**1.** Would Sofaer's representation violate Rule 1.11? Explain the arguments about how the rule would apply in this case. In particular:

   a. Was Sofaer's role at the State Department in connection with the bombing a "matter" under Rule 1.11?
   b. Was his participation "personal and substantial"?

**2.** Apart from whether Sofaer violated the rule, consider whether it was wrong for him to take on representation of Libya. If you think so, consider whether you believe the problem is that he was the former legal advisor of the State Department or that no American lawyer should represent Libya with

---

100. In fact, the rule in effect was a little bit different from the current Rule 1.11.

respect to this bombing. If Sofaer had never served in the government, would there be any problem with his taking on this work?

## 2. Conflicts of government lawyers who formerly worked in private practice

We have explored the successive conflicts rules that apply to lawyers who worked for government agencies and then switched jobs. Now we take up the opposite question, about how a government lawyer should evaluate conflicts that arise because of work that the lawyer did in a previous private law job. Former client conflicts are addressed by Rule 1.11(d).[101]

> **Rule 1.11(d)**
> Except as law may otherwise expressly permit, a lawyer currently serving as a public officer or employee:
> > (1) is subject to Rules 1.7 and 1.9; and
> > (2) shall not: . . . participate in a matter in which the lawyer participated personally and substantially while in private practice or nongovernmental employment, unless the appropriate government agency gives its informed consent, confirmed in writing. . . .

Unlike former government lawyers, who are to evaluate successive conflicts under Rule 1.11(a) through (c) *instead of* Rule 1.9(a), present government lawyers who may have conflicts resulting from their previous work in private practice are subject to the restrictions of Rules 1.7, 1.9 and 1.11. So a present government lawyer could be precluded from working on a matter based on Rule 1.7 (concurrent conflicts), Rule 1.9(a), which prohibits a lawyer from working on "the same or a substantially related matter in which that person's interests are materially adverse to the interests of a *former,* client unless that client gives informed consent, confirmed in writing,"[102] or Rule 1.11.

Both present and former government lawyers are subject to Rule 1.9(c) on protecting confidences of former clients. The differences in the rules governing these two groups are in the standards used to evaluate other successive conflicts and in who must consent.

If the work would be adverse to a former client, the lawyer must ask whether it is both substantially related and involves material adversity. If so, the lawyer can't do the work without the consent of the former client. Even if the new work is not adverse to the interests of a former client but involves a matter that the lawyer did a lot of work on in private practice, the government lawyer is precluded from working on it unless the current employing agency gives its consent.

---

101. Rule 1.11(d)(2)(ii) deals with a different question, of restrictions on government lawyers who wish to apply for jobs with persons who are involved in matters on which the government lawyers are working. This question is discussed below in connection with a similar provision for former judges in Rule 1.12.

102. Rule 1.9(a).

# J. Conflicts involving judges, arbitrators, and mediators

Up to this point, Chapters 5 and 6 have addressed concurrent, successive, and imputed conflicts of interest of lawyers. Here we shift gears and offer a brief introduction to some of the conflicts issues that arise for present and former adjudicators. While there is not time in a survey course on the law that governs lawyers to treat judicial ethics issues in any depth, some discussion is needed. Perhaps the most important judicial rules for law students and new lawyers to study are the rules on when a judge must decline to hear a matter because of a conflict. (Law students who become law clerks to judges can help to protect their employers by being familiar with these limitations.) We also examine the conflicts rules for judicial law clerks and certain other professionals.

## 1. Conflicts rules for sitting judges

Like lawyers, judges are subject to rules of conduct adopted by the courts. The judicial rules have extensive provisions on conflicts of interest, which specify the circumstances under which a judge may not hear a matter because of a conflicting interest or a possible bias. About 20 states have adopted, in whole or part, the ABA Rules of Judicial Conduct, while about 16 additional states have adopted some provisions of this code.[103] The United States Judicial Conference has adopted a code of ethics for federal judges that includes some of the same provisions as appear in the ABA Code of Judicial Conduct.[104] One of the most important topics covered in the Code of Judicial Conduct is: When should a judge disqualify himself from hearing a particular matter because of a conflict of interest?

The Code directs a judge to disqualify herself if her "impartiality might reasonably be questioned." It also specifies several particular situations in which a judge should disqualify herself from deciding a matter, including those in which the judge

- has a personal bias toward a party or lawyer;
- knows about disputed facts in the case from personal experience;
- has an economic interest in a case;

---

103. In 2003, the American Bar Association established a Joint Commission to Evaluate the Model Code of Judicial Conduct, chaired by Mark I. Harrison of Phoenix, to review the ABA Model Code of Judicial Conduct and to recommend revisions for possible adoption in August 2005. For information about the status of this effort, see http://www.abanet.org/judicialethics/about.html (last visited Oct. 23, 2004).

104. Stephen Gillers & Roy D. Simon, Regulation of Lawyers: Statutes and Standards 622 (Aspen L. & Bus. 2003) (referencing a survey of states that have adopted the ABA Code by the American Judicature Society).

- is related to a party, a lawyer, or someone with a substantial stake in the case;
- knows that she has received campaign contributions of more than a specified amount from a party or lawyer; or
- has made a public statement that appears to commit her with respect to an issue in the case.[105]

Suppose you are a lawyer handling a matter that is assigned to a judge who has a clear conflict of interest (for example, a personal injury suit against the judge's wife) and the judge does not recuse himself. You must file a motion for recusal with the judge whose recusal is sought. Awkward, don't you think? Suppose the judge disagrees with you that recusal is required, turns down your motion, and insists on hearing the case. Will your client be disadvantaged by your having more or less accused the judge of unethical behavior? Despite the awkwardness of the procedure for challenging the impartiality of a judge, it is the usual path by which lawyers seek recusal of judges who appear to have a conflict of interest in particular matters.

## PROBLEM 6-6  THE JUDGE'S FORMER PROFESSOR

*This problem is based on a news report about a judge who was presiding over a case involving a prominent public figure.*

You are a lawyer for Carl Ahr, a government official who is a defendant in a suit for sexual harassment. The suit was filed in federal court and was assigned to Mindy Lynch, a respected judge. There might be a problem, however.

Your client did a brief stint as a law professor many years ago, before becoming a public official. The judge was actually a student in one of his classes. He says the judge was a very good student and he enjoyed having her in class, so maybe the former relationship will have a positive impact on the outcome of the case.

There's a possible hitch, however. Just after the end of the semester in which Mindy Lynch took his class, Ahr went away on vacation. He says he still doesn't know what happened, but he mislaid a pile of bluebooks from the course in which Lynch was enrolled.

After Ahr established that the exams were gone, never to be seen again, he consulted with the dean and offered the students whose bluebooks he had lost grades of B+ in the class. Every student accepted the offer except for Lynch. She urged that her grade point average was higher than B+, and she felt she deserved a higher grade. After some negotiation, Ahr gave her an A.

---

105. ABA Code Jud. Conduct, Canon 3E, Disqualification (as amended 2003).

There's another funny coincidence as well. Judge Lynch's husband is now a law professor at the same law school where Ahr once was a professor. Mr. Lynch joined the faculty after Ahr left, but because Ahr returns to the law school for various events, Ahr knows the Lynches personally. Even weirder, when the lawyers went to meet with the judge for a status conference a couple of weeks ago, Mr. Lynch was present during the meeting and participated in the discussion of the issues in the case. There are rumors that Mr. Lynch helps his wife to evaluate and decide the cases before her.

---

## Questions about the Judge's Former Professor

**1.** What impact does the prior relationship between Lynch and Ahr have on the case? If the plaintiff's lawyer learns about the prior relationship between Ahr and Lynch, is he likely to file a motion requesting that the judge recuse herself? Why or why not? If the plaintiff's lawyer does not file such a motion, should you do so?

**2.** Assuming that the ABA Code of Judicial Conduct applies, if a motion requesting recusal is filed, will the judge have to disqualify herself? (Review Canon 3 to answer this question.)[106]

**3.** Canon 2B prohibits a judge from allowing "family, social, political or other relationships to influence the judge's conduct or judgment." Canon 3B(7)(b) allows a judge to obtain the advice of "a disinterested expert" on the law that applies to a particular matter if the judge notifies the parties as to who is consulted and of the substance of the communication and allows the parties to respond. Has Judge Lynch violated either of these rules? If so, should you object to Mr. Lynch's involvement on behalf of your client? (Review the relevant canons before you answer this question.)

## 2. Conflicts rules for former judges, law clerks, arbitrators, and mediators

Some judges remain on the bench for the duration of their professional lives. Others return to practice after a period of judicial service. Many other lawyers do part-time or occasional adjudicative work as special masters, arbitrators, or mediators.[107] An even larger group of lawyers have worked as law clerks for

---

106. If you have a statutory supplement, the code may appear there. Otherwise you can find it and the proposed revisions at http://www.abanet.org/judicialethics/drafts.html#canon3 (last visited Oct. 23, 2004).

107. Rule 1.12, Comment 1, explains, "The term 'adjudicative officer' includes such officials as judges pro tempore, referees, special masters, hearing officers, and other parajudicial officers, and also lawyers who serve as part-time judges."

judges or as staff attorneys (professional law clerks) for courts. Consequently, a considerable number of lawyers have had adjudicative responsibility on various matters. Rule 1.12 lays out conflicts rules for those lawyer-adjudicators.[108]

> **Rule 1.12(a)**
> ... [A] lawyer shall not represent anyone in connection with a matter in which the lawyer participated personally and substantially as a judge or other adjudicative officer or law clerk to such a person or as an arbitrator, mediator or other third-party neutral, unless all parties to the proceeding give informed consent, confirmed in writing.[109]

## a. Personal and substantial participation

The "personal and substantial participation" standard is the same as that used for conflicts of government lawyers in Rule 1.11.

> **FOR EXAMPLE:** Suppose a lawyer had been a law clerk for a judge on a state court of appeals that has nine sitting judges and hears cases in panels of three. The former clerk would be considered to have participated personally and substantially in a case in which he drafted the opinion or for which his judge sat on the three-judge panel, but not one that was handled by another panel.[110] He could not thereafter "represent anyone in connection with" the matter "unless all parties to the proceeding give informed consent, confirmed in writing."[111]

## b. Imputation

What if a former judge leaves the bench and, a year later, joins a firm that represents one of the parties in a complex matter on which he handled the early motions? The former judge would be disqualified under Rule 1.12(a). Would his conflict be imputed to the firm? Rule 1.12(c) says no, so long as the judge "is timely screened from any participation in the matter and is apportioned no part of the fee therefrom; and ... written notice is promptly given to the parties and any appropriate tribunal" so that they can check whether the rule is observed. The prohibition on receiving profits from conflicted work "does not prohibit the screened lawyer from receiving a salary or partnership share established by prior independent agreement."[112]

---

108. We use this term to refer to people who have occupied any of the judicial or quasi-judicial roles covered by this rule.

109. The rule makes an exception from this prohibition for "an arbitrator selected as a partisan of a party in a multi-member arbitration panel." Rule 1.12(d).

110. This example is adapted from the explanation in Rule 1.12, Comment 1. The comment also makes clear that the exercise of "remote or incidental administrative responsibility that did not affect the merits" would not constitute personal and substantial participation. Id.

111. Rule 1.12(a).

112. Rule 1.12, Comment 4.

### c. Employment negotiation

Like Rule 1.11(d)(2)(ii), applicable to government lawyers, Rule 1.12(b) prohibits lawyer-adjudicators from negotiating for employment with any party or lawyer for a party to a matter in which the adjudicator is "participating personally and substantially."[113]

> **Rule 1.12(b)**
>
> A lawyer shall not negotiate for employment with any person who is involved as a party or as lawyer for a party in a matter in which the lawyer is participating personally and substantially as a judge or other adjudicative officer or as an arbitrator, mediator or other third-party neutral. A lawyer serving as a law clerk to a judge or other adjudicative officer may negotiate for employment with a party or lawyer involved in a matter in which the clerk is participating personally and substantially, but only after the lawyer has notified the judge or other adjudicative officer.

This language uses the present tense; it appears not to prohibit the lawyer-adjudicator from employment negotiation after the adjudication has concluded.

Law clerks, fortunately, are permitted to apply for jobs, even with parties or lawyers involved in matters that are pending before their judges, but "only after the lawyer has notified the judge or other adjudicative officer."[114] This may be especially important in smaller communities, in which every firm in town may have matters before each judge in town.[115] Since most clerkships are one or two years in duration, law clerks need more latitude in applying for new jobs.


# K. Conflicts involving prospective clients

A last topic for Chapter 6 is the conflicts that involve prospective clients who consult lawyers while seeking representation but who do not engage those lawyers. During a preliminary discussion with a potential client, a lawyer may learn various confidences for the purpose of assessing whether the lawyer will represent the client. Even if this lawyer ultimately does not represent

---

113. A similar prohibition is imposed on government lawyers by Rule 1.11:

(d) Except as law may otherwise expressly permit, a lawyer currently serving as a public officer or employee: . . . shall not . . . negotiate for private employment with any person who is involved as a party or as lawyer for a party in a matter in which the lawyer is participating personally and substantially, except that a lawyer serving as a law clerk to a judge, other adjudicative officer or arbitrator may negotiate for private employment as permitted by Rule 1.12(b) and subject to the conditions stated in Rule 1.12(b).

114. Rule 1.12(b).

115. When the authors taught in Morgantown, West Virginia, for example, two judges and four magistrates served the community of 40,000.

the client, the lawyer may possess confidential information that could be used adversely to that former prospective client on behalf of another client. Therefore, Rule 1.18 lays out a set of standards by which to evaluate conflicts with prospective clients.[116] Prospective clients obtain some protection from conflicts with the lawyer's other clients, but not as much protection as actual clients. In particular, even if a lawyer is disqualified by this rule because the lawyer received confidential information from a prospective client, the rule permits screening (along with other procedural requirements) to avoid imputing the conflict to other lawyers in the firm. This is the third instance in which the rules permit screening to avoid imputation of conflicts to other lawyers.

## Rule 1.18    Duties to Prospective Client

| Rule language* | Authors' explanation |
|---|---|
| (a) A person who discusses with a lawyer the **possibility of forming a client-lawyer relationship** with respect to a matter **is a prospective client.** | Not everyone who communicates with a lawyer is protected — unilateral communication without the expectation of a possible representation doesn't make someone a prospective client. Comment 2. |
| (b) **Even when no client-lawyer relationship ensues**, a lawyer who has had discussions with a prospective client **shall not use or reveal information** learned in the consultation, except as Rule 1.9 would permit with respect to information of a former client. | If a lawyer learns confidences to assess the possibility of representation, this rule prohibits use or revelation (except per Rule 1.9) regardless of the brevity of the contact. Comment 3. |
| (c) A lawyer subject to paragraph (b) **shall not represent a client with interests materially adverse to those of a prospective client in the same or a substantially related matter if** the lawyer **received information** from the prospective client that **could be significantly harmful** to that person in the matter, except as provided in paragraph (d). If a lawyer is disqualified from representation under this paragraph, no lawyer in a firm with which that lawyer is associated may knowingly undertake or continue representation in such a matter, except as provided in paragraph (d). | "Even in the absence of an agreement, . . . the lawyer . . . [may represent] a client with interests adverse to those of the prospective client in the same or a substantially related matter unless the lawyer has received . . . information that could be significantly harmful. . . ." Comment 6.<br><br>This sets a higher standard for what information is disqualifying than does Rule 1.9. |

*Continued*

---

116. This rule makes explicit the duty to protect confidences received from and to avoid representation that conflicts with the interests of a prospective client (depending on how much adverse confidential information the lawyer received). Lawyers have other duties to prospective clients also, such as the duty of competence and duties with respect to papers or other property that a prospective client leaves in the lawyer's care. See Rule 1.18, Comment 9.

| Rule language* | Authors' explanation |
|---|---|
| (d) When the **lawyer has received disqualifying information as defined in paragraph (c), representation is permissible if:** (1) both the affected client and the prospective client have given **informed consent**, confirmed in writing, or: (2) the lawyer who received the information **took reasonable measures to avoid exposure to more disqualifying information** than was reasonably necessary to determine whether to represent the prospective client; and (i) the disqualified lawyer is **timely screened** from any participation in the matter and is apportioned no part of the fee therefrom; and (ii) **written notice** is promply given to the prospective client. | "A lawyer may condition conversations with a prospective client on the person's informed consent that no information disclosed during the conversation will prohibit the lawyer from representing a different client in the matter. . . . [T]he prospective client may also consent to the lawyer's subsequent use of the information received from the prospective client." Comment 5. Imputation also may be avoided if the lawyer obtains informed consent or if the relevant lawyers are screened and written notice is sent to the prospective client. Comment 7. |

*All emphasis added.

## PROBLEM 6-7 **THE MINE EXPLOSION**

You are one of seven plaintiffs' personal injury lawyers in a small city. You know from newspaper accounts that last month an explosion in the coal mine on the outskirts of town injured several miners. You do not know any of the injured miners.

Last week, you received a telephone call from Robert Boggle, owner of the mine. You know from an employment suit that you settled against his company some years ago that he is usually represented by a large downtown firm. The conversation went like this:

BOGGLE: Hey there. Listen, I might want to have you represent my company in this mine explosion thing. There are bound to be suits by some of the miners.

YOU: Mr. Boggle, you already have a lawyer.

BOGGLE: Yeah, but my lawyer doesn't know beans about personal injury cases. You're an expert.

YOU: I've never represented a defendant before.

BOGGLE: The first time's always the best.

YOU: I'm not sure it would be good for my reputation.

BOGGLE: But I might just make it worth your while. Besides, there's a reason I really need you.

YOU: What's that?

BOGGLE: I'm in real trouble. I just got a report from our chief engineer suggesting that our safety inspection process was "less than adequate." And he says that our exhaust pipes were too narrow.

YOU: I don't think I want to get into this, Mr. Boggle. I appreciate your call, but if I represented your company, I might never get another personal injury client.

A series of phone calls quickly revealed to you that, as you had begun to suspect, Boggle had called each of the other plaintiffs' lawyers in town and had a similar conversation.

This morning, Wade Schultz, one of the injured miners, was released from the hospital. He called you and asked you to represent him in a suit against Boggle's company.

## Questions about the Mine Explosion

**1.** May you agree to represent Schultz? You can bet your life that Boggle won't consent.

**2.** If you can't handle the matter, can your partner Oswald take on the matter?

**3.** Could you have avoided this problem? If so, how?

# 7 CONFLICTS OF INTEREST BETWEEN LAWYERS AND CLIENTS

"My fees are quite high, and yet you say you have little money.
I think I'm seeing a conflict of interest here."

Lawyers encounter conflicting interests nearly as often as they breathe. Consider the following absurd scenario. Imagine a lawyer who wants to make certain that he never has a conflict of interest. To avoid possible conflicts with other present or former clients, this lawyer would represent only one client for her entire career. To avoid possible conflicts between the client's interests and the lawyers, the lawyer might

- work for the client without charging a fee since fee agreements involve some level of conflicts of interest between lawyer and client (the lawyer wants to be paid more, the client wants to pay less);
- avoid any acquisitions of property from or business arrangements with the client, or with anyone whose property or business interests might have some interest for or impact on the client; or
- make no other time commitments to activities such as family vacations or hobbies that might interfere with the lawyer's ability to devote her full attention to the client's interests.

The point is that lawyers encounter conflicts between their interests and the interests of clients all the time. The ethical rules, liability rules, and disqualification rules on conflicts of interest tend to identify conflicts that may harm the representation of a client or the client's interests. To be a good and loyal representative of clients, a lawyer must learn the law on conflicts of interest, but the lawyer also must develop sensitivity to the whole spectrum of possible conflicts of interest that are not discussed in formal rules. A lawyer, of course, is not expected to forgo having a family, taking vacations, or representing other clients to avoid conflicts of interest. A lawyer is expected, however, to be aware of and attentive to the constant collision of these various competing interests and to exercise judgment about how she juggles them. It is the essence of professionalism to exercise care, judgment, and restraint that goes far beyond the boundaries set by ethical or legal rules.

In this chapter, we explore some of the possible conflicts between the interests of client and lawyer. Most of these conflicts are financial in nature. Indeed, many of the most potentially troublesome conflicts between client and lawyer are financial ones.

Many of these problems involve lawyers' pursuit of financial self-interest by setting fees without adequate consultation with or disclosure to clients. Some situations involve deliberate theft and deception. Others involve standard practices in contracting between lawyers and clients that allow lawyers almost unfettered discretion in setting fees.

The first part of this chapter looks at lawyer-client fee contracts. It explains the types of fee arrangements lawyers use, the rules requiring that fees be reasonable, the principle that lawyers should communicate with clients about fees, and the requirements for modification of fee agreements. We then examine regulation of billing practices by lawyers, explaining some of the developing law in this area and offering practical guidance for new lawyers. We next look at restrictions on use of contingent fees by lawyers. We consider some particular fee and expense arrangements that have been prohibited or restricted, such as providing financial assistance to clients during representation. This part of the chapter continues with a discussion of the law relating to fee disputes between lawyers and clients and collection of fees by lawyers. Next we look at the rules governing division of fees between lawyers who are not in the same firm and limits on fee-sharing with non-lawyers. Then we turn to restrictions on payment of legal fees by someone other than the client.

The second part of the chapter examines other conflicts between the interests of lawyers and clients. We explain the restrictions on business transactions and sexual relationships between lawyers and clients, the handling of situations in which two opposing lawyers are family members, and the imputation of lawyer-client conflicts to other lawyers in a firm.

The final part of the chapter looks at rules governing lawyers who have custody of clients' documents or property. We discuss the rules on management of client trust accounts, on duties relating to client property, and on rules for lawyers who administer estates and trusts for clients.

# A. Legal fees

## 1. Lawyer-client fee contracts

When a client hires a lawyer to represent him, the client and the lawyer enter into a contract. The contract may involve a formal written agreement, or it may involve a conversation followed by a perfunctory letter in which the lawyer confirms how much she will charge for each hour of her time. Regardless of whether the terms are written or even stated, the hiring of a lawyer creates a contract that is subject to all the usual rules of contract law. If the client fails to pay the fee, the lawyer may sue the client for breach of contract. Likewise, if the lawyer was hired to file a lawsuit and fails to do so, the client may sue for breach of contract. If, in the course of making a contract, a lawyer deceives a client about the cost or nature of the service to be provided, the contract might be voidable for misrepresentation.[1]

In addition to the rules of contract law, lawyer-client fee contracts are governed by the ethical rules in the relevant jurisdiction and are sometimes constrained by other law as well. In bankruptcy, probate, public benefits, and other areas, additional rules are imposed by legislatures, agencies, and courts about how billing is done and how much a lawyer can charge.[2]

### a. Types of agreements

The most common basis for fees of American lawyers is the amount of time the lawyer spends on the matter. About 70 percent of legal services are billed on an hourly basis.[3] Some firms charge only for lawyer time, but other firms charge by the hour also for the time of paralegals and secretaries. In personal injury cases, lawyers often charge a contingent fee in which the lawyer gets a percentage of the damages (if any) that are paid to the client. If the client receives no recovery, the lawyer gets nothing. In recent years, some lawyers have begun to experiment with other methods of billing. Some charge flat fees for certain standard services. Some use a schedule of fees in which a particular amount is charged for various tasks performed.

Since the early 1990s, corporate clients have become much more concerned about controlling expenditures on outside counsel fees. Some have issued

---

1. Restatement (Second) of Contracts §§ 162, 164 (1981).

2. For example, a federal law provides a lawyer who helps a veteran to obtain benefits from the Department of Veterans Affairs may not charge *any* fee for advocacy services rendered prior to a final decision by the Board of Veterans Appeals. For appellate services rendered after that decision, in which a fee agreement specifies that the fee shall be paid directly to the lawyer out of past-due benefits, the lawyer's fee is limited to 20 percent of those benefits. 38 U.S.C. § 5904 (2004). The apparent premises of this law are: (1) that veterans do not need lawyers to obtain just resolutions of their claims for federal benefits, and (2) that if they need to appeal, they need only inexpensive legal services. Perhaps the restriction on legal fees for appeals is an effort to protect veteran's benefits from being used up to pay lawyers. One authority has stated that "few attorneys" have been willing to handle veterans' appeals under these conditions. Barton F. Stichman, The Impact of the Veterans' Judicial Review Act on the Federal Circuit, 41 Am. U. L. Rev. 855, 868 (1992).

3. William Ross, The Honest Hour: The Ethics of Time-Based Billing by Attorneys (Carolina Academic Press 1996).

policies restricting what outside counsel may bill for. Some invite competitive bidding by law firms for various projects. Contracts between large corporations and law firms sometimes involve extensive negotiation in which the client has significant bargaining power.

In contracts between lawyers and nonaffluent individual clients, however, lawyers commonly inform new clients of their hourly rates and require an initial payment from the client against which the first hours will be charged. Typically, however, they give little information about the projected cost of the service. Some lawyers defend this practice on the basis that it is difficult to predict how much time any legal work will take. On the other hand, this practice requires a client essentially to sign a blank check for whatever amount the lawyer charges for the work. A client can dissolve the relationship and stop the meter at any time, but hiring a replacement lawyer is costly because a new lawyer will have to learn the case afresh and may in the long run charge just as much. Many clients wind up feeling blind-sided by the steep legal bills and angry that they were not given more information at the outset.

## b. Reasonable fees

The ethical rules impose a few "bright line" restrictions on legal fees, and case law imposes some additional boundaries, but lawyers have wide discretion in deciding how much to charge. Rule 1.5(a) requires that fees be reasonable and gives a shopping list of criteria that lawyers should use to evaluate whether they are charging reasonable fees.[4]

> **Rule 1.5(a)**
> A lawyer shall not make an agreement for, charge, or collect an unreasonable fee or an unreasonable amount for expenses. The factors to be considered in determining the reasonableness of a fee include the following:
> > (1) the time and labor required, the novelty and difficulty of the questions involved, and the skill requisite to perform the legal service properly;
> > (2) the likelihood, if apparent to the client, that the acceptance of the particular employment will preclude other employment by the lawyer;
> > (3) the fee customarily charged in the locality for similar legal services;
> > (4) the amount involved and the results obtained;
> > (5) the time limitations imposed by the client or by the circumstances;
> > (6) the nature and length of the professional relationship with the client;
> > (7) the experience, reputation, and ability of the lawyer or lawyers performing the services; and
> > (8) whether the fee is fixed or contingent.[5]

---

4. The Restatement (Third) of Law Governing Lawyers, similarly, states that a lawyer may not charge a fee "larger than reasonable under the circumstances." Restatement § 34.

5. This is the text of the relevant Delaware Rule of Professional Conduct. Unless specified otherwise, all of this book's quotations from rules of professional conduct are quotations from

Some lawyers have been disciplined for charging unreasonable fees, but the guidance offered by this rule would make it difficult for any lawyer to know that a particular fee would be considered to violate the rule. However, in evaluating whether a fee is reasonable, the courts tend to ask whether the fee is comparable to fees charged by other lawyers in similar cases, and whether the fee makes sense in light of the work performed and the results obtained.[6] A fee might be found unreasonable if the lawyer does not have records to show how much time was spent and what was done during that time.[7] Or a fee might be found improper because the fee is disproportionate to the services provided.[8] There have been cases in which relatively small fees have been found unreasonable,[9] and others in which very large fees have been found reasonable.[10]

Much of the calculus of what is reasonable depends on the norms in the legal community in question and in a particular area of practice. To some extent, lawyers are permitted to charge whatever fees the market will bear. While there is some price competition in the legal profession, the market is not effective in controlling price through competition. One reason is that legal services are intangible, so it is difficult for clients to compare the quality of services offered by different firms. Also it is difficult for clients to compare the cost of hiring one firm or another. In most cases, price is determined by the number of hours spent on the task, so price is determined after the service is rendered. In addition, most clients have limited information about the firms that they hire. Although some information may be obtained from advertising or other materials published by a firm, comparison is difficult. In many industries, there are services and publications that evaluate and compare the services provided by different vendors. A local consumer magazine, for example, might publish a comparative survey of the auto mechanics in a particular community. No comparable consumer information is routinely available about lawyers.

---

the Delaware Rules of Professional Conduct. In a few instances, we quote from rules or from published proposed rules in other states. Except where we note otherwise, however, the text of all state rules that we quote is the same as the text of the ABA Model Rules of Professional Conduct. See the note in the Introduction for a more detailed explanation.

6. ABA, Annotated Model Rules of Professional Conduct 65 (5th ed. 2003).

7. See, e.g., In re O'Brien, 29 P.3d 1044 (N.M. 2001). "Client files must contain work to justify the fee. Whether the evidence of work is in notations of research, time sheets, copies of depositions, evidence of time spent in hearings or meetings; such evidence is essential. Respondent's file contained scant documentation to justify her fee." Id. at 1047.

8. See, e.g., In re Dorothy, 605 N.W.2d 493 (S.D. 2000) (lawyer charged over $47,000 for representation of client on a standard child custody and support matter).

9. See, e.g., People v. Hohertz, 926 P.2d 560 (Colo. 1996) (fee of $5,200 found unreasonable for representation of a domestic relations client in light of lawyer's failure to answer a discovery request and failure to perform other needed work).

10. See, e.g., Bauermeister v. McReynolds, 571 N.W.2d 79 (Neb. 1997) (fee agreement that could produce a fee of $4 million was found to be not excessive. A business venture was unlikely to succeed and no fee would be paid unless it succeeded. Also, lawyer had already expended $250,000 worth of time on the project, and had lost other business as a consequence.).

The *Brobeck* and *Fordham* cases, excerpted below, explore when a fee may be considered excessive. The *Brobeck* case began after Telex sued IBM for antitrust violations and won an enormous judgment of nearly $260 million. That decision was reversed by the Court of Appeals for the Tenth Circuit, which also affirmed an $18.5 million counterclaim against Telex. Then Telex hired Moses Lasky of the Brobeck law firm, on a contingent fee basis, to prepare a petition for certiorari. After the firm filed the petition, IBM and Telex settled their dispute with neither paying anything to the other. Brobeck sent Telex a bill for $1 million, which it claimed under the contingent fee agreement. When Telex refused to pay, Brobeck sued, and the district court ruled for Brobeck, granting it a $1 million judgment. Telex appealed.

## Brobeck, Phleger & Harrison v. Telex Corp.

602 F.2d 866 (9th Cir.), *cert. denied*, 444 U.S. 981 (1979)

PER CURIAM: . . .

To maximize Telex's chances for having its petition for certiorari granted, they [Telex official] decided to search for the best available lawyer. They compiled a list of the preeminent antitrust and Supreme Court lawyers in the country, and Roger Wheeler, Telex's Chairman of the Board, settled on Moses Lasky of the Brobeck firm as the best possibility. . . .

When asked about a fee, Lasky stated that, although he would want a retainer, it was the policy of the Brobeck firm to determine fees after the services were performed. Wheeler, however, wanted an agreement fixing fees in advance and arranged for Lasky to meet in San Francisco on February 10th to discuss the matter further with Telex's president, Stephen Jatras, and Floyd Walker, its attorney in the IBM litigation.

The San Francisco meeting was the only in-person meeting between Lasky and the Telex officials on the subject of Brobeck's compensation. Jatras told Lasky that Wheeler preferred a contingency fee arrangement. Lasky replied that he had little experience with such arrangements but proposed a contingency fee of 5% of either the judgment or settlement. Jatras thought there should be a ceiling and someone proposed that the ceiling be set at 5% of the first $100 million. Jatras also proposed that anything due IBM on its counterclaim judgment be deducted before calculating the 5% fee. Lasky rejected this, but suggested as a compromise that the amount of the counterclaim judgment be deducted if Telex received $40 million or less in judgment or settlement.

Lasky added that if there was to be ceiling on the contingent fee, there ought to be a minimum fee as well, and suggested that the minimum fee be $1 million. In his deposition, Jatras acknowledged that Lasky proposed a minimum fee, but disputed the other participants' account of the remainder of the discussion. According to Jatras, he told Lasky that Telex would not pay a minimum fee "unless we got something to pay it from." Lasky denied hearing such a proposal. The parties reached no final agreement at the San Francisco meeting. . . .

The next day Walker drafted a . . . proposed fee agreement [which was reviewed and modified by Jatras and sent to Lasky]. . . . The pertinent portion of this proposal, paragraph three, is set forth below:

> Once a Petition for Writ of Certiorari has been filed with the Clerk of the United States Supreme Court then Brobeck will be entitled to the payment of an additional fee in the event of a recovery by Telex from IBM by way of settlement or judgment in excess of the counterclaim judgment; and, such additional fee will be 5% of the first $100,000,000.00 of such recovery, the maximum contingent fee to be paid is $5,000,000.00 and the minimum is $1,000,000.00.

On the day he received the letter and proposed fee agreement, Lasky telephoned Jatras to tell him the proposal was not acceptable and [he drafted and sent an agreement]. . . . This agreement, which Lasky had already signed, is set forth in full:

> MEMORANDUM
> 1. Retainer of $25,000.00 to be paid. If Writ of Certiorari is denied and no settlement has been effected in excess of the Counterclaim, then the $25,000.00 retainer shall be the total fee paid; provided however, that
> 2. If the case should be settled before a Petition for Writ of Certiorari is actually filed with the Clerk of the Supreme Court, then the Brobeck firm would bill for its services to the date of settlement at an hourly rate of $125.00 per hour for the lawyers who have worked on the case; the total amount of such billing will be limited to not more than $100,000.00, against which the $25,000.00 retainer will be applied, but no portion of the retainer will be returned in any event.
> 3. Once a Petition for Writ of Certiorari has been filed with the Clerk of the United States Supreme Court then Brobeck will be entitled to the payment of an additional fee in the event of a recovery by Telex from IBM by way of settlement or judgment of its claims against IBM; and, such additional fee will be five percent (5%) of the first $100,000,000.00 gross of such recovery, undiminished by any recovery by IBM on its counterclaims or cross-claims. The maximum contingent fee to be paid is $5,000,000.00, provided that if recovery by Telex from IBM is less than $40,000,000.00 gross, the five percent (5%) shall be based on the net recovery, i.e., the recovery after deducting the credit to IBM by virtue of IBM's recovery on counterclaims or cross-claims, but the contingent fee shall not then be less than $1,000,000.00.
> 4. Once a Writ of Certiorari has been granted, then Brobeck will receive an additional $15,000.00 retainer to cover briefing and arguing in the Supreme Court.
> 5. Telex will pay, in addition to the fees stated, all of the costs incurred with respect to the prosecution of the case in the United States Supreme Court.

Jatras signed Lasky's proposed agreement, and on February 28 returned it to Lasky with a letter and a check for $25,000 as the agreed retainer. To "clarify" his thinking on the operation of the fee agreement, Jatras attached a set of hypothetical examples to the letter. This "attachment" stated the amount of the fee that would be paid to Brobeck assuming judgment or settlements in eight different amounts. In the first hypothetical, which assumed a settlement of $18.5 million and a counterclaim judgment of $18.5 million, Jatras listed a "net recovery" by Telex of "$0" and a Brobeck contingency fee of "$0."[11]

Lasky received the letter and attachment on March 3. Later that same day he replied:

> Your attachment of examples of our compensation in various contingencies is correct, it being understood that the first example is applicable only to a situation where the petition for certiorari has been denied, as stated in paragraph 1 of the memorandum.

No Telex official responded to Lasky's letter.

Lasky, as agreed, prepared the petition for certiorari and filed it in July 1975. . . . [A] meeting was held on September 5. Lasky told the assembled Telex's officials that the chances that the petition for certiorari would be granted were very good. Wheeler, however, was concerned that if the petition for certiorari was denied, the outstanding counterclaim judgment would threaten Telex with bankruptcy. Wheeler informed Lasky that Telex was seriously considering the possibility of a "wash settlement" in which neither side would recover anything and each would release their claims against the other. Lasky responded that in the event of such a settlement he would be entitled to a fee of $1,000,000. Wheeler, upon hearing this, became emotional and demanded to know from the others present whether this was what the agreement provided. Walker agreed that it had. Jatras said he didn't know and would have to read the correspondence.

Two days later Jatras wrote a memorandum for the Telex Board of Directors in which he stated: "Lasky claims that his deal guarantees him $1 million fee in the event that Telex settles after the Petition for Writ is filed if the settlement is at least a 'wash' with the counterclaim judgment.

"Wheeler doesn't agree that the Lasky interpretation is correct and has asked Jatras to review his notes and recollections of this matter. Jatras has done so and has no independent knowledge beyond the documents. . . ."

---

11. [Court's footnote 1.] The attachment in full provided:

| Assumed gross judgment or settlement on antitrust case | Assumed judgment or settlement on counterclaim | Net recovery by Telex | Brobeck contingent fee | Comment |
|---|---|---|---|---|
| $ 18,500,000 | $18,500,000 | $ 0 | $ 0 | |
| 20,000,000 | 18,500,000 | 1,500,000 | 1,000,000 | Minimum Fee |
| 30,000,000 | 18,500,000 | 11,500,000 | 1,000,000 | Minimum Fee |
| 39,000,000 | 18,500,000 | 20,500,000 | 1,025,000 | 5% of Net |
| 40,000,000 | 18,500,000 | 21,500,000 | 2,000,000 | 5% of Gross |
| 60,000,000 | 18,500,000 | 41,500,000 | 3,000,000 | 5% of Gross |
| 100,000,000 | 18,500,000 | 81,500,000 | 5,000,000 | Maximum Fee |
| 150,000,000 | 18,500,000 | 131,500,000 | 5,000,000 | Maximum Fee |

Having returned to San Francisco, Lasky, at Telex's request, prepared a reply brief to IBM's opposition to the petition for certiorari, and sent it to the Supreme Court on September 17th for filing. In the meantime, Wheeler opened settlement discussions with IBM. He telephoned Lasky periodically for advice.

On October 2 IBM officials became aware that the Supreme Court's decision on the petition was imminent. They contacted Telex and the parties agreed that IBM would release its counterclaim judgment against Telex in exchange for Telex's dismissal of its petition for certiorari. On October 3, at the request of Wheeler and Jatras, Lasky had the petition for certiorari withdrawn. Thereafter, he sent a bill to Telex for $1,000,000. When Telex refused to pay, Brobeck filed its complaint. . . .

### [Is the fee contract ambiguous, precluding disposition on summary judgment?]

Paragraph three of the memorandum agreement provided that Brobeck was entitled to an additional fee "in the event of a recovery by Telex from IBM by way of settlement or judgment of its claims against IBM." Telex contends that the wash settlement reached by IBM and Telex was not such a recovery because the contract contemplated that Brobeck would be entitled to its contingent fee only if Telex actually received money in settlement of its suit with IBM. . . .

The extrinsic evidence advanced by Telex to support its interpretation of the contract consists almost exclusively of Jatras' belief that an additional fee would be paid only if there was a net recovery (i.e., a settlement in excess of the counterclaim judgment). Jatras claims that he expressed his belief to Lasky on several occasions.

To the extent that Telex is relying on Jatras' subjective belief to establish the meaning of the contract, we must disagree. Under the modern theory of contracts we look to objective, not subjective, criteria in ascertaining the intent of the parties. Even when we view Jatras's protestations as part of the objective circumstances surrounding the formation of the contract, we find that they do not make the contract reasonably susceptible to Telex's interpretation, because Jatras's words are contradicted by his later actions. . . .

Two days after the stormy September 5 meeting, Jatras wrote the previously quoted memorandum for the Telex Board of Directors in which Jatras stated:

> Wheeler doesn't agree that the Lasky interpretation is correct and has asked Jatras to review his notes and recollections of this matter. Jatras has done so and has no independent knowledge beyond the documents. . . .

Telex proposed a contract whereby it would pay Brobeck only if Telex recovered an amount in excess of the amount owed on the counterclaim judgment. Brobeck, however, by excluding this limitation in its version sent Telex and to which the parties finally agreed, specifically rejected such a contract. We think that the only correct inference to be drawn from the omission of Telex's proposal in the final contract is that the parties agreed that Brobeck would be entitled to its additional fee in the event of a settlement between IBM and Telex, without regard to whether the amount of settlement was greater than the counterclaim judgment.

The events surrounding the cryptic "attachment" that Jatras sent to Brobeck after the contract was signed also belie Telex's interpretation of the contract. The first example in the series of eight hypotheticals supports Jatras's interpretation that the contingent fee would be paid only if there was a net recovery to Telex. Lasky, by a return letter, promptly disagreed with this interpretation, stating that it applied only in the situation when the petition for certiorari was denied. As Telex admitted in a request for admission:

> neither Mr. Jatras nor anyone else connected with defendants at any time wrote or spoke to Mr. Lasky concerning any statement in the letter of March 3, 1975, and particularly concerning the last paragraph. . . .

We regard Telex's inaction as acquiescing to Brobeck's interpretation of the contract.

### [Was the fee excessive?]

Finally, Telex contends that the $1 million fee was so excessive as to render the contract unenforceable. Alternatively it argues that unconscionability depends on the contract's reasonableness, a question of fact that should be submitted to the jury.

Preliminarily, we note that whether a contract is fair or works an unconscionable hardship is determined with reference to the time when the contract was made and cannot be resolved by hindsight.

There is no dispute about the facts leading to Telex's engagement of the Brobeck firm. Telex was an enterprise threatened with bankruptcy. It had won one of the largest money judgments in history, but that judgment had been reversed in its entirety by the Tenth Circuit. In order to maximize its chances of gaining review by the United States Supreme Court, it sought to hire the most experienced and capable lawyer it could possibly find. After compiling a list of highly qualified lawyers, it settled on Lasky as the most able. Lasky was interested but wanted to bill Telex on hourly basis. After Telex insisted on a contingent fee arrangement, Lasky made it clear that he would consent to such an arrangement only if he would receive a sizable contingent fee in the event of success.

In these circumstances, the contract between Telex and Brobeck was not so unconscionable that "no man in his senses and not under a delusion would make on the one hand, and as no honest and fair man would accept on the other." This is not a case where one party took advantage of another's ignorance, exerted superior bargaining power, or disguised unfair terms in small print. Rather, Telex, a multi-million corporation, represented by able counsel, sought to secure the best attorney it could find to prepare its petition for certiorari, insisting on a contingent fee contract. Brobeck fulfilled its obligation to gain a stay of judgment and to prepare and file the petition for certiorari. Although the minimum fee was clearly high, Telex received substantial value from Brobeck's services. For, as Telex acknowledged, Brobeck's petition provided Telex with the leverage to secure a discharge of its counterclaim judgment, thereby saving it from possible bankruptcy in the event the Supreme Court denied its petition for certiorari. We conclude that such a contract was not unconscionable.

The judgment of the district court is affirmed.

## Questions about *Brobeck*

**1.** When first contacted, Lasky explained that his firm's policy was to set fees after the services were performed. He may have meant only that when a firm bills by the hour, the amount of the fee is unknown until the firm knows how many hours the work required. But perhaps Lasky meant that he would not bill by the hour, and that after the case was over, he would judge the value of the services he had performed and charge a "reasonable" price for those services. Would a contract that included no information about the price of a service be valid and enforceable?

**2.** Perhaps the dispute about the agreement could have been avoided if it had been drafted more clearly. Suppose that you were Lasky and you wanted paragraph 3 of the agreement to provide (as years later, the court held it did) for a $1 million payment to be made even if the petition were withdrawn. But you wanted the text to be so clear that Jatras would have no doubt about its meaning. Redraft paragraph 3 to achieve this result.

**3.** Telex was assisted by counsel in negotiating this fee agreement. If (given the later flap) you assume that some senior Telex officials did not understand that the agreement provided for a $1 million minimum fee in the event of a wash settlement (in which neither party pays damages), does this suggest that Walker, Telex's lawyer, erred in not explaining it?

**4.** The court concluded that the $1 million minimum fee for filing a petition for certiorari was neither excessive nor unconscionable. Do you agree with the court's reasoning in reaching these conclusions?

## In the Matter of Fordham

668 N.E.2d 816 (Mass. 1996)

O'CONNOR, Justice.

This is an appeal from the Board of Bar Overseers' (board's) dismissal of a petition for discipline filed by bar counsel against attorney Laurence S. Fordham. On March 11, 1992, bar counsel served Fordham with a petition for discipline alleging that Fordham had charged a clearly excessive fee . . . for defending Timothy Clark (Timothy) in the District Court against a charge that he operated a motor vehicle while under the influence of intoxicating liquor (OUI) and against other related charges. . . .

After five days of hearings, and with "serious reservations," the hearing committee concluded that Fordham's fee was not substantially in excess of a reasonable fee and that, therefore, the committee recommended against bar discipline. Bar counsel appealed.... By a vote of six to five, with one abstention, the board accepted the recommendation of the hearing committee and dismissed the petition for discipline.... [The case was eventually appealed to the state supreme court.]

### [Fordham's representation of Timothy]

On March 4, 1989, the Acton police department arrested Timothy, then twenty-one years old, and charged him with OUI, operating a motor vehicle after suspension, speeding, and operating an unregistered motor vehicle.... The police discovered a partially full quart of vodka in the vehicle. After failing a field sobriety test, Timothy was taken to the Acton police station where he submitted to two breathalyzer tests which registered .10 and .12 respectively....

Timothy ... and his father, Laurence Clark (Clark) consulted with three lawyers, who offered to represent Timothy for fees between $3,000 and $10,000. Shortly after the arrest, Clark went to Fordham's home to service an alarm system which he had installed several years before. While there, Clark discussed Timothy's arrest with Fordham's wife who invited Clark to discuss the case with Fordham. Fordham then met with Clark and Timothy.

At this meeting, ... Fordham, whom the hearing committee described as a "very experienced senior trial attorney with impressive credentials," told Clark and Timothy that he had never represented a client in a driving while under the influence case or in any criminal matter, and he had never tried a case in the District Court. The hearing committee found that "Fordham explained that although he lacked experience in this area, he was a knowledgeable and hard-working attorney and that he believed he could competently represent Timothy. Fordham described himself as 'efficient and economic in the use of [his] time.' ...

"Towards the end of the meeting, Fordham told the Clarks that he worked on [a] time charge basis and that he billed monthly.... In other words, Fordham would calculate the amount of hours he and others in the firm worked on a matter each month and multiply it by the respective hourly rates. He also told the Clarks that he would engage others in his firm to prepare the case. Clark had indicated that he would pay Timothy's legal fees." After the meeting, Clark hired Fordham to represent Timothy.

According to the hearing committee's findings, Fordham filed four pretrial motions on Timothy's behalf, two of which were allowed. One motion ... [to suppress evidence] was based on the theory that, although two breathalyzer tests were exactly .02 apart, they were not "within" .02 of one another as the regulations require.... [After a bench trial on October 10 and October 19, 1989,] the judge found Timothy not guilty of driving while under the influence.

## [Fordham's bills]

Fordham sent the following bills to Clark:

"1. April 19, 1989, $3,250 for services rendered in March, 1989.
"2. May 15, 1989, $9,850 for services rendered in April, 1989.
"3. June 19, 1989, $3,950 for services rendered in May, 1989.
"4. July 13, 1989, $13,300 for services rendered in June, 1989.
"5. October 13, 1989, $35,022.25 revised bill for services rendered from March 19 to June 30, 1989.
"6. November 7, 1989, $15,000 for services rendered from July 1, 1989 to October 19, 1989."

The bills totaled $50,022.25, reflecting 227 hours of billed time, 153 hours of which were expended by Fordham and seventy-four of which were his associates' time. Clark did not pay the first two bills when they became due and expressed to Fordham his concern about their amount. Clark paid Fordham $10,000 on June 20, 1989. At that time, Fordham assured Clark that most of the work had been completed "other than taking [the case] to trial." Clark did not make any subsequent payments. Fordham requested Clark to sign a promissory note evidencing his debt to Fordham and, on October 7, 1989, Clark did so. In the October 13, 1989, bill, Fordham added a charge of $5,000 as a "retroactive increase" in fees. On November 7, 1989, after the case was completed, Fordham sent Clark a bill for $15,000.

Bar counsel and Fordham have stipulated that all the work billed by Fordham was actually done, . . . that Fordham and his associates spent the time they claim to have spent, [and] that Fordham acted conscientiously, diligently, and in good faith in representing Timothy and in his billing in this case. . . .

The board dismissed bar counsel's petition for discipline against Fordham because it determined, relying in large part on . . . [the hearing committee report], that Fordham's fee was not clearly excessive. "A fee is clearly excessive when, after a review of the facts, a lawyer of ordinary prudence, experienced in the area of the law involved, would be left with a definite and firm conviction that the fee is substantially in excess of a reasonable fee." [The court quotes from the Massachusetts rule the same eight factors listed in Rule 1.5(a) that determine whether a fee is reasonable.] . . .

## [The expert testimony]

Four witnesses testified before the hearing committee as experts on OUI cases. One of the experts, testifying on behalf of bar counsel, opined that "the amount of time spent in this case is clearly excessive." He testified that there were no unusual circumstances in the OUI charge against Timothy and that it was a "standard operating under the influence case." The witness [acknowledged the novel argument and that the good result was unusual]. . . . The witness estimated that it would have been necessary, for thorough preparation of the case including the novel breathalyzer suppression argument, to have billed twenty to thirty hours for preparation, not including trial time.

A second expert, testifying on behalf of bar counsel, [concurred that the case was not very difficult, but that Fordham's legal theory was novel].... Nonetheless, the witness concluded that "clearly there is no way that [he] could justify these kind of hours to do this kind of work." He estimated that an OUI case involving these types of issues would require sixteen hours of trial preparation and approximately fifteen hours of trial time. He testified that he had once spent ninety hours in connection with an OUI charge against a client that had resulted in a plea ... [but] it was a case of first impression, in 1987, concerning new breathalyzer equipment and comparative breathalyzer tests.

An expert called by Fordham testified that the facts of Timothy's case presented a challenge and that without the suppression of the breathalyzer test results it would have been "an almost impossible situation in terms of prevailing on the trier of fact." He ... believed that Fordham's hours were not excessive and, in fact, he, the witness, would have spent a comparable amount of time. The witness later admitted, however, that within the past five years, the OUI cases which he had brought to trial required no more than a total of forty billed hours. ... [Even so, he thought that] Fordham ... had spent a reasonable number of hours on the case. ...

The fourth expert witness, called by Fordham, ... testified that, although the time and labor consumed on the case was more than usual in defending an OUI charge, the hours were not excessive ... because the case was particularly difficult due to the "stakes [and] the evidence." She conceded, however, ... that the issues presented in this case were not unusual. ... She thought she may have known of one person who might have spent close to one hundred hours on a difficult OUI case; ... but she had never heard of a fee in excess of $10,000 for a bench trial.

### [The reasonableness of the fee]

In considering whether a fee is "clearly excessive" ... the first factor ... is "the novelty and difficulty of the questions involved, and the skill requisite to perform the legal service properly." ... The number of hours devoted to Timothy's OUI case by Fordham and his associates was substantially in excess of the hours that a prudent experienced lawyer would have spent. ... The novel and successful motion to suppress the breathalyzer test results ... cannot justify a $50,000 fee in [this] type of case. ...

The board determined that "[b]ecause [Fordham] had never tried an OUI case or appeared in the district court, [Fordham] spent over 200 hours preparing the case, in part to educate himself in the relevant substantive law and court procedures." Fordham's inexperience in criminal defense work and OUI cases in particular cannot justify the extraordinarily high fee. It cannot be that an inexperienced lawyer is entitled to charge three or four times as much as an experienced lawyer for the same service. ...

[The court said another factor is the comparability of the lawyer's fee to that charged by others in the community for similar services. The court reviewed the expert testimony generally suggesting that fees for OUIs were substantially lower than Fordham's.]

Although finding that Fordham's fee was [much higher than that charged by other lawyers] . . . the hearing committee nevertheless determined that the fee . . . was not clearly excessive because Clark "went into the relationship with Fordham with open eyes," Fordham's fee fell within a "safe harbor," and Clark acquiesced in Fordham's fee by not strenuously objecting to his bills. . . .

Testimony . . . revealed that the fee arrangement had been fully disclosed to Clark including the fact that Fordham "would have to become familiar with the law in that area." . . . The hearing committee [also] found that "[d]espite Fordham's disclaimers concerning his experience, Clark did not appear to have understood in any real sense the implications of choosing Fordham to represent Timothy. Fordham did not give Clark any estimate of the total expected fee or the number of $200 hours that would be required." [This] . . . finding . . . directly militates against the finding that Clark entered into the agreement "with open eyes." . . .

The hearing committee reasoned that as long as an agreement existed between a client and an attorney to bill a reasonable rate multiplied by the number of hours actually worked, the attorney's fee was within a "safe harbor" and thus protected from a challenge that the fee was clearly excessive. The board, however, . . . correctly rejected the notion "that a lawyer may always escape discipline with billings based on accurate time charges for work honestly performed."

The "safe harbor" formula would not be an appropriate rationale in this case because the amount of time Fordham spent to educate himself and represent Timothy was clearly excessive despite his good faith and diligence. [The rule] . . . creates explicitly an objective standard by which attorneys' fees are to be judged. . . . [The rule] plainly does not require an inquiry into whether the clearly excessive fee was charged to the client under fraudulent circumstances, and we shall not write such a meaning into the disciplinary rule. . . .

Finally, bar counsel challenges the hearing committee's finding that "if Clark objected to the numbers of hours being spent by Fordham, he could have spoken up with some force when he began receiving bills." Bar counsel notes, and we agree, that "[t]he test . . . is whether the fee 'charged' is clearly excessive, not whether the fee is accepted as valid or acquiesced in by the client." Therefore, we conclude that . . . Fordham's fee was clearly excessive. . . .

[The court then rejects an argument by Fordham that the imposition of discipline would violate his due process rights.]

The ABA Model Standards for Imposing Lawyer Sanctions § 7.3 (1992) endorses a public reprimand as the appropriate sanction for charging a clearly excessive fee. We deem such a sanction appropriate in this case. Accordingly, a judgment is to be entered in the county court imposing a public censure. . . . So ordered.

## Questions about *Fordham*

**1.** No one would quibble with a lawyer who devoted extra time to increase the odds of getting a desired result for a client. The issue in this case is whether a lawyer may bill for that time. There is no indication that Fordham was lying about the amount of time he actually worked, and in fact the parties stipulated that he and his associates really spent 227 hours on the case. Do you think that Fordham billed Clark for too many hours on Timothy Clark's matter?

**2.** If Fordham's fee was excessive, what about the fee charged by the Brobeck firm to Telex? If one lawyer can charge $1 million for writing a petition for certiorari, should another lawyer be disciplined for charging $50,000 for getting his client acquitted on a criminal charge after a trial?

**3.** Review the standard for a reasonable fee under Rule 1.5(a). This was the standard that was applied in the *Fordham* case. Is the guidance provided by the rule clear enough to be a basis for discipline? Draft some changes that could clarify this rule.

**4.** In the paragraph after the list of fees, the court explains that Clark objected to the amount of Fordham's fee, but then signed a promissory note acknowledging the debt. If Clark did not object more strongly, should that have led the court to conclude that the fee was reasonable?

**5.** In the same paragraph mentioned in the previous question, the court notes that one of the bills included an additional amount for a retroactive rate increase. Assuming this was the first that Clark knew about the rate increase, was this proper?

**6.** The court rejects the "safe harbor" idea, at least as applied to this case, because Fordham billed for hours he spent learning a new area of law. The concept is that if a lawyer contracts to bill by the hour, and honestly and diligently works the actual number of hours billed to the client, the resulting fee should be regarded as reasonable. Should the courts follow this principle as to lawyer bills that do not bill for "initial study time"?

**7.** Several years after the *Fordham* case was decided, the attorney general of Massachusetts hired several law firms, on a contingent fee basis, to assist it in novel and highly uncertain litigation against several tobacco companies, in which it claimed damages for its expenses in providing medical treatment for cancer victims over many decades. At the time, the tobacco industry had won 800 court cases and had never lost a case. The law firms declined to work on the case unless the state was willing to pay 25 percent of any damages that the state was awarded. They urged that this fee was appropriate because they would have to devote the time of more than 100 lawyers to this work with no certainty that they would ever be paid. The state agreed to these terms, in writing. Eventually, the state won an $8.3 billion dollar settlement from the tobacco companies, but the public (and the state government) balked at paying approximately $2 billion to the lawyers. If the firms had charged by the hour, at their normal rates, the bill would have been about $20 million. The state agreed to pay only $775 million, and two law firms sued the state for

$1.2 billion, their share of the balance owed under the contingent fee agreement.[12] Should the lawyers have won their suit against the state?

### c. Communication about fee arrangements

As we explained above, many conflicts between lawyers and clients over fees are caused by inadequate disclosure about fees at the outset of the representation or inadequate consultation with the client about fees as the representation progresses. Rule 1.5(b) requires lawyers to make some disclosures to clients about the fees they intend to charge.

> **Rule 1.5(b)**
> The scope of the representation and the basis or rate of the fee and expenses for which the client will be responsible shall be communicated to the client, preferably in writing, before or within a reasonable time after commencing the representation, except when the lawyer will charge a regularly represented client on the same basis or rate. Any changes in the basis or rate of the fee or expenses shall also be communicated to the client.

Let's examine what this rule requires.

### What must be disclosed?

A lawyer must disclose information about the scope of the representation. What does this mean? A comment says that the lawyer must disclose "the general nature of the legal services to be provided." Perhaps this comment isn't very helpful to lawyers who are trying to draft letters to their clients. The term "general nature" doesn't add very much to the term "scope."

A lawyer must disclose the "basis or rate of the fee and expenses." The comments suggest disclosure of information about "the lawyer's customary fee arrangements" and "the basis, rate, or total amount of the fee and . . . any costs or expenses or disbursements" that will be charged to the client. If the lawyer is billing by the hour, then, the lawyer should tell the client what is his hourly rate. If the client will be billed 25 cents a page for photocopying or charged for the cost of hiring a court reporter for a deposition, the client should be informed.[13]

### Must the disclosure be in writing?

No, unless the lawyer intends to charge a contingent fee (see below). The rule recommends but does not require that the disclosure be in writing. The Ethics

---

12. Thanassis Cambanis, Law Firms Accuse State of Breaching Tobacco Deal, Boston Globe, Nov. 5, 2003.

13. See ABA Comm. on Ethics & Prof. Resp., Formal Op. 94-389 (1994) (before entering into a contingent fee arrangement with a client, a lawyer should discuss possible choices of fee arrangements).

2000 Commission recommended that the word "preferably" be eliminated from the rule; this change would have required a written disclosure. The ABA House of Delegates, however, rejected this suggestion, preferring to give lawyers the discretion to decide whether to disclose information about fees and expenses in writing.

## Does the lawyer have to disclose fee and expense information before starting work on the matter?

No. The rule says the disclosure must occur "before or within a reasonable time after commencing the representation." In some cases, the client needs services on an emergency basis. For example, a client who is in jail may need legal assistance to be released, and it might be appropriate to postpone discussion of fee information until after the work has begun. Absent such circumstances, principles of contract law require articulation of terms before an enforceable fee agreement comes into existence.[14] In addition, disclosure of information about fees is good business practice. A client who commits time and money to a relationship with a lawyer but only learns the price when the bill arrives may feel that he was manipulated into an agreement.

## Must the lawyer estimate the amount of time she will spend or the total fee?

No. Such estimates are required for plumbers and auto repair people (who also bill by the hour),[15] but not for lawyers. Some lawyers urge that such estimation is impossible because the amount of time that will be consumed by a matter cannot be predicted. Even though such disclosure is not required, it is good business practice to provide clients with a realistic assessment of the possible cost of the representation. One reason why people don't trust lawyers is that so many clients have been blind-sided by legal fees far higher than they had been led to expect.[16] If there is uncertainty about the amount of time a matter will consume, the lawyer could provide an estimate that includes a high and low prediction. A lawyer who wants good relations with clients whose resources are limited would be well advised to disclose more information in advance and perhaps to commit to a ceiling on what he will charge for a specified service.

14. Restatement § 38, comment b, notes, for example, that if a lawyer says "I will charge what I think fair, in light of the hours expended and the results obtained," this might be part of a valid contract, but it "does not bind the client or tribunal to accept whatever fee the lawyer thinks fair."

15. See, e.g., Colo. Rev. Stat. Ann. § 42-9-104 (2003) (requiring auto repair shops to give customers specific written price estimates before performing repair work).

16. ABA Formal Op. 93-379 explains that "One major contributing factor to the discouraging public opinion of the legal profession appears to be the billing practices of some of its members." ABA Comm. on Ethics & Prof. Resp., Formal Op. 93-379 (1993). See generally Marc Galanter, The Faces of Mistrust: The Image of Lawyers in Public Opinion, Jokes, and Political Discourse, 66 U. Cin. L. Rev. 805 (1998); Leonard E. Gross, The Public Hates Lawyers: Why Should We Care? 29 Seton Hall L. Rev. 1405 (1999).

PROBLEM 7-1  **AN UNREASONABLE FEE?**

*A lawyer called one of the authors for advice about a situation similar to the one described in this problem.*

Ingrid Sanders hired a lawyer, Colin Horlock, to settle a dispute with her landlord about who was responsible for the cost of clean-up and renovation following a flood in her luxury apartment. The landlord had refused to cover the repairs. The work cost Ingrid $70,000. Colin told Ingrid that his rate was $250 per hour, and she agreed that he should pursue the matter. He did so vigorously, devoting so much time to the matter that he billed Ingrid for $60,000. Initially Colin spent many hours on legal research into a landlord's responsibility for repairs caused by flooding. He spent even more time on fact investigation. He interviewed many other tenants in Ingrid's building to determine what, if any, problems they had with the landlord, what costs they had incurred as a result of the flood, and who had paid for those costs. Then he persuaded the landlord's lawyer to participate in a mediation process, which took many hours of time but which unfortunately produced no settlement. Eventually, Colin filed a lawsuit and deposed the landlord and the landlord's accountant. During the course of the work, Colin did not consult with Ingrid about whether she wanted him to expend this much time on the matter.

When Ingrid got the bill from Colin, she was aghast. She went to consult another lawyer, Nadia Neruda, about whether Colin's bill was excessive. Ingrid pointed out to Nadia that even if she ultimately collected the full $70,000 from the landlord for the repair work, she would have spent nearly the same amount on the legal fees to obtain this recovery. Nadia called Colin, and she expressed outrage at the size of his fee. As authority for her view, she cited the *Fordham* decision. Colin retained you to negotiate with her and to try to preserve as much of his fee as possible.

## Questions

**1.** How would you evaluate whether your client actually has charged an excessive fee?

**2.** What information would you want to collect before talking to Ingrid's lawyer?

**3.** Colin complied with the requirement in Rule 1.5 that a lawyer who has not regularly represented a client disclose the "basis or rate" of the fee. The rule says this should be done "preferably in writing," but it does not require a writing unless the fee is contingent on the outcome, which this is not. What, if any, additional information about fees should the rule require lawyers like Colin to disclose to their clients?

**4.** Apart from the application of Rule 1.5, has Colin violated any other duties to Ingrid under the rules of professional responsibility or other law?

## d. Modification of fee agreements

If a lawyer represents a client over a long period of time, the lawyer's regular hourly rate might increase during that period. May the lawyer simply begin billing an existing client at the increased rate? In contractual terms, the lawyer is seeking a modification of an ongoing contract. An agreement modifying an initial contract is enforceable if it is "fair and equitable in view of circumstances not anticipated by the parties when the contract was made."[17]

The courts vary in the standards imposed for enforcement of fee modification contracts. Some cases hold that a lawyer may not simply notify a client of an increase in the hourly rates charged.[18] Others require client consent before a lawyer increases the percentage of a settlement retained as a contingent fee.[19] If a lawyer holds up distribution of a settlement until the client consents, the consent may be invalid.[20]

PROBLEM 7-2  **RISING PRICES**

> You are representing Ahmed Halim in a civil lawsuit against Melinda Ramirez. You have filed a complaint and deposed Ramirez, but much remains to be done. Last week your landlord notified you that he will soon raise your office rent by 20 percent. Yesterday, your secretary asked for a substantial raise. These and other recent events have led you to decide that you must increase your hourly rate from $200 to $215. Besides Halim's case, you have over 100 other current clients.
>
> How should you handle the rate increase? Should you
>
> ■ simply include a notice in your next month's bills, explaining why your hourly rate has increased;

---

17. Restatement (Second) of Contracts § 89(a) (1981). The Restatement (Third) of the Law Governing Lawyers asserts that "the client may avoid [such an agreement] unless the lawyer shows that the contract and the circumstances of its formation were fair and reasonable to the client." Restatement § 18(1)(a). Some case law presumes that modifications of legal fee agreements are "presumptively fraudulent" unless the lawyer "demonstrates full disclosure of all the relevant information, client consent based on adequate consideration, and client opportunity to seek independent legal advice before agreeing to the modification." Durr v. Beatty, 491 N.E.2d 902 (Ill. App. 1986). See also Corti v. Fleisher, 417 N.E.2d 764 (Ill. App. 1981); Christian v. Gordon, 2001 WL 883551 (Terr. V.I. June 20, 2001).

18. See, e.g., Severson, Werson, Berke & Melchior v. Bolinger, 1 Cal. Rptr. 2d 531 (Ct. App. 1991) (where a fee agreement provided that law firm would charge client its "regular hourly rates," the law firm was not permitted to raise its rates without the client's consent).

19. See, e.g., In re Thayer, 745 N.E.2d 207 (Ind. 2001) (lawyer violated Rules 1.5(a) and 1.8(a) by presenting client with a fee modification agreement on the day of settlement which increased his fee from 40 percent to 50 percent).

20. Id.

■ send a letter to all your clients explaining that you must increase your hourly rate and notifying them of the reasons and when the prospective increase will take effect;

■ send the same letter as in (2), but also asking the clients to indicate, if they want to continue to use your services, that they assent to the modification by signing and returning the letter; or

■ maintain your present rate for current clients and charge the higher rate only to new clients?

## 2. Regulation of hourly billing and billing for expenses

Until about 1990, many lawyers sent their clients bills that said "for professional services rendered" and then listed an amount to be paid. Few clients inquired as to how the number was arrived at. Since then, however, it has become apparent that some lawyers who agree to bill clients by the hour inflate the amount of time recorded, work more hours than is necessary to complete the task, or bill for time spent doing ministerial tasks. Some also bill clients for personal expenses or bill for legitimate expenses but at a higher rate than the actual cost of those expenses. Although very many lawyers are scrupulously honest about how they calculate fees, some lawyers engage various forms of chicanery to generate higher bills.[21]

### How many lawyers engage in unethical billing practices?

No one really knows how many lawyers have engaged in occasional "padding" or in even more serious misrepresentation of their time or expenses. Some scholars have collected valuable empirical data, which provide a few tentative answers to this question.

Survey data collected by Professor William Ross in 1991 suggests that a majority of lawyers who bill by the hour at least occasionally inflate their hours, and that a smaller percentage of them anonymously admit to larger-scale inflation of hours or fabrication of time records.[22] Most lawyers report that other lawyers engage in billing fraud more often than they themselves do.[23]

In 1994-1995 Ross conducted a second survey to collect information about lawyer billing practices. This one elicited responses from 106 lawyers in private

---

21. One authority has called bill padding "the perfect crime . . . [because] much padding of hours is simply impossible to detect." William G. Ross, The Honest Hour: The Ethics of Time-Based Billing by Attorneys 23 (Carolina Academic Press 1996). In Chapter 9, we consider some cultural and economic factors in law firms that encourage these practices.

22. Professor William Ross of Cumberland School of Law surveyed 500 lawyers and received responses from 272. Of that group, 49 percent of the respondents said that they either "rarely" or "occasionally" billed two clients for the same period of time (engaged in double-billing), while 1.2 percent admitted to "frequent" double-billing. William G. Ross, The Ethics of Hourly Billing by Attorneys, 44 Rutgers L. Rev. 1, 78-83 (1991).

23. Ross asked how often the respondents thought that other lawyers "padded" their hours (recording more time than actually worked), and found that 12.3 percent said other lawyers pad their hours "frequently"; 80.4 percent said "rarely" or "occasionally"; 7.3 percent said "never." Id. at 16.

practice and 91 lawyers who work for corporations.[24] In the second survey, Ross asked what percentage of the time billed by American lawyers "consists of 'padding' for work not actually performed?" Of the lawyers in private practice who responded, 16 percent estimated that 25 percent or more of the hours billed reflected "padding."[25] Ross asked again in the second survey whether the lawyers had ever engaged in "double-billing" (billing two clients for the same period of time) or billed for "recycled" work (billing one client for work that was originally done for another). Seventy-seven percent of the lawyers said they had "never" engaged in double-billing, but 23 percent admitted that they had done so. In this same group, 65.1 percent said they had never billed a client for recycled work, but 34.9 percent reported that they had done so.[26]

In 1999-2000, Professor Susan Saab Fortney asked some questions similar to Ross's in her survey of randomly selected law firm associates in Texas. She received responses from 487 lawyers. Eighty-six percent of her respondents

reported that they had not engaged in double-billing, and 83 percent reported that they had not billed clients for recycled work,[27] meaning that about one in six lawyers in this group indirectly admitted to double-billing or billing for recycled work.

These careful surveys suggest that a very high percentage of lawyers are careful to avoid unethical billing practices, but that a significant percentage of American lawyers at least occasionally engage in unethical billing practices.

*Professor Susan Saab Fortney*

Some law firms have responded to emerging data on improper billing practices by setting policies for the lawyers in their firms and conducting training of their employees to implement those policies. But many lawyers still make decisions about what is proper without the benefit of firm policy or training. In Fortney's 1999-2000 survey, she asked how many respondents worked at law firms that "had written billing guidelines other than those imposed by clients." Forty percent responded affirmatively. "Thirty-six percent of the respondents reported that their firms had no such guidelines. . . . 24 percent . . . checked 'I don't know.'"[28]

Once clients and jurists became aware that some lawyers were taking liberties with their time sheets and expense records, some clients demanded more detailed information about how they spent their time. Judges and ethics committees began

24. William G. Ross, The Honest Hour: The Ethics of Time-Based Billing by Attorneys 6 (Carolina Academic Press 1996).

25. Id. at 265-266. Of the corporate counsel who responded, 17.4 percent estimated that 25 percent or more of the hours billed reflected padding. Id. at 269.

26. Id. at 267. On the double-billing question, 15 percent checked "rarely," 7 percent checked "a moderate number of times," and 1 percent checked "often." On the recycled work question, 18.8 percent checked "rarely," 11.3 percent checked "a moderate number of times," and 4.8 percent checked "often." Id.

27. Susan Saab Fortney, Soul for Sale: An Empirical Study of Associate Satisfaction, Law Firm Culture, and the Effects of Billable Hour Requirements, 69 UMKC L. Rev. 239, 258 (2000).

28. Id. at 253.

to produce opinions spelling out some boundaries on permissible and impermissible billing practices. Some of these boundaries are summarized below.

### No padding or time inflation: A lawyer billing by the hour may not bill for more hours than she actually worked

A lawyer who has agreed to bill based on time worked may not increase the amount of time recorded above the actual time recorded for any reason.[29] Sometimes lawyers pad their hours because they think their work is "worth" more than the amount that would be billed based on time. Sometimes they do it to meet firm demands that they bill a certain number of hours. The ABA Ethics Committee made it clear, however, that this is impermissible: "It goes without saying that a lawyer who has undertaken to bill on an hourly basis is never justified in charging a client for hours not actually expended."[30]

A question remains, however, about whether a lawyer may bill a tenth of an hour for working only one or two minutes. The ABA Ethics Committee clearly stated that an hour is an hour, and a lawyer may not bill more hours than she actually works, except for rounding up to a minimum billing increment. "In matters where the client has agreed to have the fee determined with reference to the time expended by the lawyer, a lawyer may not bill more time than she actually spends on a matter, except to the extent that she rounds up to minimum time periods (such as one-quarter or one-tenth of an hour)."[31] If the ABA intended to require lawyers to conform their practices to consumers' and statisticians' usual expectations about how numbers are rounded, it should have required lawyers to round up only if they used more than half of their usual time increment for a client and to round down if they used less than half of that increment.[32] Lawyers who want to avoid deceiving clients should adopt this method of rounding. However, since the opinion refers only to "rounding up," some lawyers may interpret the opinion to allow lawyers to behave like owners of parking lots, charging their customers for an additional increment of time if they provide even one additional minute of service beyond the previous unit of time changed.

---

29. ABA Comm. on Ethics & Prof. Resp., Formal Op. 93-379 (1993).

30. Id.

31. Id.

32. One typical definition of rounding is found at Rules for Rounding, at http://www.uop.edu/cop/psychology/Statistics/Rounding.html (last visited Oct. 24, 2004):

There are three general rules for rounding:

Rule 1 — If the remainder *beyond the last digit* to be reported is less than 5, drop the last digit. Rounding to one decimal place, the number 5.3467 becomes 5.3.

Rule 2 — If the remainder is greater than 5, increase the final digit by 1. The number 5.798 becomes 5.8 if rounding to 1 digit.

Rule 3 — To prevent rounding bias, if the remainder is exactly 5, then round the last digit to the *closest even number*. Thus the number 3.55 (rounded to 1 digit) would be 3.6 (rounding up) and the number 6.450 would round to 6.4 (rounding down) if rounding to 1 decimal.

See also Russell Hurlburt, Comprehending Behavioral Statistics 12 (Wadsworth 1994).

FOR EXAMPLE:   Lawyer Gerald F. Phillips reported that in California, a senior partner who billed $175 per hour used 18-minute increments as his routine billing period. He "recorded a one-minute telephone call as eighteen minutes, [and] billed the client $52.50 for work that should have cost only $3 if billed for the time actually spent."[33]

Some authorities believe that undisclosed rounding up combined with large billing increments impose on clients millions of dollars of unearned legal fees every year.[34] Perhaps the ABA should revisit this issue and amend its opinion so that clients are better protected.

## No inventing hours that weren't really worked

The ABA opinion made clear that padding hours is unethical. Another related practice reported by some lawyers is simply to fabricate time records out of thin air and then bill for them as if the hours were real.

FOR EXAMPLE:   Bill Duker was a very successful New York lawyer. Duker got a Ph.D. from the University of Cambridge, England, and then a law degree from Yale. After a clerkship, he spent several years as an associate at Cravath, Swain & Moore. After a few years as a law professor, he started his own firm and became an expert in litigation involving professional misconduct. Between 1990 and 1995, he earned between $1 million and $5 million per year. As managing partner, Duker reviewed the time records of all the other lawyers in his firm. As he reviewed them, he wrote instructions to his bookkeeper as to how many hours should be added to those recorded by the lawyers, systematically increasing the number of hours billed out to the federal banking agency that was his biggest client. In this fashion, he overbilled his client by at least $1.4 million. After this was discovered, Duker was indicted and plead guilty to charges of mail fraud, filing false claims, making false statements, and obstructing a federal audit. He was sentenced to 33 months in prison. In a related civil settlement, Duker agreed to pay the agency over $2.5 million. He was disbarred in 1997.[35]

At least a few lessons emerge from Duker's story. One is that if a lawyer inflates his hours and then transmits the resulting bill to a client, he may be charged with federal mail fraud or other crimes. This has happened to a surprising number of lawyers in recent years.[36] Another is that some highly

---

33. Gerald F. Phillips, Time Bandits: Attempts by Lawyers to Pad Hours Can Often Be Uncovered by a Careful Examination of Billing Statements, 29 W. St. U. L. Rev. 265, 273 (2002). Phillips is in a position to speak with authority on where the bar should draw the line between acceptable and fraudulent billing methods. He practiced for 38 years in the firm of Phillips, Nizer, Benjamin, Krim & Ballon.

34. Id at 273 n. 38.

35. This story is recounted in Lisa G. Lerman, Blue-Chip Bilking: Regulation of Billing and Expense Fraud by Lawyers, 12 Geo. J. Leg. Ethics 205 (1999).

36. Id.

educated, intelligent, and successful lawyers — some of whom even specialize in professional responsibility — don't obey the rules.

Some lawyers who bill for fictitious hours are not detected or punished. One large-firm associate related these examples:

> I used to prepare the bills for a client. . . . I was working on a bill . . . and . . . one of the managing partners of the firm was written down [as having spent] ten or twenty hours [working for that client that] month. I went in to my boss . . . and said, "Did [Steve Whitman] work on this case?" . . . And he said, "No, no. He didn't. . . . He . . . [explained] that [Steve] spends so much time managing the firm and not doing client business, that in order to justify his existence and salary every month, he just sort of [picks] some clients that are decent-sized clients and throws a few hours onto their bills. This was known in the firm as the [Whitman] Tax. Someone later [asked], "Oh, you didn't know about the Whitman Tax" — "Oh, that was the first time you got socked with the Whitman Tax?" And you had to hide it in the bill. You couldn't put this guy's name [down] at a billing rate of $285 an hour — and you just sort of had to swallow it. There were lots of things like that where you were really in a tough spot. You were told to do it, . . . you couldn't run and tell the management of the firm . . . because they were the ones doing it. And if you tattled to the client, . . . [you would get] fired. So you really were really [stuck].
>
> Another partner that I worked for [he was the billing partner] — used to . . . just twiddle his thumbs most of the time and read magazines in his office. [Occasionally he really worked hard, but not most of the time.] . . . At the end of the month, he would ask for my time sheets and [those of] another associate who worked on cases for him. . . . He would manufacture his own [time sheets] based on how many hours we were working and when our peak times were — just sort of pro-rated and figured what his own time should have been. A total fabrication, but sort of "What would be a reasonable thing for me [to charge for] . . . supervising these two?" And that's how he would construct his month.
>
> [A third partner I worked for] used to have . . . a sort of warped sense of the value of his services, [which] had nothing to do with hours or time, which is, of course, what the client was being told they were billed for. So, for example, if we had a really good phone call with the Department of Energy . . . and felt it furthered the client's cause, that was a ten hour phone call. Sometimes, curiously enough, there were more than twenty-four hours in a day if he'd had a really good day. . . . He had grandiose notions . . . about the value of his work. . . .[37]

### No profits on costs: A lawyer may not bill for "overhead" or mark up costs

A lawyer may bill a client for costs incurred in the course of representation, such as postage or messenger service. However, a lawyer may not bill the client more than the actual cost of the service to the lawyer. The ABA Ethics Committee said very clearly that turning your copy room into a profit

---

37. Lisa G. Lerman, Gross Profits? Questions about Lawyer Billing Practices, 22 Hofstra L. Rev. 645, 646-647 (1994) (quoting from a confidential interview with a lawyer).

center is prohibited. "The lawyer's stock in trade is the sale of legal services, not photocopy paper, tuna fish sandwiches, computer time or messenger services."[38] It also concluded that while a lawyer may bill a client at cost for disbursements and for services provided in-house, it is improper to bill clients for general overhead costs, which should be covered by lawyers' ample hourly fees.[39] What counts as non-billable overhead? The Committee offered as examples the cost of running a library, purchasing malpractice insurance, or paying for office space, heating, or air conditioning.

The ABA opinion was triggered in part by a 1991 article in *American Lawyer* reporting a fee dispute involving Skadden Arps, Meagher & Flom in which the client had discovered that the law firm had added surcharges onto many costs billed to clients. For example, the firm billed the client $33.60 for coffee and pastries for four people, which in 1991 seemed like an outrageous sum. But the firm also billed for faxes (both incoming and outgoing) by the page, as well as $35-45 per hour for the staff person who watched over the fax machine.[40]

Once the ABA made clear that lawyers might earn profits from legal services but not by marking up other costs, one would have assumed that law firms, especially large prominent law firms, would have changed policy to comply with this interpretation of the ethics rules. Apparently this isn't what happened. In 1995, one large firm surveyed 30 others and found that markups on costs were still commonplace. The results of the survey were leaked to *American Lawyer*, which reported:

> Eleven of the 30 firms charged at least $2 per page for an outgoing domestic fax. Twenty-one of the firms marked up telephone charges. Eighteen firms charged 20 cents or more a page for photocopying. And 13 of the 30 firms admitted to marking up LEXIS charges, five by as much as 50 percent.[41]

## No double-billing: A lawyer may not bill two clients for one period of time

If a lawyer does work that benefits two clients, and the lawyer is billing both clients based on time, the lawyer may bill each client for half the time expended or, with their consent, may allocate the time in some other way. But the lawyer may not bill the block of time twice. This may seem obvious and logical, but double-billing has been common practice in some firms.[42] A former paralegal at a large firm remembered this story:

> In preparation for litigation and anticipated discovery on behalf of Client A, I was sent on a trip . . . to the client's HQ to review document files. . . . Meanwhile,

---

38. See also In re Zaleon, 504 S.E.2d 702 (Ga. 1998) (lawyer disciplined for charging client above cost for disbursements without disclosing to the client that the lawyer was doing so).

39. ABA Comm. on Ethics & Prof. Resp., Formal Op. 93-379 (1993); see also Restatement § 38(3)(a).

40. Skaddenomics, Am. Law., Sept. 1991, at 3.

41. Karen Dillon, Dumb and Dumber, Am. Law., Oct. 1995, at 5.

42. See, e.g., Kevin Hopkins, Law Firms, Technology, and the Double-Billing Dilemma, 12 Geo. J. Leg. Ethics 93 (1998).

a matter involving Client B was heating up. . . . The partner handling the Client B matter was also handling Client A. He asked that I take some of the [Client B] depositions with me and digest them while on the road. He also said something to the effect, "Besides, it will give you something to do on the plane." Apprising the partner of the firm policy to bill transportation time to the client (in this case Client A), I asked how I should bill the time I spent digesting the depositions for Client B. He responded that I should bill the total transportation time to Client A and the time spent digesting depositions to Client B. In other words, double bill. . . . [L]ater, in similar situations, the senior paralegal in charge of assignments let it be known that this is how billing was to be handled.[43]

This incident took place before the ABA ethics opinion made clear that double-billing was unethical. This practice is less common than it used to be, but it still happens.

### No billing a second client for recycled work

ABA Opinion 93-379 asks, what if a lawyer does "research on a particular topic for one client that later turns out to be relevant to an inquiry from a second client. May the firm bill the second client, who agreed to be charged on the basis of time spent on his case, the same amount for the recycled work product that it charged the first client?" The ABA says that it may not:

> A lawyer who is able to reuse old work product has not re-earned the hours previously billed and compensated when the work product was first generated. Rather than looking to profit from . . . the luck of being asked the identical question twice, the lawyer who has agreed to bill solely on the basis of time spent is obliged to pass the benefits of these economies on to the client. The practice of billing several clients for the same time or work product, since it results in the earning of an unreasonable fee, therefore is contrary to the mandate of . . . Model Rule 1.5.

### No churning or running the meter: A lawyer may not do unnecessary extra work in order to justify billing more hours

One of the biggest problems with hourly billing is that it provides lawyers with an enormous incentive to be inefficient. The more time the work takes, the more they get paid. Often the judgment of what "needs" to be done is extremely subjective, so a lawyer can err on the side of thoroughness, spend lots of extra time, and be well within the range of normal professional conduct. One lawyer whom we call "Winston Hall" described this problem:

> The most common [type of deception], by far, is makework that the client pays for but that didn't lead very directly to the result. That describes an enormous percentage of the activity that I think goes on in law firms.[44]

---

43. This story is recounted in Lisa G. Lerman, Lying to Clients, 138 U. Pa. L. Rev. 659, 710 (1990).

44. Id. at 706-708, quoting an associate at a large firm. The subsequent quotes from the Hall interview are excerpted from this article.

One partner in Hall's firm had explained to him that

> [L]aw practice is somewhat supply-side driven. You can decide how heavily you are going to bill on a matter. There is a wide range of acceptability. If you've got the people, you do more work; if you don't have the people, then you don't.

Hall described a major lobbying matter that his firm handled for a big industry. "We spent half a million dollars tracking this legislation — eight people working on it essentially full-time." The firm billed this time primarily to two clients. The firm hoped to attract additional clients in this area, so part of the work product (reports analyzing the legislation) was sent to 300 people. The reports covered many issues that would have no impact on the clients who were paying for the work. Hall thinks that "it was all done without the client knowing that it was being billed to them." Several months into this project, representatives of the client companies began coming to the law firm to work with the lawyers on preparation of testimony and other tasks. Disaster struck:

> It was like a customer going to the kitchen of a restaurant. They saw eight people running around . . . [who] didn't have carefully defined ends and means. We didn't know all that they expected us to know, didn't have the

access that they expected us to have. . . . They just saw what was actually going on and they were utterly horrified. The shit hit the fan and there were lots of fights. Ultimately we had a reconciliation, and we kept doing the work. But not too long after that . . . they said enough . . . no more . . . no more time billed to this matter.

If clients understood the broad scope of the lawyer's discretion, they might exercise more control over what work was to be done. Hall elaborates:

The worst clients from the point of view of a lawyer are the ex-partners from the firm . . . who know damn well . . . [that lawyers do work to run the meter]. One lawyer . . . who [left to become general counsel of a client bank] would say, "I don't want a single memo written about this" . . . because he knew exactly what happens.

Comment 5 to Rule 1.5 says: "A lawyer should not exploit a fee arrangement based primarily on hourly charges by using wasteful procedures." ABA Opinion 93-379 also addressed this question with an unequivocal "don't do it."

Continuous toil on or overstaffing a project for the purpose of churning out hours is also not properly considered "earning" one's fees. . . . Just as a lawyer is expected to discharge a matter on summary judgment if possible rather than proceed to trial, so too is the lawyer expected to complete other projects for a client efficiently. A lawyer should take as much time as is reasonably required to complete a project, and should certainly never be motivated by anything other than the best interests of the client when determining how to staff or how much time to spend on any particular project.

## No billing clients or the firm for personal expenses or marking up expense receipts

Lots of lawyers have gotten in bad trouble (discipline, prosecution, civil liability, loss of employment, to name a few) for charging their clients or their firms for personal expenses or for inflating their claimed business expenses.

Some cases involve small amounts. A first-year associate named Thomas Schneider simply added a "1" in front of eight receipts for under $100. He claimed he was just doing that to get reimbursed for some expenses for which he didn't have receipts. He was suspended from practice for 30 days.[45]

Other cases involve much larger amounts of money. Webster Hubbell, while managing partner of his firm, paid personal credit card bills on ten different cards out of firm accounts. These were among over 400 instances of financial fraud, which also included inflation of hours billed, that amounted to $480,000 in billing and expense fraud. The discovery of this misconduct required his resignation from his position as associate attorney general in the Clinton administration. Hubbell was also disbarred and plead guilty to criminal charges of mail fraud. He was sentenced to 21 months in prison.[46]

---

45. In re Schneider, 553 A.2d 206 (D.C. 1989). Curiously, like Bill Duker, Mr. Schneider had earned a Ph.D. in addition to his law degree; Duker's was from Cambridge, Schneider's was from Oxford.

46. Lerman, supra n. 35, at 213.

## No billing by the hour at lawyer rates for administrative services

Lawyers charge high hourly rates compared to plumbers, electricians, psychiatrists, auto mechanics, and anyone else who bills by the hour. The idea is that the high hourly rate is justified by the notion that the lawyer is using a high level of professional skill during the hours billed. The high rates are also justified by reference to the overhead and staff salaries that must be paid out of legal fees. Clients may assume that lawyers delegate to staff work that could be done by nonlawyers and that senior lawyers delegate simpler work to less experienced (and cheaper) lawyers. But most lawyers spend some time doing administrative work that does not involve a high level of professional skill. Is this time billable? A lawyer whom we call "Madeline Stein" offered this example:

> After days of working nearly non-stop on a large case for a large corporate client, the ... entire office becomes inundated with documents, drafts of pleadings, xeroxed cases, and notes. Cleaning up becomes imperative, and most of it involves sorting, filing and throwing away, with no more thought involved than the discretion of one who is intimately involved with the case. . . . Is [this time] billable? If so, does one write "straighten office" on the billing sheet?
>
> I would most normally bill the time, perhaps discounting it a bit for sorting other clients' papers and for the nature of the work. But I would not let the client or the billing partner know I was billing for cleaning my office — it just doesn't sound right. And besides, it is necessary work that must be done for proper case management . . . by the person who created the mess. . . . So I bill it to "case management" or "legal research" or "draft pleadings."[47]

The ABA opinion did not address whether this type of work is legitimately billable at lawyer rates. However, as Stein pointed out, this cleanup work really needs to be done by the lawyer who did the work because she knows which documents must be retained and how to assemble them.

While some administrative services may be legitimately billable at lawyer rates, query whether lawyers should bill for administrative tasks that could be delegated to a staff person. In 2000, the Colorado Supreme Court held that lawyers should not bill hourly rates for clerical services. In the case before the court, there were "multiple entries reflecting the faxing of documents to the client and opposing counsel, entries for calls made to the court of appeals clerk's office, and the delivery of documents to opposing counsel." Applying Colorado's Rule 1.5, the court concluded that "charging an attorney's hourly rate for clerical services that are generally performed by a non-lawyer, and thus for which an attorney's professional skill and knowledge add no value to the service, is unreasonable as a matter of law."[48]

---

47. Lerman, supra n. 43, at 719.

48. In re Green, 11 P.3d 1078, 1088-1089 (Colo. 2000). The court cited other decisions that reached similar conclusions.

### Billing for time spent billing

If a lawyer bills by the hour, may the lawyer bill the client for time she spends explaining her billing practices to the client? What about the time she spends preparing the bills? Or time spent writing or calling clients to urge them to pay their bills? One opinion from the Indiana Supreme Court suggests that billing for time spent billing is improper, but this opinion is ambiguous.[49]

## Billing Irregularities: A Case Study

You are about to read a story about one associate's unhappy experience in a law firm. Some of the themes raised in this story are revisited in the discussion of professional satisfaction in Chapter 9. Here, however, we focus on evaluating the many billing practices that the lawyer found troubling.

### Lisa G. Lerman, Scenes from a Law Firm[50]

50 Rutgers L. Rev. 2153 (1998)

*The real "Nicholas Farber"*

What follows is one lawyer's description of his experiences at a law firm [an insurance defense firm of about 50 lawyers] where he worked. . . . The lawyer, whom I call "Nicholas Farber," . . . agreed to allow me to publish the stories only if neither he nor the firm would be identified, because some of the stories involve serious misconduct. . . .

#### An idealistic beginning

When I started at the firm it was ten years old. The firm began as an offshoot of another firm. . . . The founding partner at my firm disagreed with the

---

49. The holding is ambiguous because, in that case, the lawyer had never done the work he had been hired to do:

> The respondent billed the client $943 for writing two letters to him: one outlining the procedure that might be employed in collecting the debt [due to the client] (and supporting the initial charged fee of $583), the second demanding payment of the bill incurred for the preparation of the first letter. That the respondent never got around to making a bona fide attempt actually to collect the debt (i.e., contacting the debtor) reflects the unreasonable nature of charging the $943 fee. We therefore find that the respondent attempted to exact from his client an unreasonable fee, . . . in violation of Prof. Cond. R. 1.5(a). In re Schneider, 710 N.E.2d 178, 181 (Ind. 1999).

50. [Article's note.] This article was co-authored with the lawyer whom I call "Nicholas Farber." Because of the sensitivity of the material and the need for confidentiality, he decided not to identify himself as a co-author. Initially Farber told me these stories during a tape-recorded interview. I transcribed portions of the tape, edited the transcript, and organized the stories into a draft. Farber then reviewed the draft and made some stylistic and other changes. Small factual changes have been made to obscure the identity of the firm and the lawyers discussed. In every important respect, however, this narrative is faithful to Farber's account. The interview with "Nicholas Farber" was conducted on May 8, 1996. I reproduced portions of the transcript of the interview with minor editing.

philosophy of the firm he came from. . . . He didn't think that they were pro-moting young associates to equity partner quickly enough. He thought he could do a better job of building a firm where people would have lives as well as jobs. . . .

### How many hours were associates expected to bill each year?

2000 hours for associates. Partners always billed at least 2000. 2000 was your target. They would always say, "If you fall short it's no big deal." But that was a lie. . . . Those who got significant bonuses typically billed well over 2000. . . . I heard the highest number of hours a lawyer at the firm billed in a year was 2600. . . .

### You've got to "add value"

From the very beginning . . . I was told that "We are not out to churn out five Cadillacs or Mercedes-Benzs a year, what we are here to churn out is 150 Fords." "We'd rather that you would do a C job on 150 cases than an A job on fifty cases." "You have to 'add value' to the firm." . . . "We're paying you X amount of dollars and it's costing us this much to keep you on board, so you have to find a way to make yourself profitable." . . . "Adding value" meant churning out as many billable hours as you could and doing as much market-ing as you could.

### A "discount law firm"

We were told by the partners . . . that we could do a lot of this billing that we did . . . because our rate was so low. . . . The client was only paying $75 or $80 per hour for associates, so what did you care if you padded the bill for three times that because that is what we are worth. The firm was a "discount law firm" for this one insurance company. That is why we got so many of their cases. . . . We were supposed to be billing at rates much lower than most places. . . .

[The partners always told me my hours were too low.] I billed honestly. . . . I billed 1600 to 1800 hours a year. . . . At one point they told me that I had the lowest billable hours in the firm. I didn't think that was possible, because I had just had a conversation with another associate who told me that her hours only added up to 1450. But that was part of their game, . . . to tell you that you are the lowest in your group and maybe the lowest in the firm. I guess they thought that news like this would shame me into billing more hours.

I was always in the office by seven and I tried to leave by five-thirty. I rarely took a full hour for lunch. I just closed my door and tried to work as much as I could. I didn't want to spend evenings and weekends there if I didn't have to. Nobody spent as much time at work as I did, but they billed more. When I asked, "I'm here all the time, why don't my hours add up to as much as the other associates' do?" The partners would say, "Well they are taking work home."

### "Okay, here's the deal"

The partners were very careful not to instruct us to do dishonest billing. Early on, a partner came to see me and said, "Your hours are the lowest in the practice group, maybe the lowest in the firm." The partner said: "So and so's billing 2200 hours, why don't you go and talk to him? See if he can show you anything. Maybe you are not writing things down, or maybe you are not billing for things that you should be. Go find out what he's doing." And . . . they sent me to the most senior associates in the group, who had played the game. . . . I went to see two people. They each closed the door behind me and said, "Okay here's the deal."

The first lawyer gave me this tip: "You have . . . fifty or sixty files. . . . You need to find a reason to make a telephone call to somebody involved in each file." He said something like: "You think about it, you've got the client, you've got experts, you've got opposing counsel. Think of all the people you can call. Find a reason to call somebody. Make the call. You bill for the call. When you hang up the phone you immediately do a confirmatory letter. Then you bill for the letter. And if the adjuster will let you, you do a memo to the adjuster . . . on what transpired during the call. Then bill for the memo. So you bill three times per call." And he said, "A month shouldn't go by without this happening at least once to every case." In other words, create a reason, and then create a bunch of work to go with it, and it looks like you are just being on top of the situation. . . .

### [Was the timekeeping fairly precise?]

The timekeeping wasn't really that accurate. You'd get on the phone and talk, but . . . you'd bill the telephone call and confirmatory letter . . . at .5. Some people would actually put .6 for this, the senior associate told me. .5 you could get away with, .4 would be unquestioned. . . . He was telling me how to gauge how much I could squeeze out of each piece of work by thinking about how it looked rather than how much time it actually took.

### The magic number

The other associate said . . . he just kept a list of the tasks that he did each day and tried to keep an estimate of the time it took for each task. At the end of the day he would add it all up. If it didn't equal 8.6, he would just inflate it so that it did. I said, "Why the magic number 8.6?" He said, "Well, that's the number of hours you need to bill every day in order to get three weeks paid vacation and all your holidays off. That's how you make sure you make your 2000 hours." . . . So there's a technique.

### Crank out the forms

Many people told me that a good technique to increase one's billable hours was to crank out these forms — discovery requests, interrogatories, requests for production of documents — they are on the machine. . . . We use them for every single case. You change a few things specific to the case that you are working on and you bill as if you had created it from scratch. . . . You could really make some money billing there.

### How did you decide how much to bill for each task? . . .

I would ask another lawyer: "How much did you bill for that?" and he would say "Oh, .8." I would ask: "Well how did you arrive at that?" The other lawyer would say, "That's just what we bill. Everybody does." I think if you bill too many .5s and 1.0s, it looks as if you are faking it. Therefore they used smaller fractions.

### Easy billing

One lawyer told me . . . he was happy because he was involved in one case in which there were a lot of parties. He would get a lot of pleadings that didn't require him to do much of anything except to read them and know what was happening. . . . If one party filed a motion . . . and he was not going to oppose it, . . . he would read the documents, and bill for that time. Sometimes . . . they would serve discovery on other parties, and he wouldn't even read the documents, but he would bill for it: . . . "receipt and review of the following:" That's how he made up his time, by whatever came in the mail. He could bill as if he had read it.

   This associate got the highest merit bonus that year. . . . He's playing the game the way they wanted him to play it, so he'll be made a non-equity partner at some point.

### Triple billing

I was routinely told to double and triple bill my time. If I spent an hour doing one thing, the partner would urge me to find a way to do three things in that hour. Then I could bill three different hours to three different clients. For example, the partner told me that he wanted me to get a car phone and carry a Dictaphone with me all the time because I spent a lot of time driving . . . to depositions, court hearings, and things like that. That time in the car, he said, was wasted time. I said, "I bill for the travel time." He said, "You could be billing for the travel time, reviewing things at stop lights, making telephone calls, or dictating deposition summaries. You could be billing for all of that." . . .

   I didn't want to get a Dictaphone and a car phone. . . . I didn't want to have a traffic accident. I felt I had enough on my mind going to and from court. . . . But beyond that, I need to think to do work well. . . . I wanted to be able to close the door and sit down in my office and do a good solid depo summary. . . . Because I was inexperienced, I wanted to think things through, do a thorough job. It seems all they were concerned about was volume. . . .

### Fifteen hours of paralegal time

There was a rule for this particular client that no more than fifteen hours of paralegal time could be billed for a single case. If you had to use more than that, you had to get permission in advance from an adjuster. . . . The lawyers often got too busy and they asked paralegals to do work that lawyers were supposed to do. . . . In some cases the paralegals would come in and say, "I've hit my fifteen hour limit" and stop. . . . Other times they would work and work and work, and bill and bill and bill. Then you'd get a pre-bill that said "Paralegal time: 65 hours." If the bill went to the insurance company that way, the adjuster would just . . . subtract fifty hours. . . . So when the pre-bill came out, if there were more than fifteen hours of paralegal time, we were told to turn them into attorney time. In other words, you didn't do the work, but just say you did.

I am not sure whether the client was billed at attorney rates for the same number of hours worked or whether the firm computed the difference in the billing rate and reduced the number of hours accordingly . . . but I think they didn't bother to change the rate. . . .

On one occasion I went to my partner and said, "There's all this paralegal work on the pre-bill that is over the fifteen hour limit. . . . What should I do about it?" He said, "Well whatever is over, just make sure that the narrative describing the work reads properly and then change the initials to yours." I said, "But I wasn't even at the firm when this work was done!" He said, "Well then, bill it as the attorney who was here during that time period so there won't be any question." . . .

### Billing off the secretaries

People routinely billed off their secretaries. . . . They'd give their secretaries a list of phone calls to make . . . and tell them to keep a list of how long it took for each call. Then at the end of the day, the secretary would hand the attorney a list of telephone calls. . . . The attorney would bill his time sheets for all of them . . . as if he had done the work.

### Are you sure?

Absolutely.

### How do you know?

They told me how to do it. In fact, I shared a secretary with another associate, and she said, "Do you want me to keep track of my time?" I said, "Why would you keep track of your time?" "So you can bill on it," she said.

### Did they bill for secretarial time?

No.

### So the only reason that a secretary would have been keeping time . . .

. . . would be so that her attorney . . . could bill for the time. . . . That's how they made their 2000 hours.

### Pressure to pad

The associate merit bonus program was completely tied to billable hours. . . . The partners denied that. They would say, "It's a wide range of factors that we take into consideration . . . pro bono work, . . . bar functions, . . . community service, . . . marketing, . . . all these . . . wonderful things that make you a well-rounded spirited participant here at the firm." But when the list came out, anybody under 2000 didn't get a bonus, and almost everybody over 2000 got a bonus. The more an associate's hours exceeded 2000, the bigger the bonus. . . . The associates who got the biggest bonuses . . . were some of the ones who had taught me some of these tricks.

### Did you pad your bills at all in response to that pressure?

I did, to a certain extent. I remember thinking, "I'm going to have to do something here so I don't get fired." . . . I'd pad them enough that I felt I wasn't going to get fired but . . . it wasn't going to put me in contention for a massive bonus. . . .

### Is there anybody who wasn't padding bills?

Oh yes. They were usually the lawyers who quit on their own, or who were constantly being harped on (like I was) for not meeting the billing requirements. It usually took people about a year to figure out what it is that they were trying to get you to do. And then you either stay and play the game or you leave.

There were two partners who billed honestly. They routinely billed in the 2000-2100 range each year. But they had no lives — they [usually] worked seven days a week, ten to twelve hour days. . . .

### Hit it for .5

If you thought about a file while you were mowing the lawn over the weekend, you were to come in Monday and bill it .5, because you were thinking about that file. . . . If you woke up in the middle of the night because you were worrying about a case, and you couldn't get back to sleep because you were thinking about things that had to be done, . . . the first thing you were supposed to do when you woke up in the morning was "hit" that file for .5. . . . Half an hour. "Well, what do you call it?" I would ask. "Review of file, plan strategy for discovery," I was told.

If you and some of the other associates at the firm went to a ball game, and at the ball game you talked about a file, . . . you could bill for that time. . . .

### Thwarting the auditors

We were told to bill for travel time. . . . None of us were supposed to bill more than 8.6 hours in any given day. . . . The insurance company would be very suspicious of an eleven hour day. So we were told sometimes to move hours. If you did the work on that Thursday but Friday was a lower day, then move some of those hours over there. But make sure [the work you are billing for is] not a letter, because the date has to match. But if it's legal research, then move it, but you need to fit it in so that the client doesn't become suspicious.

One insurance company client had hired a company to go over its bills. All of the time manipulation was designed to thwart the guy checking the bill.

### Billing envy

This is how warped I became there — I remember thinking it would be so wonderful to work on one of the other litigation teams because they had really huge cases that lasted five years. The lawyers in that group would routinely bill eight hours a day to nothing but legal research. Their bills would never be questioned because there was so much research to be done that you could bill a forty hour week to legal research. . . .

If I had worked in that group it would have been so much easier to meet my billables. There wouldn't have been so much pressure. . . .

I know plenty of ethical attorneys. . . . I know people who . . . cut their bills just to be fair to clients. There are people out there like that, but you have got to search for them. They are not so common. . . .

## Questions about Scenes from a Law Firm

**1.** Consider each problem that Farber identifies. Do you agree with Farber that the behavior described is unethical? If you do, think about why. If some of Farber's examples seem ethically proper, consider why your judgment differs from Farber's.

**2.** Suppose you are an associate in the firm where Nicholas Farber once worked, and you are experiencing the same pressures and observing the same problems that he observed. What would you do? Do the ethical rules mandate any particular response?

**3.** What if you are a partner in Farber's old firm? Would your reaction to the situation be different? Would your duties under the ethical rules be different?

**4.** Lerman interviewed Farber and published a longer version of the edited transcript of the interview. She promised Farber that she would not identify him or his law firm to anyone. Did she violate the rules by not reporting Farber or his colleagues to the disciplinary authorities?

**5.** If you have worked in a law firm, how does the conduct Farber described compare with conduct you have observed? If you have seen examples of conduct that might involve billing or expense fraud, write down these examples so that you can evaluate what you observed in light of what you have learned in the previous section. Consider whether they differ from those that Farber observed, and think about why. If you have worked in a law firm whose "ethical culture" was very different from that at Farber's firm, what accounts for the difference in firm cultures?

## 3. Contingent fees

### a. In general

Though the ethical rules impose relatively few constraints on lawyers regarding legal fees, they impose more restrictions if the fee is contingent on the result achieved for the client. A common type of contingent fee is one that is calculated as a percentage of the client's recovery. Another type of contingent fee is one in which the client pays an hourly fee or a flat fee, but pays the lawyer an additional fee if a specified result occurred.[51]

Our discussion above of misconduct in relation to hourly fees suggests that there is reason for concern about dishonesty or overreaching by lawyers billing by the hour. Historically, however, the bar has been more concerned about lawyers who have a financial stake in their clients' recoveries since they may engage in improper tactics to make sure their clients get good recoveries (in which they will share).[52]

Until the latter part of the twentieth century, contingent fees were viewed with suspicion and frowned upon by the bar. Over time, the use of contingent fees has become more accepted. One reason is that many clients who do not have the funds to hire lawyers cannot obtain representation unless the fee is paid out of the client's recovery. Contingent fees allow access to justice for people who are not wealthy. Also, while the use of an hourly fee sets up a conflict between the lawyer's interests and the client's, the use of a contingent fee usually aligns the interests of lawyer and client. If the lawyer is to be paid a percentage of the client's recovery, the better the client does, the better the lawyer does. While some ethical concerns about contingent fees persist, the rules allow lawyers to charge contingent fees except if the fee is contingent on achieving a particular outcome in a criminal case or a domestic relation case.[53] Still, the rules impose more specific disclosure requirements for contingent fees than for other legal fees.

### Rule 1.5(c)

| Rule language* | Authors' explanation |
| --- | --- |
| A fee **may be contingent** on the outcome of the matter for which the service is rendered, except in a matter in which a contingent fee is **prohibited by paragraph (d) or other law.** | Rule 1.5(d) bars contingent fees in many criminal and domestic relations cases. See p. 444. Other law sometimes bars such fees. Rule 1.5(a) requires that contingent fees be reasonable. Comment 3. |

*Continued*

---

51. Restatement § 35, comment a.

52. See Rule 1.8(i) restricting lawyers from acquiring a proprietary interest in litigation, discussed in Section A4a.

53. See Restatement § 35(1).

| Rule language* | Authors' explanation |
| --- | --- |
| A contingent fee agreement shall be **in a writing signed by the client** and shall **state the method by which the fee is to be determined,** including the **percentage** or percentages that shall accrue to the lawyer in the event of settlement, trial or appeal;<br><br>**litigation and other expenses to be deducted** from the recovery;<br><br>and **whether such expenses are to be deducted before or after the contingent fee is calculated.** | The agreement must specify the percentage of the recovery to be earned by the lawyer and indicate whether the percentage to be charged depends on how the case proceeds.<br><br><br><br>The agreement must explain whether expenses are to be deducted from the total settlement or judgment before or after the lawyer's fee is calculated. |
| The agreement must clearly **notify** the client of any **expenses for which the client will be liable** whether or not the client is the prevailing party. | The agreement needs to explain which expenses the client must pay even if she gets no recovery. |
| Upon **conclusion** of a contingent fee matter, the lawyer shall provide the client with a **written statement stating the outcome of the matter and, if there is a recovery, showing the remittance to the client and the method of its determination.** | When the matter is concluded, the lawyer must provide this client with another writing explaining what fee and expenses were charged and how they were calculated. |

*All emphasis added.

## What difference does it make whether expenses are deducted from the client's recovery before or after the lawyer's fee is calculated?

This is best explained by example. Suppose a client is injured in a car accident. The lawyer sues the other driver, who was at fault, and obtains a verdict for the client of $100,000. Litigation expenses were $10,000. The lawyer is to receive a contingent fee of 40 percent of the recovery. If the lawyer's fee is calculated before expenses are taken out, here's what happens:

### Fee calculated before expenses subtracted

| | |
| --- | --- |
| Total recovery: | $100,000 |
| Lawyer's fee: | 40,000 |
| Expenses: | 10,000 |
| Client's recovery: | 50,000 |

Suppose instead that the expenses are deducted from the total amount before the lawyer's fee is calculated. Here's what happens:

### Fee calculated after expenses subtracted

| | |
|---|---|
| Total recovery: | $100,000 |
| Expenses: | 10,000 |
| Lawyer's fee: | 36,000 |
| Client's recovery: | 54,000 |

If the litigation expenses are higher, the client's recovery would be affected even more than in this example by whether the fee is calculated before or after expenses are taken out. The rule requires a lawyer to disclose to a client how the lawyer intends to calculate the fee. Note that the rule does not require lawyers to deduct expenses before calculating their fees or to offer clients an option to do so.

## Is there any limit on what percentage of the recovery a lawyer may charge as a contingent fee?

The rule does not specify a maximum percentage that may be charged, but contingent fees, like other fees, are subject to the requirement of Rule 1.5 that they be "reasonable." In some jurisdictions, however, other law imposes a ceiling on the percentage that may be charged or imposes other restrictions.

## Is it fair for a lawyer to take 30 or 40 percent of a client's recovery as a contingent fee?

That depends. One justification for the use of contingent fees is that, in some cases, it is very uncertain whether the client will obtain any recovery. The lawyer takes a risk in such cases that he will invest substantial time and obtain no fee for the work. If the contingent fee in successful cases is generous to the lawyer, it compensates for the risk of obtaining no fee in unsuccessful cases.

In some cases, it is fair for the lawyer to get 30 or 40 percent of the client's damages because the lawyer has invested substantial time to obtain that recovery. In other cases, however, the risk of nonrecovery is minimal or nonexistent, and the work required to obtain the recovery is modest. In such cases, some scholars argue, it is not fair for a lawyer to take such a hefty percentage of the recovery. They assert that the norm of a one-third contingent fee in the legal profession allows lawyers to take more than their fair share of the recovery in some percentage of these cases.[54] Other scholars suggest that contingent fee lawyers do not earn higher fees than those of other lawyers.[55] If, however, legal fees are

---

54. See Lester Brickman, Contingent Fees without Contingencies: Hamlet without the Prince of Denmark? 37 UCLA L. Rev. 29, 105-111 (1989).

55. See Herbert M. Kritzer, The Wages of Risk: The Returns of Contingency Fee Legal Practice, 47 DePaul L. Rev. 267, 290-299, 302 (1998).

unreasonably high, it's not much comfort if contingent fees are comparable to others.[56]

Another justification often offered for large contingent fees is that many lawyers who handle contingent fee matters earn fees in some matters but not others. The relatively high fees in some cases cross-subsidizes lawyers to handle matters that generate no fees at all.[57] The notion is that it is valuable for plaintiffs to have access to contingent fee lawyers since so many people could not afford to hire lawyers otherwise. If these lawyers were limited to lower percentage contingent fees across the board, they might decline to accept cases that posed a risk of nonrecovery. Some of these cases are meritorious but risky. Or these lawyers might cease handling contingent fee matters altogether. The 30 to 40 percent contingent fee is urged to be fair because lawyers need the cross-subsidy to maintain viable practices.

## b. Criminal and domestic relations cases

Rule 1.5 prohibits lawyers from charging contingent fees in criminal and in most domestic relations cases.

> **Rule 1.5(d)**
> A lawyer shall not enter into an arrangement for, charge, or collect:
>> (1) any fee in a domestic relations matter, the payment or amount of which is contingent upon the securing of a divorce or upon the amount of alimony or support, or property settlement in lieu thereof; or
>> (2) a contingent fee for representing a defendant in a criminal case.

One concern underlying the bar on contingent fees in domestic relations cases is that lawyers should not have a financial stake in their clients' ultimate divorce. Traditionally, lawyers were obliged to make efforts to encourage a divorcing couple to reconcile. If the lawyer's fee depended on the parties actually divorcing, lawyers might foment further discord between the parties to ensure that they would get paid. However, after a divorce has been granted, a lawyer may charge a contingent fee to collect past due alimony or child support.[58]

There are several potential problems with the use of fees that are contingent on successful outcomes in criminal cases. The concerns are primarily with possible conflicts between the interests of lawyer and client, and with the possibility that the lawyer will charge an excessive fee.

**FOR EXAMPLE:** Suppose that a criminal defense lawyer agrees that her client will pay her a substantial fee if the client is acquitted. Suppose

---

56. See Ted Schneyer, Empirical Research with a Policy Payoff: Market Dynamics for Lawyers Who Represent Plaintiffs for a Contingent Fee, 80 Tex. L. Rev. 1829, 1831 n. 15 (2002) (making this point at n. 15 but also providing a lucid review of the empirical analysis of contingent fees).

57. See Restatement § 35, comment b.

58. Rule 1.5, Comment 6.

then that the client wants to go to trial and give false testimony as to her alibi. The lawyer's financial stake in the acquittal might tempt the lawyer to allow the client to give false testimony. What if, instead, the client wanted to accept a favorable plea agreement in which the client would plead guilty to a criminal charge in exchange for the dismissal of other charges and a light penalty? The lawyer might be tempted to discourage the client from pleading guilty because her doing so would result in the lawyer not getting paid.

Another possible problem with the use of contingent fees in criminal cases is that clients facing criminal charges may be vulnerable and may accept fee agreements that overcompensate the lawyer. Because a contingent fee is uncertain, a client might agree to a high contingent fee, doubting that it would ever come due.[59]

## 4. Forbidden and restricted fee and expense arrangements

### a. Buying legal claims

**Can a collection lawyer purchase claims from a client and then pursue collection on his own behalf?**

Some lawyers do collection work for retailers and lenders, suing purchasers and borrowers who have not paid their bills. Rule 1.8(i) prohibits lawyers from acquiring an interest in litigation on behalf of a client, except for permitted liens and contingent fees.[60] Under this rule, a lawyer may not purchase an interest in a claim on which the lawyer is representing the client. However, if a lawyer purchases a claim from a client and ceases to represent the client in the collection of that claim, the transaction would no longer violate Rule 1.8(i). However, it still could present conflicts between the interests of the lawyer and the client. Suppose the lawyer, to collect on the claim, needed to have the client testify about matters that the client preferred to keep private? The ABA Ethics Committee opined that a lawyer may purchase collection claims from a client, so long as the lawyer complies with Rule 1.8(a) and (j). Compliance with Rule 1.8(a), as we have explained, requires that the terms be reasonable, that the client have the opportunity to seek independent legal

---

59. Criminal defendants are often vulnerable regardless of the nature of the fee arrangement. It is not uncommon, for example, for a criminal defense lawyer to insist that a client pay, for example, $10,000 before the lawyer will agree to accept the case. For an indigent client, the amount may be enormous, but the stakes are so high that a client may feel tremendous pressure to produce the cash.

60. Rule 1.8(i):

> A lawyer shall not acquire a proprietary interest in the cause of action or subject matter of litigation the lawyer is conducting for a client, except that the lawyer may:
> (1) acquire a lien authorized by law to secure the lawyer's fee or expenses, and
> (2) contract with a client for a reasonable contingent fee in a civil case.

See In re Rivera-Arvelo, 830 F. Supp. 665 (D.P.R. 1993) (in which a lawyer was disbarred because he had acquired an interest in property that was the subject of a lawsuit in which he was representing a client).

advice, that the lawyer disclose any possible conflicts clearly and in writing, and that the client consent in writing.[61]

## b. Financial assistance to a client

The same concerns that led lawyers to look askance at contingent fees have led to restrictions on lawyers providing financial assistance to clients during the course of litigation. These are stated in Rule 1.8(e).

> Rule 1.8(e)
> A lawyer shall not provide financial assistance to a client in connection with pending or contemplated litigation, except that:
>> (1) a lawyer may advance court costs and expenses of litigation, the repayment of which may be contingent on the outcome of the matter; and
>> (2) a lawyer representing an indigent client may pay court costs and expenses of litigation on behalf of the client.

One goal of this rule is to prevent lawyers from having too big a stake in the outcome of litigation, for fear that this will produce an improper level of zeal. Likewise, if a lawyer offers to pay a client's living expenses while the lawsuit is going on, a client might pursue a frivolous suit to obtain the offered financial support.[62]

Despite these concerns, the rule allows lawyers to pay court costs and litigation expenses, including the cost of needed medical examinations or other costs to obtain evidence.[63] If the client is not indigent, the client is ultimately responsible for paying these costs, but they may be taken out of the client's recovery. If the client is indigent, the lawyer need not attempt to collect these sums from the client.

### PROBLEM 7-3  AN IMPOVERISHED CLIENT

*This problem is based on a real case handled by students who were supervised by one of the authors.*

You have your own private practice. One of your clients is Gerald Mahoney, a 62-year-old man who recently lost his job as a night security guard at a local mall. According to Mr. Mahoney, the manager who fired him said that Mahoney seemed to be "slowing down" and that "it was time to get some younger blood around here." He was given two weeks' notice. He came to see you because he has no pension plan and almost no savings.

You brought suit against Mahoney's employer under the Age Discrimination in Employment Act. In its answer to your complaint, the employer admitted that it fired Mahoney, but said that the

---

61. ABA Comm. on Ethics & Prof. Resp., Formal Op. 00-416 (2000), discussing lawyer's purchase of accounts receivable from a client.

62. Rule 1.8, Comment 10.

63. Id.

firing was justified because he was sitting around too much and not making rounds often enough. Nevertheless, your preliminary investigation suggests that other employees have been fired because of their age. You think there is a decent chance that Mahoney will win his case. The case probably will come to trial in about three months. If he prevails, Mahoney could be awarded $50,000 in damages, of which you would collect one-third under your contingency fee agreement.

Yesterday, Mahoney showed up in your office. He said that he had used up his savings and was no longer able to pay his $400 per month rent. He had been served with an eviction notice. His telephone had been disconnected because he had no money to pay the phone bill. Mahoney said that because he has no living relatives, if he is evicted next month, he will have to live on the streets.

If Mahoney is evicted, it will be difficult for you to continue to represent him because it will be hard to stay in contact. Even if he stays in his apartment, the fact that he no longer has a phone will make it difficult for you to prepare him for trial. More important, probably, is that unless he gets some emergency funds while the case is pending, he may not have enough to eat.

You would like to give Mahoney some money to help him to get by while the case is pending and avoid his having to drop the case for lack of funds. You would like to buy him a prepaid cell phone so that you can call him when you need to talk to him about the case, and you would like to pay his rent for the next three months so that he is not put on the street before his case gets to trial. Also, you'd like to give him some cash for groceries.

May you pay these expenses?

## c. Publication rights

Suppose a famous pop star asks you to represent him in a criminal case. His fortune is spent, his financial situation disastrous. Can you agree to take on the matter in exchange for a promise that when it is all over, you will have exclusive rights to publish a book about the case? Rule 1.8(d) says that you may not.

> **Rule 1.8(d)**
> Prior to the conclusion of representation of a client, a lawyer shall not make or negotiate an agreement giving the lawyer literary or media rights to a portrayal or account based in substantial part on information relating to the representation.

Why not? Isn't this just another version of a contingent fee? The drafters of the rules think not. The problem is that if the case is quickly settled in a quiet plea bargain, no one will want to read the book. On the other hand, if there is a lengthy trial that makes lots of headlines in the newspaper, the book might be a bestseller. A lawyer in such a situation might be tempted to do things that would be bad for the client and good for the book.

The prohibition is on the making of such an arrangement before the case is over. If after the case has concluded the pop star owes you a hefty fee, you and the client could agree to forgive part or all of the debt in exchange for transfer of literary or media rights.

This rule applies to transfer of literary or media rights to the story of the representation. It does not restrict lawyers representing clients in book or movie contracts where the book or movie is not about a case handled by the lawyer.

FOR EXAMPLE: If a cartoonist makes a contract with an independent film company to write a screenplay based on one of her graphic novels, the lawyer who negotiates the contract on her behalf may make an agreement that her fee will be a percentage of the royalties paid to the cartoonist for the movie. However, such an agreement would be subject to Rule 1.8(a), so the lawyer would have to comply with its disclosure requirements.[64]

## d. Advance payment of fees and nonrefundable retainers

Lawyers often ask clients to pay a portion of the lawyer's fee for a specified service before the service is performed. This payment is often referred to as a retainer. However, contracts for services between lawyers and clients also are referred to as retainer agreements, even if the client is making no advance fee payment and even if the client is being represented pro bono. Here we use the word to refer to the advance payment of fees.

When a client pays a retainer at the outset, the lawyer has some protection against the client if he becomes unwilling or unable to pay for services that the lawyer has already rendered. The lawyer will charge fees against the advance payment as she earns them. The advance is deposited in the lawyer's client trust account (discussed below), and the lawyer withdraws portions of the advance as they are earned. If the lawyer does not earn the whole amount advanced, the unearned portion of the advance must be returned to the client.[65] After the advance payment has been exhausted, if the lawyer continues to do work for the client, the lawyer usually bills the client periodically.

Another type of fee paid in advance is a lump-sum payment to secure the lawyer's availability for a period of time or for a particular task. For example, a company might pay a lawyer some thousands of dollars each month to advise the company on tax matters if and when the company needed tax advice. This type of retainer, sometimes called a classic retainer or a general retainer, may be treated by the lawyer as having been earned when it is received. The reason is that the payment secures the lawyer's availability but does not depend on the

---

64. Rule 1.8, Comment 9.
65. Rule 1.16(d).

performance of any particular task.[66] The lawyer may have to forgo other obligations to maintain his availability.[67]

### May a lawyer require a nonrefundable advance payment from an individual client with whom the lawyer has no prior relationship?

This practice is controversial. Such a payment, it is argued, locks the client into the relationship with the lawyer and tends to constrain the client from firing the lawyer if, for example, the lawyer fails to perform adequately. Courts consider it very important to protect the right of clients to fire their lawyers. Public policy disfavors nonrefundable retainers as inconsistent with a lawyer's fiduciary obligations to his client.[68]

A New York lawyer was suspended for two years because he charged non-refundable retainers to his divorce clients.[69] One of the respondent's written fee agreements with his clients read as follows:

> My minimum fee for appearing for you in this matter is fifteen thousand ($15,000) dollars. This fee is not refundable for any reason whatsoever once I file a notice of appearance on your behalf.[70]

## 5. Fee disputes

### a. Prospective limitations of lawyers' liability and settlement of claims against lawyers

Time was when clients almost never sued their lawyers for malpractice. These days, legal malpractice suits are common. Suppose a lawyer decides it is not worth practicing law with a risk of liability hanging over his head. He wants to ask each client to agree in advance not to sue the lawyer for malpractice, no matter what. Can the lawyer do that? Rule 1.8(h) says yes, but only if each client

---

66. If a lawyer accepts such a payment and then fails to perform his duties under the agreement, he would be subject to suit for breach of contract and might be obliged to return the payment.

67. See In re Lochow, 469 N.W.2d 91, 98 (Minn. 1991) (explaining that most advance payments of fees should be placed in the client trust account, but if a lawyer must forgo other opportunities to be available to serve a client, a retainer may be considered to be earned when paid. The purpose of this type of retainer must be recorded in writing and approved by the client.).

68. See Wong v. Michael Kennedy, P.C., 853 F. Supp. 73 (E.D.N.Y. 1994).

69. In re Cooperman, 591 N.Y.S.2d 855 (App. Div. 1993), aff'd, 633 N.E.2d 1069 (N.Y. 1994). While the law is not entirely settled about which, if any, nonrefundable retainers are enforceable, most judges and ethics committees scrutinize such fee arrangements with a skeptical eye. For discussion of nonrefundable retainers, see Lester Brickman & Lawrence A. Cunningham, Nonrefundable Retainers Revisited, 72 N.C. L. Rev. 1 (1993); Steven Lubet, The Rush to Remedies: Some Conceptual Questions About Nonrefundable Retainers, 73 N.C. L. Rev. 271 (1994).

70. Another one used this language:

This is the minimum fee no matter how much or how little work I do in this investigatory stage . . . and will remain the minimum fee and not refundable even if you decide prior to my completion of the investigation that you wish to discontinue the use of my services for any reason whatsoever.

Cooperman, 591 N.Y.S.2d at 856.

has independent legal representation in making that agreement. This means that in most cases, it is impractical to include a waiver of malpractice liability in a contract for legal services.

### If a lawyer and a client settle a malpractice claim against the lawyer, does the client have to be separately represented?

If a lawyer makes a mistake for which the lawyer might be liable, the lawyer might contact her malpractice insurance company and/or notify the client. The lawyer and client might well work out a settlement of the potential claim short of litigation. A lawyer may settle with a client who does not have independent legal advice, but the lawyer must advise the client in writing that it is a good idea to get advice from another lawyer before making such a settlement. The lawyer also must give the client a chance to consult another lawyer. Rule 1.8(h) explains.

> Rule 1.8(h)
> A lawyer shall not:
>> (1) make an agreement prospectively limiting the lawyer's liability to a client for malpractice unless the client is independently represented in making the agreement, or
>> (2) settle a claim or potential claim for such liability with an unrepresented client or former client unless that person is advised in writing of the desirability of seeking and is given a reasonable opportunity to seek the advice of independent legal counsel in connection therewith.

### Are lawyers allowed to organize law firms in ways that limit their liability for acts or omissions of their partners?

To answer this question, we need to ask a prior question: To what extent are law partners liable for the acts of others?[71] A partnership involves "[a] voluntary contract between two or more competent persons to place their money, effects, labor and skill . . . in lawful commerce or business, with the understanding that there shall be a proportional sharing of profits and losses between them."[72] Until the 1960s, most lawyers who practiced with other lawyers formed general partnerships.[73] In a general partnership, "each partner in the firm [is] vicariously liable, jointly and severally, for the malpractice of each other partner or lawyer-employee. 'Vicarious' liability . . . means that the

---

71. While one thinks of most lawyers working in sizeable firms with many partners, Professor Tom Morgan notes that "as recently as 1980 '[a]lmost two thirds of all private practitioners practice[d] law on a solo basis or in association with one or two other lawyers.'" Thomas D. Morgan, Conflicts of Interest and the New Forms of Professional Associations, 39 S. Tex. L. Rev. 215, 216 (1998), quoting Barbara A. Curran et al., The Lawyer Statistical Report: A Statistical Profile of the U.S. Legal Profession in the 1980s 13 (ABA 1985).

72. Black's Law Dictionary 1120 (6th ed., West 1990), cited in Susan Saab Fortney, Professional Liability Issues Related to Limited Liability Partnerships, 39 S. Tex. L. Rev. 399, 400 n. 4 (1998).

73. Morgan, supra n. 71, at 216.

plaintiff [is] not required to demonstrate any personal wrongdoing of a particular firm lawyer in order to hold the firm lawyer [liable]."[74]

Other organizational structures allow lawyers to invest resources together and share profits but limit their liability for the acts or omissions of their partners.[75] One common structure is a "limited liability partnership" or "LLP."[76] This form of organization offers lawyers a degree of protection from malpractice liability for their partners' actions. The point is to "make their pockets shallower."[77] If a firm is organized as an LLP, one partner is liable for his own conduct and that of others he supervises, but is otherwise not vicariously liable for the conduct of his partners.[78] As of the late 1990s, the District of Columbia and every state but Wyoming had passed legislation allowing lawyers to organize firms as LLPs.[79]

So are lawyers prohibited from these organizational limitations of liability? Though the LLP might protect lawyers to some extent from liability for the malpractice of their partners, Rule 1.18 does not prohibit this arrangement, "provided that each lawyer remains personally liable to the client for his or her own conduct" and provided that the firm complies with other restrictions imposed by law.[80]

## b. Fee arbitration

Many bar associations have established committees to intermediate between lawyers and clients who have disputes over fees. The lawyer might initiate this process in connection with a client who refuses to pay. A client might initiate

---

74. Charles W. Wolfram, Inherent Powers in the Crucible of Lawyer Self-Protection: Reflections on the LLP Campaign, 39 S. Tex. L. Rev. 359, 365 (1998).

75. Morgan, supra n. 71, at 216-217.

76. The LLP structure was authorized by state statutes in the early 1990s in the wake of the savings and loan scandals, which had resulted in many cases in which law partners at elite firms such as Kaye, Scholer and Jones Day found themselves personally liable for millions of dollars because of the misfeasance of certain of their partners in representing the savings and loans. See John S. Dzienkowski, Legal Malpractice and the Multistate Law Firm: Supervision of Multistate Offices; Firms as Limited Liability Partnerships; and Predispute Agreements to Arbitrate Client Malpractice Claims, 36 S. Tex L. Rev. 967, 981-982 (1995) (recounting how the savings and loan mess led to the creation of LLPs). See generally James O. Johnson Jr. & Daniel Scott Schecter, In the Matter of Kaye, Scholer, Fierman, Hays & Handler: A Symposium on Government Regulation, Lawyer's Ethics, and the Rule of Law, 66 S. Cal. L. Rev. 977 (1993); Susan Beck & Michael Orey, They Got What They Deserved, Am. Law., May 1992, at 68 (describing the settlement in which the partners of Kaye, Scholer agreed to pay $41 million to resolve allegations of misfeasance by firm lawyers representing Lincoln Savings and Loan).

77. Dennis E. Curtis, Old Knights and New Champions, Kaye, Scholer, the Office of Thrift Supervision, and the Pursuit of the Dollar, 66 S. Cal. L. Rev. 985, 1014 (1993).

78. Fortney, supra n. 72, at 402.

79. Id. at 403-404. A related development is the creation of limited liability companies, which offer similar benefits for corporate entities. LLCs differ from LLPs in that the LLCs are subject to more regulatory formalities than LLPs. Id. at 402 n. 18.

80. Rule 1.8, Comment 14. Similarly, Restatement § 58 acknowledges that lawyers who are partners in LLPs may be protected from the vicarious liability imposed on general partners. Some drafters of the Restatement preferred to articulate a general rule of vicarious liability for law partners. See Wolfram, supra n. 74, at 370 n. 32.

this process because the client believes the lawyer is charging too much. A comment to Rule 1.5 notes that if a jurisdiction has set a mandatory mediation or arbitration process for resolution of fee disputes, a lawyer must comply with it. If the available process is voluntary, the comment urges that a lawyer "should conscientiously consider submitting to it."[81]

### Can a lawyer ask clients to agree in advance to arbitrate any disputes about the lawyer's services?

Many lawyers include clauses in their retainer agreements with clients in which both parties agree to go to binding arbitration in the event of a fee dispute. Some of these also require clients to agree to binding arbitration of any malpractice claims. Some have questioned the use of such clauses because clients are asked to waive their right to sue before the service is provided. However, the ABA Ethics Committee concluded that such an agreement is proper if the client is carefully advised of the advantages and disadvantages of arbitration, the client gives informed consent, and the provision does not insulate the lawyer from liability that might otherwise be imposed by law.[82] For example, the lawyer should explain that in agreeing to arbitration, the client would waive her right to a jury trial, some of her discovery rights, and her right to appeal. Some other ethics committees, however, have declared that it is unethical for a lawyer to require a client to sign an agreement to arbitrate any dispute before a dispute has arisen, unless the client has the advice of independent counsel before signing the agreement.[83]

### c. Collection of fees

### What if your client doesn't pay?

If a client doesn't pay a fee that is due, a lawyer may contact the client to request payment. The lawyer may file suit against the client to collect the fee (though it is a good idea to think carefully before doing so because some clients counterclaim for malpractice). A lawyer may use a collection agency or hire another lawyer to collect a fee owed by a client, but it is important to be sure that the agency or lawyer will not use improper methods of fee collection (see below). As discussed in Chapter 4, many jurisdictions allow lawyers to withhold documents prepared by the lawyer for which payment has not been received, but only if doing so will not unreasonably harm the client.[84]

---

81. Rule 1.5, Comment 14 [Delaware]. In the ABA's Model Rules, it is Comment 9.

82. ABA Comm. on Ethics & Prof. Resp., Formal Op. 02-425 (2002).

83. Jean Fleming Powers, Ethical Implications of Attorneys Requiring Clients to Submit Malpractice Claims to ADR, 38 S. Tex. L. Rev. 625, 633 (1997) (citing ethics opinions in Washington, D.C., Maryland, and Michigan).

84. See Chapter 4, section on "Terminating a Lawyer-Client Relationship"; see also Restatement § 43, comment c.

## Does state or federal law restrict lawyers' methods of fee collection?

Lawyers are subject to the Fair Debt Collection Practices Act[85] if they regularly engage in consumer debt collection activities.[86] This means they may not make "false or misleading representations" or engage in various abusive and unfair practices.[87] Violators are subject to civil liability in claims by harassed debtors and subject to enforcement actions by the Federal Trade Commission.[88]

Several state consumer statutes (including those in Connecticut, Louisiana, Massachusetts, and Texas) apply to lawyers and forbid various unfair and deceptive practices.[89] Some of the consumer statutes impose quite specific prohibitions, and violation may result in the award of double, treble, or punitive damages. In addition, some allow the award of attorneys' fees against the violator.[90]

While the application of the state consumer statutes to lawyers is variable, lawyers are well advised to avoid some of the debt collection practices prohibited by those statutes. For example, a lawyer should not

- commit any acts of harassment against a debtor or make a frivolous claim,
- retain documents or unearned fees that should be turned over to a client as leverage to secure payment of fees,
- make any false or misleading statements about the fee claim,
- reveal information to a third party (or threaten to do so) to get a client to pay a fee.[91]

## May lawyers obtain liens on client property?[92]

As we explained earlier, there is a historical prohibition in the rules on a lawyer acquiring a "proprietary interest" in a client's case. However, Rule 1.8(i) allows a lawyer to charge an otherwise permitted contingent fee or to "acquire a lien authorized by law to secure the lawyer's fee or expenses."

---

85. 15 U.S.C. § 1692 et seq. (2004).

86. Heintz v. Jenkins, 514 U.S. 291 (1995). The act, one version of which was enacted in 1977, exempted lawyers from coverage, but in 1986, Congress repealed this exemption. Id. at 294-295.

87. Id. at 292.

88. Id. at 293.

89. Susan P. Koniak & George M. Cohen, Under Cloak of Settlement, 82 Va. L. Rev. 1051, 1079 n. 88 (1996). These authors also state that

Courts in four other states — Montana, Oregon, South Carolina and Washington — have suggested such claims would be upheld in appropriate circumstances. . . . Three states — Maryland, North Carolina and Ohio — have statutes that exclude lawyers from coverage. . . . Cases in three more states — Illinois, New Hampshire and New Jersey — have rejected the application of consumer protection statutes to lawyers. . . . Cases in Arkansas, Idaho and Pennsylvania suggest that lawyers may be exempt from liability under consumer protection statutes in those states.

Id.

90. See John A. Spanogle et al., Consumer Law 79 (2d ed., West 1991).

91. Restatement § 41, comment c, reporter's note (listing cases in which lawyers were alleged to have engaged in the listed behavior as methods of fee collection).

92. This section refers to client property other than documents that the client provided to the lawyer or that the lawyer created during the course of the representation. The lawyer's obligation to return documents is discussed in Chapter 4, in the section on termination of representation.

### How would a lawyer acquire a lien on a client's property?

Each state has law that authorizes liens — some by statute, some by common law, and some by contract. A lawyer who agreed to represent a client in a matter might contract with the client to secure the payment of the legal fee by a lien on the client's summer home. If the client did not pay the fee, the lawyer might assert a claim against the client's summer home.

The comments following Rule 1.8 explain that such a lien, acquired by contract, constitutes a business transaction with a client and is covered by Rule 1.8(a).[93] This means that the client is entitled to fair terms, a clear explanation of the terms in writing, and written encouragement and opportunity to seek the advice of an independent lawyer before the client agrees to give the lawyer a lien on the property.

A lawyer who acquires a lien on client property in violation of the law is subject to discipline.

> **FOR EXAMPLE:** A sole practitioner in Minnesota named Brian Peterson "filed an attorney's lien against a client's homestead without a signed waiver of the homestead exemption." (Minnesota prohibits the filing of a lien against a residence occupied by its owner.) When this was discovered and disciplinary charges were filed against him, he "fabricated a waiver of the homestead exemption by cutting and pasting together a photocopied signature block and notarization block from other documents and submitted the document in an ethics investigation." He was suspended from practice for six months.[94]

### d. Fees owed to a lawyer who withdraws or is fired before the matter is completed

If a lawyer withdraws from representing a client before the representation is completed, whether the lawyer is entitled to payment for the work done depends on the reason she withdrew. This most often comes up in contingent fee cases, where the lawyer generally receives no payment until after the case is settled or tried. If the client has breached the contract with the lawyer — by failing to cooperate in the representation, for example — the lawyer may be considered justified in withdrawing. (See Rule 1.16(b) for a list of reasons a lawyer would be justified in withdrawing.) In such a case, the lawyer would be entitled to compensation on a quantum meruit basis (an equitable assessment of the value of the work done). On the other hand, if the lawyer withdraws from representing the client without good cause, then the lawyer is breaching the contract and may forfeit her right to recover any fees for the work done.[95]

---

93. The Restatement also provides that "Acquisition of . . . a security interest [in property not connected to the representation] is a business or financial transaction with a client within the meaning of § 126." Restatement § 43(4).

94. In re Peterson, 620 N.W.2d 29 (Minn. 2000).

95. See, e.g., Augustson v. Linea Aera Nactional-Chile, S.A., 76 F.3d 658 (5th Cir. 1996) (whether a lawyer is entitled to quantum meruit compensation upon withdrawal depends on whether the lawyer can prove that there was just cause for withdrawal).

If a client fires his lawyer in a contingent fee case, the lawyer may get a quantum meruit fee award, assuming that the services provided are deemed to have some value. A retainer agreement that provides for payment of more fees than would be recovered on a quantum meruit basis would violate the prohibition on charging excessive fees.[96]

# 6. Dividing fees with other firms or with nonlawyers

## a. Division of fees between lawyers not in the same firm

### If two lawyers in different firms work on a case, can they split the fee?

Two lawyers in different firms may work on a single matter for various reasons. An inexperienced lawyer might enlist an expert in a certain field to assist her on a matter. A lawyer might ask another lawyer to assist because a matter must be litigated in a jurisdiction in which she is not licensed to practice. One lawyer might collaborate with another because of the amount of work that needs to be done or to ensure that counsel would be available during the vacation or sick leave of one of the lawyers.

If two lawyers in different law firms work on a case, both should be paid for their services. If the fee agreement provides for hourly fees, it is easy to calculate which lawyer is entitled to be paid what amount. However, if the agreement provides for a contingent fee, the allocation of the fee is less obvious, especially because some contingent fee lawyers do not keep time records, so it is not easy to measure the relative contributions of the two lawyers. Rule 1.5(e) allows the lawyers to share a fee, but the rule imposes conditions to protect clients.

> Rule 1.5(e)
> A division of a fee between lawyers who are not in the same firm may be made only if:
> (1) the division is in proportion to the services performed by each lawyer or each lawyer assumes joint responsibility for the representation;
> (2) the client agrees to the arrangement, including the share each lawyer will receive, and the agreement is confirmed in writing; and
> (3) the total fee is reasonable.[97]

---

96. See, e.g., Fla. B. v. Hollander, 607 So. 2d 412 (Fla. 1992) (fee agreement that provided for substantial fees upon discharge of lawyer was found improper because it provided for excessive fees; lawyer suspended for six months); see generally Lester Brickman, Setting the Fee When the Client Discharges a Contingent Fee Attorney, 41 Emory L.J. 367 (1992).

97. This is North Carolina's version of Rule 1.5(e). This rule is one as to which there is considerable state variation, reflecting policy differences. Although this book usually quotes the Delaware Rules of Professional Conduct, because Delaware adopted most of the Model Rules after those rules were revised in 2002, Delaware did not adopt the revised version of Rule 1.5(e). North Carolina did adopt the ABA's revised wording for Rule 1.5(e).

### If one lawyer refers a case to another lawyer, may the first lawyer be paid a referral fee?

Suppose a client seeking a divorce approaches a lawyer who handles only medical malpractice cases. This lawyer refers the client to another lawyer who does domestic relations work. Under the rule quoted above, the referring lawyer may indeed collect a referral fee, and it could be a large part of the total fee, provided that she meets various conditions. First, she must take on "financial and ethical responsibility for the representation as if the lawyers were associated in a partnership."[98] In addition, the proposed share that each lawyer receives must be disclosed to and approved by the client, the fee-sharing arrangement must be confirmed in writing, and the total fee must be reasonable.

If the referring lawyer is planning to do some work on the case, the lawyers and the client may agree in writing that the lawyers will divide the fee based on the proportion of time spent or work done. In that case, each one will have to take financial and ethical responsibility for that lawyer's work, but not for the case as a whole.

### What does it mean for a lawyer to take "financial and ethical responsibility for the representation"?

This phrase means that in the event of disciplinary action or a malpractice suit, the lawyers agree to share responsibility as if they were law partners. It follows from their equal responsibility that each lawyer has a duty of supervision under Rule 5.1. That rule makes lawyers in supervisory positions responsible to ensure compliance with the rules and makes them responsible for some violations of the ethics rules by others working on a matter.[99]

A lawyer who collects a fee for referring a case and who does not plan to collaborate on the case is well advised to follow the referred case closely because if the lawyer to whom the case is referred commits an ethical breach or is negligent, the referring lawyer could be disciplined or sued. The Utah State Bar Ethics Advisory Opinion Committee explained:

> Lawyers contemplating a joint-responsibility arrangement must realize that each lawyer's responsibility is significant. The lawyer receiving a referral fee under a joint-responsibility arrangement cannot simply "hand off" the client

---

98. Rule 1.5, Comment 8 [North Carolina]. The corresponding comment in the Model Rules is Comment 7.

99. While lawyers in different firms are not partners, the "joint responsibility" fee-sharing arrangement gives them responsibility for the work of the other as if they were partners. See ABA Informal Ethics Op. 85-1514 (1985) (joint responsibility means that each lawyer assumes responsibility to client "comparable to that of a partner in a law firm under similar circumstances, including financial responsibility [and] ethical responsibility to the extent a partner would have ethical responsibility for actions of other partners in a law firm in accordance with Rule 5.1"). When Rule 1.5 was amended in 2002, Comment 7 was amended to delete a reference to the obligations stated in 5.1, but this was replaced by a reference to "financial and ethical responsibility for the representation as if the lawyers were associated in a partnership." This language was based on Opinion 85-1514. ABA Center for Professional Responsibility, Model Rule 1.5, Reporter's Explanation of Changes, Comment 7, available at http://www.abanet.org/cpr/e2k-rule15rem.html (last visited Oct. 24, 2004).

to the receiving lawyer. . . . [A] referring and receiving lawyer must work out arrangements that give reasonable assurance that neither will violate the Rules of Professional Conduct in the matter in question. Partners are responsible for each others' violations of the rules if they order the violations, knowingly ratify them, or knowingly fail to take reasonable, potentially effective remedial action. Under these circumstances, therefore, both referring and receiving lawyers would be responsible for each others' ethical violations.[100]

It is not uncommon for lawyers to make fee-splitting agreements that do not comply with Rule 1.5(e). Some courts refuse to enforce such agreements because they violate the public policy stated in the rule.[101] Some have found that a lawyer may recover a share of the fees on a quantum meruit basis even if the fee-splitting agreement is unenforceable.[102]

## b. Sharing fees with nonlawyers

While lawyers are allowed to share legal fees with other lawyers, they are not allowed to share legal fees with nonlawyers, except in certain narrow circumstances.[103] As to splitting fees with nonlawyers in general, Rule 5.4(a) provides that "A lawyer or law firm shall not share legal fees with a nonlawyer, except that: . . . (3) a lawyer or law firm may include nonlawyer employees in a compensation or retirement plan, even though the plan is based in whole or in part on a profit-sharing arrangement." The purpose of the rule is to protect the lawyer's independent judgment from being affected by influence or pressure from nonlawyers. We return to this rule in Chapter 10, where we consider its social consequences.

Law firms may pay salaries and bonuses to nonlawyer employees but may not routinely divide profits among lawyers and nonlawyers. So, for example, if a firm employed a paralegal with skills like those of Erin Brockovich and made millions as a result of her work, it could give her a big bonus but not a share of the annual profits.[104]

## Can lawyers pay "runners" who find them clients who are accident victims?

In most states, lawyers may not pay referral fees to nonlawyers who send them clients,[105] except that they may pay lawyer referral services for making information available about their practices.[106] Some personal injury lawyers

---

100. Utah State Bar, Ethics Advisory Op. Comm., Op. No. 121 (approved Aug. 26, 1993).

101. See, e.g., Post v. Bregman, 707 A.2d 806 (Md. 1998).

102. Daynard v. Ness, Motley, Loadholt, Richardson & Poole, P.A., 178 F. Supp. 2d 9 (D. Mass. 2001).

103. One exception relates to payments made by a lawyer's firm to the estate of a deceased lawyer. Another relates to the purchase of the law practice of a no-longer-practicing lawyer. Another involves a lawyer sharing fees with a nonprofit organization. See Model Rule 5.4.

104. See a brief biography of Erin Brockovich-Ellis, at http://www.wma.com/erin_brockovich/bio/ERIN_BROCKOVICH_ELLIS.pdf. (last visited Oct. 24, 2004).

105. Restatement § 10, comment d.

106. See ABA Comm. on Ethics & Prof. Resp., Informal Op. 85-1510 (1985).

nevertheless employ "runners" to go to the scene of accidents or to hospital emergency rooms to distribute business cards or brochures; some of them have been disbarred.[107] Likewise, a lawyer may not pay an accountant, real estate broker, or anyone else who comes into contact with a potential client group for sending potential clients her way.

## 7. Payment of fee by a third party

The principle of maintaining a lawyer's independent judgment has produced restrictions on allowing one person to pay a lawyer to represent another person. As a practical matter, it is necessary to allow parents to pay for the representation of minor children who need lawyers. Likewise, some employers pay for the legal representation of employees in matters that arise out of workplace activities. Consequently, the rules allow a third party to pay a lawyer's fee, but only if the client consents after being advised, the third person does not direct the lawyer's decisions or otherwise interfere in the representation, and the lawyer avoids sharing with the third person any confidences learned in the course of the representation.[108]

## B. Conflicts with lawyers' personal or business interests

### 1. In general

Rule 1.7(a)(2) states that a lawyer has a conflict of interest if "there is a significant risk that the representation of one or more clients will be materially limited . . . by a personal interest of a lawyer." If the lawyer's personal or business interest in a matter is at odds with the interests of her client, she might be unable to provide disinterested advice or advocacy.[109] If such a conflict exists, a lawyer must not represent the client unless all of the conditions in Rule 1.7(b) are met.[110] Here are some hypothetical examples of such conflicts:

- ■ A lawyer is engaged in settlement negotiations with a lawyer from another firm. The other lawyer happens to be the hiring partner of a

---

107. See In re Pajerowski, 721 A.2d 992 (N.J. 1998) (lawyer who used runners, provided financial assistance to clients, and committed other ethical violations disbarred).

108. Rule 1.8(f). The Restatement articulates similar restrictions but provides that a third person may direct the lawyer's judgment if the client consents and the direction is reasonable. Restatement § 134. See generally Nancy Moore, Ethical Issues in Third-Party Payment: Beyond the Insurance Defense Paradigm, 16 Rev. Litig. 585 (1997) (exploring the relationship of lawyers to third parties who pay their fees such as parents of children represented by the lawyers, employers who pay legal fees of employees, and other examples).

109. Rule 1.7, Comment 10.

110. The lawyer must reasonably believe that she will be able to provide competent and diligent representation despite the conflict; the representation must not be prohibited by law; the matter

firm to which the first lawyer has applied for a job. The lawyer's advocacy on behalf of his client might be compromised by his efforts to appear cooperative to the adverse lawyer.[111]

- A lawyer who handles Social Security disability cases often refers his clients to a physical therapy clinic. He is part owner of the clinic but does not mention this. The lawyer's obligation to look out for his client's best interests might be compromised by his interest in the profitability of the clinic.[112]

- A state attorney general is in charge of an investigation of a large corporation whose main offices are located in the state capital. The investigation could lead to criminal fraud charges against the corporation and its officers. This particular corporation was the largest contributor to a campaign fund that assisted the attorney general in his last campaign for election and is likely to do so again—depending on the outcome of the investigation. The attorney general's obligation to the citizens of his state may be compromised by his concerns about the impact of the investigation on his campaign funds.[113]

## 2. Business transactions between lawyer and client

Sometimes, lawyers and clients have strong incentives to do nonlegal business with each other. A client may benefit from doing business with his lawyer because his lawyer may give him loans or equity investments, reduced fees for legal services, and sophisticated business and legal advice. A lawyer may benefit from a business deal with a client by getting in on the ground floor of a new and promising company or by obtaining compensation in the form of an equity investment in a client who is too short of cash to pay legal fees. For decades, real estate lawyers have bought interests in their clients' ventures. More recently, many lawyers who helped in the formation of new dot-com companies were paid with company stock rather than with cash. The attitude of the bar toward deals like these has gradually become more permissive, although both the practices of the bar and the ABA's imprimatur on these practices has been the subject of criticism, including the following from Professors John Dzienkowski and Robert Peroni:

> The traditional view in the legal profession until the late 1990s was that lawyer equity investments in clients should generally be avoided because they pose special risks and conflicts. . . . Beginning in 1995, several bar associations,

---

must not involve a lawyer in representing two clients on opposite sides in litigation; and each of the clients must give written informed consent. See Rule 1.7(b).

111. This example is adapted from Rule 1.7, Comment 10.

112. Id.

113. This example was drawn from a story about fund-raising by Alabama Attorney General William Pryor Jr. when he was being considered for a federal judicial appointment. R. Jeffrey Smith & Tania Branigan, GOP Attorneys General Asked for Corporate Contributions, Wash. Post, July 17, 2003, at A1.

ultimately including the ABA in 2000, issued ethics opinions that basically place their stamp of approval on lawyers obtaining equity interests in clients, subject to a few exceptions and provided that they meet certain requirements. [But] lawyers throughout the country have used these opinions to justify aggressive and even arrogant demands for client equity. . . . These practices have significant potential to undermine the independent judgment of lawyers and adversely change the relationship of the lawyer to the client.[114]

The traditional view is that lawyers should avoid doing business with clients. Lawyers have fiduciary obligations to clients. If a lawyer does business with or invests financially in a client, the lawyer's interest in making money or gaining other advantages is likely to conflict with his ability to look out for his client's interests. Because clients trust their lawyers' judgment, it is easy for lawyers to take advantage of that trust in a business deal. It is better to maintain clear boundaries as to the lawyer's role and not to muddy the provision of legal services with other transactions.

Rule 1.8(a) does not flatly prohibit lawyers from doing business with clients but strongly discourages them from doing so.

### Rule 1.8(a)

(a) A lawyer shall not enter into a business transaction with a client or knowingly acquire an ownership, possessory, security or other pecuniary interest adverse to a client unless:

(1) the transaction and terms on which the lawyer acquires the interest are fair and reasonable to the client and are fully disclosed and transmitted in writing to the client in a manner that can be reasonably understood by the client;[115]

(2) the client is advised in writing of the desirability of seeking and is given a reasonable opportunity to seek the advice of independent legal counsel on the transaction; and

(3) the client gives informed consent, in a writing signed by the client, to the essential terms of the transaction and the lawyer's role in the transaction, including whether the lawyer is representing the client in the transaction.

**FOR EXAMPLE:** You have a client named Masha. You helped Masha to get her green card and are helping her to adopt her husband's son by a previous marriage. Masha is from Belarus. She's been in the United States for four years. She came to America in part because she inherited a lovely home from her great-aunt Sonia. Masha decides to sell the house. It happens to be in a part of town where you and your family would like to move. May you offer to buy the house?

---

114. John S. Dzienkowski & Robert J. Peroni, The Decline in Lawyer Independence: Lawyer Equity Investments in Clients, 81 Tex. L. Rev. 405 (2002).

115. The phrase "to the client" in this part of Rule 1.8(a) appears in the Delaware rule but does not appear in the ABA's Model Rule 1.8(a).

The answer (as usual) is maybe. There are some problems. Suppose Masha asks you what you think the house is worth. As a prospective customer, you might give her a low number. As your client, she might assume that you have her best interests at heart and that she can trust your judgment. Because she is an immigrant and has not had much experience employing lawyers, she may be more likely to defer to you. You helped her with some important matters. She feels indebted to you. If you express interest in buying her house, she might feel constrained not to explore whether another buyer would pay her more money.[116]

If you want to buy a client's house, or undertake any such transaction, you need to satisfy the conditions articulated in Rule 1.8(a).

---

**Before you make a deal with a client, ask these questions:**
- Are the terms fair to the client?
- Have you explained the terms to the client clearly and in writing?
- Have you advised the client in writing that she should get legal advice about the deal from a lawyer not associated with you?
- Has the client had a chance to get advice from another lawyer?
- Has the client given informed consent in writing to the terms of the deal and to the lawyer's role in the deal?

---

### Do the restrictions on lawyer-client business deals apply to every lawyer-client contract?

No. The rule applies to contracts for goods and services regardless of whether the lawyer is the buyer or the seller. There are a couple of exceptions. The restrictions do not apply

- to a contract for legal services, unless part or all of the fee is to be paid by the transfer of property to the lawyer; so a standard contract for legal services in which the client pays a fee is not covered;
- to a contract in which the client sells the lawyer some product or service that the client normally sells to others. For example, a lawyer may go to a doctor who is his client and pay for the doctor's services without worrying about Rule 1.8(a).[117]

The rule covers business deals between lawyers and clients whether the contracts are related or unrelated to the matter on which the lawyer represents the client.[118] For example, a real estate lawyer who sells title insurance must

---

116. See Rule 1.8, Comment 1, which says that "A lawyer's legal skill and training, together with the relationship of trust and confidence between lawyer and client, create the possibility of overreaching when the lawyer participates in a . . . transaction with a client."

117. Id.

118. Id.

comply with this provision for the sale of the title insurance.[119] Likewise, if the same lawyer sold his golf clubs to the client, he must comply with the rule.

The rule does not apply to all contracts made by lawyers, only to those in which another party to the contract is a client. As we have observed in Chapters 4, 5, and 6, it may be unclear whether a particular individual is a client of a lawyer. The relationship may be tenuous, the legal services may have been completed, or the relationship may involve a mix of business and legal advice.

The cases in which lawyers have been disciplined for violating Rule 1.8 are a gallery of stupid mistakes by lawyers who took advantage of their access to clients' funds or took advantage of their clients' trust. Here are some rules of thumb that can save you from an untimely professional demise.

## Several simple steps to avoid inadvertent professional suicide

**Don't borrow money from your clients or lend money to your clients unless you take great care to comply with Rule 1.8** (except for litigation expenses, discussed above). Some lawyers have been disbarred for making loans to or from clients without making adequate disclosures.[120] Especially in dealing with noninstitutional clients, a good rule of thumb is: If you or your client needs to borrow money, get it from a bank.

**Don't ever borrow a penny from client funds that are entrusted to you.** Not even just for a day. Many lawyers with cash flow problems have junked their careers by temporary appropriation of client funds. Most disciplinary agencies regard this as an extremely serious offense — a sure path to disbarment.

**Don't sell your house, your wife's old car, or anything else to a client.** Find another buyer. While you can make such a sale to a client if you jump through the hoops listed above, it is risky.[121] What if you sell the car to a client, it dies a week later, and the client accuses you of having made inadequate disclosures?

---

119. Id.

120. ABA, Annotated Model Rules of Professional Conduct 149 (5th ed. 2003), citing, among others, In re Cordova-Gonzalez, 996 F.2d 1334 (1st Cir. 1993) (Cordova was disbarred because, among other things, he "violated ABA Model Rule 1.8(a) when he borrowed $100,000 from his client Jose Lopez-Nieves. . . . Cordova borrowed money from Lopez-Nieves without disclosing to his client (a) that he did not own the property pledged as collateral, (b) that his wife — who did own the collateral — and he were involved in bankruptcy proceedings, and (c) that the collateral was subject to the jurisdiction of the bankruptcy court, which had not approved the pledge."); People v. Johnson, 35 P.3d 168 (Colo. O.P.D.J. 1999) (Court syllabus explained that "disbarment was appropriate sanction for attorney who, along with misconduct involving two other clients, obtained two loans totaling $50,000 from client during pendency of an estate proceeding, having been aware that the client had received a bequest from the estate, and failed to advise client to seek independent advice concerning the loan, or obtain her written consent to the loan, and after having made some initial repayment, he thereafter knowingly misled client into believing that he would repay the loan.").

121. See In re Hartke, 529 N.W.2d 678 (Minn. 1995) (lawyer suspended indefinitely for selling his wife's car to a client without making adequate disclosures, and other offenses).

**Don't ask your client to invest in your business.**    Suppose your client just got a hefty personal injury settlement. She's got cash on hand. How about suggesting that you and she buy some real estate together? Or maybe you and she could buy old Coca-Cola paraphernalia and then sell it for a profit? Forget it! One lawyer in Indiana got an 18-month suspension for various instances of unethical behavior, including trying out this idea.[122]

### Can a lawyer accept stock or stock options as payment for legal services instead of cash?

A lawyer may be paid in the form of stock or stock options, but this type of transaction requires compliance with Rule 1.8.[123] This means that the terms of the transfer must be fair to the client. The lawyer must make a full written disclosure of the terms to the client and must explain that the lawyer's ownership of stock in a client corporation could cause a conflict of interest between the lawyer and the client that would require the client to withdraw from representing the client. The problem is that if the lawyer becomes a shareholder, the lawyer has a personal financial stake in the entity that might be at odds with the interests of the entity as a whole. The lawyer-shareholder, for example, might want short-term financial benefits that could be had only if needed research was forgone. The client must be given a chance to get independent legal advice before the stock transfer. The client's consent must be in writing.[124]

### PROBLEM 7-4  **STARTING A BUSINESS**

*Events similar to these occurred in Rhode Island.*

Ten years ago, you successfully defended Jose Lopez against a misdemeanor charge. As a result, the two of you became friends. You have never represented him on a legal matter since then, and he has never paid you any money since that time, although from time to time you have given him advice about buying and selling property.

A few months ago, Lopez, who is expert in appliance repair, decided to set up his own appliance repair company, and he asked you to help him in various ways. Together, you found a suitable building, which is the only asset owned by the 1404 Forest Street Corporation (Forest). That corporation is owned by Pasha Harari (she owns all 100 shares).

---

122. In re Davis, 740 N.E.2d 855 (Ind. 2001).

123. The transaction also requires compliance with Rule 1.7 and it may be subject to regulations of the Securities and Exchange Commission. See Dzienkowski & Peroni, supra n. 114, at 477.

124. See ABA Comm. on Ethics & Prof. Resp., Formal Op. 00-418 (2000); D.C. Bar, Ethics Op. 300 (2000); N.Y.C. Bar Assoc., Ethics Op. 2000-3 (2000).

You are planning to make the following arrangements:

- You will provide $25,000 in start-up money to buy all of the stock in the corporation from Harari. Lopez will put up only a small amount of money, but he will work full-time running the company. You expect to own 20 percent of the company, and Lopez will own 80 percent.
- When you pay the money to Harari, you will have her transfer 80 shares of Forest to Lopez and 20 shares to yourself.
- You and Lopez have agreed orally that Lopez will get another lawyer to represent him in connection with the purchase of the stock from Harari, but you will prepare the relevant documents.
- Lopez will serve as the president and sole director of Forest. You will serve as its general counsel and will handle its legal matters. You will be paid a salary.

You would prefer to enter into these arrangements without having to make any special disclosures to Lopez. He gets nervous about complicated legal information, so if you go overboard on disclosure, he might back out of this deal with you.

What, if any, warnings or disclosures do you have to give to Lopez?

## 3. Gifts from clients

Gifts from clients to lawyers can be problematic.[125] A gift from a client to a lawyer could represent a disguised fee in excess of the "reasonable" limit imposed by Rule 1.5. Or a client could make a gift in response to unfair pressure by the lawyer. For example, a lawyer might suggest to a client that in lieu of paying overdue bills for legal services, the client should change his will to leave his house to the lawyer. Rule 1.8(c) prohibits a lawyer from soliciting substantial gifts or bequests from a client. It also prohibits a lawyer from preparing for a client any instrument (such as a will) giving a gift to the lawyer or his relatives.[126] The rule allows a lawyer to prepare such an instrument on behalf of a close relative, however.

> **Rule 1.8(c)**
> A lawyer shall not solicit any substantial gift from a client, including a testamentary gift, or prepare on behalf of a client an instrument giving the lawyer or a person related to the lawyer any substantial gift unless the lawyer or other recipient of the gift is related to the client. For purposes of this paragraph, related persons include a spouse, child, grandchild, par-

---

125. Also, Rule 1.8(e), discussed earlier in this chapter, bars certain types of financial assistance to clients by lawyers.

126. The practice of writing a client's will in the lawyer's favor is prohibited unless the lawyer is a close relative. For example, in Clements v. Ky. B. Assn., 983 S.W.2d 512 (Ky. 1999), a lawyer was suspended from practice for preparing a will under which she would inherit $50,000.

ent, grandparent or other relative or individual with whom the lawyer or the client maintains a close, familial relationship.

The rule does not bar lawyers from receiving unsolicited gifts from clients. However, if the gift is too large, the client could later sue for its return.[127]

Therefore, if your client offers you a holiday gift or some other modest thank you gift, you may accept it. But you may not ask a client for a substantial gift or prepare a document transferring client property to you or one of your relatives, unless the client is a close relative or the functional equivalent of a close relative. This rule reflects a concern that some lawyers might take advantage of their clients' trust and appreciation by persuading clients to give them property.

## 4. Sexual relationships with clients

Lawyers and clients sometimes develop sexual relationships. It is obvious that if a lawyer coerces a client into a sexual relationship (for example, in lieu of paying a fee), the relationship is improper because it is exploitative.[128] However, it is not as clear that there is anything wrong with a truly consensual sexual relationship between a lawyer and a client, especially if there is no harm to the quality of the legal representation. Perhaps there is always a possibility of adverse impact, if only because the romance might end and then the professional relationship would become strained. In 1996, the ABA Committee on Ethics and Professional Responsibility declined to conclude that sexual relationships with clients were inherently unprofessional, but it advised lawyers to avoid them "because of the danger of impairment to the lawyer's representation." The Committee wrote that "the lawyer would be well advised to refrain from such a relationship. If such a sexual relationship occurs and the impairment is not avoided, the lawyer will have violated ethical obligations to the client."[129]

Some states have suspended lawyers from practice because of consensual lawyer-client sexual relations, even though no disciplinary rule explicitly prohibited the relationship and even though there was no evidence of harm to the client. In one case, a male lawyer was disciplined because he had a sexual relationship with a female client while handling a matter for her. Then,

---

127. Rule 1.8, Comment 6.

128. See, e.g., Cleveland B. Assn. v. Feneli, 712 N.E.2d 119 (Ohio 1999) (lawyer suspended from practice after having oral sex with client and telling her that "she had certain other methods of payment that he would enjoy more than money"). Many reported cases involved clients who retained lawyers for divorce proceedings, at a time when they may have been particularly vulnerable. See, e.g., In re Halverson, 998 P.2d 833 (Wash. 2000) (former president of the state bar was a divorce specialist who had edited a book discussing the adverse consequences of lawyer-client sexual relationships but was suspended for one year for having sex with six female divorce clients).

129. ABA Comm. on Ethics & Prof. Resp., Formal Op. 92-364 (1992).

after the work and the romance ended, she hired him to handle another matter for her. In imposing a one-month suspension, the court reasoned:

> First, because of the dependence that so often characterizes the attorney-client relationship, there is a significant possibility that the sexual relationship will have resulted from the exploitation of the lawyer's dominant position and influence and, thus, breached the lawyer's fiduciary obligations to the client. Second, a sexual relationship with a client may affect the independence of the lawyer's judgment. Third, the lawyer's engaging in a sexual relationship with a client may create a prohibited conflict between the interests of the lawyer and those of the client. Fourth, a non-professional, yet emotionally charged, relationship between attorney and client may result in confidences being imparted in circumstances where the attorney-client privilege is not available, yet would have been, absent the personal relationship.[130]

In 2002, at the recommendation of the Ethics 2000 Commission, the ABA amended the Model Rules to prohibit sexual relationships with clients, even if the client is not prejudiced, except for sexual relationships that existed before the lawyer-client relationship began. If a lawyer represents a corporation, Rule 1.8(j) bars the lawyer from a sexual relationship with any person in the corporation "who supervises, directs, or regularly consults with that lawyer concerning the organization's legal matters."[131]

Note that the rule does not prohibit lawyers from having romances with former clients. However, a lawyer who wishes to initiate a romantic relationship with a client might first assist the client in finding new counsel.

## 5. Intimate or family relationships with adverse lawyers

One common "personal interest" conflict occurs when two lawyers who are members of the same family represent clients with adverse interests in a matter. If the relationship between the two lawyers is that of "parent, child, sibling or spouse," they normally may not represent clients who are adversaries unless the clients have been informed of the relationship, advised of the possible problems, and given informed consent.[132]

> **FOR EXAMPLE:** Sandra is a district attorney prosecuting a murder case. Her husband, Abdul, is a public defender who has been assigned to represent the defendant. Both lawyers must inform their clients (or, in Sandra's case, the representative of an institutional client) of their relationship and

---

130. Matter of Tsoutsouris, 748 N.E. 2d 856 (Ind. 2004). See also Fla. B. v. Bryant, 813 So. 2d 38 (Fla. 2002) (lawyer suspended for one year for sex with client even though the referee had found that the relationship was not exploitative because the client was a prostitute).

131. Rule 1.8, Comment 17.

132. Rule 1.7, Comment 11. This type of conflict is not imputed to members of the lawyers' firms. Id. If two adverse lawyers have an intimate relationship that is not one of those listed in Comment 11, it may be advisable nevertheless to seek consent before going forward.

the possible ways that it could compromise their work on behalf of their clients (for example, through sharing of confidences) and seek consent.

As with other personal interest conflicts, this type of conflict is not imputed to other lawyers in the firm, so if one of the clients is not willing to consent, another lawyer in the firm may take over the representation.

# 6. Imputation of personal interest conflicts to other lawyers in a firm

## a. Financial interest conflicts

Rule 1.8 lays out rules on many particular situations in which lawyers' financial interests may conflict with those of clients. Rule 1.8(k) provides that financial interest conflicts of one lawyer in a firm are imputed to all other lawyers in the firm. This means, for example, that "one lawyer in a firm may not enter into a business transaction with a client of another member of the firm without complying with paragraph (a), even if the first lawyer is not personally involved in the representation of the client."[133]

## b. General rule on imputation of conflicts with a lawyer's interests

While the imputation provision in Rule 1.8 governs imputation of particular financial conflicts between the interests of client and lawyer, Rule 1.10(a) addresses imputation of other conflicts between a client's interests and a lawyer's interests to other lawyers in a firm.

As we discussed in Chapter 5, Rule 1.10(a) imputes to all lawyers in a firm any conflicts of one *client* with the interests of another present or former *client* of another lawyer in the firm. The rule also imputes some conflicts created by the personal interests of a *lawyer* in the firm. However, if a "personal interest" conflict "does not present a significant risk of materially limiting the representation of the client by the remaining lawyers in the firm," the conflict is not imputed to other lawyers in the firm.[134] A comment explains that whether a personal interest conflict is imputed depends on whether it presents "questions of client loyalty [or] protection of confidential information."[135]

> FOR EXAMPLE: One lawyer in a firm wants to represent an organization that advocates for the rights of Palestinians in Israel. Another lawyer in the firm neither wants nor is able to handle this work because he has family in

---

133. Rule 1.8, Comment 20.
134. Rule 1.10(a).
135. Rule 1.10, Comment 3. If the personal interest of the affected lawyer involves a prohibition to undertake certain transactions under Rule 1.8, one should refer to Rule 1.8(k) rather than Rule 1.10 to determine whether that conflict is imputed to other lawyers in the firm. Rule 1.10, Comment 8.

Israel and is unsympathetic to this organization. This conflict would not be imputed to the other lawyers in the firm so long as the conflicted lawyer would not do any work on the matter.

**FOR EXAMPLE:** One lawyer in a firm wishes to represent a worker at a thermos factory who was injured on the job while operating a machine. One of the partners in the firm owns the thermos factory and therefore is not able to handle the suit. This conflict would be imputed to the other lawyers in the firm because the other lawyers in the firm "would be materially limited in pursuing the matter because of loyalty to that lawyer."[136]

From these examples, it is apparent that one must evaluate each such conflict on its facts rather than attempting to make categorical distinctions. Suppose that the first example involved a small firm of five lawyers and that the lawyer with the conflict had lost a family member to a Palestinian suicide bomber. In that case, the loyalty of the other lawyers to the first might require imputation of this conflict for the same reasons as in the second example.

# C. Lawyer as custodian of client property and documents

Lawyers very often have responsibility for money, documents, and other valuables that belong to clients. They have a fiduciary duty to protect their clients' possessions and to turn money and property over to clients upon request or, in some cases, promptly after receiving it.

## 1. Client trust accounts

One important aspect of the lawyer-client relationship involves a lawyer's management of the client trust account, the bank account in which the lawyer keeps funds that belong to various clients. If a lawyer takes possession of money from a client or third party in connection with a representation, she must keep it "separate from the lawyer's own property. Funds shall be kept in a separate account maintained in the state where the lawyer's office is situated, or elsewhere with the consent of the client or third person."[137]

Property other than money must be "appropriately safeguarded," and the lawyer must keep "complete records" of the funds or other property for a period specified in state rules (the ABA recommends five years) after the events that they record.[138]

---

136. Rule 1.10, Comment 3. Both of these examples are elaborations on the examples offered in Comment 3.

137. Rule 1.15(a).

138. Id.

This rule permits a lawyer to keep funds that belong to multiple clients in a single account, but the funds that belong to clients must be kept in a separate account from any funds that belong to the lawyer.[139] This rule seeks to ensure that the lawyer does not spend client funds improperly and that the lawyer's creditors are not able to seize funds held by the lawyer that belong to clients.

If a client pays a lawyer in advance a sum against which the lawyer may charge fees, this sum should be deposited into the client trust account. The lawyer may withdraw funds against this payment only as fees are earned or expenses incurred.[140]

Rule 1.15 bars lawyers from depositing their own funds into the client trust account, to ensure that lawyers do not attempt to hide their own monies from creditors in their client accounts.

**FOR EXAMPLE:** J. Kevin Lund, a Kansas lawyer, was divorced from his wife and ordered to pay child support. When he fell behind in his payments, his wife obtained a judgment for some past-due amounts. Lund deposited some of his personal funds into his client trust account, thus protecting them from attachment by his wife. He was suspended from practice for a year.[141]

The rule also requires lawyers to keep detailed records of deposits into and withdrawals from the client trust account. Many state bars have initiated programs to conduct random audits of client trust accounts to ensure that lawyers comply with these rules.

Once you have a license to practice law, one of the quickest and surest ways to lose it is to put funds that belong to a client into your own account (not the client trust account) or to "borrow" funds from the client trust account that you have not yet earned. In many jurisdictions, these offenses are considered most grave and are grounds for disbarment. A lawyer may be disciplined for commingling or misappropriation even if the violation was unintentional, even if no client funds were lost, and even if the lawyer's mental capacity is compromised by illness.[142]

# 2. Responsibility for client property

## a. Prompt delivery of funds or property

When a lawyer receives a settlement check or other funds that should be paid (at least in part) to a client, the lawyer is obliged to notify the client and to make prompt payment of all funds due to the client. If the client asks, the lawyer must provide a record of the amount received and of how much was

---

139. Rule 1.15, Comment 1.

140. Rule 1.15, Comment 7(b) [Delaware]; Rule 1.15(c) [ABA Model Rules].

141. In re Lund, 19 P.3d 110 (Kan. 2001).

142. ABA, Annotated Model Rules of Professional Conduct 252 (5th ed. 2003); see generally Irene Ricci, Client Trust Funds: How to Avoid Ethical Problems, 11 Geo. J. Legal Ethics 245 (1998).

paid to whom.[143] The same obligation applies if the person who has an interest in the funds is someone other than a client. This sounds fairly routine, but some lawyers contrive to obtain funds that belong to others as a result of settlement negotiations; they then conceal their misconduct by giving clients inadequate or inaccurate information.

> **FOR EXAMPLE:** James O'Hagan was a partner at Dorsey & Whitney, one of the largest firms in Minneapolis. One of his clients was the famous Mayo Clinic, which he represented in medical malpractice cases. O'Hagan settled some cases but was not always honest with his client about the amounts of the settlements. O'Hagan reportedly settled one case for $270,000, but then told the Mayo Clinic that it had settled for $595,000. The Mayo Clinic gave O'Hagan a check for $595,000. He paid $270,000 to the plaintiff's attorney and used the remainder to pay off personal loan obligations. For this and other similar offenses that added up to alleged theft of $3 million, O'Hagan was fined and sentenced to 30 months in prison.[144]

### b. Disputes about money or property in lawyer's possession

Suppose a lawyer and her plaintiff client make a contingent fee agreement under which the lawyer will receive one-third of the amount of any settlement. The case then settles for $25,000. The defendant writes a check and sends it to the lawyer, who deposits it in the trust account. The client, upon learning of the settlement, points out to the lawyer that the settlement took place after the lawyer had done only a few hours' work on the matter. The client claims that the original agreement would overcompensate the lawyer. Can the lawyer withdraw her one-third from the trust account?

Rule 1.15(c) provides that if there is a dispute about the amount of the fee, the lawyer is to distribute undisputed portions of the settlement and keep the disputed portion in the client trust account. So the lawyer should pay out to the client two-thirds of the settlement amount and should not transfer the

---

143. Rule 1.15(d):

> Upon receiving funds or other property in which a client or third person has an interest, a lawyer shall promptly notify the client or third person. Except as stated in this Rule or otherwise permitted by law or by agreement with the client, a lawyer shall promptly deliver to the client or third person any funds or other property that the client or third person is entitled to receive and, upon request by the client or third person, shall promptly render a full accounting regarding such property.

144. State v. O'Hagan, 474 N.W.2d 613 (Minn. App. 1991). O'Hagan's conduct also would violate Rule 1.15 because he arranged to be in possession of funds that belonged to his client and neither notified the client nor distributed the funds to the client. This conduct also would violate the prohibition against dishonesty in Rule 8.4. O'Hagan was disbarred in the wake of these allegations, but no findings were made as to which Minnesota rules were violated. Instead, O'Hagan was disbarred because he failed to respond to the disciplinary action filed against him. In re O'Hagan, 450 N.W.2d 571 (Minn. 1990). In 1994, O'Hagan was also convicted on federal mail fraud, securities fraud, and money laundering charges and sentenced to 41 months in prison. U.S. v. O'Hagan, 521 U.S. 642 (1997).

remaining third to herself until the dispute is resolved. Even if the lawyer thinks that the client is wrong and that the lawyer is entitled to one-third, the client's inquiry places that amount in dispute.[145]

### c. Lawyers' responsibilities to clients' creditors

Suppose that you receive a settlement check for $10,000 for a client. What if you then get a notice from a local department store indicating that your client owes it $5,000 and asking you to remit the amount due?

A comment to Rule 1.15 explains that if a third party has a "lawful claim" against funds that are in the lawyer's custody, the lawyer might have some obligation to the third party. The lawyer is not supposed to try to arbitrate such a claim, but if the claim is not "frivolous," the lawyer should hold the property until the claims are resolved. Does the example given above fall within this ambit?

It does not. A lawyer is not a collection agency for all his clients' creditors. The department store has no right to ask the lawyer to give it money that the client owes, even if the debt is legitimate and overdue. If, on the other hand, the department store sues the client for the money, obtains a judgment, and then obtains an order against the lawyer to surrender the funds, that is another matter. Such situations are not very common. The main thing to know is that unless the creditor has a legitimate claim to the particular funds in the lawyer's possession, the lawyer's duty is to his client, not to the third party.[146]

## 3. Administering estates and trusts

### May a lawyer act as executor of a client's estate?

A lawyer may accept appointment as executor of a client's estate. Executors often are paid substantial sums for their services in settling estates, but this is not prohibited by Rule 1.8(c) because the payment would be for services rendered, not an outright gift. However, a lawyer giving advice about whom to appoint as executor or carrying out the functions of executor for a client might be improperly biased by self-interest in doing so. A lawyer must comply with Rule 1.7 in giving such advice or in acting as executor for a client's estate.[147]

---

145. See In re Haar, 698 A.2d 412 (D.C. App. 1997) (a lawyer who withdrew a legal fee that was disputed by the client because he believed he was entitled to the payment was found to have engaged in negligent misappropriation).

146. See generally D.C. Bar, Ethics Op. 293 (2000) (explaining what might constitute a legitimate claim by a third party to client funds in a lawyer's possession).

147. Rule 1.8, Comment 8.

# 8 LAWYERS' DUTIES TO COURTS, ADVERSARIES, AND OTHERS

A. Being a good person in an adversary system
B. Investigation before filing a complaint
   1. Required investigation by lawyers filing civil cases
   2. Required investigation by prosecutors before charges are filed
C. Truth and falsity in litigation
   1. The rules on candor to tribunals
   2. Which rule applies when? A taxonomy of truth-telling problems in litigation
   3. A lawyer's duties if a client or witness intends to give false testimony
   4. False impressions created by lawyers during litigation
   5. Lawyers' duties of truthfulness in preparing witnesses to testify
D. Concealment of physical evidence and documents
   1. Duties of criminal defense lawyers with respect to evidence of crimes
   2. Concealment of documents and evidence in civil cases
E. The duty to disclose adverse legal authority
F. Disclosures in ex parte proceedings
G. Improper influences on judges and juries
   1. Improper influences on judges
   2. Improper influences on juries

So far we have examined the obligations that lawyers owe to their clients — the duties of confidentiality, competence, diligence, communication, deference, loyalty, and fair dealing. Our system of justice also requires lawyers to behave in certain ways toward people who are not their clients. Those other people include judges and other government officials, adversary parties and their lawyers, potential witnesses, and other members of society with whom lawyers have contact.

Now we explore those obligations to nonclients and how they may conflict with the duties that lawyers owe to clients. Conflicting duties are inherent in an adversary system of justice. In the interest of justice, lawyers are directed to be fiercely loyal to their clients. But if there were no bounds on such loyalty, lawyers could subvert justice, for example, by helping clients to commit crimes or by supplying courts with false evidence.

We begin the chapter with a famous defense of zealous advocacy, even when that practice necessarily causes pain to others, and with an observation about the extent to which our profession's ethical rules encourage, or at least tolerate, making a client's interests primary, particularly in situations of conflict such as litigation. We then turn to how rules of law constrain such advocacy in the interest of fair adjudication and decent treatment of adversaries and others. The first sections consider the duties imposed on lawyers in court proceedings. We then examine duties that lawyers owe to other lawyers and to third parties even when no formal proceeding has begun.

# A. Being a good person in an adversary system

The conflicting ethical demands on lawyers in an adversary system have provoked dozens of books and articles that explore the dilemmas faced by conscientious lawyers and possible resolutions of the conflicting pressures. These articles and books ask whether a lawyer should seek every advantage for his client short of violating the law or violating a clearly defined ethical prohibition. They ask whether a lawyer should also look out for the interests of other persons, even when no law or rule compels it.

The laws and rules occasionally require or forbid particular conduct, but very often they allow lawyers to act as they think best. On many issues on which the rules give lawyers discretion, lawyers differ in their view of what is proper. For example, most lawyers would agree that a lawyer representing a defendant in a civil case may, but is not required to, assert an available technical defense to defeat a plaintiff's claim, even if that tactic would defeat an otherwise legitimate lawsuit.[1] All lawyers occupy a place on a spectrum in their attitudes about to whom they owe duties. At one end are the "hired guns" who pursue every possible tactic on behalf of their clients. At the other end are lawyers who believe that their duties as "officers of the court" are as important as their duties to their clients. One of these public-spirited lawyers might decline to pursue a technical argument if it might produce what the lawyer believed to be an unfair outcome on the merits. Or such a lawyer might not hesitate to disclose to a judge information that might harm his client's case if he believed that he had a higher duty to the system of justice than to his client.

Those who subscribe to the hired gun approach to lawyering urge that if the adversary system tilts too strongly toward loyalty to clients, perhaps the system should be changed, but in the meantime, they should not be faulted for serving their clients within that system. The public-spirited lawyers believe that other values should sometimes override their clients' goals. Somewhere in the middle of the spectrum we might find a group of lawyers whose decisions reflect concern for clients but also a concern to maintain good personal relationships with judges, adversary lawyers, or adversary clients. Some client-centered lawyers also forgo aggressive tactics because they think that their clients will best be served, in the long run, if lawyers do not press for every possible advantage.

Some lawyers believe that the hired gun model may be appropriate for representation of criminal defendants to counter the immense resources that the state can bring to bear on their clients, but that a less client-centered approach is more suitable for all other kinds of legal work.

The debate about where lawyers should place themselves on the spectrum described above is sometimes couched in terms of whether a good lawyer can also be a good person, or conversely whether a lawyer must sometimes relinquish lawful tactics that would help his clients.

---

1. An example of such a technical defense would be that the process server was not a resident of the forum state as required by that state's law. Some lawyers might say that if a client wants the lawyer to use such a defense, the lawyer is bound to follow the client's wishes. However, most would say either that this question is one of means rather than objectives, requiring the lawyer only to consult the client under Rule 1.2, or that the issue is so technical that not even client consultation is needed before the lawyer decides either to assert or not to assert the defense.

## Charles Fried, The Lawyer as Friend: The Moral Foundations of the Lawyer-Client Relation

85 Yale L.J. 1060 (1976)

[Professor Fried is Beneficial Professor of Law at Harvard Law School. He served as the U.S. solicitor general during the Reagan administration and as an associate justice of the Supreme Judicial Court of Massachusetts.]

Can a good lawyer be a good person? . . . Does the lawyer whose conduct and choices are governed only by the traditional conception of the lawyer's role . . . lead a professional life worthy of moral approbation, worthy of respect—ours and his own? . . . [Lawyers are frequently criticized because their ethic of loyalty to clients] appears to authorize tactics which procure advantages for the client at the direct expense of some identified opposing party. Examples are discrediting a nervous but probably truthful complaining witness or taking advantage of the need or ignorance of an adversary in a negotiation. . . . [A] classic case is the interposition of a technical defense such as the running of the statute of limitations to defeat a debt that the client admits he owes.[2] . . .

I will argue in this essay that it is not only legally but also morally right that a lawyer adopt as his dominant purpose the furthering of his client's interests. . . . Charles Curtis made the perspicacious remark that a lawyer may be privileged to lie for his client in a way that one might lie to save one's friends or close relatives. I do not want to underwrite the notion that it is justifiable to lie even in those situations, but there is a great deal to the point that in those relations—friendship, kinship—we recognize an authorization to take the interests of particular concrete persons more seriously and to give them priority over the interests of the wider collectivity. One who provides an expensive education for his own children surely cannot be blamed because he does not use these resources to alleviate famine or to save lives in some distant land. . . .

How does a professional fit into the concept of personal relations at all? He is, I have suggested, a limited-purpose friend. A lawyer is a friend in regard to the legal system. He is someone who enters into a personal relation with you—not an abstract relation as under the concept of justice. That means that like a friend he acts in your interests, not his own; or rather he adopts your interests as his own. I would call that the classic definition of friendship. . . . When I say the lawyer is his client's legal friend, I mean the lawyer makes his client's interests his own insofar as this is necessary to preserve and foster the client's autonomy within the law. . . .

---

2. [Fried's footnote 13.] For a striking example, see Zabella v. Pakel, 242 F.2d 452 (7th Cir. 1957), where the debtor asserting the technical defenses was a savings and loan association president, and the creditor was a man who had worked for him as a carpenter and had lent him money in earlier, less fortunate days.

The lawyer acts morally because he helps to preserve and express the autonomy of his client vis-à-vis the legal system. It is not just that the lawyer helps his client accomplish a particular lawful purpose. Pornography may be legal, but it hardly follows that I perform a morally worthy function if I lend money or artistic talent to help the pornographer flourish in the exercise of this right. What is special about legal counsel is that whatever else may stop the pornographer's enterprise, he should not be stopped because he mistakenly believes there is a legal impediment. . . . to assist others in understanding and realizing their legal rights is always morally worthy. . . .

Is there not something odd about analogizing the lawyer's role to friendship when in fact his so-called friendship must usually be bought? If the lawyer is a public purveyor of goods, is not the lawyer-client relationship like that underlying any commercial transaction? My answer is "No." . . . [Under the rules of professional responsibility, a lawyer's duty to a client continues, even if the client no longer can afford to pay] if withdrawal of their services would prejudice that individual. . . . It is undeniable that money is usually what cements the lawyer-client relationship. But the content of the relation is determined by the client's needs, just as friendship is a response to another's needs. . . .

I come now to what seems to me one of the most difficult dilemmas of the lawyer's role. It is illustrated by the lawyer who is asked to press the unfair claim, to humiliate a witness, to participate in a distasteful or dishonorable scheme. . . . Consider . . . asserting the statute of limitations or the lack of a written memorandum to defeat what you know to be a just claim against your client. . . . [I]f an injustice is worked, it is worked because the legal system not only permits it, but also defines the terms and modes of operation. . . . [A] lawyer is morally entitled to act in this formal, representative way even if the result is an injustice, because the legal system which authorizes both the injustice (e.g., the result following the plea of the statute of limitations) and the formal gesture for working it insulates him from personal moral responsibility. . . .

[The lawyer] may explain the system for his client even if the system consequently works injustice. He may, but must he? . . . [I]f you are the last lawyer in town, is there a moral obligation to help the finance company foreclose on the widow's refrigerator? If the client pursues the foreclosure in order to establish a legal right of some significance, I do not flinch from the conclusion that the lawyer is bound to urge this right. So also if the finance company cannot foreclose because of an ideological boycott by the local bar. But if all the other lawyers happen to be on vacation and the case means no more to the finance company than the resale value of one more used refrigerator, common sense says the lawyer can say no. One should be able to distinguish between establishing a legal right and being a cog in a routine, repetitive business operation, part of which just happens to play itself out in court.

---

Professor Stephen Gillers explores the same issue. He constructs a pair of interesting hypotheticals and suggests that a lawyer who uses permitted (but not required) tactics to produce unjust results can properly be criticized, along with her client, for immoral conduct.

## Stephen Gillers, Can a Good Lawyer Be a Bad Person?

84 Mich. L. Rev. 1011, 1011–1022 (1986)[3]

[Professor Gillers is vice dean and the Emily Kempin Professor of Law at New York University School of Law.]

Assume a just legal system in a constitutional democracy. Assume a person wishing to achieve a lawful goal. Assume a lawyer who agrees to assist her. If the lawyer uses only legal means, can a coherent theory of moral philosophy nevertheless label the lawyer's conduct immoral? Can a good lawyer be a bad person? . . . [Some argue that the legal system] is so special that as long as a lawyer acts within it, he or she must be insulated from moral accountability. . . . The lawyer is [morally] unaccountable not because the client's ends or means are lawful, but because of the lawyer's instrumental status. . . . Skeptics might call this explanation facile. No lawyer is required to accept a client and generally does so for no noble purpose. The lawyer's concern with helping society fulfill a promise is belied by the fact that clients unable to purchase the lawyer's time are ordinarily turned away. . . .

[Consider these hypotheticals. First,] a man whose lifelong dream has been to open a restaurant persuades a wealthy cousin to lend him $50,000. The man is unsophisticated in business matters while the cousin is not. The man signs a demand note for the loan and opens the restaurant. Food critics give it excellent reviews; great success is predicted. Seeing this, the cousin calls the note, then brings an action on it, intending to acquire the restaurant in a foreclosure sale. The man goes to a lawyer who sees improbable defenses on the merits and who proceeds to make a series of nonfrivolous procedural motions calculated to gain time for her client until either the restaurant's cash flow is great enough to pay the note or a bank loan can be obtained. The motions are either weak, with the lawyer expecting them to fail, or they are highly technical.

[Second,] while on her way home from a job as a housekeeper, a single mother of three children is hurt by falling debris at a construction site. She suffers permanent injuries that prevent her from resuming gainful employment. She sues the construction company. Its lawyer, recognizing only weak defenses on the merits, makes [similar] procedural motions. . . . These have the effect of increasing pressure on the financially desperate plaintiff to settle for a tenth of what she could reasonably expect to recover at trial.

[These are] two situations in which lawyers, with no realistic defense on the merits, make weak or technical procedural motions in order to delay plaintiffs' efforts to vindicate their legal rights. Assume the motions are addressed to the sufficiency of service of process. One motion alleges that service was made by

---

3. A revised version of this article appears at 2 J. Inst. Study Leg. Ethics 131 (1999).

someone a month under eighteen years of age. If true, service was improper, but the motion must be counted as highly technical. Another motion makes a weak assertion that the agent served with process was not one identified in applicable law.

If the Code and the rules mean to forbid this sort of "indirect" strategy, they certainly say so obscurely. I assume they permit the motions on the posited facts. The rules that identify the minimum age of a process server and the agents eligible to receive service either mean what they say or they do not. If they do, then a defendant must be able to challenge service when there is reason to believe these rules were ignored. The right to challenge, furthermore, does not accrue only to those defendants who can, in good faith, demonstrate a probable defense on the merits. Nevertheless, even if law and the governing ethical document permit the motions, does the lawyer who makes them act immorally by "frustrating an opposing party's attempt to obtain rightful redress or repose?" I believe she does. On these facts, a good lawyer may be a bad person. . . .

A lawyer may refrain from making the motions, even if requested to do so by her client, without violating [ethical norms]. Because the tactic is discretionary, the lawyer who invokes it by making the motions is as morally accountable as the client on whose behalf she acts. I do not mean to say that the lawyer who makes the motions will necessarily have acted badly, but only that she stands in no better position than her client. Whether the conduct of a lawyer and client may be morally criticized hinges on the entire factual context, including the particular circumstances of the case and the behavior of the opposition. It may be that the conduct in [the first hypothetical] can be defended, while the conduct in [the second] cannot.

### Question about the Fried and Gillers Articles

These articles use examples of lawyers interposing valid but technical defenses, such as a defense based on the age of the process server, to defeat otherwise valid legal claims. Do you expect to use such tactics? If your answer is yes, do you expect to have any moral qualms about doing so? In particular, consider the example that Fried suggests in his footnote based on the *Zabella* case. A man borrows money from a generous person who once worked for him as a carpenter. The borrower becomes a wealthy executive and fails to repay the money, although he admits owing it. When the carpenter sues him, his lawyer invokes the statute of limitations to avoid repayment. Would you do the same thing if your client were the executive and wanted to avoid repayment? Why or why not?

## B. Investigation before filing a complaint

Fried and Gillers ask whether a good lawyer can be a good person if the lawyer uses all of the permitted tools of the legal system on behalf of a client. Often the legal rules do not draw clear lines between what is permitted and what is forbidden. Lawyers often must interpret imprecise regulatory language or apply that language to unique facts to know whether they may take particular actions on behalf of clients. If they make judgments with which others disagree, they may find themselves subject to bar discipline, civil suits, or even (like Belge in Chapter 2) criminal indictments.

**How much fact investigation must a lawyer do before filing a lawsuit?**

One ethical problem lurks at the threshold of every lawsuit: Does the lawyer for the party initiating the proceedings have enough of a factual and legal basis to justify starting a case that will impose burdens of time and expense on others? Lawyers are not expected to limit themselves to filing "sure winners," but they are not allowed to file "frivolous" lawsuits — those that have virtually no chance of succeeding.

## 1. Required investigation by lawyers filing civil cases

> **Rule 3.1    Meritorious claims and contentions**
> A lawyer shall not bring or defend a proceeding, or assert or controvert an issue therein, unless there is a basis in law and fact for doing so that is not frivolous, which includes a good faith argument for an extension, modification or reversal of existing law. A lawyer for the defendant in a criminal proceeding, or the respondent in a proceeding that could result in incarceration, may nevertheless so defend the proceeding as to require that every element of the case be established.[4]

Rule 3.1 prohibits the filing of "frivolous" claims, but it does not define that term. A lawyer may not file a suit on the basis of mere speculation that a prospective defendant has done something wrong. But how much more is required? Comment 2 states that the facts need not be "fully substantiated" before suit is filed. It recognizes that a lawyer may need to use discovery to "develop vital evidence." On the other hand, lawyers must "inform themselves about the facts of their clients' cases and the applicable law and determine that they can make good faith arguments in support of their clients' positions."

Some court rules further elaborate a lawyer's duty before filing a case. In federal civil cases, Federal Rule of Civil Procedure 11(b) is similar to Rule 3.1, but it is more detailed.[5] Under Rule 11, a party's legal theory must be "warranted by existing law or by a nonfrivolous argument for the extension,

---

4. This is the text of the relevant Delaware Rule of Professional Conduct. Unless specified otherwise, all of this book's quotations from rules of professional conduct are quotations from the Delaware Rules of Professional Conduct. In a few instances, we quote from rules or from published proposed rules in other states. Except where we note otherwise, however, the text of all state rules that we quote is the same as the text of the ABA Model Rules of Professional Conduct. See the note in the Introduction for a more detailed explanation.

5. All states have similar rules, and most are modeled on Fed. R. Civ. P. 11.

modification, or reversal of existing law or the establishment of new law.[6] Factual assertions must "have evidentiary support or, if specifically so identified, [be] likely to have evidentiary support after a reasonable opportunity for further investigation or discovery."[7]

This standard is subject to widely ranging interpretation. Evidence can consist of documents or testimony. Even unpersuasive statements of a witness who is willing to testify may constitute "evidentiary support." Juries are allowed to draw inferences, so evidence can be circumstantial. And for some factual assertions, the pleader need not have evidentiary support if the lawyer justifiably believes (and asserts) that discovery will "likely" produce such support.[8] On the other hand, FRCP 11 also may be interpreted to require a party to have some evidence in hand with respect to every element of the case for which the party has the burden of pleading. This interpretation would require considerable prefiling investigation in some cases.

We do not have definitive answers to these questions about how to interpret Rule 3.1 or FRCP 11. FRCP 11 was amended in 1993.[9] Most of the cases decided since then are very fact-specific trial court decisions. This makes it difficult to generalize about what lawyers need to do in other cases.

Here are summaries of some recent decisions interpreting Rule 11.

**Boyer v. KRS Computer & Business School**[10]   Boyer was fired. He claimed that his employer had invaded his privacy by electronically eavesdropping on his conversation with other employees about his complaints against his employer. His lawyer was sanctioned for (among other failures) filing the suit without having checked with the other employees to find out whether the employer learned about Boyer's complaints from one of those people. In fact, the employer had not eavesdropped. The employer had learned of Boyer's complaints from one of the employees in question.

**Parker v. Vigo County School Corp.**[11]   Jill Parker, a public school cafeteria worker, sued the Indiana School Food Service Association. She claimed

---

6. Fed. R. Civ. P. 11(b)(2). The importance of permitting good faith arguments for outcomes that are inconsistent with existing law cannot be understated. If lawyers were not permitted to make such arguments, they could not urge changes in the common law and could not ask courts to correct erroneous or outdated precedents. The law would become frozen. Because ethical standards encourage American lawyers to challenge even recent precedents if they seem wrongly decided, courts, including the Supreme Court, can correct their own mistakes relatively quickly. See, e.g., Lawrence v. Texas, 539 U.S. 558 (2003) (statutes making it a crime for persons of the same sex to engage in private sexual activity violated the due process clause), *overruling* Bowers v. Hardwick, 478 U.S. 186 (1986) (because it was incorrectly decided).

7. Fed. R. Civ. P. 11(b)(3).

8. Lawyers are not fond of conceding that they don't currently have critically needed support for their claims and need discovery to obtain it. That admission could invite the opposing party to resist discovery more strongly.

9. Among other changes, the 1993 amendment added the section allowing lawyers to file cases that include identified allegations for which they do not yet have evidentiary support.

10. 171 F. Supp. 2d 950 (D. Minn. 2001).

11. 2000 WL 33125132 (S.D. Ind., Dec. 20, 2000).

that the association had interfered with her employment contract. Parker had refused to join the local chapter of ISFSA. In addition, she had not become certified by the county for employment as a cafeteria worker. The case turned on whether her refusal to join the association had affected the county's decision not to certify her. Some time after she refused to join the association, Parker's supervisor, Nancy Snedeker, told her that her work hours were being reduced. Snedeker mentioned that she had decided to reduce Parker's work hours after consultation with Pam Drake, the county's certification director. At the time, Snedeker was president of the local chapter of ISFSA, and Drake was a member. However, when Parker sued, neither she nor her lawyer had any evidence that ISFSA had told Snedeker to cut her work hours. ISFSA won summary judgment, but the judge denied sanctions against Parker's lawyer. The court said that Snedeker and Drake's memberships in ISFSA and the conversation between Snedeker and Drake amounted to a "scintilla of evidence" that Parker's hours were cut because she had not become certified and that she was not certified because she refused to join ISFSA. This scintilla, while not enough to avoid summary judgment, was enough "evidentiary support" to avoid FRCP 11 sanctions.

**Jimenez v. Madison Area Technical College**[12]  Elvira Jimenez hired Willie Nunnery to represent her in a claim of employment discrimination based on race and sex. She gave Nunnery several e-mails she had allegedly received from her employer over the years; they said, for example, "I guess you are merely a stupid mexican [sic] after all . . . your [sic] nothing more than a little, bitchy, money-hungry spic." She also provided him with copies, but not originals, of discriminatory memoranda. Nunnery's practice was "to accept what [his clients] tell him, incorporate the allegations in a complaint and let the crucible of cross-examination and discovery lead to the truth," while also warning his clients about the penalties for perjury. Nunnery met with a representative of the employer, but he did not believe the employer's denials because he expected the employer to deny discriminating. The e-mails turned out to be forgeries. The court punished Nunnery by dismissing the case and requiring Nunnery to pay $16,000. The judge acknowledged that it is hard to say whether a lawyer could ever rely solely on his client's version of the facts as a basis for filing suit, and that this might be more justifiable if the statute of limitations was about to expire. But, the court said, the lawyer should have realized that it was very unlikely that several professionals would make ungrammatical written discriminatory statements. He should have "subjected his client to rigorous questioning" and "insisted on seeing the original documents."

---

12. 2001 WL 34392042 (W.D. Wis. Aug. 13, 2001). Nunnery appealed the dismissal. The court of appeals not only affirmed the lower court decision but found that the appeal was frivolous, and it imposed additional monetary sanctions. Jimenez v. Madison Area Tech. Coll., 321 F.3d 652 (7th Cir. 2003). Both courts also ordered that Nunnery's conduct be brought to the attention of the bar disciplinary authorities.

## What are the differences between Rule 3.1 and FRCP 11?

Rule 3.1 and FRCP 11 articulate similar standards, but there are important distinctions between them.

- **Sanctions.** Violation of Rule 3.1 can result in bar disciplinary action against an attorney. A violation of FRCP 11 is punished not by the state bar but by the judge in the civil action, and it can result in nonmonetary directives or monetary sanctions against a lawyer or a party.
- **Safe harbor.** FRCP 11 has a "safe harbor" provision not found in Rule 3.1. If an opposing party makes a motion complaining that a lawyer has violated FRCP 11, the lawyer may withdraw the allegedly frivolous pleading within 21 days after opposing counsel's motion and suffer no sanction other than having to pay the attorneys' fees that the opposing party incurred for making the motion. Although Rule 3.1 has no safe harbor provision, a bar counsel would be unlikely to file a charge against a lawyer for filing a frivolous case or defense that the lawyer withdrew pursuant to the safe harbor provision of the FRCP.[13]

## What penalties may apply to lawyers who bring unsubstantiated suits?

**Rule 11 penalties** A lawyer who initiates a federal court lawsuit in good faith and later finds out (for example, through discovery) that the lawsuit is groundless may be subject to sanctions under FRCP 11.

**Attorneys' fees** A federal statute provides that a lawyer who "multiplies the proceedings in any case unreasonably and vexatiously" may be required to pay the other party's attorneys' fees.[14]

FOR EXAMPLE: In one famous case, two U.S. journalists were seriously injured when a bomb was detonated at a press conference in Nicaragua. Their lawyer relied on unreliable hearsay evidence as the basis for the claim that CIA operatives who were "main figures in the Irangate scandal"[15] (often referred to as the Iran-Contra affair) had set the bomb as part of a conspiracy to assassinate a Nicaraguan opposition leader. The lawyer continued the case even though he could not substantiate the claims through discovery. Relying on Rule 11 and on the federal sanctions statute, the court imposed counsel fees and other sanctions of more than $1 million against the lawyer

---

13. In 2004, the House of Representatives approved H.R. 4571, which would have eliminated the safe harbor provision from FRCP 11 and would also have imposed new types of sanctions on lawyers who violate that rule. During 2004, the bill was not approved by the Senate and did not become law, but Congressional efforts to make FRCP 11 more strict will probably continue until a bill like H.R. 4571 is enacted.

14. 28 U.S.C. § 1927 (2004).

15. Mark Tan, Appeal Against 1 Million Dollars Costs in Irangate Case, Guardian (London), Feb. 7, 1989. During the Reagan administration, it was revealed that federal government officials had used profits from secret arms sales to Iran to fund an off-the-books insurgency against the government of Nicaragua.

and the nonprofit organization that employed him.[16] This sanction bankrupted the nonprofit organization.[17]

**Liability for malicious prosecution**    In some states, a defendant who has been sued on the basis of virtually no evidence may sue the plaintiff or the plaintiff's lawyer for the tort of malicious prosecution.[18] Most courts impose higher burdens of proof for winning such cases than for granting sanctions under FRCP 11. A plaintiff usually must prove

- that she won the previous suit in which she was a defendant,
- that the prior suit was brought without probable cause,
- that the prior suit was brought with malice (a motivation other than obtaining a proper adjudication of the case), and
- that the plaintiff was injured despite having won the prior suit.[19]

Some states, such as Michigan, also require a plaintiff to show "special injury" — that is, that he was injured in his reputation, his person, or his liberty. It is not enough to claim only that the suit was costly or time-consuming.[20]

A lawyer can prove that there was "probable cause" for the previous suit, defeating a claim for malicious prosecution, if the lawyer had a "reasonable belief" that facts could be established and that, under those facts, the client had a valid claim.[21]

## PROBLEM 8-1  YOUR VISIT FROM PAULA JONES

*The facts of this problem are drawn from the complaint filed in Jones v. Clinton, 858 F. Supp. 902 (E.D. Ark. 1994).*

Paula Jones, an employee of a state agency in Arkansas, comes to see you at your law office. She wants you to file a lawsuit against the president of the United States for sexually harassing her while he was the governor of Arkansas. She tells you the following story.

She claims that she was working at the conference registration desk at a hotel where the governor was speaking. The governor's bodyguard appeared at her desk with a piece of paper with a hotel suite number on it

---

16. Avirgan v. Hull, 932 F.2d 1572 (11th Cir. 1991). The court probably would have imposed a sanction if this case had arisen under the 1993 version of FRCP 11 because the plaintiffs did not withdraw the case when discovery failed to provide the necessary evidence.

17. Gregg Easterbrook, Blond Ghost: Ted Shackley and the CIA's Crusades, Wash. Monthly, Sept. 1994 (bankruptcy of the Christic Institute); Nick Schou, Who Killed Col. James Sabow? Orange County Weekly, Feb. 18-24, 2000 (plaintiff in suit charged lawyer with poor work, tried to get him disbarred, and sued him to recover investigative material he collected during the litigation).

18. In some states, the tort is called "wrongful use of civil proceedings." See, e.g., Northwestern Nat'l Casualty Co. v. Centry III Chevrolet, 863 F. Supp. 247 (W.D. Pa. 1994); In re Smith, 989 P.2d 165 (Colo. 1999); Morse Bros. v. Webster, 772 A.2d 842 (Me. 2001).

19. See Wal-Mart Stores Inc. v. Goodman, 789 So. 2d 166, 174 (Ala. 2000).

20. See Friedman v. Dozorc, 312 N.W.2d 585 (Mich. 1981).

21. Restatement § 57, comment d.

*Paula Jones*

and told her that the governor (whom she had never met) wanted to meet her. She thought she might be considered for promotion, so she went to the governor's suite. He closed the door, told her that her superior in the state government was his good friend and appointee, and said "I love your curves." Then he put his hand on her leg and attempted to kiss her. She walked away from him, but he lowered his trousers and underwear and asked her to kiss his erect penis. She fled but feared that her job would be jeopardized by her having refused his advances. She was so afraid of being fired for reporting the incident that she did not even tell her best friends about it. Some years later, after she had taken maternity leave, she was transferred to a position from which she could not earn a promotion. She was told that her previous position had been abolished, but in fact it had not been abolished.

What, if anything, must you do to corroborate Jones's allegations before you may sue the president?

In answering this question, assume that a jury could infer from these facts, *if proved*, that the president committed the tort of sexual harassment. Also assume, as is the case, that the president is not constitutionally immune from being sued for his unofficial acts.[22] Finally, exclude from your consideration any knowledge of Monica Lewinsky, the White House intern whose sexual liaison with President Clinton became the subject of an impeachment proceeding. At the time Jones visits you (and at the time the actual lawsuit on which this problem is based arose), Lewinsky is not yet on the scene.

## 2. Required investigation by prosecutors before charges are filed

Rule 3.8(a)   Special responsibilities of a prosecutor
The prosecutor in a criminal case shall . . . refrain from prosecuting a charge that the prosecutor knows is not supported by probable cause.

Rule 3.8(a) is the prosecutor's analogue to Rule 3.1. The Restatement elaborates the special responsibility of prosecutors articulated in Rule 3.8, explaining that a prosecutor may not file a criminal case without a "belief, formed after due investigation, that there are good factual and legal grounds" for it.[23] This

---

22. Clinton v. Jones, 520 U.S. 681 (1997).

23. Restatement § 97(3). The ABA's Standards Relating to the Administration of Criminal Justice, The Prosecution Function (1992) are not binding on officials, but they would impose a higher standard. They provide that a prosecutor should not institute a criminal charge in the absence of "sufficient admissible evidence to support a conviction." Standard 3-3.9(a). At least some

rule imposes a standard for filing of criminal charges similar to the standard imposed by Rule 11 for civil plaintiffs' lawyers. Professor Fred Zacharias explains that prosecutors are rarely disciplined for initiating proceedings based on skimpy evidence because "so long as some evidence supports a criminal charge, observers typically disagree over the propriety of a prosecutor's decision to support a police arrest pending further investigation."[24] Despite the relative infrequency of discipline, it is particularly important for prosecutors to conduct independent investigations into the evidence before initiating criminal charges. If a prosecutor files charges without adequate basis, then even if the defendant is ultimately acquitted, the charges may damage the reputation of the person charged and disrupt the person's life.[25]

# C. Truth and falsity in litigation

Once a case has been filed, the lawyers are bound by court rules and ethical rules to be honest with the tribunal. The rules vary from one state to another. The lawyers' duties also vary depending on the stage of the proceeding and whether the lawyer herself or a witness is communicating to the court.

## 1. The rules on candor to tribunals

Rules 3.3 and 8.4(c) are the starting points for analysis.

### Rule 3.3   Candor Toward the Tribunal

| Rule language* | Authors' explanation |
|---|---|
| (a) **A lawyer shall not knowingly:** (1) make a **false statement of law or fact** to a tribunal or **fail to correct a false statement of material fact or law previously made to the tribunal by the lawyer;** | • Rule 3.3(a)(1) bars false statements to courts by lawyers themselves, as opposed to false testimony by clients or other witnesses. • If a lawyer discovers that she has made a false statement, the lawyer must correct it. |
| (2) **fail to disclose** to the tribunal **legal authority** in the **controlling jurisdiction** known to the lawyer to be **directly adverse** to the position of the client and not disclosed by opposing counsel; | • Rule 3.3(a)(2) requires more than avoiding falsehood. Lawyers must affirmatively disclose directly adverse law in the controlling jurisdiction if the opponent doesn't do so. |

*Continued*

commentators argue, however, that a prosecutor may appropriately bring a charge even though on the basis of the evidence the prosecutor herself, applying the "beyond a reasonable doubt" standard, would not, in the role of a juror, vote to convict. Thus, where a prosecutor knows from years of experience that identification of a black defendant by an elderly white robbery victim who glimpsed him only briefly may be flawed despite the victim's apparent certainty and would vote to acquit on this basis, the prosecutor, it is argued, may nevertheless bring the robbery charge. H. Richard Uviller, The Virtuous Prosecutor in Quest of an Ethical Standard: Guidance from the ABA, 71 U. Mich. L. Rev. 1145 (1973).

24. Fred Zacharias, The Professional Discipline of Prosecutors, 79 N.C. L. Rev. 721, 736 (2001).
25. Restatement § 97, comment h.

| Rule language* | Authors' explanation |
|---|---|
| (3) **offer evidence that the lawyer knows to be false.** If a lawyer, the lawyer's client, or a witness called by the lawyer, **has offered material evidence and the lawyer comes to know of its falsity, the lawyer shall take reasonable remedial measures, including, if necessary, disclosure to the tribunal.** A lawyer may refuse to offer evidence, other than the testimony of a defendant in a criminal matter, that the lawyer reasonably believes is false. | • A lawyer who knows that his client or other witness is going to lie to the court may not allow the witness to do so.<br>• If the witness does lie, the lawyer must call on the witness to correct the lie, and if he won't, the lawyer must disclose the lie.<br>• This rule applies to trial testimony, depositions, and other testimony related to adjudication. Comment 1.<br>• If a lawyer reasonably believes, but is not certain, that evidence is false, the lawyer "may" (or may not) refuse to offer the evidence.<br>• In a criminal case, a lawyer must allow the defendant to testify if the lawyer reasonably believes but is not certain that the evidence is false. |
| (b) A lawyer who **represents a client** in an **adjudicative proceeding** and who knows that a person intends to engage, is engaging or has engaged in **criminal or fraudulent conduct related to the proceeding shall take reasonable remedial measures,** including, if necessary, disclosure to the tribunal. | This rule imposes on lawyers a duty to prevent not only false testimony but also "criminal or fraudulent conduct" in connection with a case before a tribunal. |
| (c) The duties stated in paragraphs (a) and (b) continue **to the conclusion of the proceeding,** and apply **even if compliance requires disclosure of information otherwise protected by** Rule 1.6. | • If a lawyer learns that a witness gave false testimony, the lawyer must take steps to correct the record unless the case, including any appeals, has been completed.<br>• The duty to correct the record overrides the duty of confidentiality. |
| (d) In an ex parte proceeding, a lawyer shall inform the tribunal of all material facts known to the lawyer that will enable the tribunal to make an informed decision, whether or not the facts are adverse. | • In a proceeding in which only one side makes a presentation to the court, the lawyer has a duty to tell the court about adverse facts as well as adverse law. |

*All emphasis added.

## Rule 8.4(c)    Misconduct

| Rule language* | Authors' explanation |
|---|---|
| It is professional misconduct for a lawyer to . . . engage in conduct involving **dishonesty, fraud, deceit or misrepresentation.** | This rule applies to *all* conduct by lawyers, including conduct before tribunals. The bans on "deceit" and "misrepresentation" may be broader than the Rule 3.3(a)(1) ban on false statements. |

*All emphasis added.

## 2. Which rule applies when? A taxonomy of truth-telling problems in litigation[26]

Rules 3.3, 4.1, and 8.4 apply to many different situations. One way to understand these rules is to inventory some of the situations in which these obligations arise and to explain which rule applies in each circumstance.

### Which Truth-telling Rule Applies

| Who might lie or deceive | Situation (Court, administrative hearing, or discovery) | Lawyer's obligation |
|---|---|---|
| Lawyer | Lawyer *is considering* making a false statement of fact or law to a judge. | The lawyer must not do it. Rules 3.3(a)(1), 8.4. |
| Client | Lawyer *knows*[27] that her client is considering testifying falsely in court or in a deposition. | Lawyer must counsel client and refrain from asking client questions that would elicit the false testimony. Rule 3.3(a)(3). |
| Civil client or witness in any proceeding | Lawyer *suspects* but does not know that planned testimony may be false; witness is not criminal defendant. | If lawyer "reasonably believes" it is false, lawyer may refuse to offer the testimony — or may allow it. Rule 3.3(a)(3). |
| Criminal defendant | Lawyer *suspects* but does not know that planned testimony may be false; witness is a criminal defendant. | If defendant insists on testifying, the lawyer must allow it even if the lawyer "reasonably believes it is false." Rule 3.3(a)(3). |
| Client or witness | Lawyer *knows* that her client or other witness has testified falsely during direct or cross-examination. | Lawyers must counsel client to correct the record; consider withdrawing; correct record if necessary to undo the effect of the false evidence. Rule 3.3(b) and (c), and Comment 10. |

*Continued*

26. As noted in Chapter 2, Rules 1.2(d), 1.6(b), and 4.1 impose additional obligations in settings unrelated to litigation.

27. How does a lawyer "know" that testimony will be false? See discussion of intended false testimony below. For a discussion of when a lawyer should seek to learn all of the facts of a client's case and when a lawyer might properly warn a client not to reveal adverse information that the lawyer would be obliged or would have discretion to reveal, see Stephen Ellman, Truth and Consequences, 69 Ford. L. Rev. 895 (2000).

| Who might lie or deceive | Situation (Court, administrative hearing, or discovery) | Lawyer's obligation |
|---|---|---|
| **Client or witness** | Witness has *misled* the court by making statements that are literally true but deceptive. | Lawyer may have duty to counsel client and correct the record. Rules 3.3(b), 8.4(c). |
| **Lawyer** | Lawyer *knows* of directly adverse controlling *legal authority* that has not been disclosed by opposing counsel. | Lawyer must bring it to court's attention (and distinguish it or explain why it is not authoritative). Rule 3.3(a)(2). |
| **Lawyer** | Lawyer *knows* of *facts adverse* to client's interest, not requested in discovery or required to be disclosed by a court rule. | No need to disclose unless the proceeding is ex parte. Rule 3.3(d). |

## 3. A lawyer's duties if a client or witness intends to give false testimony

### a. When the lawyer believes that a criminal defendant intends to lie on the stand

Rule 3.3 states that a lawyer may not present testimony that the lawyer knows to be false. On the other hand, a client expects a lawyer's assistance in presenting his version of the facts to a court, and nowhere is the lawyer's assistance more important than in criminal cases. What should a lawyer do when a criminal defendant wants the lawyer to help him present a patently false case?

### Nix v. Whiteside

475 U.S. 157 (1986)

Chief Justice BURGER delivered the opinion of the Court.
We granted certiorari to decide whether the Sixth Amendment right of a criminal defendant to assistance of counsel is violated when an attorney refuses to cooperate with the defendant in presenting perjured testimony at his trial.

### [Whiteside's plan to lie]

Whiteside was convicted of second-degree murder by a jury verdict which was affirmed by the Iowa courts. [The Court of Appeals for the Eighth Circuit later granted Whiteside a writ of habeas corpus, and Iowa sought review in the Supreme Court.] The killing took place on February 8, 1977, in Cedar Rapids, Iowa. Whiteside and two others went to one Calvin Love's apartment late that night, seeking marihuana. Love was in bed when Whiteside and his companions arrived; an argument between Whiteside and Love over the marihuana ensued. At one point, Love directed his girlfriend to get his "piece," and at another point got up, then returned to his bed. According to Whiteside's testimony, Love then started to reach under his pillow and moved toward Whiteside. Whiteside stabbed Love in the chest, inflicting a fatal wound. . . .

[Whiteside was charged with murder, and Robinson was appointed to represent him.] Whiteside gave him a statement that he had stabbed Love as the latter "was pulling a pistol from underneath the pillow on the bed." Upon questioning by Robinson, however, Whiteside indicated that he had not actually seen a gun, but that he was convinced that Love had a gun. No pistol was found on the premises . . . [and none of] Whiteside's companions who were present during the stabbing . . . had seen a gun during the incident. Robinson advised Whiteside that the existence of a gun was not necessary to establish the claim of self-defense, and that only a reasonable belief that the victim had a gun nearby was necessary even though no gun was actually present.

Until shortly before trial, Whiteside consistently stated to Robinson that he had not actually seen a gun, but that he was convinced that Love had a gun in his hand. About a week before trial, during preparation for direct examination, Whiteside for the first time told Robinson and his associate Donna Paulsen that he had seen something "metallic" in Love's hand. When asked about this, Whiteside responded: "[In] Howard Cook's case there was a gun. If I don't say I saw a gun, I'm dead."

### [Robinson's threat to expose his client]

Robinson told Whiteside that such testimony would be perjury and repeated that it was not necessary to prove that a gun was available but only that Whiteside reasonably believed that he was in danger. On Whiteside's insisting that he would testify that he saw "something metallic" Robinson told him, according to Robinson's testimony:

"[We] could not allow him to [testify falsely] because that would be perjury, and as officers of the court we would be suborning perjury if we allowed him to do it; . . . I advised him that if he did do that it would be my duty to advise the Court of what he was doing and that I felt he was committing perjury; also, that I probably would be allowed to attempt to impeach that particular testimony." Robinson also indicated he would seek to withdraw from the representation if Whiteside insisted on committing perjury.

Whiteside testified in his own defense at trial and stated that he "knew" that Love had a gun and that he believed Love was reaching for a gun and he had acted swiftly in self-defense. On cross-examination, he admitted that he had not actually seen a gun in Love's hand. Robinson presented evidence that Love had been seen with a sawed-off shotgun on other occasions, that the police search of the apartment may have been careless, and that the victim's family had removed everything from the apartment shortly after the crime. Robinson presented this evidence to show a basis for Whiteside's asserted fear that Love had a gun.

[After Whiteside was convicted, he claimed] that he had been deprived of the assistance of his appointed counsel by Robinson's admonitions not to state that he saw a gun or "something metallic." [The Court of Appeals for the Eighth Circuit agreed with his view that Whiteside's constitutional right to counsel implied a duty by Robinson to allow Whiteside to testify as he desired, even if it was untruthful.] . . .

In Strickland v. Washington,[28] . . . , we held that to obtain relief by way of federal habeas corpus on a claim of a deprivation of effective assistance of counsel under the Sixth Amendment, the movant must establish both serious attorney error and prejudice. To show such error, it must be established that the assistance rendered by counsel was constitutionally deficient in that "counsel made errors so serious that counsel was not functioning as 'counsel' guaranteed the defendant by the Sixth Amendment." To show prejudice, it must be established that the claimed lapses in counsel's performance rendered the trial unfair so as to "undermine confidence in the outcome" of the trial.

In Strickland, we acknowledged that the Sixth Amendment does not require any particular response by counsel to a problem that may arise. Rather, the Sixth Amendment inquiry is into whether the attorney's conduct was "reasonably effective." To counteract the natural tendency to fault an unsuccessful defense, a court reviewing a claim of ineffective assistance must "indulge a strong presumption that counsel's conduct falls within the wide range of reasonable professional assistance." In giving shape to the perimeters of this range of reasonable professional assistance, Strickland mandates that "[prevailing] norms of practice as reflected in American Bar Association Standards and the like, . . . are guides to determining what is reasonable, but they are only guides."

Under the Strickland standard, breach of an ethical standard does not necessarily make out a denial of the Sixth Amendment guarantee of assistance of counsel. When examining attorney conduct, a court must be careful not to narrow the wide range of conduct acceptable under the Sixth Amendment so restrictively as to constitutionalize particular standards of professional conduct and thereby intrude into the state's proper authority to define and apply the standards of professional conduct applicable to those it admits to practice in its courts. . . .

We turn next to the question presented: the definition of the range of "reasonable professional" responses to a criminal defendant client who informs counsel that he will perjure himself on the stand. We must determine whether, in this setting, Robinson's conduct fell within the wide range of professional responses to threatened client perjury acceptable under the Sixth Amendment.

---

28. [Authors' footnote.] Strickland v. Washington is excerpted in Chapter 4.

## [The propriety of Robinson's threat]

In *Strickland,* we recognized counsel's duty of loyalty and his "overarching duty to advocate the defendant's cause." Plainly, that duty is limited to legitimate, lawful conduct compatible with the very nature of a trial as a search for truth. Although counsel must take all reasonable lawful means to attain the objectives of the client, counsel is precluded from taking steps or in any way assisting the client in presenting false evidence or otherwise violating the law. . . .

[B]oth the Model Code and the Model Rules do not merely authorize disclosure by counsel of client perjury; they require such disclosure. . . . These standards confirm that the legal profession has accepted that an attorney's ethical duty to advance the interests of his client is limited by an equally solemn duty to comply with the law and standards of professional conduct; it specifically ensures that the client may not use false evidence. This special duty of an attorney to prevent and disclose frauds upon the court derives from the recognition that perjury is as much a crime as tampering with witnesses or jurors by way of promises and threats, and undermines the administration of justice. . . .

It is universally agreed that at a minimum the attorney's first duty when confronted with a proposal for perjurious testimony is to attempt to dissuade the client from the unlawful course of conduct. The commentary [to the Model Rules] also suggests that an attorney's revelation of his client's perjury to the court is a professionally responsible and acceptable response to the conduct of a client who has actually given perjured testimony. . . . Withdrawal of counsel when this situation arises at trial gives rise to many difficult questions including possible mistrial and claims of double jeopardy. . . .

Considering Robinson's representation of respondent in light of these accepted norms of professional conduct, we discern no failure to adhere to reasonable professional standards that would in any sense make out a deprivation of the Sixth Amendment right to counsel. Whether Robinson's conduct is seen as a successful attempt to dissuade his client from committing the crime of perjury, or whether seen as a "threat" to withdraw from representation and disclose the illegal scheme, Robinson's representation of Whiteside falls well within accepted standards of professional conduct and the range of reasonable professional conduct acceptable under *Strickland.* . . .

The Court of Appeals' holding that Robinson's "action deprived [Whiteside] of due process and effective assistance of counsel" is not supported by the record since Robinson's action, at most, deprived Whiteside of his contemplated perjury. Nothing counsel did in any way undermined Whiteside's claim that he believed the victim was reaching for a gun. . . . Robinson divulged no client communications until he was compelled to do so in response to Whiteside's post-trial challenge to the quality of his performance. We see this as a case in which the attorney successfully dissuaded the client from committing the crime of perjury. . . .

Whatever the scope of a constitutional right to testify, it is elementary that such a right does not extend to testifying falsely. . . . On this record, the accused enjoyed continued representation within the bounds of reasonable professional conduct and did in fact exercise his right to testify; at most he was denied the right to have the assistance of counsel in the presentation of false testimony. Similarly, we can discern no breach of professional duty in Robinson's admonition to respondent that he would disclose respondent's perjury to the court.

Reversed.

Justice BRENNAN, concurring in the judgment:
This Court has no constitutional authority to establish rules of ethical conduct for lawyers practicing in the state courts. Nor does the Court enjoy any statutory grant of jurisdiction over legal ethics.

Accordingly, it is not surprising that the Court emphasizes that it "must be careful not to narrow the wide range of conduct acceptable under the Sixth Amendment so restrictively as to constitutionalize particular standards of professional conduct and thereby intrude into the state's proper authority to define and apply the standards of professional conduct applicable to those it admits to practice in its courts." I read this as saying in another way that the Court cannot tell the States or the lawyers in the States how to behave in their courts, unless and until federal rights are violated.

Unfortunately, the Court seems unable to resist the temptation of sharing with the legal community its vision of ethical conduct. But let there be no mistake: the Court's essay regarding what constitutes the correct response to a criminal client's suggestion that he will perjure himself is pure discourse without force of law. As Justice Blackmun observes, that issue is a thorny one, but it is not an issue presented by this case. Lawyers, judges, bar associations, students, and others should understand that the problem has not now been "decided."

Justices BLACKMUN, BRENNAN, MARSHALL and STEVENS, concurring in the judgment:
. . . The only federal issue in this case is whether Robinson's behavior deprived Whiteside of the effective assistance of counsel; it is not whether Robinson's behavior conformed to any particular code of legal ethics.

Whether an attorney's response to what he sees as a client's plan to commit perjury violates a defendant's Sixth Amendment rights may depend on many factors: how certain the attorney is that the proposed testimony is false, the stage of the proceedings at which the attorney discovers the plan, or the ways in which the attorney may be able to dissuade his client, to name just three. The complex interaction of factors, which is likely to vary from case to case, makes inappropriate a blanket rule that defense attorneys must reveal, or threaten to reveal, a client's anticipated perjury to the court. Except in the rarest of cases, attorneys who adopt "the role of the judge or jury to determine the facts" . . . pose a danger of depriving their clients of the zealous and loyal advocacy required by the Sixth Amendment.

I therefore am troubled by the Court's implicit adoption of a set of standards of professional responsibility for attorneys in state criminal proceedings. The States, of course, do have a compelling interest in the integrity of their criminal trials that can justify regulating the length to which an attorney may go in seeking his client's acquittal. But the American Bar Association's implicit suggestion in its brief amicus curiae that the Court find that the Association's Model Rules of Professional Conduct should govern an attorney's responsibilities is addressed to the wrong audience. It is for the States to decide how attorneys should conduct themselves in state criminal proceedings, and this Court's responsibility extends only to ensuring that the restrictions a State enacts do not infringe a defendant's federal constitutional rights. Thus, I would follow the suggestion made in the joint brief amici curiae filed by 37 States at the certiorari stage that we allow the States to maintain their "differing approaches" to a complex ethical question. The signal merit of asking first whether a defendant has shown any adverse prejudicial effect before inquiring into his attorney's performance is that it avoids unnecessary federal interference in a State's regulation of its bar. Because I conclude that the respondent in this case failed to show such an effect, I join the Court's judgment that he is not entitled to federal habeas relief.

## Notes and Questions about *Nix*

**1.** Once the Supreme Court decided that a lawyer's compliance with Rule 3.3 does not violate his client's constitutional rights, the application of that rule to the situation presented in Nix v. Whiteside becomes a relatively "easy" case. Whiteside virtually admitted to his lawyer that he was going to lie about having seen "something metallic" in Love's hand. Rule 3.3(a)(3) prohibits a lawyer from introducing evidence (through testimony, documents, or other exhibits) that the lawyer "knows" to be false, so a lawyer in Robinson's position may not present Whiteside's false story.

**2.** The two concurring opinions express concerns that the majority opinion is trying to dictate standards of professional responsibility for lawyers. They assert that the Supreme Court has no authority to do so. Did the Supreme Court overstep its authority?

**3.** The Court held that "Whatever the scope of the constitutional right to testify, it is elementary that such a right does not extend to testifying falsely." Do you agree with this interpretation of defendants' constitutional right to testify? If so, who should be the judge of whether a defendant's planned testimony is truthful or false?

*"O.K.—let's review what you didn't know and when you didn't know it."*

## b. A lawyer's "knowledge" of a client's intent to give false testimony

In most cases, lawyers are presented with more ambiguous facts than those presented in Nix. It is very common for witnesses in a case to disagree with each other about what happened. Often, a lawyer cannot tell which of them is telling the truth. The rules of professional responsibility do not require lawyers to present only truthful evidence, so a lawyer may present evidence about which he is unsure. But if the lawyer "knows" that the evidence is false, he may not present it.

Under the rules, a lawyer's obligation depends on her belief as to the truth or falsity of a witness's statement. It depends also on whether the witness is a criminal defendant. If the lawyer thinks (or reasonably believes) that the intended testimony of a witness is true, the lawyer may offer it to the court. In a civil case, if the lawyer reasonably believes that the testimony is false, the lawyer may refuse to offer it. Alternatively, the lawyer may give the client or other witness the benefit of the doubt and agree to present the testimony. Only if the lawyer *actually knows* that the witness is going to testify falsely must the lawyer refrain from offering the testimony. On the other hand, if the person testifying is a criminal defendant, the lawyer must not present false testimony if the lawyer *knows* that it is false, but *must allow* the testimony if he does not *know* but *only reasonably believes* it to be false.

How can a lawyer ever know that planned testimony is false? The most obvious case is one, like Whiteside, in which the client essentially admits to the lawyer that his planned testimony is a lie. But suppose that the facts were slightly different, as follows:

Suppose that in his first statement to Robinson, Whiteside had said only that he knew that Love owned a gun and that he saw Love reach under his pillow. Whiteside did not mention seeing an object there. Robinson didn't ask whether Whiteside saw one. Suppose that in his second statement to Robinson, two weeks later, Whiteside said that he saw something metallic under Love's pillow.

In these circumstances, could Robinson allow Whiteside to testify about seeing "something metallic" because Robinson cannot be certain that Whiteside simply omitted that detail in his first statement? Or would anyone in Whiteside's shoes have reported seeing something metallic in his very first statement if indeed he had really seen such an object?

This question about a variation on the Whiteside theme is merely hypothetical. But consider this problem from an actual case.

### PROBLEM 8-2   **FLIGHT FROM SUDAN, SCENE 1**

*This problem is based on a case handled by two students in a law school clinic who were supervised by Professor Schrag. As usual, we have changed the names of the individuals, but in this case we have also changed the country, the name of the newspaper, and a few other details to protect the identity of the client.*

You are a staff lawyer for the Immigrants' Rights Center. You represent Joseph Barragabi, an applicant for political asylum. You met him two months ago when he was referred to your office by a human rights organization. You interviewed him and accepted his case. He seemed terrified that he might lose his case and be forcibly returned to Sudan, which he had fled. In fact, he seems to be one of the most frightened clients you had ever met. You have interviewed him at five different meetings. He has always seemed very anxious about his case. You suspect that if he loses and all his appeals fail, he might commit suicide rather than return home.

Sudan is ruled by a brutal dictator. Political opponents of the regime are tortured and killed. Barragabi says that for a year, in 2003-2004, he was a staff member for the underground opposition newspaper, *Democracy*. He did not write any articles under his own name, however. He worked on several articles with other staff members, but they were published under a fictitious name so that the authors would be less at risk of government reprisal.

In April 2004, the government raided and closed the newspaper and arrested several of the editors. Barragabi says he escaped, left his family, and went into hiding with a friend in a small village. Some of the editors who were arrested have been in jail ever since.

Eventually, Barragabi made it out of the country into Ethiopia, where he worked under a false name and earned enough money to buy a counterfeit passport and an airline ticket to New York City. When he got to the airport in the United States, he admitted having a false passport and he requested asylum. As a result, he was automatically placed in deportation proceedings.

If a person in such proceedings persuades a judge that he qualifies for asylum, the person can remain in the United States. To qualify, the person must show a "well-founded fear" of political or religious persecution in his home country. If the person fails to persuade the judge (either because his story doesn't seem true or because his fear of returning is based on a nonpolitical reason, such as fear of reprisals from a creditor), he will be deported.

Only about one-third of asylum applicants are successful. A major barrier to victory is a series of court decisions on "corroboration." They provide that although a judge may believe an asylum applicant's story based only on the applicant's testimony, applicants ordinarily should corroborate their stories through the testimony of other witnesses or through documentation.

It is easy to corroborate some of the facts of Barragabi's case through newspaper accounts and respected human rights reports. You find published accounts of the crackdown on the opposition press in Sudan, the closing of *Democracy*, and the incarceration of some of the editors. You have documents showing Barragabi's travel through Ethiopia to the United States. However, Barragabi has been unable to document that he ever worked for *Democracy*. He has no employment card, payroll stub, or other such documents. This is not surprising, however. Refugees often leave most of their documents behind when they are fleeing their home countries.

During the last month, you have done two things. First, you have prepared a detailed affidavit (sworn statement) that your client will sign and file in court, telling his whole story. Under court rules, the affidavit must be filed the day after tomorrow. In a hearing in two weeks, he will be expected to testify consistently with the affidavit. Second, you have been searching for some corroboration of his employment with the newspaper. The other editors seemed to be either in jail or in hiding.

This morning, you had a major breakthrough. You discovered that the editor in chief of *Democracy*, Hamid Al-Parah, escaped from jail and from Sudan, and is now living in Canada. You called him right away to ask him to supply an affidavit and perhaps to come to the United States to testify regarding your client's former employment. Much to your surprise, Al-Parah told you that he had never heard of Barragabi. You described your client's appearance. Al-Parah insists that he knew all of his employees and that Barragabi never worked for him, either under the name Barragabi or any other name.

## Questions about Flight from Sudan, Scene 1

**1.** Should you tell Barragabi about your conversation with Al-Parah?

**2.** Should you file the affidavit?

**3.** Should you ask the court for permission to withdraw from representing Barragabi?

**4.** Did you make a mistake by doing your job too well? After learning that Al-Parah was in Canada, should you have said to Barragabi, "I've found a number for Al-Parah in Canada. Of course I only want to call him if he will corroborate your story. Should I call Al-Parah?"

### c. A lawyer's duties if a client intends to mislead the court without lying

Many issues involving possible deception of tribunals involve partial truths rather than bald-face lies. The ethics rules prohibit false statements but permit some less direct forms of deception. A partial truth is a statement that may literally be true but that deceives another person by omitting relevant information or twisting information in a way that distorts it. Many people believe that partial truths and deception by omission are morally more defensible than false affirmative assertions.[29] As we are about to see, the criminal law of perjury makes a sharp distinction between the two types of deception.

Perjury — lying under oath — is a crime. If a lawyer knowingly puts on perjured testimony, the lawyer might be disbarred[30] or even convicted of the crime of subornation of perjury.[31] The crime of perjury is a very extreme form of dishonesty, and precisely because it is a crime, the definition of what constitutes perjury is quite narrow. The leading case is Bronston v. United States.[32] Bronston had a personal bank account in Switzerland for five years, which he closed just before filing for bankruptcy. In the bankruptcy proceeding, he was being questioned about his assets, and he testified as follows:

Q. Do you have any bank accounts in Swiss banks, Mr. Bronston?

A. No sir.

Q. Have you ever?

A. The company had an account there for about six months in Zurich.

---

29. One scholar attempts to explain this difference by arguing that "a victim who is deceived by a [deliberate] non-lie feels foolish and embarrassed, presumably because he believes he has contributed to his own harm by drawing unwarranted inferences from misleading premises. By contrast, a victim of lies is much more likely to feel "brutalized" . . . by some external force." Stuart P. Green, Lying, Misleading and Falsely Denying: How Moral Concepts Inform the Law of Perjury, Fraud, and False Statements, 53 Hastings L.J. 157, 167-168 (2001).

30. Matter of Mitchell, 262 S.E.2d 89 (Ga. 1979).

31. Sheriff v. Hecht, 710 P.2d 728 (Nev. 1985) (subornation of perjury where a lawyer advised a witness to testify falsely that he did not remember a fact); Butler v. Texas, 429 S.W.2d 497 (Crim. Ct. App. Tex. 1968).

32. 409 U.S. 352 (1973).

Bronston was charged with perjury under a federal statute that made it a crime when a witness under oath "states or subscribes any material matter which he does not believe to be true." Prosecutors argued that Bronston's evasive answer tended to mislead his creditors into thinking that he had never had a personal Swiss bank account. He was convicted. The Supreme Court unanimously reversed the conviction. The Court noted that Bronston may well have intended to mislead his questioner by giving a "nonresponsive" answer. But his answer was not literally a false statement, and the Court declined to interpret the federal perjury law to prohibit intentionally misleading nonresponsive statements:

> Under the pressures and tensions of interrogation, it is not uncommon for the most earnest witnesses to give answers that are not entirely responsive. Sometimes the witness does not understand the question, or may in an excess of caution or apprehension read too much or too little into it. It should come as no surprise that a participant in a bankruptcy proceeding may have something to conceal and consciously tries to do so, or that a debtor may be embarrassed at his plight and yield information reluctantly. It is the responsibility of the [examining] lawyer to probe; testimonial interrogation, and cross-examination in particular, is a probing, prying, pressing form of inquiry. If a witness evades, it is the lawyer's responsibility to recognize the evasion and to bring the witness back to the mark, to flush out the whole truth with the tools of adversary examination.[33]

Under the *Bronston* standard, deliberately false statements by lawyers or witnesses may be prosecuted as perjury under federal and state perjury statutes, and lawyers who commit perjury can be disciplined for making false statements to courts.[34] But under *Bronston*, many of the corners that lawyers and witnesses cut do not involve actual perjury. The disciplinary standards, however, require a more exacting degree of truthfulness from lawyers than does the criminal law of perjury.

The most relevant ethics rules are the state rules corresponding to Rule 3.3(b) (requiring lawyers to correct "fraudulent" conduct by their witnesses) and Rule 8.4(c) (barring "deceit"). But neither these nor other rules deal expressly with the problem of half-truths. Rule 7.1, which mainly regulates lawyer advertising but which uses very general language about lawyers' communications, bars lawyers from making false or misleading statements about themselves or their services. It provides that when a lawyer communicates about himself or about his services, the statement "is false or misleading if it contains a material misrepresentation of fact or law, or omits a fact necessary to make the statement considered as a whole not materially misleading." That explanation does not appear in Rule 3.3 or Rule 8.4.

---

33. Id. at 358-359.

34. See, e.g., People v. Cardwell, 2001 WL 1174299 (Colo., July 11, 2001) (lawyer suspended for three years for falsely telling court that his client had no prior convictions for driving under the influence of alcohol).

Curiously, very little case law speaks to whether lawyers can be disciplined because they or their witnesses mislead courts with partially true but deceptive testimony. We did a LEXIS search of 201 bar disciplinary cases that mentioned "deceit" and "omission," together with either "3.3" or "8.4." Nearly all these cases involved deceptive conduct by lawyers outside of the context of litigation before tribunals — for example, tax fraud, embezzlement of client funds, false statements on bar applications, or misrepresentation of the lawyer's own qualifications. Not one of the cases resulted in discipline of a lawyer because the lawyer or a witness called by the lawyer misled a tribunal or an opposing lawyer without actually making a false statement of fact.[35]

Even if lawyers are never or rarely disciplined or sanctioned for the half-truths of their testifying clients or witnesses, what should lawyers do when their clients engage in nonperjurious deceptive behavior?

## PROBLEM 8-3  FLIGHT FROM SUDAN, SCENE 2

*This problem is also based on a case handled by two law students in an immigration clinic. Actually, it involved a client other than the one on whose case Scene 1 is based.*

---

Al-Parah, the former editor in chief of *Democracy*, told you that Barragabi, your asylum client, never worked for him. After some reflection, you decide that you have no basis to believe him over your client. You decide to continue to represent Barragabi in his deportation proceeding.

Barragabi said that during the months while his asylum application was pending, he participated in three demonstrations against the government of Sudan outside of the embassy of Sudan. This tends to support his claim that he is an opponent of the government. You have evidence that embassy officials photograph demonstrators so that the government can punish them if they ever return to Sudan. Therefore, if you can prove that he participated in the demonstrations, this would help to demonstrate that he would be at risk if he were deported.

The only person who can corroborate Barragabi's participation in the demonstration is his roommate, Farik Massariah, another Sudanese refugee whom Barragabi met after he came to the United States. You interviewed Massariah and learned that he, too, had

---

35. Although not a lawyer discipline case, Technomed v. Santiago imposed a monetary sanction of $1,000 against attorney Emilio Santiago for misleading a New York trial court by a half-true statement. On behalf of a client, Santiago moved for (and received) a default judgment, representing to the court that the defendant had neither filed an answer to his complaint nor moved for an extension of time. Those statements were true, but Santiago failed to mention that the defendant had moved to dismiss. Anthony Lin, Lawyer Liable in Bronx Case, N.Y.L.J, July 1, 2003.

applied for asylum. He had been a dissident leader in Sudan. The government's interviewer provisionally recommended that he be granted asylum, subject to the results of an FBI fingerprint check. The FBI report stated that there was an outstanding arrest warrant from Pennsylvania for Massariah. The government directed Massariah to supply a certificate from the Pennsylvania state police showing that he did not have a criminal record in that state. He did so, but the government nevertheless withdrew the provisional recommendation and initiated deportation proceedings against Massariah. His hearing is scheduled in six months.

At Barragabi's asylum hearing, you put Massariah on the stand. He testifies that Barragabi and he participated in three demonstrations outside of the Sudanese embassy. The government lawyer cross-examined Massariah as follows:

Q. What is your own immigration status, Mr. Massariah?
A. I was provisionally recommended for asylum. But there was something wrong with my fingerprints, and I had to get some records from the police in Pennsylvania showing that I had not been convicted of any crimes there. I got those records and I supplied them to the immigration officials.
Q. How many people attended the first demonstration in which you and Mr. Barragabi participated?

The government lawyer asked more questions about the demonstrations but never returned to the subject of Massariah's immigration status. Massariah never stated that he himself was still a respondent in deportation proceedings.

Should you take steps (including your own disclosure, if necessary) to inform the government or the court that immigration officials withdrew the provisional recommendation that Massariah be given asylum and instead put Massariah into deportation proceedings?

---

## d. Variations in state rules on candor to tribunals

Most states have adopted language similar to Rule 3.3. Under some conditions, a lawyer may not allow his client or any other witness to testify falsely and must disclose confidential information to correct false testimony if the client will not do so. Several jurisdictions have adopted different rules for some or all types of cases. For example, in the District of Columbia, a lawyer who is not able to dissuade a criminal defendant client from giving testimony that the lawyer believes to be false may allow the client to give the testimony in a "narrative" fashion. The client may tell his story without the lawyer asking questions that would elicit the false testimony.[36] During closing argument, the lawyer must not refer to the facts stated by the defendant as if they were true. The D.C. approach protects a defendant whose lawyer may have misjudged him and protects his right to a day in court. At the same time, a lawyer who uses this approach signals the trial judge that the client is lying. However, if the case is tried to a jury, the judge's perception may be irrelevant because many jurors would not realize that the different style of providing testimony has a hidden meaning.[37]

As for lawyers who did not expect their clients to lie but discover that clients are lying or did lie, a few jurisdictions prohibit them from "ratting" on their clients rather than requiring them to do so.[38] These jurisdictions appear to put a higher value on preserving the lawyer-client relationship than on making the lawyer a warrantor that a client is not lying.

### Why don't the rule writers agree about what lawyers should do when clients lie in court?

*Professor Monroe Freedman*

At the root of differences among these approaches is what Professor Monroe Freedman calls a legal "trilemma." Every jurisdiction must balance three important values. We want lawyers to investigate cases thoroughly, so that they can represent their clients (particularly criminal defendants) well. We want to preserve lawyer-client confidentiality. And we don't want lawyers to become part of a system that makes decisions on the basis of false evidence. Freedman says we can't have it all three ways.

---

36. D.C. R. Prof. Conduct 3.3(b) (lawyer must first try to dissuade the client from lying and, if that fails, must move to withdraw, but if the motion is denied, the lawyer may allow the client to testify "in a narrative fashion"). See Mass. R. Prof. Conduct 3.3(e) (lawyer who cannot dissuade defendant from lying should make a motion to withdraw, to a judge other than the trial judge, but if a trial has already started, the lawyer need not make the motion if that would prejudice the defendant. If the motion is denied, lawyer may allow "narrative testimony" in which the defendant tells his story without the usual question-and-answer participation of his lawyer.). Although the client initially tells his story in this unusual manner, he is still subject to ordinary cross-examination.

37. Note that *Nix* decided only that a lawyer's refusal to permit perjured testimony doesn't violate the defendant's constitutional rights. *Nix* therefore left states free to adopt ethics rules, such as this one, that direct other solutions to the problem of expected false testimony by clients.

38. D.C.R. Prof. Conduct 3.3(d) (lawyer should call upon client to rectify a fraud on the tribunal, but if the lawyer is unsuccessful, the lawyer should abide by the ban imposed by Rule 1.6 on disclosing confidential information); Mass. R. Prof. Conduct 3.3(e) (in a criminal case, if client will not rectify false testimony, lawyer shall not reveal the falsity to the tribunal).

The lawyer is required to know everything, to keep it in confidence, and to reveal it to the court. . . . If we recognize that professional responsibility requires that an advocate have full knowledge of every pertinent fact, then the lawyer must seek the truth from the client, not shun it. That means that the attorney will have to dig and pry and cajole, and, even then, the lawyer will not be successful without convincing the client that full disclosure to the lawyer will never result in prejudice to the client by any word or action of the attorney. This is particularly true of the indigent defendant, who meets the lawyer for the first time in the cell block or the rotunda of the jail. The client did not choose the lawyer, who comes as a stranger sent by the judge, and who therefore appears to be part of the system that is attempting to punish the defendant. . . . [Even when the client is a wealthy businessperson with a tax problem,] truth can be obtained only by persuading the client that it would be a violation of a sacred obligation of the lawyer ever to reveal a client's confidence. Of course, once the lawyer has thus persuaded the client of the obligation of confidentiality, that obligation must be respected scrupulously. . . .[39]

Freedman queries what a lawyer should do if her client, a criminal defendant, denies his guilt but also plans to testify (falsely) that he was at the scene of the crime. Freedman urges that a lawyer in that situation should counsel her client that the testimony he plans to give would violate the law. Then, Freeman urges, the lawyer should proceed to put the client on the stand in the normal way. He urges that the "narrative approach" illustrated by the DC rule discussed above is a poor solution to the trilemma because the jury often will intuit the meaning of the lawyer's arm's-length conduct. Likewise, Freedman urges, it is not a good solution to require lawyers to tell their clients in advance that they will have to reveal any false testimony. That solution, while it allows the lawyer to be candid with the court, sacrifices the lawyer's ability to learn all the relevant facts.[40]

## 4. False impressions created by lawyers during litigation

Up to this point, we have considered the duties of a lawyer whose witness may lie or mislead a tribunal, or has already done so. Most lawyers take their obligations of candor to tribunals very seriously and would not themselves mislead an adjudicator. However, because many lawyers also take their obligations to their clients very seriously, it sometimes does happen that a lawyer gives a false impression to a court. Furthermore, the problems that arise for lawyers, like those that arise for witnesses, are rarely as simple as making clearly false statements to courts. Lawyers often must decide whether their efforts to shade or embellish the truth in favor of their clients represent good advocacy or punishable deception. The editorial that follows provides an example for your consideration.

---

39. Monroe Freedman, Lawyers' Ethics in an Adversary System 28-38 (Bobbs-Merrill 1975).
40. Id.

## How Simpson Lawyers Bamboozled a Jury

Omaha World Herald, Oct. 10, 1996

[O. J. Simpson is a famous African American football player and actor who was charged with murdering his ex-wife, Nicole Brown Simpson, and her friend, Ronald Goldman. During the trial, the court allowed the jury to visit Brown Simpson's house, the scene of her murder. Over the objection of the prosecutor, the court also allowed the jury to tour Mr. Simpson's nearby house, where some of the evidence had been found.]

Another sordid revelation for the O. J. Simpson file: A soon-to-be-published book about Simpson's criminal trial says that defense lawyers did some redecorating at Simpson's home before the jury toured the home during the trial.

The book says a nude photo of Simpson's white girlfriend, Paula Barbieri, was removed from his bedroom and a framed picture of Simpson's mother was placed by his bed. Pictures of other white friends were taken down and replaced by pictures of black friends.

Defense attorney Johnnie Cochran took from his own office a Norman Rockwell print of a black girl being escorted to school by federal marshals and hung it in Simpson's home in a place where the jury would be sure to see it.

Any sensible defense attorney wants his client to make a favorable impression on the jury. Granted, having an unkempt lout shave, get a haircut and put on a new suit is a little disingenuous if the defendant has seldom done so. But a fellow ought to be allowed to put himself in the best possible light. And the argument can be made that everyone ought to clean up out of respect for the court.

If the pictures of Ms. Barbieri and others had been replaced with pictures of football highlights or scenic landscapes, that might have been branded sneaky but similar to cleaning up oneself for a court appearance.

The replacement of white people's pictures with pictures of black people takes on a more sinister quality because race was a major issue in the Simpson trial. Some African Americans had questioned Simpson's commitment to fellow blacks. Nine of the 12 jurors were black. Cochran would later call the case against Simpson a conspiracies of lies and doctored evidence produced by a racist police force that was jealous of Simpson's wealth and fame.

In that context, the attempt to give the jury a different picture of Simpson through the swapping of pictures and the display of a civil-rights poster becomes a contemptible, despicable fraud that tarnishes the reputations of all involved.

## Question about Omaha World Herald Editorial

Do you agree that Cochran's substitution of the pictures was a "contemptible, despicable fraud" in the murder trial of O. J. Simpson?

Did it violate any rule of professional conduct? Or was it a good and ethically responsible piece of lawyering, similar to providing the defendant with a nice suit? Would you have done the same thing?

## PROBLEM 8-4  **THE DRUG TEST**

*This problem is based closely on a case that was decided in a midwestern state early in the twenty-first century.*

---

You work in a small law firm and represent Frederic Krause in a divorce action against his wife, Maria. Maria's lawyer has made a motion to suspend Frederic's right to visit the couple's three-year-old daughter, Darlene. Maria claims that Frederic uses methamphetamines. Under the law, a judge may suspend the visitation rights of any parent who currently uses illegal drugs.

The judge scheduled a hearing on Maria's motion in five days. In preparing for the hearing, you asked Frederic whether he was using methamphetamines. He said that he did so at one time while living with Maria, but that he had not used this drug in more than four years. You advised him to get a drug test to prove that he was not using methamphetamines. Frederic then went to your town's hospital and asked to have his urine tested for methamphetamines. He instructed the hospital to send the report on the drug test to you.

The hospital's laboratory technician telephoned you and reported that Frederic tested negative for methamphetamines. However, the test screened for eight substances, and Frederic had tested positive for marijuana. She faxed you a copy of the printout.

There were no allegations of marijuana use in Frederic's legal case, so you told the technician that you needed a report showing only the methamphetamine results. You asked for a new test, for methamphetamines only. She said that she could do only a multisubstance screen, but she could provide you with a second report, omitting the marijuana results.

You asked her to do that. She mailed you part of the original printout. In comparing the report she mailed you with the technician's earlier fax, you saw that she had simply used a scissors to cut off the bottom portion of the original report and sent you only the top portion showing that your client tested negative for methamphetamines.

---

## Questions about the Drug Test

**1.** When you received the telephoned report from the laboratory, would it have been proper for you to thank the hospital, dispense with a written report, and advise Frederic to get a new test at another hospital, making sure to find a laboratory that uses a test for methamphetamines only and not for other substances?

**2.** Now that you have received the partial report in the mail, would it be ethically proper for you to send a copy of it to Mrs. Krause's lawyer and then offer it as an exhibit that will be part of the evidence?

**3.** Assume that you do introduce it as evidence. The judge then asks you (as the judge in the real case did), "Is this the entire report?" Which of the following possible responses is best? (If you don't approve of any of these responses, devise a better one.)

a. "Yes, your honor."

b. "That's what I have, judge. That's what I asked them to screen for."

c. "No, your honor. Mr. Krause tested positive for marijuana, but I asked the lab technician to exclude that result from the report since Mrs. Krause accused Mr. Krause only of using methamphetamines."

d. "Actually, your honor, I have just decided to withdraw the exhibit."

## PROBLEM 8-5 **THE BODY DOUBLE**

*This problem is closely based on a case that was decided by a state supreme court in 1994.*

You represent Jaden Pomfrey, who is facing criminal charges of failing to yield while making a left turn and driving with a revoked license. Pomfrey has told you that he is guilty, but of course, the state has the burden to prove its case.

When Pompfey made his ill-fated left turn, he hit another car. The police officer who responded to the scene interviewed Pomfrey and asked him for identification, but Pomfrey did not have any identification with him, partly because his driver's license had been revoked. He gave the police officer his name, but the police officer had no proof that the person he ticketed was in fact Pomfrey.

One day, while you are preparing Pomfrey for the trial, you notice that Fred Stalnaker, one of your law firm's messengers, looks a lot like Pomfrey. An idea occurs to you. Under the court's rules, Pomfrey has to be in court for his trial, but no rule requires him to sit at the counsel table. If Stalnaker sits next to you at the counsel table, the arresting officer might well identify him as the person who failed to yield and turned out not to have a valid driver's license. Then you could put on evidence showing that Stalnaker wasn't driving the car in question and wasn't anywhere near the incident. This would demonstrate that the arresting officer could not identify the defendant beyond a reasonable doubt, and he would have to be acquitted.

You consider the possibility of advising the judge about this tactic before the trial. You know that you are not allowed to have any one-side communications about the case with the judge. You'd have to tell the prosecutor too. Then the prosecutor would alert the arresting officer, and your tactic would fail. The only way to pull it off would be to give it a try without advance notice to anyone.

Should you do it?

## 5. Lawyers' duties of truthfulness in preparing witnesses to testify

A lawyer is not permitted to offer evidence known to be false, so it follows that a lawyer may not advise a client or other witness to give false evidence. But what about more subtle advice? For example, may a lawyer who is preparing a witness for trial urge the witness to use particular truthful words or phrases that the witness normally would not use? Alternatively, may a lawyer coach a witness on nonverbal behavior such as facial expressions and tone of voice?[41] What about rehearsing testimony so that the witness hesitates less and is less likely to contradict herself? All of these methods of preparation may enhance the credibility of the witness or the clarity of the testimony, but they also may give a misleading impression of the witness or of the events at issue.

Even if lawyers do not try to distort the testimony of a witness, preparation for a trial may inevitably change how a witness recalls events and therefore change the substance of the testimony. Professor Richard C. Wydick of the University of California illustrates the problem with this pretrial dialogue:

Q. When Bloggs came into the pub, did he have a knife in his hand?
A. I don't remember.
Q. Did you see him clearly?
A. Yes.
Q. Do people in that neighborhood often walk into pubs with knives in their hands?
A. No, certainly not.
Q. If you had seen Bloggs with a knife in his hand, would you remember that?
A. Yes, of course.
Q. And you don't remember any knife?
A. No, I don't remember any knife.

---

41. This discussion focuses on the ethical propriety of coaching while preparing a witness who is going to testify in a trial or a deposition. Coaching a witness who has already taken the stand or begun to give testimony during a deposition, particularly while a question is pending, may violate the rules of a tribunal. See, e.g., Hall v. Clifton Precision, 150 F.R.D. 525 (E.D. Pa. 1993) (analogizing depositions to trials and prohibiting coaching during either type of proceeding); S.C. R. Civ. P. 30(j)(5) and (6) (prohibiting coaching during depositions). Only a few courts have taken this position, however.

During the days or months between the interview and the trial, the story can harden, and what started as "I don't remember" may come out like this at trial:

Q. When Bloggs came into the pub, did he have a knife in his hand?
A. No, he did not.[42]

Wydick points out, however, that American law tolerates a considerable amount of coaching because uncoached witnesses often ramble and contradict themselves. Lawyers help courts to process cases efficiently by preparing witnesses to give clearer and more cogent, coherent, and pertinent testimony than the witnesses would give without preparation.[43]

## What do the ethics rules say about coaching?

There is very little "law" on the subject of coaching.[44] The ethical rules address this subject only in the most general terms.

> Rule 3.4 Fairness to Opposing Party and Counsel
> A lawyer shall not . . .
> (b) falsify evidence, counsel or assist a witness to testify falsely, or offer an inducement to a witness that is prohibited by law.[45] . . .

The focus on false testimony may imply that if lawyers avoid conduct that leads witnesses to testify falsely, coaching is ethically unobjectionable. Alternatively, perhaps the drafters were simply in such disagreement about the propriety of coaching that they decided not to address the issue.

The Restatement more explicitly allows coaching that does not induce false evidence:

> In preparing a witness to testify, a lawyer may invite the witness to provide truthful testimony favorable to the lawyer's client. Preparation . . . may include discussing the role of the witness and effective courtroom demeanor; discussing the witness's recollection and probably testimony; revealing to the witness other testimony or evidence that will be presented and asking the witness to reconsider the witness's recollection or recounting of events in that light. . . . Witness preparation may include rehearsal of testimony. A lawyer may suggest choice of words that might be employed to make the witness's meaning clear. However, a lawyer may not assist the witness to testify falsely as to a material fact.[46]

---

42. Richard C. Wydick, The Ethics of Witness Coaching, 17 Cardozo L. Rev. 1, 11-12 (1995).
43. Id. at 12-13.
44. There may be relatively little law because information about coaching takes place in private, and no one who might complain about it really knows what coaching took place. If someone did complain, communications between lawyers and their clients are effectively shielded by the attorney-client privilege, and even communications with nonclient witnesses are usually protected by the more limited work product doctrine. As a result, courts and disciplinary authorities are not likely to learn the nature of any pretrial coaching, and it is difficult to find reported cases with information about such coaching.
45. In the ABA Model Rules, this section ends with a semicolon rather than a period.
46. Restatement § 116, comment b. The Restatement adds that this comment "is supported by relatively sparse authority but, it is believed, by the uniform practice of lawyers in all jurisdictions." Id. at comment b, reporter's note.

*"I love my testimony. You've really captured my voice."*

The D.C. Bar Legal Ethics Committee took the view, consistent with the Restatement, that lawyers may suggest answers to witnesses even when the basis for the answers did not derive from the witnesses themselves, provided that the substance of the testimony given "is not, so far as the lawyer knows or ought to know, false or misleading."[47] Some experts criticize this approach. Professors Fred Zacharias and Shaun Martin argue that "attorneys who 'coach' their clients or witnesses to fashion a story that is consistent with the written record can simultaneously foster the introduction of false testimony while remaining ignorant of the true set of facts." "Under the D.C. Bar Opinion's approach," they write, "lawyers are justified in introducing the altered testimony on the grounds that the lawyers do not 'know' that it is false."[48] Wydick states that if "the lawyer uses [a] role-playing session as an occasion for scripting the witness's answers, then it is unethical."[49]

## PROBLEM 8-6 **REFRESHING RECOLLECTION**

You represent Nancy Magill, who is being sued by the Superior Mortgage Company. The company is attempting to take Magill's house from her because she became unable to keep up her mortgage

---

47. D.C. Bar Leg. Ethics Comm., Formal Op. 79 (1979).
48. Fred C. Zacharias & Shaun Martin, Coaching Witnesses, 87 Ky. L.J. 1001, 1015 n. 59 (1998).
49. Wydick, supra n. 41, at 16.

payments. She said she never realized that the interest rate for the mortgage would be so high, so she didn't anticipate how hard it would be to make the payments.

When you interviewed Magill initially, you asked her whether the loan agent, Spencer Martinelli, made any statements to her about what interest rate Superior would charge for the loan. She said that he did not. In fact, although the loan documents show that Martinelli was her loan agent, she does not remember him very well and is not able to describe him.

After you began to work on the Magill case, you agreed to represent several other homeowners in the neighborhood who also had obtained mortgages from Superior. Nearly all of your other clients said that Martinelli had falsely asserted that "Superior's interest rates were the lowest in the region." Actually, they were a quarter of a percentage point higher than the rates offered by City Mortgage Company.

When you took Martinelli's deposition in the Magill case, he denied having made such statements. You have settled two cases on favorable terms after Superior's lawyer deposed your clients and heard their credible testimony about Martinelli's lies. You are about to meet with Magill to prepare her for her own deposition.

If you remind Magill to testify truthfully, during this meeting may you do any of the following?

a. May you ask Magill whether Martinelli made any statements to her to the effect that Superior's rates were lower than those of other companies?

b. May you tell her that Superior settled other cases favorably because the borrowers remembered that Martinelli said that "Superior's interest rates were the lowest in the region." (Assume that you could share this information without disclosing any confidences of other clients.)

c. May you remind her what Martinelli looks like?

d. Suppose you tell her that other customers of Martinelli have testified that he told them that Superior's rates were lower than those of other companies, and she then recalls that he told her the same thing. May you advise her to sound forceful and confident about this fact when she testifies?

---

# D. Concealment of physical evidence and documents

Of course, a lawyer should not conceal evidence. Do we need to discuss this topic? Consider the duty of confidentiality, which requires lawyers to conceal quite a lot of information. In the missing bodies case considered in Chapter 2, a lawyer felt pinned between his duty of confidentiality to his clients and his duty (reinforced by a criminal statute) to reveal to authorities the location of undiscovered cadavers. In that case, the client told the lawyer where the bodies of two murder victims were located. The lawyer saw the physical evidence but did not come into the possession or control of it.[50] Sometimes lawyers are given or independently discover physical evidence or documents related to an impending or ongoing case. This section explores how lawyers should balance their duty to protect client confidences against their responsibilities to the system of justice.

As we shall see, the relevant ethics rules are painted with a broad brush. They do not distinguish between civil and criminal cases, or between physical evidence and documentary evidence, or between material generated for purpose of obtaining legal assistance and material that would have been created even if no lawyer were involved. In practice, these distinctions are important.

# 1. Duties of criminal defense lawyers with respect to evidence of crimes

### What should a lawyer do when a criminal defendant hands the lawyer a weapon or other tangible evidence of a crime?

In criminal cases, prosecutors may not use discovery to obtain information from defendants. If a prosecutor requires a suspect to answer questions before a grand jury, the suspect may refuse to testify to avoid self-incrimination. But law enforcement officials may obtain search warrants to look for physical evidence (which law enforcement officials and judges sometimes refer to as "real evidence"). If a lawyer for a suspect in a criminal case were to take possession of physical evidence, the lawyer could help the client to avoid prosecution by hiding it. On rare occasions, judges grant warrants to search lawyers' offices, but because such searches could breach attorney-client privilege in all of the lawyer's cases, prosecutors are reluctant to ask for such searches and judges hesitate to authorize them.[51] The rules of professional

---

50. Actually, Mr. Belge, one of the two lawyers for defendant Robert Garrow, had not only seen and photographed the evidence, but touched part of it, when he moved some bones that had been carried away by animals. Did he thereby conceal evidence, make it easier to discover, or neither? This aspect of his actions apparently was not discussed in the judicial opinions on the case. Was it ethically significant? Perhaps so: An opinion of the New York State Bar, released four years after the case was over, stated that "there could be an appearance of impropriety . . . in moving a part of one of the bodies" even if the only purpose in doing so was to bring the body part within camera range and not to conceal any evidence." N.Y. State Bar Assn., Formal Op. 479 (prepared in 1974 but publication withheld until Feb. 28, 1978).

51. The U.S. Department of Justice has issued rules that prosecutors must follow before lawyers' offices are searched. 28 C.F.R. § 59.4 (2004). In addition, Rule 3.8(e) bars a prosecutor from issuing subpoenas to lawyers to try to force them to present evidence against their clients unless the prosecutor reasonably believes that the information is not protected by privilege, is essential to an investigation or prosecution, and is not obtainable by other means.

responsibility therefore restrict lawyers from hiding evidence of criminal misconduct.

**Rule 3.4(a)    Fairness to Opposing Party and Counsel**
**A lawyer shall not: . . . unlawfully obstruct another party's access to evidence or unlawfully alter, destroy or conceal a document or other material having potential evidentiary value. A lawyer shall not counsel or assist another person to do any such act.**

This rule does not prohibit all concealment or destruction of evidence but only "unlawful" concealment or destruction. Nor does the rule prohibit concealment or destruction of every object or document in the possession of a suspect or other witness, but only material having "potential evidentiary value." In a state that adopts this rule, the ban applies only if some other law makes the concealment or destruction unlawful. The word "unlawful" is not defined in the rules, but the ABA Annotated Model Rules of Professional Conduct explains that concealment or destruction of evidence is a violation of the ethical rule

> only if the lawyer already has some obligation to disclose it, such as if the evidence is the subject of a discovery request to which no objection has been made, or is the fruit or instrumentality of a crime and the lawyer is required by law to turn it over to law enforcement officials. (5th ed., p. 350)

If the conduct at issue would violate a criminal obstruction of justice statute, the destruction or concealment is unlawful. If the conduct violates a court order, it is unlawful because it is a contempt of court. Similarly, a lawyer may violate Rule 3.4(a) by failing to comply with a discovery request or with discovery rules imposing an ongoing duty of disclosure.[52]

Concealment or destruction of evidence also may be unlawful under Rule 3.4 if it would constitute a tort, but this is less clear than the above cases in which the lawyer has a legal duty to protect or to disclose certain evidence. For example, in some jurisdictions, destroying or concealing documents for the purpose of preventing an adversary from using them constitutes the tort of spoliation.[53] If certain conduct is tortious, then one who engages in that conduct may be obliged to pay damages. But that doesn't necessarily mean that the act in question is illegal or unlawful.

So one problem with Rule 3.4 is the lack of clarity about the meaning of "unlawful." Another problem is that some state obstruction of justice and

---

52. See, e.g., Briggs v. McWeeny, 796 A.2d 516 (Conn. 2002) (affirming a trial court finding that "the plaintiff had violated Rule 3.4 by suppressing relevant, discoverable evidence to which the opposing parties and their counsel were entitled in accordance with the plaintiff's continuing duty to disclose under [Connecticut's] Practice Book § 3-15").

53. The development of this tort appears to have begun with a case decided by an intermediate appellate court in California, Smith v. Super. Ct., 151 Cal. App. 3d 491 (1984), but 14 years later, the Supreme Court of California held that the tort does not exist in that state except, perhaps, in favor of a party who could not have known about the spoliation during the underlying lawsuit (the suit for which the evidence was concealed) and who therefore could not have moved for sanctions or other remedies in that case. Cedars-Sinai Med. Ctr. v. Super. Ct., 954 P.2d 511 (Cal. 1998). Meanwhile, other states recognized the tort. See, e.g., Hazen v. Anchorage, 718 P.2d 456 (Alaska 1996); Oliver v. Stimson Lumber Co., 993 P.2d 11 (Mont. 1999).

evidence tampering statutes are very ambiguous, which makes it hard to know what is prohibited.[54]

Two other problems make enforcement of this rule quite difficult. To begin with, violations are often difficult to detect. If a lawyer is destroying or concealing evidence, who will find out? In addition, even if a prosecutor accuses a lawyer of concealing evidence for a defendant, the lawyer inevitably cites the attorney-client and work product privileges to avoid revealing information. The prosecutor must find some way to prove the misconduct without any admission by the lawyer.

The conflict between loyalty to clients and loyalty to the justice system with respect to real evidence relevant to criminal investigations has arisen and been adjudicated in a variety of procedural contexts.

**State v. Olwell**[55]   Warren was stabbed to death, and Gray was arrested for murder. Gray admitted killing Warren but said he didn't know what happened to the knife. Two days later, he retained Olwell to represent him. The coroner subpoenaed Olwell to attend an inquest and asked whether Olwell had a knife belonging to Gray. Olwell refused to answer, claiming attorney-client privilege. He was held in contempt. The appellate court reversed the contempt order because the subpoena had not been drafted properly, but it offered guidance for lawyers who are given evidence by their clients. The court said that Olwell, who had come into possession of a knife that he believed belonged to Gray, could have kept it for a reasonable period of time for purposes of examining it and conducting tests on it. After that, he should have turned it over to the prosecution at his own initiative, "as an officer of the court," without being asked or issued a subpoena. "The attorney should not be a depository for criminal evidence (such as a knife, other weapons, stolen property, etc.), which in itself has little, if any, material value for the purposes of aiding counsel in the preparation of the defense of his client's case." To encourage lawyer-client confidentiality, however, the prosecutor "when attempting to introduce such evidence at the trial, should take extreme precautions to make certain that the source of the evidence is not disclosed in the presence of the jury. . . ." If Olwell had given Gray's knife to the prosecutor, law enforcement officials would have been more certain that Gray was the murderer. This could have made it more likely that they would charge Gray with the crime or that they would demand more in a plea bargain.

---

54. For example, the D.C. Code makes it a crime to destroy or conceal a record, document, or other object "with intent to impair its integrity or its availability" for use in an "official proceeding" if the defendant knew or had reason to believe that the proceeding had begun or was "likely to be instituted." D.C. Code Ann. § 22-723 (2001). A defendant accused of violating this law, or a lawyer accused of violating a state rule based on Rule 3.4(a), could dispute her intent, the likelihood that a proceeding would be instituted, her knowledge or reason to believe that it would be instituted, and whether whatever process was foreseeable was an "official proceeding." Obviously a criminal prosecution is such a proceeding, but what if all that was in the offing was a legislative investigation, the inquiry of a commission, or the institution of a civil lawsuit?

55. 394 P.2d 681 (Wash. 1964).

However, if the prosecutor refrained from informing the jury that the knife came from Olwell, the jury would not be able to use the lawyer's cooperation to convict his client. (It turned out that the knife in Olwell's possession did belong to Gray, but it was not the murder weapon! Gray was convicted anyway.)

**In re Ryder**[56]   A man robbed a bank, using a sawed-off shotgun, and stole $7,500, including a number of marked $10 bills. Two days later, a man named Cook rented a safe deposit box. Later that day, FBI agents visited Cook at his home. At their request, Cook gave the agents some money in his possession, probably not realizing that it was marked. Also he called his lawyer, whose name was Ryder. (Ryder was admitted to the bar in 1953 and served for five years as an assistant U.S. attorney before he embarked on the private practice of law.) After the agents left (without arresting Cook), Cook persuaded Ryder that he had won the money gambling. Despite this conversation, Ryder asked the FBI whether Cook's money had been stolen. The FBI told Ryder that Cook's money included some of the marked bills. Now disbelieving Cook, Ryder asked Cook to authorize Ryder to have access to Cook's safe deposit box. Ryder went to the bank and transferred the money and the gun from Cook's safe deposit box to his own. He apparently intended to prevent Cook from disposing of the evidence. Soon after that, Cook was arrested. The FBI obtained a warrant and searched Ryder's box (this was one of those rare searches of a lawyer's property), and it found the evidence.

Ryder was barred from practicing before the federal court because he had engaged in unethical conduct.[57] His motivation for moving the money was deemed to be irrelevant because he had helped to conceal the evidence. "Ryder knew that the law against concealing stolen property and the law forbidding receipt and possession of a sawed-off shotgun contain no exemptions for a lawyer who takes possession with the intent of protecting a criminal from the consequences of his crime." The appellate court, affirming his suspension, said that Ryder made himself an "accessory after the fact" to the robbery.[58]

**People v. Meredith**[59]   Scott helped to rob and kill Wade. After Scott took the money out of Wade's wallet, he tried to burn the wallet. Unable to do that, he threw the partially burned wallet, with Wade's credit cards, into a trash can behind his house. He told Schenk, his lawyer, where it was. Schenk sent his investigator to retrieve the wallet, turned it over to the police, and withdrew as counsel. The prosecutor called the (former) defense lawyer's investigator to testify as to where he had found the wallet. Scott was convicted. In appealing

---

56. 263 F. Supp. 360, 361 (E.D. Va), *aff'd*, 381 F.2d 713 (4th Cir. 1967).
57. Ryder was charged with violation of Canons 15 and 32 of the Canons of Professional Ethics of the Virginia State Bar. (Most states at this time had adopted a set of canons of ethics, which were later replaced by a Code of Professional Responsibility and later by Rules of Professional Conduct.)
58. 381 F.2d at 714.
59. 631 P.2d 46 (Cal. 1981).

his conviction, Scott argued that the investigator's testimony violated the attorney-client privilege. The court held that the testimony was proper. Schenk could have left the wallet in place. Then the communication about its location would have been fully privileged. But when Schenk's investigator removed the wallet, the privilege was partly abrogated. When he removed the wallet, the investigator prevented the police from finding it in the trash and testifying about the find. The only way the prosecution could prove the location of the evidence was to call the defense investigator as a witness. Furthermore, the prosecutor properly protected what was left of the privilege by not asking the investigator, in the presence of the jury, to reveal that he was employed by Scott's lawyer.

### Are documents treated differently from other physical evidence?

No. Rule 3.4(a) applies both to physical evidence and to documents. Different rules apply to documents created by or for lawyers, but documents such as maps or plans used in the perpetration of crimes are just one type of physical evidence. Just as a lawyer may not conceal incriminating physical evidence, the lawyer may not destroy such evidence or counsel the client to do so. Destruction would be even more problematic than concealment, because there would be no possibility of recovering the evidence.

**Morrell v. State**[60]    A document was at the center of Morrell v. State. Morrell was charged with kidnaping and rape, and Cline, a public defender, was appointed to represent him. A friend of Morrell cleaned out Morrell's car and found a written kidnap plan. He gave it to Cline, who consulted the Ethics Committee of the Alaska Bar Association about what to do with it. On the committee's advice, he returned the plan to the friend and resigned from the case. With some assistance from Cline (who telephoned the police), the friend gave the plan to the police, and it was used as evidence against Morrell, who was convicted. On appeal, Morrell claimed that Cline's actions violated his constitutional right to counsel. The Alaska Supreme Court applied the rule from *Olwell* and held that Cline had a duty to turn over the plan to the prosecutor, even without having been asked for it. If Morrell's friend had not been willing to turn it over, Cline would have had to do so himself. This duty derived from Alaska's statute prohibiting concealment of evidence.[61]

It is difficult to say whether the *Morrell* case implies that a lawyer would have to reveal to authorities a document (for example, an exchange of documents between a client and his competitor conspiring to fix prices in violation of the antitrust laws) revealing that her client has committed a white-collar crime. Morrell's kidnap plan was a "document," but it was not the kind of

---

60. 575 P.2d 1200 (Alaska 1978).

61. Since the plan was not part of a privileged communication from Morrell to Cline, the caution in *Olwell* that the prosecutor should avoid telling the jury that the lawyer was ultimately the source of the information was inapplicable.

document that a lawyer might receive from a business client. We are not aware of any cases requiring lawyers to give prosecutors documentary evidence of such crimes. The Restatement, however, makes no distinction between physical and documentary evidence.[62]

These decisions appear to establish the following guidance for lawyers:[63]

- If a client tells a lawyer about the location of evidence, the lawyer may inspect the evidence but should not disturb it or move it unless doing so is necessary to examine or test the evidence.[64]
- If the lawyer merely inspects the evidence without disturbing it, the lawyer's knowledge of its location remains privileged.[65]
- In many states, a lawyer may "take temporary possession of physical evidence of client crimes for the purpose of conducting a limited examination that will not alter or destroy material characteristics of the evidence. . . . Applicable law may require the lawyer to turn the evidence over to the police or other prosecuting authority. . . ."[66]
- If a client delivers physical evidence of a crime to a lawyer, the lawyer must turn the evidence over to the law enforcement authorities within a reasonable period of time — at least in some jurisdictions.[67] This rule applies to documents as it does to other physical evidence.[68]
- A prosecutor who receives evidence of a crime from the lawyer for a suspect should take steps to avoid revealing to a jury the fact that the incriminating evidence came from the defendant's lawyer.[69]

### Do all jurisdictions require lawyers to contact prosecutors about physical evidence in their possession?

No. In the District of Columbia, a lawyer may turn evidence over to the DC Bar Counsel, who then gives it to the prosecutor. Under this system, the prosecutor would not learn the identity of the lawyer from whom the real evidence came, much less the identity of the client. A DC lawyer who receives incriminating physical evidence from a client may return it to its rightful owner (the client or a third party) if it is not yet under subpoena and if it can be done without revealing client confidences or violating other law. If returning the evidence

---

62. The duty to turn physical evidence over to prosecutors "includes such material as documents and material in electronically retrievable form used by the client to plan the offense, documents used in the course of a mail-fraud violation, or transaction documents evidencing a crime." Restatement § 119, comment a.

63. Note, however, that none of these opinions directly construe Rule 3.4. All of them predate the ABA's initial adoption of Rule 3.4 in 1983. Also, these decisions arise from only a few jurisdictions. Most jurisdictions do not have reported decisions on these issues. Nevertheless, these three cases have been important in establishing the principles articulated here.

64. People v. Meredith, 631 P.2d 46, 53 (Cal. 1981).

65. Id.

66. Rule 3.4, Comment 2.

67. State v. Olwell, 394 P.2d 681, 684 (Wash. 1964).

68. Morrell v. State, 575 P.2d 1200 (Alaska 1978).

69. Olwell, 394 P.2d at 685.

would give away confidences, the lawyer may ask the D.C. bar counsel to turn it over to the owner.[70]

---

**How cases involving a lawyer's concealment of physical evidence may arise**
These cases reveal the many fora and procedural postures in which issues about lawyers and physical evidence can arise.

- *Olwell*: A lawyer was resisting a coroner's subpoena.
- *Ryder*: The FBI obtained a warrant to search a lawyer's safe deposit box. As a result of the lawyer's concealment of evidence, federal trial court imposed severe sanctions on the lawyer.
- *Meredith*: A defendant appealed his conviction based on an alleged violation of the rules of evidence (specifically, attorney-client privilege).
- *Morrell*: A defendant appealed his conviction alleging that his lawyer's revelations deprived him of the effective assistance of counsel.

The issue could also arise in other contexts, such as state bar disciplinary proceedings against a lawyer who either did or did not reveal evidence to a prosecutor.

---

## PROBLEM 8-7  A REVEALING PORTFOLIO

You are in private law practice. For a year, you have represented the Cameron Company, owned by Joan Cameron. The company makes nutritional supplements.

Cameron comes into your office and tells you that she has heard a rumor, through industry sources, that the staff members in state attorney general's office are urging the attorney general to allow them to open an investigation of false advertising (a crime under state law) in the herbal products industry.

Cameron is carrying a thick portfolio. She says that she would like you to review the set of documents that she has brought with her to see whether her company could be in trouble. You ask what the documents are. She says that before marketing Synthpro, a protein supplement, the company did tests on its nutritional value. The sales manager, worried about falling profits, grossly exaggerated the results in the company's advertising. The portfolio contains the only copies of the original test results and copies of the advertising that reported on this testing. You tell your client that you will read the documents and then give her a call.

After Cameron leaves your office, you review the portfolio. The test results are clear. The advertising copy blatantly distorts the test results. It appears that the company's false advertising was deliberate.

A statute in your state makes it a crime if a person "knowing or having reason to believe that an official proceeding has begun or is

---

70. D.C. R. Prof. Conduct 3.4(a) and Comments 5, 6, and 7.

likely to be instituted, ... alters, destroys, mutilates, conceals or removes a record, document or other object, with intent to impair its integrity or its availability for use in the official proceeding."

No government agency has asked you for these documents or issued a subpoena for them.

Are you legally obliged to turn the file over to the attorney general or to keep it confidential? May you return it to Cameron or, if you choose, keep it in your office? What will you do?

---

### If a lawyer acquires evidence of wrongdoing by someone who is not a client, should the lawyer always reveal it to public authorities?

Up to now, we have been concerned with balancing the duties to a client with those to tribunals and investigating authorities. It might seem that if a lawyer learns that a person who is not a client may be engaged in wrongdoing, no such balancing of interests is necessary. However, Rule 4.4 articulates some duties that lawyers owe to third parties. In addition, in some situations, a lawyer might be civilly or criminally liable for failure to respect the rights of a third party (for example, if the lawyer tortiously invades the privacy of the third party or takes possession of property stolen from the third party). Before analyzing the next problem, read Rule 4.4.

> Rule 4.4   Respect for Rights of Third Persons
>
>    (a) In representing a client, a lawyer shall not use means that have no substantial purpose other than to embarrass, delay, or burden a third person, or use methods of obtaining evidence that violate the legal rights of such a person.
>
>    (b) A lawyer who receives a document relating to the representation of the lawyer's client and knows or reasonably should know that the document was inadvertently sent shall promptly notify the sender.
>
> Comment
>    [1] Responsibility to a client requires a lawyer to subordinate the interests of others to those of the client, but that responsibility does not imply that a lawyer may disregard the rights of third persons. It is impractical to catalogue all such rights, but they include legal restrictions on methods of obtaining evidence from third persons. . . .
>    [2] Paragraph (b) recognizes that lawyers sometimes receive documents that were mistakenly sent or produced by opposing parties or their lawyers. If a lawyer knows or reasonably should know that such a document was sent inadvertently, then this Rule requires the lawyer to promptly notify the sender in order to permit that person to take protective measures. . . . [T]his Rule does not address the legal duties of a lawyer who receives a document that the lawyer knows or reasonably should know may have been wrongfully obtained by the sending person. . . .

PROBLEM 8-8 **THE BREAK-IN**

*This problem is based on a case that Professor Lerman handled many years ago.*

You represent Cheryl Gardner in a suit against her ex-husband Ron to obtain sole custody of her two daughters, Evie and Rachel, who are five and seven. Cheryl believes that Ron has been molesting the girls during visitation and that he is about to kidnap them and take them to Iran, where he is going to work for a petroleum company. You are worried about the children's safety, but it is not clear whether or to what extent Cheryl's fears are well grounded. You have ascertained that Ron has obtained passports for the children. Neither girl says that her father has molested her, and the county's sex abuse program has examined the girls and found no evidence of abuse. Ron's lawyer has been arguing vigorously that Ron should have at least joint custody.

One day Cheryl bursts into your office looking furious but excited. For months she's been saying that her ex-husband was molesting the girls, but Department of Social Services officials have not believed her, and she hasn't had a shred of tangible evidence. She opens her tote bag and produces a stack of documents. She reports that she broke into Ron's house, climbing in through an unlocked window, and "borrowed" the originals of these documents, which she photocopied and then returned to the house. Cheryl leaves the documents with you to review.

You have examined the product of Cheryl's expedition. One set of documents consists of photocopies of photos of the two girls, both nude and posed in positions that might be considered titillating. Another is a photocopy of Ron's girlfriend's diary, including an entry observing that Ron often crawls into bed with his daughters to sleep. A third is a draft of a novel by Ron in which the population of the planet has been annihilated by a nuclear war, except for two people, a father and his young teenage daughter. During the course of the novel, the daughter persuades the father that they must procreate for the preservation of the human race. Then she seduces him.

What should you do with these documents? Your client is willing to allow you to make whatever use of them you think best. But these are private documents containing information that Cheryl stole from Ron's house. Consider Rules 1.2(d), 3.4(a), 4.4, and 8.4 (Assume that the state's child abuse reporting statute does not apply to lawyers. Evaluate the following options:

**Return?** Does any disciplinary rule require you to return the documents to Ron or to notify him that you have received them?

**Negotiate?** Would it violate any rules to use these documents in negotiating with Ron's lawyer about custody or to push for a better financial settlement for Cheryl?

## Note: Stolen documents as evidence

Some courts have excluded evidence that was improperly or illegally obtained from the opposing party.[71] When such evidence is excluded, the court may also disqualify the lawyer who received the evidence from representing her own client. But some courts have excluded the improperly obtained evidence without disqualifying the lawyer.[72] Uncertainty about whether the evidence would be excluded at trial may be a factor in each side's judgment about terms on which to settle a case.

# 2. Concealment of documents and evidence in civil cases

## a. A more limited obligation to reveal

**May a lawyer hide or destroy, or counsel a client to hide or destroy, potential evidence when only a civil lawsuit is likely?**

Rule 3.4(a) applies both to civil and criminal cases, but as noted above, it bans only "unlawful" concealment. Some state laws allow lawyers to keep possession of tangible evidence, including documents, that are not pertinent to criminal investigations. The standard for civil cases is different (in some states) because the possession of such documents may not cover up a crime. Also, in a civil case, discovery can be used to obtain the evidence, even if it is in the physical custody of an opposing party's lawyer.

**At what point in a criminal or civil matter does the lawyer's obligation not to conceal or destroy objects or documents begin?**

It is not possible to state these rules succinctly or with accuracy on a national basis, both because state laws vary considerably and because there is very little case law on this subject. In general, however, the rules break down as follows.

### Criminal matters
■ If a lawyer has no knowledge that a violation of law has been committed and no criminal investigation is foreseeable, a lawyer has no duty to turn evidence over to a prosecutor.[73]

---

71. In re Shell Oil Refinery, 143 F.R.D. 105 (E.D. La. 1992) (ordering the suppression of documents obtained by the plaintiff outside of the discovery process from an anonymous employee of the defendant). See also Lipin v. Bender, 644 N.E.2d 1300 (N.Y. 1994) (plaintiff's action dismissed because during a deposition, while lawyers were arguing outside of the room, plaintiff took and copied documents left sitting on deposition table).

72. Restatement § 60, comment m, reporter's note, cites, among others, Cooke v. Super. Ct., 83 Cal. App. 3d 582 (1978) (evidence excluded, but lawyer for wife in dissolution action not required to be disqualified despite receipt of confidential information about husband, including confidential communications between husband and his lawyer, purloined and passed to lawyer by husband's unfaithful agent without complicity of receiving lawyer). The problem in the text involves theft from the husband, not the husband's lawyer, but the result could be the same.

73. Cf. Restatement § 119 (affirming the lawyer's duty to turn over physical evidence of "a client crime" to authorities).

- In some states, the lawyer's duty not to conceal tangible evidence takes effect as soon as the lawyer believes that an official investigation is about to be instituted. In other states, it does not begin until an investigation has actually started.[74]

## Civil matters

- Obligations in civil cases are governed by civil discovery rules[75] as well as by professional responsibility rules.[76] Soon after a civil case is commenced, a lawyer may have a duty under the pertinent rules of procedure to turn over some information to the opposing party, even in the absence of a discovery request.[77]
- Some state laws require the preservation of business records for specified periods of time even if no dispute is on the horizon. In general, when a lawsuit is pending or foreseeable, individuals and businesses have more stringent duties to protect and eventually to disclose relevant material.[78]
- As in the case of tangible evidence, where no specific record preservation statute applies but a lawyer has some reason to believe that wrongdoing has occurred, state law varies as to when the duty to preserve evidence "kicks in" (that is, whether a lawsuit or government investigation must have begun, be imminent, or merely be foreseeable).[79]
- In any event, once a duty to preserve documents applies, relevant records and objects should be retained even if they could otherwise routinely be destroyed.

Even within a particular jurisdiction, a lawyer may need to do serious research to understand when documents or objects may be destroyed. The Restatement warns:

> It may be difficult under applicable criminal law to define the point at which legitimate destruction becomes unlawful obstruction of justice. Under crim-

---

74. Deborah L. Rhode & David Luban, Legal Ethics 342-343 (4th ed., Found. Press 2004).

75. E.g., Fed. R. Civ. P. 26 et seq., and particularly R. 26 and R. 34.

76. Rule 3.4(a), discussed in the text, prohibits destruction of documents, and Rule 3.4(c) bars a lawyer from knowingly disobeying an obligation under the rules of a tribunal (including discovery rules), except for an open refusal based on an assertion that no valid obligation exists.

77. See, e.g., Fed. R. Civ. P. 26(a)(1), requiring disclosure without a prior request of a copy of, or a description by category and location of, all documents, data compilations, and tangible things in the possession and control of the party and that the disclosing party may use to support its claims and defenses, unless solely for impeachment, and any liability insurance agreement that may make an insurance company liable to satisfy a judgment. Note that the party is *not* obligated to disclose the existence of documents that would *contradict* its claims and defenses (that is, the damaging documents that the other side's lawyers would most like to inspect).

78. See generally Restatement § 118, comment c.

79. Id.

inal law, a lawyer generally is subject to constraints no different from those imposed on others. Obstruction of justice and similar statutes generally apply only when an official proceeding is ongoing or imminent. For example, the American Law Institute Model Penal Code Sec. 241.7 (1985) provides that the offense of tampering with or fabricating physical evidence occurs only if "an official proceeding or investigation is pending or about to be instituted. . . ."

Difficult questions of interpretation can arise with respect to destruction of documents in anticipation of a subpoena or similar process that has not yet issued at the time of destruction. . . . No general statement can accurately describe the legality of record destruction; statutes and decisions in the particular jurisdiction must be consulted. In many jurisdictions, there is no applicable precedent. Legality may turn on such factual questions as the state of mind of the client or a lawyer.[80]

The bottom line is that a lawyer should never assume that documents that are or could be pertinent to a civil lawsuit may be concealed or destroyed, even if a suit has not yet been filed. Obstruction of justice or evidence tampering statutes may still apply. These laws may trigger obligations under Rule 3.4(a).

## b. A lawyer's duties in responding to discovery requests

Once documents or tangible evidence have been requested through discovery procedures, lawyers involved in civil litigation are subject to court rules that require litigants to comply with discovery requests or else to object to make formal objections to the requests.[81] The courts may enforce their rules by sanctioning the parties or their lawyers.[82] Discovery abuse is also punishable by bar discipline under Rule 3.4.

> Rule 3.4(d)  Fairness to Opposing Party and Counsel
> A lawyer shall not . . . in pretrial procedure, make a frivolous discovery request or fail to make reasonably diligent efforts[83] to comply with a legally proper discovery request by an opposing counsel.

Despite the discovery rules and the rules of professional conduct, lawyers in practice often seek discovery of many more documents than they really need. This increases the cost of litigation. Also, many lawyers work hard to avoid disclosing embarrassing or damning information or documents that an opponent dearly wants to discover. In the 1970s, Wayne Brazil did a huge empirical study of discovery practices. He reported the results of interviews with 180 Chicago attorneys.

---

80. Id.
81. See, e.g., Fed. R. Civ. P. 26.
82. See, e.g., Fed. R. Civ. P. 26(g), 30(d)(2), and 37.
83. In the ABA Model Rule, this word is "effort" rather than "efforts."

## Wayne D. Brazil, Views from the Front Lines: Observations by Chicago Lawyers About the System of Civil Discovery

1980 ABA Found. Research J. 219

*Magistrate Judge Wayne D. Brazil*

[Wayne D. Brazil, formerly a law professor, later became a federal magistrate judge in California.]

Evasive or incomplete responses to discovery requests, while apparently less often a source of difficulty for small case lawyers than for their large case counterparts, nevertheless reportedly impede discovery in almost one out of every two smaller lawsuits. As significant a problem as evasion seems to be, however, smaller case litigators complained more frequently and vehemently about two other problems: difficulty in scheduling discovery events and delay. One [plaintiffs'] personal injury lawyer claimed (and had his secretary verify that, on the average, each deposition in his cases is continued (rescheduled) between 15 and 20 times. . . . Some of the interviewed attorneys said one cause of delay is intentional tactical jockeying by counsel. One attorney volunteered, in describing the factors he considered when plotting the sequence of his discovery demands that when he wanted to "slow things down" he would make discovery demands that would provoke time-consuming disputes with his opponents. Another lawyer proudly recounted how, by manipulating the discovery process, he had "horsed around" opposing parties so as to create enough time for a financially troubled client to collect outstanding debts and thus avoid bankruptcy. . . .

Many larger case litigators complained that much of the information requested by opposing parties is either wholly irrelevant to matters in dispute or of only marginal utility. . . . As in smaller case litigation, delay is a significant problem. Many larger case lawyers appear routinely to overcommit themselves. . . . [In large cases] the problem of delay appears to be more often a product of the intentional tactical jockeying. . . . In one lawyer's words, the "sophisticated clients know what the discovery system is all about and they know that discovery is a business. In big cases the goal is to delay the resolution. . . ." More colorfully, another respondent admitted that as a defense attorney he "just loves delay" and that he "drags these babies out forever." . . .

Attorneys whose practices revolve primarily around larger cases more often complain than do their smaller case counterparts about harassment, overdiscovery (quaintly characterized by some as discovery by "avalanche"), overproduction (referred to variously as the "warehouse" tactic or the "Hiroshima" defense) and other efforts to distract an opponent attention from important information.

Evasive or incomplete responses to discovery are also a persistent and serious source of frustration and difficulty. . . . One attorney admitted that he "schools" his deponents to answer in the subjunctive [for example, "I would lock the safe every evening" rather than "I locked the safe every evening"] and to be as evasive as possible in order to decrease the possibility of their being impeached through their deposition testimony. The game of evasion reportedly is played most studiously, however, in "answering" interrogatories. . . . [Many attorneys reported that these practices continue because the judges don't want to become enmeshed in demands for sanctions.] A large number of attorneys reported that many judges respond to discovery conflicts with an air of undisguised condescension, impatience, or open hostility — implying that involvement in these kinds of disputes is either beneath their dignity or an unjustifiable intrusion on their time. . . . The judiciary's lack of hospitality to discovery problems reportedly is accompanied too often by incompetence in solving them. . . . Many litigators complained that most courts are transparently reluctant to impose sanctions at all and that when sanctions are imposed they often are too mild to serve as significant deterrents to future abuses. . . . In fact, some judges reportedly are known to require at least three failures to respond to the same clearly legitimate discovery request before they will consider seriously a motion for sanctions.

### Do lawyers today engage in wily discovery tactics?

Twenty years after Brazil published his study, the ABA Section on Litigation convened a group of ten partners and nine associates from major law firms who typically represented large corporate defendants in two cities. The conveners invited this group to discuss hypothetical discovery problems and to talk about their own experiences within their law firms. The researchers intended to report the content of the discussion but promised the participants anonymity. The conveners also held discussions with 10 judges, 16 plaintiffs' lawyers, and 16 inside counsel. Some of the lawyers' observations were reported by the researchers in a series of related articles in the *Fordham Law Review*. They suggest that not much had changed in 20 years.[84]

## Ethics: Beyond the Rules

67 Fordham L. Rev. 697 (1998) (symposium)

### Douglas N. Frenkel, Robert L. Nelson & Austin Sarat:[85]

To one degree or another, all of the researchers saw the problems in this area as inseparable from . . . the adversary system and its expectation of partisan conduct amidst a neutral, amoral stance — the so called "dominant" or "standard" conception. They saw and heard the adversary norm as alive and well, some opining that nothing short of basic structural change will alter the climate

---

84. Nor were the 1970s very different from the 1960s. For a first-person account of one of the authors' personal encounters with the horrors of a broken discovery system (in the New York state courts), see Philip G. Schrag, Bleak House 1968: A Report on Consumer Test Litigation, 44 N.Y.U. L. Rev. 115 (1969).

85. Bringing Legal Realism to the Study of Ethics and Professionalism, 67 Fordham L. Rev. 697, 703 (1998). Professor Frenkel teaches and directs the clinical programs at the University of Pennsylvania. Professor Nelson is a sociologist at Northwestern University. Professor Sarat is a professor of jurisprudence and political science at Amherst College.

of litigation. In this world, information is marshaled competitively, competence is paramount, and advantages in resources or ability are to be exploited in the name of honoring the primacy of the duty to favor one's client. The greater the stakes, the harder the fight. Attention to the functioning of the system or to the justice of outcomes is secondary at best. Ethics is a matter of steering, if necessary, just clear of the few unambiguous prohibitions found in rules governing lawyers, i.e., that which is not unlawful is required if the client wants it.

Each group of lawyers sought to shift responsibility for systemic problems onto others with whom they interact. Plaintiffs' lawyers attacked the aggressive information withholding of defense counsel. The latter pointed to their disloyal, unreasonable clients and to frivolous, extortionate filings by, or incompetence of, plaintiffs' lawyers. Corporate clients complain about the over-aggressiveness of both lawyers, with everyone reactive in a system approximating a prisoner's dilemma. All blamed trial judges for failing to police the system. They, in turn, blamed the participants' and appellate courts' lack of support for tough sanctions.

### Robert L. Nelson:[86]

The upshot of our probes and discussions was that problematic behavior was an

*Professor Robert L. Nelson*

infrequent, but persistent part of large firm litigation. It was perceived as more common now than in previous years. . . . Conversations with large-firm litigators suggest that large firms are experiencing a set of fundamental transformations [described in footnote 87] that make uncivil and unethical behavior more likely to occur.[87] . . .

The shift in the balance of power between inside counsel and outside counsel may affect the possibility for ethical breaches. . . . [One lawyer] argued that [he] would not advise a client to destroy documents.

> People have too much respect for their law licenses to ever tell somebody to destroy anything, you would be insane to give that advice. [But] I've seen it

---

86. The Discovery Process as a Circle of Blame: Institutional, Professional and Socio-economic Factors that Contribute to Unreasonable, Inefficient, and Amoral Behavior in Corporate Litigation, 67 Fordham L. Rev. 773, 776, 782, 801 (1998). Professor Nelson is a professor of sociology at Northwestern University and Director of the American Bar Foundation.

87. Later in his article, Professor Nelson described some of the changes, including new insistence by corporations' inside counsel during discovery that outside counsel could obtain information only from a limited number of the corporation's personnel; more lawyers in practice and more "one-shot" litigation, so that lawyers and judges in any city do not have ongoing relationships with each other; more work at a "frenetic pace" under the pressure of imminent deadlines; less training and guidance of associates than previously because firms expect younger lawyers to move from one firm to another, causing partners to think of discovery work as "deposition camp" for associates; the lack of information flow within firms (referred to as the absence of "deposition police"); the hierarchical structure of large firms, which made some associates reluctant to report misconduct for fear of adverse effects on their careers; and the decline in loyalty: by clients to particular firms, partners to partners, and law firms to their associates, causing everyone to care less about law firms' institutional reputations for ethical conduct, Id. at 782-787.

happen all the time. You don't know most of the time when they've destroyed documents. You only know when they're withholding documents. I'm telling you it's done all the time. It's done by in-house counsel, a lot and it occurs a lot, the destruction of documents.

The group disagreed about the general issue about how likely lawyers in their firms would be to destroy documents. . . .

We pushed defense counsel to consider the scope of their obligations in discovery by asking whether they were obligated to turn over a relevant, "smoking gun" document to a plaintiff if defense counsel came into possession of it on the eve of reaching a settlement with the plaintiff. In our hypothetical, the document clearly fell within a standing discovery request, but there was no other deadline that compelled delivery of the document to the plaintiffs. None of the inside counsel said they would feel compelled to produce before completing the settlement. When asked to explain why not, several inside counsel said that "this system is screwed up." They reported that if they litigated in that fashion they would be crucified. "If we thought the system were just, we would be more inclined to disclose such information" [but] plaintiffs' lawyers [were] unreasonable. . . . A few lawyers told how they had let local counsel go because they did not feel the lawyers were sufficiently zealous in their representation.

### Austin Sarat:[88]

Many of the participants in this project said that . . . narrowing discovery responses [and] delaying production [of requested documents] was typical. One of the judges [said that] ". . . the fact that documents are often hidden never comes out. There is usually no consequence at all to an attorney for hiding documents. What matters is keeping the client and winning the case." And, as an in-house counsel said, . . . "The norm is that one generally responds as narrowly as possible. You don't volunteer anything in the hope they'll wear down." . . . As one judge put it, "Discovery rules are supposed to facilitate truth seeking, but in practice that is the last thing they are. They are a cash-cow for lawyers for whom discovery is about hiding the pea."

### Mark C. Suchman:[89]

[W]hile large-firm associates felt that informal role-modeling was generally more effective than formal instruction, they did not necessarily feel that the most commonly modeled behaviors were particularly conducive to ethical practice. Said one . . .

> You're taught these things when you walk into the firm. You're taught to be aggressive and to not just hand things over. The attitude is almost that they have to rip it out of your hands, otherwise we're going to build up all sorts of road blocks. . . . At my firm from the time I was a baby associate in my

---

88. Enactments of Professionalism: A Study of Judges' and Lawyers' Accounts of Ethics and Civility in Litigation, 67 Fordham L. Rev. 809, 822-823 (1998).

89. Working Without a Net: The Sociology of Legal Ethics in Corporate Litigation, 67 Fordham L. Rev. 837, 863, 872 (1998). Professor Suchman teaches sociology at the University of Wisconsin.

first couple of weeks I've had a number of partners who've said, "This document... it's absolutely nothing. It's the employment application or something!... This document was not specifically called for, so we're not going to produce it." Certainly, the aggressive attitude was communicated in those kinds of situations.

If judges fail to fulfill their ethical obligations — such as the duty to impose sanctions for discovery abuse — they tend to justify these actions (or inactions) as efforts to short-circuit the litigation game. As one judicial informant commented: "Our response is to stop playing the game. If we impose sanctions, then we have litigation within litigation. And how have we advanced the case? If we award sanctions, we are saying, 'Keep this game going.'"

## PROBLEM 8-9  **THE DAMAGING DOCUMENTS**

*This problem is closely based on an actual document request that was received by the lawyer for a drug manufacturing company in the northwest United States.*

You are an associate at the law firm representing Bison Corporation, a drug manufacturing company. Your immediate supervisor is a partner, Harris Whittaker.

*Theophylline*

On behalf of Bison, your firm is defending a $15 million lawsuit brought in state court by the family of Joanne Sargent, a girl who, four years ago at the age of two, suffered seizures caused by an excessive amount of theophylline in her system while she had a virus. Theophylline is the technical name for a drug used as a standard treatment for asthma. The seizures resulted in severe and permanent brain damage. Bison's theophylline product is an oral liquid called Somophyllin, which is made from theophylline and some inactive ingredients such as flavorings. Bison's defense is that it did not know, at the time of the incident, that theophylline could be hazardous to children suffering from viral infections.

You have been given primary responsibility for handling this case, under Whittaker's supervision. You know that how well you do with this case will significantly affect your promotion within the law firm. The plaintiff served a request under Rule 34 for production of documents.[90] The request for production began with this definition:

> Definition: The term "the product" as used hereinafter shall mean the product which is claimed to have caused damage to Joanne Sargent as alleged in pleadings filed on her behalf, namely, to wit: Somophyllin liquid.

---

90. Like its federal counterpart, State Court Rule 34 says that any party may serve a request on another party to inspect and copy any designated documents. Under Rule 26, the documents must

The requests for production of documents included these items:

(1) Produce all documents pertaining to any warning letters including "Dear Doctor letters" or warning correspondence to the medical professions regarding the use of the product.

(2) Produce all documents of any clinical investigators who at any time stated to the defendant that the use of the drug Somophyllin liquid might prove dangerous.

(3) Produce all documents regarding tests done on the product to determine its safety.

You met with Bison officials and searched the files to prepare your response to the plaintiff's discovery request. You learned several things.

a. The company includes two divisions. The Traditional Products Division has for decades manufactured Intal, a product based on the chemical compound cromolyn sodium, a product that has been used for decades to treat people who have asthma. Intal competes with the newer products that are based on theophylline, including Bison's own Somophyllin. The New Products Division has been manufacturing Somophyllin for about ten years.

b. The files of the New Products Division consist of approximately 60,000 pages of documents pertaining to tests for the safety of theophylline and another 60,000 pages pertaining to tests for the safety of Somophyllin liquid, including thousands of pages that were supplied to the Food and Drug Administration (FDA). All of these files show that theophylline and Somophyllin are safe for children to use.

c. The files of the Traditional Products Division include even more material, most of it related to cromolyn sodium. However, one document in that file is a letter, written five years before the incident in this lawsuit, by a Traditional Products Division official, Audrey Quine, to a small number of influential doctors. Quine's letter disparaged theophylline and promoted Intal, based on cromolyn sodium, as an alternative to theophylline. Quine enclosed a published study that included reports of "life-threatening theophylline toxicity when pediatric asthmatics contract viral infections." However, Quine's letter did not itself quote from or summarize the study.

d. The FDA occasionally asks a pharmaceutical company to send a "Dear Doctor" letter to all U.S. physicians to warn them of some

---

be relevant to the claim or defense of any party. The party who is served must either state that inspection and copying will be permitted as requested or object and state the reasons for the objection (for example, that the request is not relevant to the issues in litigation or that compliance would be overly burdensome). If an objection is made to part of the request, the inspection must go forward as to the remainder. If the requested party objects or fails to respond to any part of the request, the requesting party may move to compel discovery. Finally, under Rule 26(g), if a party makes a disclosure that is not complete and correct, the court may order "an appropriate sanction."

risk presented by a particular medication. Some executives at Bison and at other drug companies use the term "Dear Doctor letter" more loosely, to refer as well to promotional literature sent to doctors. Quine's letter promoting cromolyn sodium was not sent at government request. It did not go to a mailing list of all doctors known to be using cromolyn sodium or theophylline, much less to all doctors in the United States.

e. A second document in the Traditional Products Division file is an interoffice memorandum, written a year before the incident, from the company's director of medical communications, Walter Lall, to the director of marketing.

The Lall memo says that there had been a "dramatic increase in reports of serious toxicity to theophylline." It also warned that many doctors who follow the usual dosage recommendation "may not be aware of this alarming increase in adverse reactions such as seizures, permanent brain damage, and deaths."

Lall explained that this increase was apparently the result of a mistaken judgment about the proper dosage of the drug. The dosage of theophylline currently recommended by all drug companies, Lall explained, was based on a poor clinical judgment that had been published by one prominent physician. That doctor was regarded as the most knowledgeable doctor in the field. He was also a consultant to and investor in one of Bison's competitors.

After you completed your review of the Bison files, you wrote a memo to your boss, Whittaker, to tell him what you had learned, especially about the troubling documents, and to get his guidance about how to respond to the document request. In reply, he left the following message on your voice mail:

> I got your memo. I suggest that you make sure that those two documents are not produced in discovery. The plaintiff's lawyer would ignore Bison's many studies showing that Somophyllin was safe and would just play up those two papers. A jury focused on those two documents could think our client's defense was full of holes. I wouldn't be surprised if they granted a $15 million verdict for the plaintiff.
>
> We don't have to produce them, anyway. The plaintiff's lawyer defined the product to mean only Somophyllin, not theophylline. We certainly should send them some documents, maybe even all 60,000 documents on Somophyllin in the files of the New Products Division, and maybe even more than that, but not the two documents in the Traditional Products file. Maybe you could draft a response in the form of a letter covering thousands of documents that we ship over to them. You could write the covering letter in a way that could be read, if they ever find out about the two documents and complain about it later, as indicating that we are cooperatively supplying what they asked for. Just make sure it can't be read to suggest that the

documents it covers include, as well, everything we have about theophylline. After all, that's not what they asked for.

Of course, this covering letter should not be so revealing about our having still more materials that the plaintiff will then make a second document request, one that actually covers the two documents. As you know, interpreting a discovery request narrowly and only supplying what was asked for is pretty standard practice.

What will you do in response to the document request? If your answer includes writing something, such as a covering letter of the type suggested by Whittaker, a motion for a protective order, or any other paper, draft the key paragraph and bring it to class. If your answer involves some action other than drafting (such as ignoring the request, destroying the two documents, or sending them to the plaintiff in response to the request for production of documents), write down what you would do and bring what you write to class. During class, you might be asked to read what you have written.

---

## E.  The duty to disclose adverse legal authority

Unless a court disclosure or discovery rule applies,[91] or a lawyer is required to remedy false testimony or some other ethical breach,[92] a lawyer representing a client in litigation need not inform an adversary of adverse facts. However, Rule 3.3(a)(2) prohibits a lawyer from knowingly failing to disclose legal authority in the controlling jurisdiction that the lawyer knows is directly adverse to her client's position, if an opponent has not already informed the judge of the adverse authority.

### Isn't this backwards? Shouldn't a lawyer have a stronger duty to disclose adverse facts than adverse law?

At first it may seem strange that a lawyer has a duty to reveal adverse law but not adverse facts. After all, if a lawyer hides the law, the court and the opposing party can find it by doing research. If the lawyer hides the facts, the court might never find out about them.

There is a certain logic to the idea that the lawyer's first duty should be to ensure that the facts are on the table. However, the idea of a lawyer

---

91. "Disclosure" refers to lawyers' revelations of fact that are required by court rules even when no discovery has been requested, such as disclosure under Fed. R. Civ. P. 26(a)(1) of documents on which a party will later rely. As a matter of professional responsibility, prosecutors also must disclose any exculpatory evidence to criminal defendants. Rule 3.8(d). The term "discovery" refers to providing information, as required by court rules, in response to requests.

92. See Rule 3.3(a)(1), (a)(3), and (b).

volunteering facts that are adverse to a client is contrary to the principles of confidentiality and client loyalty. Disclosure and discovery rules also require lawyers to give away inculpatory information about their clients, but those rules are subject to the attorney-client and the work product doctrine.

But why does the rule require lawyers to disclose adverse legal authority? The premise of this rule is that cases should be decided within the framework of the law — the whole body of law, not only the favorable parts of it that parties told the judge about or about which the judge learned through independent research.[93] Neither judges nor opposing counsel always find relevant adverse authority: hence, this duty of disclosure.

### How often do lawyers actually have to disclose adverse legal authority?

This provision of the rules doesn't create very many problems for lawyers. Most of the time, an opponent will tell the judge of any authority adverse to your position. If the opponent has not yet done so but has the right to file another brief, such as a reply brief, the lawyer may not (yet) have a duty to disclose.[94] Even if the opponent has filed her last permitted brief without disclosing some legal authority adverse to a lawyer's client, the lawyer still may have no duty of disclosure.

- If the adverse law is from another jurisdiction, it need not be disclosed because only law from the controlling jurisdiction matters.
- Only authority that is "directly adverse" need be disclosed. Dicta and holdings that are applicable only by analogy do not have to be disclosed.
- Persuasive authority, such as statements in treatises and law review articles, need not be disclosed.

### Can a lawyer be disciplined for overlooking a directly adverse case?

No, because the prohibition is for "knowingly" failing to reveal the adverse authority. On the other hand, knowledge under the ethics rules can be inferred from circumstances.[95]

# F. Disclosures in ex parte proceedings

Rule 3.3(d) requires that in ex parte (one-sided) proceedings, a lawyer must inform the tribunal of "all material facts known to the lawyer that will enable the tribunal to make an informed decision, whether or not the facts are adverse."

---

93. Restatement § 111, comment c.
94. Id.
95. Rule 1.0(f).

## Doesn't this exception violate the client's expectation of confidentiality?

Yes, the duty overrides the obligation to protect confidences under Rule 1.6.[96] However, lawyers are not required to reveal information protected by the attorney-client and the work product doctrine.[97]

## Why are lawyers required to disclose known adverse facts in ex parte proceedings?

The ethics rules illustrate the need for disclosure of facts in an ex parte proceeding through the example of a request for a temporary restraining order, in which one party rushes into court to try to stop an irreparable injury that may occur before the opposing party can even be notified that the matter will be contested in court.[98]

> FOR EXAMPLE: If a mother has reason to believe that her former husband, with whom she has had a great deal of conflict, is about to take their 12-year-old daughter to another country, the mother might seek a court order prohibiting the father from leaving the country with the child. The mother might seek a temporary restraining order ex parte, without first alerting the father, because advance disclosure might trigger immediate departure.

Under circumstances like these, it is plain why the petitioner's lawyer arguably should disclose all known adverse facts. Suppose that the father and mother in the previous example are living separately and are bitterly angry at each other. Suppose the father has been threatening to take the daughter abroad for a long period of time. Suppose further that the mother's lawyer knows, however, that the father is not planning to leave the country permanently but is going to give a lecture in Paris and has invited his daughter to accompany him. Since the father's lawyer will not be in court, his side of the story would not come out unless the mother's lawyer is required to reveal it.

## Does a lawyer have to disclose adverse facts in nonemergency ex parte hearings?

There are other types of ex parte proceedings. Some of them, such as patent applications and Social Security disability hearings, are hearings on the merits of the cases, as opposed to preliminary matters. The application of this rule to those proceedings might be unfair.

---

96. Technically, a state court that has promulgated Rule 3.3(d) and created the legal obligation to disclose under these circumstances has excused lawyers from the obligation of confidentiality because Rule 1.6(b)(6) allows disclosures that are required "to comply with other law."

97. Restatement § 112, comment b. The Restatement doesn't cite authority, but presumably the theory is that the privileges are ordinarily understood to trump other law, as in the Belge case, discussed in Chapter 2, unless the state legislature explicitly narrows their scope.

98. See, e.g., Fed. R. Civ. P. 65(b).

In a state that has adopted Rule 3.3, an advocate who represents claimants in Social Security disability hearings may be in a serious bind. The lawyers' clients are going to hearings because government officials claim that they are not truly disabled. In a hearing before a federal administrative law judge (ALJ), the lawyer must prove that the client is disabled. The hearing consists of an examination of documentary evidence and searching questioning by the ALJ. It is formally ex parte; that is, the government does not send a lawyer to argue that the claimant is able to work. In preparing for such a hearing, the claimant's lawyer collects all of her client's medical records, which often include conflicting reports about the degree of disease or injury.[99] The ALJ can order his own "consultative examination," but most do not do so.

Must the lawyer provide the ALJ with all the medical reports, including those that would justify denying disability benefits? If so, might the client have a valid complaint that the lawyer failed to act as her advocate? Comment 14 after Rule 3.3 explains that the purpose of Rule 3.3(d) is to allow the judge to "accord the absent party just consideration." This suggests that if the matter is not truly adversarial, perhaps 3.3(d) does not apply. The bar authorities that have considered these questions in the context of Rule 3.3(d) are divided. Some read the rule literally as requiring disclosure. Others conclude that "a lawyer has no duty to defeat his own case."[100] Some jurisdictions have not adopted Rule 3.3(d).[101]

# G.  Improper influences on judges and juries

The goal of lawyers who litigate is to persuade judges and juries. But some methods of persuasion are improper. All states make it a crime to bribe a judge,

---

99. The documentation may be equivocal, for example, if the client's doctor was trying to minimize his description of an illness to encourage his patient to get back on her feet, or if the client was injured on the job and was examined by a doctor hired by the employer who was trying to show that the injury was minor.

100. The quotation is from an unpublished opinion of the chairman of the Missouri Bar Administration Advisory Committee, while the general counsel of the Alabama State Bar Disciplinary Commission held that Rule 3.4(d) compels disclosure. Robert E. Rains, The Advocate's Conflicting Obligations Vis-a-Vis Adverse Medical Evidence in Social Security Proceedings, 1995 B.Y.U. L. Rev. 99, 113-114. Rains concludes that the law is "totally unsettled." Id. at 135. He recommends that a lawyer should produce the adverse evidence because that plan "is not only prudent in terms of the attorney's good standing with the bar, but also as a litigation strategy." Id. at 134. He suggests, however, that the lawyer should seek to subpoena any doctor who wrote the adverse report and then move to exclude the report if (as will often be the case) the doctor does not honor the subpoena. Id. at 134-135. After Rains published his article, North Carolina issued Formal Ethics Op. 98-1 (1998), concluding that Rule 3.3(d) does not apply to Social Security hearings. Vermont concluded that a lawyer need not disclose medical opinions harmful to a Social Security client if there is "reasonable justification for rejecting the opinion and accepting another" and the judge has not asked for such materials. Vt. B. Assn., Op. 95-8 (1995). Vermont apparently distinguishes between medical "fact," which should be disclosed, and medical "opinion," which need not be disclosed. Rains points out in an update to his article that "anyone who has ever dealt with forensic medicine will readily understand that the distinction between a medical fact and a medical opinion is an elusive one at best." E-mail from Professor Raines to the authors (Aug. 2, 2003).

101. See, e.g., D.C. R. Prof. Conduct 3.4; N.Y. Code Prof. Resp. (2002).

for example. Likewise Rule 3.5(a) states that a lawyer may not "seek to influence a judge, prospective juror or other official by means prohibited by law."

# 1. Improper influences on judges

## a. Ex parte communication with judges

A lawyer must not communicate with a judge about a pending case, orally or in writing, unless the lawyers for all parties to the case are privy to the communication. Rule 3.5(b) states that a lawyer shall not "communicate . . . ex parte with [a judge, juror, prospective juror, or other official] during the proceeding unless authorized to do so by law or court order. . . ."[102]

### Should lawyers avoid becoming friends with judges?

The lawyers and judges in any community often have attended the same law schools and belong to the same professional associations, so friendships are commonplace. Rule 3.5 prohibits only communications related to particular proceedings, not personal communications. However, a lawyer who has a case pending before a judge who is a friend, or who even works with a lawyer who has a case pending, should be careful to avoid communications that could touch on the subject of the case.[103]

### May a lawyer contact a judge's chambers to ask a procedural question, such as whether a motion is likely to be decided soon?

Lawyers are allowed to call judges' secretaries or clerks to make minor, routine procedural inquiries about pending cases without having to notify the other parties. Under the Model Code of Judicial Conduct, "ex parte communications for scheduling, administrative purposes or emergencies that do not deal with substantive matters are authorized," but only if the judge reasonably believes that no party will gain an advantage from the contact. Even then, the judge must promptly "notify all other parties of the substance of the ex parte communication" and allow them to respond.[104]

---

102. A similar provision in the judges' code of professional responsibility imposes on them the obligation to avoid ex parte communications. Model Code Jud. Conduct canon 3(B)(7) (as amended through 2003).

103. In one case, John Gerstle, a lawyer who was a friend of Judge Russell, stopped by Russell's chambers and suggested that they have a beer. Judge Russell was putting the finishing touches on an opinion and Gerstle asked her about it. Judge Russell said she was working on a case involving Subway Restaurants and a party named Kessler, and that he was imposing sanctions on a lawyer named Duree. Gerstle told Judge Russell that Duree was a "great guy" who had paid Gerstle's fees to represent Kessler in a different case. Judge Russell had to recuse herself from the case, and, citing Rule 3.5, the Supreme Court of Kansas said that Gerstle's questioning had been inappropriate. Subway Restaurants Inc. v. Kessler, 970 P.2d 526 (Kan. 1998).

104. Model Code Jud. Conduct canon 3(B)(7)(a) (as amended through 2003). In 2003, the ABA began a major overhaul of the Model Code of Judicial Conduct, which it expects to complete in 2005. See ABA Joint Commission to Evaluate the Model Code of Judicial Conduct, Commission Home, at http://www.abanet.org/judicialethics/home.html (last visited Oct. 27, 2004).

**Are these limits scrupulously observed?**

Every community has its own norms, and in some communities, some ex parte communication is accepted. The chief justice of Indiana reports that

> during the course of a busy day in a courthouse, all sorts of administrivia [sic] passes between various actors that no objective observer would deem to violate [the goals of even-handedness and fair process]. "Judge, my client says he'll plead if the prosecutor recommends probation. Is that a deal you might approve?" "Yes, probably, but I'd like to hear what the prosecutor says about it. Subject to reading the presentence report it sounds all right." While we tend to label such communications as improper, they advance the practice of litigation. Our profession not only condones these conversations, it relies on them. We usually sanction the participants when some unexpected force arises, like a runaway client who complains loudly.[105]

### b. Campaign contributions

In many states, state court judges have to run for election.[106] Lawyers are often the main contributors to judicial election campaigns. It is not improper for a lawyer to make a contribution to a judge's campaign. However, the ABA recommends that states set limits on the amount of money that a judge may receive from a lawyer without having to disqualify herself from all proceedings in which that lawyer is involved.[107] The state judges' response to this suggestion has been muted. Many states have not adopted the suggested provision of the Model Code of Judicial Conduct. Some states have contribution limits applicable to all contributors.[108]

## 2. Improper influences on juries

### a. Lawyers' comments to the press

Pick up almost any newspaper or watch TV news for a few days, and you will see lawyers commenting to the press about pending cases. Although the practice is common, the ethics rules impose some limits, particularly when a case is going to be tried by a jury. Courts must balance the free speech rights of lawyers

---

105. Randall T. Shepard, Judicial Professionalism and the Relations Between Judges and Lawyers, 14 Notre Dame J.L. Ethics & Pub. Policy 223, 228 (2000).

106. For an analysis of the merits of various state judge selection systems, see Judith L. Maute, Selecting Justice in State Courts, 41 S. Tex. L. Rev. 1197 (2000).

107. See Model Code Jud. Conduct canon 3(E)(1)(e) (as amended through 2003).

108. A Wisconsin statute limits individual contributions to campaigns for trial judges in large cities to $3,000. Wis. Stat. § 11.26 (2002). By contrast, Texas allows a political action committee to contribute $52,000 to a trial judge's campaign. American Judicature Society, Judicial Selection in the States — Texas, at http://www.ajs.org/js/TX_elections.htm (last visited Oct. 27, 2004). Critics charge that large campaign contributions by lawyers influence the outcomes of litigation there. See Texans for Public Justice, Pay to Play: How Big Money Buys Access to the Texas Supreme Court (2001) at http://www.tpj.org/press_releases/paytoplay.html (last visited Oct. 27, 2004) (Texas Supreme Court justices receive 52 percent of their campaign contributions from litigants and lawyers, and contributors account for 70 percent of the petitions that the court accepts for review).

and their clients against the possibility that jurors would base decisions on what they learned about the case from the media rather than on the evidence they heard in court. The ethical rules reflect concerns about comments that might prejudice a finder of fact and they reflect constitutional concerns.

## The Gentile Case

In 1987, the Las Vegas police discovered large amounts of money and cocaine missing from their safe deposit box at Western Vault Corporation. (The funds and drugs had been used as part of an undercover operation.) Other people also reported that property was missing from their safe deposit boxes. The thief

*Dominic Gentile*

could have been a police detective with access to the vault or the owner of the vault company, Grady Sanders. The sheriff spoke to the press, announcing his faith in the police officers. The deputy police chief eventually announced that two detectives who had access to the vault had been cleared. Seventeen major newspaper stories and several television reports cast suspicion on Sanders. The police leaked that Sanders was about to be indicted. With the indictment imminent but a trial at least six months away, Sanders's lawyer, Dominic Gentile, held a press conference. He hoped to counter the publicity directed against Sanders. He said that when the case was tried, the evidence would show that Sanders was innocent and that one of the detectives was most likely to have taken the property. He asserted that his client was being made into a scapegoat and that four of the other victims of the alleged theft were known drug dealers who might be currying favor with the police.

Six months later, Gentile represented Sanders in the jury trial. Sanders was acquitted. The jury foreman called Gentile to say that if the detective had been charged, the jury would have found him guilty.

The state bar then accused Gentile of violating Nevada's rule against pretrial publicity, prohibiting public comments that "will have a substantial likelihood of materially prejudicing an adjudicative proceeding," but nevertheless allowing a lawyer to "state without elaboration . . . the general nature of the . . . defense." Gentile was reprimanded, but he appealed to the U.S. Supreme Court.

By a 5-4 vote, the Supreme Court held the disciplinary rule void because the "elaboration" and "general nature" clauses were too vague to convey clear information about what was prohibited, so the state bar might enforce the rule in a discriminatory manner.[109] Four of the five justices who sided with Gentile said that an attorney may "take reasonable steps to defend a client's reputation and reduce the adverse consequences of indictment . . . [and] attempt to demonstrate in the court of public opinion that the client does not deserve

---

109. Gentile v. St. B. Nev., 501 U.S. 1030 (1991).

to be tried."[110] The ABA amended its Model Rule to delete the clause that the Supreme Court had criticized.

Rule 3.6 governs pretrial publicity for lawyers. Rule 3.8(f) imposes some additional restrictions on prosecutors.[111]

## Rule 3.6(a) and (b)   Trial Publicity

| Rule language* | Authors' explanation |
| --- | --- |
| (a) A **lawyer** who is participating or has participated in the investigation or litigation of a matter **shall not make** an **extrajudicial statement** that the lawyer knows or reasonably should know will be disseminated by means of public communication and will have a **substantial likelihood of materially prejudicing** an adjudicative proceeding in the matter. | |
| (b) Notwithstanding paragraph (a), a **lawyer may state:**<br>(1) the **claim, offense or defense involved** and, except when prohibited by law, the identity of the persons involved;<br>(2) information contained in a **public record**;<br>(3) that an investigation of a matter is in progress;<br>(4) the scheduling or **result of any step in litigation**;<br>(5) a **request for assistance in obtaining evidence** and information necessary thereto;<br>(6) a **warning of danger** concerning the behavior of a person involved, when there is reason to believe that there exists the **likelihood of substantial harm to an individual or to the public interest**; and<br>(7) in a **criminal case**, in addition to subparagraphs (1) through (6):<br>(i) the identity, residence, occupation and family status of the accused;<br>(ii) if the accused has not been apprehended, information necessary to aid in apprehension of that person;<br>(iii) the fact, time and place of arrest; and<br>(iv) the identity of investigating and arresting officers or agencies and the length of the investigation. | "Paragraph (b) is not intended to be an exhaustive listing of the subjects upon which a lawyer may make a statement, but statements on other matters may be subject to paragraph (a)." Comment 4.<br><br>Comment 5 lists some "subjects that are more likely than not to have a material prejudicial effect on a proceeding" including, for example, the credibility or reputation of a party, the expected testimony of a witness, the possibility of a guilty plea or the contents of a confession or admission, the nature of evidence to be presented, an opinion as to guilt or innocence, or any information that is likely to be inadmissible as evidence.[112] |

*All emphasis added.

---

110. Id. at 1043.

111. Rule 3.8(f) requires prosecutors to "refrain from making extrajudicial comments that have a substantial likelihood of heightening public condemnation of the accused and exercise reasonable care to prevent investigators, law enforcement personnel, employees or other persons assisting or associated with the prosecutor in a criminal case from making an extrajudicial statement that the prosecutor would be prohibited from making under Rule 3.6 or this Rule."

112. The Nevada rule that was declared void for vagueness by the Supreme Court (and which was almost identical to the ABA Model Rule at that time) included this list of potentially prejudicial

Rule 3.6(c) allows a lawyer to make a statement that a "reasonable lawyer would believe is required to protect a client from the substantial undue prejudicial effect of recent publicity" initiated by others. Subsection (d) makes clear that if one lawyer in a firm or organization cannot make a statement, the others in the organization may not do so either.

### How can a lawyer know when a statement to the press is likely to "materially prejudice a proceeding"?

Lawyers should take care in their public statements to restrict their comments to topics on the "permitted" list in subsection (b), and to avoid comments on the more likely prejudicial topics listed in Comment 5. Also, the type and timing of the proceeding matters. A lawyer should be most judicious about speaking to the press when a criminal jury trial is likely. Prejudice is less likely in civil jury trials because they tend to be less sensational and also because a person's life or liberty is not at stake. Extrajudicial statements are least likely to prejudice nonjury cases because, as professional adjudicators, judges are less likely to be swayed by such statements.

The second rule about pretrial publicity applies only to prosecutors. Rule 3.8(f) bars prosecutors from making comments that are likely to heighten "public condemnation of the accused." They also must take "reasonable care" to prevent law enforcement personnel from making any out-of-court statement that either rule would prohibit a prosecutor from making.

> **FOR EXAMPLE:** Jose Padilla, a U.S. citizen, was arrested in May 2002 on a "material witness" warrant, based on fears that he was involved in a terrorist plot. President Bush declared him an "enemy combatant," and for two years Padilla was placed in solitary confinement in a naval brig. No evidence was presented to a grand jury, and no criminal charges were filed against him. In December 2003, the Second Circuit Court of Appeals declared that the government had no legal basis for detaining Padilla. The court ordered that he should be released. The Department of Justice appealed the order to the U.S. Supreme Court.
>
> In June 2004, while the appeal of the order to release Padilla was pending before the Supreme Court, Deputy Attorney General James Comey held a press conference at which he detailed the government's evidence (based on statements by informants and on Padilla's statements while in custody). The point of the press conference was to "allow the American people to understand the threat [Padilla] posed." Comey described in detail allegations that Padilla had met with senior members of al Qaeda in which he had proposed to explode a dirty bomb in the United States. Comey reported that the al Qaeda officials disapproved this idea and that what

---

types of statements in the black-letter rule rather than in the comment, but also stated that information on the list "ordinarily is likely to" result in material prejudice. 501 U.S. at 1060-1061.

Padilla was actually setting forth to blow up some apartment buildings using natural gas.[113]

Would Comey's comments during the press conference violate Rule 3.6 or 3.8(f)? If you think the answer is yes, try to explain why the deputy attorney general of the United States might have thought otherwise.

## PROBLEM 8-10  **A LETTER TO THE EDITOR**

*This problem is closely based on a case that occurred in the Midwest in the late 1990s. The letter to the editor in the problem is the letter that the lawyer actually wrote, except that the names have been changed.*

You are a criminal defense lawyer and have just succeeded in winning a retrial for a Louanne Baker, who was convicted of neglecting her daughter Alice. The charge was brought because her boyfriend beat her daughter to death in a motel room. The prosecution charged that Baker should not have left her daughter in the care of a man she knew to be violent. Baker was found guilty and sentenced to 20 years in prison, of which she served 18 months before you won your appeal. You have just heard that the district attorney, who could have chosen not to reprosecute the case, is planning to have another trial. Your client was just freed, and you would like to avoid a retrial. You've drafted the following letter to the editor about the case, but you haven't mailed it yet:

> I thought that your readers would be interested to know that here in Clark County, the prosecutor has elected to retry my client Louanne Baker. Baker's boyfriend, Bram Cabell, murdered her daughter Alice four years ago. Baker was subsequently charged with neglect of a dependent because she allegedly knew that leaving Alice with Cabell would endanger her life.
>
> She was sentenced to 20 years but her conviction was recently reversed by the Court of Appeals because it said that she didn't r-eceive a fair trial due to the judge's refusal to allow her to present evidence that Cabell had battered her.
>
> In the weeks preceding Alice's murder, Cabell had beaten Alice and allegedly raped Baker at knife point. She reported the beating and rape to the police who, because they were friendly with Cabell, released him. The police gave Baker a lie detector test, which she passed. She moved away from Cabell, but she returned to him a week later when he promised her that he would get help. Two weeks later, Alice was brutally murdered.

---

113. The information in this example is drawn from Scott Turow, Trial by News Conference? No Justice in That, Wash. Post, June 13, 2004, at B1. On jurisdictional grounds, the Supreme Court eventually reversed the decision that had ordered Padilla's release. Rumsfeld v. Padilla, 124 S. Ct. 2711 (2004).

Baker has spent the last 18 months in jail for a crime she did not commit. All too often, a battering victim accepts the batterer's words, even after a child has been injured, and they (sic) have trouble leaving their attackers. The decision to reprosecute her is abominable. She has lost the dearest thing to her, and our citizens should voice their concern that she continues to be penalized for being a victim.

## Questions about a Letter to the Editor

1. Should you mail the letter?
2. What, if any, changes would you make in the letter before sending it, how would you change the letter?

### Do lawyers who are not involved in criminal trials ever get in trouble for pretrial publicity?

Disciplinary proceedings against lawyers for talking to the press in civil cases are not common, but they do occur. Consider the following case.

## Scott Brede, A Notable Case of Exceptionally Unsafe Sex

*Conn. L. Trib., July 10, 2000*

Glastonbury trial attorney Donald P. Guerrini's glib remark to a newspaper reporter regarding a suit brought by a man injured in his motel room while having sex has . . . earned Guerrini a reprimand from the state's attorney-ethics police. . . . The reprimand stems from a 1997 action brought by Shawn Ervin, a Waterbury resident who holds Red Roof Inns responsible for an injury he sustained while a guest of one of its lodgings. Ervin alleged that he and his girlfriend were engaged in sex when the headboard of his motel bed came loose and crushed his finger. . . . A reporter at the *Waterbury Republican-American* . . . dialed up Guerrini [who represents the insurer of Red Roof Inns. He commented] that the plaintiff had to be engaged in "serious acrobatics" for the headboard to come loose. . . . Guerrini also maintained that the gist of his statement was part of the public record already available to the reporter in the form of Red Roof Inns' June 12, 1998 answer to Ervin's complaint . . . that Ervin "failed to take reasonable and proper care in the performance of sexual activity." . . . At its June meeting the [state grievance committee] upheld the reviewing committee's finding that Guerrini violated ethics rules barring attorneys from making extrajudicial statements that would likely prejudice a court proceeding.

The grievance committee reprimanded Guerrini for violating Rule 3.6, but the superior court later remanded the case because the committee had not specified how he should have known that his statement would materially prejudice a trial that was still "several years" in the future.[114] Still, who would want to have to defend and appeal a disciplinary proceeding because of a flip remark to an inquiring reporter?

## b. Impeachment of truthful witnesses

**If a lawyer believes that an opposition witness is truthful, may the lawyer cross-examine the witness in a way that suggests that the witness is lying?**

The rules of professional conduct do not explicitly address a problem sometimes faced by criminal defense lawyers and sometimes by others. A lawyer defending a client whom the lawyer knows to be guilty may assist the client in pleading not guilty and may force the state to present its evidence. The lawyer may object to proffered evidence that may be inadmissible (for example, unlawfully seized evidence). May the lawyer cross-examine the victim (or some other witness) in a way that implies that the victim may be lying if the lawyer in fact believes that the victim is telling the truth? The ethics rules do not address this question directly. Rule 4.4(a) states that a lawyer may not use means that "have no substantial purpose other than to embarrass, delay, or burden a third person. . . ." Of course, the tactic of discrediting an honest witness is not undertaken merely to embarrass or burden the witness but to make the testimony of the witness seem false.

Although this question comes up frequently, there are no reported disciplinary or other cases that address it.[115] The Restatement terms this problem "particularly difficult," but it takes the position that a lawyer may "cross-examine a witness with respect to testimony that the lawyer knows to be truthful, including harsh implied criticism of the witness's testimony, character or capacity for truth-telling."[116] But the Restatement notes that "even if legally permissible, a lawyer would presumably do so only where that would not cause the lawyer to lose credibility with the tribunal or alienate the factfinder."[117]

## Harry I. Subin, The Criminal Defense Lawyer's "Different Mission": Reflections on the "Right" to Present a False Case

1 Geo. J. Leg. Ethics 125, 129-135 (1987)[118]

*Professor Harry I. Subin*

[Professor Subin is Professor of Law Emeritus at New York University Law School.]

About fifteen years ago I represented a man charged with rape and robbery. The victim's account was as follows: Returning from work in the early morning hours, she was accosted by a man who pointed a gun at her and took a watch from her wrist. He told her to go

---

114. Guerrini v. Statewide Grievance Comm., 2001 WL 417337 (Conn. Super. Nov. 28, 2001).

115. Restatement § 106, comment c, reporter's note.

116. Id. at comment c.

117. Id.

118. The reference in the title is a quotation from Justice Byron White: "[D]efense counsel has no . . . obligation to . . . present the truth. Our system assigns him a different mission. . . . If he can

with him to a nearby lot, where he ordered her to lie down on the ground and disrobe. When she complained that the ground was hurting her, he took her to his apartment, located across the street. During the next hour there, he had intercourse with her. Ultimately, he said that they had to leave to avoid being discovered by the woman with whom he lived. The complainant responded that since he had gotten what he wanted, he should give her back her watch. He said that he would.

As the two left the apartment, he said he was going to get a car. Before leaving the building, however, he went to the apartment next door, leaving her to wait in the hallway. When asked why she waited, she said that she was still hoping for the return of her watch, which was a valued gift, apparently from her boyfriend.

She never did get the watch. When they left the building, the man told her to wait on the street while he got the car. At that point she went to a nearby police precinct and reported the incident. She gave a full description of the assailant that matched my client. She also accurately described the inside of his apartment. [The man was arrested, and a gun was found, but the woman was unable to identify the gun as the weapon he had used.] No watch was recovered. . . .

[The client had an alibi, which I investigated and was unable to corroborate. Then he came up with an entirely different alibi, which was obviously false. Finally he confessed to me that he had committed the crime. Meanwhile, at a preliminary hearing, the complainant testified and told her story under oath] in an objective manner that, far from seeming contrived, convinced me that she was telling the truth. She seemed a person who, if not home with the meanness of the streets, was resigned to it. To me that explained why she was able to react in what I perceived to be a non-stereotypical manner to the ugly events in which she had been involved. . . .

[Since consent is a defense to a rape charge, and the robbery charge would fail if the woman seemed to be a liar, the best defense would be] to raise a reasonable doubt as to whether he had compelled the woman to have sex with him. The doubt would be based on the scenario that the woman and the defendant met, and she voluntarily returned to his apartment. Her watch, the object of the alleged robbery, was either left there by mistake or, perhaps better, never there at all.

The consent defense could be made out entirely through cross-examination of the complainant, coupled with argument to the jury about her lack of credibility on the issue of force. I could emphasize the parts of her story that sounded the most curious, such as the defendant's solicitude in taking his victim back to his apartment, and her waiting for her watch when she could have gone immediately to the nearby precinct that she went to later. I could

---

confuse a witness, even a truthful one . . . that will be his normal course. . . . [A]s part of the duty imposed on the most honorable defense counsel, we countenance or require conduct which in many instances has little, if any, relation to the search for truth." U.S. v. Wade, 388 U.S. 218, 256-258 (1967) (White, J., concurring).

point to her inability to identify the gun she claimed was used (although it was the one actually used), that the allegedly stolen watch was never found, that there was no sign of physical violence, and that no one heard screaming or other signs of a struggle. . . . The defendant would not have to prove whether the complainant made the false charge to account for her whereabouts that evening, or to explain what happened to her missing watch. If the jury had reason to doubt the complainant's charges it would be bound to acquit the defendant.

## Question about the Subin Article

In Subin's account of this case, he reports that he considered cross-examining this complaining witness to make the points listed above. Would it be proper for him to cross-examine the complainant in a manner that implies that she consented to go to the defendant's apartment and have sex with him, even though the defendant has privately confessed that he raped her?

## c. Statements by lawyers during jury trials

**The advocate-witness rule**  In general, lawyers may not testify as witnesses in cases that they are handling. Rule 3.7 explains this rule and states some important exceptions.

### Rule 3.7   Lawyer as Witness

| Rule language* | Authors' explanation |
|---|---|
| **(a) A lawyer shall not act as advocate** at a trial in which the lawyer is likely to be a necessary witness **unless:** | The rule purports to apply only to trials, but the advocate-witness rule has been held to apply to all contested proceedings, including hearings on motions at which evidence is taken and evidentiary administrative proceedings.[119] This rule is often enforced through motions by opposing parties either to disqualify a lawyer or to prevent her from testifying for her client. |
| (1) the testimony relates to an **uncontested issue;** | Example: If the issue is not contested, a lawyer attempting to introduce a letter into evidence may testify that she received the letter from her client's brother. |
| (2) the testimony relates to the **nature and value of legal services** rendered in the case; | Example: If a lawyer wins a case and is filing a petition for attorneys' fees to be paid by the losing party, the lawyer may testify about how much time he spent on the case. |

*Continued*

---

119. Restatement § 108, comment c. The version of the rule in §108 is slightly different from the version in the Model Rules. For example, the Restatement version would apply to any case in which the lawyer "is expected to testify for the lawyer's client" or the lawyer does not intend to testify but (i) the lawyer's testimony would be material to establishing a claim or defense of the client, and (ii) the client has not consented . . . to the lawyer's intention not to testify." Rule 3.7 applies where the lawyer "is likely to be a necessary witness."

| Rule language* | Authors' explanation |
|---|---|
| (3) disqualification of the lawyer would work **substantial hardship on the client.** | Example: A lawyer who has handled the financial affairs of a client with a mental disability might seek to testify for the client in a small tax claim where the lawyer had personal knowledge of the issues, was representing the client pro bono, and no other lawyer would accept a case involving such a small amount. |
| (b) A lawyer **may act as advocate in a trial in which another lawyer in the lawyer's firm is likely to be called** as a witness unless precluded from doing so by Rule 1.7 or Rule 1.9. | • If another lawyer in the advocate's firm has the same information as the advocate, the other lawyer usually is not barred from being a witness.<br>• None of the exceptions to the advocate-witness rules excuses a lawyer from the conflict of interest rules, although those rules include their own exceptions (e.g., for consent under some conditions). See Comment 7. |

*All emphasis added.

The advocate-witness rule has two purposes. First, it seeks to avoid a situation that could "prejudice the tribunal and the opposing party."[120] This concern apparently relates primarily to jury trials, for it is said that "it may not be clear whether a statement by an advocate-witness should be taken as proof or as an analysis of the proof."[121] Second, it seeks to avoid "a conflict of interest between the lawyer and client"[122] because a lawyer who has unprivileged, personal knowledge of a case might give testimony that was adverse to the client. This could arise even if the lawyer is called as a witness on behalf of the client. If there is a conflict, the lawyer must assess whether it is consentable, and if so, "the lawyer must secure the client's informed consent, confirmed in writing."[123]

**Comments by lawyers appealing to racial or other prejudice of jurors**   Lawyers should avoid attempting to appeal to jurors' racial or other prejudices. The rules of professional conduct address this issue in one of the comments that follows Rule 8.4, explaining that manifestation of prejudice could be a basis for discipline.

> A lawyer who, in the course of representing a client, knowingly manifests by words or conduct, bias or prejudice based upon race, sex, religion, national origin, disability, age, sexual orientation or socioeconomic status, violates paragraph (d) when such actions are prejudicial to the administration of justice. Legitimate advocacy respecting the foregoing factors does not violate paragraph (d). . . .[124]

---

120. Rule 3.7, Comment 1.
121. Id. at Comment 2.
122. Id. at Comment 1.
123. Id. at Comment 6.
124. Rule 8.4, Comment 3.

Some judges will declare a mistrial or order a new trials if a lawyer makes a discriminatory appeal to a jury.

> **FOR EXAMPLE:** Smrokers and their survivors sued tobacco companies in a Florida state court class action, claiming that the nation's tobacco companies had tortiously caused widespread disease, including cancer. The court certified the class, estimated to consist of 700,000 Floridians, and the case proceeded to trial by a six-person jury that included four African Americans.[125] During the closing argument, the plaintiffs' lawyer, Stanley Rosenblatt, told the jury that the tobacco companies "study races" and divide consumers into "white" and "black." He told the jury that it could fight "unjust laws" as Martin Luther King had done, implying that they could ignore the judge's instructions about the legality of cigarette sales. Also, he informed the jury that in the 1960s, the courtroom in which they now sat had white-only drinking fountains.
>
> The jury ruled in favor of the plaintiffs and granted damages to the class in the amount of *$145 billion.* this verdict, one of the largest in american history, was reversed on appeal. the principal ground for reversal was that the court had improperly certified a class. the appellate court also noted that the case had to be reversed because "plaintiffs' counsel's improper race-based appeals for nullification caused irreparable prejudice."[126]

**Other restrictions**   Rule 3.4(e) imposes further limits on what lawyers may say in court — particularly restricting comments that might prejudice the judgment of juries.

## Rule 3.4(e)   Fairness to Opposing Party and Counsel

| Rule language* | Authors' explanation |
| --- | --- |
| A lawyer shall not: . . . in trial, allude to any matter that the lawyer does not reasonably believe is relevant | Example: Even if a witness blurted out that he was the father of twins, and even though that fact might endear the witness to the jury, the lawyer who put the witness on the stand should not mention the fact unless it is relevant to the case. |
| or that will not be supported by admissible evidence, | Example: Police officer Justin Volpe was tried for raping Abner Louima with a broom handle and causing severe internal injuries. Volpe's lawyer, Marvyn Kornberg, said in his opening statement that the DNA of another man was found in the feces of |

*Continued*

---

125. Robert A. Levy, Tobacco Class Decertified in Florida, Sanity Restored, The Hill, June 11, 2003.

126. Liggett Group Inc. v. Engle, 853 So. 2d 434 (Fla. Dist. App. 2003).

| Rule language* | Authors' explanation |
|---|---|
| | Louima, implying that the injuries were the result of consensual gay sex. Volpe pled guilty during the trial after four eyewitnesses testified against him.[127] |
| **assert personal knowledge of facts** in issue except when testifying as a witness, | A lawyer should not evade the advocate-witness rule by providing factual information to the jury. If the lawyer must state facts within her unique personal knowledge, she should attempt to take the stand under one of the exceptions to the advocate-witness rule. |
| or **state a personal opinion** as to the justness of a cause, the credibility of a witness, the culpability of a civil litigant or the guilt or innocence of an accused. | • Example: In a closing statement, a lawyer should not say that she believes that her client is telling the truth.<br>• The reason for this rule is probably the concern that juries may trust lawyers more than they should, given the lawyer's partisan role; also, the views of nontestifying lawyers are not subject to cross-examination. |

*All emphasis added.

### Can a lawyer communicate his own knowledge or opinions if he includes them in questions posed to witnesses?

No. A jury can obtain information by hearing a question as well as by listening to its answer, so a lawyer should not ask an improper or objectionable question to plant an idea in the minds of the jurors.

> **FOR EXAMPLE:** When two defendants are being tried separately for a crime they allegedly committed together, a prosecutor may not call one of them to the stand in the trial of the other and ask whether he participated in the crime, knowing that the witness will invoke his right not to incriminate himself.[128] That tactic could suggest to the jury that the witness was guilty even though a jury is not entitled to draw that inference from invocation of the right.[129]

---

127. Laura Mansneris, When the Job Requires a Walk on the Ethical Line, N.Y. Times, May 30, 1999.

128. Douglas v. Alabama, 380 U.S. 415 (1965). *Douglas* was not a disciplinary proceeding. The issue arose in the context of a criminal trial. The prosecutor called co-conspirator Loyd to the stand, had him sworn, and then after Loyd invoked his right not to incriminate himself, had him declared a hostile witness. Then the prosecutor read the alleged confession of Loyd, under the guise of asking Loyd questions about it, even though he knew that Loyd would refuse to answer. Douglas, of course, was unable to cross-examine either the prosecutor or Loyd because the prosecutor was not a witness and Loyd refused to answer any questions. The court held that Douglas' Sixth Amendment rights had been violated.

129. See Restatement § 107, comment c.

**What consequences might a lawyer face for violating the rules against making personal comments on the evidence or asking improper questions to prejudice a jury?**

Improper conduct in violation of these rules is usually punished by the trial judge. The judge may sustain objections to the lawyer's improper statements, order them stricken from the record, and give corrective instructions to the jury (for example, to disregard the statements). That remedy may not be sufficient if jurors have already heard the lawyer's improper statements or questions. In that event, the court may declare a mistrial, or an appellate court might order a new trial. If the conduct is repeated, the trial court may order sanctions against the lawyer or hold the lawyer in contempt of court. The state bar might bring disciplinary proceedings against the lawyer.

**Are there still other limitations on what lawyers may say in court?**

Rule 3.5(d) commands that lawyers should not "engage in conduct intended to disrupt a tribunal." Comment 4 elaborates that lawyers should refrain from "abusive or obstreperous" conduct. Even if a judge screams at a lawyer or otherwise acts in inappropriate ways, a "judge's default is no justification for similar dereliction by an advocate." This rule applies during depositions as well as in hearings.[130]

In addition to the ethical rules, rules of evidence, procedural rules of particular courts, and the substantive law of a jurisdiction may impose further limitations on what lawyers may say in court.[131] For example, lawyers are generally permitted to discuss the law in closing statements but not in opening statements. In practice, however, most judges do not strictly enforce this rule but allow lawyers to "steer a middle course" and permit them to "frame the legal issues" for the jury.[132]

**Are lawyers permitted to interview jurors after trials to find out why they were successful or unsuccessful?**

Rule 3.5 regulates contacts between lawyers and jurors outside of the courtroom. Lawyers may not influence jurors (or judges) illegally (for example, by bribing them), and they may not communicate with jurors during a proceeding unless permitted by law or by the judge. After a case is over and the jury has been discharged, a lawyer may talk to any juror who is willing to talk to the lawyer. However, such communication is prohibited if barred by law or a court order, or if the juror has stated that she does not want to communicate. Finally, a lawyer may not mislead, coerce, pressure, or harass jurors. For example, a lawyer may not pretend to be a member of the press in order to find out what happened during jury deliberations.

---

130. Rule 3.5, Comment 5.
131. Restatement § 107, comment a.
132. Steven Lubet, Modern Trial Advocacy 315 (student ed., Natl. Inst. Tr. Advoc. 2000).

# H. Lawyers' duties in nonadjudicative proceedings

Up to this point, we have considered only the rules governing lawyers who appear in courts or other adjudicative[133] proceedings. However, under Rule 3.9, some of these rules also apply when lawyers represent clients in legislative hearings, in rulemaking, or in other nonadjudicative proceedings before government agencies "in which the lawyer or the lawyer's client is presenting evidence or argument."[134] The idea is that if a lawyer is involved in presenting factual or legal material to a decision maker, the lawyer has a responsibility to the decision maker to assure the accuracy of the information presented and to conduct himself in a manner that assists the administration of justice.[135]

> **Rule 3.9    Advocate in Nonadjudicative Proceedings**
>
> **A lawyer representing a client before a legislative body or administrative agency in a nonadjudicative proceeding shall disclose that the appearance is in a representative capacity and shall conform to the provisions of Rules 3.3(a) through (c), 3.4(a) through (c) and 3.5(a) and (c).[136]**

Rule 3.9 does not apply all of these rules to negotiations with or inquiries to government agencies that are unconnected to an "official hearing or meeting." Comment 3 explains:

> It does not apply to representation of a client in a negotiation or other bilateral transaction with a governmental agency or in connection with an application for a license or other privilege or the client's compliance with generally applicable reporting requirements, such as the filing of income-tax returns. Nor does it apply to the representation of a client in connection with an investigation or examination of the client's affairs conducted by government investigators or examiners. Representation in such matters is governed by Rules 4.1 through 4.4.

The internal cross-references make this rule a little hard to follow, but this chart clarifies which prohibitions apply to nonadjudicative proceedings.

---

133. Adjudication refers to a proceeding whose purpose is to decide a case involving a specific set of persons or facts. Rule 3.3 specifically refers to proceedings before "tribunals." Rule 1.0(m) defines "tribunal" to refer to

> a court, an arbitrator in a binding arbitration proceeding or a legislative body, administrative agency or other body acting in an adjudicative capacity. A legislative body, administrative agency or other body acts in an adjudicative capacity when a neutral official, after the presentation of evidence or legal argument by a party or parties, will render a binding legal judgment directly affecting a party's interests in a particular matter.

134. Rule 3.9, Comment 3.
135. Id. at Comment 1.
136. Delaware Rule 3.9 differs from ABA Model Rule 3.9 only in its reference to Rule 3.5. The Delaware rule obliges lawyers in nonadjudicative proceedings to comply only with Rule 3.5(a) and (c), whereas the Model Rule obliges such lawyers to comply with all of the provisions of Rule 3.5. This means Delaware lawyers need not attend to Rule 3.5(b) (ex parte communications) and (d) (conduct intended to disrupt a tribunal) in their representation of clients in nonadjudicative proceedings.

## Application of Rule 3.9 to nonadjudicative proceedings

| Rule | Mandates that apply to nonadjudicative proceedings |
|------|----------------------------------------------------|
| **3.3(a)** | • Lawyer may not make false statements of fact or law.<br>• Lawyer must correct own previous statements if false.<br>• Lawyer must disclose directly adverse controlling law.<br>• Lawyer may not offer evidence that the lawyer knows is false.<br>• Previously offered false evidence must be corrected. |
| **3.3(b)** | • Lawyer may not allow client to engage in criminal or fraudulent conduct related to the proceeding.<br>• If such conduct has taken place, lawyer must take remedial measures including disclosure, if needed. |
| **3.3(c)** | • The duty to correct overrides the duty of confidentiality.<br>• The duty continues to the end of the proceedings. |
| **3.4(a)** | • Lawyer may not unlawfully alter, destroy, or conceal documents with potential evidentiary value. |
| **3.4(b)** | • Lawyer may not falsify evidence, advise a witness to testify falsely, or give an unlawful inducement to a witness to procure testimony. |
| **3.4(c)** | • Lawyer may not disobey an obligation under the rules of a tribunal (unless the lawyer openly discloses he is doing so because he or she disputes the obligation). |
| **3.5** | • Lawyer may not attempt to influence officials illegally.<br>• Lawyer may not illegally communicate ex parte with "judge, juror or prospective juror" during the proceedings. (Note, however, that ex parte contact with legislators or their staffs in connection with proposed or pending legislation is normal, not illegal, and protected by the First Amendment. This prohibition does not apply in Delaware.)<br>• Lawyer may not communicate with jurors after a case is over by using misrepresentation or coercion or if barred by law.<br>• Lawyer may not intentionally disrupt a tribunal. (This prohibition does not apply in Delaware.) |

The incorporation by reference of all of these rules into Rule 3.9 isn't entirely logical.[137] The Restatement simply provides that in administrative proceedings that are adjudicative in nature or that involve a government agency as a participant, lawyers have the same responsibilities that they do in courts. In other types of government proceedings, the Restatement concludes that lawyers have the same duties that they have when they deal with private persons.[138] The

---

137. For example, the bar on certain communications with jurors in nonadjudicative proceedings is difficult to reconcile with the fact that jurors work in courts.

138. Agency adjudications (such as proceedings before a zoning board to determine the proper zoning for a client's property) are of the first type, while consideration of legislation is of the second variety. Restatement § 104.

Restatement candidly notes that "few decided cases have considered a lawyer's obligations in dealing with legislative bodies and administrative agencies" and that "the proper classification of a particular proceeding may be unclear."[139]

# I. Communications with lawyers and third parties

When lawyers communicate with others on behalf of clients outside of "proceedings," Rules 4.1 through 4.4 apply. Some of the obligations are very similar to those that apply in proceedings, but others are quite different.

## 1. Deception of third parties

### a. The duty to avoid material false statements to third parties

> Rule 4.1(a)   Truthfulness in Statements to Others
> In the course of representing a client a lawyer shall not knowingly . . . make a false statement of material fact or law to a third person. . . .

Rule 4.1(a) is similar to the first part of Rule 3.3(a)(1) — both rules instruct lawyers not to lie. While Rule 3.3 applies only to proceedings before tribunals, Rule 4.1(a) applies whenever a lawyer is representing a client, such as when the lawyer is talking to a potential witness or to an opposing lawyer. Rule 4.1 also differs from Rule 3.3 in that Rule 3.3 bars a lawyer from making any false statements to tribunals, while Rule 4.1 prohibits only "material" false statements of fact or law to third parties. Rule 8.4(c), which prohibits lawyers from engaging in conduct involving "deceit or misrepresentation," has no qualifier excusing false statements that are not "material."

**PROBLEM 8-11  EMERGENCY FOOD STAMPS**

> *William Simon, a former legal services advocate, is William W. and Gertrude H. Saunders Professor of Law at Stanford University. This problem is his own account of one of his cases, excerpted from a law review article.*[140]

One Friday in 1980, a man named Jessie Rogers walked into our legal aid office in Boston to complain that he had just been denied "emergency" food stamps by the neighborhood welfare office. He had been released from prison the prior day. The prison authorities had arranged temporary lodging for him in a small room with primitive cooking facilities, given him a little cash, and told him he could receive food stamps on application at the welfare office. A social service agency would assess him for employment the following week.

---

139. Id. at comments b and d.
140. William H. Simon, Virtuous Lying: A Critique of Quasi-Categorical Moralism, 12 Geo. J. Leg. Ethics 433, 433-439 (1999).

The prison authorities' expectation that he would receive food stamps was not unreasonable. Statutes and regulations entitled financially eligible people in Rogers' residential circumstances to an "over-the-counter" issue of stamps on application if they were in "immediate need." The application process called for various documents, such as proof of residence and a Social Security card, which Rogers had satisfied. He was, however, unable to satisfy one of the demands: He did not have a "picture ID," and neither he nor the welfare worker to whom he applied knew how he could get one in less than five days. Although the regulations stated that documentation requirements should be waived in cases of "immediate need" where there was a reasonable explanation of inability to comply, the worker told Rogers that he could not receive any benefits until he could produce the "picture ID."

On hearing Rogers' story, our paralegal telephoned the welfare worker to argue that Rogers was entitled to a waiver of the ID requirement. While the paralegal waited, the welfare worker went to consult the office director and returned to confirm the office's refusal to provide benefits. When Rogers and the paralegal told me their stories, I called the office. The welfare worker told me that the director had instructed her not to grant benefits without a "picture ID." I asked to speak to the director. The worker, after hesitating suspiciously, said that the director had "left for the day." The paralegal did not believe this: "They're stonewalling. They hate to waive documentation. On Monday, when we finally get to see the director, he'll claim that the worker never told him Mr. Rogers was in immediate need. In the meantime, they'll have had the satisfaction of jerking Mr. Rogers and us around."

I proposed that the paralegal call the office back and, in a secretarial tone, tell the receptionist that Theresa Taylor wished to speak to the director. Theresa Taylor was the welfare department district manager to whom the office director reported. It worked. Within seconds, the office director came on the line. His initially obsequious tone became first irritated and then sheepish as I explained who I was and why his office was clearly obliged to issue stamps immediately to Mr. Rogers. Vindicating our paralegal, the director said with ineptly feigned surprise, "Oh, he's in immediate need! He should have told us that." He finally agreed to yield up the stamps that afternoon.

---

## Questions about Emergency Food Stamps

**1.** A Massachusetts rule in effect at the time these events took place imposed the same obligation that Rules 4.1 and 8.4(c) impose now. Did Professor Simon violate those rules?

**2.** If so, did he do the right thing?

**What about false statements by clients? If a lawyer knows that her client is lying in her presence to someone other than a court, must the lawyer ask the client to tell the truth or tell the third party herself?**

As we have seen, if a lawyer knows that her client or any witness she presents is lying to a tribunal or in a pretrial deposition, Rule 3.3(b) requires the lawyer to take remedial measures, which could include informing the tribunal if the client refuses to correct the record herself. Also, even if the client is not testifying before a tribunal, the lawyer must withdraw from representing a client who is using the lawyer's services (such as documents prepared by the lawyer) to perpetrate a fraud.[141] But suppose that no proceeding has commenced, and the client is not using the lawyer's services to perpetrate a fraud, but the lawyer nevertheless knows that the client is providing false information to a third party. For example, suppose that in the course of a criminal investigation, the police question a suspect in his lawyer's presence, and the lawyer knows that her client is providing incorrect information.

The lawyer would probably be foolish to allow her client to lie under these circumstances because the client could be charged with a crime such as obstructing justice. To serve her client well, the lawyer should interrupt the questioning, take her client aside, and advise her to tell the truth. However, if the lawyer does not do so, or if the lawyer does so and the client refuses to accept her advice, no rule appears to require the lawyer to correct the record.

It could be argued that the lawyer's presence during an event at which the client provides false information is a "use" of the lawyer's services to commit a fraud, permitting disclosure under Rule 1.6(b) and therefore perhaps requiring the disclosure under Rule 4.1(b). However, we are unaware of any holding to that effect.

Nevertheless, a lawyer might be disciplined for sitting by silently while a client perpetrates a fraud, particularly if any action by the lawyer could be construed as participation in the fraud.

> **FOR EXAMPLE:** In the case of In re Austern, a lawyer was serving as an escrow agent at a real estate closing. The buyers feared that once they closed the sale, the seller would not complete work on the apartment units it was selling. They insisted that the seller give the lawyer a check for $10,000 to guarantee completion. The lawyer accepted the check, but his client told him privately that there was no money in the account and that the check was therefore worthless. Nevertheless, the lawyer went ahead with the closing, without informing the buyers that the check had no backing. Austern delayed opening the escrow account until two months later, when he received a good check. He was publicly censured for assisting his client in a fraud; the District of Columbia Court of Appeals said that he should have withdrawn, but instead he "used his status as an attorney to lend legitimacy to a transaction which had none."[142]

---

141. See the discussion in Chapter 2.

142. 524 A.2d 680, 687 (D.C. 1987). This case is somewhat different from the hypothetical question posed in the text in which the lawyer is entirely passive, because Austern did more than sit

## b. Lawyers' duties of truthfulness in fact investigation

A lawyer is obliged to undertake a "reasonable" inquiry before filing a suit. Even if this were not required, simple economics would compel most lawyers to investigate potential suits before filing them to avoid investing time and money in lawsuits that have little chance of success. Discovery under court rules is unavailable before a case begins, so lawyers must investigate cases privately. Sometimes the needed investigation can be accomplished through interviews with witnesses and collection of available documents. But in some cases, lawyers or their investigators believe that they can obtain the required information only by misrepresenting their identity or the purpose of their inquiry.

> FOR EXAMPLE:   An aspiring tenant believes that the landlord of a desirable building rejected his application to rent an apartment because the tenant is African American. If questioned, the landlord would almost surely deny that his motivation was unlawful racial discrimination. A lawyer might want to *test* the landlord's willingness to rent to African Americans by sending, for example, four investigators — two of them white and two of them black — to pose as possible tenants and fill out rental applications, giving similar family information and credit histories. If the landlord agreed to sign leases with the white applicants but not the black applicants, this would substantiate the claim of discrimination. Some courts have recognized such practices as a legitimate method to identify violations of the civil rights laws.[143]

The testing process requires that the lawyer direct his investigators to lie about their interest in renting apartments in the building, and probably also about their identities, families, and credit histories. Rule 8.4(a) states that it is professional misconduct for a lawyer to violate one of the rules or to "knowingly assist or induce another lawyer to do so" or to "do so through the acts of another." So if the lawyer could not ethically do this work himself, he cannot enlist another person to do it either. Do Rules 4.1 and 8.4(c) preclude the use of testers?[144]

### Apart from use of testers, are lawyers ever justified in using deception in the course of investigation?

This question comes up often but is evaluated by courts infrequently. One court looked at some deceptive investigation tactics used by a lawyer for Yoko Ono

---

silently while his client committed a fraud. The court found that he signed the escrow agreement after knowing of the fraud. Nevertheless, the case is a warning that even more subtle activity by a lawyer in connection with a client's false representations to third parties could subject the lawyer to discipline. The sanction imposed on Austern was light because of his excellent professional reputation and achievements.

143. Havens Realty Corp. v. Coleman, 455 U.S. 363 (1982).

144. For discussion of the ethical issues relating to use of testers, see David B. Isbell & Lucantonio N. Salvi, Ethical Responsibility of Lawyers for Deception by Undercover Investigators and Discrimination Testers: An Analysis of the Provisions Prohibiting Misrepresentation Under the Model Rules of Professional Conduct, 8 Geo. J. Leg. Ethics 791 (1995).

Lennon. The International Collectors Society (ICS) sold foreign postage stamps bearing pictures of celebrities, including the Beatles. Lennon sued ICS to enjoin the sales, claiming that the stamps included copyrighted photographs. In court, ICS agreed to a judgment ordering it to terminate the sales. Under this consent decree, however, ICS could sell off a few thousand stamps to persons who had already become members of the "Beatles/Lennon Club" by having purchased Beatles stamps in the past. Two months later, Dorothy Weber, one of Lennon's lawyers, called ICS, posing as a consumer by using her married name, Dorothy Meltzer. She said that her husband was a John Lennon fan. She bought stamps over the phone. At Weber's direction, her secretary and several investigators also posed as consumers who were not Beatles/Lennon club members, and they too were able to buy stamps over the phone. Lennon then sought to hold ICS in contempt for violating the consent decree. ICS defended, partly relying on the theory that Lennon should not be able to enforce the court's order because Weber had violated Rule 8.4(c). Professor Bruce Green, who teaches professional responsibility at Fordham Law School, filed a statement with the court on behalf of Lennon, arguing (as an ethics expert) that Weber had not violated the rule. The court concluded as follows.

## Apple Corps, Ltd. v. International Collectors Society

### 15 F. Supp. 2d 456 (D.N.J. 1998)

[Rule] 8.4(c) does not apply to misrepresentation solely as to identity or purpose and solely for evidence-gathering purposes. Undercover agents in criminal cases and discrimination testers in civil cases, acting under the direction of lawyers, customarily dissemble as to their identities or purposes to gather evidence of wrongdoing. This conduct has not been condemned on ethical grounds by courts, ethics committees or grievance committees. This limited use of deception, to learn about ongoing acts of wrongdoing, is also accepted outside the area of criminal or civil rights enforcement. . . . See . . . Green Declaration.[145] The prevailing understanding in the legal profession is that a public or private lawyer's use of an undercover investigator to detect ongoing violations of the law is not ethically proscribed, especially where it would be difficult to discover the violations by other means. (Green Declaration) . . . If the drafters of [Rule] 8.4(c) intended to prohibit automatically "misrepresentations" in all circumstances, [Rule] 4.1(a) would be entirely superfluous. As a general rule of construction, however, it is to be assumed that the drafters of a statute intended no redundancy. . . . Accordingly, Plaintiffs' counsel and investigators did not violate [Rule] 8.4(c).

---

145. [Authors' footnote.] Professor Green's declaration, on file with the authors, cited one authority that did not involve civil rights testing or criminal law enforcement—Alabama Ethics Op. RO-89-31 (1989) suggesting (in Green's words) that "a lawyer may direct an investigator to pose as a buyer for the plaintiff's machine in order to determine whether the plaintiff can lift the machine and must therefore have lied about the extent of his injuries."

Across the country, however, lawyer Daniel Gatti got in trouble for misrepresenting his identity while investigating whether to file a civil lawsuit.

## The Gatti Case

Gatti represented chiropractors. One chiropractor told him that he suspected that a company called California Medical Review (CMR), which reviewed medical claims submitted to insurance companies, was using people who lacked medical training to evaluate insurance claims. When one of Gatti's chiropractor clients had a claim rejected based on a recommendation from a "Dr. Becker" who worked for CMR, Gatti began to investigate a possible fraud case against CMR. He called Becker, pretended to be a chiropractor, and asked Becker to describe his qualifications. He also called a Mr. Adams at CMR, stated (falsely) that he was a doctor,[146] that he'd been referred to CMR by Becker and an insurance company, and said he was interested in working as a claims reviewer and wanted to learn about CMR's educational programs for insurance adjusters.

*Daniel Gatti*

Adams at CMR filed a complaint against Gatti. The Oregon Bar filed disciplinary proceedings against Gatti for misrepresenting his identity in violation of its version of Rule 8.4(c). Gatti defended in part by quoting from a letter he had once received from the Oregon Bar, stating that government prosecutors could use deception in undercover investigations. The trial panel in Gatti's disciplinary proceeding might have exonerated Gatti under a theory like that used by the court in the Beatles case, or it might have distinguished his case from that of prosecutors, allowing the latter but not the former to use deception. But it did neither. It held that there was no implicit law-enforcement exception, either for private lawyers like Gatti or for government lawyers such as prosecutors. On the other hand, it dismissed the case against Gatti because it believed that he had reasonably relied on the letter from the bar.

The bar appealed to the Oregon Supreme Court. The U.S. attorney for Oregon and the Oregon attorney general urged the court at least to uphold the use of undercover tactics by public law enforcement officials, a practice that the trial panel had said would violate professional standards. Gatti also cited the Beatles case in defense of undercover tactics by private lawyers who were investigating frauds.

## In re Gatti

8 P.3d 966 (Or. 2000)

[T]his court is aware that there are circumstances in which misrepresentations, often in the form of false statements of fact by those who investigate violations

---

146. Gatti claimed that this particular assertion was not actually false since he held the degree of Juris Doctor.

of the law, are useful means for uncovering unlawful and unfair practices, and that lawyers in both the public and private sectors have relied on such tactics. However, Oregon Revised Statutes 9.490(1) [authorizing this court to issue rules for lawyers] provides that the rules of professional conduct "shall be binding upon all members of the bar." . . . In our view, this court should not create an exception to the rules by judicial decree. . . . By misrepresenting his identity and purpose and making other false statements when he called Becker and Adams with the intention of deceiving them, the accused violated his duty to the public to maintain personal integrity. . . .

Statements by parties *amici* indicate that lawyers in both private practice and those who work in the public sector in good faith have held the mistaken belief that they ethically are permitted to misrepresent their identity and purpose, and to encourage others to do so, to acquire information. Thus, it is a fortuity that the accused in this case, rather than some other Oregon lawyer, is the subject of these proceedings. . . . Under the circumstances of this case, therefore, we conclude that a public reprimand is the appropriate sanction.

## Notes about *Gatti*

1. The law enforcement community in Oregon was shocked by the outcome in *Gatti,* which jeopardized all prosecutor-directed undercover investigations of criminal activity in the state. A year after the case was decided, law enforcement officials persuaded the legislature to pass an emergency law allowing any lawyer working for any federal, state, or local government agency to "provide legal advice and direction to" and to "participate in" covert law enforcement activities, "even though the activities may require the use of deceit or misrepresentation."[147] The statute made no such exception for private lawyers. Subsequently, the Oregon Supreme Court drew the line between permitted and prohibited conduct in a quite different place. It amended its rules of professional responsibility to allow both government lawyers and private lawyers to supervise undercover investigations involving deception, but the amendment did not authorize lawyers of either type to participate personally in the deceptions.[148]

---

147. Or. Rev. Stat. Ann. § 9.528 (2003). The Utah State Bar ethics committee evaluated the question and reached a conclusion similar to the Oregon legislature, carving an exception for governmental lawyers but reserving for another day the question of whether the exception would also apply to private lawyers who were attempting to investigate fraud or other wrongdoing. Utah St. Bar, Ethics Advisory Op. Comm., Op. 02-05 (2002).

148. The new rule permits lawyers to "advise clients or others about or to supervise lawful covert activity in the investigation of violations of civil or criminal law or constitutional rights, provided the lawyer's conduct is otherwise in compliance with these disciplinary rules." "Covert activity" is defined as an "effort to obtain information on unlawful activity through the use of misrepresentations or other subterfuge." The rule added that covert activity could be commenced or supervised by a lawyer "only when the lawyer in good faith believes there is a reasonable possibility

**2.** Daniel Gatti's reprimand stood. He published a novel, *White Knuckle,* and said that he wished that a reformed disciplinary rule "could have come about another way."[149]

## c. Lawyers' duties of truthfulness in negotiation

The text of Rule 4.1 does not allow lawyers to lie for the purpose of bargaining. More precisely, it does not allow a lawyer knowingly to "make a false statement of material fact or law." A lawyer reading this rule might conclude, therefore, that she would engage in professional misconduct if she told her opposing counsel that her client would not accept a settlement of less than $80,000, knowing that, in fact, her client would be quite happy to walk away with $75,000. But Comment 2 qualifies the rule:

> This Rule refers to statements of fact. Whether a particular statement should be regarded as one of fact can depend on the circumstances. Under generally accepted conventions in negotiation, certain types of statements ordinarily are not taken as statements of material fact. Estimates of price or value placed on the subject of a transaction and a party's intentions as to an acceptable settlement of a claim are ordinarily in this category, and so is the existence of an undisclosed principal except where nondisclosure of the principle would constitute fraud.[150]

The contrary messages in the rule and the comment may reflect a profession that is deeply divided about the acceptability of certain lies during negotiations (for example, about acceptable levels of settlement or about a lawyer's authority to settle for a certain amount). One author surveyed 15 leading academics, practitioners, and judges about whether they could, consistently with the ethical rules, falsely state that they were not authorized by their defendant client to settle for the amount that the plaintiff wanted to receive. Six said that the rules would not allow such a statement, and seven said that such a statement was permissible. All but one said that for tactical reasons or because of their personal ethics, they would evade the question rather than lie.[151]

Several academic authorities have criticized the comment to Rule 4.1, arguing that it enshrines, without justification, an overly adversarial model of negotiation.

---

that unlawful activity has taken place, is taking place or will take place in the foreseeable future." Or. Code Prof. Resp., DR 1-102(D) (2004).

149. Ashbel S. Green, Lawyers' No-lying Dispute Comes to a Close, Oregonian, Jan. 30, 2002.

150. The last part of this comment refers to a situation in which the person on the other side of the negotiation from the lawyer thinks that the lawyer is representing a particular person or institution, but the lawyer is really representing other interests, perhaps entities that could afford to pay much more to the unwitting person.

151. Larry Lempert, In Settlement Talks, Does Telling the Truth Have Its Limits? 2 Inside Litig. 1 (1988).

## Carrie Menkel-Meadow, Ethics, Morality and Professional Responsibility in Negotiation

Dispute Resolution Ethics: A Comprehensive Guide 119, 127-128, 134-135, 144-145, 154
(Phyllis Bernard & Bryant Garth eds., ABA 2002)

[Professor Menkel-Meadow is Professor of Law at Georgetown University.]

*Professor Carrie Menkel-Meadow*

Following the crisis of credibility the legal profession suffered after Watergate, the ABA's Kutak Commission [which drafted the proposal that evolved into the 1983 Model Rules] suggested in 1980 that an enhanced duty of care, candor and conscionability might be appropriate in legal negotiations. Proposed Rule 4.2 would have required lawyers to be "fair" in their dealings with third parties in negotiation. . . . These proposals were defeated by an active professional debate that sought to preserve the caveat emptor culture of both the litigator and the transactional dealmaker. A zealous advocate protects his or her client and does not do the work of protecting the other side. As one commentator has put it, the adopted version of Rule 4.1, prohibiting only "material" misrepresentations of fact or law, "unambiguously embraced 'New York hardball' as the official standard of practice." . . .

[F]or those who are "tough negotiators" or who see legal negotiation as an individual maximization game, [most deceptions, such as those explicitly permitted by the comment, or other common practices such as falsely stating that a client intends to sue if the other party doesn't settle] can be justified by reference either to "expectations" about how the legal-negotiation game is played, or to the lawyer's obligation to be a zealous advocate. . . . Who decides what "generally accepted conventions" [the phrase used in the ABA's comment] are? The drafters of the ethics rules, without empirical verification? And, more importantly, why should "generally accepted conventions" prevail in an ethics code? Are we looking at "generally accepted conventions" in other areas of the Rules? . . . The answer is usually "no" — we require lawyers appearing before tribunals to reveal adverse authority without regard to what "accepted conventions" of advocacy might suggest, e.g., that each side should do its own research and it is up to the judge or clerk to find the cases. . . .

Guides to negotiation often advise negotiators to "deflect" questions or "answer different questions" or "change the subject" as a way of avoiding giving an incomplete or untruthful answer to a specific request for information. Increasingly these tactics can give rise to post-hoc fraud or misrepresentation claims, especially if there is evidence that a negotiator deliberately refused to answer, "recklessly" gave incomplete or incorrect responses or allowed some incorrect fact or information to stand. . . . Both case law and ethics opinions now make it clear that negotiators cannot take advantage of incorrect assumptions or mistakes of the other side when they know such mistakes are being made. In what has become standard fare for both contracts classes and negotiation courses, the case of Stare v. Tate[152] demonstrates what can happen when one side knowingly takes advantage of another. After a hotly contested divorce negotiation, especially focused on the value of some stock, the wife's lawyer made an arithmetic error in the final agreement, undervaluing the stock to be divided. The husband's lawyer knew about the error but didn't say anything. Later when the husband gleefully told his ex-wife he had gotten the better of her in the negotiation, the court was so offended it reformed the divorce agreement. . . .

*Stare* was an easy case because of the husband's need to get his "last licks" in. More often, such fraud will be harder to prove, dependent on often-conflicting testimony about what was said, and in these cases such questions often go to a jury for factual determination. Nevertheless, lay juries have often proven to have lower tolerance for hardball negotiation tactics than judges or lawyer disciplinary bodies who may be inured to "conventional" lawyer negotiation tactics. . . .

Consider the objections consistently made to proposals that lawyers approach each other in negotiation with an obligation to affirmatively tell the truth. (1) The obligation would be unfair to the lawyer of greater technical skill or his client. Heaven forbid that outcomes in negotiation turn on the "merits" rather than the lawyer's exercise of technical skill. (2) The requirement would reduce incentives to investigate information. If a negotiator could trust the disclosures of the other side, information costs could actually decrease because each negotiator would have to investigate only that about which the other side wouldn't have superior knowledge. (3) It would be impossible to monitor whether someone was telling the truth (and what is "truth" in negotiation anyway?). Perhaps. It would be difficult, but who knows? We have never tried it. We do, however, allow legal actions for fraud and misrepresentations in all other forms of contracting (not to mention medical malpractice, corporate securities and a variety of other specific contexts). Should lawyers be less subject to monitoring than others who negotiate (real estate agents, stockbrokers)? What is wrong with this picture? . . .

Consider how much more efficient and just, as well as fair, negotiations might be if the presumptive expectations about information and the purposes of negotiation were reversed. Clients would say what they really wanted and be required to produce what information they had to support their claims. . . . Shouldn't we aim for "generally accepted conventions" that seek to do the best for all parties, rather than only a few? Perhaps then we could, in the words of one modern ethicist, "live so that we can look other people, even outsiders [as well as ourselves] in the eye."

### d. Obligations of disclosure to third parties

Rule 4.1(b) imposes on lawyers a limited duty to make affirmative disclosures to others when necessary to avoid assisting a criminal or fraudulent act by a client. However, the duty to disclose is subordinate to the duty to protect

---

152. [Menkel-Meadow's footnote 81.] 98 Cal. Rptr. 264 (Cal. App. 1971).

confidential information. The issues raised by the obligation and its limitation are explored in Chapter 2 as part of the discussion of when a lawyer may reveal a crime or fraud.

## 2. Restrictions on contact with represented parties

We move on from a series of questions about deception to explore what should be a lawyer's relationship to a nonlawyer who is involved in a matter in which the lawyer is representing a client. The ethical rules impose some restrictions on communication between lawyers and adverse parties out of concerns about possible overreaching. The rules first address restrictions on contact with a person (not just an adverse party) who is represented by a lawyer.

> **Rule 4.2   Communication with Person Represented by Counsel**
> **In representing a client, a lawyer shall not communicate about the subject of the representation with a person the lawyer knows to be represented by another lawyer in the matter, unless the lawyer has the consent of the other lawyer or is authorized to do so by law or a court order.**

A major purpose of this rule is to prevent lawyers from making "end runs" around other lawyers to get information from the other lawyers' clients.[153] If a lawyer contacts a represented person without his lawyer's consent, the represented person might make disclosures or concessions that his lawyer would have counseled him to avoid. The rule applies to all contacts with represented persons, not only to parties in litigation.[154]

Comments to Rule 4.2 and an ABA opinion elaborate and qualify these restrictions:

■ Rule 4.2 applies whether the lawyer or the represented initiates the conversation.[155]

**FOR EXAMPLE:**   Two parties dispute the bill that the seller sent the buyer. Each has a lawyer who is known to negotiate all such disputes. The buyer personally calls the seller's lawyer to ask her to have the seller revise the bill. The seller's lawyer should refuse to discuss the matter and should instruct the buyer that she would be willing to talk to the buyer's lawyer about it, or to the buyer personally if the buyer's lawyer agrees to that procedure.

---

153. Another purpose is to prevent lawyers from interfering with the lawyer-client relationships of their adversaries. Rule 4.2, Comment 1.

154. The ABA revised Rule 4.2 and its comments in 2002. Professor Carl A. Pierce has written three articles exhaustively exploring the effect of the changes. Variations on a Basic Theme: Revisiting the ABA's Revision or Model Rule 4.2, 70 Tenn. L. Rev. 121 (2002) (Part I); 70 Tenn. L. Rev. 321 (2003) (Part II); 70 Tenn. L. Rev. 643 (2003) (Part III).

155. Rule 4.2, Comment 3. Another way to state this proposition is that a client's consent is not sufficient to overcome the "anti-contact" rule; the consent of the client's lawyer is necessary to permit the contact. Restatement § 99, comment b.

- If a represented client contacts a second lawyer to obtain a second opinion or to explore changing lawyers, the second lawyer may talk to the represented client.[156]
- If a lawyer starts a conversation with another person erroneously believing that the person is unrepresented, the lawyer must end the conversation upon learning that the person has a lawyer.[157]
- The rule applies only to communications with persons known to be represented by a lawyer in "the matter" that is the subject of the communication. The lawyer may communicate with the person about other subjects, even closely related subjects, if they involve a different "matter," as in the following situation.

FOR EXAMPLE: A lawyer for the Jonquil Corporation knows that the Romero Corporation uses the law firm of Hampton & Kim for all of its legal matters. The lawyer may nevertheless call the president of the Romero Corporation directly to ask whether the Romero Corporation would sell one of its subsidiaries to the Jonquil Corporation. Even though the lawyer knows that Hampton & Kim always represents Smith on its legal matters, it does not know that Hampton & Kim represents Smith on the new matter of the possible transfer of its subsidiary.[158]

## May a lawyer get around this rule by having a paralegal or investigator call the opposing party?

No. A lawyer may not circumvent any of the rules by directing anyone else to do so. Rule 8.4(a) states that a lawyer may not attempt to violate any rule "through the acts of another."

## May the lawyer suggest that her client call the represented person directly, even if that person is represented?

Two people who are represented by lawyers may talk with one another without their lawyers' permission. Rule 4.2 applies to lawyers, not to clients. However, if a lawyer *tells* her client to call the opposing party *for some particular purpose*, the lawyer might be violating Rule 4.2 through the acts of another, as described above. On the other hand, since a client may contact the opposing party directly, a lawyer may advise a client that *she may* do so.

Perhaps the line between proper and improper lawyer involvement in a client's direct contact with a represented person is this: If the lawyer initiates the discussion with the client and essentially uses the client to obtain from the

---

156. Restatement § 99, comment c.

157. Rule 4.2, Comment 3.

158. ABA Comm. on Ethics & Prof. Resp., Formal Op. 95-396 (1995). This conclusion seems philosophically although not technically at odds with the ABA's view that if a lawyer has reason to believe, but does not know for certain, that a lawyer is representing a person in a particular matter, the lawyers may not evade the rule "by closing eyes to the obvious." Rule 4.2, Comment 8.

other party information that the lawyer wants to obtain, the lawyer's involvement is not proper. On the other hand, if a client asks the lawyer, for example, "Can't I just call my ex-husband to try to straighten out the visitation arrangements?" the lawyer may advise the client that she may do so. The client is not acting as the agent of the lawyer to circumvent the rule.[159]

### Do prosecutors' undercover investigations (for example, those that infiltrate police officers into criminal conspiracies) violate this rule?

Such investigations raise questions about compliance with this rule as well as about compliance with Rule 4.1. Some prosecutors argue that the "authorized by law" exception at the end of the rule excuses compliance with Rule 4.2. However, the Restatement notes that undercover operations sometimes may violate suspects' constitutional rights. It takes the view that such operations should be neither categorically permitted or categorically banned under the rule. It adds that "organizations of prosecutors and lawyers are elaborating rules governing specific situations."[160]

Federal prosecutors have fought, unsuccessfully to date, for an exemption from state ethics' rules limitations on their investigative contacts with use of deceptive tactics in undercover investigations. In 1994, the Department of Justice adopted a policy allowing its prosecutors to communicate directly with suspects who were known to have lawyers without first informing the lawyers or getting permission from a court.[161] This practice was challenged by Representative Joseph McDade (R-Pa.), who "had been out to harness federal prosecutors since he was acquitted of bribery and racketeering charges."[162]

In 1998, Congress passed the McDade Amendment, which provides that "an attorney for the Government shall be subject to State laws and rules, and local Federal court rules, governing attorneys in each State where such attorney engages in that attorney's duties, to the same extent and in the same manner as other attorneys in that State."[163] The executive branch of the federal government has tried to persuade Congress to repeal the McDade Amendment, arguing that "abiding by state ethics rules . . . would hamper use of undercover agents and informants,"[164] but Congress has not done so.

The enactment of the McDade Amendment has not resolved the question of whether federal prosecutors may communicate with represented suspects. Federal and state prosecutors continue to argue that such contact, in the course of legitimate criminal investigations, falls within the "authorized by law" exception to state rules that use the language of Rule 4.2. The relevant court

---

159. For a discussion of this issue, see St. B. Cal., Standing Comm. on Prof. Resp. & Conduct, Formal Op. 1993-131 (1993), and Restatement § 99, comment k.

160. Restatement § 99, comment h.

161. 28 C.F.R. §§ 77.1-77.5 (2004).

162. Walter Pincus, Revisiting Rules for Federal Prosecutors; Senate Bill Aims to Resolve Long-Running Dispute Between Justice Dept., State Bars, Wash. Post, Feb. 10, 1999, at A6.

163. 28 U.S.C. § 530B (2004).

164. Pincus, supra n. 162.

decisions and other authorities are inconsistent.[165] The Justice Department believes that, in most states, it is an open question whether law enforcement officers who are working with prosecutors and arrest an indicted suspect known to be represented may give the suspect Miranda warnings and then question him, or whether they may communicate only through his lawyer.[166]

### Does Rule 4.2 mean that lawyers representing clients who have disputes with government agencies must contact the general counsel's office of the agency and may not make direct contact with government officials?

No. The First Amendment's guarantee of the right to petition government overrides any state ethical rule. However, in that situation, an ABA ethics opinion urges that the lawyer must first notify the government's lawyer of her intent to talk directly with the policy official or officials, to give the lawyer a chance to advise them not to talk to the lawyer, or to advise them what to say.[167]

### What if a lawyer wants to contact an employee of a corporation represented by another lawyer?

Here we explore some issues that are related to those addressed in our discussion of the *Upjohn* case in Chapter 3. That case dealt with the extent to which a corporation is entitled to the protection of attorney-client evidentiary privilege. There a plaintiff suing a corporation sought access through discovery to the paper records of an internal investigation of the corporation that had been conducted by the corporation's lawyers. The question was whether the corporation was entitled not to disclose the documents based on a claim that they were privileged communications.

Rule 4.2 imposes certain constraints on lawyers who want to interview employees of an adverse corporation without permission of counsel for the corporation. In deciding the scope of the attorney-client privilege for corporations and in interpreting Rule 4.2 as it applies to corporations, judges and rule writers must strike a balance between the desire not to intrude on the attorney-client relationship and the desire to provide litigants, the public, and the courts with access needed to investigate disputed facts. Here is a diagram of the relationship between these two sets of issues, and a summary of the relevant rules.[168]

---

165. The Restatement reports that it "has been extensively debated whether . . . the anti-contact rule independently imposes all constraints . . . on prosecutors or, to the contrary, whether the authorized-by-law exception . . . entirely removes such limitations. Both polar positions seem unacceptable." Restatement § 99, comment h.

166. U.S. Dept. of Justice, Professional Responsibility Advisory Office, Legal Ethics for Investigative Agents? 5 Q. Rev. 6 (2003), available at http://www.fletc.gov/legal/qr_articles/LEGALETHICS.pdf (last visited Oct. 27, 2004).

167. ABA Comm. on Ethics & Prof. Resp., Formal Op. 97-408 (1997).

168. As you will see when you read the *Messing* case, the extent to which corporations should be allowed to invoke the protection of Rule 4.2 has been much debated, and the states have adopted divergent interpretations of their versions of Rule 4.2.

## Comparison of corporate attorney-client privilege and Rule 4.2

| Applicable law | If a party that is in litigation with a corporation wants to: | The corporation may deny access as follows: |
|---|---|---|
| **Attorney-client privilege**, after Upjohn v. US, 449 U.S. 383 (1981) | Compel the corporation to produce documents prepared by the corporation's lawyer as part of an internal investigation. | To documents reflecting communications between the corporation's lawyers and employees "so long as the communication relates to the subject matter of the representation." Restatement § 73, comment d. |
| **Rule 4.2, Comment 7** (Comment 4 in previous editions of the rules) | Interview employees of the corporation to learn facts relevant to the litigation without permission from the corporation's lawyer. | To the employee in question if he or she:<br>• "supervises, directs or regularly consults with the organization's lawyer concerning the matter,"<br>• "has authority to obligate the organization with respect to the matter," or<br>• is one "whose act or omission in connection with the matter may be imputed to the organization for purposes of civil or criminal liability." |

Comment 7 to Rule 4.2 attempts to balance two competing policies. One objective is to enable lawyers to conduct inexpensive fact gathering before and after initiating lawsuits. The other is to protect clients from overreaching by opposing lawyers. Because states have different views of which policy is more important, the proper test for barring lawyers from speaking with organizational employees has been "extensively debated."[169] Some states have adopted divergent formal standards on when lawyers may contact corporate employees, but these standards vary from state to state.[170] Other states have evolved their own interpretations of Comment 7 or similar language, through bar ethics opinions or case law.

## Messing, Rudavsky & Weliky, P.C. v. President & Fellows of Harvard College

764 N.E.2d 825 (Mass. 2002)

COWIN, J. . . .

### [The lawyers' interviews with Harvard employees]

In August of 1997, MR&W [Messing, Rudavsky & Weliky] filed a complaint against President and Fellows of Harvard College (Harvard) with the

---

169. Restatement § 100, comment b, reporter's note.
170. See, e.g., Va. Rules of Prof. Conduct 4.2, Comment 4 (2003); Tex. Disc. R. Prof. Conduct 4.02 (1989).

Massachusetts Commission Against Discrimination (commission) on behalf of its client, Kathleen Stanford. Stanford, a sergeant with the Harvard University police department (HUPD), alleged that Harvard and its police chief, Francis Riley, discriminated against her on the basis of gender and in reprisal for earlier complaints of discrimination. MR&W represented Stanford, and Harvard was represented before the commission by in-house counsel, and thereafter by a Boston law firm. Following the institution of the suit, MR&W communicated ex parte with five employees of the HUPD: two lieutenants, two patrol officers, and a dispatcher. Although the two lieutenants had some supervisory authority over Stanford, it was not claimed that any of the five employees were involved in the alleged discrimination or retaliation against her or exercised management authority with respect to the alleged discriminatory or retaliatory acts.

In response to a motion by Harvard, the commission ruled that MR&W's ex parte contacts with all five employees violated rule 4.2, but declined to issue sanctions for these violations. MR&W removed the case to the Superior Court, where Harvard filed a motion seeking sanctions for the same violations of rule 4.2 on which the commission had previously ruled. The Superior Court judge then [held] that MR&W violated the rule with respect to all five employees, prohibiting MR&W from using the affidavits it had procured during the interviews, and awarding Harvard the attorney's fees and costs it had expended in litigating the motion, in a later order calculated as $94,418.14. . . .

### [How other courts have interpreted Comment 4 of Rule 4.2]

When the represented person is an individual, there is no difficulty determining when an attorney has violated the rule; the represented person is easily identifiable. In the case of an organization, however, identifying the protected class is more complicated.

Because an organization acts only through its employees, the rule must extend to some of these employees. However, most courts have rejected the position that the rule automatically prevents an attorney from speaking with all employees of a represented organization. . . .

According to comment [4] to rule 4.2, an attorney may not speak ex parte to three categories of employees: (1) "persons having managerial responsibility on behalf of the organization with regard to the subject of the representation"; (2) persons "whose act or omission in connection with that matter may be imputed to the organization for purposes of civil or criminal liability"; and (3) persons "whose statement may constitute an admission on the part of the organization."[171]

---

171. [Court's footnote 6.] Massachusetts adopted the commentary to rule 4.2 proposed in the ABA Model Rules of Professional Conduct, except that the Massachusetts version adds the phrase "with regard to the subject of the representation" to the first category of the comment.

*[Authors' note: The language quoted above is similar to the language of Model Rule 4.2, Comment 4, before the ABA amended the comment in 2002. In 2002, the ABA deleted the language that barred a lawyer from contacting persons "whose statement may constitute an admission." Many courts interpreted this word "admission" as that word was used in the law of evidence.[172]]*

The Superior Court judge . . . held that all five employees interviewed by MR&W were within the third category of the comment. He reached this result by concluding that the phrase "admission" in the comment refers to statements admissible in court under the admissions exception to the [evidence] rule against hearsay. . . . We have held that a court may admit a "statement by [the party's] agent or servant concerning a matter within the scope of [the] agency or employment, made during the existence of the relationship" [quoting a rule of evidence]. Because the comment includes any employee whose statement may constitute an admission, this interpretation would prohibit an attorney from contacting any current employees of an organization to discuss any subject within the scope of their employment. This is, as the Superior Court judge admitted, a rule that is "strikingly protective of corporations regarding employee interviews". . . .

However, other jurisdictions that have adopted the same or similar versions of rule 4.2 are divided on whether their own versions of the rule are properly linked to the admissions exception to the hearsay rule, and disagree about the precise scope of the rule as applied to organizations. . . . Some jurisdictions have adopted the broad reading of the rule endorsed by the judge in this case [because they believe the rule should be interpreted in accordance with the evidence rule].

At the other end of the spectrum, a small number of jurisdictions has interpreted the rule narrowly so as to allow an attorney for the opposing party to contact most employees of a represented organization. These courts construe the rule to restrict contact with only those employees in the organization's "control group," defined as those employees in the uppermost echelon of the organization's management. . . .

Other jurisdictions have adopted yet a third test that, while allowing for some ex parte contacts with a represented organization's employees, still maintains some protection of the organization. The Court of Appeals of New York articulated such a rule in Niesig v. Team I, 559 N.Y.S.2d 493 (N.Y. 1990), rejecting an approach that ties the rule to Fed. R. Evid. 801(d)(2)(D). Instead, the court defined a represented person to include "employees whose acts or omissions in the matter under inquiry are binding on the corporation . . . or imputed to the corporation for purposes of its liability, or employees implementing the advice of counsel." In addition, the Restatement (Third) of the Law Governing Lawyers endorses this rule.

---

172. [Authors' footnote.] Thus if the employee could possibly make a statement admissible against the corporation under the "admission" exception to the hearsay rule of evidence, the opposing lawyer or her investigator could not talk to that employee.

### [Balancing fairness concerns]

We adopt a test similar to that proposed in Niesig v. Team I, supra. Although the comment's reference to persons "whose statement may constitute an admission on the part of the organization" was most likely intended as a reference to Fed. R. Evid. 801(d)(2)(D), this interpretation would effectively prohibit the questioning of all employees who can offer information helpful to the litigation. We reject the comment as overly protective of the organization and too restrictive of an opposing attorney's ability to contact and interview employees of an adversary organization.

We instead interpret the rule to ban contact only with those employees who have the authority to "commit the organization to a position regarding the subject matter of representation." See [Restatement § 100]. See also Ethics 2000 Commission Draft for Public Comment Model Rule 4.2 Reporter's Explanation of Changes (Feb. 21, 2000) (recommending deletion of the third category of the comment). The employees with whom contact is prohibited are those with "speaking authority" for the corporation who "have managing authority sufficient to give them the right to speak for, and bind, the corporation." Employees who can commit the organization are those with authority to make decisions about the course of the litigation, such as when to initiate suit, and when to settle a pending case. We recognize that this test is a retrenchment from the broad prohibition on employee contact endorsed by the comment.

This interpretation . . . would prohibit ex parte contact only with those employees who exercise managerial responsibility in the matter, who are alleged to have committed the wrongful acts at issue in the litigation, or who have authority on behalf of the corporation to make decisions about the course of the litigation. This result is substantially the same as the *Niesig* test because it "prohibits direct communication . . . 'with those officials . . . who have the legal power to bind the corporation in the matter or who are responsible for implementing the advice of the corporation's lawyer' . . . or whose own interests are directly at stake in a representation."

Our test is consistent with the purposes of the rule, which are not to "protect a corporate party from the revelation of prejudicial facts," but to protect the attorney-client relationship and prevent clients from making ill-advised statements without the counsel of their attorney. . . . The Superior Court's interpretation of the rule would grant an advantage to corporate litigants over nonorganizational parties. It grants an unwarranted benefit to organizations to require that a party always seek prior judicial approval to conduct informal interviews with witnesses to an event when the opposing party happens to be an organization and the events at issue occurred at the workplace. . . .

Fairness to the organization does not require the presence of an attorney every time an employee may make a statement admissible in evidence against his or her employer. The public policy of promoting efficient discovery is better advanced by adopting a rule which favors the revelation of the truth by making it more difficult for an organization to prevent the disclosure of relevant evidence.

Harvard argues that adopting the Superior Court's interpretation of rule 4.2 will not prevent parties from conducting informal interviews with an organization's employees, but will instead simply force them to seek prior judicial approval. However, if we adopt such a rule, too often in cases involving a corporate party the court will be asked to decide the extent of informal interviews permitted. This will result in extensive litigation before the underlying case even begins, and would clearly favor the better-financed party. . . .

## [Application of the new test to the lawyers' interviews]

The five Harvard employees interviewed by MR&W do not fall within the third category of the comment as we have construed it. As employees of the HUPD, they are not involved in directing the litigation at bar or authorizing the organization to make binding admissions. In fact, Harvard does not argue that any of the five employees fit within our definition of this category. . . . All five employees were mere witnesses to the events that occurred, not active participants.

We must still determine, however, whether any of the interviewed employees have "managerial responsibility on behalf of the organization with regard to the subject of the representation." Mass. R. Prof. C. 4.2 comment [4]. Although the two patrol officers and the dispatcher were subordinate to Stanford and had no managerial authority, the two lieutenants exercised some supervisory authority over Stanford. However, not all employees with some supervisory power over their coworkers are deemed to have "managerial" responsibility in the sense intended by the comment. "Supervision of a small group of workers would not constitute a managerial position within a corporation."

Even if the two lieutenants are deemed to have managerial responsibility, the Massachusetts version of the comment adds [to the Model Rules version] the requirement that the managerial responsibility be in "regard to the subject of the representation." Mass. R. Prof. C. 4.2 comment [4]. Thus, the comment includes only those employees who have supervisory authority over the events at issue in the litigation. There is no evidence in the record that the lieutenants' managerial decisions were a subject of the litigation. The affidavits of the two lieutenants indicate that they did not complete any evaluations or offer any opinions of Stanford that Chief Riley considered in reaching his decisions. . . . We vacate the order of the Superior Court judge . . . . and remand the case for the entry of an order denying the defendant's motion for sanctions.

CORDY, J. (concurring in part and dissenting in part). . . .

I concur that the financial sanction levied against Messing, Rudavsky & Weliky, P.C., must be set aside, but do so for reasons different from those set forth in the court's opinion. I disagree with the court's interpretation of Mass. R. Prof. C. 4.2. . . .

Our ruling today upsets the balance created by the rule and commentary and creates a distinct disadvantage to the organizational parties. . . .

[I think it was permissible for the plaintiff's lawyers to talk to Harvard's patrol officers and dispatcher.] I view the plaintiff's communications with the Harvard police lieutenants, however, as more problematic. Those employees clearly had a measure of supervisory responsibility over Stanford, whose job performance was to be a central issue in her discrimination litigation. Thus, those interviews run afoul not only of the prohibition against communicating with employees about matters within the scope of their employment but also the prohibition against communicating with employees having managerial responsibility regarding the subject of the representation. . . .

## Notes about *Messing*

**1. Amendment to Rule 4.2.** As noted above, the ABA revised Model Rule 4.2 in 2002. It changed Comment 4 (now Comment 7) to eliminate the restriction on contacting those whose statements could be "admissions on the part of the organization." In explaining this deletion, the Ethics 2000 Reporter's memo stated that "This reference has been read by some as prohibiting communication with any person whose testimony would be admissible against the organization as an exception to the hearsay rule."[173]

*Ellen Messing*

**2. The nexus between the rule change and the *Messing* case.** The ABA's House of Delegates actually adopted the change in current Comment 7 in January 2002, two months before the Massachusetts Supreme Court issued the *Messing* opinion. Note that in support of its conclusion in favor of interpreting the Massachusetts rule to allow more investigative activity by plaintiffs' lawyers, the court actually cites the fact that the ABA is moving in that direction. In fact, the House of Delegates acted in response to a coalition of employment and civil rights lawyers led by Ellen Messing, one of the named partners of the law firm that was appealing the sanction against it.[174] Messing told the *National Law Journal* that under the rules established by the pre-2002 comment, some

---

173. ABA Ethics 2000 Commission, Reporter's Explanation of Changes to Rule 4.2, http://www.abanet.org/cpr/e2k-rule42rem.htm (last visited August 13, 2004). The ABA also amended the comment to narrow the language restricting access to "persons having a managerial responsibility on behalf of the organization" to restrict access only to those who had managerial authority over the matter at issue. The Ethics 2000 Reporter's memo explaining the changes noted that the previous language had been criticized as "vague and overly broad." Id.

174. Marcia Coyle, Mass. High Court Adds Wrinkle to Worker Contact, National Law Journal at A8, March 25, 2002.

lawyers were being sanctioned for investigating cases against corporations. Others, fearing sanctions, were "simply forgoing investigating their cases by interviewing current employees out of fear they would get in trouble."[175] James Cott of the NAACP Legal Defense and Educational Fund added that Rule 4.2 had prevented lawyers from obtaining information from their clients' co-workers about their employers' racial discrimination. He said that the rule also had prevented lawyers from talking to guards in prisoner rights cases and from talking to police officers in racial profiling cases.[176]

## 3. Restrictions on contact with unrepresented persons

On behalf of clients, lawyers routinely contact people who do not have lawyers of their own. When a lawyer or the lawyer's agent contacts an unrepresented person to obtain information or to negotiate, there is a risk that the lawyer will take advantage of his greater knowledge and sophistication. Also there is a risk that the unrepresented person will not understand if the lawyer is representing a client whose interests are adverse to his. The unrepresented person may provide information or agree to settlement terms that he would have rejected if he had obtained the advice of a lawyer. These risks are particularly worrisome when lawyers deal with unrepresented people who are indigent or who have limited education.[177] Rule 4.3 imposes some limits on lawyers' contacts with such persons. The unrepresented persons protected by this rule include, among others, those with whom a client has a dispute, potential witnesses, and experts.

### Rule 4.3   Dealing with Unrepresented Person

| Rule language* | Authors' explanation |
| --- | --- |
| In dealing on behalf of a client with a person who is not represented by counsel, **a lawyer shall not state or imply that the lawyer is disinterested.** | • This part of the rule tells a lawyer what *not* to do. The lawyer should not mislead the person into thinking that the lawyer doesn't represent a client.<br>• The lawyer should not state or imply that the lawyer is looking out for the interests of both the client and the unrepresented person. |
| **When the lawyer knows** or reasonably should know that the **unrepresented person misunderstands** the lawyer's role in the matter, the **lawyer shall** make reasonable efforts to **correct the misunderstanding.** | • This part of the rule imposes an affirmative duty on lawyers.<br>• If the lawyer should know that the person doesn't understand the lawyer's role, the lawyer should correct any misimpression. |

*Continued*

---

175. Marcia Coyle, The Long Road to Changing a Controversial Ethical Rule, Natl. L.J. Feb. 25, 2002, at A8.

176. Id.

177. See Russell Engler, Out of Sight and Out of Line: The Need for Regulation of Lawyers' Negotiations with Unrepresented Poor Persons, 85 Cal. L. Rev. 79, 81-82 (1997).

| Rule language* | Authors' explanation |
|---|---|
| The **lawyer shall not give legal advice to an unrepresented person,** other than the advice to secure counsel, **if** the lawyer knows or reasonably should know that the interests of such a person are or have a **reasonable possibility of being in conflict with the interests of the client.** | • If there may be a conflict of interest between the client and the person with whom the lawyer is communicating, the lawyer must refrain from giving any legal advice except the advice to obtain independent counsel.<br>• In some states, such as Colorado and Pennsylvania, Rule 4.3 bars the lawyer from giving any advice, not just legal advice, to such an unrepresented party. |

*All emphasis added.

## How would a lawyer know that an unrepresented person misunderstands the lawyer's role?

The lawyer has to be alert to the circumstances. For example, suppose a lawyer meets with an unrepresented person on behalf of a client to negotiate a contract. If the unrepresented person says, "I have a few legal questions about this transaction that you are handling for me," it would be obvious that the unrepresented person thinks the lawyer is *his* lawyer.[178] The statement, "I have a few legal questions about this transaction," while not as clear a warning sign, at least raises the possibility that the person thinks that the lawyer's role was to serve the speaker's interests.

## Does this rule mean that a lawyer representing a client must refrain from negotiating a deal or the settlement of a lawsuit with an unrepresented person?

No. The lawyer may even prepare the relevant documents for both parties to sign. The rule requires only that the lawyer not mislead the unrepresented party about the fact that the lawyer is representing a client.[179] The lawyer has no affirmative duty to clarify her role unless she knows or should know that the other person is confused. And if the other person's interests are at odds with those of the lawyer's client, she should not give advice to the unrepresented person except for advising the person to get a lawyer.

## Does Rule 4.3 apply to a lawyer for a corporation who is dealing with employees of the corporation?

Yes. Employees of the corporation may not understand that the lawyer's duties are to the corporation, not to its officers or employees.

FOR EXAMPLE: Suppose a corporation lawyer is investigating possible wrongdoing by an employee, and she plans to interview the employee. Because the lawyer represents the company that employs the person

---

178. See Restatement § 103, comment d, illus. 2.
179. See Restatement § 103, comment d.

being interviewed, the employee may think that he and the lawyer are "on the same side."

### What disclosures should a lawyer make to an employee of an organization to clarify her role?

Rule 4.3 doesn't specify what disclosures a lawyer should make to an employee of her client organization. Professor Sarah Duggin studied internal corporate investigations and offered these and other suggestions.

- The lawyer should advise the employee at the beginning of the interview that the lawyer represents the organization rather than the individual.
- The lawyer should explain that she may share any information that the employee reveals with officers of the corporation or with law enforcement personnel or other third parties, if such disclosure is in the interest of the organization.
- The lawyer should periodically assess whether there is a risk of criminal liability for the employee being interviewed or others, and if so, whether she should advise the employee of the option of hiring his own lawyer and of having his lawyer present during the interview.[180]

### Can a lawyer encourage an unrepresented witness not to talk to her opposing counsel?

Suppose a criminal defense lawyer interviews a witness about the event that led to charges against his client. Assume the witness understands the lawyer's role and that there is no conflict or potential conflict between the client's interests and those of the witness. May the lawyer tell the witness that someone from the prosecutor's office might seek to interview the witness, but the witness doesn't have to talk to that person?

Yes. Rule 4.3 prohibits a lawyer dealing on behalf of a client with a third person who has no lawyer from giving advice to that person if the interests of the witness may conflict with those of the client. If there is no such conflict, the lawyer may give this advice.

### What if the witness is a friend of the lawyer's client and the lawyer merely asks him, as a favor to the client, not to talk to the prosecutor?

This is not allowed. Rule 4.3 does not address this situation, but Rule 3.4(f) precludes such advice. A lawyer may not ask a person other than the lawyer's own client "to refrain from voluntarily giving relevant information to another party" unless the unrepresented "person is a relative, employee, or other agent of the lawyer's client" and the lawyer believes that the witness'

---

180. Sarah Helene Duggin, Internal Corporate Investigations: Legal Ethics, Professionalism and the Employee Interview, 2003 Colum. Bus. L. Rev. 859, 958 (recommending several proposed ground rules for "investigative employee interviews." (A different part of this article is excerpted in Chapter 3.)

interests won't be harmed by his clamming up. So if the witness is a friend of the client, such advice is not permitted. Even if the witness were a relative, employee, or agent of the client, a lawyer should not advise him not to talk to the prosecutor unless the lawyer is sure that there would be no harm to the witness from his doing so.[181]

### If a lawyer conducts a witness interview on the telephone, may the lawyer secretly tape-record the conversation?

In some states, it is a crime to record a conversation without the consent of *all* parties. In most states, however, the consent of *one* party (for example, the lawyer) is sufficient.[182] In 1974, the ABA issued an ethics opinion stating that secretly recording conversations was professionally improper regardless of state law.[183] Few jurisdictions agreed with the ABA opinion, however, and in 2001, the Committee on Ethics and Professionalism withdrew the old opinion and issued a new one that concluded only that lawyers should not make secret recordings in violation of state law and that secretly recording one's own client is "at the least, inadvisable."[184] The more recent opinion explained that "it is questionable whether anyone today justifiably relies on an expectation that a conversation is not being recorded by the other party, absent a special relationship with or conduct by that party inducing a belief that the conversation will not be recorded."

## PROBLEM 8-12  **THE PROSECUTOR'S MASQUERADE**

*This problem is closely based on actual events in a western city.*

---

You are the district attorney in a small city. The police have called you to a crime scene in an apartment. Three women lie brutally murdered. Their heads have been split open with an axe. Stacey Blankenwell, an eyewitness to the murders, is in the apartment.

Stacy recounts the following story. A man abducted her and the other women and took them, one by one, to the apartment. He identified himself as Ward Flood. Then he tied Blankenwell to a bed, raped her, and forced her to watch as he killed the others. He also dictated details of his crimes into a tape recorder. Finally, he left the apartment,

---

181. Comment 4 to Rule 3.4 notes that the rule "permits a lawyer to advise employees of a client to refrain from giving information to another party," but it does not advert to the Rule 3.4(f)'s second clause, allowing such advice only if the person's interests apparently would not be adversely affected.

182. Stacy L. Mills, Note, He Wouldn't Listen to Me Before, But Now . . . : Interspousal Wiretapping and an Analysis of State Wiretapping Statutes, 37 Brandeis L.J. 415, 429 (1998). For discussion of restrictions on surreptitious recording, see Clifford S. Fishman & Anne T. McKenna, Wiretapping and Eavesdropping (2d ed., Clark Boardman Callaghan 1995).

183. ABA Comm. on Ethics & Prof. Resp., Formal Op. 94-337 (1994).

184. ABA Comm. on Ethics & Prof. Resp., Formal Op. 01-422 (2001).

instructing Blankenwell to call the police and to page him by calling a specified telephone number when they arrived. She followed his instructions. Flood then telephoned the apartment from a cell phone.

When Flood called, a police officer who was in the apartment answered the phone and talked with him for three and a half hours. Flood told the officer all the details of his crimes. The police recorded the call but were unable to trace Flood's location.

Flood told the police that he could still kill more people and that he would not surrender until he had legal representation. He demanded guarantees that if he turned himself in, he would be isolated from other prisoners and would be allowed cigarettes. He wanted assistant public defender Harrison Biaggi to be his lawyer. Biaggi had represented him on a previous criminal charge.

The police told Flood that they would try to locate a public defender for him. Then they consulted you about whether they should call any lawyer for Flood while he was still at large and capable of killing more people. You were ambivalent about doing so because you knew that any lawyer would tell Flood not to continue talking with the police. You found Biaggi's number in a telephone book that was in the apartment. He was now apparently in private practice. You called the number and felt relieved when a recording stated that the number was no longer in service.

Suddenly, a plan occurred to you. You could get on the telephone and tell Flood that you were an assistant public defender. You could then "negotiate" with the police and arrange for his peaceful surrender in exchange for the promises he sought of isolation and cigarettes. You will see to it that he in fact receives those minor benefits after he surrenders.

Should you do it? If so, should you simply negotiate the terms of the surrender or should you try to get information during your conversation with Flood that would assist in obtaining his conviction?

---

Few lawyers will face dilemmas as dramatic as those described in the preceding problem. Many lawyers, however, will find themselves in situations in which they must consider the conflict between their duty to their clients and their duty to unrepresented parties under Rule 4.3. The next problem reflects such a circumstance.

### PROBLEM 8-13  **THE COMPLAINING WITNESS**

*This problem is based on a hypothetical that was considered by a bar ethics committee in response to an inquiry involving facts like these.*

---

You are a criminal defense lawyer. The court has appointed you to represent Nick Krutko, who has been charged with contempt of court by violating a civil protection order.

Krutko's ex-girlfriend, Lucille DiBello, claimed that Krutko had repeatedly beaten her. She went to court without a lawyer and obtained a civil protection order prohibiting Krutko from visiting or communicating with her in any way. Three weeks later, she went back to court, still with no lawyer. She claimed that Krutko had violated the order by calling her several times, pleading with her to resume their relationship, and threatening that if she did not take him back, he would beat or kill her. The judge signed the forms that initiated the pending contempt case. If DiBello can prove that Krutko threatened her after she obtained the protection order, Krutko could go to jail.

Krutko denies that he ever beat DiBello. He also denies that he called or threatened DiBello after she obtained the order. He says that she often lies. You aren't sure whether you believe him, but it is your job to represent him, and DiBello has the burden of proof.

Your office employs Sally Fox as a part-time investigator to interview witnesses in upcoming cases. Sally is a 19-year-old college student. She is five feet tall and very friendly; nobody ever feels threatened by her. She is very congenial and charming in dealing with witnesses. Usually the people she interviews give her the information she seeks.

You are planning to send Fox to interview DiBello. She will tell DiBello that she works for Krutko's court-appointed counsel. She will ask DiBello for a detailed, signed written statement of what Krutko said and did to her. When Fox testifies at Krutko's trial, you will use any inconsistencies between her testimony and her written statement to impeach her testimony. This is standard procedure for criminal defense lawyers.

You also would like Fox to get DiBello's signature on a medical release form so that you can obtain copies of her recent medical records. This will allow you to identify any inconsistencies between the injuries she claims occurred and those, if any, that appear in the medical records.

You ask Krutko whether DiBello is likely to slam the door in Fox's face. He says that DiBello is likely to talk to Fox. DiBello once refused to talk to a guardian ad litem that the court had appointed for her son. When she went to a hearing on the matter, the judge chastised her for not cooperating. This really shook her up.

## Questions

**1.** May Fox visit DiBello at all? (As your investigator, Fox must live by any ethical rules that apply to you.[185])

---

185. The ethical rules bind only lawyers. But lawyers are required under Rule 5.3 to "make reasonable efforts to ensure" that their employees comply with the rules. A lawyer could be

**2.** If Fox may visit DiBello, must she advise DiBello that DiBello has no obligation to speak to her, that anything that DiBello says may be used against her in court, or that DiBello should obtain a lawyer?

**3.** May Fox say that she works for a lawyer who is Krutko's "court-appointed" counsel?

**4.** Does your knowledge of DiBello's prior chastisement by a judge for not speaking with a guardian ad litem impose any greater duty on you or Fox to make sure that DiBello knows that you represent Krutko and that she does not have to give a statement?

**5.** May Fox not only interview DiBello but also ask her to sign a written statement?

**6.** May Fox say that DiBello "needs" to sign the release form so that you can obtain her medical records?

# J. Conduct prejudicial to the administration of justice

In this chapter, we have considered many duties that lawyers owe to people whom they encounter, including judges, adversaries, and witnesses. Some of the rules governing lawyers' conduct are quite specific, like the advocate-witness rule; others are very general, like the prohibition of "deceit" in Rule 8.4(c). Lawyers should also be aware of the most general of all of the rules, Rule 8.4(d), which provides that it is professional misconduct for a lawyer to "engage in conduct that is prejudicial to the administration of justice." Under this rule, lawyers have been disciplined for improper actions relating both to clients and to other persons.

This provision is a kind of catch-all that exhorts people to act honorably, without defining the behavior that could cause a lawyer to be disciplined or even disbarred. It has been challenged repeatedly on the ground that it is unconstitutionally vague, but all of the challenges have been rejected by the courts.[186]

The comments that follow Rule 8.4 mention that a lawyer who knowingly manifests bias or prejudice on such grounds as race, sex, religion, and sexual orientation "in the course of representing a client" violates the rule if "such actions are prejudicial to the administration of justice."[187] Lawyers have been disciplined under the standard of Rule 8.4(c) for a very wide range of conduct. Here are some examples.[188]

---

disciplined for not giving an employee proper guidance. Lawyers are responsible for rules violations by their employees if they order the misconduct or ratify it. Also, Rule 8.4(a) prohibits a lawyer from violating an ethical rule through the acts of another.

186. See cases cited in Restatement § 5, comment c, reporter's note; ABA, Annotated Model Rules of Professional Conduct 614 (5th ed. 2003).

187. Rule 8.4, Comment 3.

188. The same standard appeared in the Model Code of Professional Responsibility, and some of the following decisions are from states whose rules follow the Model Code.

- A lawyer heard that a police drug raid was likely to be conducted in a Wooster, Ohio. She called a former client and advised him to "clean up his act." The grateful client agreed to cooperate with the police and to testify against his lawyer, who was then convicted of attempted obstruction of justice. (One-year suspension, six months stayed.)[189]
- In an Internet chat room, a male lawyer asked girls between the ages of 13 and 16 to meet him for the purpose of having sex. Some of them met him, but he did not have sex with any of them. (Indefinite suspension.)[190]
- After a client won a judgment against her lawyer requiring him to refund her $5,000 retainer, the lawyer did not pay the money he owed her. There was no finding that the lawyer intended to obstruct the suit against him, merely that he failed to pay violated the provision. (Reprimand.)[191]
- President Bill Clinton, a member of the Arkansas bar, "knowingly gave evasive and misleading answers" regarding his relationship with Monica Lewinsky while being deposed in the lawsuit brought by Paula Jones. (Five-year suspension.)[192]

## K. Are lawyers really too zealous?

We began this chapter with Professor Fried's defense of the adversary system against the charge that in such a system, a person cannot be both a good lawyer and a moral human being. We conclude with some reflections by Professor Ted Schneyer about the behavior of lawyers who are confronted by problems like those we have considered throughout the chapter. After reviewing several empirical studies on lawyers, Professor Schneyer argues that the profession's ethical rules do not require that lawyers put clients' interests above societal interests to the extent charged by critics of the legal profession. Schneyer also suggests that lawyers who face conflicts between the interests of their clients and those of others often give careful consideration to the interests of others. Schneyer says that lawyers may actually give the interests of others *too much* weight.[193]

---

189. Off. of Disc. Counsel v. Klaas, 742 N.E.2d 612 (Ohio 2001).

190. Atty. Grievance Commn. of Md. v. Childress, 770 A.2d 685 (Md. 2001).

191. Daniels v. Statewide Grievance Comm., 804 A.2d 1027 (Ct. App. CT 2002).

192. American Bar Association, 17 Lawyers' Manual on Professional Conduct 73 (2001).

193. Schneyer's counterexamples do not review the empirical literature on civil discovery, an arena in which, according to writings such as those excerpted in this book, the prevailing legal culture may be particularly directed toward adversary behavior.

## Ted Schneyer, Moral Philosophy's Standard Misconception of Legal Ethics

1984 Wis. L. Rev. 1529, 1532-1533, 1536-1538, 1544-1548, 1555-1556, 1567-1569

[Professor Schneyer is Milton O. Riepe Professor of Law at the University of Arizona.]

*Professor Ted Schneyer*

[Certain moral philosophers who write about lawyers] claim that lawyers routinely do things for clients that harm third parties and would therefore be immoral, even in the lawyers' eyes, if done for themselves or for non-clients. Such actions constitute "role-differentiated behavior" in the sense that the actors, if asked to justify themselves, would claim that their role as a lawyer required them to "put to one side [moral] considerations ... that would otherwise be relevant if not decisive." A lawyer's role-differentiated behavior could involve helping a client pursue a morally objectionable aim, or using a hurtful or unfair tactic to give a client an advantage. Specific examples might include invoking the statute of frauds to help a client avoid paying a debt he really owes, attacking an honest person's veracity in order to discredit him as a witness, [or] taking advantage of an opponent's misunderstanding of the applicable law in settlement negotiations. . . .

[T]he philosophers claim that lawyers do this to conform to their profession's ethical principles and not just to make money, earn a promotion, win a contest, pick a fight, or be doggedly loyal to someone in trouble. . . . The debate between Charles Fried and others about whether a lawyer should act toward clients according to the principles she would act upon in her capacity as friend, like so many in professional ethics, is couched exclusively in role terms. The participants score points by comparing and contrasting two specific roles — lawyer and friend — each of which, compared to still other spheres in one's life, may call for the application of distinct moral principles.

In any event, though the concept of role-differentiated behavior does little to strengthen their indictment, the philosophers still conclude that the principles of legal ethics encourage lawyers to do things that cost society too much. . . . When it comes to proposing remedies for all this, the philosophers cannot be accused of thinking small. Most do not suggest changes in the Code or make proposals for the new Model Rules in order to correct what they perceive to be an imbalance in the weights traditionally assigned to client and third-party interests. Instead, [some of them suggest that duties should be] determined by each practitioner in the light of his general moral experience and his own assessment of the profession's legitimate functions. In other words, only when the legal profession abandons its ethical canon or orthodoxy in favor of a priesthood of all believers can lawyers be restored to a state of grace. . . .

[They argue that] ethical principles fashioned collectively by the legal profession in our society (i.e., by bar organizations such as the ABA) inevitably give undue weight to the interests of clients (not to mention lawyers themselves) at the expense of third parties. On this theory ethics codes do nothing to buffer lawyers against morally inappropriate client demands; they legitimize conduct that accedes to these demands. . . .

[The sociological literature does not support the critics' claims.] Take criminal defense work. Sociologist Abraham Blumberg found, in what remains one of the most important empirical studies of the field, that defense lawyers sometimes behave more like professional wrestlers than zealous combatants.[194] Generally, criminal defense lawyers represent their clients on a one-shot basis and are paid by a third party. For these structural reasons, Blumberg found, defense lawyers are understandably tempted to sacrifice individual clients, or even their clients as a class, in order to maintain good personal relations with the prosecutors, police, and court and jail personnel with whom they must deal on a long-term basis. Moreover, they sometimes succumb to the temptation, foregoing meritorious defenses to avoid antagonizing busy prosecutors and judges, and even acting as "double agents" for the criminal justice bureaucracy by advising clients to cop pleas when it might not be in their interest and by "cooling out" clients who fail at first to see the wisdom of the advice. . . .

The vivid and influential ties Blumberg observed between criminal defense lawyers and third parties can sometimes be found in civil litigation as well. Sociologist Donald Landon recently interviewed 200 trial lawyers who practice in small communities and often know an opposing party or counsel personally.[195] Landon began by supposing that lawyers are strongly influenced by the Code and that the Code tilts sharply toward the client in defining the lawyer's proper role as advocate. He was therefore surprised to find that his lawyers were far from single-minded advocates willing to push to the hilt any and all of a client's legally defensible positions.

Landon's advocates were sometimes reluctant to accept cases, not because of moral qualms, but because it would make them unpopular in their community and be bad for business; one lawyer, for instance, called his decision to handle a malpractice suit against the local doctor a ruinous mistake he would never repeat. . . . Landon's advocates were unwilling to use sharp tactics to gain an advantage over a lawyer they knew and regularly dealt with. As one said: "You don't file a five-day motion on Charley Jones when he's on a two-week vacation, or try to take advantage of him. If he's forgot to file an answer, you don't ask the judge for default. You call him. . . . [F]airness is more important than winning." . . .

Putting criminal and civil litigation aside, consider the way lawyers behave as negotiators, advisers and draftsmen. Regarding negotiations, several years

---

194. [Schneyer's footnote 54.] Abraham Blumberg, The Practice of Law as Confidence Game: Organizational Cooptation of a Profession, 1 Law and Socy. Rev. 16 (1967).

195. [Schneyer's footnote 64.] Donald Landon, Clients, Colleagues, and Community: The Shaping of Zealous Advocacy in Country Law Practice, [1985 Am. B. Found. Res. J. 81].

ago my colleague Stewart Macaulay surveyed 100 Wisconsin lawyers practicing in a wide range of settings who had experience representing buyers or sellers in the settlement of minor consumer complaints.[196] His conclusions about the way lawyers behave in the negotiation process were these:

> Rather than playing hired gun for one side, lawyers often mediate between their client and those not represented by lawyers. They seek to educate, persuade and coerce both sides to adopt the best available compromise rather than to engage in legal warfare. Moreover, in playing all of their roles, . . . lawyers are influenced by their own values and self-interest. . . .

[It is true that the profession's ethical rules] tolerate many litigation tactics that can not only harm witnesses or adverse parties, but make judicial decisionmaking less reliable to boot. Examples include discrediting a truthful witness on cross-examination; counseling a client not to retain certain records because they could be damaging in future litigation; cultivating an expert witness by feeding her only favorable information until she is locked in to supporting the client's position; and using pre-trial motions, refusals to stipulate and discovery requests to exploit a client's greater staying power. Since lawyers will surely be tempted to use these tactics, and since the Code is a lawyers' product, the question remains: Can't moral philosophers justly charge the legal profession with giving partisanship more than its due, even if the Code merely tolerates such tactics?

Perhaps the answer is "yes," but let me suggest five reasons why it is not clearly so. . . .

[1. Some unsociable behavior may be tolerated not because it is desirable but only because prohibitions on it would be counterproductive or impossible to enforce.
2. Some prohibitions might be hard to write in ways that give fair notice to lawyers that they could be disciplined.
3. Some unfair behavior need not be prohibited in the ethics code because it is banned in court rules, and judges can enforce those bans better than bar officials.
4. The suggestion by some philosophers that more difficult decisions should be relegated to the individual moral judgments of the affected lawyers is likely to make things worse, not better.
5. To the extent that lawyers try to justify unfair tactics, they don't really cite codes like the Model Rules; they rely on concepts, like Charles Fried's notion of the lawyer as a "friend," quite removed from the profession's ethical rules.]

I suspect that philosophers and legal scholars alike have fallen prey to the notion that legal ethics must, as an intellectual field, be dominated by a single overarching theory or set of principles — a paradigm. . . . Whatever may be the

---

196. [Schneyer's footnote 72.] Stewart Macaulay, Lawyers and Consumer Protection Laws, 14 Law and Socy. Rev. 115 (1979).

case in other fields, legal ethics has no paradigm, only some fragmentary conceptions of the lawyer's role vying inconclusively for dominance — the lawyer as "hired gun," to be sure, but the lawyer also as "officer of the court," "counsel for the situation," "friend," "minister," and so forth. As a result the organized bar, for all its attention to ethics rules, has been able to do very little "predetermining" of the individual lawyer's responsibilities, at least when it comes to reconciling his duties to clients and to third parties.

## Notes and Questions about the Schneyer Article

**1.** In Chapters 2 through 7, we have explored lawyers' duties to their clients, many of which appear to require loyalty of various kinds. In this chapter, we have examined lawyers' duties to others, some of which may conflict with or override the duties of loyalty to clients.

Lawyers are often criticized for being too loyal to clients — for being their hired guns. But according to Schneyer, the empirical literature on how lawyers actually behave suggests that most lawyers do not press every advantage and that many lawyers, particularly criminal defense lawyers, do not take their duties to their clients seriously enough.

What do your own observations of lawyers among your friends, family, and employers suggest about this question? Do the lawyers you know move heaven and earth for their clients, perhaps even to the point of unfairness to adversaries or third parties, as in some of the problems in this chapter? Or are they sometimes disrespectful or disdainful of their clients' rights, desires, or finances, as in some of the problems in earlier chapters, particularly Chapters 4 and 7?

**2.** In your experience, does how lawyers treat their clients and how assiduously they advocate for them depend on who the clients are or how much money they are paying?

**3.** To what extent is the ethical behavior of lawyers and their loyalty to clients influenced by the economic and social settings in which the lawyers are employed? This is one of several important issues raised by the last two chapters of this book.

# 9 | THE LEGAL PROFESSION

**A. Origins and development of the U.S. legal profession**
  1. Pre-revolutionary America
  2. The nineteenth century
  3. Growth of large firms in the twentieth century

**B. A short history of American legal education**

**C. Race, sex, and class in the legal profession**
  1. Women
  2. People of color

**D. The legal profession today**
  1. Large firms
  2. Small firms
  3. Government and nonprofit organizations

**E. The ethical climate of the legal profession**
  1. Mass production
  2. Pressure to pad bills
  3. Pressure from clients to help them commit fraud
  4. Ethics and substance abuse
  5. Public perceptions of lawyers
  6. How to find a law firm or other employer that has high ethical standards and humane work conditions

Most of the preceding chapters have focused on dilemmas of professional responsibility, exploring the application of the ethics rules and other law to those problems. This chapter and the next one take a different direction, exploring historical, sociological, and economic issues relating to the legal profession. These issues also have ethical dimensions, but the primary goal of the next two chapters is to provide you with a range of information about what goes on (and what has gone on) in the American legal profession. In this chapter, we first offer a thumbnail history of the legal profession and of legal education. Then, turning to the modern legal profession in America, we examine the sociological characteristics of lawyers. Who are we (collectively), and what do we do? We inquire into professional relationships in law firms and other settings in which lawyers work. We look at some literature on management practices, personnel practices, and the plight of lawyers who for reasons of conscience, refuse to follow dubious orders. Along the way, we consider the extent to which lawyers are satisfied with their work lives and barriers to satisfaction such as preoccupation with money, abusive behavior by superiors, bias within firms, and substance abuse.

Before we continue, we offer this warning to our readers: This chapter includes some quite discouraging information about the profession you have chosen to enter. As Professor Patrick Schiltz (in an article excerpted later in this chapter) puts it: "Dear Law Student: I have good news and bad new. The bad news is that the profession that you are about to enter is one of the most unhappy and unhealthy on the face of the earth — and, in the view of many, one of the most unethical. The good news is that you can join this profession and still be happy, healthy and ethical."[1]

Some students get pretty depressed when they realize how many problems young lawyers confront and how little the real life of law practice resembles the romantic TV depictions. One said, "If I had learned all this stuff before I came to law school, I wouldn't have bothered racking up $100,000 in debt." We present this chapter with some hesitancy, knowing that it will feel like a cold shower to some students. However, like Professor Schiltz, we firmly believe that you are better off going in with your eyes open. If you are aware of some of the pitfalls that may await you, you may clarify your life goals, choose your path more carefully, and investigate much more carefully before you accept a job offer.

# A. Origins and development of the U.S. legal profession[2]

## 1. Pre-revolutionary America

Early America had very few lawyers. Particularly in New England, the primary lawmakers were members of the clergy. One of the first English-trained lawyers

---

1. Patrick J. Schiltz, On Being a Happy, Healthy, and Ethical Member of an Unhappy, Unhealthy, and Unethical Profession, 52 Vand. L. Rev. 871, 872 (1999).

2. We are grateful to Keith Palfin, J.D., Georgetown University Law Center 2004, for contributing an earlier draft of this historical summary to our book.

in the Massachusetts Bay colony, Thomas Lechford, had only recently hung out his shingle when he was caught tampering with a jury and promptly tossed out of the colony. The colony's leaders decided that they could get along just fine without lawyers and, in 1641, they passed a law prohibiting the collection of money for legal services.

Massachusetts Bay's attitude toward lawyers was by no means unique. At around the same time, both Virginia and Connecticut passed laws barring lawyers from appearing in courtrooms. The Fundamental Constitutions of the Carolinas declared that it was "a base and vile thing" to be a lawyer.[3] As Professor Lawrence Friedman succinctly concludes, "the lawyer was unloved in the 17th century."[4]

The colonial public didn't trust lawyers and saw no need for them. Many people believed that justice was best served if the parties to legal disputes presented their cases themselves. The popular view was that lawyers made disputes more complicated than they needed to be, swelling their wallets in the process. Professor Friedman notes that colonial Americans often said of Pennsylvania: "They have no lawyers. Everyone is to tell his own case. . . . 'Tis a happy country."[5]

Colonial America was an "era of law without lawyers, a time when law was shaped by theologians, politicians, farmers, fishermen, and merchants."[6] There was only one task lawyers were thought equipped to handle — courtroom advocacy. And few at the time believed that lawyers really made the world a better place when they performed this task.

## 2. The nineteenth century

Between 1800 and 1830, manufacturing and transportation grew dramatically. By 1860, 30,000 miles of railroad track had been laid, a tenfold increase over a mere 20-year period. Soon thereafter, the telegraph revolutionized communications. These advances transformed the American economy and society. Agriculture is one example of this transformation; agricultural

---

The following sources contributed to this section: Arlin M. Adams, The Legal Profession: A Critical Evaluation, 74 Judicature 77, 79 (1990); Jerold S. Auerbach, Unequal Justice: Lawyers and Social Change in Modern America 63 (Oxford U. Press 1976); Deborah A. Ballam, The Evolution of the Government-Business Relationship in the United States: Colonial Time to Present, 31 Am. Bus. L.J. 553, 580-582 (1994); Clara N. Carson, The Lawyer Statistical Report (Am. B. Found. 1999); Lawrence M. Friedman, A History of American Law 94-97, 303-313, 633-651 (2d ed., Simon & Schuster 1985); Geoffrey C. Hazard, The Future of Legal Ethics, 100 Yale L.J. 1239 (1991); James W. Hurst, The Growth of American Law: The Law Makers 9-11, 285-287 (Little, Brown & Co. 1950); Thomas D. Morgan & Ronald D. Rotunda, Professional Responsibility: Problems and Materials 2-3, 601-602 (Found. Press 2000); Richard B. Morris, The Legal Profession in America on the Eve of the Revolution, in ABA, Political Separation and Legal Continuity, 4-11 (Harry W. Jones ed., 1976); Deborah L. Rhode, Keynote: Law, Lawyers, and the Pursuit of Justice, 70 Fordham L. Rev. 1543, 1557 (2002); Deborah L. Rhode & David Luban, Legal Ethics 61-62 (3d ed., Found. Press 2001).

3. Friedman, supra n. 2, at 94.
4. Id. at 95.
5. Id. at 94.
6. Morris, supra n. 2, at 5.

goods suddenly could be sold wherever the railroad went, and previously remote lands could be developed as farms and towns.

As industry developed, so did the law. For example, to facilitate the development of railroads, state legislatures and courts had to deal with issues involving rights of way and railway accidents. One historian notes that the revolution in American technology "could not have occurred had there not been equally revolutionary changes in American business law."[7] There were major upheavals in nearly all areas of law including "torts, contracts, corporations, property, and government regulation of business."[8] There were more laws, more types of law, and more complexity within the law — all of which demanded more people specially trained in the law; in other words, more lawyers.

*Daniel Webster*

The growth of the legal profession did not improve the public's opinion of lawyers; lawyers were grudgingly accepted as "a necessary evil."[9] Before the Civil War, a typical lawyer was a courtroom lawyer, and a showman at that. The most famous lawyers of the time were those who delivered dramatic performances at trial or appellate arguments. Judges expected and allowed a level of oratorical flamboyance that is seldom seen today. Attorneys arguing before the U.S. Supreme Court in 1824 were often "heard in silence for hours, without being stopped or interrupted."[10] For example, in Dartmouth College v. Woodward[11] lawyer Daniel Webster delivered an emotionally charged four-hour-long argument before the Supreme Court. His oration was so moving that, at its end, Chief Justice John Marshall's eyes were filled with tears.[12]

The rapid growth of enormous railroad projects and large financial trusts and industrial corporations in the latter half of the nineteenth century witnessed the birth of the "Wall Street" transactional lawyer who "made more money and had more prestige than any courtroom lawyer could."[13] The rise of the Wall Street lawyer "was the most important event in the profession during this period."[14] Lawyers began to practice law without ever seeing the inside of a courtroom. This was unheard of before the mid-1800s. The work of some lawyers was no longer primarily to try lawsuits but to prevent them from being necessary in the first place. Some businesses started hiring lawyers full time. By the end of the nineteenth century, hiring in-house counsel had become a common practice.

---

7. Ballam, supra n. 2, at 582.

8. Id. at 583. For a detailed discussion of the actual changes that took place in the law at this time, see id. at 583-598.

9. Friedman, supra n. 2, at 96.

10. Id. at 313.

11. 4 Wheat. 519 (1819).

12. Id.

13. Friedman, supra n. 2, at 633.

14. Id. at 636.

Between 1850 and 1900, the population of lawyers in the United States grew by over 500 percent, significantly outpacing general population growth. The size of law firms also grew. In 1872, almost no firms had more than five members. Thirty years later, there were nearly 70 firms with more than five lawyers.[15]

## 3. Growth of large firms in the twentieth century

During the twentieth century, the profession continued to grow rapidly. The United States had 300,000 practicing lawyers in 1970. That number has swelled to over a million today. Large law firms also have also continued to flourish. In 1975, only 4 U.S. law firms had more than 200 lawyers. At first, "they were viewed with great skepticism."[16] By 1990, there were more than 150 such firms.[17]

# B. A short history of American legal education[18]

Until the twentieth century, most American lawyers entered the profession through an apprenticeship with a practicing lawyer; the trainee paid fees for this privilege. There were few law schools in the eighteenth and early nineteenth centuries. In theory, the apprentice learned the law on the job while receiving guidance from the more experienced practitioner.

In fact, however, apprenticeships were often grueling and unrewarding for the apprentices. Apprentices often performed countless hours of thankless grunt work (such as copying documents by hand) and had little time left to study legal skills or substantive law.

Slowly, the apprenticeship system gave way to legal education. The first law schools were independent institutions. Many of them eventually affiliated with universities. Many law schools opened and then closed during the first half of the nineteenth century, but they gained a more stable foothold during the latter part of the century. By 1860, the nation had 21 law schools or university law departments.[19] During most of the rest of the century, law "was taught by the Dwight Method, a combination of lecture, recitation, and drill named after a

---

15. Id. at 640.

16. Adams, supra n. 2, at 79.

17. The figures in this paragraph are based on figures from the Statistical Abstract of the United States (2003); see also Hazard, supra n. 2, at 1259.

18. The following sources contributed to this section: Friedman, supra n. 2, at 98, 318, 606-618; David A. Garvin, Making the Case, Harvard Magazine 56-65 (Sept.-Oct. 2003); George B. Shepherd & William G. Shepherd, Scholarly Restraints? ABA Accreditation and Legal Education, 19 Cardozo L. Rev. 2091, 2111 (1998); Robert Stevens, Law School: Legal Education in America from the 1850s to the 1980s (U.N.C. Press 1983); Robert Stevens, Democracy and the Legal Profession: Cautionary Notes, Learning & Law 15 (Fall 1976); Herb D. Vest, Felling the Giant: Breaking the ABA's Stranglehold on Legal Education in America, 50 J. Leg. Educ. 494, 496-497 (2000).

19. Stevens, Democracy in the Legal Profession, supra n. 18, at 21.

professor at Columbia. Students prepared for class by reading 'treatises,' dense textbooks that interpreted the law and summarized the best thinking in the various fields. They were then tested, orally and in front of their peers."[20] Students were asked to recite what they had read and memorized. They learned real legal skills later in apprenticeships or actual practice.

In the mid-to-late 1800s, academic law schools became more respected due in no small part to Dean Christopher Columbus Langdell of Harvard Law School. Langdell revolutionized legal education, and many of his reforms have survived into the twenty-first century. Langdell expanded the then-standard one-year curriculum into a three-year law school program. He required that students pass final exams before they advanced to the next level of courses. He pioneered the use of "casebooks" in place of the treatises. Finally, he replaced the then-pervasive use of lectures in class with an early version of the Socratic method.

*Christopher Columbus Langdell*

Langdell advocated a number of views that have since gone out of fashion. He thought that the common law possessed elegance and wisdom that resulted from hundreds of years of slow, careful sculpting at the hands of skilled and sagacious judges. Statutory and other lesser forms of law, he believed, were the hurried work of easily swayed politicians and were therefore unworthy of study in a law classroom. Langdell opposed the teaching of constitutional law because he felt it had more in common with the vulgarity of statutes than with the beauty of common law. He insisted that "the law" (meaning, of course, common law) was a science. He believed that legal education should focus on the internal logic of the law, not on the relationship between law and society. Social, economic, and political issues were excluded from the classroom.[21]

Initially students and professors reacted negatively to Langdell's reforms. Students cut Langdell's classes in unprecedented numbers. When word of Langdell's wacky new teaching style got out, the enrollment at Harvard significantly declined. The Boston University Law School was founded in 1872 partly "as an alternative to Harvard's insanity."[22]

In the end, Langdell's philosophy and approach won out. Some of Langdell's better students were hired as instructors at other schools; they brought Langdell's "insanity" with them. Eventually, however, law professors evolved Langdell's methods to teach critical analysis of law. For example, they began to assign cases with inconsistent outcomes to allow students to examine conflicting values in society and to question whether law is objective or scientific. A modified version of Langdell's case method of teaching remains the

---

20. Garvin, supra n. 18, at 58.

21. In fact, the field of political science originated from the generally unsuccessful attempts of early law professors to introduce lessons in politics, government, and society into law classrooms. Friedman, supra n. 2, at 611.

22. Id. at 615.

dominant mode of legal education more than a century later. Not until the 1970s, when clinical legal education was introduced into the curricula of most law schools, did any other type of law teaching become even a significant part of most law schools' curricula. Clinical education started when the Ford Foundation offered American law schools $11 million to experiment with student representation of live clients.[23]

Another innovation of the 1970s was the advent of courses in professional responsibility. Ethics education was required at most law schools after several lawyers were convicted of criminal charges for their roles in the Watergate cover-up during the Nixon administration.[24] The nation was horrified to find that so many elite lawyers had facilitated a tangle of corruption in government.

## C. Race, sex, and class in the legal profession[25]

If you look around your law school classrooms, you may see men and women, people of all races and many nationalities, people with diverse religious affiliations (or with no affiliation), gay and straight people, old and young people, and people with disabilities.

This diversity in the legal profession is of relatively recent vintage. During most of our collective professional history, wealthy white Protestant men from prominent families dominated the American legal profession and excluded others. During the latter half of the nineteenth century, middle-class Protestant men entered the profession in increasingly large numbers. They in turn resisted admission of immigrants, Jews, Catholics, nonwhites, and women.[26] This exclusionary behavior may have been rooted in economic self-interest as

---

23. Ford's principal purpose was to improve legal education by connecting students' learning with reality, but providing more assistance for poor people was an additional benefit. See Philip G. Schrag & Michael Meltsner, Reflections on Clinical Legal Education 3-10 (Northeastern U. Press 1998).

24. Frank S. Block et al., Filling in the Larger Puzzle: Clinical Scholarship in the Wake of the Lawyering Process, 10 Clin. L. Rev. 221, 228 (2003). The Watergate scandal (1972-1974) resulted from the gradual revelation that with the help of many government officials (some of whom were lawyers), President Richard M. Nixon first authorized criminal acts to spy on his perceived political enemies and then attempted to cover up the crimes. The Supreme Court eventually upheld an order requiring Nixon to deliver records of his crimes to federal prosecutors. The Judiciary Committee of the House of Representatives voted to impeach the president, and he resigned from office. See U.S. v. Nixon, 418 U.S. 683 (1974); Carl Bernstein & Bob Woodward, All the President's Men (2d ed., Simon & Schuster 1994). One leading authority on ethics in government argues that legal ethics courses would not have prevented some of the lawyers, such as Nixon himself, from committing crimes, but they might have helped to keep subordinate lawyers from participating in the scandal. Kathleen Clark, Legacy of Watergate for Legal Ethics Instruction, 51 Hastings L.J. 673 (2000).

25. The following sources contributed to this section: Friedman, supra n. 2, at 100, 304-305, 619-654; Stevens, Democracy and the Legal Profession, supra n. 18.

26. In the first third of the twentieth century, corporate and patent law were "the exclusive domains of white Christian males. Lawyers who were Jewish essentially were confined to practicing real estate and negligence law." The entry of Jews into the legal profession was "strewn with obstacles of exclusion and discrimination set by law schools and law firms." Jerome Hornblass, The Jewish Lawyer, 14 Cardozo L. Rev. 1639, 1641 (1993).

much as in social elitism: competition from more lawyers would produce lower fees for everyone.

As a practical matter, most people could be excluded from the legal profession in its early years because the procedures for entry depended on personal connections. When apprenticeship was the primary method of becoming a lawyer, people from disfavored racial, ethnic, or religious groups could not easily find established lawyers willing to apprentice them. As law schools and other advances opened the bar to a greater number of people, other barriers were imposed. Some laws prohibited admission of members of certain groups. For example, California in the 1800s barred nonwhites, women, and noncitizen immigrants from becoming lawyers.[27]

Even after the overtly exclusionary laws were repealed, efforts by bar associations in the late 19th and early 20th centuries to raise the standards of the profession often resulted in exclusion of applicants from marginalized groups. Bar associations sought to protect the public from unscrupulous or incompetent practitioners by requiring attendance at law school as a condition of bar admission, by requiring some college study as a condition of law school admission, by imposing character and fitness requirements, and so on. While the stated purpose of these initiatives was to protect the public, practicing lawyers may have been motivated also by economic and social self-interest. Some lawyers probably viewed the resulting exclusion of women and minorities as a beneficial side effect.[28]

## 1. Women[29]

The first female lawyer in America was Margaret Brent, who practiced law in the 1630s and 1640s. She was born in England to a wealthy and powerful family. She received an education in the law at a time when education was

---

27. Act Concerning Attorneys and Counsellors at Law, ch. 4, § 1, 1851 Cal. Stat. 48 (limiting admission to the bar to "white male citizen[s]").

28. Richard L. Abel concludes that "professional associations . . . did deliberately construct entry barriers to affect the social composition of the profession. . . . Indeed, supply control may have been as much a project of controlling who became a lawyer, in order to elevate the collective status of the profession, as of controlling how many did so, in order to enhance their financial rewards — although the two goals are obviously interrelated. . . . At the beginning of [the twentieth] century, the professional elite were quite open about their desire to exclude Jewish and Catholic Eastern and Southern European immigrants and their sons, whose entry into the profession had been greatly facilitated by the shift from apprenticeship to academic training. The introduction of prelegal educational requirements, the attack on unapproved and part-time law schools, the requirement of citizenship, and the introduction of 'character' tests were all directed toward this end, in whole or part." Richard L. Abel, American Lawyers 85, 109 (Oxford U. Press 1989).

29. The following sources contributed to this section: Dawn B. Berry, The 50 Most Influential Women in American Law 1-5, 53-54 (RGA 1996); Carson, supra n. 2; Virginia G. Drachman, Sisters in Law: Women Lawyers in Modern American History 38-43, 178 (Harvard U. Press 1998); Deborah L. Rhode, ABA Commission on Women in the Profession, The Unfinished Agenda: Women and the Legal Profession (ABA 2001); Rhode & Luban, supra n. 2, 25-34 25-34; Charles W. Wolfram, Toward a History of the Legalization of American Legal Ethics — II The Modern Era, 15 Geo. J. Leg. Ethics 205 n. 62 (2002).

denied to most women. She arrived in America in 1638 and set up what became a thriving litigation practice. Brent was involved in more than 100 court cases between 1638 and 1646, including many jury trials, and reportedly never lost a single one. Her skill caught the attention of Governor Leonard Calvert of Maryland, who appointed her to be his legal counsel. After the governor died, Brent served as the executor of his estate. Her skillful handling of the estate earned her a public commendation from the Maryland Assembly. She was particularly successful in finding food to satisfy the claims of a group of former soldiers who had been loyal to Calvert and who threatened to mutiny if they were not paid overdue wages. Many judges at the time apparently could not fathom the concept of a female attorney. Many addressed her as "Gentleman" Margaret Brent. However, there is little evidence that Brent suffered much discrimination as a result of her sex. She was regarded as an anomaly, not as a threat to the patriarchal organization of society. After Brent, not a single female attorney was permitted to practice law in America for more than 200 years.[30]

During the last half of the nineteenth century, an increasing number of women tried to enter the profession. This time, judges, law school administrators, and others saw female lawyers as a threat to the social order. In an 1875 court opinion, the chief justice of the Wisconsin Supreme Court wrote that any woman who attempted to become a lawyer was committing "treason" against "the order of nature."[31] Similarly, in 1872, three U.S. Supreme Court justices (in a concurring opinion) opined that it was against "the divine ordinance" for women to enter the legal profession and insisted that the "paramount destiny and mission of woman" was to "fulfill the noble and benign offices of wife and mother." (See box on page 592.)

After three women attempted to enter the law school at Columbia University in 1868, trustee and law school founder George Templeton Strong wrote in his diary, "No woman shall degrade herself by practicing law, in N.Y. especially, if I can save her."[32] Needless to say, all three were denied entry.[33]

Some of those who supported admission of women to law school offered peculiar justifications. In 1872, attorney George C. Sill wrote a letter to Yale

---

30. This paragraph is primarily based on the account of the life of Margaret Brent in Berry, supra n. 29, at 1-5; see also Karen B. Morello, The Invisible Bar: The Woman Lawyer in America: 1638 to the Present 3-9 (Random House 1986).

31. In re Goodell, 39 Wis. 232, 240 (1875).

32. Drachman, supra n. 29, at 41, quoting The Diary of George Templeton Strong: Post-War Years, 1865-1875, at 256 (Allan Nevins & Milton H. Thomas eds., Macmillan 1952).

33. One of the three women denied entry was Lemma Barkeloo, who later went on to become the first American woman to formally study at a law school when admitted to Washington University in 1869. She completed one year of legal education at the top of her class and then went on to take, and pass, the state's bar exam. After she died a biographical publication reported that the cause of her death was "overmental exertion." (She actually died of typhoid only a few months after beginning her legal career, but not before she became "the first female attorney of official record to try a case in court."). Berry, supra n. 29, at 53-54.

**Bradwell v. State**
**83 U.S. 130 (1873)**

*Myra Bradwell*

Myra Bradwell applied for a license to practice law. She met all the requirements, but the Illinois court denied her application. Although state law did not explicitly preclude women from becoming lawyers, the court concluded that legislators could not have contemplated their admission to the bar. The court said "that God designed the sexes to occupy different spheres of action, and that it belonged to men to make, apply, and execute the laws, was regarded [when the statutes were passed] as an almost axiomatic truth." Application of Bradwell, 55 Ill. 535, 539 (1869).

The Supreme Court affirmed the denial on the ground that the privileges and immunities clauses of the Constitution did not give Bradwell the right to practice. Three concurring justices added: "Man is, or should be, woman's protector and defender. The natural and proper timidity and delicacy which belongs to the female sex evidently unfits it for many of the occupations of civil life. The constitution of the family organization, which is founded in the divine ordinance, as well as in the nature of things, indicates the domestic sphere as that which properly belongs to the domain and functions of womanhood. . . . The paramount destiny and mission of woman are to fulfil the noble and benign offices of wife and mother."

Law School, from which he had graduated, recommending that it admit women, but he did so with this curious endorsement: "Are you far advanced enough to admit young women to your school? . . . I am in favor of their studying & practicing law, provided they are ugly."[34] Yale, apparently, was not as "far advanced" as the progressive Mr. Sill and continued to refuse law school admission to women.[35]

Many nineteenth-century experts opposed all professional activity and even higher education for women. In 1873, for example, Harvard University physician Dr. Edward H. Clarke published a book warning of the adverse medical consequences that could result from women pursuing higher education. He wrote that female reproductive physiology made it dangerous for women to engage in strenuous intellectual activity. Such activity, in his medical opinion, would divert energy from female reproductive organs to the brain, harming the health of women and their children. This, he warned ominously, could cause irreparable harm to the future of America.

---

34. Drachman, supra n. 29, at 43, quoting from Frederick C. Hicks, Yale Law School: 1869-1894, Including the County Court House Period 72 (Yale U. Press, 1937).

35. Id.

Dr. Clarke's writings were very influential at the time, spawning criticism of women's colleges, even from within the colleges. One president of a women's college wondered when the college opened "whether woman's health could stand the strain of education."[36]

Despite the controversy, some law schools opened their doors to women. The University of Iowa and Washington University admitted women as early as the late 1860s. Other schools continued to deny admission to women. Harvard Law School, for example, admitted only men until 1950.[37] Some accredited schools maintained restrictions on female enrollment (quotas) even into the early 1970s. But during the second half of the twentieth century, the percentage of women law students climbed from trivial numbers to about 48 percent. By the end of the twentieth century, though sexist attitudes and discrimination remained, more than one in four American lawyers was female. Sixteen percent of U.S. Circuit Court judges were female, and two women sat on the Supreme Court.[38]

## 2. People of color[39]

Like women, African Americans and members of other racial minority groups were largely excluded from the practice of law until relatively recently. During the period when lawyers were trained through apprenticeship, few black people could find established lawyers willing to train them, and few could afford the fees even if a willing lawyer was available. Until the late nineteenth century, law school doors were largely closed to blacks as well. Because black students could not enroll in "white" law schools, law schools were set up to serve the black community. About a dozen black law schools were established before 1900.[40] Of those, only Howard University's law school raised enough funds to stay open. Many Howard law graduates became prominent in private practice, government, and public interest law. One of them was Thurgood Marshall, who began as a civil rights lawyer (he argued Brown v. Board of Education) and was later appointed to become the first black Supreme Court justice.[41]

---

36. Id. at 39, quoting M. Carey Thomas, Present Tendencies in Women's Colleges and University Education, 25 Educ. Rev. 68 (1908).

37. Celebration 45: Waiting for the HLS Door to Open, Harvard L. Bull. (Spring 1999).

38. ABA Commission on Women in the Profession and the Stanford Law School Library, Statistics and Data on Women in the Legal Profession, at http://womenlaw.stanford.edu/womenlawyerstats.html (last visited Nov. 14, 2004).

39. The following sources contributed to this section: ABA Task Force Report on Minorities in the Legal Profession (Jan. 1986); Auerbach, supra n. 2, at 266; Berry, supra n. 29, at 55-58; Rhode & Luban, supra n. 2; Geraldine R. Segal, Blacks in the Law: Philadelphia and the Nation 1-17 (U. Penn. Press 1983).

40. See J. Clay Smith Jr., Emancipation: The Making of the Black Lawyer, 1844-1944, at 33-40 (U. Penn. Press 1993).

41. Marshall, who grew up in Baltimore, wanted to attend the University of Maryland Law School but was barred from admission there because of racial segregation. In 1936, his first significant court victory, Pearson v. Murray (before correction in 1961, reported as Univ. of Md. v. Murray), 182 A. 590 (Md. 1936), forced the desegregation of that school. Randall Kennedy, Schoolings in Equality, New Republic, July 5, 2004.

Thurgood Marshall

Efforts to "raise standards" for admission to the practice of law in the first third of the twentieth century made it more difficult for African Americans to enter the profession. Because black Americans experienced disproportionately high levels of poverty and lack of access to quality education, they often could not satisfy requirements for entry to the bar or to law school. In the 20 years before 1947, not a single black applicant to the Louisiana Bar was accepted. By 1960, although 32 percent of the people in Louisiana were black, only 1 percent of Louisiana lawyers were black.

Starting in 1896, the Supreme Court's "separate but equal" ruling in Plessy v. Ferguson[42] was relied on by some law schools to justify discrimination. For example, a black applicant applied for admission to the University of Texas Law School after the *Plessy* decision. Rather than admit the student, the state of Texas added law classes at a nearby "impoverished black institution," which offered college credit for "mattress and broom-making" and other vocational training for menial jobs.[43] Two of the three law classrooms "lacked chairs and desks."[44] Nevertheless, the Texas state court held that this hastily created "law school" was "substantially equal" to the University of Texas Law School.[45] Thurgood Marshall argued for the black students in the Supreme Court case that reversed this decision.[46]

Black women suffered double discrimination. Those not excluded because of their race were often excluded because of their sex. In the 65 years before 1940, fewer than 50 black women practiced law in the United States. By 1960, only a few more black women had been able to obtain a legal education. Those who succeeded often had to go to extraordinary lengths to secure training.

In the late nineteenth century, Charlotte Ray applied to Howard University Law School under the name C. E. Ray to disguise her sex. At the time, Howard excluded women. Ray's appearance on the first day of class caused some commotion and debate, but the school ultimately allowed her to stay. She graduated with honors. In 1872, she became the first black woman to practice law in America and the first woman to practice in Washington, D.C.

Bar associations often were hostile to aspiring black lawyers. In 1912, three black lawyers were accidentally given memberships in the ABA. After much controversy, these three lawyers were allowed to retain their memberships, but the ABA amended its application form to ask applicants to state their race and sex. Only in 1943 did the ABA declare that membership did not depend on these factors.[47]

---

42. 163 U.S. 537 (1896).
43. Rhode & Luban, supra n. 2, at 887.
44. Id.
45. Sweatt v. Painter, 210 S.W.2d 442 (Tex. Civ. App. 1948).
46. Sweatt v. Painter, 339 U.S. 629 (1950).
47. Segal, supra n. 39, at 17-18.

As a result of the work of Thurgood Marshall and others on the legal staff of the NAACP, law school admissions barriers fell across the country. Brown v. Board of Education,[48] was decided in 1954. Plessy v. Ferguson's "separate but equal" doctrine was overturned, and the Supreme Court strongly proclaimed "separate" education to be "inherently unequal."[49] Ten years later, no accredited law school reported denying admission to an applicant on the basis of race.

By 1970, most law schools had established programs to recruit and retain minority students. But the legal struggle over admission policies did not end then. Organizations opposed to affirmative action supported lawsuits challenging affirmative action policies, particularly by public law schools. In 2003, the U.S. Supreme Court sustained the affirmative action plan of University of Michigan Law School, holding the creation of a diverse educational community was a compelling state interest.[50]

Despite a great deal of progress, the integration of the legal profession has been slow. In California, for example, Latinos comprised more than a third of the state's population in 2001 but less than 4 percent of the state bar. Asian and Pacific Islanders constituted 11 percent of the population but only 6 percent of the bar. African Americans comprised 6.4 percent of the population but less than 3 percent of the bar.[51]

Barriers related to socioeconomic status also have disproportionately impacted minority groups. As a result of poor educational opportunities and financial difficulties, law school was "out of reach for the vast majority of minorities" even when discrimination was not an issue.[52] However, social, legal, and economic progress has resulted in significant increases. The number of minority law students jumped from approximately 3 percent in 1968 to 20 percent in the late 1990s. Recent national figures show that minorities comprise 10 percent of lawyers, 10 percent of full professors, and 3 percent of partners at large law firms.[53]

# D. The legal profession today

The American legal profession today is larger and more diverse than ever. Although many different kinds of people are lawyers, much social stratification

---

48. 347 U.S. 483 (1954).

49. Id. at 495.

50. Grutter v. Bollinger, 539 U.S. 306 (2003).

51. Survey Finds Bar Makeup Is Shifting, but Slowly, Cal. St. B.J. (Nov. 2001), quoted in Edward M. Chen, The Judiciary, Diversity, and Justice for All, 10 Asian L.J. 127, 130 (2003).

52. Rhode & Luban, supra note 2, at 28.

53. Id. at 28-43, 888; Break the Glass Ceiling Foundation, Diversity in the Legal Profession, at http://www.breaktheglassceiling.com/statistics-minorities.htm (last visited Nov. 14, 2004) (minority enrollment in law schools has held steady at about 20 percent for years, and African-Americans are about 7 percent of law students and 12 percent of the population. However, in the 77 largest law firms in New York, fewer than 1 percent of the partners are African-Americans).

remains. In addition, serious questions have been raised about whether the profession meets the needs either of most of its members or of large segments of the public.

Let's start with some numbers. At the beginning of the twenty-first century, there were about 1 million lawyers in the United States. Perhaps because large firms have grown so dramatically, many people erroneously think that most of these lawyers work for large corporate firms. In fact, a majority of lawyers today do not work in multilawyer law firms at all; they work alone, for the government, or in some other capacity. Specifically, in 1995, 74 percent of American lawyers were in private practice. The more detailed breakdown is as follows:

| | |
|---|---|
| Private practice | 74% |
| Corporations | 8% |
| State and local government | 7% |
| Federal government | 4% |
| Nonprofit organizations | 2%[54] |
| Education | 1% |
| Retired | 5%[55] |

Only 53 percent of the lawyers in private practice (39 percent of all American lawyers) worked in law firms of two or more lawyers. The lawyers in multilawyer firms were distributed as follows.

## Distribution of Lawyers in Private Law Firms, by Firm Size, 1995[56]

| Size of firm | Percentage of Lawyers in Multilawyer Firms Who Work in Firms of This Size[57] |
|---|---|
| 2 | 11 |
| 3-5 | 17 |
| 6-10 | 14 |
| 11-20 | 13 |
| 21-50 | 14 |
| 50-100 | 8 |
| more than 100 | 23 |

54. This category includes, among other organizations, trade associations, public defenders, and legal aid agencies.

55. Carson, supra n. 2, at 7.

56. Id. at 7-8.

57. This table shows a percentage breadown of the 53 percent of lawyers in private practice who work in multilawyer firms. The other 47 percent of lawyers in private practice are sole practitioners.

Where a lawyer works and what type of work a lawyer does seems to be determined at least in part by who the lawyer is — not just ability and interest but race, sex, religion, socioeconomic background, and so on. John P. Heinz, a law professor, and Edward O. Laumann, a sociologist, published an important study of Chicago lawyers in 1982.[58] The researchers believed that Chicago lawyers were typical of lawyers in other major American cities in terms of social stratification.[59] They found that lawyers in private practice were divided into two very different professions. There was one large group of wealthy lawyers in large firms, mostly drawn from 12 "elite" and "prestige" law schools, who mainly represented corporations. A slightly smaller group consisted of much less wealthy lawyers, drawn mainly from regional and local law schools, who primarily represented individual clients. Heinz and Laumann explain:

> [M]uch of the differentiation within the legal profession is secondary to one fundamental distinction — the distinction between lawyers who represent large organizations (corporations, labor unions, or government), and those who represent individuals. The two kinds of law practice are the hemispheres of the profession. Most lawyers reside exclusively in one hemisphere or the other and seldom, if ever, cross the equator. . . . [Also, in doctrinal areas that the adversary system divides into opposing fields, such as environmental plaintiffs vs. environmental defense,] the side of the case that characteristically represents corporate clients is consistently assigned higher prestige [in the estimation of the public] than is the side that more often represents individuals. . . . This suggests the thesis that prestige within law is acquired by association, that it is "reflected glory" derived from the power possessed by the lawyers' clients. . . .
>
> The patterns were divided into readily identifiable . . . networks, one area being composed disproportionately of WASPs who serve the largest corporate clients and another having a great preponderance of Catholics who do trial work for individuals and smaller businesses. . . .
>
> Any profession will surely include disparate parts, but we doubt that any other is so sharply bifurcated as the bar. . . . The two sectors of the legal profession . . . include different lawyers, with different social origins, who were trained at different law schools, serve different sorts of clients, practice in different office environments, are differentially likely to litigate (when and if they litigate) in different forums, have somewhat different values, associate with different circles of acquaintances, and rest their claims to professionalism on different sorts of social power. . . . Only in the most formal of senses, then, do the two types of lawyers constitute one profession.[60]

---

58. John P. Heinz & Edward O. Laumann, Chicago Lawyers: The Social Structure of the Bar (Am. B. Found. 1982). The book is based on data collected in 1975.

59. Id. at 28.

60. Id. at 319, 331, 354, 379, 384. Heinz and Laumann found that 45 percent of the securities lawyers in Chicago had gone to law school at Chicago, Columbia, Harvard, Michigan, Stanford, or Yale, while only 8 percent of personal injury plaintiffs' lawyers, 4 percent of criminal defense lawyers, and none of the prosecutors, had attended these schools. Id. at 113.

Heinz and Laumann updated their study in 1998 with data collected 20 years after the original study. During that 20-year period, the size of the profession had doubled, and women flocked into the profession for the first time.[61] The new data showed that by 1995, the two hemispheres were no longer approximately equal in size. By then, 64 percent of all lawyers' services were delivered to corporations and other large organizations while only 29 percent of lawyers' services were provided to individuals and small businesses.[62] In addition, the authors described a "middle group of [seven] fields [such as income tax work]" in which some lawyers represented both business and individual clients.[63] Also, Heinz and Laumann concluded that specialization among lawyers had greatly increased. As a result of this and other factors:

> [There are] several reasons to suppose that Chicago lawyers might be less cohesive in the 1990s than they were in the 1970s, and urban lawyers may now have become subdivided into smaller clusters. But the division between the two classes of clients — between large organizations, on the one hand, and individuals and small businesses, on the other — endures. . . . We think it unlikely that the present organizational structures provide enough interchange among the specialties to produce a bar that functions as a community of shared fate and common purpose.[64]

## 1. Large firms

Only about 10 percent of lawyers in private practice work in firms of more than a hundred lawyers. Even so, the big firms are important because they often have a disproportionate influence over what happens in the profession. Also, the big firms keep getting bigger, so this percentage may grow.

**Many law students hope to get jobs with large firms. Why is this such a popular choice?**

Probably the main reasons are the high salaries and social status. Large law firms pay much higher salaries and bonuses than small firms. NALP, an organization of legal employers that collects data reports that "the legal profession has had the highest levels of income inequality among the leading professions."[65] Salary

---

61. In addition, the authors realized that the questionnaire that they used in their original study did not sufficiently divide some areas of law, such as tax work, into corporate or personal representation, an error they corrected in the 1995 survey instrument.

62. John P. Heinz, Edward O. Laumann, Robert L. Nelson & Ethan Michelson, The Changing Character of Lawyers' Work: Chicago in 1975 and 1995, 32 L. & Socy. Rev. 751, 767 (1998).

63. The fields in this middle group were personal tax, plaintiffs' environmental work, municipal law, residential real estate, personal civil litigation, probate, and civil rights. Id. at 763-764. In 1995, the authors considered only what work lawyers performed; they did not reassess the socioeconomic or educational separation of practitioners as they had in their first study.

64. Id. at 773-775.

65. Robert L. Nelson, The Futures of American Lawyers: A Demographic Profile of a Changing Profession in a Changing Society, 44 Case W. Res. L. Rev. 345, 373 (1994).

differentiation begins with entry-level jobs. In 2002, the national median starting salaries for new lawyers were as follows.

- $125,000 (not including signing and end-of-year bonuses) for those at firms with over 250 lawyers
- $52,000 for those at firms with 11 to 25 lawyers
- $42,000 for government lawyers
- $36,000 for public interest lawyers[66]

NALP concluded in 2003 that "the prevalence of high salaries in large law firms, in concert with the relatively stable salaries among other employers, has resulted in a salary distribution with two distinct peaks: one at the high end and one in the $35,000-$55,000 range."[67]

The allure of large firms may be enhanced by the astronomical earnings of their most senior lawyers. In 2002, at 50 of the nation's largest law firms, partners' average compensation exceeded $600,000 per year. At 22 firms, the average compensation for partners exceeded $1 million. At Wachtell, Lipton, Rosen & Katz, the 77 partners averaged just under $3 million.[68]

Some law students aspire to work in large law firms not only because of the money but also because the big firm jobs are very prestigious. Many students also expect that large firms offer superior training or mentoring. This used to be the norm and may still be the case at some firms, but — as we explain below — the economic pressure of private practice has greatly reduced the amount of time that partners spend doing training or mentoring. Also, many law graduates seek positions in large firms so that they can repay their enormous student loans in the years after graduation. In 2002, the median debt of recent graduates of the nation's private law schools[69] was $86,378.[70] Repayment over 10 years would amount to $12,780 per year; or, if the debt is repaid over 20 years, the payments would be $9,000 per year.[71] By definition, half of the graduates owe more than the median amount. In 2002, 20 percent of U.S. law school graduates finished school owing more than $120,000.[72]

---

66. NALP Foundation for Research and Education, Jobs and JDs: Employment and Salaries of New Law Graduates, Class of 2002, at 30 (2003). Eighty-three percent of starting salaries at law firms with more than 250 lawyers were higher than $95,000, while only 5 percent of starting salaries at the small firms exceeded that level. Id. at 18. In 2002, the national median starting compensation (including bonuses) for all new graduates who were starting jobs as associates at law firms of all sizes was $70,350. Altman Weil, Inc., Press Release, Law Firm Profits Up Despite Uncertain Economy, Survey Reports, at http://www.altmanweil.com/news/release.cfm?PRID=32 (last visited Nov. 5, 2003).

67. NALP, supra n.66 at 18.

68. Rounding Out the Pay Picture, Am. Law., July 2003, at 157-158.

69. About two-thirds of U.S. law schools are "private" (usually nonprofit) law schools. The others are taxpayer-subsidized state universities, which generally have lower tuition.

70. ABA, Lifting the Burden: Law Student Debt as a Barrier to Public Service: The Final Report of the ABA Commission on Loan Repayment and Forgiveness 20-22 (2003).

71. Id.

72. Id. at 24.

## What are the disadvantages of large firm practice?

Several writers suggest that the financial rewards of large firm practice are outweighed by some of the downsides. Some large firms tend to exploit associates and unwittingly to deprive them of the normal benefits of living in families or society. In some firms, cut-throat competition among associates undermines morale.[73] Professor Michael Asimow focuses, in particular, on the exceedingly long hours that the large firms require,[74] and on the stressful and sometimes unfair competition for promotion within the firms.

## Michael Asimow, Embodiment of Evil: Law Firms in the Movies

48 UCLA L. Rev. 1339, 1376-1380 (2001)

[Professor Asimow is Professor of Law Emeritus at UCLA Law School. In 1965-1967, before beginning his teaching career, he practiced at a Los Angeles law firm that at the time had 17 lawyers. In this article, he investigates whether the negative portrayal of large law firms in many movies reflects the reality of life within those institutions.]

*Professor Michael Asimow*

Numerous statistical studies [indicate] that big firm lawyers earn the most money, work the most hours, and they are the least satisfied with their work. . . . It appears that the biggest culprits are the killingly long hours of work combined with arbitrary work demands, a lack of autonomy, and poor inter-personal communications between associates and partners. Many associates feel they are working in nicely decorated sweatshops. Billable hours have become the raison d'etre of law firm existence. High numbers of billable hours are essential to maximize the benefits of leverage for equity partners as well as to pay for the sharply increased levels of associates' compensation. Consequently, associates must bill very high hours to receive bonuses and to be considered for advancement to partnership. Even partners (at least non-rainmaking partners) must maintain high rates of billable hours or risk being pruned.

---

73. "Some people are of the mindset that if you get rid of the other associates around you, you have a better chance of making partner," reported a Chicago lawyer who said that "associate backstabbing was rampant" at his former firm. Stephanie Francis Ward, Betrayals of the Trade, ABA J., Aug. 2003, at 34 (also reporting some associates try to steal other associates' clients; e.g., male associates invite female associates' male clients to go on all-male hunting trips).

74. Law firms regularly raise the number of hours that they demand from their associates, but they almost never lower them. One survey found that between 1999 and 2000, 28 percent of law firms raised their billable hour targets, while not a single firm reduced them. NALP Foundation for Research and Education, Beyond the Bidding Wars: A Survey of Associate Attrition, Departure Destinations, and Workplace Incentives 35 (2000).

In order to bill 2000 hours a year, most lawyers need to be physically present at the office for close to 3000 hours.[75] Given a thirty-minute commute each way, a 3000-hour work year requires the lawyer to be out of the house and away from family or friends around eleven hours per day, six days a week, fifty weeks a year. That means leaving home at 8:00, returning at 7:00, Monday to Saturday. Want to work half day on Saturday? Then return home at 8:30 or 9:00 during the week or work Sundays. In any event, there will be many late-nighters or Sundays at work; time demands are erratic and unpredictable and can change on an hourly basis. If the firm requires associates (or the associates drive themselves) to bill 2400 hours per year, which is not unusual, add on at least another two hours per day, six days a week. The destructive consequences on personal health and on family or relationships from working anything like these kinds of hours are painfully obvious. They are particularly unbearable for lawyers with child-care responsibilities. Many lawyers report that they see only their offices, their cars, and their beds. There is little time for a personal life, let alone a lifestyle.

Not every law firm associate feels exploited by the long hours. Many young lawyers in big firms believe that long hours at work are an acceptable tradeoff for the stunningly high compensation they receive, especially given the crushing levels of debt that burden most law school graduates. Many believe that young lawyers in smaller firms or young people in other professions (such as medicine) work just as hard but get paid much less.

Traditionally, big firms offered additional payoffs beyond generous compensation and lavish fringe benefits. For example, at large law firms, associates can do interesting and challenging work of a sort that small firm lawyers may never encounter. Big firms are supposed to offer excellent training and mentoring. . . . There is the sense that big firm lawyers will work as part of a team; good friends and colleagues will toil together. Those associates who want to depart or who are not made partners could count on the firm to provide them with excellent lateral mobility. They could move to partnership at a smaller firm or an in-house position with the firm's clients.

However, these traditional benefits of big firm practice appear to be withering away in the contemporary environment. Every possible minute of every working day must translate directly into billable hours and money, so partners at many firms do not have time to provide training and mentoring to all or most of their young associates, even assuming they have the inclination and the skills to do so. Because clients will not pay for time spent on training, mentoring, or tag-alongs, such time becomes nonbillable. Firms may only provide training and mentoring to associates perceived as running on the partnership track. Colleagueship seems elusive in the stressful, intensely competitive, totally exhausting environment of the big firms. Some firms provide excellent

---

75. [Asimow's footnote 165.] By general consensus, most lawyers need to work (or at least be away from home) about three hours to bill two, given the substantial nonbillable claims on their time such as client development, associate recruiting, bar association activity, personal calls or errands, keeping up with the law, training, lunch or coffee breaks, schmoozing with colleagues, and so on [citing studies].

training and maintain a more traditional, friendly, and supportive atmosphere for their associates. Others, concerned with high attrition rates, have tried to improve associate life style with casual dress codes or tolerating work from home. Nevertheless, the accounts available to us indicate that the work life of many associates in big city megafirms is quite miserable.

Another traditional element of associate life in big firms was the tournament of partnership.[76] As described by Galanter and Palay, the rules of this tournament are assumed to be fair and transparent. The winners of the tournament could anticipate a lavishly rewarded and highly secure law firm partnership. The losers would at least understand that they had lost out in a fair competition.

Tournament theory, however, is in need of significant modification. Wilkins and Gulati[77] explain that law firms engage in a system of tracking the most promising associates based on the quality of work during their early associate years. They also give preference to associates that graduated from the better law schools or who have the best connections. Those fortunate enough to be placed on the partnership track receive most of the interesting work. The boring but necessary work is allocated to those identified as probable losers in the partnership competition. Because of such favoritism, associates perceive that the rules of the tournament are opaque. They soon realize that success depends less on hard work and dedication and more on nurturing relationships with senior lawyers.

### Why do large law firms require lawyers to work such long hours?

One theory is that law firms get into "bidding wars" for a small number of highly credentialed law school graduates. This means they have to pay really high salaries. To generate the income needed to pay such salaries and to generate profits to pay lavish partner salaries, they encourage or require lawyers to bill vast numbers of hours per year. The following article explains this phenomenon.

## Patrick J. Schiltz, On Being a Happy, Healthy, and Ethical Member of an Unhappy, Unhealthy, and Unethical Profession

52 Vand. L. Rev. 871, 898-903 (1999)

[Patrick J. Schiltz, a former law clerk to Justice Antonin Scalia, worked as an associate and then as a partner in a large law firm before resigning to begin teaching at Notre Dame Law School. He is currently the St. Thomas More Professor at the University of St. Thomas School of Law. Although we can reprint only short excerpts from his article here, we recommend the full article to law students considering the pros and cons of different types of law practice.]

---

76. [Authors' footnote.] Marc Galanter & Thomas Palay, Tournament of Lawyers: The Transformation of the Big Law Firm (U. Chi. Press 1991).

77. [Authors' footnote.] David B. Wilkins and G. Mitu Gulati, Reconceiving the Tournament of Lawyers: Tracking, Seeding, and Information Control in the Internal Labor Markets of Elite Law Firms, 84 Va. L. Rev. 1581 (1998).

*Professor Patrick J. Schiltz*

[B]ig firms do get into bidding wars — all the time — and, as a result, the salaries of first year associates get pushed to extraordinary levels. . . . As the salaries of first year associates go up, the salaries of senior associates must rise to keep pace. After all, no sixth year associate wants to be paid less than a first year associate. And as the salaries of senior associates go up, the salaries of junior partners must rise to keep pace. After all, no junior partner wants to be paid less than a senior associate. And, of course, as the salaries of junior partners go up, so must the salaries of senior partners.

How do firms pay for this ever-spiraling increase in salaries? In theory, they have two options: First, they can raise billing rates. Instead of charging, say, $100 per hour for the time of first year associates, they can charge $115, and instead of charging, say, $225 per hour for the time of junior partners, they can charge $250. Second, they can bill more hours. Instead of demanding 2000 billable hours per year from first year associates, they can demand 2100, and instead of demanding 1900 billable hours per year from junior partners, they can demand 1950.

In reality, though, firms have only one option: They have to bill more hours. The market for lawyers' services has become intensely competitive. As the number of lawyers has soared, competition for clients has become ferocious. Clients insist on getting good work at low hourly rates. They also insist that lawyers minimize the amount of time that they devote to each file to hold down costs. If clients do not get what they want, they will move their business to one of the thousands of other lawyers who are chomping at the bit to get it. Raising billing rates to pay for spiraling salaries is simply not much of an option for most firms. As a result, firms get the extra money to pay for the spiraling salaries in the only way they can: They bill more hours. Everyone has to work harder to pay for the higher salaries. . . .

I am leaving out one wrinkle — an important wrinkle that you should know about if you are contemplating joining a large law firm (or a firm that acts like a large law firm). The partners of a big firm have a third option for making more money. This option involves what big firm partners euphemistically refer to as "leverage." I like to call it "the skim." Richard Abel calls it "exploitation."[78] The person being exploited is you. . . .

At some firms, profits per partner approach or exceed $2 million per year, meaning that some partners are paid more than $2 million (because profits are not divided equally among partners). Not one of these highly paid partners could personally generate the billings necessary to produce such an income. Even a partner billing 2000 hours per year at $500 per hour, "both of which figures [according to Professor Abel] lie at the outer limits of physical and economic possibility," would generate only $1 million in revenue, "a good

---

78. [Authors' footnote.] Richard L. Abel, American Lawyers 193 (Oxford U. Press).

proportion of which would be consumed by overhead." So how can big firm partners take home double or triple or quadruple the revenue they generate? They can do so because partner compensation reflects not only the revenue that partners themselves generate, but also "the surplus value law firms extract from associates." Alex Johnson puts the point more dramatically: "The blood and sweat of new associates line the pockets of the senior members of the firm."

Basically, what happens is that big firms "buy associates' time 'wholesale and sell it retail.'" Here is how it works: As a new associate in a large firm, you will be paid about one-third of what you bring into the firm. If you bill, say, 2000 hours at $100 per hour, you will generate $200,000 in revenue for your firm. About a third of that — $70,000 or so — will be paid to you. Another third will go toward paying the expenses of the firm. And the final third will go into the pockets of the firm's partners. Firms make money off associates. That is why it's in the interests of big firms to hire lots of associates and to make very few of them partners. The more associates there are, the more profits for the partners to split, and the fewer partners there are, the bigger each partner's share.

After you make partner (if you make partner — your chances will likely be about one in ten), you will still be exploited, although somewhat less. You may take home 40% or so of what you bring into the firm as a junior partner. Your take will gradually increase with your seniority. At some point, you will reach equilibrium — that is, you will take home roughly what you bring into the firm, minus your share of the firm's overhead. And, if you stick with it long enough, some day you will reach Big Firm Nirvana: You will take home more than you bring into the firm (minus your share of overhead). You will become the exploiter instead of the exploited.

It should not surprise you that, generally speaking, the bigger the firm, the more the leverage. . . . As a result of the disparity in leverage between big and small firms, partners in big firms make dramatically more money than partners in small firms. . . . The stark relationship between firm size and partnership compensation cannot be explained by differences in hourly rates, hours billed, or quality of legal services. Rather, it results from the skim.

This, then, is life in the big firm: It is in the interests of clients that senior partners work inhuman hours, year after year, and constantly be anxious about retaining their business. And it is in the interests of senior partners that junior partners work inhuman hours, year after year, and constantly be anxious about retaining old clients and attracting new clients. And it is in the interests of junior partners that senior associates work inhuman hours, year after year, and constantly be anxious about retaining old clients and attracting new clients and making partner. And most of all, it is in everyone's interests that the newest members of the profession — the junior associates — be willing to work inhuman hours, year after year, and constantly be anxious about everything — about retaining old clients and attracting new clients and making partner and keeping up their billable hours. The result? Long hours, large salaries, and one of the unhealthiest and unhappiest professions on earth.

### Are these firms' associates actually unhappy?

In 1997, the Boston Bar Association studied the relative professional satisfaction of lawyers in various types of jobs. It concluded that "most associates are overwhelmed by the tension between the typical large firm's billable hourly requirements and the need to devote additional time to develop one's practice, generate business, attend seminars, and participate in firm administrative matters."[79]

The conclusion that junior lawyers' incomes are inversely related to their happiness is echoed in several other reports. Among law graduates of the University of Michigan, for example, "lawyers who make the most money are the least happy."[80] The Michigan alumni were surveyed five years after graduation about their levels of satisfaction. Among those at firms of over 50 lawyers, 54 percent of those the classes of 1978 and 1979 rated their level of satisfaction either "1" or "2" on a 7-point scale, levels that Michigan's analyst for this data, Professor David Chambers, interpreted as "quite satisfied." Of the same group in the classes of 1990 and 1991, only 30 percent said they were quite satisfied.[81] While even 54 percent may seem like a low number, the decline suggests that something has gone very wrong in the work lives of large firm lawyers.

Some people might expect that those who go to elite law schools can get jobs where they will be happy. A survey of Yale alumni, like the Michigan study, suggests that these lawyers may indeed be able to earn high incomes, but that happiness is a different story. Five years after graduating, 72 percent of Yale Law School graduates employed by large firms earned more than $150,000. Yet only 24 percent of them report being very satisfied. "Law firm respondents cite billable hour expectations, lack of control over work, and poor professional development opportunities as reasons for their lack of satisfaction. As one law firm practitioner said, 'Don't assume you can balance your life with work at a law firm. They take everything you can give.'" In contrast, 57 percent of the Yale respondents in business and 58 percent in public service report being very satisfied, despite much lower incomes.[82]

Schiltz reports that lawyers' unhappiness is not merely a subjective phenomenon. He summarizes a study of workers in 104 occupations done by Johns Hopkins researchers, which concluded that the incidence of major depressive disorder was higher for lawyers than among workers in any of

---

79. Boston B. Assn., Task Force on Professional Fulfillment, Expectation, Reality, and Recommendations for Change 9 (1997).

80. Tina King, Survey Shows Money Can't Buy Lawyer Happiness, Ind. Law., Feb. 17, 1999, at 11.

81. Patrick Schiltz, On Being a Happy, Healthy, and Ethical Member of an Unhappy, Unhealthy, and Unethical Profession, 52 Vand. L. Rev. 871, 882 (1999); see also e-mail from Professor David Chambers to Philip G. Schrag (Oct. 30, 2003) (stating that "1" and "2" equate to "quite satisfied").

82. Kelly J. Voight, Class of 1996 Fifth Year Career Development Survey Results, Yale L. Rep. (Winter 2002). The survey produced a very high (55 percent) response rate. Forty-one percent of the 99 respondents worked for large firms; 35 percent were in public service, 16 percent in business, and 8 percent in academia.

the other 103 occupations.[83] Also, lawyers have a much higher rate of obsessive-compulsiveness (21 percent for male lawyers, 15 percent for female lawyers) than the general population (1.4 percent).[84] Nearly 20 percent of lawyers abuse alcohol (twice the rate in the general population).[85] "The divorce rate for female lawyers was twice the divorce rate for female doctors,"[86] and the suicide rate for white male lawyers is double the rate for other white males.[87]

### Are senior lawyers happier?

Recent literature suggests that senior lawyers in large firms are not much better off, despite earning vastly more money. Lawyers in law firms used to spend their whole careers at the firms at which they started. Their partnerships were lifelong relationships. The idea that a partner could be fired from a firm was unthinkable only a few decades ago. But in the last 20 years, all this has changed. Many firms are now managed by younger lawyers who are more concerned than their seniors with increasing profits. Law partners often pack their bags to move on to more lucrative arrangements at new firms. Law firms often terminate the employment of lawyers who have not generated enough income for the firm. Some of the lawyers who may lose out are those who spend more time doing pro bono work or some other community service work and those who are more attentive to their families.

Professor Marc Galanter has elaborated on this trend:

> Within the large firm sector the 1970s saw the dissolution of the world of assured tenure, infrequent lateral movement, and enduring retainer relationships with loyal, long-term clients. In its place rose a world of rapid growth, mergers and breakups, overt competition, aggressive marketing, attorney movement from firm to firm, fears of defection, and pervasive insecurity. . . . Partners . . . are expected to bring in business as well as to contribute to firm revenues by billing long hours. As firms accumulate ever-larger cadres of partners, there is increasing pressure on lawyers over fifty, apart from rainmakers and a few specialists and superstars, to make way for younger partners and eventually to leave. . . . As with professional athletes, there are real possibilities of late-career downward movement. . . . By the early 1980s, there were reports of partners having their prerogatives or shares reduced or even being "de-equitized" or "departnerized" or pushed off the iceberg altogether. . . . A 1991 survey of large law firms found that 60 percent of those that responded had asked partners to leave during the previous eighteen months. . . . In such a volatile atmosphere, collegiality gives way to distrust.[88]

---

83. Schiltz, supra n. 81, at 874.

84. Id. at 876.

85. Seventeen percent of lawyers in a North Carolina study admitted to drinking three to five alcoholic beverages a day. N.C. B. Assn., Report of the Quality of Life Task Force and Recommendations 4 (June 1991). Schiltz, supra n. 81, at 876-877 collects other sources with consistent findings.

86. Schiltz, supra n. 81, at 878.

87. Id. at 880.

88. Marc Galanter, Old and In the Way: The Coming Demographic Transformation of the Legal Profession and Its Implications for the Provision of Legal Services, 1999 Wisc. L. Rev. 1081, 1094-1096.

Lawrence J. Fox, a very successful and well-respected senior partner, notes with obvious dismay that

> Partners are victims of a new mentality that asks not what contributions they have made during their careers, but what they have done for the firm this year, and which values a migratory lawyer with a sexy satchel of business over a loyal partner who has dedicated a lifetime to the enterprise. And, like the devastating effect of capital punishment on the executioner, the result of this new trend is not only exile for the departing partners, but an overwhelming sense of remorse and regret among the "lucky" ones who retain their positions, prompted in part by the concern that the next round of down-sizing might send them packing as well.[89]

Law firm associates are well aware that their chances of becoming partners at large firms are poor, and that even if they do, their professional lives are not likely to be improved significantly by the advance.[90] Many associates no longer want to become partners. In a major survey by NALP, many law firm associates "indicated that partnership was either not a priority or that it was not a goal to which they aspired.... The disillusionment is not just with the life and lot of an associate but with partnership that is its reward."[91] As a result, associates have been leaving large law firms in droves. In firms with more than 250 lawyers, 56 percent of new associates leave their employer firms within the first four years.[92] The percentage who leave large firms after only a few years is even higher for women and minorities.[93] Although U.S. law firms hire equal numbers of men and women, firms have an average of 63 white male partners and an average of 13 female partners, according to a recent study by the Equal Employment Opportunity Commission.[94]

---

89. Lawrence J. Fox, Money Didn't Buy Happiness, 100 Dick. L. Rev. 531, 534 (1996).

90. One authority suggests that there are barely any differences between most partners and associates. "[Except for a small subgroup of partners who control a large firm], differences ... are minimal. The partner has a monthly drawing account and a share of net profits at the end of the year. The associate has a monthly salary and a bonus at the end of the year. Both can be fired. On termination a partner receives whatever share he has of partnership capital.... An associate receives termination pay.... Yet in law firms the rigid difference in status, inherited from an earlier epoch, continues in form.... [A]ssociates may feel they are like squeezed oranges, to be thrown away after their juice has been extracted [while the] nonmanagement partner may feel apprehensive about the reality of his status...." Macklin Fleming, Lawyers, Money, and Success: The Consequences of the Dollar Obsession 126 (Quorum 1997).

91. NALP Foundation for Research and Education, Keeping the Keepers: Strategies for Associate Retention in Times of Attrition 14 (1998).

92. NALP, supra n. 74, at 23.

93. NALP, supra n. 91, at 54-55. The gender differential held true in the Foundation's later study. NALP, supra n. 74. The Foundation apparently did not include ethnicity data when it published its updated study.

94. Kimberly Blanton, Few Women Reach Top at Law Firms: Glass Ceilings, Family Duties Seen Taking Toll, Boston Globe, Oct. 24, 2003, at D2. This same study showed that U.S. firms had an average of only one African American partner, one Latino, and one Asian. Id.

### Is there still discrimination and sexual harassment in law firms?

Researchers with the American Bar Association have documented continuing problems in both areas. In all sectors of private practice, from sole practitioners through law firm partners, women "feel much more dissatisfied than their male colleagues."[95] The ABA reported six reasons for the difference:

■ More women than men (30 percent to 21 percent) report not having a good chance to advance and that advancement is not determined by the quality of work.

■ More women than men (33 percent to 28 percent) report that political intrigue and backbiting abounds in their firms.

■ More women than men (21 percent to 15 percent) report that the work atmosphere is not warm and personal.

■ More women than men (61 percent to 55 percent) report not having enough time for themselves.

■ More women than men (13 percent to 7 percent) report that they are not respected by superiors.

■ Women are paid less for the same work. For example, in 1989, 11 percent of male junior associates were paid more than $75,000, but only 3 percent of female junior associates were in this salary group. Forty-seven percent of male partners but only 33 percent of female partners were paid more than $100,000.[96]

Firms' different treatment of women begins at the moment of their first contact with law firms: the job interview. Thirty-five percent of female law students but only 18 percent of male students are asked about their marital status or marriage plans. Twenty-four percent of women but only 6 percent of men are asked about their plans for having children.[97]

Sexual harassment of women in law firms is also common, despite decades of federal and state legislation and public education aimed at prevention. Twenty-six percent of female lawyers report unwanted sexual teasing from superiors, and 20 percent report unwanted sexual looks, gestures, touching, or cornering by superiors. Men confirm these reports: 75 percent of male

---

95. ABA Young Lawyers Division, The State of the Legal Profession 1990, at 54 (1991).

96. Id. at 64. A separate set of data, from California, confirms these differences. Among lawyers in practice between 10 and 19 years, 53 percent of males but only 35 percent of females and 31 percent of minorities earned more than $100,000. Nelson, supra n. 65, at 380. NALP's extensive statistics on starting salaries do include comparisons across gender and race but do not break down that data by size of firm. Among all law firms, large and small, the median starting salary for men graduating in 2001 was $60,000 and for women, $51,000. NALP, supra n. 66, at 58. Median starting salaries also vary by race: Asian Americans/Pacific Islanders had the highest median ($85,000). This figure was $55,000 for Caucasians and $52,000 for African Americans. Id. at 57. These numbers may not represent discrimination within any particular firm or even any practice setting. For example, a higher proportion of Asian Americans may have decided to apply for or have been accepted for jobs in the large firms that pay the highest starting salaries.

97. Id. at 67.

junior associates have observed at least five types of sexual harassment of women in their offices within a two-year period.[98]

One scholar reports that "gender and race continue to matter for lawyers. . . . Women in high pressure, corporate practices report being penalized for taking maternity leave. Many women have withdrawn from corporate firms to avoid such tensions. Others have foregone marriage and motherhood, in part because they saw the demands as irreconcilable."[99]

## PROBLEM 9-1  THE REFORMING PARTNER

You have just become a partner at a large firm in which the compensation levels and working atmosphere are similar to those described in the preceding pages. Your firm is respected in your community and represents most of the large corporations in town. You were paid more than $300,000 last year, but you worked so hard that you rarely saw your family. You know that many associates in the firm are stressed and unhappy because they have even less leisure time than you do. More than half of them leave within four years after they arrive. You once mentioned this fact to one of the senior partners. He replied, "That's as it should be. Sure, we've invested some money in training them, but that cost is less than the salary difference between first-year associates and fifth-year associates." Clearly, not everyone at the firm shares your opinion that something should be changed. Nevertheless, you are considering making a proposal to your partners that something should be done to make working conditions more pleasant for all of the lawyers. What might you propose?

## PROBLEM 9-2  THE JOB INTERVIEW

You are a recently married female in your second year of law school. When you graduate, you will owe $95,000 on your student loans, and you need to contribute to the medical care of your elderly parents. The solution to these problems seems to be to work for Challam & Tate, the largest and best-known law firm in your city. The starting salary is $120,000, and bonuses to valuable associates are reputed to exceed $40,000. The firm has invited you to interview for a summer job. Nearly all of the firm's postgraduation hiring is done from among the firm's former summer associates.

You know what large law firms are like and you are going down this career path with your eyes open. You don't expect to spend more than

---

98. Id. at 67-68.
99. Nelson, supra n. 65, at 380.

three or four years with a large firm. You expect that you will be ready to start a family in a few years.

The interviewer is a female junior partner. She appears to be in her late thirties. She asks some standard questions, such as why you want to work at Challam & Tate and what areas of law interest you the most. Near the end of the interview, she asks, "Are you planning to start a family in the next few years?"

What will you say?

## 2. Small firms

### a. Salaries and attrition

Large firms have gotten more research attention than small firms, so we know less about the benefits and burdens of working as a lawyer in a small law firm. As we explain above, the compensation scales are lower at most small firms than at large firms. The NALP figures show a steady reduction in national median (and mean) starting salaries as the size of law firms declines.[100] Attrition rates of new associates are about the same at small and large firms for associates during their first three years. For fourth-year associates, attrition rates at small firms are slightly lower; this is also true for seventh-year associates.[101] This lower rate could indicate greater satisfaction, or it could reflect fewer opportunities for exit.

### b. Setting one's own schedule

*Professor Carroll Seron*

Relatively little has been written about lawyers' work lives in small firms. The principal work is sociologist Carroll Seron's study based on in-depth interviews with 102 lawyers in firms ranging from 1 to 15 lawyers in the New York metropolitan area.[102] Seron looked at several aspects of small-firm practice. One of the major subjects of her attention was how professional life in these firms affected the lawyers and their families. She learned that lawyers in small firms, like those in large firms, struggle to find enough time for personal and family time. For some of the lawyers who were setting up practices, the conflict between work and family life may have been even more severe than for their large-firm counterparts. As one male lawyer reported:

My typical day when I first started practicing. . . . I'd be up at eight o'clock. I'd go into the court here in Hauppage [about 75 miles from Manhattan].

---

100. NALP, supra n. 66, at 30.

101. Forty-eight percent of associates in firms smaller than 50 lawyers, as opposed to 56 percent in large firms, leave within four years. After seven years, 71 percent as opposed to 79 percent have left their firms. NALP, supra n. 74, at 23.

102. Carroll Seron, The Business of Practicing Law (Temple U. Press 1996).

Cover the calendar. Drive into the city, because you had to drive; you can't take the trains. . . . I'd be home at two-thirty in the morning. . . . [I hardly] saw the kids in the first five years of practice. . . . Sometimes I wondered how I *had* kids in the first five years. After that when [I moved my practice to my hometown] I was coming home after a twelve-hour day. It was great. [Now I work] twelve-, fourteen-hour day[s with] no commuting [though my wife cares for the home and my four children and I bring home a briefcase of work that I may or may not do when I get home].[103]

Many small-firm lawyers reported that they were satisfied with their professional lives, despite 12- to 14-hour workdays, because a small-firm lawyer "can set [her] own hours — even if those hours turn out to be extremely demanding."[104] But Seron's interviews reveal that married male lawyers can put in those long workdays because their wives do nearly all the housework and child care. Seventy-one percent of the married men in these firms worked "expanded" professional hours, and 87 percent of those respondents did less than equal child rearing.[105] Seron's concludes that "work committed males" in small firms selected careers that "offered an opportunity to work independently and to set one's own hours" but that they "enjoy a support system that permits them to bring this same mind-set to the task demands at home."[106]

By contrast, among the married female lawyers who worked expanded hours, their husbands did not take over at home. Seventy-one percent of these women did most of the housework.[107] Seron concluded that a "female commitment to professionalism . . . includes overtime at the workplace in conjunction with a full-time job at home as well as affective demands to care for a family's well being."[108] In other words, women working in small firms risked having to work the equivalent of at least two jobs.

Not surprisingly, the small-firm attorneys who were least stressed by the conflicting demands of home and work were those who were not married or living with partners. They too had very long workdays "but they did not convey a rushed or harried quality" and they built relaxation into their days. One single female practitioner reported, for example, that "she does have time for 'personal things' — reading, watching TV, working in the garden, something like that."[109]

Although small-firm life may be different for men and men, small firms may offer greater satisfactions and opportunities than big firms. Professor Schiltz lists nine such advantages:

---

103. Id. at 31.

104. Id.

105. Id. at 33. In fact, among the 30 married male respondents who worked expanded hours, 13 of their spouses did all of the housework and child care. Id. at 34.

106. Id. at 36.

107. Id. at 34. Only four women in the study had children and worked expanded hours. Two of them did all of the child care. Id.

108. Id. at 38.

109. Id. at 39.

**Advantages of Small Firm Practice**

1. Lawyers are closer to their colleagues and have a better chance of obtaining good mentoring.
2. There is a greater chance of becoming a partner, because there are fewer associates per partner.
3. To a greater extent, small firms allow more flexible work schedules.
4. The attrition rate is lower.
5. Small firms have more freedom to choose their clients.
6. Young lawyers get substantial responsibility for cases sooner.
7. New lawyers have more client contact.
8. Small firms demand fewer billable hours. (The ABA's 1990 study found that only 25% of firms with 4-9 lawyers had written or unwritten billable hours requirements, compared with 78% of firms with more than 200 lawyers.)
9. Surveys show that small firm lawyers are happier with their careers.[110]

Schiltz, who worked only in a large firm, may err in thinking that the grass is greener in small firms. The ABA noted in 1990 that

> in the past six years, the extent of lawyer dissatisfaction has increased through-out the profession. It is now reported in significant numbers by lawyers in all positions — partners as well as junior associates. It is now present in firms of all sizes, not just the largest and smallest firms. This increased dissatisfaction is directly caused by a deterioration of the lawyer workplace, by the increasing number of lawyers who have experienced negative work environments. In particular, the amount of time lawyers have for themselves and their families has become an issue of major concern for many lawyers.[111]

## c. Bringing in business

Small-firm lawyers always have to think about bringing in business. As one lawyer explained to Carroll Seron, "In any small firm . . . you join what I call the animal clubs. You join the Elks. . . . In my case it was the Jaycees and the B'nai Brith and the local Democratic Party. One purpose of this activity is to get client referrals from other professionals." Another lawyer told Seron, "I do more socializing with people who might send me referrals, such as accountants [than with former clients, who are also a source of referrals]. . . . I [get a third of my referrals from other attorneys because] lots of attorneys don't want to handle matrimonial work." As Seron puts it, "club activities are an extension of some friendship networks for men and, in turn, evolve into client-getting resources."[112]

## d. Promotion in small firms

Schiltz observed that because small firms have fewer associates per partner, the prospect of partnership should be better in a small firm than in a large firm.

---

110. Schiltz, supra n. 81, at 940.

111. ABA Young Lawyers Division, supra n. 95, at 81.

112. Seron, supra n. 102, at 52-55. Seron reports that female attorneys are less likely to view business-getting as part of their jobs. Id. at 56.

However, the small-firm associates interviewed by Seron didn't see it that way. Instead, associates at these firms "view their work as training and preparation for setting up their own practices. . . . [A]ssociates in small firms *may* become partners, but there are no cues, no time frames, no ground rules, no clear expectations."[113]

### e. Other features of small-firm life

Lawyers in small firms tend to spend more time with clients than do large-firm lawyers. The lawyers in Seron's study emphasized the importance of social skills in their work. One reported, "It's definitely business and social acumen as opposed to legal knowledge [that makes a difference with clients]. It's *not* legal knowledge! It's people."[114] In a practice that depends on personal relationships, clients make demands on the lawyers' time. Some clients call often to insist that their lawyers "be more aggressive and move the case, . . . keep an eye on the bottom line, or . . . sympathize with the emotional turmoil caused by a legal battle." Clients also increasingly insist on speedy results at a low price.[115] The lawyers' days are "driven by the demands of clients who want the work done, are scared, or have questions that compel answers."[116]

Unlike their counterparts in large law firms, most lawyers in small firms do not have fixed hourly rates. Instead, they negotiate a fee individually with each client. Often the client's ability to pay affects the lawyer's decision about how much to charge.[117]

### f. Urban versus rural practice

Seron's study was based in New York City and its suburbs. Sociologist Donald Landon studied 201 lawyers practicing in small firms in small Missouri towns in the 1980s. He found that

> the rural bar, by contrast [to solo practitioners in large cities] is generally content. When asked to identify the practice situation in which they would most like to find themselves, 87 percent selected "my current situation." When asked how satisfied they were with the community in which they were practicing, 71 percent indicated an unqualified yes. . . . [Many urban legal entrepreneurs] view the practice of law as more of a business than a profession. Many feel like parasites. Most feel that they are not respected by the public. They are at the bottom of a hierarchical order, and they know it. By contrast, morale among rural lawyers was found to be consistently high. . . . They saw their broad general practice as the standard by which professional performance should be measured. While many of their attitudes are self-serving, there was no apparent dissatisfaction regarding their place in the professional system.[118]

---

113. Id. at 70-71 (emphasis in the original).
114. Id. at 112 (emphasis in the original).
115. Id. at 115.
116. Id. at 125.
117. Id. at 116-117.
118. Donald D. Landon, Country Lawyers: The Impact of Context on Professional Practice 62-63 (Praeger 1990). It should be noted that Landon's interviews took place in 1982 and 1983. The

## g. Gender bias in small firms

Apparently gender bias affects women in small firms much as it does in large firms. A careful sociological study found that the "two practice settings from which women most often move (large law firms and solo/small firms) require significantly more hours worked than the two settings in which women are overrepresented (government practice and internal counsel positions)," probably because of the "competing demands of practice and family." It turned out that "work-family tension had a significant negative effect on the odds of making partner [in a firm], but only for women. We also found that having children significantly increases the odds of being a partner in a law firm, but separate models for men and women reveal that this is significant and positive only for men."[119]

## h. The future of small firms

Work in small firms may be less pressured than in large firms, or at least, lawyers may feel less distressed if they sense that they are creating their own pressures rather than having double- and triple-time obligations foisted upon them. And partners in small firms may be less likely to push each other into early retirement than partners in large firms. However, the future of small firms as a whole may not be promising. Professor Marc Galanter warns that even if demand for the services of small-firm lawyers continues to grow at a moderate rate, small firms may not do so well. He notes that every year, the law schools produce large numbers of additional lawyers, most of whom go to small firms where they compete for the business of a limited number of clients. As a result, small-firm lawyers have experienced a decline in "real income" (earnings adjusted for inflation) for several decades.[120]

Professor Leslie Levin of the University of Connecticut explains that lawyers in small firms still "occupy the mid-to-lower rungs of the legal profession's hierarchy." They "tend to receive significantly less income and substantially more [professional] discipline than their big firm colleagues."[121]

More recently, an article in the *ABA Journal* warned that "midsize firms" (defined as those of about 25 lawyers in relatively small cities such as Kansas City and 50 to 200 lawyers in cities like Chicago) "are becoming an endangered species" that "may not be able to match either the multiskilled resources of large firms or the specialized focus of boutique operations." It quoted the managing partner of a midsize Chicago firm who believed that "what's

---

ABA's studies suggest that, in general, dissatisfaction among lawyers increased between 1984 and 1990. ABA Young Lawyers Division, supra n. 95, at 81. It is not known whether this trend, occurring after Landon collected his data, also affected rural lawyers.

119. Kathleen E. Hull & Robert L. Nelson, Assimilation, Choice, or Constraint? Testing Theories of Gender Differences in the Careers of Lawyers, 79 Soc. Forces 229, 252 (2000).

120. Galanter, supra n. 88, at 1099-1100.

121. Leslie C. Levin, Preliminary Reflections on the Professional Development of Solo and Small Law Firm Practitioners, 70 Fordham L. Rev. 847-848 (2001).

going on with midsize firms is a shakeout that isn't going to leave a lot of firms left doing the kind of work they want to do."[122]

### i. Small firms and the Internet

The Internet is changing the nature of small-firm practice, notes Levin. At many firms, lawyers work at home and communicate with clients and with other lawyers through e-mail.[123] This allows lawyers to be available to children and other family members, and allows those lawyers more personal time and flexibility that they do not have if they spend 50 or more hours a week at the office.

The telecommuting lawyer may experience some professional disadvantages, however. Professor Levin urges that "the abbreviated and immediate nature of e-mail communication discourages more nuanced discussion about client matters and more expansive advice giving. . . . Virtual firms reduce the opportunities for strong mentoring relationships [and] opportunities to convey a clear and consistent ethical culture."[124] No doubt the loss of daily direct contact with colleagues would result in some loss in relationship and communication. On the other hand, the scholars quoted earlier in this chapter have noted that even when they practically live at the office, lawyers don't talk to each other nearly as much as they once did because of pressure to bill so many efficient hours. Furthermore, it is quite possible that some lawyers' interactions might be more thorough, careful, and nuanced by e-mail than in person. Some people actually think more clearly when they are writing, so a written conversation might produce higher quality ideas than an oral one. In any event, the Internet undoubtedly will have a massive impact on the structure and quality of law practice in the twenty-first century. It may be too early to see all that might be lost or gained by this development.

## 3. Government and nonprofit organizations

About 13 percent of all lawyers, and a similar percentage of lawyers in their first jobs (not including clerkships),[125] work for governments and nonprofit organizations. Because government and nonprofit jobs are so varied, it is not possible to describe the working conditions of lawyers in any depth. There are, however, several narrative accounts written by public sector lawyers.[126]

---

122. Martha Neil, Caught in the Middle, ABA J., July 2003, at 37-41 (quoting Jerry H. Biederman, managing partner of Chicago's Neal, Gerber & Eisenberg).

123. While neither of the authors of this book is a small-firm lawyer, we note that while we worked on this chapter, one of us worked primarily at the office and the other worked at home, mainly to be available to our children. (Can you guess which author had which role?) We used e-mail to exchange drafts and edit one another's work.

124. Levin, supra n. 121, at 899.

125. The data on initial jobs appears in NALP, supra n. 66, at 12.

126. See, e.g., Milner Ball, The Word and the Law 7-72 (U. Chi. Press 1993) (short profiles of 7 public interest lawyers); Serving the Public: A Job Search Guide 15-31 (14th ed., Harv. L. Sch. 2003)

These stories suggest that some lawyers obtain immense, daily satisfaction from legal work. Most of these stories involve lawyers who care about a cause or a particular type of client or work setting and who are willing to trade money for professional fulfillment. Here are two representative passages from the *Harvard Law School Handbook*:

> [At the National Center for Youth Law] I represent [clients who are 9 to 13 years old] in legal guardianship proceedings and assist in getting the financial support and social services that their relatives need to care for them. Such assistance can often mean the difference between a stable home with a relative or a long struggle in a foster home. . . . There has not been a day that I have regretted not working at a large, private law firm. It is nice that I do not need to find 2,100 billable hours somewhere under a stack of trade secret documents. Admittedly, I do not own the house I live in; I have not bought that Mercedes yet; I may never make $150,000 a year. On the other hand, I have not missed a loan payment; I still eat like a pig; and, damn, I'm happy. It is hard to believe that I wake up each morning and get paid for doing what I do.[127]
>
> Fresh from graduating and not yet sworn in to any bar, I began [my career] in the Tax Division, Criminal Enforcement Section [of the U.S. Department of Justice]. [As soon as I finished some work on my first case,] I was pulled onto a special Waco task force where the Criminal Division responded frantically to Congressional subpoenas and weighing executive privilege claims in a highly politicized atmosphere. And then I got sworn into the bar. A couple of weeks later I had my first trial while on detail to the Domestic Violence and Sex Offense Unit of the D.C. United States Attorney's office. With a caseload of over 200 matters, the trials came fast and furious. Early on I tried a child abuse case. . . . I am not sure if anything will compare to the feeling of winning this misdemeanor case: receiving the thanks of the children (including my own hand-drawn picture of Barney), their mother and grandmother, the defense attorney storming out saying "I never lose," and the competitive thrill of advocacy. . . . I took this job in part because of a belief in an ethic of public sacrifice over private gain. As it turns out, sacrifice has not been part of the equation as my nascent career has exceeded not only my expectations of working in the ominous "real world" but also, in truth, my imagination.[128]

# E. The ethical climate of the legal profession

In the preceding section of this chapter, we talked about what life is like for practicing lawyers — where they work, how hard they work, how much

---

(16 first-person narratives by public interest lawyers describing their jobs; includes two accounts of work as a prosecutor, one federal and one state).

127. Katina Ancar, in Serving the Public, supra n. 126, at 28-29.

128. John Carlin, id. at 30-31.

they earn, what they like and don't like about their professional lives. In this section, we focus on another dimension of lawyers' work lives — the ethical climate in legal organizations. As in the previous section, our primary focus is on private practice because most lawyers are in private practice and because more information is available about the ethical climate of private law firms.

One way to approach this question is to look at some examples of flagrant unethical conduct by lawyers (like the one discussed in the Reese's Leases problem in Chapter 2) and to ask: Do those stories represent "just a few bad apples" in the profession, or are those lawyers who get caught "the tip of an iceberg" of pervasive and egregious unethical conduct? The answer, of course, lies somewhere in between. It used to be thought that most unethical behavior by lawyers involved alcoholic or drug-addicted sole practitioners, and that the vast majority of lawyers were ethical Mr. Cleans. In recent decades, however, many senior government lawyers and leaders of fine law firms have been disciplined or prosecuted for gross unethical and criminal behavior.[129] Most lawyers really care about honesty, integrity, professionalism, public service, and compliance with legal and ethical rules. As more cases of unethical behavior have come to light, law firms and other organizations have instituted staff and structures to offer training, set policy, and provide guidance to lawyers on compliance with legal and ethical rules. Things may be getting worse, but they are also getting better.

Our primary concern in this text is with the types of unethical conduct that lawyers may encounter or be pressured into early in their years of practice. There is some evidence that the pressures for ever higher profits within many law firms may lead frequently to more subtle kinds of ethical improprieties. In some highly pressured work environments, lawyers may take more cases than they can handle competently or they may work on cases without doing the time-consuming work of interviewing, investigation, and legal research that could turn failure into success. Second, lawyers may experience pressures to pad clients' bills and even tacit approval from others in their firm for billing for more time than they actually worked, billing a different client than the one for whom the work was done, or working extra hours just to be able to bill for them.[130] Third, lawyers who are competing to obtain clients sometimes have a hard time turning anyone away, and some clients pressure lawyers to help them to engage in illegal or immoral conduct. Finally, lawyers may neglect clients' cases or engage in financial misconduct because the lawyers become addicted to alcohol or other substances.

---

129. See the descriptions of several major thefts and frauds by large firm lawyers in Lisa G. Lerman, Blue Chip Bilking: Regulation of Billing and Expense Fraud by Lawyers, 12 Geo. J. Leg. Ethics 205 (1999). Likewise, during Watergate and since, some senior government lawyers engaged in fraud, theft, and other misconduct.

130. There are many variations on the kinds of billing and expense fraud that occur. Some are discussed in Chapter 7.

# 1. Mass Production

### PROBLEM 9-3  SMALL CLAIMS

You grew up poor, in the slums of this city, living in rat-infested housing. Your younger brother has a mental disability as a result of having eaten lead paint that was chipping off the walls. You can recall people coming to your door to take back the appliances that your mother had bought on credit when she missed a payment or two — your family's television set, living room furniture, and the refrigerator. You vowed that some day, you would do something to make life better for the people inhabiting the huge grim blocks of apartments of the inner city.

After years of work, you achieved this ambition. Now you practice law in a two-lawyer office in a large industrial city. You and your partner specialize in defending cases brought against low-income consumers who used credit to buy automobiles and other goods and services. The suits are brought against your clients in the city's small claims court, which hears cases involving less than $5,000.

You love serving the low-income community. In half of your cases, you charge no fees because the clients cannot afford to pay you at all. In the other half, you charge only what the client can pay, which is very little. Because you charge such low fees, to make a modest living, you represent a large number of clients. Usually you have an active case load of about 700 cases. After expenses but before taxes, you took home $39,000 last year, plus small gifts from grateful clients. The money barely supports your family. Your spouse stays home to take care of your three children, and you also help support your aging father.

You do the best you can for your clients. Most of them are undocumented immigrants. Their incomes are low enough to make them eligible for government-funded legal services, but Congress passed a law prohibiting the use of public funds for representation of undocumented immigrants.

Because of your large case load, you don't have enough time to do thorough fact investigation for most of your cases. Typically, a used car dealer suing one of your clients will assert that the defendant missed one or more payments, triggering an "acceleration" clause in the contract that made the entire balance come due. Your client's defense is usually that something is wrong with the car. Often you don't have time to determine exactly when payments were made, how many were missed, or to learn about all of the defects in the car. You do a good interview, but your answers mainly report what your clients say. There is no money to have cars evaluated mechanically by experts, nor to pay experts for the time that would be required to testify about the defects that were discovered.

Fortunately, the sellers' lawyers are usually in a rush because they also make their money from high volume legal work. The creditors' lawyers, to save time, usually offer to settle for half of what they claim they are owed. Discovery is allowed in small claims court, but usually neither you nor your opposing counsel request discovery. You haggle a little. Every case is settled. Your clients always consent to have judgment entered against them, usually for about half of the amount originally demanded in the lawsuit.

If you did a more careful job on each case, you would have to change the nature of your practice. You might be able to retool yourself as a commercial lawyer and represent small corporations in contract disputes. But you prefer to represent the people who most need services. If you did not assist them, your clients would have no legal representation. They would default in their lawsuits and would be ordered to pay the entire amount for which they were sued plus interest and attorneys' fees. They wouldn't be able to pay, so the creditors would seize part of their weekly wages until the entire amount was collected.

In conducting your practice in this way, are you doing anything wrong?

## 2. Pressure to pad bills

Professor Schiltz, whom we quoted earlier in this chapter, offers a dire warning that law firms pressure lawyers to exaggerate the number of hours that they work for clients so that they can meet the unrealistic billing quotas that the firms impose on them. Unlike some other portions of Schiltz's work, his views seem to follow from his own experience and observations rather than from published empirical studies. Perhaps the firms he has seen or heard about are not typical of the profession. We hope this is the case, but reports from other lawyers with whom we have talked tend to confirm Schiltz's worst fears.

### Patrick J. Schiltz, On Being a Happy, Healthy, and Ethical Member of an Unhappy, Unhealthy, and Unethical Profession

52 Vand. L. Rev. 871, 916-918 (1999)

Unethical lawyers do not start out being unethical; they start out just like you — as perfectly decent young men or women who have every intention of practicing law ethically. They do not become unethical overnight; they become unethical just as you will (if you become unethical) — a little bit at a time. And they do not become unethical by shredding incriminating documents or bribing jurors; they become unethical just as you are likely to — by cutting a corner here, by stretching the truth a bit there.

Let me tell you how you will start acting unethically: It will start with your time sheets. One day, not too long after you start practicing law, you will sit down at the end of a long, tiring day, and you just won't have much to show for your efforts in terms of billable hours. It will be near the end of the month. You will know that all of the partners will be looking at your monthly time report in a few days, so what you'll do is pad your time sheet just a bit.

Maybe you will bill a client for ninety minutes for a task that really took you only sixty minutes to perform. However, you will promise yourself that you will repay the client at the first opportunity by doing thirty minutes of work for the client for "free." In this way, you will be "borrowing," not "stealing."

And then what will happen is that it will become easier and easier to take these little loans against future work. And then, after a while, you will stop paying back these little loans. You will convince yourself that, although you billed for ninety minutes and spent only sixty minutes on the project, you did such good work that your client should pay a bit more for it. After all, your billing rate is awfully low, and your client is awfully rich.

And then you will pad more and more — every two minute telephone conversation will go down on the sheet as ten minutes, every three hour research project will go down with an extra quarter hour or so. You will continue to rationalize your dishonesty to yourself in various ways until one day you stop doing even that.

And, before long — it won't take you much more than three or four years — you will be stealing from your clients almost every day, and you won't even notice it.

You know what? You will also likely become a liar. A deadline will come up one day, and, for reasons that are entirely your fault, you will not be able to meet it. So you will call your senior partner or your client and make up a white lie for why you missed the deadline. And then you will get busy and a partner will ask whether you proofread a lengthy prospectus and you will say yes, even though you didn't. And then you will be drafting a brief and you will quote language from a Supreme Court opinion even though you will know that, when read in context, the language does not remotely suggest what you are implying it suggests. And then, in preparing a client for a deposition, you will help the client to formulate an answer to a difficult question that will likely be asked — an answer that will be "legally accurate" but that will mislead your opponent. And then you will be reading through a big box of your client's documents — a box that has not been opened in twenty years — and you will find a document that would hurt your client's case, but that no one except you knows exists, and you will simply "forget" to produce it in response to your opponent's discovery requests.

Do you see what will happen? After a couple years of this, you won't even notice that you are lying and cheating and stealing every day that you practice law. None of these things will seem like a big deal in itself — an extra fifteen minutes added to a time sheet here, a little white lie to cover a missed deadline there. But, after a while, your entire frame of reference will change. You will still be making dozens of quick, instinctive decisions every day, but those decisions, instead of reflecting the notions of right and wrong by which you conduct your personal life, will instead reflect the set of values by which you will conduct your professional life — a set of values that embodies not what is right or wrong, but what is profitable, and what you can get away with. The system will have succeeded in replacing your values with the system's values, and the system will be profiting as a result.

Does this happen to every big firm lawyer? Of course not. It's all a matter of degree. The culture in some big firms is better than in others. . . . The big firm at which I practiced was as decent and humane as a big firm can be. Similarly, some big firm lawyers have better values than others. I owe a lot to a partner who sacrificed hundreds of hours of his time and tens of thousands of dollars of income to act as a mentor to me and to many other young lawyers like me. At the same time, you should not underestimate the likelihood that you will practice law unethically. It is true, for example, that not every lawyer knowingly and blatantly lies on his time sheets. But there is a reason why padding time sheets has been called "a silent epidemic."[131]

## 3. Pressure from clients to help them commit fraud

In a recent study based on interviews of 41 small-firm lawyers in New York, Professor Leslie C. Levin found that "one of the most common ethical challenges . . . was the problem of a client who wished to engage in some form of fraud." She elaborates:

> One attorney stated, "I've had clients ask me to change documents, change dates, change amounts." . . . A lawyer who specialized in estate planning [said] . . . "I'm constantly confronted with what my client is going to report." He observed, "basically, my clients are hiring me to do things that are unethical. For this reason, if you want to be a lawyer and you want to practice [tax] law, sometimes you have to bend the law." . . . Matrimonial lawyers reported that clients often sought to underreport their income on financial disclosure statements; real estate and commercial lawyers said that money "under the table" in purchase and sale transactions was common; and personal injury lawyers reported clients who faked the cause of their injury. . . . The lawyers responded that clients simply expected this of lawyers . . . that a lawyer can help you hide and cheat better than you can yourself . . . [but some added that] the decision to refuse to take certain clients . . . is, however, a difficult one because of the challenges of making a living.[132]

---

131. The ethics counsel at a large Minneapolis law firm asserts that Professor Schiltz's "characterizations of large law firms [particularly Schiltz's claims about the unethical conduct they tolerate] miss or distort several fundamental points." William J. Wernz, The Ethics of Large Law Firms — Responses and Reflections, 16 Geo. J. Leg. Ethics 175, 176 (2002).

132. Leslie C. Levin, The Ethical World of Solo and Small Law Firm Practitioners, 41 Houston L. Rev. 309, 337-339 (2004). Levin sent letters to 181 lawyers "randomly selected from a list of lawyers registered with the New York Office of Court Administration." The 41 interviews, which Levin conducted in 2001, were "semi-structured interviews, which lasted on average from ninety minutes to two hours." Id. at 318.

## 4. Ethics and substance abuse

As noted above, about 20 percent of lawyers abuse alcohol,[133] and other lawyers are addicted to unlawful narcotics and other substances.[134] This is a

human tragedy, but it also has ethical implications. Can a lawyer who is suffering from alcohol addiction provide competent representation to clients? Between 40 and 75 percent of major disciplinary cases against lawyers involve lawyers with substance abuse problems.[135] It is obvious at least that substance abuse creates a risk of serious misconduct. Some lawyers with addiction problems "borrow" from their trust accounts to pay for their habits. Some lawyers accept representation of many more clients than they have time to serve. They ask each client for a retainer (perhaps several thousand dollars) when the client hires the lawyer. The lawyer cashes the checks but—in part because of the impairment caused by addiction—never manages to follow through on many of the matters she has taken on. Lawyers with addiction problems miss deadlines, lose files, fail to return phone calls. Any lawyer might do one of those

133. See n. 85 and accompanying text.

134. See G. Andrew H. Benjamin, Elaine J. Darling & Bruce Sales, The Prevalence of Depression, Alcohol Abuse, and Cocaine Abuse Among United States Lawyers, 13 Intl. J.L. & Psych. 233 (1990).

135. Linda Himelstein, Defense for Misconduct: Addiction to Legal Drugs, Leg. Times, Jan. 15, 1990, at 1 (60 percent); Report of the AALS Special Committee on Problems of Substance Abuse in the Law Schools, 44 J. Leg. Educ. 35, 36 (1994) (50 to 75 percent).

things from time to time, but lawyers with addiction problems usually make these mistakes repeatedly.

Alcoholism is also a serious problem for many law students. In 1993, a study by the Association of American Law Schools asked law students whether they had abused alcohol, defining abuse to mean "in a manner that does physical, psychological or emotional harm to yourself and/or others." Thirty-one percent of law students responded that they had done so, including 12 percent who had abused alcohol while in law school. Three percent of the students reported that they "often" drove under the influence of alcohol.[136]

Alcoholism or drug addiction is a disease, not the product of a moral failing. Lawyers with addiction problems need help to overcome their addictions. Most state bar associations sponsor programs that offer free evaluation and counseling to lawyers and law students who have substance abuse problems, depression, other mental illness, or learning disabilities. The services provided are strictly confidential. The counseling programs do not share information with bar admissions, disciplinary authorities, or anyone else. Some bar associations also sponsor offices that provide training and assistance to lawyers who have difficulty with the management of their law practices. These services are designed to prevent and to remedy some of the problems that most often lead to disbarment and suspension of lawyers.

## PROBLEM 9-4  "I'M NOT DRIVING"

*This problem is based on a situation that one of the authors encountered as a law student.*

Dominick was in his first year of law school. He enjoyed classes but, like most of his friends, found the workload overwhelming. He and his pals worked in the library until eleven on Monday through Thursday. They studied during weekend days also, but Friday and Saturday evenings they tried to forget about school and have some fun. They went to parties, movies, and bars. One of Dominick's friends was a guy named Ryan. Ryan was one of the most considerate guys Dominick knew — he went way out of his way for his friends, helped people move apartments, shared outlines, and the like. Dominick noticed that whenever he went out with Ryan, Ryan just couldn't wait to get his hands on a large supply of alcohol. One night, they were on their way to a party at another friend's place. Ryan wanted to stop to buy beer. They went into a convenience store and bought a couple of six-packs. Dominick thought "gosh, what a nice guy, doesn't want to show up empty-handed." But then as soon

---

136. Id. at 43. Ten years later, the ABA saw "no firm evidence of improved sobriety." Thomas Adcock, Substance Abuse Persists at Law Schools, N.Y. Law., June 27, 2003.

as they left the store, Ryan pulled out a beer, offered one to the other guys, and proceeded to gulp down three or four beers before they even got to the party. "Slow down, man," Dominick said to him. Ryan said "Don't worry, I'm not driving." Dominick has tried a few times to talk to Ryan about how much he drinks, but has gotten nowhere.

What should he do?

---

## 5. Public perceptions of lawyers

In this chapter, we have quoted some lawyers who are critical of the contemporary American legal profession. Unfortunately, the public's perception of our profession is even worse.

- In 1995, a *U.S. News and World Report* poll found that 69 percent of Americans believe that lawyers are "only sometimes honest or are not usually honest," and 56 percent thought that lawyers "used the system to protect the powerful and enrich themselves." Only 35 percent believed that lawyers played "an important role in holding wrongdoers accountable."[137]

- In a 1995 Gallup poll, lawyers ranked 17th among 26 professions in terms of the public's view of their honesty and ethics. Lawyers beat out car salespeople but ranked below funeral directors and building contractors. Opinions of lawyers were higher among those with less education, but only 11 percent of college-educated people gave lawyers high or very high ethical ratings. Only 2 percent of the population believed that lawyers were excellent role models.[138]

- In 1997, a Harris Poll found that public confidence in lawyers had fallen more rapidly than public opinion about any other occupation. Only 7 to 10 percent of the public had a great deal of confidence in the people running law firms. This was the lowest of any institution that was the subject of the poll, the lowest recorded for any institution over a 30-year period, and lower than "such commonly despised institutions as Congress, organized labor, and the press."[139] The prestige of lawyers

---

137. Stephen Budiansky, Ted Gest & David Fischer, How Lawyers Abuse the Law, U.S. News & World Report, Jan. 30, 1995, at 50.

138. Amy E. Black & Stanley Rothman, Shall We Kill All the Lawyers First? Insider and Outsider Views of the Legal Profession, 21 Harv. J.L. & Pub. Policy 835, 852-854 (1998). By 1999, lawyers ranked 37th among 45 professions rated for the honesty, with only 13 percent of the public regarding them as having very high or high honesty and ethical standards. Leslie McAneny, Nurses Displace Pharmacists at Top of Expanded Honesty and Ethics Poll, Gallup Poll Monthly, Nov. 16, 1999, at 41.

139. Michael Asimow, Embodiment of Evil: Law Firms in the Movies, 48 UCLA L. Rev. 1339, 1372 (2001).

also fell dramatically over a 20-year period, with the percentage of people who thought they had very great prestige falling from 36 percent in 1977 to 21 percent in 2000.[140] By 2004, the percentage had fallen further, to 17 percent.[141]

■ A 2002 Harris poll found that only 24 percent of the public would trust lawyers to tell the truth, far lower than the percentage who would trust an "ordinary man or woman" (65 percent), and the lowest percentage for any profession except stockbrokers (23 percent).[142]

## 6. How to find a law firm or other employer that has high ethical standards and humane work conditions

Most graduating law students want to find jobs that will not require them to participate in unethical or illegal activities. Most aspire to find employers who

140. Harris Interactive, Scientists, Doctors, Teachers and Military Officers Top the List of Most Prestigious Occupations, Oct. 16, 2002, at http://www.harrisinteractive.com/harris_poll/index.asp?PID=333 (last visited Nov. 5, 2004).

141. Harris Interactive, Doctors, Scientists, Firemen, Teachers and Military Officers Top List as "Most Prestigious Occupations" (Sept. 15, 2004), at http://www.harrisinteractive.com/harris_poll/index.asp?PID=494 (last visited Nov. 14, 2004).

142. Harris Interactive, Trust in Priests and Clergy Falls 26 Points in Twelve Months, Nov. 27, 2002, at http://www.harrisinteractive.com/harris_poll/index.asp?PID=342 (last visited Nov. 5, 2004).

will treat them with respect. And most want positions that will leave them time for their personal lives. Achieving all of these objectives is a surprisingly tall order. Tall, but not necessarily impossible.

The first thing to notice is that there seems to be an inverse relationship between money and overall satisfaction. Lawyers in government and the non-profit sector make less money than those in firms, particularly large firms, but they tend to work fewer hours and to be more satisfied with their professional lives. Most lawyers want to work in firms or corporations. Therefore, although the government and nonprofit sectors comprise only about 15 percent of the jobs in the profession, any law graduate who wants to work in a government agency or a nonprofit organization and is willing to pursue this objective for a period of time can probably secure such employment.

A law graduate who prefers the private sector should notice that there are significant differences between large and small firms, and also differences in the cultures of individual firms. Some lawyers mistakenly assume that they should accept the highest-paying job that is offered to them. They may not have realized that money often is not a proxy for happiness (at least among lawyers). They may not have thought carefully about how much money they really need.

A new law graduate may be aware of the risks of accepting a job without knowing much about it but may not realize that it is possible to research the hours, pressures, ethical practices, and other aspects of the culture of a law firm.

One fact of life about recruiting of associates by law firms is that many firms sell themselves to inexperienced lawyers by giving out information that isn't accurate. It's marketing — puffery. It's not that people in law firms actually lie to new recruits. They just put everything in a positive light. The point is that to get a less rose-colored picture, you need to be skeptical about what you are told and to dig a bit.

Professor Schiltz writes eloquently on why money is a poor proxy for happiness.[143] He also describes the process by which lawyers lose sight of the value of money, becoming obsessed, instead, with having to make *more* money than other lawyers they know, so that their needs can almost never be satisfied.[144]

### How can one find out what goes on inside a firm without working there?

It is quite possible for a new lawyer to research the culture of a law firm where she is thinking of working. One can learn some things before being offered a job, but after the offer is made and before it is accepted, the offeree is in the catbird's seat. The firm wants her, so it has an interest in allowing her to meet with lawyers and staff members in the firm and to ask candid questions. Since the offer is in hand, it is unlikely that asking questions would jeopardize the offer.

---

143. See Patrick Schiltz, On Being a Happy, Healthy, and Ethical Member of an Unhappy, Unhealthy, and Unethical Profession, 52 Vand. L. Rev. 871, 921-924 (1999).

144. Id. at 905-906.

Here are some things a lawyer can do to research what life is really like in a law firm that may hire her.

Before receiving an offer:

- If you have a summer or term-time job at the firm, make friends with people who will talk honestly about the good and bad aspects of work at the firm. Try to notice how much time associates are able to spend with friends and family.
- Compare old and current editions of the Martindale-Hubbell directory of lawyers to learn the names of lawyers who have left the firm. Try to figure out (through this method or another) what is the rate of associate attrition at the firm.[145] A high attrition rate is a serious red flag. Interview a few former associates on the telephone. Even a lawyer who may have an axe to grind because she was fired may speak candidly about life with her former employer.
- Look on Lexis or Westlaw for reported cases involving public disciplinary proceedings against lawyers working in the firm or suits for malpractice, wrongful discharge, discrimination, and the like. The absence of discipline doesn't mean very much since most respondents in disciplinary proceedings are sole practitioners or in very small firms. If there is a reported disciplinary matter or opinion, however, it could be a revealing window into the firm.
- Research the firm on the Web and in electronic newspaper files to learn whether it has been the subject of favorable or unfavorable news. The *National Law Journal* and *American Lawyer* magazine are loaded with data and stories about law firms.
- Look for gossip on the firm from associates who participate in Web chatter such as http://www.greedyassociates.com.

After receiving an offer:

- Ask for a reasonable amount of time to consider the offer and ask whether you may visit the firm and chat with associates, paralegals, and other support staff. (Often, you can judge the character of an institution by how well it treats the members of the staff who are lowest in the hierarchy. If they feel respected at the institution, that is a very good sign.)
- Check with your law school alumni office to identify lawyers who went to your law school who work or worked at the firm. Recent graduates, especially, may be eager to share what they have learned.

---

145. Lerman's article, "Scenes from a Law Firm," which is excerpted in Chapter 7, Section A of this book, involved a firm at which about half the associates had quit and been replaced within an 18-month period.

- Go to lunch with some associates. If they say that they don't have time to have lunch with you, that's not a good sign. If you do go to lunch with them, go someplace quiet, assure them of confidentiality, and try to find out what life is really like. Ask specific questions.

Regarding hours and pressures:

- Does the firm have an explicit or informal billable hours requirement?
- If so, what is it, and what happens to lawyers who fail to meet it?
- What time do associates come to work every day, and what time do they leave?
- Do associates take work home?
- How much work do associates do on weekends?
- How does the firm treat lawyers with children or other outside obligations? Are there part-time lawyers?

Regarding mentoring:

- Are partners and senior associates able to sit down with junior associates to really discuss assignments, offer suggestions, and give guidance?
- Do they sit down to go over draft memos page by page, line by line?
- Are the senior lawyers so busy that they spend only the minimal time giving supervision and feedback?

Regarding how the firm handles ethical problems:[146]

- Has the firm designated at least one partner as "ethics counsel" charged with advising any lawyer on ethical issues?
- Does this person (or an ethics committee) do anything besides screen incoming matters for conflicts of interest?
- Does the ethics counsel advise all the lawyers in the firm? What about nonlawyers?
- Does the ethics counsel participate in developing policy? (If there are ethics policies in writing, ask for copies.)
- Does the ethics counsel do training?
- If the firm has an ethics counsel, is he a senior partner or a low-level contract lawyer? If he expresses doubt about a course of action, is his advice generally followed or overruled?
- What would happen if an associate went to the firm's ethics counsel to complain about possible unethical behavior by a partner?

---

146. The most ethically sensitive firms devote significant resources to monitoring developments in the law, providing advice on ethics issues to lawyers and nonlawyers, setting policy, and doing training.

147. See Elizabeth Chambliss & David B. Wilkins, The Emerging Role of Ethics Advisors, General Counsel, and Other Compliance Specialists in Large Law Firms, 44 Ariz. L. Rev. 559 (2002).

Regarding pro bono work:

- How much time and money does the firm put into pro bono practice?
- Are lawyers allowed to do pro bono work of their choice?
- Do pro bono hours count toward the target or the minimum?
- Is there a cap on the number of pro bono hours that "count"?

Service to clients who cannot afford to pay for it is an important aspiration of the profession. It is a source of significant pride to some law firms, but it is discouraged by others. We explore this subject further in the next chapter.

# 10 | THE PROVISION OF LEGAL SERVICES

A. The unmet need for legal services

B. Unauthorized practice and the role of lay advocates

C. Other legal restrictions on the free market for legal services
   1. Advertising and solicitation
   2. Interstate law practice
   3. Ownership of law firms
   4. Multidisciplinary practice
   5. Limited representation

D. Beyond the free market: expanding legal services
   1. The right to counsel for indigent litigants
   2. Civil legal aid
   3. Fee-shifting statutes
   4. Pro bono representation
   5. Loan forgiveness and scholarships for public service lawyers

This chapter examines the extent to which the legal profession is meeting the public's needs for legal services. It considers whether laws that restrict access to legal services should be reevaluated in the light of unmet public needs. It also examines the laws and institutions that benefit clients who cannot afford to pay for legal services.

We begin with a survey of the empirical literature on the need for legal services in the United States. Then we turn to an important limitation on the provision of legal services: state laws that prohibit persons other than licensed lawyers from providing such services. We also examine laws and rules governing advertising and solicitation, law firm ownership, interstate practice, multidisciplinary practice, and the provision of less expensive, partial legal services (by both lawyers and nonlawyers). All of these restrictions protect the public from overreaching by lawyers, but they also restrict a free market for legal services by lawyers.

In the last portion of the chapter, we examine rules and institutions that act to expand the supply of legal services available to those who cannot afford to pay. These include the constitutional guarantee of legal services to indigent criminal defendants (but not to impoverished civil litigants), legal aid organizations, fee-shifting statutes, the rule of professional conduct that encourages pro bono service to the poor, and loan repayment assistance to low-salaried individual lawyers who offer legal services to those in need.

## A. The unmet need for legal services

In the mid-1990s, for the first time in 20 years, the American Bar Association conducted a comprehensive empirical assessment of the extent to which Americans' needs for legal services were being met. The study was based on interviews with adults in 3,000 randomly selected American households.[1]

The research assumed that the wealthiest one-fifth of Americans were able to afford legal services, so the study focused on households with incomes in the lowest 80 percent of the population.[2] Each person interviewed was asked a battery of questions to determine whether that person's family had experienced, during the previous year, problems involving any of 67 specific sets of circumstances that might have required legal assistance.

The researchers concluded that "Each year about half of all low- and moderate-income households in the United States face a serious situation that raises a civil legal issue. But neither low-income nor moderate-income households bring the overwhelming proportion of such situations to any part of the justice system."[3] About half of the surveyed households had more than one legal need during the year. The most common problems, affecting

---

1. The results were published in 1994. ABA, Legal Needs and Civil Justice: A Survey of Americans (1994). The text of the report is available online at http://www.abanet.org/legalservices/downloads/sclaid/legalneedstudy.pdf. The ABA published a follow-up report two years later. ABA, Agenda for Access: The American People and Civil Justice (1996). The text of the report is available online at http://www.abanet.org/legalservices/downloads/sclaid/agendaforaccess.pdf.

2. This excluded households with 1992 incomes above $60,000. ABA, Legal Needs, supra n. 1, at 1.

3. ABA, Agenda for Access, supra n. 1, at vii.

17 percent of both poor and moderate-income households, involved personal finances, including "problems with creditors, insurance companies, inability to obtain credit, and tax difficulties." In five other categories (real estate transactions, community problems such as environmental hazards, employment problems such as compensation or benefits disputes, personal injuries, and wills or estate administration), at least 10 percent of the moderate-income households (those above the poorest 20 percent of the population) also had legal needs.[4] Moderate-income people were more likely than low-income people to seek legal assistance. Yet in both categories, most people did not turn to lawyers, paralegals, or courts for help. Only 39 percent of the moderate-income households and 29 percent of the low-income households turned to the civil justice system for assistance. The majority either tried to solve the problems themselves, sought help from someone other than a lawyer (for example, a real estate agent or a neighborhood association), or took no action. Twenty-six percent of moderate-income households and 38 percent of low-income households did not act on the problem at all.[5]

## Action taken by people with legal needs in 1992

| Action taken | Low income (bottom 20% of population) | Moderate income (middle 60% of population) |
| --- | --- | --- |
| Used lawyer or judicial system | 29% | 39% |
| Sought assistance from nonlegal helper | 8% | 12% |
| Tried to solve problem without help | 24% | 23% |
| Took no action on problem | 38% | 26% |

For low-income households, the main reason for not consulting lawyers or courts was that "it would not help and it would cost too much." For moderate-income households, "the three dominant reasons . . . were that the situation was not really a problem, that they could handle it on their own, and that a lawyer's involvement would not help."[6]

Among low-income people who tried to solve their legal problems on their own, only about 27 percent were satisfied with the outcomes. This percentage rose to about 40 percent for moderate-income people who tried to solve their

---

4. ABA, Legal Needs, supra n. 1, at 5.

5. Interestingly, the highest proportion of problems on which no action was taken involved community problems — that is, issues of concern beyond the respondent's immediate family. Id. at 13.

6. Id. at 15.

own legal problems. But among people who sought help from the legal system, these figures rose to 48 percent and 64 percent.[7]

The researchers concluded that "even counting the efforts many people make to handle problems on their own or to get help from outside the legal system, substantial proportions of low- and moderate-income households still may need legal help. Meanwhile, over the last twenty years, legal services to individuals and households have declined as a proportion of all legal services provided by the civil justice system."[8]

Several studies on a smaller scale have echoed the findings of the ABA study. The California Bar Association found that "the legal needs of approximately three-quarters of all poor people are not being met at all," and that persons in the middle one-fifth of the state's population "are often unable to afford representation," causing "harm and injustice to these families of moderate means."[9] A Florida Bar Association study found that 70 percent of the legal needs of low- and moderate-income residents were unmet.[10] An Oregon study found that low- and moderate-income residents of that state were able to obtain legal assistance for only 20 percent of their legal problems, which tended to concentrate in the areas of housing issues, public services, family law issues, employment disputes, and consumer problems. However, 76 percent of those who did obtain legal services were satisfied with the outcome, while only 24 percent of those who did not seek a lawyer's help were satisfied. The study concluded that the "current legal services delivery system cannot meet the critical legal needs" of low- and moderate-income Oregonians.[11]

We can also look at the distribution of legal services in the United States by estimating the value of legal services for different demographic groups, and by calculating the number of clients per lawyer for each of these groups. Professor David Luban has done the arithmetic, focusing particularly on those most in need:

> Law is a $100 billion per year industry. Of that $100 billion, however, less than $1 billion is dedicated to delivering [civil] legal services to low-income Americans. Put in terms of people rather than dollars, there is about one lawyer for every 240 nonpoor Americans, but only one lawyer for every 9000 Americans whose low income would qualify them for legal aid.[12]

---

7. Id. at 17-19.

8. ABA, Access to Justice, supra n. 1, at vii.

9. Commn. on Access to Justice, Cal. B. Assn., And Justice for All: Fulfilling the Promise of Access to Civil Justice in California (1996). The text of the report is available online by going to http://www.calbar.ca.gov/ and searching on the report's title.

10. Mark D. Killian, Legal Needs Going Unmet, Fla. B. News, at http://www.afn.org/~afn 54735/legalneeds1.html (last visited Dec. 17, 2004).

11. D. Michael Dale, The State of Access to Justice in Oregon Part I (2000). The text of the report is available online at http://www.osbar.org/_docs/resources/LegalNeedsreport.pdf.

12. David Luban, Taking Out the Adversary: The Assault on Progressive Public-Interest Lawyers, 91 Cal. L. Rev. 209, 211 (2003).

## What do these studies prove?

Most people think that the studies demonstrate that ordinary Americans have an immense, unmet need for legal services.[13] On the other hand, maybe the researchers took account of trivial problems and inflated the perceived need. Or maybe the research shows that many people really don't need lawyers because they find other ways, such as enlisting the help of neighbors or clergy, to address their legal problems, or that it is reasonable for most people to accept a certain amount of unredressed injustice as a normal part of life or at least as a reasonable alternative to an abundance of lawyers.[14]

One could also conclude that the problem of insufficient legal resources for those with less money is, in reality, not so much a problem about the distribution of legal services but about the distribution of income and wealth in America. Perhaps if wealth were distributed more evenly, each person could decide how to spend his money, and we would be less troubled if some elected to have more consumer goods and fewer legal services.

But wealth is not distributed very evenly. In 1998, the richest 20 percent of American families owned 83 percent of all household wealth and 91 percent of household financial wealth.[15] The richest 1 percent owned 38 percent of the net worth of the nation, while the bottom 40 percent owned two-tenths of 1 percent.[16] In a nation with so much inequality, the available data on the legal needs of the poor — the one-fifth of the population with the lowest income — suggests that they have at least as many needs for legal assistance as the middle class but are much less able to afford it.[17] Attorney General Janet

---

13. Roger C. Cramton, Delivery of Services to Ordinary Americans, 44 Case W. Res. L. Rev. 531, 542 (1994) (discussing the "prevailing consensus").

14. Some argue that what the nation needs is fewer lawyers. David Gergen, who served as communications director for President Ronald Reagan and as counselor to President Bill Clinton, argues that "we need to de-lawyer our society." David Gergen, America's Legal Mess, U.S. News & World Report, Aug. 19, 1991, at 72. Paul W. McCracken, chairman of the Council of Economic Advisors under President Richard M. Nixon, complained that "law schools have been flooding the nation with graduates who are suffocating the economy with a litigation epidemic of bubonic plague proportions." Paul W. McCracken, The Big Domestic Issue: Slow Growth, Wall St. J. Oct. 4, 1991, at A14.

15. Household wealth refers to all marketable assets, less debts. Financial wealth refers to net worth minus net equity investment in owner-occupied housing, an asset that is difficult to convert quickly into cash when a need arises. Edward N. Wolff, Recent Trends in Wealth Ownership, 1983-1998, at http://www.levy.org/ (last visited Nov. 5, 2004).

16. See id.; Edward N. Wolff, Top Heavy: The Increasing Inequality of Wealth in America and What Can Be Done About It (Norton 1996).

17. ABA, Legal Needs, supra n. 1. See also Md. B. Assn., Advisory Council on Family Legal Needs of Low Income Persons, Increasing Access to Justice for Maryland's Families (1992) (only 11 percent of Maryland's poor who have domestic problems receive legal assistance); Mass. B. Assn., Family Law Section, Committee on the Probate and Family Court, Changing the Culture of the Probate and Family Court 26 (1997) (in probate and family court, at least one party is unrepresented in approximately 80 percent of cases); Jane C. Murphy, Access to Legal Remedies: The Crisis in Family Law, 8 B.Y.U. J. Pub. L. 123 (1993) (summary of several surveys); William P. Quigley, The Unmet Civil Legal Needs of the Poor in Louisiana, 19 S.U. L. Rev. 273 (1992) (85 percent to 92 percent of the low-income people in Louisiana who had civil legal needs in 1991 were unrepresented).

Reno noted in 1994 that "eighty to ninety percent of the poor and the working poor in America do not have access to legal services."[18]

Wealth inequalities affect access to all types of goods and services. But at least some types of legal services are not like other consumer needs. In some situations, people desperately need lawyers. If a person is arrested and faces possible imprisonment, she must have access to counsel. Criminal defendants have a right to state-subsidized counsel if they cannot afford to pay attorneys. The payment often is too low or the lawyer's caseload too high to provide adequate representation, but at least society accepts the principle of providing help to indigent criminal defendants. Other situations also present "legal emergencies." If someone is about to be evicted or have her heat shut off, the need for legal help is urgent. That is also true where a person faces domestic violence or termination of parental rights or child custody. Even if a situation is not a legal emergency, the need for legal services may be much greater than the need for ordinary consumer goods or services. If a person has to go to court for any reason, he is much more likely to obtain a favorable outcome if he is represented by a lawyer because lawyers are much more likely to understand the culture of the court, the strategies of successful advocacy, and the rules of procedure and evidence.[19]

Some laws expand or subsidize legal services, particularly for the poor. But these access-expanding laws are often limited in scope and full of restrictions that take back some of what they seem to promise. In other ways, American laws make it difficult for people to obtain help with legal problems. State statutes bar nonlawyers from helping people to solve relatively simple problems that have legal components. State laws and ethical rules also restrict lawyers from working collaboratively with nonlawyers unless the lawyers employ the nonlawyers. In addition, the ethical rules on competence and diligence and the doctrines governing malpractice may deter lawyers from agreeing to represent clients who cannot afford expensive, comprehensive services.

# B. Unauthorized practice and the role of lay advocates

If most people need legal help but cannot afford it, and if the government is not willing to pay enough lawyers to meet the need, perhaps we should allow trained paralegals or other nonlawyers to provide some basic legal services.

---

18. Janet Reno, Speech, Address Delivered at the Celebration of the Seventy-Fifth Anniversary of Women at Fordham Law School (Fordham L. Sch., N.Y., N.Y., May 19, 1994), in 63 Fordham L. Rev. 5, 12 (1994).

19. See Frank I. Michelman, The Supreme Court and Litigation Access Fees: The Right to Protect One's Rights — Part I, 1973 Duke L.J. 1153, 1172-1177.

That is the essential issue in the debate over the proper role for nonlawyers in the solution of routine legal problems.

From 1914 to 1940, professional bar associations, including the ABA, organized successful campaigns that often resorted to litigation to bar non-lawyers from competing with lawyers.[20] Today nearly every state has a statute barring nonlawyers from practicing law or a court doctrine permitting the state bar association or state officials to bring suits to enjoin unauthorized practice.[21]

A central question in the prohibition of unauthorized practice of law (UPL) is the definition of "practice of law." The ABA tried to craft a uniform national definition of what activities constitute the "practice of law, but it eventually abandoned this project."[22] The wording of the UPL statute varies from state to state, but Connecticut's somewhat circular law is representative.

> **Conn. Gen. Stat. § 51-88 (2003)**
> A person who has not been admitted as an attorney . . . shall not: (1) Practice law or appear as an attorney-at-law for another, in any court of record in this state, [or] (2) make it a business to practice law, or appear as an attorney-at-law for another in any such court. . . . Any person who violates any provision of this section shall be fined not more than two hundred and fifty dollars or imprisoned not more than two months or both.

In Delaware, unauthorized practice is restricted by court-made doctrine, rather than by statute. The Delaware Supreme Court has promulgated Rule 86, creating a Board on the Unauthorized Practice of Law. The board has issued these "guidelines," published in its Rule 4(c), in an effort to determine what work is "unauthorized" to be performed by a nonlawyer:

> (i) giving legal advice on matters relating to Delaware law, (ii) drafting legal documents or pleadings for a person or entity (other than one's self) reflecting upon Delaware law, for use in a Delaware legal tribunal or governmental agency, unless the drafting of such documents or pleadings has been supervised by a person authorized to practice law in the State of Delaware, (iii) appearing as legal counsel for, or otherwise representing, a person or entity (other than one's self) in a Delaware legal tribunal or governmental agency, (iv) holding one's self out as being authorized to practice law in the State of Delaware, (v) engaging in an activity which has traditionally been performed exclusively by persons authorized to practice law, and (vi) engaging in any other act which may indicate an occurrence of the unauthorized practice of law in the State of Delaware as established by case law, statute, ruling, or other authority. The foregoing description of types of conduct are

---

20. Derek A. Denckla, Nonlawyers and the Unauthorized Practice of Law: An Overview of the Legal and Ethical Parameters, 67 Fordham L. Rev. 2581, 2583-2584 (1999).

21. Id. at 2585-2586.

22. Utah and Arizona Define Practice of Law; ABA Group Opts Not to Set Model Definition, 71 U.S.L.W. 2642, Apr. 15, 2003. The ABA abandoned its effort after the U.S. Department of Justice and the Federal Trade Commission warned that its draft rule would reduce consumer choice.

to be used as general guidelines for evaluation by Disciplinary Counsel, and not as definitions of the unauthorized practice of law.[23]

Some experts have criticized unauthorized practice laws and rules because they make it virtually impossible for low- and moderate-income persons to obtain essential legal assistance.

## David C. Vladeck, Statement Before the ABA Commission on Non-lawyer Practice

June 25, 1993

*Professor David Vladeck*

[When he delivered this statement to an ABA Commission that was considering recommending changes to state unauthorized practice rules, David Vladeck was an attorney with Public Citizen Litigation Group. He is currently Associate Professor of Law at Georgetown University.]

Lawyers are simply unwilling to provide services that low and moderate income people can afford. Yet, the lawyer monopoly on the provision of legal services bars non-lawyers from filling this void, placing legal services out of reach for too many Americans.

In the past, the Bar has fought tooth and nail against any inroad on the lawyer monopoly. The Bar has erected every barrier imaginable to non-lawyers directly serving the public. . . . To mask the Bar's self-interest in excluding non-lawyer representation, the Bar's arguments have always been couched in terms of consumer protection; namely shielding the client from "inferior" assistance. . . .

Most [state unauthorized practice] restrictions contain no definition of precisely what it is that constitutes the "practice of law." This indeterminacy has sparked efforts by the organized Bar to define the term as broadly as possible in order to prevent non-lawyers from performing a range of functions, including many that most lawyers eschew: representing clients before administrative agencies; filling out standard forms for wills, trusts, deeds, non-contested divorces, name changes, spousal protective orders, and other routine legal matters; and providing basic legal information to poor and middle income people who are trying to protect their rights. . . . Take the cases involving the most routine of legal services. In the divorce context, for example, does it violate the unauthorized practice rules to tell someone that residence and domicile may be the same thing? Or what state law provides in terms of distribution of property? Most state Bars would argue "yes." . . . In my view, . . . as to the most routine of legal matters, the risk to the public of getting

---

23. Office of Disciplinary Counsel, Supreme Court of Delaware, Rules of the Board on the Unauthorized Practice of Law, Rule 4(c), at http://courts.state.de.us/odc/uplr.htm (last visited Nov. 5, 2004).

incorrect or misleading advice is generally marginal, and what the Bar often characterizes as legal "advice" is really little more than the provision of basic information about legal rights. . . .

---

In some areas of work, however, there may be a greater risk to clients than Vladeck suggests. For example, the American Immigration Lawyers Association notes that "there are numerous instances of people being victimized by fraudulent immigration consultants. . . . [They] extract thousands of dollars to prepare applications that are not filed or that are incorrectly filed. The stakes are high when dealing with immigration law. Filing the wrong documents, missing a deadline, or failing to fully disclose all the facts in a case can mean the difference between legal status, deportation, and in the case of some asylum seekers, even death." AILA supports "jurisdiction at the federal level to prosecute fraudulent consultants."[24]

After Vladeck and others criticized the rules on UPL in the 1990s, the ABA's Commission on Non-lawyer Practice recommended reforming the rules. For example, it recommended that states should consider allowing nonlawyer representation of individuals in state administrative agency proceedings and that the ABA should examine its own ethical rules regarding unauthorized practice. It also recommended that the ABA examine, for each type of prohibition of nonlawyer activity, whether the benefits of regulation were outweighed by the negative consequences.[25] "The report was sent to a committee of the Board of Governors but was never presented to the House of Delegates. Its recommendations were never implemented."[26]

### Are nonlawyers ever allowed to help people with their legal problems?

Yes. Lawyers are allowed to hire and train nonlawyers as paraprofessionals (termed "nonlawyer assistants" by Rule 5.3). These employees may help clients with routine legal problems, such as filling out forms, and they may offer routine advice. However, the employing lawyer must supervise the paraprofessionals and take responsibility for their advice and other work. If a paraprofessional violates a rule of professional responsibility, the supervising lawyer may be disciplined for the violation.[27] Lawyers who employ paraprofessionals often bill clients for their time at an hourly rate.

Some statutes, courts rules, and administrative agencies explicitly permit lay advocacy. For example, the Social Security Administration allows unsuccessful claimants to obtain hearings to challenge denials of benefits (such as

---

24. Consumer Protection and the Unauthorized Practice of Law, AILA Dispatch, July/Aug. 2003, at 7.

25. ABA, Non-lawyer Activity in Law-Related Situations: A Report with Recommendations 8-10 (1995) (copy on file with the authors).

26. Debra Baker, Is This Woman a Threat to Lawyers? ABA J., June 1999, at 54.

27. Rule 5.3. The standards for disciplining the supervising lawyer are very similar to the standards for disciplining supervisors of associates under Rule 5.1, which is discussed in Chapter 1.

disability benefits). In those hearings, the claimants may be represented by persons of their choice.[28] Similarly, the Department of Homeland Security has a process of certifying nonlawyer staff members of "religious, charitable, social service, or similar" organizations to represent immigrants claiming certain immigration benefits.[29] Also, many courts and agencies allow law students to provide free representation to indigent clients. The students must be supervised by clinical teachers or (in some cases) legal aid lawyers.

Finally, the prohibition against unauthorized practice of law is more blurry in some commercial contexts than in noncommercial contexts. For example, accountants routinely prepare tax returns for their clients, even though the tax code is very complex and almost any judgment about how income or expenditures should be treated for tax purposes involves interpretation of law. Similarly, in many states, realtors prepare deeds to property and manage the execution of the closing documents.

### Is it a violation of the unauthorized practice laws to publish a manual on how to write a will or a lease?

Maybe. A federal district court in Texas enjoined the publication of the software Quicken Family Lawyer, which included forms for wills, leases, premarital agreements, and 100 other situations. The software itself (but not the packaging) cautioned that the program did not provide individualized information and that purchasers should use their own judgment about whether to consult lawyers. The court found that publication of the software constituted unauthorized practice of law, and that the Texas UPL rule did not violate the First or Fourteenth Amendments.[30] The Texas legislature overturned the result by passing a statute that stated that the publication of "computer software or similar products" does not constitute unauthorized practice if the products state conspicuously that they are not a substitute for the advice of a lawyer.[31] After the legislature enacted this new law, the U.S. Court of Appeals dissolved the injunction.[32]

### May a lawyer provide guidance to a nonlawyer who helps people with their legal problems?

Suppose a community organizer who is not a lawyer but who is an expert on landlord-tenant problems advises poor people about their problems with their landlords. Suppose this person has a lawyer friend whom she calls for advice when questions come up that she can't answer. If she has the advice of her

---

28. 20 C.F.R. § 404.1705 (2004).

29. 8 C.F.R. §§ 292.1-292.2 (2004).

30. Unauth. Prac. L. Comm. v. Parsons Tech., 1999 WL 47235 (N.D. Tex., Jan. 22, 1999).

31. Tex. H.B. 1507, 76th Leg., Reg. Sess. (Feb. 16, 1999), enacted as Tex. Govt. Code Ann. § 81.101 (1998 & Supp. 2004).

32. Unauth. Prac. L. Comm. v. Parsons Tech., 179 F.3d 956 (5th Cir. 1999).

friend, is her assistance of tenants still unauthorized practice of law? Or does the lawyer's "on-call" assistance solve the problem?

If the lawyer employs the nonlawyer, takes and accepts responsibility for the quality of the work that is performed, and subjects herself to malpractice liability and bar discipline if the work is performed incompetently, the organizer's work is not unauthorized practice. But if the organizer is independent, either she or the lawyer could get into trouble. Rule 5.5(a) states that a lawyer may not practice law in any jurisdiction in violation of the laws regulating the practice of law in that jurisdiction or "assist another in doing so."[33]

## PROBLEM 10-1    SPECIAL EDUCATION

*This problem is based on an actual Delaware case.*

---

You are a clerk to a judge of the Delaware Supreme Court. The judge wants you to recommend whether she should vote to affirm or dissolve an order by the Board on the Unauthorized Practice of Law, a statutory body whose members are appointed by the State Supreme Court. The order prohibited personnel from the Disabled Students Resource Center from assisting families with hearings to determine what services the public school system would provide to their children.

A federal statute called the Individuals with Disabilities Education Act (IDEA) provides that children with disabilities are entitled to accommodations that would assist them in obtaining an education. Parents of a child who qualifies for "special education" are entitled to "an impartial due process hearing" if they wish to challenge the child's placement or the services provided to the child.[34] A hearing, which is held by a three-person panel that includes a lawyer (as chair), a special education expert, and one other person, usually lasts from two to four days. The proceedings are adversarial. The school board, defending its decision about the child's services, is represented by a lawyer. The parents may be represented by a lawyer, but the government does not supply a free lawyer.

The hearing begins with opening statements by each side. Then evidence is presented through the direct and cross-examination of

---

33. This is the text of the relevant Delaware Rule of Professional Conduct. Unless specified otherwise, all of this book's quotations from rules of professional conduct are quotations from the Delaware Rules of Professional Conduct. In a few instances, we quote from rules or from published proposed rules in other states. Except where we note otherwise, however, the text of all state rules that we quote is the same as the text of the ABA Model Rules of Professional Conduct. See the note in the Introduction for a more detailed explanation.

34. 20 U.S.C. § 1415(f) (2004).

witnesses. The chair rules on legal issues, the qualification of expert witnesses, and objections to questions. The hearing ends with formal closing statements.

Aileen Babajanian's daughter Melissa has a neurological condition that causes a severe visual impairment and limits her control of her fingers. When Melissa reached public high school, Ms. Babajanian asked her school to purchase a special, expensive computer that would respond to vocal commands, scan her daughter's textbooks, and read them aloud to her. The school refused, saying that lending Melissa books on tape would be sufficient. Ms. Babajanian and Melissa contended that Melissa can not consistently operate a tape recorder. A hearing was scheduled at which doctors, experts on Melissa's impairments, and technology consultants would testify. Ms. Babajanian could not find a lawyer who would represent her for less than $8,000. She could not afford to pay that fee.

Through friends, however, Ms. Babajanian heard of the Disabled Students Resource Center, founded and staffed by parents of disabled children who had been through the hearing process. They had learned how difficult it is to go through the hearing process, opposing an experienced lawyer for the school board, without representation. After losing their cases, the parents formed the Center so that they could train themselves as lay advocates to help future parents in need. After months of study and training, they advertised their availability to assist parents who wanted help. The Center charges a flat $3,000 fee for its services in a case, which includes assistance at the hearing. This is less than half of what lawyers in the community charge for representation. The Center does not employ any lawyers.

The Center would like to represent Ms. Babajanian. But recently, after the Center's staff had represented five parents (and obtained satisfactory results for the parents in four of them, which cost the school system a great deal of money), the attorney for a school board complained to the Board on the Unauthorized Practice of Law. The Board has ordered the chairpersons of all hearing panels not to allow the Center to participate in hearings. It based its order on the Center's violations of Rule 4(c)(iii) and (v) of the Delaware Rule (which is reprinted in the text preceding this problem).

Ms. Babajanian and the Center have appealed the Board's order. On this appeal, the Center claims that advising parents and representing them before the Board is not practicing law, and that if it is, it is not "unauthorized" practice because it is permitted by a federal law, 20 U.S.C. § 1415(h)(1), which says that any party to a special education hearing "shall be accorded . . . the right to be accompanied and advised by counsel and by individuals with special knowledge or training with respect to the problems of children with disabilities." Therefore, they say, the Board's order should be dissolved. The Board wants its order affirmed.

Taking into account all plausible legal and policy arguments for each side in this controversy, what result will you recommend to the judge for whom you work, and why?

# C. Other legal restrictions on the free market for legal services

Some critics of the organized bar complain that in the name of quality control, the rules against unauthorized practice preserve an unwarranted "monopoly" for lawyers. Other rules governing lawyers may also constrain competition within the legal profession, keeping the cost of legal services artificially high. The pertinent restrictions are those on advertising and solicitation, the ownership of law firms, the interstate practice of law, collaborative practice with members of other disciplines, and limited representation of clients.

## 1. Advertising and solicitation

### a. General advertising

Today, lawyers advertise on billboards, on local television stations, and in the yellow pages of the phone book. But as recently as the 1970s, lawyers didn't advertise at all. In fact, advertising by lawyers was considered both unseemly and unethical.

Everything changed as a result of Bates v. State Bar of Arizona, decided by the U.S. Supreme Court in 1977.[35] Like most states, Arizona banned advertising by lawyers:

> A lawyer shall not publicize himself, or his partner, or associate, or any other lawyer affiliated with him or his firm, as a lawyer through newspaper or magazine advertisements, radio or television announcements, display advertisements in the city or telephone directories or other means of commercial publicity, nor shall he authorize or permit others to do so in his behalf.[36]

Some Arizona lawyers who wanted to offer routine, low-cost legal services set up a legal clinic. They advertised their low rates in a daily newspaper, willfully violating the disciplinary rule. The Arizona Supreme Court suspended them from practicing law. They appealed to the Supreme Court, claiming that the court's advertising ban violated the First Amendment. By a 5-4 vote, the Supreme Court agreed with their position, invalidated the Arizona rule, and ushered in an age of advertising by lawyers. The Court noted, however, that a

---

35. 433 U.S. 350 (1977).
36. Ariz. D.R. 2-101(B) (1976), quoted at 433 U.S. 350, 355.

state could prohibit false advertising by lawyers, just as it could prohibit false advertising by any type of merchant.[37]

## b. In-person solicitation

In 1978, the Court held that although a state may not prohibit truthful advertising aimed at the general public, it may ban in-person solicitations by lawyers (for example, approaching accident victims and suggesting that they hire the lawyers to make claims on their behalf). Such restrictions serve "to reduce the likelihood of overreaching and the exertion of undue influence on lay persons, to protect the privacy of individuals, and to avoid situations where the lawyer's exercise of judgment on behalf of the client will be clouded by his own pecuniary self-interest."[38] In the court's view, the "potential for overreaching" was "significantly greater when a lawyer, a professional trained in the art of persuasion, personally solicits an unsophisticated, injured, or distressed lay person."[39]

## c. Direct-mail solicitation

Individualized mailed solicitations lie somewhere between mass advertising and in-person solicitation. In 1988, in Shapero v. Kentucky Bar Association,[40] a divided Supreme Court invalidated a Kentucky rule that barred lawyers from sending letters to people known to need legal services. Kentucky argued that a targeted letter was merely a written version of in-person solicitation. The Court decided, however, that a writing does not involve the "coercive force of the personal presence of a trained advocate" or the "pressure on the potential client for an immediate yes-or-no answer. . . . A letter, like a printed advertisement (but unlike a lawyer) can readily be put in a drawer to be considered later, ignored, or discarded."[41] But while the Court rejected a blanket prohibition on mailed solicitations, it invited states to "require the letter to bear a label identifying it as an advertisement or directing the recipient how to report inaccurate or misleading letters.[42]

---

37. Despite the Supreme Court's ruling, advertising by lawyers continues to be controversial. When the Staten Island ferry crashed into a pier in New York in 2003, injuring many passengers, lawyers published television and newspaper advertisements to recruit clients. One TV commercial showed a "ghostly image of a ferry washed over by a tidal wave of green dollar signs" and proclaimed "If you were injured, you may be entitled to money damages." The New York Times quoted legal experts and personal injury lawyers as saying that some of these ads "dangle at the edge of what is morally and ethically appropriate after a fatal accident." Susan Saulny, Lawyers' Ads Seeking Clients in Ferry Crash, N.Y. Times, Nov. 4, 2003, at A1.

38. Ohralik v. Ohio St. B. Assn., 436 U.S. 447, 461 (1978). In an observation notable for its double negative, the Court elaborated its concern about possible conflicts of interest between lawyer and client: "lapses of judgment can occur in any legal representation, but we cannot say that the pecuniary motivation of the lawyer who solicits a particular representation does not create special problems of conflict of interest." Id. at 461 n. 19.

39. Id. at 464-465.

40. 486 U.S. 466 (1988).

41. Id. at 475-476.

42. Id. at 477-478.

## d. The ethics rules

The rules reflect the decisions in these cases. Rule 7.1 prohibits a lawyer from making "a false or misleading communication about the lawyer or the lawyer's services" and defines such a communication to include both one that includes a "material misrepresentation" and one that "omits a fact necessary to make the statement considered as a whole not materially misleading." Rule 7.2(a) permits advertising "through written, recorded or electronic communication, including public media." Rule 7.3 prohibits "in-person, live telephone or real-time electronic contact" to solicit professional employment "when a significant motive for the lawyer's doing so is the lawyer's pecuniary gain," unless the person contacted is a lawyer or has a family, close personal, or prior professional relationship with the lawyer. The "significant motive" clause appears to permit real-time solicitation by legal aid lawyers who do not charge fees for their services. Rule 7.3 does not bar mailed solicitation, but it requires the sender to include the words "Advertising Material" on the outside envelope.

In 1990, after the *Shapero* case was decided, Florida enacted a more restrictive rule than Rule 7.3 to limit solicitation by mail.

> **Florida Rule 4-7.4**
> (1) A lawyer shall not send . . . a written communication directly or indirectly to a prospective client for the purpose of obtaining professional employment if . . . the written communication concerns an action for personal injury or wrongful death or otherwise relates to an accident or disaster involving the person to whom the communication is addressed or a relative of that person, unless the accident or disaster occurred more than 30 days prior to the mailing of the communication. . . . The first page of such written communications shall be plainly marked "advertisement" in red ink, and the lower left corner of the face of the envelope containing a written communication likewise shall carry a prominent, red "advertisement" mark.

Before Florida adopted the rule, the state bar had conducted a public opinion poll on lawyer solicitation. Fifty-four percent of respondents said that for a lawyer to contact accident victims invades the privacy of those contacted. Forty-five percent of respondents who had received direct-mail advertising from lawyers believed that these letters were "designed to take advantage of gullible or unstable people," and 24 percent reported that the letters "made [them] angry." Twenty-seven percent of direct-mail recipients reported that their regard for the legal profession and for the judicial process as a whole was "lower" as a result of receiving the direct mail. One man who responded to the survey was "appalled and angered" by a letter he received after he was injured and his fiancee was killed in an auto accident. Another found it "despicable and inexcusable" that a Pensacola lawyer wrote to his mother three days after his father's funeral. One person wrote, "I consider the unsolicited contact from you after my child's accident to be of the rankest form of ambulance chasing and in incredibly poor taste. . . . I cannot begin to express with my limited vocabulary the utter contempt in which I hold you and your kind."

## PROBLEM 10-2  DO YOU NEED A LAWYER?

*This problem is based on an actual Florida case.*

You are a member of the Florida bar. Your speciality is plaintiffs' personal injury work. Before Rule 4-7.4 was passed, you got about 30 percent of your cases through word of mouth from previous clients, 30 percent through general advertising, and 30 percent through mailings addressed to accident victims. You learned the names and addresses of these victims through police accident reports, which are public records. Because you contact and represent a large number of clients, you are able to charge lower rates than lawyers who do not advertise.

You would like to continue to send mailings to accident victims. You don't object to putting a red "advertising" notice on the envelope, but the 30-day waiting period is likely to destroy your law firm. Insurance adjusters rush in to settle claims well before 30 days after an accident occurs, and the settlements extinguish any further rights that might be asserted by accident victims. The state bar's ban on contact applies only to lawyers, not insurance agents, and the state bar has no authority to regulate insurance agents.

You are thinking of bringing a lawsuit, based on *Shapero*, to challenge the constitutionality of Florida's rule.

## Questions

1. What arguments might you make, and what would you expect the state bar to argue?
2. What outcome would you predict if the case goes all the way to the Supreme Court?

## 2. Interstate law practice

Suppose that a man who lives in New Jersey and works in New York asks his regular lawyer, who is licensed to practice only in New York, for advice about whether New Jersey would impose a tax on the sale of his New Jersey home. If the New York lawyer knows or can easily obtain the answer, may he give this advice about New Jersey law? If so, does it matter where he or his client is when he gives the advice? May the New York lawyer provide the advice while having dinner at his friend's New Jersey home? May the lawyer give the advice on the telephone from his Manhattan office if his friend is at his home in New Jersey?

Or suppose a lawyer who is admitted to practice in New York wants to advertise for clients in New Jersey newspapers. May New Jersey prohibit such advertising even though it could not ban ads by New Jersey lawyers?

Although most Americans identify themselves as citizens of the United States rather than of their states, individual states still regulate the practice of law. In the name of consumer protection, state bars protect their lawyers from "outside" competition and regard poaching by out-of-state lawyers as unauthorized practice, just as if an out-of-state lawyer were not a lawyer at all.[43]

Europe imposes fewer geographic restrictions on law practice. European lawyers may practice throughout their own countries and in other countries that are part of the European Union. One expert explains: "Lawyers and law firms from any EU [European Union] state are able to represent clients on a continuous basis throughout the European Union, practice in almost all commercial law fields in any EU country, and form multinational law firms with offices as desired in any EU commercial center."[44]

Contrast this European flexibility with Birbrower, Montalbano, Condon & Frank v. Superior Court of Santa Clara.[45] A California company retained New York lawyers to help it make claims against another California company. The lawyers went to California, met with their client's accountants, and advised them about how to settle the dispute. Over a period of two days, they also met with representatives of the other California company. On a second trip, they discussed settlement with both parties. Arbitration was contemplated, but the case was eventually settled without going to arbitration. When the New York lawyers sued their client for their fee, the client defended against payment by objecting that the New York lawyers' work in California was unauthorized practice. The California Supreme Court held that the fee agreement was unenforceable because the New York lawyers had not been admitted to practice in California. The court stated that unauthorized practice included not only court appearances but also advice-giving and other lawyerly activities. The court noted that an out-of-state lawyer could commit unauthorized practice in California without even setting foot in the state by advising a California client by telephone or e-mail about California law. The court also observed that California law made no exception that would permit

---

43. All states, however, have traditionally allowed their courts to permit an out-of-state attorney to represent a particular client in a particular proceeding, provided that an in-state lawyer also represents the client in the proceeding. Lawyers appearing under these "pro hac vice" court rules sometimes have difficulty finding local lawyers with whom to associate, particularly if they are handling the cases for no fee or a low fee. See Gerald M. Stern, The Buffalo Creek Disaster 64 (Vintage 1976).

44. Roger J. Goebel, The Liberalization of Interstate Legal Practice in the European Union: Lessons for the United States? 34 Intl. Law. 307, 308 (2000). When a European lawyer wants to appear before a tribunal in another country in the EU, he may (depending on the law of the host country) have to comply with a requirement that he appear "in conjunction with" a host state lawyer, but the host state lawyer need not take the leading role in the case or even be continuously present in court. Rather, the two lawyers should decide on their roles in a manner "appropriate to the client's instructions." Commission v. Germany, Case 427/85, 1988 E.C.R. 1123 (1988); Goebel at 315. A law firm in one country may also establish an office with nonlegal staff in another country and send lawyers for work in that office for moderately long periods of time, but the lawyers may not permanently work out of the office in the second country. Id. at 317 n. 65.

45. 949 P.2d 1 (Cal. 1998).

out-of-state lawyers to give advice or perform other legal services in California even if they affiliated themselves with local California law firms.

This decision shocked the organized bar into initiating a modest effort to allow attorneys from one state to perform some services in another state, eventually provoking an amendment to Model Rule 5.5, which is explained in the article excerpted below.

## Stephen Gillers, It's an MJP World: Model Rules Revisions Open the Door for Lawyers to Work Outside Their Home Jurisdictions

ABA J., Dec. 2002, at 51

*Professor Stephen Gillers*

[Stephen Gillers, Emily Kempin Professor and Vice Dean at NYU Law School, was a member of the ABA's Commission on Multijurisdictional Practice.]

Tension has long existed between the jurisdictional limits on where a lawyer may practice — generally restricted to states in which the lawyer is licensed — and the cross-border needs of clients.

Is a Michigan attorney still entitled to practice, for instance, when she is temporarily in Illinois on client business? And will her conduct in Illinois be governed by that state's professional conduct rules for lawyers — or by those of Michigan? And if she violates the rules in Illinois, can she even be disciplined there? These questions, once largely academic, have assumed practical importance as client matters increasingly cross state boundaries. The need to resolve these issues was underscored in 1998 when the California Supreme Court [decided *Birbrower*]. . . .

Reaction to *Birbrower* was quick. The California General Assembly effectively overruled it by granting most arbitrators authority to permit appearances by out-of-state lawyers. The authority sunsets in 2006, but a court-appointed committee is expected to make recommendations addressing this and other cross-border questions before then.

On the national level, then-ABA President Martha W. Barnett of Tallahassee, Fla., appointed a Commission on Multijurisdictional Practice in 2000 to study the issue and develop proposed amendments to the ABA Model Rules of Professional Conduct. The commissioners would have to weigh concerns over effective lawyer regulation with the imperatives of a changing legal landscape in which many attorneys find that they cannot properly serve clients if they confine their practices to just the one or two states in which they are licensed. . . . The House approved every one of the MJP Commission's proposed amendments to the Model Rules.

Previously, Rule 5.5 consisted primarily of a prohibition against a lawyer practicing law "where doing so violates the regulation of the legal profession in that jurisdiction." As amended, Rule 5.5 sets forth conditions under which lawyers may represent clients outside the states in which they are licensed.

The amended Rule 5.5 permits a lawyer otherwise in good standing to perform legal services in another host state on a temporary basis if any one of four factors applies:

The lawyer is affiliated with another lawyer licensed in the host state who actively participates in the matter.

The lawyer is preparing for pending or potential litigation and is admitted to appear in the proceedings or reasonably expects to be admitted.

The lawyer's work in the host state is incident to a pending or potential alternative-dispute-resolution proceeding and is reasonably related to the lawyer's practice in a state in which he or she is admitted.

The lawyer's work arises out of practice in a jurisdiction in which the lawyer is licensed. Among the types of legal services that would qualify under this provision are work for a home-state client, work on a matter with a significant connection to the home state, and work in the lawyer's area of concentration.[46]

The temporary practice authority granted by amended Rule 5.5 does not permit a lawyer to engage in a systematic and continuous presence in the host state. . . .

The MJP amendments to the ABA model rules protect the regulatory interests of host states in three primary ways:

Rule 8.5 was amended to give host states disciplinary jurisdiction over any lawyers who perform or offer to perform legal services in the state. Previously, the rule did not expressly grant states authority to discipline lawyers from outside the jurisdiction.

Under a new choice-of-law provision in Rule 8.5, the ethics rules of the jurisdiction in which a tribunal sits will apply to conduct in connection with matters pending before that tribunal. For any other conduct, a lawyer may be subject to the rules of the jurisdiction in which the conduct occurred or the rules of a jurisdiction in which the conduct had its predominant effect.

Under stronger rules on reciprocal discipline, a lawyer will not be able to evade discipline by retreating to his or her home state. With narrow exceptions, the lawyer's home state would have to credit the sanctioning decision of the host state's disciplinary proceeding.

The MJP amendments to the ABA Model Rules will go a long way toward enabling the regulatory structure for lawyers to catch up with the reality of modern practice, while ensuring that states retain the ability to protect their residents and punish lawyer misconduct within their borders.

---

Note that the ABA's new rule, if approved by California, might not even have protected the New York lawyers in *Birbrower* from committing

---

46. [Authors' footnote.] This is Professor Gillers' paraphrase of Model Rule 5.5.

unauthorized practice. They were not affiliated with a California firm. They did not contemplate litigation for which they expected to be admitted by a court. The case did involve a potential alternative dispute resolution, but the proceeding was not related to the firm's New York practice. Possibly the work was "reasonably related" to their New York practice.[47] Gillers states that this test of the rule encompasses "work in the lawyer's area of concentration," so if the New York lawyers made a specialty of the type of work they were doing in California, they might be excused by this exception to the unauthorized practice rules. However, Gillers's gloss is broader than that stated in the text of the rule and in Comment 14 explaining the fourth exception. That comment interprets the "reasonably related" test to cover situations in which the out-of-state lawyer has "recognized expertise developed through the regular practice of law on behalf of clients in matters involving a particular body of federal, nationally-uniform, foreign or international law."

In any event, amended Rule 5.5 does not go nearly as far in permitting cross-border practice in the United States as Europe has gone in permitting cross-border international practice. It remains to be seen whether the states will adopt, modify, or reject this ABA recommendation.

## 3. Ownership of law firms

Rule 5.4 bars lawyers from sharing fees with nonlawyers or from forming partnerships with nonlawyers to provide legal services. It also prohibits lawyers from practicing law for profit in an association in which a nonlawyer owns any interest or of which a nonlawyer is an officer or director. The stated purpose of this rule is to protect "the lawyer's professional independence of judgment."[48]

This rule bars lawyers from practicing in a firm in which a nonlawyer has any ownership interest or in which a nonlawyer has a leadership role. This rule, while it formally governs lawyers, effectively precludes corporations and all individuals other than lawyers from investing in or owning law firms.[49] Therefore, a corporation or large investor may not make increased legal services available to a community by creating or investing in a for-profit law firm.

Professor Gillers is a critic of the ban on lay investment in law firms because he believes that the primary purpose and effect is to reduce price competition in the legal profession. He notes the ABA's client-protection justification for the rule but replies that "I do not find that justification credible. Rule 5.4 must be counted as serving the interests of some critical mass of lawyers, numerous and powerful enough" to block proposed reforms of this rule. Gillers urges that one main effect of the rule "is to exclude a major source of capital for new firms. Established firms, with accumulated capital and clientele, are protected

---

47. This is the test under Rule 5.5(c)(4).
48. Rule 5.4, Comments 1 and 2.
49. It should be noted that this rule does permit nonlawyers to serve as officers or directors of nonprofit organizations that practice law, such as union-based prepaid legal services plans.

from the rapid growth of new competitors that private investment might encourage."[50] Gillers argues that Rule 5.4 increases the cost of legal services to the public because it

> suppresses competition on the supply side. The fewer the consumer alternatives, the more lawyer-employers can charge for their employees' time. In addition to the predictable downward pressure on fees that would accompany increased competition, lay investors might be willing to accept a lower return on their money. The rule of thumb has been that a law firm associate's time should be billed at a rate that nets a profit of one-third after deduction of salary and overhead. That's a pretty good margin, one other investors might be willing to undersell.[51]

Professor Gillers is not alone in claiming that the rule exists for the protection of lawyers more than the protection of clients. Professor Bruce Green explains that the rule originated as a criminal statute enacted in New York in 1909 at the behest of lawyers. At that time, a small number of corporations had contracts with thousands of lawyers throughout the world to provide legal advice to subscribers who paid $10 a year for the privilege of receiving legal advice. These companies asked an appellate court to interpret the law to permit them to continue to hire lawyers to serve their clients, but the president of the Brooklyn Bar Association's Committee on Grievances argued that such an interpretation "is disadvantageous and unfair to me as a practicing member of the bar of this state and others similarly situated" because they had spent time and money to become licensed as lawyers. The court ruled in favor of the bar and against the corporations, and its ruling was affirmed by the highest court of New York.[52] Green points out that the corporations wanted to be able to *hire* lawyers, not to compete with them by using nonlawyers to give advice. The real issue was that corporate employment of lawyers probably would have lowered prices, in part because corporations knew how to advertise the services they supplied, and, unlike lawyers, they were willing to advertise the availability of legal services.[53]

# 4. Multidisciplinary practice

Lawyers may hire other professionals to assist them. These might be doctors, engineers, accountants, or others who work as expert witnesses, analysts, lobbyists, or in some other capacity. But just as Rule 5.4 bars nonlawyers from even part ownership of law firms, it also bars lawyers from forming multidisciplinary

---

50. Stephen Gillers, What We Talked About When We Talked About Ethics: A Critical View of the Model Rules, 46 Ohio St. L. Rev. 243, 266-268 (1985).

51. Id. at 268.

52. In re Co-op. L. Co., 92 N.E. 15 (N.Y. 1910).

53. Bruce A. Green, The Disciplinary Restrictions on Multidisciplinary Practice: Their Derivation, Their Development, and Some Implications for the Core Values Debate, 84 Minn. L. Rev. 1115, 1126-1128 (2000).

partnerships that might, for example, offer legal services, social work, and medical services from a single office. Neither may lawyers and accountants partner to offer legal and financial services. A person who is both a lawyer and a certified public accountant may not even offer both types of service from his office if he works in an accounting firm owned by nonlawyers.[54] The controversy around this issue has been driven mainly by accounting firms that would like to expand the range of their services (and expand their profits) by having lawyers in their employ advise their clients on a variety of financial matters. The nonprofit sector is interested in this issue as well because the public might benefit from partnerships or other entities in which people from various disciplines collaborate.

## Stacy L. Brustin, Legal Services Provision Through Multidisciplinary Practice: Encouraging Holistic Advocacy While Protecting Ethical Interests

73 U. Colo. L. Rev. 787, 792, 798, 801-802, 812-815 (2002)

[Stacy Brustin is Associate Professor of Law at the Catholic University of America.]

*Professor Stacy L. Brustin*

A multidisciplinary model can respond to the myriad needs of those who are poor or marginalized by their social, medical, or psychological circumstances. Those who live in poverty are often isolated and lack access to resources and support systems. Offering a package of services in one accessible location allows for greater efficiency and continuity of care. Clients do not have to travel from one agency to another to receive services, but can take care of all or most of their needs in a single, familiar place. Clients who would otherwise forego services because they do not have the time or money to follow up on referrals to agencies throughout the city or region can receive the services they need.

A multidisciplinary approach provides an ideal way to address complex social issues such as domestic violence, HIV, concerns facing the elderly, community economic development, and poverty more generally. Professionals from different disciplines can use their skills to develop more comprehensive solutions for clients. Doctors and other medical professionals can use their expertise to provide quality prenatal care for women, basic preventative primary care to children, ongoing treatment for those who are HIV-positive, and pain management services for elderly clients with chronic illnesses. Psychologists and social workers can provide therapy and counseling to individuals in crisis. These services complement the types of remedies a lawyer might secure for a client. For example, a lawyer who obtains a restraining order for a client experiencing domestic violence has addressed one narrow aspect of

---

54. See, e.g., Utah St. B. Ethics Advisory Op. Comm., Op. 02-04 (2002).

the problem. The client will most likely need counseling, financial assistance, and possibly medical treatment — all services a lawyer cannot provide. . . .

Despite the numerous benefits clients can reap from non-profit MDPs [multidisciplinary practices] offering direct legal and non-legal services, the model raises concerns. First, some scholars have argued that organizations dominated by a variety of professionals run the risk of re-creating the types of intractable bureaucracies they were designed to counter. . . . Second, and perhaps of greater concern, these MDP organizations arguably violate current ethical prohibitions on partnership and fee-sharing between lawyers and non-lawyers. These prohibitions exist in every state, and the extent to which they apply to non-profit MDPs engaged in direct legal services provision is some-what unclear. . . . At a minimum, it is likely that these ethical prohibitions inhibit the widespread development of MDP non-profits. . . .

[Rule 5.4] appears to target the for-profit sector, but ambiguity remains because neither the Model Rules nor the Model Code squarely addresses whether the restrictions on MDP apply to lawyers providing direct legal ser-vices in non-profit, multidisciplinary organizations. The recent revision to Rule 5.4, authorizing lawyers to share court-awarded legal fees with a non-profit organization, suggests that, in all other respects, the restrictions of Rule 5.4 apply to lawyers in non-profit organizations.

For example, the prohibition in section (a), forbidding a lawyer or law firm from sharing fees with a non-lawyer, applies to fees charged for services. Attorneys representing low-income clients in non-profit multidisciplinary centers often do not collect fees for their services; however, there are non-profit organizations that charge modest fees. These fees may be shared with non-lawyer personnel in organizations governed by boards comprised of law-yers and non-lawyers. By its breadth, Rule 5.4(a) suggests that such fee-sharing between lawyers and non-lawyers in a non-profit setting is prohibited, unless the fees are court-awarded.

Section (b) of Rule 5.4, prohibiting lawyers from forming partnerships with non-lawyers, seems to be directed toward formal partnerships created to gen-erate profit. Nevertheless, partnership is not defined. The Rule and the comments do not explicitly exempt lawyers who partner with non-lawyers and form a non-profit organization from the prohibition. In fact, section (d) of Rule 5.4 specifically limits the applicability of that particular provision to lawyers practicing for a profit. One could argue, therefore, that because 5.4(b) makes to such mention of profit status, its applicability is broader in scope. The third provision of the rule, section (c), mandates that a lawyer must not allow a person who recommends, employs, or pays the lawyer to provide legal assistance for others to influence the lawyer's professional judgment. A disciplinary committee interpreting the scope of this provision conceivably could determine that lawyers representing clients in a full-scale MDP offering non-legal services independent of legal assistance were violating the ethical proscriptions in Rule 5.4 requiring lawyers to maintain sufficient independence of professional judgment. This scenario is even more likely where the executive director and/or senior managers in the organization are non-lawyers. . . .

[For years, the ABA has debated easing or eliminating restricting on multidisciplinary practice. Some] small firm lawyers and solo practitioners, however, express fears that MDPs will obliterate small practice. They argue that large companies and franchises will offer a multitude of services, including legal services, and small practices will not be able to compete.

Opponents of MDPs also argue that the proposed changes will compromise client confidentiality, particularly given the differing duties non-legal professionals have to preserve confidentiality. . . . There is further concern that non-lawyers in MDPs might be compelled by law or subpoena to divulge information that a lawyer would be prohibited from divulging. Clients who are the victims of domestic violence or elder abuse, for example, might disclose the situation to an attorney believing that the information will remain confidential. A social worker partnering with the attorney in an MDP might discover such information and be obligated by state statute to report the information. . . . [55]

Opponents also fear that the independence lawyers have to make judgments and devise strategies for their cases will be compromised by the involvement of other professionals. Some believe that the sharing of fees, for example, may allow the bottom line to control, rather than concern for clients. These opponents believe that market forces should not take precedence over core principles of the legal profession. There is a worry that lawyers may develop conflicting fiduciary duties, one to the client and one to the non-lawyer partner. Further, some express concern that the proliferation of MDPs will result in non-lawyers engaging in the unauthorized practice of law.

After two years of public hearings and investigation, the Commission recommended, in its July 2000 report, that the ABA revise the Model Rules of Professional Conduct to allow lawyers and non-lawyers to engage in limited forms of multidisciplinary practice. Once again, however, the ABA rejected the proposal and, on July 11, 2000, upheld the ban on multidisciplinary practice. The ABA House of Delegates urged jurisdictions around the country to resist the move toward MDP and to revise their ethical rules so as to "preserve the core values of the legal profession." [In 2002, the ABA relaxed its rule in just one minor respect, permitting lawyers to share court-awarded fees (but not client-paid fees) with a nonprofit organization that employed or retained the lawyer.]

---

Because the ABA rules are only models, states are free to liberalize their rules despite the ABA's rejection of multidisciplinary practice. In recent years, several states have appointed commissions to study possible reforms, but for the most part, the states have not changed their rules. District of Columbia

---

55. [Authors' footnote.] For a discussion of the problems caused when different degrees of privilege apply to lawyers and social workers or other mental health professionals with whom they are collaborating, particularly in abuse cases, see Jacqueline St. John, Building Bridges, Building Walls: Collaboration Between Lawyers and Social Workers in a Domestic Violence Clinic and Issues of Client Confidentiality, 7 Clin. L. Rev. 403 (2001).

Rule 5.4 goes furthest in allowing multidisciplinary practice. The D.C. Rule allows lawyers in a firm or organization engaged solely in legal practice to share fees with nonlawyers (provided certain other conditions are also met), but it does not allow the firm or organization to provide other types of services. The D.C. Bar's Special Committee on Multidisciplinary Practice has recommended that this rule be changed to permit fee-sharing by "lawyers and non-lawyers who wish to practice their respective professions together in the same firm."[56] New York, by contrast, decided to allow only "contractual relationships" between lawyers and nonlawyers. A "contractual" relationship is one in which the other professional would receive a salary but would not be a partner entitled to a share of the profits. New York prohibits fee-sharing, and the contractual relationships are prohibited unless the other professionals are licensed by a government entity and are bound by an enforceable code of ethical conduct.

The president of the New York State Bar explained, "We wanted to make sure it wasn't going to lead to 'John Smith, Attorney at Law and Nail-Wrapping Salon.'"[57] (Smith's concept appears unseemly at first blush, but consider whether there is any good reason to disallow any such collaborative ventures. If a divorce lawyer thought she could draw clients by joining up with a manicurist, what exactly is the problem?)

Some experts believe that although the ABA disfavors creating separate ethics rules for particular types of lawyers (such as lawyers serving in nonprofit organizations),[58] at least nonprofit organizations should be permitted to undertake multidisciplinary practice, particularly in view of the apparent difficulty of persuading the ABA and the states to reform Rule 5.4 for profit-making firms.[59] Law professor Louise G. Trubek and sociology student Jennifer J. Farnham advocate still another approach: liberalized rules for government-approved "social justice collaboratives." (See Brustin at 835.) Trubek and Farnham urge that these should be allowed even if they charge fees and make profits, so long as they serve people unable to pay the full cost of legal services. Such entities would be subject to oversight (for example, they would have to administer client satisfaction surveys), but they would be permitted to offer multidisciplinary services and would be protected by evidentiary privileges from having to disclose confidences.

---

56. Report and Recommendation of the District of Columbia Bar Special Committee on Multidisciplinary Practice, at https://www.dcbar.org/inside_the_bar/structure/reports/special_committee_on_multidisciplinary_practice/summary.cfm (last visited Nov. 5, 2004).

57. New York Courts Modify Ethics Rules to Allow Multidisciplinary Alliances, 70 U.S.L.W. 2070-2071 (2001).

58. The Model Rules do incorporate several provisions or exceptions that deal specifically with criminal defense, such as Rule 3.3(a)(3), which generally allows a lawyer to refuse to offer evidence that the lawyer reasonably believes is false but makes an exception for the testimony of a criminal defendant. Generally speaking, these special exceptions derive from constitutional protections for defendants. In 2002, the ABA amended the Model Rules in a limited way to facilitate service by nonprofit legal organizations, allowing them to offer "short-term limited legal services." See Rule 6.5, discussed below.

59. Stacy Brustin recommends this approach. Legal Services Provision Through Multidisciplinary Practice: Encouraging Holistic Advocacy While Protecting Ethical Interests, 73 U. Colo. L. Rev. 787, 832 (2002). Compare with Louise G. Trubek & Jennifer J. Farnham, Social Justice Collaboratives: Multidisciplinary Practices for People, 7 Clinical L. Rev. 227, 229 (2000).

## 5. Limited representation

If car dealers sold only Lexuses, few people could have cars. Some authorities believe that the Model Rules essentially restrict the availability of legal services by requiring lawyers to sell only Lexuses. Rule 1.2(c) allows a lawyer to "limit the scope of the representation if the limitation is reasonable under the circumstances and the client gives informed consent." Even so, many lawyers believe that whenever a lawyer agrees to represent a client, he must provide the best-quality services that he can. They fear that if they offer brief, off-the-cuff advice, without thorough research, because a particular client can afford only an hour's consultation, they might do poor work and face charges of incompetence or malpractice liability.[60] Consider, for example, the Washing Machine problem in Chapter 4. Imagine that the lawyer in that problem was billing the client by the hour. Would it have been appropriate for the lawyer and client to have agreed at the outset that the lawyer would negotiate only a payment plan for the client and that the lawyer would not

---

60. Margaret Graham Tebo, Loosening Ties: Unbundling of Legal Services Can Open Door to New Clients, ABA J., Aug. 2003, at 35.

investigate the client's possible defenses and counterclaims?[61] Another barrier to limited representation is that some lawyers fear that judges would disapprove should the lawyers attempt to help a litigating party without full responsibility for their work. These fears are reinforced by several recent developments.

- ■ In Nichols v. Keller,[62] a California court held that a lawyer who filed a workers' compensation claim for a client, without also advising the client that he might be able to sue someone other than his employer for tort, could be sued for malpractice, "even when a retention [of the lawyer] is expressly limited," at least if the lawyer did not "make such limitations in representation very clear to his client."[63]
- ■ Several recent ethics opinions have stated that although a lawyer may offer some assistance to a pro se litigant and help him to prepare pleadings, if the lawyer offers a litigant "active and extensive" help before and during a trial without disclosing that fact to the court, the lawyer may be acting unethically.[64]
- ■ In a few cases, judges have admonished lawyers for "improper" conduct after they wrote portions of briefs for pro se litigants.[65]
- ■ State court rules often provide that once a lawyer enters an appearance in a case, the lawyer may not withdraw without court approval.[66] Some lawyers worry that if a lawyer tried to represent a client in a court case for a limited purpose (for example, helping with pleadings or with

---

61. See Mary Helen MacNeal, Redefining Attorney-Client Roles: Unbundling and Moderate-Income Elderly Clients, 32 Wake Forest L. Rev. 295 (1997). Professor MacNeal suggests that at least when representing elderly clients, lawyers should tread cautiously before offering limited services. She suggests several guidelines that they should follow before considering offering less than full service representation. For example, she urges that "to avoid ethical breaches for the lack of competency and diligence, the lawyer must engage in sufficient factual investigation to identify relevant legal issues, such as potential counterclaims." Id. at 336.

62. 15 Cal. App. 4th 1672 (1993).

63. Id. at 1687.

64. ABA Informal Op. 1414 (1978) (applying the Model Code of Professional Responsibility) (the lawyer observed the trial and advised the litigant without formally becoming the litigant's lawyer for purposes of the case). See also state bar opinions collected in Maryland Legal Assistance Network, Informal National Survey of Ethical Opinions Related to "Discrete Task Lawyering" (2003) at http://www.unbundledlaw.org/thinking/ethicsurvey.htm (last visited Nov. 6, 2004), which hold it unethical for lawyers to write pleadings for pro se clients, to sell do-it-yourself divorce forms, or to advise clients while disclaiming the creation of an attorney-client relationship.

65. Ricotta v. California, 4 F. Supp. 2d 961, 974-977 (S.D. Cal. 1998) (reviewing prior cases and agreeing that (a) ghost-writing a pleading is an evasion of a lawyer's responsibility under Fed. R. Civ. P. 11 to sign pleadings and personally represent that there are grounds to support them, and (b) such behavior implicates the ethical prohibitions against dishonesty, fraud, deceit, and misrepresentation).

66. See, e.g., Mich. Ct. R. 2.117(c)(2). Washington State, however, now permits a lawyer to represent a client for one stage of the case and to withdraw without court permission when that limited representation has been completed. Wash. Ct. R. 70.1.

discovery), the court might refuse to allow the lawyer to withdraw from the case before trial, even if the lawyer and client so desired.[67]

Defenders of a Lexus-only rule of full-service representation of clients might respond that no automobile can be driven unless it meets minimum safety requirements, enforced through state vehicle inspections. The ethical rules protect the public by requiring basic levels of competence, diligence, conflict-avoidance, and so on.

In recent years, several state bar committees have urged that the unmet need for legal services could be satisfied in part by making "unbundled" services more available and changing ethical rules to permit this practice. (The metaphor refers to treating full-scale legal services as a complete "bundle.") In Michigan, for example, such a group made the following recommendations.

- Because commercial and corporate lawyers already often provide limited advice, lawyers who represent ordinary individuals and families should also be permitted to do so.
- Court rules should be changed to allow lawyers to represent clients for some aspects of a case (at the request of a client) and then to withdraw without court permission.
- Ethics rules should expressly permit lawyers to draft pleadings for pro se clients, provided that the pleading includes a phrase stating that it was "prepared by" a specified lawyer who is not representing the client in the case.[68]

An ABA Task Force recommended greater use of "limited scope legal assistance," because "in the great majority of situations some legal help is better than none. An informed pro se litigant is more capable than an uninformed one."[69] The Task Force noted with approval two modest changes in the 2002 Model Rules amendments that would facilitate limited representation.

- Comment 6 to Rule 1.2 was amended to make clear that a lawyer could legitimately offer limited service to a client to "exclude actions that the client thinks are too costly."[70]
- New Rule 6.5 allows a lawyer providing short-term services such as advice or form completion "under the auspices of a program sponsored by a non-profit organization or court" to do so without having

---

67. State Bar of Michigan, Access to Justice for All Task Force, Service Delivery Subcommittee Work Group B, Unbundling Report 9 (2000). The full text of the report is available online at http://www.unbundledlaw.org/program / 1%20-%20Developing%20%20-%20Deming.pdf (last visited Nov. 14, 2004).

68. Id.

69. ABA Section of Litigation, Modest Means Task Force, Handbook on Limited Scope Legal Assistance 12 (2003).

70. The new text in Rule 1.2 and in Comment 7 is qualified by the statement in Comment 6 that the "limitation must be reasonable under the circumstances."

to perform an extensive check for conflicts of interests with other clients.

However, despite the very limited scope of these reforms, the Task Force did not recommend additional changes in the Model Rules. It did recommend amending court rules to allow lawyers to draft pleadings anonymously for pro se clients.[71]

# D. Beyond the free market: expanding legal services

Although the legal profession has not moved as quickly as it might to make low-priced services available to poor and middle-class individuals and families, many professional groups have advocated vigorously in favor of programs that provide free legal services to indigent people.

## 1. The right to counsel for indigent litigants

### a. Criminal defendants

Most criminal defendants are too poor to hire lawyers.[72] In 1938, the Supreme Court held that the Constitution requires the government to provide counsel for indigent defendants in federal criminal cases.[73] It later extended that ruling to felony defendants in state prosecutions,[74] misdemeanor defendants who could be subjected to imprisonment,[75] and juveniles.[76]

States and counties spend about 3.3 billion dollars annually for criminal defense services.[77] This amount is about 3 percent of the amount spent for local police, judicial services, and corrections.[78] State and local governments provide service to indigent criminal defendants in three ways. Some fund a municipal or regional public defender's office staffed by salaried lawyers and support staff. In some states, lawyers are appointed to represent the defendants pro bono, without fees. Some states make contracts with lawyers who provide defense

---

71. Modest Means Task Force, supra n. 69, at 144-145.

72. In 1991, three-quarters of state prison inmates had been represented by lawyers who were appointed for them. U.S. Department of Justice, Bureau of Justice Statistics, Indigent Criminal Defense: A National Perspective, at http://justice.uaa.alaska.edu/forum/f132su96/b_indigen.html (last visited May 15, 2004).

73. Johnson v. Zerbst, 304 U.S. 458 (1938).

74. Gideon v. Wainwright, 372 U.S. 335 (1963).

75. Argersinger v. Hamlin, 407 U.S. 25 (1972).

76. In re Gault, 387 U.S. 1 (1967).

77. The Spangenberg Group, State and County Expenditures for Indigent Defense Services in Fiscal Year 2002 (2003). The text of the full report is available at http://www.abanet.org/legalservices/downloads/sclaid/indigentdefense/indigentdefexpend2003.pdf (last visited Nov. 6, 2004).

78. U.S. Department of Justice, Bureau of Justice Statistics, Indigent Defense Statistics, at http://www.ojp.usdoj.gov/bjs/id.htm (last visited Nov. 6, 2004).

services to indigents for a fixed fee per case or for an hourly rate. These fees can be very low. According to the Criminal Justice Section of the ABA, "The compensation currently received by most CJA lawyers [lawyers appointed for indigent defendants and funded under the federal Criminal Justice Act], $45 [per hour] for out-of-court time and $65 for in-court time, is so low that it threatens to eviscerate the constitutional guarantee of effective representation to all regardless of economic circumstances."[79] States often pay even lower hourly rates, even for representation in capital cases. Some jurisdictions "impose shockingly low maximum hourly rates or arbitrary fee caps for capital defense (Alabama $20-40 an hour, up to $2,000 cap, meaning that an attorney devoting 600 hours to pretrial preparation in Alabama would earn $3.33 an hour; Tennessee, $20-30 an hour; Mississippi, a $1,000 cap)."[80]

In urban areas, public defender offices account for 73 percent of the funds spent on indigent defense.[81] However, the percentage of services provided through contracts with private attorneys is growing. Critics of the contract system are concerned about this trend because contract lawyers are often paid such low fees that the quality of the services rendered is often poor. A Justice Department report urged that some of the contract programs may not be "ethically sound" because they "place cost containment before quality, create incentives to plead cases out early rather than go to trial, result in lawyers with fewer qualifications and less training doing a greater percentage of the work . . . provide unrealistic caseload limits or no limits at all [and] do not provide support staff or investigative or expert services."[82]

As we mentioned in Chapter 4, some judges appoint lawyers to represent indigent criminal defendants even if there are no funds available to pay

---

79. ABA, Criminal Justice Section, Report to the House of Delegates (1998), reprinted in Terence F. McCarthy, Unanimous Resolution, Champion Magazine of the Natl. Assn. of Crim. Def. Lawyers, April 1999.

80. Testimony of Beth Wilkinson, Co-Chair of the Constitution Project's Death Penalty Initiative, Before the U.S. Senate, Committee on the Judiciary, Hearing on Protecting the Innocent: Ensuring Competent Counsel in Death Penalty Cases (June 27, 2001). Virginia pays attorneys only $112 (per case, not per hour) to represent a child charged with a juvenile offense. ABA Juvenile Justice Center, Virginia: An Assessment of Access to Counsel and Quality of Representation in Delinquency Proceedings 5 (2002). A chart showing the rates paid in the ten most populous states in 1999 appears as Table 1 in House Research Organization, Texas House of Representatives, The Best Defense: Representing Indigent Criminal Defendants (1999), at http://www.capitol.state.tx.us/hrofr/focus/indigent.pdf (last visited Nov. 6, 2004).

81. U.S. Department of Justice, Indigent Defense Statistics, supra n. 78 (based on expenditures for defense and the other listed services in the nation's 100 most populous counties).

82. See U.S. Department of Justice, Office of Justice Programs, Contracting for Indigent Defense Services: A Special Report at 13 (2000). The text of the full report is available online at http://www.ncjrs.org/pdffiles1/bja/181160.pdf (last visited Nov. 6, 2004). When Clark County, Washington, moved from public defender's office to a contract system, there was "a decline in the quality of representation, including a decline in the number of cases taken to jury trial, an increase in guilty pleas at first appearance hearings, a decline in the filing of motions to suppress, a decline in requests for expert assistance, and an increase in complaints received by the court from defendants." Id. at 10.

them. Rule 6.2 urges lawyers to accept such appointments except for "good cause."

> **Rule 6.2    Accepting Appointments**
>
> A lawyer shall not seek to avoid appointment by a tribunal to represent a person except for good cause, such as:
>
> > (a) representing the client is likely to result in violation of the Rules of Professional Conduct or other law;
> >
> > (b) representing the client is likely to result in an unreasonable financial burden on the lawyer;
> >
> > (c) the client or the cause is so repugnant to the lawyer as to be likely to impair the client-lawyer relationship or the lawyer's ability to represent the client.

### Do judges often simply assign lawyers to represent indigent criminal defendants?

No. We don't know of any state in which judges just call lawyers at random and assign them to criminal cases. Some courts poll lawyers periodically and ask whether they are willing to volunteer to be on panels of attorneys who could be assigned if their services are needed.[83]

### How do the U.S. rules compare to the British rules on lawyers' discretion about whom to represent?

Much of U.S. law is modeled on the British law, but the British rule on accepting new clients is different from ours. British barristers are supposedly bound by the "cab rank rule,"[84] requiring them to accept as a client any criminal defendant who wants help, provided that the compensation is adequate. Britain's publicly funded compensation for indigent criminal defendants is automatically deemed adequate.[85] A barrister is permitted to refuse a case if he or she lacks the "competence to handle the matter."[86] In fact, despite the cab rank rule, in half of the publicly funded British cases, barristers "return the briefs" (which means they decide, a day or two before trial, that they cannot try the cases because of scheduling difficulties). This practice forces the defendants' solicitors to "search, often frantically, for a replacement, or accept a substitute chosen by the clerk from the withdrawing barrister's chambers."[87]

---

83. Cait Clarke, Problem-Solving Defenders in the Community: Expanding the Conceptual and Institutional Boundaries of Providing Counsel to the Poor, 14 Geo. J. Leg. Ethics 401, 420 (2001).

84. Barrister's Code of Conduct, Part VI, § 602.

85. Peter W. Tague, Representing Indigents in Serious Criminal Cases in England's Crown Court: The Advocates' Performance and Incentives, 36 Am. Crim. L. Rev. 171, 172 (1999).

86. Teresa Stanton Collett, The Common Good and the Duty to Represent: Must the Last Lawyer in Town Take Any Case? 40 S. Tex. L. Rev. 137, 155 n. 69 (1999).

87. Tague, supra n. 85, at 205. See also Maree Quinlivan, The Cab Rank Rule: A Reappraisal of the Duty to Accept Clients, 28 Victoria U. Wellington L. Rev. 113, 137 (1998).

### Is there any reason to force lawyers to take on clients they don't want to represent?

One problem with giving lawyers total freedom to turn down clients is that some lawyers are able to limit their practices to very rich clients. This means that access to legal services in America may depend on wealth. We return to the subject of the distribution of legal services later in this chapter.

Rule 6.2 doesn't distinguish between civil and criminal cases. What would happen if a court appointed a lawyer to represent a poor person in a civil case, and the lawyer didn't want to handle the matter?

### PROBLEM 10-3 AN INDIGENT PRISONER

*This problem is based on a real situation that a young midwestern lawyer encountered during the 1980s.*

You are a recent law school graduate. For the past year, you have practiced securities and corporate law at a three-member firm; that is your only legal experience. You like the type of work you do. You have never handled or assisted any litigation, and you have always preferred other less adversarial areas of law practice.

In your jurisdiction, the federal district court has set up a system in which the judges receive requests from indigent litigants — both civil and criminal — for the appointment of free lawyers. Then judges screen these requests. If a civil case brought by an indigent person appears meritorious, the judge assigns the case randomly to a member of the bar. The judge makes this assignment pursuant to 28 U.S.C. § 1915, which provides that a federal court "may request an attorney to represent" any impoverished person who is "unable to employ counsel." The local bar has a committee that provides training and materials for lawyers who are assigned cases in areas of law with which they are not familiar.

This week, the court assigned you to represent Calvin Rivers, an inmate of the local prison, who has sued several of his guards. Rivers's pro se complaint alleges that the guards abused him and filed false disciplinary charges against him. You think that somebody should represent Mr. Rivers — but it shouldn't be you. Your firm would allow you to take the case without reducing your pay, but you don't want to do it.

You wrote a letter to the judge, explaining your lack of experience in civil rights work, your dislike of litigation, and your opinion that you could not adequately represent Mr. Rivers. You asked to be taken off the case. You offered, as an alternative, to be assigned to represent any indigent who needs assistance in a case involving corporate, securities, or bankruptcy law.

This morning, the court denied your request to be relieved of the assignment and directed you to meet promptly with Mr. Rivers in the prison where he is incarcerated, and to begin work on the case.

## Questions

**1. An obligation?** Do you have an ethical responsibility under the Model Rules to handle Rivers's case?

**2. Your options.** Identify your options and the advantages and disadvantages of each option.

---

Despite the right to counsel and the creation of state-funded programs for criminal defense, states have not always provided counsel for indigent defendants with sufficient resources to investigate and defend cases, even when their clients face the death penalty.

## Richard C. Dieter, With Justice for Few: The Growing Crisis in Death Penalty Representation[88]

Death Penalty Information Center, 1995

[Richard C. Dieter is the Executive Director of the Death Penalty Information Center.]

Compensation rates for court-appointed attorneys in capital cases are well below the rates for comparable work by experienced attorneys in almost every state. And the U.S. Congress, while imposing new deadlines and draconian restrictions on death row appeals,

*Professor*
*Richard C. Dieter*

has failed to impose any conditions on the representation afforded capital defendants at trial.

### Inadequate Pay Brings Inadequate Results

Although, in theory, the fee that an attorney is paid should not figure into the quality of representation, it usually does. Some lawyers can work for free or are not concerned about meeting office expenses, making a profit and paying their staff, but most attorneys have to keep their eye on the bottom line if they are to remain in practice. If the court allows only $2,000 to prepare for a death penalty trial, then a lawyer who puts in 20 hours will be making about $100 per hour, which is a minimal fee in many kinds of practice. (Of course, 20 hours is a seriously deficient amount of time to prepare for a death penalty trial.) An attorney who decides to devote 200 hours of preparation, however,

---

88. The full text of the article is available online at http://www.deathpenaltyinfo.org/article.php?scid=45&did=544 (last visited Nov. 6, 2004).

would be making only $10 per hour, and someone who was diligent enough to put in the 500 to 1,000 hours which experts estimate is often needed to prepare a capital case would be working for *below* minimum wage.

Yet, fees in the range of $2,000 for preparing a death penalty case are not unusual. Justice Blackmun pointed to the "perversely low" compensation offered to attorneys appointed to these cases as one of the principal reasons for poor representation. "Kentucky pays a maximum of $2,500 for [*all* pretrial and trial proceedings]. Alabama limits reimbursement for out-of-court preparation in capital cases to a maximum of $1,000 each for the trial and penalty phases." (Kentucky's fee cap was recently raised to $5,000, still abysmally low.)

In other states, the arrangement between the courts and the attorneys they appoint may be less constrained but still totally inadequate. A survey by the Mississippi Trial Lawyer's Association found that death penalty lawyers were paid an estimated $11.75 per hour. In the . . . Texas case of Federico Macias [in which the lawyer based his trial decisions on a misunderstanding of Texas law and did no presentencing investigation other than speaking to the defendant during a lunch break of the sentencing proceedings], the U.S. Court of Appeals overturned his conviction and death sentence because of the poor representation he received at trial. The Court directly linked the attorney's failure to present evidence of Mr. Macias's innocence to the inadequate pay:

> We are left with the firm conviction that Macias was denied his constitutional right to adequate counsel in a capital case in which actual innocence was a close question. The state paid defense counsel $11.84 per hour. Unfortunately, the justice system got only what it paid for.[89] . . .

Some states have sought to deal with the crisis in death penalty representation by assigning these cases to the public defender's office, under the assumption that the attorneys there are already adequately funded by the state and presumably screened for competence. This might work where caseloads can be adjusted for the enormous burden which even a single death penalty case places on an office, and where the public defender's office can be expanded to include attorneys specially trained to handle capital cases. However, this is clearly not a solution where the public defender's office is already overwhelmed by its non-death penalty case load. In Minnesota, Connecticut, Mississippi, Illinois and Indiana, the indigent defense systems are so overburdened that the states are being sued. . . .

### The Court's Adoption of Low Standards

The Supreme Court has abdicated responsibility for this problem by defining its notion of ineffectiveness of counsel so narrowly that only the most extreme cases of incompetence apply. They begin with a generous presumption that the attorney's conduct fits within a wide range of professional assistance. Given

---

89. [Authors' footnote.] Martinez-Macias v. Collins, 979 F.2d 1067, 1067 (5th Cir. 1992). See generally Martinez-Macias v. Collins, 810 F. Supp. 782, 814-815 (W.D. Tex. 1991).

the complexity of death penalty law, an attorney should have to establish beforehand that he or she is qualified to handle such a case. . . .

Perhaps the most often repeated story about shoddy representation in a death penalty case concerns a Georgia lawyer who was asked to name any criminal cases, from any court, with which he was familiar. The lawyer could name only *Miranda* and *Dred Scott*, the latter being a *civil* case. But the most amazing part of this sad story is not that the lawyer had such poor knowledge of criminal law, but rather that he was found competent in the case where this challenge arose and went on to try other death penalty cases while satisfying the lax standards for effective representation.

There are many similarly egregious examples of ineffectiveness in which the death sentence was upheld under the Supreme Court's lenient approach:

- John Young was represented at trial by an attorney who was addicted to drugs. Shortly after the trial in which his client was sentenced to death, the attorney himself was incarcerated on federal drug charges. However, the lawyer was not found to be ineffective, and John Young was executed in 1985.
- Jesus Romero's attorney . . . failed to present any mitigating evidence at the sentencing phase of the trial. His closing argument was 29 words. No ineffectiveness was found, and Romero was executed in 1992.
- Larry Heath's attorney failed to appear for oral argument before the Alabama Supreme Court. He filed a brief containing a one-page argument, citing only a single case. Heath was executed in 1992.
- William Garrison was defended by an attorney who "consumed large amounts of alcohol each day of the trial . . . drank in the morning, during court recesses, and throughout the evening . . . was arrested for driving to the courthouse with a .27 blood-alcohol content," and eventually died of alcohol related diseases. Garrison's conviction was affirmed, though his death sentence was overturned on other grounds.

## b. Parties in civil and administrative proceedings

Poor people who need to go to court because of family problems, landlord problems, consumer, or other "civil" problems do not have a right to have counsel appointed for them. They have no right to counsel even if they are defendants rather than plaintiffs, and even if they might be evicted from their homes, lose their children, or be deported. Any foreign national (including a lawful permanent resident who may have lived in and raised a family in the United States for decades) may be placed in deportation proceedings based on a wide range of charges of violations of law.[90] If the government prevails, the foreign national may be deported from the United States and not allowed to reenter. This is not legally a "punishment" but may be more punitive than time in prison. The respondent has a right to counsel at the deportation hearing

---

90. 8 U.S.C. § 1227(a) (2004).

if she can afford to pay a lawyer but is not entitled to have counsel provided if she is poor.[91] As a result, indigents often are unrepresented in deportation proceedings.[92]

Some indigents have claimed that denying them an appointed counsel denies them due process. Some indigent litigants also have claimed denial of due process because the courts refuse to waive fees charged for filing cases. The courts have consistently rejected these claims.

> **FOR EXAMPLE:** Robert William Kras had once worked as an insurance agent for Metropolitan Life. The company fired him when about $1,000 in premiums he had collected was stolen from his home and he could not repay his employer. For two years, he was unemployed, living in a two-and-a-half room apartment with his wife, his mother, his mother's six-year-old daughter, and his two small children, one of whom suffered from cystic fibrosis. From welfare funds, he was barely able to pay his rent. He had no car and no other assets except for $50 worth of clothing and a couch that was in storage (for which he had to pay $6 a month). He was $6,000 in debt and was harassed by his creditors. He wanted to file for bankruptcy so that he could start a new life and end the harassment. But he had no money with which to pay the $50 filing fee, even in monthly installments.
>
> The Supreme Court rejected Kras's claim that he was being unconstitutionally denied access to the court system. The Court acknowledged that it had held unconstitutional, as applied to indigents, a state statute requiring a filing fee for a divorce.[93] But it held that divorce cases were unique because "marriage involves interests of basic importance in our society" and "resort to state courts was the only avenue to dissolution of marriages." In the Court's view, "however unrealistic the remedy may be in a particular situation, a debtor [such as Kras], in theory, and often in actuality, may adjust his debts by negotiated agreement with his creditors. . . . Resort to the court, therefore, is not Kras' sole path to relief."[94] Although *Kras* involved a filing fee, this decision has been interpreted to preclude due process claims to the right to counsel in civil cases.[95]

---

91. A federal law specifies that his defense shall be "at no expense to the Government." 8 U.S.C. § 1362 (2004).

92. For example, in FY 2001, only 22 percent of the 10,703 foreign nationals who had removal hearings in the immigration court in San Antonio, Texas, had representation. Ninety percent of the 209 people who won their cases were represented, but only 11 percent of the 7,207 who lost their cases and were ordered removed were unrepresented (the remaining cases had other dispositions such as changes of venue). U.S. Department of Justice, FY 2001 Immigration Court Representation Summary, San Antonio, *at* http://www.usdoj.gov/eoir/reports/2001icrepsummary/01SanAntonio.pdf (last visited Nov. 6, 2004).

93. Boddie v. Conn., 401 U.S. 371 (1971).

94. United States v. Kras, 409 U.S. 434, 437-446 (1973). See also Ortwein v. Schwab, 410 U.S. 656 (1973) (a state need not allow an indigent to file an appeal of a civil case without paying the statutory filing fee).

95. See, e.g., Deborah L. Rhode & David Luban, Legal Ethics 725 n. 31 (3d ed., Found. Press 2001).

State courts also have been reluctant to conclude that due process requires states to spend money for indigents who seek access to the courts, except in rare circumstances.[96] In a 4-3 decision, the New York Court of Appeals held that neither indigents who sought divorces nor indigents who were sued for divorce had a right to have counsel appointed for them. The Court added that "many kinds of private litigation . . . drastically affect indigent litigants [including] eviction . . . mortgage foreclosures, [and] repossession of important assets" but "courts and litigants must make do with what exists."[97] Other states have followed New York's lead.[98]

## 2. Civil legal aid

### a. The Legal Services Corporation

Although most court decisions have denied indigents a constitutional right to counsel at government expense, Congress, state and local governments, and private donors have created a network of salaried legal aid lawyers who provide advice and representation to some poor people. The nation's largest program of civil legal aid is operated by the federally funded Legal Services Corporation (LSC). As the following article explains, however, the funds appropriated are far less than what is needed, and there are strings attached to the services that law offices funded through the corporation can provide.

### Alan W. Houseman & Linda E. Perle, Securing Justice for All: A Brief History of Civil Legal Assistance in the United States

November 2003

[Alan W. Houseman and Linda E. Perle are, respectively, the Executive Director and a Senior Attorney of the Center for Law and Social Policy.[99]]

*Alan W. Houseman*                    *Linda E. Perle*

---

96. Some states recognize an exception where the state commences a proceeding to terminate a parent's right to custody of her child on grounds of neglect. See Matter of Ella B., 285 N.E.2d 288 (N.Y. 1972).

97. Matter of Smiley, 330 N.E.2d 53, 58 (N.Y. 1975).

98. See, e.g., Kiddie v. Kiddie, 563 P.2d 139 (Okla. 1977) (divorce, and collecting other types of civil cases in which indigents have no right to counsel); Haller v. Haller, 423 N.W.2d 617 (Mich. App. 1988) (divorce where appellant loses custody of child).

99. The Center for Law and Social Policy is one of several public interest law firms founded in the 1960s to advance social justice. Houseman and Perle have spent decades litigating, lobbying, and

## The Early Years of Legal Aid: 1876-1965

Civil legal assistance for poor people in the United States began in New York City in 1876 with the founding of the German Immigrants' Society, the predecessor to the Legal Aid Society of New York. Over the years, the legal aid movement caught on and expanded into many urban areas. By 1965, virtually every major city in the United States had some kind of legal aid program, and the 157 legal aid organizations employed more than 400 full-time lawyers with an aggregate budget of nearly $4.5 million. . . .

No legal aid program had adequate resources. . . . Many areas of the country had no legal aid at all, and those legal aid programs that did exist were woefully underfunded. . . . In addition, most legal aid programs only provided services in a limited range of cases and only to those clients who were thought to be among the "deserving poor" (i.e., those who were facing legal problems through no fault of their own). . . .

Because of inadequate resources and the impossibly large number of eligible clients, legal aid programs generally gave perfunctory service to a high volume of clients. Legal aid lawyers and volunteers rarely went to court for their clients. Appeals on behalf of legal aid clients were virtually nonexistent. No one providing legal aid contemplated using administrative representation, lobbying, or community legal education to remedy clients' problems. As a result, the legal aid program provided little real benefit to most of the individual clients it served and had no lasting effect on the client population as a whole.

## The Need for "Something New"

In the early 1960s, a new model for civil legal assistance for the poor began to emerge. . . . [L]egal services advocates Edgar and Jean Cahn wrote a seminal article in the 1964 Yale Law Journal entitled "The War on Poverty: A Civilian Perspective." They argued that neighborhood law offices and neighborhood lawyers were necessary for an effective anti-poverty program because they provided a vehicle for poor residents in local communities to influence anti-poverty policies and the agencies responsible for distributing benefits. . . .

## The Early Development

In 1964, Congress passed the Economic Opportunity Act, the beginning of President Johnson's War on Poverty. . . . For the first time, Congress made federal money available for legal services for the poor. . . . The overall design for the program was fleshed out by E. Clinton Bamberger, the first director of OEO [Office of Economic Opportunity] Legal Services and his deputy (and later the second director) Earl Johnson. . . . Bamberger and Johnson worked with the National Advisory Committee. This group produced the OEO Legal

educating on behalf of efforts to expand legal assistance to the poor. The full text of the report is available online at http://www.clasp.org/DMS/Documents/1068130577.17/Legal_Aid_History.pdf.

Services Guidelines. . . . The Guidelines prohibited legal services programs from taking fee-generating cases, but required local programs to provide service in all areas of the law except criminal defense and to advocate for reforms in statutes, regulations, and administrative practices. They identified preventive law and client education activities as essential components of local programs. The Guidelines required program services to be accessible to the poor, primarily through offices in their neighborhoods with convenient hours. Unlike the legal aid systems that existed in other countries, which generally used private attorneys who were paid on a fee-for-service basis, OEO's plan for the legal services program in the United States utilized staff attorneys working for private, nonprofit entities. . . .

In addition to local service providers, OEO also developed a unique legal services infrastructure. OEO funded a system of national and state support centers, training programs, and a national clearinghouse for research and information.

### Growth and Development

In 1967, OEO legal services' second director, Earl Johnson, made a second fundamental policy decision that would also have long-term implications for the civil legal assistance program. The local OEO-funded legal services programs were facing impossible demands from clients for services with inadequate resources to meet the need. In response to this growing problem, Johnson decided to require that programs set local priorities for the allocation of resources, but established "law reform" for the poor as the chief goal of OEO legal services. He made clear that OEO would give priority in funding to proposals that focused on law reform.

In addition, Johnson wanted to create a cadre of legal services leaders who would then use peer pressure to encourage programs to provide high-quality legal services. In order to achieve this goal, OEO funded the Reginald Heber Smith Fellowship program to attract "the best and the brightest" young law graduates and young lawyers into OEO legal services. This program provided a summer of intensive training in various law reform issues, and then placed the "Reggies" in legal services programs throughout the country for one- or two-year tours of duty. Many of the Reggies became leaders in their local legal services communities, as well as on the national level. Others went on to become respected lawyers in private practice and academia, as well as important political leaders and well-known public figures.

A large investment was also made in "back-up centers" — national legal advocacy centers, initially housed in law schools, that were organized around specific substantive areas (e.g., welfare or housing) or a particular group within the eligible client population (e.g., Native Americans or elderly). These centers co-counseled with, and provided substantive support for, local programs that were engaged in key test case litigation and representation before legislative and administrative bodies on behalf of eligible clients and groups, as well as engaging directly in advocacy in significant cases with national impact. The back-up centers also provided research, analysis, and training to local legal services programs that were working on cases within the centers' areas of expertise. . . .

## Major accomplishments . . .

Legal services attorneys won major cases in state and federal appellate courts and in the U.S. Supreme Court that recognized the constitutional rights of the poor and interpreted and enforces statutes in ways that protected their interests. . . . Legal services attorneys won landmark decisions, such as Shapiro v. Thompson,[100] which ensured that welfare recipients were not arbitrarily denied benefits, and Goldberg v. Kelley,[101] which led to a transformation in the use of the concept of due process. Creative advocacy by legal services lawyers expanded common law theories that revolutionized the law protecting poor tenants and consumers, including innovative concepts, such as retaliatory eviction and implied warranty of habitability. . . . Cases like King v. Smith[102] radically changed poverty law by providing remedies in federal and state courts against those who administered the federal welfare program Aid for Families with Dependant Children (AFDC), the Food Stamp Program, public housing, and other public benefit programs.

Legal services lawyers also played critical behind-the-scenes roles in enacting or modifying federal, state, and local legislation. Legal services advocates significantly influenced the enactment of the Food Stamp Program, the Supplemental Food Program for Women, Infants and Children (WIC), and Supplemental Security Income (SSI), and they were instrumental in making changes to key federal housing legislation, Medicaid, consumer legislation, and nursing home protections. . . .

## The Reign of Howard Phillips

In January 1973, President Nixon proposed dismantling OEO and appointed Howard Phillips as the acting director of OEO to head the effort. . . . Phillips, a vocal critic of the War on Poverty in general and legal services in particular, was determined to destroy the legal services program. He declared, "I think legal services is rotten and it will be destroyed." Phillips put legal services programs on month-to-month funding, eliminated law reform as a program goal, and moved to defund the migrant legal services programs and back-up centers. The federal courts eventually stepped in and ruled that because he had not been confirmed by the Senate, Phillips lacked the authority to take such action as acting director.

While Phillips' effort to decimate legal services was ultimately thwarted by the courts, his assault made it clearer than ever that, in order for the program to

---

100. 394 U.S. 638 (1969).
101. 397 U.S. 254 (1970).
102. 392 U.S. 309 (1968).

survive, a new legal services structure, separate from the Executive branch and protected from vagaries of the political process, was essential.

### The Gestation Period

Within the organized bar, the Nixon Administration, the Congress, and the legal services community, the idea of an independent legal services entity began to take root. . . . In May 1973, President Nixon again proposed a bill to create the [Legal Services Corporation] LSC. . . . 24 restrictive amendments were appended to the bill, limiting the types of cases legal services attorneys could take, restricting lobbying and rulemaking, limiting class actions, and eliminating training and back-up centers. The back-up centers were a favorite target of conservatives because they were seen as the breeding ground for legal services activism and the incubator for law reform efforts. . . . The restrictions that remained in the [final version of the] bill dealt with representation in cases dealing with non-therapeutic abortions, school desegregation, selective service, and some instances of juvenile representation. . . .

### The Early LSC Era: Growth and Expansion

On July 14, 1975, the first of Board of Directors of LSC was sworn in by Supreme Court Justice Lewis Powell, who had led the ABA in endorsing legal services. . . . [This board] de-emphasized its regulatory role in favor of incentives, encouragement, assistance, and a spirit of partnership.

President Jimmy Carter appointed a new LSC Board to replace those members who had been appointed by President Ford. The new Board was chaired by Hillary Rodham, then a private practitioner and the wife of the young Governor of Arkansas, Bill Clinton. . . .

### Expansion

Most of the initial efforts of the new Corporation went into obtaining increased funds for the program from Congress. . . . [T]he Corporation developed a "minimum access" plan, with the goal of providing a level of federal funding for LSC programs in every area of the country, including those where no programs had been established, that would support two lawyers for every 10,000 poor persons, based on the U.S. Census Bureau's definition of poverty.

This funding and expansion strategy proved highly successful. LSC was able to transform the federal legal services program from one that had only served the predominantly urban areas of the nation to a program that provided legal assistance to poor people in virtually every county in the United States and in most of the U.S. territories. In 1975, LSC inherited a program that was funded at $71.5 million annually. By 1981, the LSC budget had grown to $321.3 million. Most of this increase went into expanding to previously unserved areas. . . . LSC had achieved, albeit briefly, the initial goal of reaching "minimum access." . . .

[T]he expansion of the program into previously unserved areas was sometimes still met with suspicion on the part of the local bar, local politicians, and business and community leaders, who feared that the business environment and social order that they had come to expect would be upset by the new breed of lawyers whose role was to assist the poor to assert their rights.

### The Late 1970s and the Beginnings of a Backlash

Two issues became particularly contentious during the late 1970s — legislative advocacy and representation of illegal aliens. In 1978, Carlos Moorhead, a Republican Congressman from California, added a rider to the legal services appropriations bill that prohibited the use of LSC funds "for publicity or propaganda purposes designed to support or defeat legislation pending before Congress or any state legislature." The Moorhead Amendment passed by a vote of 264 to 132. . . .

An alien restriction was added to the 1980 fiscal year (FY) appropriation. The provision prohibited LSC and legal services programs from using LSC funds to undertake any activity or representation on behalf of known illegal aliens. [As with the Moorhead amendment,] LSC also interpreted this rider narrowly as prohibiting representation of only those aliens against whom a final order of deportation was outstanding. Under this interpretation, representation of most aliens continued until 1983, when a much more restrictive rider was added to the FY 1983 appropriations act.

### The Reagan Era

The election of President Ronald Reagan in 1980 was a critical turning point in the history of federally funded legal services, ending the years of expansion and growth of political independence for the Corporation and its grantees. The Reagan Administration was openly hostile to the legal services program. Reagan initially sought LSC's complete elimination and proposed to replace it with law student clinical programs and a judicare system funded through block grants. In response to pressure from the White House, Congress reduced funding for the Corporation by 25 percent, slashing the appropriation from $321 million in FY 1981 to $241 million in FY 1982. The cut represented an enormous blow to legal services providers nationwide. Programs were forced to close offices, lay off staff, and reduce the level of services dramatically. . . .

In 1982, Congress enacted new restrictions on the use of LSC funds for lobbying and rulemaking and expanded the alien restriction by explicitly prohibiting the representation of certain categories of aliens using LSC funds. . . . Many of the Board members who served during that period . . . expressed outright hostility to the program they were charged with overseeing. . . . Many LSC Board members . . . expressed open disdain for the organized bar, particularly the ABA, which had emerged as a vigilant protector of the legal services program. . . .

## A Slight Resurgence

The 1990s began with a small but significant improvement in the situation of the legal services community. The Corporation's appropriation, which had been stagnant for several years, began to move upward, to $328 million for FY 1991 and $350 million for FY 1992. The first Bush Administration abandoned the overt hostility to legal services and the efforts to reduce or eliminate funding and to restrict legal services advocacy. The Bush Administration instead consistently recommended that Congress continue to appropriate money for the Corporation, albeit at level funding. . . .

In the early 1990s, for the first time in many years, Congress took up reauthorization of the LSC Act [because the Corporation's legislative authorization had expired in 1980, and only annual appropriation bills had kept it afloat]. . . . With the election of President Bill Clinton, the legal services community anticipated an end to the long period of insecurity and inadequate funding. . . . Congress also prepared to take up the LSC reauthorization bill again. . . .

## The 104th Congress

With the 1994 congressional elections, the Corporation suffered a dramatic reversal of political fortune. Conservatives included the elimination of LSC in the infamous "Contract for America." In much the same way as the Reagan Administration in the early 1980s, the leadership of the new Congress, led by House Speaker Newt Gingrich (R-GA), committed itself to the elimination of LSC and ending federal funding for legal services. . . . It seemed possible that the federal commitment to equal justice might be abandoned altogether.

Despite the efforts of the House leadership, a bipartisan majority in the Congress, led by Senator Pete Domenici (R-NM), remained committed to maintaining a federally funded legal services program. Nevertheless, key congressional decision-makers, led by Congressmen Bill McCollum (R-FL) and Charles Stenholm (D-TX), determined that major "reforms" in the delivery system would be required if the program was to survive. Grants were to be awarded through a system of competition, rather than through presumptive refunding of current recipients. A timekeeping system was imposed on all attorneys and paralegals working in programs. Programs were subject to a host of new organizational and administrative requirements. . . .

More fundamentally, the Congressional majority was determined to redefine the role of federally funded legal services by refocusing legal services advocacy away from law reform, lobbying, policy advocacy, and impact litigation and toward basic representation of individual clients. Congress set out to accomplish this goal by restricting the broad range of activities that programs had engaged in since the early days of OEO. . . . These restrictions applied to all activities that a recipient undertook, regardless of the source of the funding that was used to support the activity. Thus, with certain limited exceptions, LSC-funded programs were prohibited from using the public funds that they received from federal, state or local governments, or the private funds they received from bar associations, charitable foundations, private donations, and any other non-LSC sources for the LSC-restricted activities.

Congress prohibited representation of certain categories of clients, including prisoners, specified groups of aliens, and public housing residents who were being evicted based on drug-related charges. Perhaps even more damaging and insidious, Congress limited the kinds of legal work that LSC-funded programs could undertake on behalf of eligible clients, prohibiting programs from participating in class actions, welfare reform advocacy, and most affirmative lobbying and rulemaking activities. In addition, programs were prohibited from claiming or collecting attorneys' fees, and legal services programs were cut off from a significant source of funding and were limited in their ability to use an effective strategic tool. Finally, Congress eliminated LSC funding for national and state support centers, the Clearinghouse Review, and other entities that had provided support, technical assistance, and training to LSC-funded legal services programs. . . .[103]

Along with the new restrictions came a major reduction in funding. The LSC appropriation was cut by 30 percent, from $400 million for FY 1995 to $278 million for FY 1996. Final 1996 statistics revealed the staggering cost of the funding cuts: the number of cases that were closed fell from 1.7 million in 1995 to 1.4 million in 1996; during the same period, the number of attorneys working in LSC-funded programs nationwide fell by 900, and 300 local program offices closed. . . .

### The Legal Services Landscape from 1996 to the Present

Since 1996, the legal services landscape has undergone a dramatic transformation. Legal services has seen a reduction in the total number of LSC grantees from more than 325 programs in 1995 to 160 at the beginning of 2003, and the geographic areas served by many of the remaining programs have increased dramatically. . . .

The network of state and federal support entities formerly funded by LSC has been substantially curtailed, and some of its components have been completely dismantled. . . . Since the loss of their LSC funding, several of the national support centers that had focused solely on issues affecting the

---

103. [Authors' footnote.] Commenting on the bar's response to these restrictions, Professor David Luban notes that

> neither the Bar nor the legal-services establishment offered any organized protest when the 1996 restrictions were enacted. . . . The reason was pure fear that Congress, in the heady days of Newt Gingrich's revolution and the Contract with America, would simply abolish the LSC [Legal Services Corporation, the nation's principal source of legal aid funding]. . . . The ABA Ethics Committee's response was entirely typical: instead of writing a formal opinion insisting that the restrictions violate the ideals of the legal profession, it chose instead to write an opinion insisting that a legal-services grant recipient could practice law ethically by abandoning clients to keep its funding intact. The advice is undoubtedly accurate: declining cases is a sure-fire way to stay out of trouble.

David Luban, Taking Out the Adversary: The Assault on Progressive Public-Interest Lawyers, 91 Cal. L. Rev. 209, 225 (2003).

low-income community have broadened their focus to attract new sources of funds. Several national support centers closed their doors when they were unable to raise sufficient funds to operate effectively. . . .

At the same time, new legal services delivery systems have begun emerging in many states that include both LSC-funded programs, operating within the constraints of Congressionally imposed restrictions, as well as separate non-LSC-funded legal services providers that operate unencumbered by the LSC restrictions. Many of these non-LSC-funded providers were created specifically in response to the imposition of the restrictions. . . . In 16 states and more than 20 large- or medium-size cities, two or more parallel LSC- and non-LSC-funded legal service providers operate in the same or overlapping geographic service areas. . . .

Instead of a diverse group of separate, locally controlled and fully independent LSC-funded programs, loosely linked by a network of state and national support centers, each state is now attempting to develop a unified state justice system that includes LSC and non-LSC providers, law schools, pro bono programs, other human services providers, and key elements of the private bar and the state judicial system, working in close collaboration to provide a full range of legal services throughout the state. . . . The focus is no longer on what an individual program can do to serve the clients within its service area, but on what a state justice community can do to provide equal access to justice to all of the eligible clients within the state.

Moreover, in an increasing number of states, leadership for these state planning efforts and state justice communities is no longer concentrated in the hands of the staff and boards of individual LSC grantees but is provided by new entities that are known generically as "access to justice commissions." . . . In virtually every state, representatives of the courts, the organized bar, and the legal services provider community, . . . work together through some formal structure to expand and improve civil legal assistance. . . .

[I]n 32 states, non-LSC funds exceed LSC funds, and the ratio of non-LSC funds to LSC funds continues to increase. Although LSC funds remain the single largest source of support for civil legal services, programs in most areas of the country have become less dependent on LSC dollars in recent years.

However, this newly emerging system of delivery must be put into context. Private philanthropy is highly dependant on the state of the economy. State funding may be no more secure than federal funding, and the debate over whether there should be government funding for civil legal assistance is also occurring at the state level. In many states, efforts have been made by the legislatures . . . to impose significant restrictions on the use of their funds. For example, state funding in Missouri now includes the LSC restrictions. . . .

### Some Thoughts About the Future

The legal services system in the United States is funded far below the level of funding that is provided by most of the other Western developed nations. In the United States, the annual per capita government expenditures for civil legal assistance is $2.25, while the equivalent figure for England is $32. . . . [F]ederal funding for legal services has declined in purchasing power over the last 20 years and is a far smaller share of the overall funding for civil legal assistance in this country. . . .

[T]he political leadership of the United States 'remains deeply divided about whether there should be a federally funded legal services program, and, if so, how it should be structured. . . .

Despite the fact that the legal services community has developed mechanisms to cope with the Congressionally imposed restrictions [on federally funded legal services programs], most legal services advocates believe that the restrictions, especially as they are applied to programs' non-LSC funding, represent an unreasonable limitation on access to justice for poor people. . . .

## Questions about Legal Services for the Poor

**1.** What is the rationale for the government to provide free legal services for poor people in civil matters? Is this type of service important to the operation of our legal system, and if so, why?

**2.** What is the rationale for opposing the provision of free legal services for poor people in civil matters? Likewise, what is the rationale for restricting the available services to exclude law reform work and to exclude representation of certain groups? Why do you think that our policymakers have been so deeply divided about whether or how to fund legal services?

**3.** Some people have noted that the wealthy can afford legal assistance and the very poor (with family income less than 125 percent of the poverty level) may be eligible for legal aid subsidized by the government or by charity, but that working-class people are neither eligible for subsidized legal services nor able to afford them. Should the public subsidize or otherwise provide legal aid for working class individuals and families?

**4.** Some legal problems involve amounts of money so small that legal fees to obtain justice would exceed the amount in controversy. For example, no rational person would pay the thousands or tens of thousands of dollars that most lawyers would charge to initiate litigation, simply to recover several hundreds of dollars lost to a dishonest automobile repair shop. Many but not all states and counties have small claims courts in which individuals may bring and defend cases without lawyers, but most people do better, even in these fora, if they have experienced counsel. Should our society have a concept of "practical indigency" justifying government-subsidized legal services when the amount in controversy is so small that profit-making lawyers would not accept the case?

## PROBLEM 10-4  RESTRICTIONS ON LEGAL SERVICES

You are a staff lawyer at a policy institute concerned with helping poor people in the United States. Years have passed since Congress passed the 1996 legislation restricting the activities of neighborhood law offices funded through the Legal Services Corporation (LSC). The political climate in Congress is now more tolerant of legal services for the poor, but legal services for the poor are still unpopular or controversial in many districts, and the issue is not a high priority for most legislators. A member of Congress has advised you that a majority of members might now be willing to lift one or two of the restrictions that were imposed in 1996, but that if Congress is pressed to remove more than two restrictions at the present time, the legislation will become so controversial that Congress probably won't remove any of the limitations.

Since the 1996 law was passed, lawyers in offices that receive LSC funding may not undertake any of the following activities on behalf of a client, even with funds from nongovernmental sources:

- Attempt to influence the issuance or amendment of any local state or federal regulation
- Attempt to influence any part of a local, state, or federal adjudicatory proceeding "if such part of the proceeding is designed for the formulation or modification of any agency policy of general applicability and future effect"
- Initiate or participate in a class action
- Ask for an attorney's fee under a state or federal statute under which a judge may require the losing party to pay the prevailing party such a fee
- Participate in any suit on behalf of a person incarcerated in any prison (even, for example, an indigent prisoner who is being sued for divorce or who is defending against the state's suit to terminate her parental rights)
- Defend a person in a proceeding to evict the person from a public housing project on the ground that the person was charged with the sale or distribution of a controlled substance and the public housing agency believes that the drug activity threatens the safety of other tenants
- Participate in litigation, lobbying, or rulemaking involving an effort "to reform a Federal or state welfare system"
- Represent an alien seeking asylum in the United States
- Participate in any litigation involving abortion[104]

Which one or two of these restrictions, if any, will you advise the member of Congress to try to lift? On what basis would you argue that reversal of these particular restrictions is more urgent than reversal of others on the list?

---

104. Pub. L. No. 104-134, § 504 (1996).

## b. Other civil legal services

The federal LSC is the largest single source of funding for civil legal aid for the poor, but it pays for only about one-third of the $900 million spent annually on civil legal services in the United States. LSC funds 156 "full-service" programs (offering a range of legal services to the poor, other than those prohibited by congressional restrictions). There are also 56 full-service programs and nearly 700 specialized programs (for example, handling only one type of case) funded by foundations, charitable donations, and other sources.[105] Also, students in law school clinics contribute about 3 million hours a year (worth perhaps $150 million)[106] in uncompensated service to poor people.[107]

## c. The IOLTA controversy

The third largest source of funding for civil legal services for the poor — after LSC and contributions from state and local governments — is funds provided by a system known as IOLTA, or "interest on lawyers' trust accounts." As we have explained, most lawyers keep funds that belong to their clients in bank accounts called client trust accounts. These accounts often generate interest. Even in the electronic age, it is unduly expensive either to set up a separate account for each client or to allocate and refund the interest earned on small amounts of clients' funds when they are maintained in a single account. Since in these cases it is difficult and expensive to give the interest back to the clients, and it seems unfair to give it either to lawyers or to the banks, the state bars have set up programs to collect the IOLTA funds (which amount to millions per year in some states) and to direct these funds, under court or bar supervision, to organizations that provide legal services to indigents.

Forty-nine states have IOLTA programs. The American Bar Association has a Commission on IOLTA and has supported IOLTA programs since the early 1980s.[108]

The Washington Legal Foundation, a conservative public interest organization, has brought a series of court challenges to try to end IOLTA programs. The Foundation first argued that the system involves a taking of clients' property (the interest, however small, or the right to have a bank rather than a legal services organization obtain the benefit of the interest), in violation of the Fifth Amendment. By a 5-4 vote, the Supreme Court held that the interest, however small, was the clients' "property."[109] However, the Court later held, also by 5-4, that the proper measure of any compensation due for any taking of this

---

105. Alan W. Houseman, Civil Legal Aid in the United States: An Overview of the Program in 2003, at http://www.clasp.org/DMS/Documents/1064583480.94/view_html (last visited Nov. 6, 2004).

106. Of course, help from law students is priceless, but we are assuming a nominal billing rate of $50 per hour.

107. Luban, supra n. 103, at 236 n. 108.

108. See ABA, Commission on Interest on Lawyers' Trust Accounts, at http://www.abanet .org/legalservices/iolta/ioltcomm.html (last visited Nov. 6, 2004).

109. Phillips v. Wash. Leg. Found., 524 U.S. 156 (1998).

property was the loss to the owner, not the gain to the government. Since the net interest (the actual interest less the cost of processing it) that was lost by any client was zero, no compensation was due. The Court implied, however, that an IOLTA program might be unconstitutional if it covered client deposits that were large enough to generate "net interest" for the clients after deducting the "transaction and administrative costs and bank fees."[110]

The Washington Legal Foundation is continuing its challenge to IOLTA programs based on a second theory. It claims that because the interest on clients' funds is being used to support litigation (by the ultimate beneficiaries of the legal services) that the clients who provided those funds do not necessarily support, IOLTA programs infringe the clients' First Amendment right to free expression.[111]

## 3. Fee-shifting statutes

Under the "American Rule" that applies to litigation in the United States, each party to a lawsuit usually pays its own legal fees. Absent a statute that says otherwise, a plaintiff does not recover those fees from a defendant even when the plaintiff, as a result of prevailing, vindicates or enforces an important public policy.[112]

However, in a number of statutes, particularly civil rights and consumer protection laws, Congress and the state legislatures have included fee-shifting provisions to encourage plaintiffs to bring cases to enforce the statutes.[113] Most of these laws allow courts to order a losing party to pay the prevailing party's lawyers' fee, thereby "shifting" that cost. The Supreme Court has explained that in general, a plaintiff who prevails in such a case serves as "private attorney general" to enforce important public policies. A defendant who prevails, while entitled to his victory, does not effectuate the purposes of the relevant statute. Therefore, courts should ordinarily shift fees in favor of prevailing plaintiffs, but rarely in favor of prevailing defendants.[114]

The most important fee-shifting statute is the Civil Rights Attorney's Fees Act of 1976, often called the Fees Act.[115] It allows the court to shift fees in many federal civil rights cases, including those based on 42 U.S.C. § 1983, which is

---

110. Brown v. Leg. Found. of Wash., 538 U.S. 216, 238 (2003).

111. See Wash. Leg. Found. v. Leg. Found. of Wash., 271 F.3d 835 (9th Cir. 2001) (en banc) (remanded to district court for consideration of the First Amendment claim). Note also that under the Supreme Court's decision, as efficient computer technology reduces the level at which a client's short term deposit can earn "net interest," lawyers will have to refund that interest to clients, and IOLTA programs will be able to redirect less money to legal services programs.

112. Alyeska Pipeline Serv. Co. v. Wilderness Socy., 421 U.S. 240 (1975).

113. See 42 U.S.C. § 2000e-5(k) (2004) (employment discrimination statute); 15 U.S.C. § 1640(a)(3) (2004) (federal Truth in Lending Act); Harold J. Krent, The Fee-Shifting Remedy: Panacea or Placebo? 71 Chi.-Kent L. Rev. 415 (1995); Note, State Attorney Fee Shifting Statutes: Are We Quietly Repealing the American Rule?, 47 L. & Contemp. Probs. 321 (1984).

114. Newman v. Piggie Park Enter., 390 U.S. 400 (1968); Christiansburg Garment Co. v. EEOC, 434 U.S. 412 (1978).

115. 42 U.S.C. § 1988 (2004).

frequently invoked to redress violations of federal civil rights under color of state law.

In principle, fee-shifting statutes can help to stimulate legal services for people who cannot afford them. Even when a plaintiff who claims redress under one of these statutes is indigent, the plaintiff's lawyer may ultimately be able to recover a fee from the defendant. However, in two important rulings, the Supreme Court has made the fee-shifting statutes much less effective.

## a. Fee waiver as a term of a settlement

In Evans v. Jeff D,[116] the Supreme Court considered whether the federal fee-shifting statute was violated by a settlement offer to a client that was conditioned on the plaintiff's attorney agreeing to waive his right to have the defendant pay his attorneys' fees. The case was a class action suit handled by the Idaho Legal Aid Society, which filed a suit against a state agency for failing to provide required health services for children with emotional disabilities. The state defended the case for three years and then offered the plaintiffs a consent decree in which they would get everything they had asked for (and more than they could have expected to get as a result of a trial). However, the offer was contingent on the plaintiffs' attorney, Charles Johnson, waiving any claim for fees under the Fees Act. Johnson realized that this settlement offer created a conflict of interest between his duties to the client class and his duties to Idaho Legal Aid, which would have used the fees to pay for services to other needy clients. He decided to accept the offer for his clients, but he persuaded the state to allow court review of the fee waiver. Then he made a motion to recover the fee award notwithstanding the terms of the settlement.

The trial court denied fees. The Ninth Circuit reversed because the policy behind the Fees Act, to encourage the enforcement of certain plaintiffs' rights, would be undercut by permitting defendants to pit plaintiffs against their own lawyers.

The Supreme Court reinstated the denial, 6-3. It said that the district court could have refused to accept a consent decree that included a fee waiver, but it was not required to do so. The Court said that statutory attorneys' fees are a bargaining chip, to be negotiated like everything else in a case. The Court urged that this was good policy, for if defendants couldn't insist in a settlement offer that the fees be waived, they would offer less relief to the plaintiffs. The children in the class probably would have received less benefit from the lawsuit if the state had offered less money for health services and more for attorneys' fees. The state had to protect itself against a fee award, the magnitude of which it could not predict. Thus, according to the Court, fee waiver negotiations are, at least sometimes, good for civil rights.

The Court noted that Johnson may have experienced a conflict between the desires of his client and those of his employer, but his ethical duty ran only to his clients, not to the Legal Aid Society or its potential future clients.

---

116. 475 U.S. 717 (1986).

The Court acknowledged that if very many civil rights defendants insisted on fee waivers, the pool of lawyers willing to bring civil rights cases might dry up because nobody can work without pay for long. However, the Court urged that this concern was "premature" because there was no "documentation" of such a problem, and "as a practical matter the likelihood of this circumstance arising is remote."[117]

Justices Brennan, Marshall and Blackmun, dissenting, took issue with the idea that a study would be needed to show that fewer civil rights cases would be brought if statutory fees can be waived. They pointed out that the actual plaintiffs will always want to waive fees to get better settlements, and that only the lawyers (or legal aid societies) will lose out. They predicted that as a result of the Court's decision, defendants would always minimize liability by asking for fee waivers. The dissent noted that the U.S. Solicitor General's brief in the case implied that the United States would, in the future, ask for such fee waivers. "The conclusion that permitting fee waivers will seriously impair the ability of civil rights plaintiffs to obtain legal assistance is embarrassingly obvious."

The dissenters acknowledged that prohibiting fee waivers might discourage some settlements, but they concluded that the congressional policy of requiring fee-shifting should override the judicially created policy of encouraging settlements. They expressed hope that "Congress will repair this Court's mistake," and they also suggested another way in which the damage could be undone. "Several Bar Associations have already declared it unethical for defense counsel to seek fee waivers. Such efforts are to be commended." They also suggested that "it may be that civil rights attorneys can obtain agreements from their clients not to waive attorney's fees."

In a footnote, the dissenters said that they thought it "peculiar" that the majority "permits defendants to require plaintiff's counsel to contribute his compensation to satisfying the plaintiff's claims. In ordinary civil litigation, no defendant would make — or sell to his adversary — a settlement offer conditioned upon the plaintiff's convincing his attorney to contribute to the plaintiff's recovery."[118]

Bar associations have not acted on the dissenters' suggestion that the ethical rules should prohibit defendants from conditioning settlement on fee waivers by plaintiffs' lawyers. One bar association had issued such an opinion before the court's decision, but it withdrew the opinion after the *Evans* case was decided.[119]

---

117. Id. at 765-766.

118. Id. at 766 n. 21.

119. Bar Association of the City of N.Y., Committee on Professional and Judicial Ethics, Formal Op. 1987-4 (withdrawing Ops. 80-94 and 82-80), at http://www.abcny.org (last visited Nov. 6, 2004). The Association was persuaded by the majority opinion that the purpose of the Fees Act was only to give plaintiffs' lawyers a new bargaining chip, not to assure that they would recover fees, and that such offers were not per se unethical.

## b. Who is a "prevailing party" entitled to attorneys' fees?

Buckhannon Board and Care Home, Inc. was a facility that provided assisted living for elderly people. West Virginia sought to close down the facility because it did not conform with a state law barring such residences from housing people who would be unable to leave without help in the event of fire. Buckhannon sued the state to enjoin it from enforcing the state law, on the ground that the state law was inconsistent with the Federal Fair Housing Amendments of 1988 and the Americans with Disabilities Act. The state agreed not to close the facility until the case was resolved.

While the case was pending, the West Virginia legislature repealed the state law. Thus, Buckhannon got everything it wanted. It then sought attorneys' fees under the Fair Housing Amendments, which allowed the court to award fees to a "prevailing party." The district court and the court of appeals denied the award. They reasoned that because the state voluntarily gave up its policy before it was ordered to do so, Buckhannon was not a "prevailing party" within the meaning of the fee-shifting statute.[120]

By a 5-4 vote, the Supreme Court affirmed.[121] A "prevailing party" is one who obtains relief from a court, not through voluntary action or through an out-of-court settlement. Therefore a person whose lawsuit is merely the "catalyst" for a change in state policy cannot obtain fees unless the judgment is entered as a court order. Although the relevant Senate committee report had said that "parties may have prevailed when they vindicate rights through a consent judgment or without formally obtaining relief," the Court said that "such legislative history is clearly insufficient to alter the accepted meaning of the statutory term."[122]

Justices Ginsburg, Stevens, Souter, and Breyer, in dissent, stated that the Court's decision would "impede access to court for the less-heeled, and shrink the incentive Congress created for the enforcement of federal law by private attorneys general." They noted, by way of analogy, that Western democracies "prevailed in the Cold War even though the Soviet Union never formally surrendered."[123]

## Margaret Graham Tebo, Fee-Shifting Fallout

ABA J., July 2003, at 54

When plaintiff's lawyer William Franz thinks about [*Buckhannon*,] a 2001 Supreme Court decision on attorney fees, the image that comes to his mind is that of a neutron bomb — which kills all living things but leaves the buildings standing.

---

120. Buckhannon Board & Care Home, Inc. v. W. Va. Dept. of Health & Human Resources, 203 F.3d 819 (4th Cir. 2000).

121. Buckhannon Board & Care Home v. W. Va. Dept. of Health & Human Resources, 532 U.S. 598 (2001).

122. Id. at 608.

123. Id. at 633.

"This case effectively guts the [Americans with Disabilities Act] and other civil rights statutes, while technically not overturning them. Without the fee provisions, the statutes will continue to exist, but they'll have no teeth," says Franz, a Boca Raton, Fla., civil rights lawyer. . . .

As a result of the decision, many plaintiffs lawyers say, a host of civil rights cases will never make it to the courthouse door because plaintiffs cannot afford to pay their attorneys outright. And the attorneys cannot afford to gamble on whether they will get paid.

After *Buckhannon*, says Donald Feldman, Franz's colleague in Boca Raton, the more meritorious a plaintiff's case may be, the more likely the government will be to settle out of court — and the less likely an attorney will take it. . . . [Also,] defendants can effectively wait until it's clear that they might lose the case and then make an 11th hour settlement offer, giving the plaintiff virtually everything he asks for, except attorney fees. The plaintiff's lawyer is then left with a conflict: If he advises the client to take the settlement, which may be in the client's best interest, the lawyer risks payment. If he advises the client to reject the offer because of the lack of fees, he may be violating his ethical duty to act in the client's best interest. . . .

[The First Circuit Court of Appeals has applied *Buckhannon* and] found that the catalyst theory no longer holds for cases brought under section 1983 of the Civil Rights Act. . . . The Fees Act governs the award of fees in section 1983 cases and uses the same "prevailing party" language [as the Americans with Disabilities Act].[124]

## 4. Pro bono representation

Private lawyers' voluntary assistance to low-income clients also helps meet the legal needs of the poor. One hundred fifty-five law firms and 600 bar or other associations have formal programs through which lawyers offer assistance to indigent clients.[125] If all American lawyers offered pro bono help to those who could not afford to pay, our profession would take a huge step toward meeting the unmet need for legal services. Suppose, for example, that each of the million lawyers in the United States contributed 50 hours of their time each year to helping indigent clients. If those services were valued at $200 per hour, the value of the total contribution would be $10 billion, or about 30 times as much as the entire annual budget of the LSC.[126]

The organized bar recognizes the importance of pro bono contributions. The ABA's Model Rule 6.1 encourages — but does not require — each lawyer

---

124. [Tebo's footnote.] Richardson v. Miller, 279 F.3d 1 (2002). [Authors' note: Therefore, to the extent that other circuits or the Supreme Court agree with the First Circuit, defendants may be able to avoid having to pay plaintiffs' attorneys' fees in injunctive civil rights cases by consenting to end an illegal practice when it becomes apparent that they will lose the case.]

125. Houseman, supra n. 105.

126. This comparison may be a bit unfair because legal services lawyers who specialize in areas of law such as welfare and low-income housing may provide services more efficiently than pro bono lawyers who have to train themselves.

to spend at least 50 hours per year providing pro bono assistance to those in need. A few states have gone further, making 50 hours per year of pro bono service mandatory rather than voluntary. Consider, for example, Montana Rule 6.1,[127] which is exactly like the ABA's Model Rule 6.1 except that in title and substance, the Montana requirements are mandatory rather than voluntary.

### Montana Rule 6.1    Pro Bono Publico Service[128]

| Rule language* | Authors' explanation** |
|---|---|
| Every lawyer has a **professional responsibility to provide legal services** to those unable to pay. A lawyer **should render at least (50) hours of pro bono publico legal services per year.** In fulfilling this responsibility, the lawyer should: | The Montana Rule imposes a duty of 50 hours per year of service. The ABA Model Rule is almost identical, except that it says that a lawyer "should aspire to render" this quantity of service.<br><br>Comment 12 to the ABA Model Rule notes that disciplinary enforcement is not contemplated with respect to the voluntary requirement. It remains to be seen whether failure to perform pro bono service will be a basis for discipline in states that adopt mandatory requirements. |
| (a) provide a **substantial majority of the (50) hours** of legal services without fee or expectation of fee **to** (1) **persons of limited means** or (2) charitable, religious, civic, community, governmental and educational organizations in matters that are designed primarily to address the needs of persons of limited means; and | The ABA's comments to its corresponding Model Rule explain that the need for assistance to persons of limited means is so great that lawyers should aspire to provide at least 25 hours per year of such assistance (and at least 25 additional hours in pro bono work that could be of other types). |
| (b) **provide additional**[129] **services through:** (1) delivery of legal services at no fee or substantially reduced fee to individuals, **groups or organizations seeking to secure or protect civil rights, civil liberties or public rights,** or charitable, religious, civic, community, governmental and educational organizations in matters in furtherance of their organizational purposes, where the payment of standard legal fees would significantly deplete the organization's economic resources or would be otherwise inappropriate; | Comment 6 after ABA Rule 6.1 says that a lawyer who provides at least 25 pro bono hours a year to poor clients may satisfy the rest of her professional obligation by serving a wide variety of individuals and groups. The services might include help to religious institutions, vindication of First Amendment claims, and protection of the environment. The lawyer may charge a substantially reduced fee for these services. |

127. Available at http://www.lawlibrary.state.mt.us/dscgi/ds.py/Get/File-27482/Rules.pdf (last visited Nov. 6, 2004).

128. ABA Model Rule 6.1 is titled "Voluntary Pro Bono Publico Service."

129. Consistent with its emphasis on voluntary pro bono service, ABA Model Rule 6.1(b) is identical to the Montana rule except that the ABA inserts the word "any" before the word "additional."

| Rule language* | Authors' explanation** |
|---|---|
| (2) **delivery of legal services at a substantially reduced fee to persons of limited means; or** | Acceptance of court-appointed criminal defense work at a low rate of compensation qualifies as pro bono assistance for purposes of Rule 6.1(b). ABA Model Rule, Comment 7. |
| (3) **participation in activities for improving the law,** the legal system, or the legal profession. | Serving on bar association committees also qualifies under Rule 6.1(b). ABA Model Rule, Comment 8. |
| In addition, a lawyer should voluntarily contribute financial support to organizations that provide legal services to persons of limited means. | Lawyers' financial contributions should be made in addition to, not instead of, pro bono service. ABA Model Rule, Comment 10. |

*All emphasis added.
**Montana's rules do not include comments, but because Montana Rule 6.1 is very similar to ABA Model Rule 6.1 (except for Montana's 6.1 pro bono requirement being more than aspirational), we describe the ABA's comments to its corresponding rule.

No one knows how many lawyers meet or exceed the ABA's aspirational 50-hour standard for pro bono work, but anecdotal evidence suggests that in the competitive law firm world described in Chapter 9, the contributions are nowhere as great as they might otherwise be, and that variations based on region and type of practice are significant.[130] For example, the median annual pro bono contribution of New York lawyers is 20 hours per year, but the corresponding figure for Texas lawyers is only 5 hours per year.[131] In the most profitable large law firms, "pro bono participation . . . declined by a third during a decade [the 1990s] when their average revenues increased by over 50%," and only a quarter of the firms counted all of an associate's pro bono hours as billable hours. At many firms, "pro bono work was permissible only if it occurred 'outside the normal work hours,'" and two-thirds of associates surveyed said that pro bono work "was a negative factor in promotion and bonus decisions."[132]

## Greg Winter, Legal Firms Cutting Back on Free Services for Poor

### N.Y. Times, Aug. 17, 2000, at A1*

Many of the nation's biggest law firms — inundated with more business than they can often handle and pressing lawyers to raise their billable hours to

---

*Copyright 2000, N.Y. Times Co. Reprinted with permission.

130. Most of the reports on pro bono work concern lawyers in large firms. Apparently there are no substantial studies of pro bono work by lawyers in small and midsize firms, and there is no broad national survey of pro bono activity. E-mail from Esther Lardent, President, Pro Bono Institute, to the authors (Dec. 8, 2003).

131. Deborah L. Rhode, Pro Bono in Principle and in Practice, 53 J. Leg. Educ. 413, 429 (2003). "Only two-fifths of surveyed in-house legal departments participate in pro bono work, and the average yearly commitment is less than 8 hours per legal department employee." Id.

132. Id. at 430, 450.

pay escalating salaries — have cut back on pro bono work so sharply that they fall far below professional guidelines for representing people who cannot afford to pay.

The roughly 50,000 lawyers at the nation's 100 highest-grossing firms spent an average of just eight minutes a day on pro bono cases in 1999, according to a survey last month by *American Lawyer* magazine. That comes out to about 36 hours a year, down significantly from 56 hours in 1992, when the magazine started tracking firms' volunteer hours. Yet with the economy booming, firms are enjoying record profits, the survey also found.

"The phenomenon of being so busy that you don't have as much time for pro bono work is quite real," said Jack Londen, a partner at Morrison & Foerster. The San Francisco firm has a long tradition of taking charitable cases, but since the recession of the early 1990's, its lawyers have cut their average pro bono hours in half, the survey showed. . . .

"When there is more work than lawyers to do it, and there are not enough new lawyers out there to hire, the pro bono gets shelved," Mr. Londen said. . . .

"We're under pressure to work hard to pay for these rising salaries," said John Payton, a partner at Wilmer, Cutler & Pickering and president-elect of the Bar Association of Washington. "I don't think it's going to wipe out the tradition of pro bono, but it's clearly going to have some impact." . . .

Most firms say it is not their commitment that has waned, just their ability to take on as many cases as in the past. While lawyers typically billed 1,700 hours annually just a few years ago, today they routinely bill 2,200 to 2,300 hours, said Esther F. Lardent, director of the Pro Bono Institute. . . .

"We didn't want to be in a position where the associates would decide between doing their fee-paying work or not," said R. Bruce McLean, chairman of Akin, Gump, Strauss, Hauer & Field in Washington. Last year, the firm decided not to credit pro bono time until lawyers billed at least 2,000 hours in a given year.

## Michael Hertz, Large Law Firms: A Larger Role to Play

Pro Bono Net News, Oct. 1, 2003[133]

The total number of pro bono hours reported by the 200 largest firms in 2002 is just over 3 million hours. This number is impressive and the firms deserve the recognition that they receive for these efforts. [But] substantial room for improvement exists. For example, less than a quarter of the 200 largest firms report average pro bono hours per lawyer in excess of one common bench-mark: Model Rule of Professional Conduct 6.1, which calls for each lawyer to dedicate at least 50 hours per year to pro bono.

---

133. Available at http://www.news.probono.net/e_article000188673.cfm (last visited Nov. 6, 2004).

## Doug Campbell, Law Firms Do Little Pro Bono

Bus. J. Greater Triad Area, July 23, 2001[134]

When it comes to pro bono, some of the state's largest law firms have a long way to go. Of the largest firms in North Carolina, only [one] came even remotely close last year to reaching the "pro bono challenge" ... [an ABA standard that] calls for lawyers to put in about 60 hours of gratis legal work a year, or at least 3% of their total hours worked.[135] ... [W]ith law firms routinely shelling out $100,000 and more for associates, some legal experts say the pressure to bill as many hours as possible may have caused some lawyers to put pro bono on the back burner.

---

In 2000, the Ethics 2000 Commission debated whether the 50 hour per year goal should be converted, in the Model Rules, to a mandatory requirement (which a lawyer or firm could satisfy by contributing $25 per hour for each hour not worked to an organization that offered such services). The Commission voted, 6-5, to make the pro bono service mandatory. Then it voted to reconsider and ultimately voted 7-6 not to require lawyers to perform pro bono service.

Professor Judith Maute describes how opposition from what might seem an unlikely quarter—the community of lawyers who strongly support legal services for the poor—doomed the proposal to add a mandatory pro bono requirement to the Model Rules. While voting against this concept, it also rejected Maute's alternate suggestion for mandatory reporting of any pro bono service in lieu of mandatory service itself.

## Judith L. Maute, Changing Conceptions of Lawyers' Pro Bono Responsibilities: From Chance Noblesse Oblige to Stated Expectations

77 Tul. L. Rev. 91, 138-146 (2002)

Professor Judith L. Maute

[Judith Maute is Professor of Law at the University of Oklahoma.]

By the February 2000 ABA midyear meeting, the [Ethics 2000] Commission heard much opposition to mandatory pro bono from groups deeply committed to serving the poor. Robert Weiner, Chair of the ABA Standing Committee on Pro Bono and Public Service, predicted a "firestorm of resentment, protest, and

---

134. Available at http: //triad.bizjournals.com/triad/stories/2001/07/23/story1.html (last visited Nov. 6, 2004).

135. For information about the Pro Bono Institute's pro bono challenge, which calls on lawyers to exceed the standards of Model Rule 6.1, see http://www.probonoinst.org/challenge.php (last visited Nov. 6, 2004).

resistance," that would divert attention from the crisis in unmet legal needs to the controversial and ultimately doomed issue of compulsory service. "Forced involvement of reluctant attorneys" would present numerous practical difficulties, and "could undercut the quality of legal services to the poor." ...

I testified ... opposing mandatory service as inconsistent with the concept that law is a public calling and politically unfeasible; predictable backlash by the bar risked a public relations debacle. ... I recommended cooperative pooling arrangements and comparable financial contributions as alternatives to direct service. ... I suggested that an annual reporting requirement could achieve a sound balance between aspirational guidance and regulatory compulsion. A simple annual form, as part of the other usual compliance statements, could be designed to prompt lawyers' regular reflection on their own involvement, to obtain reliable information on volunteer services provided, to encourage increased service activity or financial support, and to create a statewide infrastructure for distribution of services for those in need. ... Thereafter, prominent members of ABA leadership weighed in, urging no change to the current rule and opposing either a service or reporting requirement. ...

Doreen Dodson testified as chair of the ABA Standing Committee on Legal Aid and Indigent Defendants (SCLAID). ... SCLAID "fervently hoped that each lawyer ... will have an internal moral compass calling ... to give something back to society." Because it had seen evidence of ineffective assistance by appointed counsel in death penalty cases, SCLAID knew "that conscripts make poor lawyers. ... Poor clients in civil matters deserve lawyers who want to represent them and who will do it with vigor." ... Dodson added: "The manner in which each state chooses to provide incentives for pro bono service should be left to those states, not dictated by a national model. Legal and bar association cultures are simply too divergent across the states for the ABA to try to promulgate a model rule on something like reporting of pro bono service." ...

After closely studying mandatory and voluntary reporting, the committee decided it was "not an appropriate strategy for every state. ... Moreover, the ethical rules are not the place to impose this type of duty to report. The Rules of Professional Conduct govern just that: the professional conduct of individual lawyers. Pro bono reporting rules are procedural. They relate to record keeping. The relationship to ethical obligations, including the ethical obligation to do pro bono work, is indirect at best. Even states that impose mandatory continuing legal education do so in court rules, not in the Rules of Professional Conduct."

Because commentators almost unanimously opposed mandatory service as "inconsistent with the needs of the indigent clientele intended to be benefitted," at its July 2000 meeting, the Commission decided to drop the idea, and propose no substantive changes to Rule 6.1. Still, the internal debate continued. At the September meeting, the Commission first voted in favor of mandatory service, then agreed to reconsider. Members debated on the

Commission listserv. Two weeks later they voted again, by teleconference; Chairman Veasey broke a tie, defeating a motion in support of the mandatory concept.

---

Professor Deborah L. Rhode has summarized some of the strongest arguments for and against a mandatory pro bono requirement, such as the one now in effect in Montana.

## Deborah L. Rhode, Cultures of Commitment: Pro Bono for Lawyers and Law Students

67 Fordham L. Rev. 2415 (1999)

[Deborah L. Rhode is the Ernest W. McFarland Professor of Law at Stanford Law School. She served as the President of the Association of American Law Schools, 1998-1999.]

While most lawyers acknowledge that access to legal assistance is a fundamental interest, they are divided over whether the profession has some special responsibility to help provide that assistance, and if so, whether the responsibility should be mandatory. One contested issue is whether attorneys have obligations to meet fundamental needs that other occupations do not share. According to some lawyers, if equal justice under law is a societal value, society as a whole should bear its cost. The poor have fundamental needs for food and medical care, but we do not require grocers or physicians to donate their help in meeting those needs. Why should lawyers' responsibilities be greater? . . .

*Professor Deborah L. Rhode*

One answer is that the legal profession has a monopoly on the provision of essential services. Lawyers have special privileges that entail special obligations. In the United States, attorneys have a much more extensive and exclusive right to provide legal assistance than attorneys in other countries. The American bar has closely guarded those prerogatives and its success in restricting lay competition has helped to price services out of the reach of many consumers. Under these circumstances, it is not unreasonable to expect lawyers to make some pro bono contributions in return for their privileged status. Nor would it be inappropriate to expect comparable contributions from other professionals who have similar monopolies over the provision of critical services.

An alternative justification for imposing special obligations on lawyers stems from their special role in our governance structure. As [a] New York [court] Report explained, . . . "Like no other professionals, lawyers are charged with the responsibility for systemic improvement of not only their own profession, but of the law and society itself."

Because lawyers occupy such a central role in our governance system, there is also particular value in exposing them to how that system functions, or fails to function, for the have nots. . . .

A final justification for pro bono work involves its benefits to lawyers individually and collectively. Those benefits extend beyond the intrinsic satisfactions that accompany public service. Particularly for young attorneys, such work can provide valuable training, trial experience, and professional contacts. . . .

Opponents raise both moral and practical objections. As a matter of principle, some lawyers insist that compulsory charity is a contradiction in terms. . . . [But] pro bono work is not simply a philanthropic exercise; it is also professional responsibility. . . .

Opponents' other moral objection [is that] it is a form of "latent fascism" and "involuntary servitude." . . .

The stronger arguments against pro bono obligations involve pragmatic rather than moral concerns. Many opponents who support such obligations in principle worry that they would prove ineffective in practice. A threshold problem involves defining the services that would satisfy a pro bono requirement. If the definition is broad, and encompasses any charitable work for a nonprofit organization or needy individual, then experience suggests that poor people will not be the major beneficiaries. Most lawyers have targeted their pro bono efforts at friends, relatives, or matters designed to attract or accommodate paying clients. A loosely defined requirement is likely to assist predominately middle-class individuals and organizations such as hospitals, museums, and churches. By contrast, limiting a pro bono requirement to low-income clients who have been given preferred status in the ABA's current rule would exclude many crucial public-interest contributions, such as work for environmental, women's rights, or civil rights organizations. Any compromise effort to permit some but not all charitable groups to qualify for pro bono credit would bump up against charges of political bias.

A related objection to mandatory pro bono requirements is that lawyers who lack expertise or motivation to serve under-represented groups will not provide cost-effective assistance. In opponents' view, having corporate lawyers dabble in poverty cases will provide unduly expensive, often incompetent services. The performance of attorneys required to accept uncompensated appointments in criminal cases does not inspire confidence that unwillingly conscripted practitioners would provide acceptable representation. Critics also worry that some lawyers' inexperience and insensitivity in dealing with low-income clients will compromise the objectives that pro bono requirements seek to advance.

Requiring all attorneys to contribute minimal services of largely unverifiable quality cannot begin to satisfy this nation's unmet legal needs. Worse still, opponents argue, token responses to unequal access may deflect public attention from the fundamental problems that remain and from more productive ways of addressing them. Preferable strategies might include simplification of legal procedures, expanded subsidies for poverty law programs, and elimination of the professional monopoly over routine legal services.

Those arguments have considerable force, but they are not as conclusive as critics often assume. . . . One option is to allow lawyers to buy out of their required service by making a specified financial contribution to a legal-aid program. Another possibility is to give credit for time spent in training. . . . A final objection to pro bono requirements involves the cost of enforcing them. Opponents often worry about the "Burgeoning Bureaucratic Boondoggle" that they assume would be necessary to monitor compliance. . . . There is, however, a strong argument for attempting to impose pro bono requirements even if they cannot be fully enforced. At the very least, such requirements would support lawyers who want to participate in public-interest projects but work in organizations that have failed to provide adequate resources or credit for these efforts.

PROBLEM 10-5 **MANDATORY PRO BONO SERVICE**

Each year, three law students are elected to serve as members of the House of Delegates of the American Bar Association, the ABA's highest governing body.[136] You have been elected to one of these positions.

Because the ABA Ethics 2000 Commission was almost evenly divided in 2000 on making pro bono service mandatory, that proposal has been brought up once again. An ABA committee has recommended that Rule 6.1 be amended to make service mandatory (with a $25/hour buyout), and the House of Delegates is scheduled to vote on the matter this afternoon.

How will you vote? Why?

# 5. Loan forgiveness and scholarships for public service lawyers

Another strategy for expanding the resources available to those who cannot pay for them is to remove the barriers to public service caused by the very high cost of attending law school.[137] Many people choose to go to law school in order to assist people in need. However, when they approach their graduation date,

---

136. See ABA Law Student Division, Position Description for the National Office of Delegate to the ABA House of Delegates, at http://www.abanet.org/lsd/elections/delegate.html (last visited Nov. 6, 2004).

137. The public interest scholarship and loan repayment programs discussed here help both the individual lawyers who receive the benefits and the clients served by the programs in which they become employed. The scholarships and loan forgiveness payments enable public service employers to hire more lawyers to carry out their missions because the benefits to the law students partially subsidize the salaries that the employers provide to their legal staffs. The benefits also enable employers to retain experienced lawyers who would otherwise have to resign after a year or two because of their debt repayment burdens.

Stu's Views © 2002 Stu All Rights Reserved www.stus.com

"Money? Ha! I'm a legal aid lawyer. The only thing in my wallet is an overdue notice for my student loans."

many feel that they cannot follow their chosen path because by that time, they owe $100,000 or more in educational loans (requiring annual repayment of about $10,000) and cannot afford to serve the poor for a salary of $36,000, more or less.[138]

138. ABA Commission on Loan Repayment and Forgiveness, Lifting the Burden: Law Student Debt as a Barrier to Public Service (2003), at http://www.abanet.org/legalservices/downloads/lrap/lrapfinalreport.pdf (last visited Nov. 6, 2004) provides a thorough discussion of this issue, replete with useful statistical information. As of 2003, the average three-year cost of attendance at the nation's private law schools was $108,113. Id. at 19. The average law student at these schools borrowed $86,378 for education, but 25 percent of the students borrowed more than $100,000. Id. at 20-24. At an interest rate of 8.25 percent, repaying an $86,378 loan over 10 years would require paying $12,780 per year; repaying over 20 years would cost only $9,000 per year but would cost a

A few law schools reduce the cost of attendance (and consequently the debt burden) for some students who want public service careers by offering them public service scholarships.[139] However, a study published by the National Association for Public Interest Law showed that in 1999, just three law schools (New York University, Georgetown, and the University of Denver) provided 76 percent of all of the funds for these scholarships. Forty-seven law schools offer loan repayment assistance, usually including partial or complete loan forgiveness, to their graduates who take low-paying public service jobs. However, in 1999 just six schools (Yale, New York University, Harvard, Columbia, Stanford, and Georgetown) provided 70 percent of all of the funds for loan forgiveness. Furthermore, more than two-thirds of American law schools had no loan forgiveness program at all.[140]

In addition, eight states have loan forgiveness programs for graduates of their state's schools, their state's public service lawyers, or both. However, funding under these programs has been very limited.[141]

Because the ability of law schools and state governments to fund loan forgiveness for public service lawyers is so limited, the ABA has recommended that the federal government provide more such assistance. As a result of an act of Congress in 1993, the federal government already offers an "income-contingent repayment" (ICR) option for student loans. Under this plan, any graduate may consolidate all undergraduate and law school government-extended or government-guaranteed loans into a loan from the government that would be repaid over 25 years. A year's repayment is never larger than 20 percent of the borrower's "discretionary income," defined to be the borrower's adjusted gross income minus the federal poverty level. (In practice, this works out to a limit of about 20 percent of after-tax income.) Any amount that would have to be paid in excess of this limit is added to the principal still owing, but compounding stops, permanently, once that amount climbs more than 10 percent above the original principal, and the entire remaining debt — principal and interest — is forgiven at the end of 25 years.[142] The plan is not

---

total of $210,000 as opposed to $106,000 in current dollars over that period of time. Id. at 21-22. For the class of 2002, the median starting salary in public interest law was $36,000. Even if a new graduate found a public service job paying $40,000 per year and repaid on a 20-year schedule, the first year's loan repayment would be more than 30 percent of her after-tax income. (On a 10-year repayment plan, it would be 43 percent of after-tax income.) Id. at 21-22.

139. As of 2000, 14 law schools had public service scholarship programs. Natl. Assn. for Public Interest Law (NAPIL), Financing the Future: NAPIL's 2000 Report on Law School Loan Repayment Assistance and Public Interest Scholarship Programs 301-358 (2000). NAPIL is now called Equal Justice Works.

140. Id. at 1-300.

141. See ABA Commission on Loan Repayment and Forgiveness, State LRAP Tool Kit: A Resource Guide for Creating State Loan Repayment Assistance Programs for Public Service Lawyers 36 (2002) (Florida's annual budget for loan repayment was $106,000 for the entire state; Texas's budget was $30,000).

142. In other words, interest continues to accrue, but interest on the interest is no longer charged. Thus, there are two potential government subsidies built into this program — the ceiling on compounding and forgiveness at the end of 25 years of payments, each year of which is capped by the income-contingent repayment formula.

dependent on taking a public service job. The repayment amount is solely a function of debt and income. The existing ICR option could subsidize public service lawyers with the highest debt-to-income ratios, but virtually no law graduates use it, both because few have ever heard of it and because those who do know about it are reluctant to sign up for a 25-year repayment plan, even though it is revocable, it can be prepaid to curtail the obligation, and for some it would eventually result in a significant subsidy.[143]

The ABA has proposed amending this law by requiring the federal government to forgive debts on the ICR plan after 15 years, rather than 25 years, for borrowers who have engaged in a specified number of years of full-time public service.[144] In 2004, Representative Rick Renzi (R-Ariz.) introduced a bill that would provide this relief for borrowers who had completed eight years of public service work.[145]

## PROBLEM 10-6  SERVICE TO THE POOR AND MIDDLE CLASS

Chapters 9 and 10 have described a legal profession that offers bountiful services to wealthy corporations and their executives at very high prices but leaves most of the legal needs of the poor and the middle class unmet. These chapters also suggest several approaches for changing doctrines and institutions in ways that might redress this imbalance.

Are you persuaded that there is a problem that needs to be solved, or is the free market for legal services, as modified by existing institutions such as Rule 6.1, sufficient?

If you think there is a problem, which solutions seem most promising? Can you suggest better or additional approaches?

---

143. Philip G. Schrag, The Federal Income-Contingent Repayment Option for Law Student Loans, 29 Hofstra L. Rev. 733 (2001).

144. See Letter from Robert D. Evans, Govt. Affairs Dir., ABA, the chairman of the Senate Committee on Health, Education, Labor and Pensions and other reflections of the ABA's continuing efforts to support this idea. These documents are posted at http://www.abanet.org/legalservices/lrap/federal/federallobbying.html (last visited Nov. 14, 2004).

145. H.R. 5270 (108th Cong.).

# ABOUT THE AUTHORS

Lisa G. Lerman is Professor of Law at The Catholic University of America, Columbus School of Law, where she has taught since 1987. She attended Barnard College (B.A.1976) and NYU School of Law (J.D. 1979). She received an LL.M. from Georgetown University Law Center in 1984. Before joining the faculty at Catholic University, Lerman was a staff attorney at the Center for Women Policy Studies, a Clinical Fellow at Antioch and Georgetown law schools, a member of the law faculty at West Virginia University, and an associate in a law firm. She also has taught at the law schools of American University, George Washington University, and Jagiellonian University (Krakow, Poland).

At Catholic University, Professor Lerman serves as Director of the Law and Public Policy Program, an academic enrichment program for students interested in careers in public interest law, government, and politics. She teaches Contracts, Professional Responsibility, and the Public Policy Practicum. She has taught clinical and externship courses as well as seminars in family law, public policy, and the legal profession. She has written many articles about lawyers, law firms, the legal profession, and legal education. Her earlier work focused on domestic violence law. Professor Lerman has served as chair of the Professional Responsibility Section of the Association of American Law Schools and as a member of the DC Bar Legal Ethics Committee. She is on the planning committee for the ABA National Conference on Professional Responsibility.

Philip G. Schrag is a professor at Georgetown University Law Center. He attended Harvard College and Yale Law School. Before he started a career in law teaching, he was Assistant Counsel of the NAACP Legal Defense and Educational Fund, Inc., and in 1970 he became the first Consumer Advocate of the City of New York. A member of the founding generation of clinical law teachers, he developed clinics at Columbia Law School and the West Virginia University College of Law, as well as at Georgetown. During the administration of President Jimmy Carter, he was the Deputy General Counsel of the United States Arms Control and Disarmament Agency.

At Georgetown, Professor Schrag directs the Center for Applied Legal Studies, an asylum and refugee clinic, and Georgetown's Public Interest Law Scholars Program. He regularly teaches Civil Procedure and has also taught Consumer Protection, Federal Income Taxation, Legislation, Administrative Law, and Professional Responsibility. He has written twelve books and many articles on public interest law and legal education. Currently, as Vice-Chair of the Government Relations and Student Financial Aid Committee of the American Bar Association's Section of Legal Education and Admissions to the Bar, he is working with other law teachers and law school deans to ask Congress to provide partial student loan forgiveness for law students who work for many years in low-paying public interest jobs.

Professors Lerman and Schrag live in Bethesda, Maryland, with their children, Sam and Sarah.

# TABLE OF ARTICLES, BOOKS, AND REPORTS

*Works that are quoted at length in the text appear in bold italic type in this table. Works that are quoted briefly or summarized appear in italics.*

# TABLE OF CASES

*Principal cases are in bold italics. Cases that have not been excerpted but have been quoted, discussed, or summarized in the text are in italics.*

# TABLE OF RULES, RESTATEMENTS, STATUTES, BAR OPINIONS, AND OTHER STANDARDS

**ABA Model Rules of Professional Conduct and Delaware Rules of Professional Conduct**

Note: As explained in the Introduction, rules of professional conduct quoted in the text are from the Delaware Rules of Professional Conduct. Except as indicated in the text, these quoted rules are identical to the ABA Model Rules of Professional Conduct. Therefore, the following list of Rules of Professional Conduct refers both to the Delaware Rules and to the Model Rules.

## Statutes and Regulations

## Bar Opinions

# INDEX

*(References are to page numbers.)*